Critical Psychology

An Introduction

Second Edition

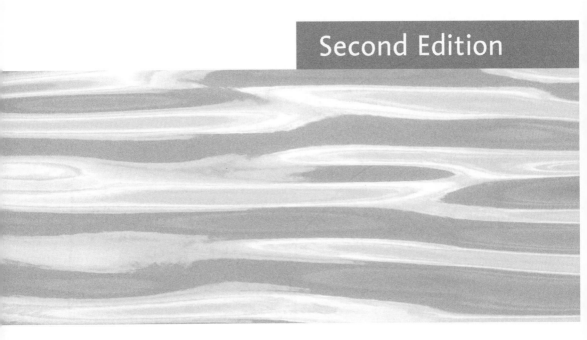

Edited by

Dennis Fox, Isaac Prilleltensky & Stephanie Austin

Los Angeles • London • New Delhi • Singapore • Washington DC

First edition published 1997
This second edition published 2009

SAGE Publications Ltd
1 Oliver's Yard
55 City Road
London EC1Y 1SP

SAGE Publications Inc.
2455 Teller Road
Thousand Oaks, California 91320

SAGE Publications India Pvt Ltd
B 1/I 1 Mohan Cooperative Industrial Area
Mathura Road
New Delhi 110 044

SAGE Publications Asia-Pacific Pte Ltd
33 Pekin Street #02-01
Far East Square
Singapore 048763

Library of Congress Control Number: 2008931103

British Library Cataloguing in Publication data

A catalogue record for this book is available from the British Library

ISBN 978-1-84787-172-5
ISBN 978-1-84787-173-2 (pbk)

Typeset by C&M Digitals Pvt Ltd, Chennai, India
Printed in Great Britain by CPI Antony Rowe, Chippenham, Wiltshire
Printed on paper from sustainable resources

FSC
Mixed Sources
Product group from well-managed forests and other controlled sources
Cert no. SGS-COC-2953
www.fsc.org
© 1996 Forest Stewardship Council

Cr

LIBRARY

This book should be returned not later than the last date stamped below.
The loan may be extended on request provided there is no waiting list.
FINES ARE CHARGED ON OVERDUE BOOKS

Contents

Contributors

Bruce A. Arrigo is Professor of Crime, Law, and Society in the Department of Criminal Justice, University of North Carolina – Charlotte. He holds additional faculty appointments in the Psychology Department, the Public Policy Programme, and the Centre for Professional and Applied Ethics. Arrigo began his career as a community organizer and social activist for the homeless and marginally housed, users of mental health services, ex-incarcerates engaged in community re-entry, and survivors of domestic violence and sexual assault. He has authored or edited 25 books and published more than 150 peer-reviewed articles, book chapters, and essays. His research addresses topics in law, medicine, and justice; critical social theory and philosophical criminology; and the sociology and psychology of deviance and violence. He is a Fellow of the American Psychological Association and the Academy of Criminal Justice Sciences.

Stephanie Austin received her PhD in psychology from York University in Toronto, Canada, in 2004. Since that time, she has been doing independent research, writing and community work on issues of social justice and human wellbeing. Stephanie was introduced to critical psychology in her MA studies with Isaac Prilleltensky and continued in her PhD with Thomas Teo. She has published collaborative work in critical psychology with Isaac Prilleltensky, Tod Sloan and Dennis Fox and currently works as a senior policy analyst at the Bureau of Women's Health and Gender Analysis at Health Canada. Stephanie is Chair of the board of directors of an organization she co-founded that inspires and promotes the empowerment, leadership, and healthy development of girls across Canada (www.powercampnational.ca). Email: astephanie@hotmail.com

Virginia Braun is Senior Lecturer in Psychology at The University of Auckland, Aotearoa/New Zealand. Her research is located within feminist and critical psychology, and relates to topics in the broad areas of sex/sexuality, sexual health, and gendered embodiment. Her primary research currently is on a relatively recent development in cosmetic surgery – female genital cosmetic surgery (the so-called 'designer vagina'). With Victoria Clarke, she is also doing work in the area of sexuality in tertiary education, and working on a book on qualitative research in psychology. She is co-editor (with Nicola Gavey) of the journal *Feminism & Psychology*. Email: v.brown@aukland.ac.nz

Heather E. Bullock is Associate Professor of Psychology and Director of the Centre for Justice, Tolerance, and Community at the University of California, Santa Cruz. Her research focuses on social psychological dimensions of poverty and economic (in)justice, particularly discrimination against low-income women and the attitudes and beliefs that predict support for anti-poverty policies. Her current research examines political mobilization among low-income women and families' pathways in and out of homelessness. Before joining the UCSC faculty, she was an American Psychological Association Congressional Fellow with the US Senate Committee on Health, Education, Labour, and Pensions – Democratic Office. She is currently chair of the APA's Committee on Socioeconomic Status. Email: hbullock@ucsc.edu

Kerry Chamberlain is Professor of Health Psychology at Massey University in Auckland. He is a critical health psychologist whose research interests focus broadly on health in everyday life, with a particular interest in projects that advance understandings and assistance to disadvantaged peoples. More specifically, his research interests include the meanings of medications and social practices in their use; food and health, and social practices around food and eating, dieting, and dietary supplementation; media and health and the mediation of health issues in contemporary society; and everyday mundane illness and its embodiment. He utilizes a variety of qualitative methodologies and methods in his research, including photo-elicitation, diaries, maps, and the use of material objects like personal possessions and photographs, to reveal the materiality and social practices of everyday life. Email: K.Chamberlain@ massey.ac.nz

Frances Cherry is Professor of Psychology and Director of the Institute of Interdisciplinary Studies at Carleton University, Ottawa, Canada. She is interested in the history and theory of psychology in general, and of social psychology in particular. Her early work is published in a book of critical research essays, *The 'Stubborn Particulars' of Social Psychology: Essays on the Research Process* (Routledge, 1995). More recently, she has been writing about the people, research practices, and organizations that linked scholarship and activism in mid-twentieth century North American social psychology. Her recent work has focused on Thomas Pettigrew's activism and research involvement in US racial desegregation, on the history of paired testing and civil rights, and on the Society for the Psychological Study of Social Issues' involvement with the United Nations (1948–2000).

Victoria Clarke is a Reader in Sexuality Studies at the University of the West of England, Bristol. Her research is located at the intersection of LGBTQ and feminist and critical psychology and focuses on lesbian and gay parenting, same-sex and heterosexual relationships, sexuality and appearance, and sexuality in education. She has co-edited two books – *Out in Psychology* (with Elizabeth Peel) (Wiley, 2007) and *British Lesbian, Gay and Bisexual Psychologies* (with Elizabeth Peel and Jack Drescher) (Haworth, 2007). She is currently writing a book on LGBTQ psychologies with Sonja Ellis, Elizabeth Peel and Damien Riggs and a book on qualitative research in psychology with Virginia Braun.

Erzulie D. Coquillon is a JD candidate at Boston College Law School. She holds a Master's degree in Counselling Psychology from Boston College and an AB, cum laude, in History from Harvard University.

Kevin Durrheim is Professor of Psychology at the University of KwaZulu-Natal, where he teaches social psychology and research methods and manages a Masters programme in applied research. He obtained his PhD in political psychology from the University of Cape Town in 1995. He has published articles and book chapters on topics related to racism, segregation and social change. He is co-author (with John Dixon) of *Racial Encounter* (2005, Routledge) and co-editor (with Martin Terre Blanche) of *Research in Practice* (1999, 2006, UCT Press).

Scot Evans is Assistant Professor in the Department of Educational and Psychological Studies at the University of Miami. He received both his MEd in Human Development Counselling and his PhD in Community Research and Action from Peabody College of Vanderbilt University. His research explores the role of community-based organizations in the promotion of social change. Scot is the 'man behind the curtain' at PsyACT – Psychologists Acting with Conscience Together (www.psyact.org) – and serves as webmaster for the Society for Community Research and Action (www.scra27.org). He has extensive practical experience in community-based organizations as a youth development worker, crisis worker, family counsellor, youth programme developer, programme evaluator and organizational consultant. Email: evanssd@mac.com

Dennis Fox is Emeritus Associate Professor of Legal Studies and Psychology, University of Illinois at Springfield. With Isaac Prilleltensky, he co-founded the Radical Psychology Network (1993) and co-edited *Critical Psychology: An Introduction* (1997). His critical essays, which frequently explore the intersection of psychology, justice, and law using insights from anarchist theory, appear in journals ranging from *American Psychologist* and *Behavioral Sciences and the Law* to *New Ideas in Psychology* and *Radical Psychology*. Since escaping full-time academic work and moving to Boston, he has written analytical, opinion, and personal essays for outlets such as the *Boston Globe, Education Week,* Salon.com, *Radical Teacher,* and *Social Anarchism*. In 2006 Fox was a consultant in Law and Society at Birzeit University, Palestinian West Bank, and a Fulbright Senior Specialist in peace and conflict resolution at Ben Gurion University, Israel. Essays, blog, photo galleries: dennisfox.net. Email: df@dennisfox.net

Rachel T. Hare-Mustin was Director of the Graduate Programme in Counselling and Consulting Psychology at Harvard University and Staff Psychologist at the Philadelphia Child Guidance Clinic and University of Pennsylvania Department of Psychiatry. She has also worked in universities in China and Nigeria, among others. As a theoretician, researcher, and practising clinician, she has published more than 120 articles and chapters and several books. She is co-author with Jeanne Marecek of *Making A Difference: Psychology and the Construction of Gender* (Yale University Press, 1990). She has published in such journals as *American Psychologist, Feminism & Psychology,* and *Family Process* and has served as President of the American Family Therapy Academy and Chair of the American Psychological Association's Ethics Committee and Committee on Women in Psychology. Her work on postmodern theory and feminist theory and practice has been recognized by numerous awards and international honours.

Ben Harris is Professor of Psychology, University of New Hampshire. He works at the intersection of the history of psychology, history of medicine, and history of science. Building on early work on the history – and mythology – of Watsonian behaviourism, he has studied the changing nature of psychological expertise throughout the century. A related interest is the transformation of psychological knowledge as presented to mass audiences – and as it returns to psychologists from the public. He is a Charter Fellow of the Association for Psychological Science and Past-President of the Society for the History of Psychology (Division 26 of the APA).

Alexa Hepburn is a Senior Lecturer in Social Psychology in the Social Sciences Department at Loughborough University. She has written a number of analytic papers on school bullying, issues of gender, violence against children, and interaction on child protection helplines. Her work has also developed a theoretical strand, focusing on issues in critical social psychology and on the relations of the philosophy of Derrida and Foucault to the theory and practice of social psychology. She has written two recent books: *An Introduction to Critical Social Psychology* (Sage, 2003) and *Discursive Research in Practice* (Sage, 2007, with Sally Wiggins). She also recently co-edited a special issue of *Discourse & Society* on developments in discursive psychology, and has taught a number of methods workshops on discursive psychology, and more recently conversation analysis, in various countries around the world.

Derek Hook is a lecturer in Social Psychology at the London School of Economics and a research fellow at the University of the Witwatersrand. The overarching focus of his research concerns the attempt to develop an 'analytics of power' sufficiently able to grapple with the unconscious and psychological dimensions of racism and ideological subjectivity. He is the author of *Foucault, Psychology & the Analytics of Power* (Palgrave, 2007) and the editor of *Critical Psychology* (University of Cape Town Press, 2004). He is one of the founding editors of the journal *Subjectivity*, and the coordinator of Psychoanalysis@LSE, a multidisciplinary research group aiming to further the use of psychoanalysis as a means of social and political analysis.

Ingrid Huygens, PhD, is a registered community psychologist and currently chairs the Institute of Community Psychology Aotearoa. A first generation Pakeha of Dutch descent, she joined the movement by anti-racism workers to educate other Pakeha about the Treaty of Waitangi signed with the indigenous Maori in 1840. She now continues this form of decolonization education with immigrant communities. She has published in the areas of feminist action, cultural racism, and discourses for decolonization. Her PhD research focused on the social and psychological processes of change experienced by a culturally dominant group in response to challenges by indigenous peoples.

Gazi Islam is Assistant Professor of Business Administration at Ibmec, São Paulo, where he teaches undergraduate and graduate courses in Leadership and Organizational Behavior, Negotiations, and International Management. He completed his PhD in Organizational Behavior at Tulane University, with research focused on organizational identity, voice, and power relations. His current research interests include the organizational antecedents and consequences of identity, and the relations between identity, group dynamics and the production of group and organizational cultures. In addition, he attempts to link identity and organizational culture to wider issues of national culture, ideology, and civil society.

Clare Jackson is a Teaching Fellow and PhD Candidate in the Department of Sociology, University of York, UK. Clare joined the sociology department in 2007, after spending many years teaching psychology to undergraduates. Her interest and teaching in critical psychology led her to explore qualitative methods, and particularly Discursive Psychology (DP). Realizing the power of DP as a radical force in psychology, she became increasingly taken by interactional research. She is now training as a Conversation Analyst, and is using Feminist Conversation Analysis to explicate how gendered identities are made relevant in talk.

Wendy M. Limbert is a Senior Associate with Collaborate Research Associates, a programme evaluation firm in Castle Rock, Colorado. Within critical psychology, her research interests centre on how economic policies in the US enhance or reduce inequality. Her current work examines the framing of US redistributive policies that affect low- versus high-income families. Her advocacy work includes several years of participation with the Supportive Parents Information Network, a grassroots anti-poverty organization, on issues such as local welfare policy, banking access, and public awareness of poverty. Email: wendy.limbert@yahoo.com

Colleen Loomis is Associate Professor of Psychology at Wilfrid Laurier University in Ontario, Canada, and Associate Director, Research of the Laurier Centre for Community Service-Learning. She has published on the psychological sense of community, service learning, and related subjects, including self-help groups, gender and power, socioeconomic class, mentoring, and bilingual education in the United States. Loomis examines the interaction between the individual and the community and its relation to positive and negative psychological and social outcomes. She conducts community-based, participatory action research studying the impact of service learning on community partners and community capacity building, as well as on student and institutional outcomes. She aims to develop new teaching models that enhance learning while addressing communities' social issues. Email: cloomis@wlu.ca

M. Brinton Lykes is Professor of Community-Cultural Psychology and Associate Director of the Centre for Human Rights and International Justice at Boston College, USA. She works with survivors of war and gross violations of human rights, using the creative arts and participatory action research methodologies to analyse the causes and document the effects of violence and develop programmes to rethread social relations and transform the social inequalities underlying structural injustices. Her activist scholarship has been published in refereed journals, edited volumes, research handbooks, and organizational newsletters. She is co-editor of three books and co-author, with the Association of Maya Ixil Women – New Dawn, of *Voces e imágenes: Mujeres Mayas Ixiles de Chajul/Voices and images: Maya Ixil women of Chajul* (Magna Terra, 2000). Brinton is a co-founder and participant in the Boston Women's Fund and the Ignacio Martín-Baró Fund for Mental Health and Human Rights. Website: www2.bc.edu/~lykes

Jeanne Marecek is the Wm. Kenan Professor of Psychology at Swarthmore College; she also teaches in Asian Studies and Gender Studies. Her interests are at the intersection of gender studies, cultural psychology, and critical psychology. She has contributed to such journals as *Feminism & Psychology*, *American Psychologist*, *Asian Journal of Counseling Psychology*, and *Psychology of Women Quarterly*, and to edited volumes. She and Rachel Hare-Mustin co-edited *Making a Difference: Psychology and the Construction of Gender* (Yale University Press, 1990). She and Michelle Fine edit the book series Qualitative Psychology (NYU Press). Her current research focuses on suicide and self-harm in rural Sri Lanka. She has served on the boards of several NGOs serving low-income women and girls in Philadelphia. In Sri Lanka, she works with Nest, an NGO working to release women incarcerated in mental hospitals, and with local humanitarian organizations active in war-affected areas.

Michael McCubbin is a researcher with a Quebec public community health and social services agency and adjunct professor at Université Laval. His education is in public policy planning and administration and economics, with a doctorate from Université de Montréal. Over the past two decades he has published in a variety of mental health and population health areas, focusing upon power, powerlessness, and empowerment. In the mental health area he has undertaken critical studies of psychoactive drugs and their iatrogenic impacts, of the organization of community mental health services, and of the oppression of those characterized as mentally ill, arguing for the individual and collective empowerment of mental health service users to advance their recovery, social inclusion and citizenship.

Elliot G. Mishler is Professor of Social Psychology in the Department of Psychiatry of Harvard Medical School. He has directed research training programmes in the social sciences, is a research consultant for the Victims of Violence programme at the Cambridge Health Alliance, and is active in the Cambridge–Boston area antiwar movement. He has applied methods of narrative analysis and other qualitative approaches to clinical and research interviews and has published over 60 articles and book chapters and six books, including *The Discourse of Medicine: Dialectics of Medical Interviews* (Ablex, 1984), *Research Interviewing: Context and Narrative* (Harvard University Press, 1986), and *Storylines: Craftartists' Narratives of Identity* (Harvard University Press, 1999). Email: emishler@comcast.net

Michael Murray is Professor of Applied Social and Health Psychology, Keele University, West Midlands, UK. He is keen to develop critical social psychological approaches to health, illness, ageing and wellbeing that are both insightful and change oriented. He locates his research within a socially dynamic theoretical and methodological framework and within a broader commitment to social justice. From a theoretical perspective he is interested in social-community psychology and social representation and narrative theory. From a methodological perspective he is interested in qualitative, participatory and arts-based research approaches. He has conducted research on the social representation and lived experience of chronic illness, the experience of health and ageing among people living in disadvantaged communities, accidents and safety in the workplace and the role of the arts in social and personal transformation. He was a founding member of the International Society of Critical Health Psychology (www.ischp.org).

Geoffrey Nelson is Professor of Psychology and a faculty member in the graduate programme in Community Psychology at Wilfrid Laurier

University, Ontario, Canada. His research and action interests in community psychology have focused on prevention and community mental health. Underlying his work in both areas is an emphasis on working in partnership with disadvantaged people, participatory action research approaches using both quantitative and qualitative methods, and value-based critical perspectives that challenge the status quo and that are oriented towards social change.

Isaac Prilleltensky is Dean of the School of Education at the University of Miami, Florida. Born in Argentina, he has studied and worked in Israel, Canada, Australia and the United States. Following practice as a school psychologist, Isaac saw the limitations of deficit-oriented, reactive, and individualistic approaches and became a community psychologist. Concerned with the role of justice in personal, relational, organizational, and collective wellbeing, he is presently working with health and human services on developing strength-based, preventive, empowering, and community change approaches. He is the author, co-author or co-editor of seven books, two special issues of professional journals and dozens of articles. He is a Fellow of the American Psychological Association and of the Society for Community Research and Action. In 2002 he was visiting fellow of the British Psychological Society. Website: www.education.miami.edu/Isaac. Email: isaacp@miami.edu

Ora Prilleltensky is a lecturer in the Department of Educational and Psychological Studies, University of Miami, after working as a lecturer in the Department of Human and Organizational Development at Vanderbilt University. Her research interests include disability studies and the promotion of wellbeing. As a person with a disability and a wheelchair user, she has both a personal and a professional interest in disability issues and disability identity. She has authored a book and several articles on motherhood and disability and co-authored articles and book chapters on promoting wellbeing. With Isaac Prilleltensky, she is co-author of *Promoting Well-Being: Linking Personal, Organizational and Community Change* (Wiley, 2006). Born in Israel, Prilleltensky has worked in Canada, Australia, and the USA. Prior to entering academia, she worked as a teacher, counsellor, behaviour consultant, and psychologist. She earned a Masters in School Psychology (University of Manitoba) and a doctorate (Ed.D) in Counselling Psychology from OISE (at the University of Toronto).

Damien W. Riggs is an Australian Research Council postdoctoral fellow in the School of Psychology, University of Adelaide, Australia. He is President of the Australian Critical Race and Whiteness Studies Association and Editor of the Australian Psychological Society journal *Gay and Lesbian Issues* and *Psychology Review*. He has published widely in the areas of lesbian and gay psychology and critical race and whiteness studies and is editor of two books:

Out in the Antipodes: Australian and New Zealand Perspectives on Gay and Lesbian Issues in Psychology (with Gordon Walker, 2004, Brightfire Press), and *Taking Up the Challenge: Critical Race and Whiteness Studies in a Postcolonising Nation* (2007, Crawford Publishers). He is also the author of two books: *Priscilla, (White) Queen of the Desert: Queer Rights/Race Privilege* (Peter Lang, 2006) and *Becoming a Parent: Lesbians, Gay Men, and Family* (Post Pressed, 2007). Website: www.damienriggs.com

Tod Sloan is Professor and Chair, Department of Counselling Psychology, Lewis & Clark College, Portland, Oregon. He is the author of *Damaged Life: The Crisis of the Modern Psyche* (Routledge, 1996a), in which he analyses the psychosocial impact of capitalist modernization and joins others in making the case for dialogue and deep democracy. He edited *Critical Psychology: Voices for Change* (Macmillan, 2000) and co-edits *The Journal for Social Action in Counseling and Psychology*. Sloan is currently developing a critical theory of dialogue, taking into account ideological and unconscious factors that systematically distort communication, drawing on a synthesis of critical hermeneutics and poststructuralist theory. He worked as US co-coordinator of Psychologists for Social Responsibility from 2001–2005 and is a founding member of A Circle Group: An Activist Support Network. Website: www.lclark.edu/faculty/sloan

Wendy Stainton Rogers is Professor in Health Psychology at the Open University in the UK, within its Faculty of Health and Social Care. She is committed to influencing policy and practice over a broad field including children's rights, safety and welfare; fair and humane youth justice services; and public health measures to counter inequalities. As well as her interest in research methodology, Wendy is developing theories about agency and action that treat people as insightful, purposeful and self-aware rather than feckless and stupid. She has contributed to NICE (the National Institute for Health and Clinical Excellence) in producing and disseminating recommendations on 'best practice' in behaviour change interventions and programmes at individual, community and population levels. Her current research looks at risk-taking in relation to health. Recent publications include co-editing (with Carla Willig) the *Sage Handbook of Qualitative Research in Psychology* (Sage, 2008); *Social Psychology: Experimental and Critical Approaches* (2003, McGraw Hill); and (with the late Rex Stainton Rogers) *The Psychology of Gender and Sexuality: An Introduction* (2001, McGraw Hill).

Vicky Steinitz was Associate Professor of Social Psychology at the College of Public and Community Service, University of Massachusetts at Boston. A co-author (with Ellen Rachel Solomon) of *Starting Out: Class and Community in the Lives of Working Class Youth* (Temple University Press, 1986) and various articles on welfare and education reform and solidarity research, she founded the Welfare and Human Rights Monitoring Project. She retired in

June 2005 to devote more time to political activism. She currently serves as a community outreach coordinator for United for Justice with Peace, the greater Boston area antiwar coalition. She is also one of the lead organizers of the Stop the BU Bioterror Lab Coalition, which aims to prevent Boston University from building a dangerous bioweapons lab in Boston.

Thomas Teo is Associate Professor in the History and Theory of Psychology programme at York University, Toronto. His research in historical and theoretical psychology is based on critical-hermeneutic analyses. In 2005 he published *The Critique of Psychology: From Kant to Postcolonial Theory* (Springer). He has also published on the transformation of psychology in nineteenth-century German philosophical psychology and on the history of race psychology and scientific racism. More recently, he has presented his concept of *epistemological violence* in psychology. He is an executive member in the historical and theoretical divisions of various national and international organizations and editor of the *Journal of Theoretical and Philosophical Psychology*. In his courses on theoretical and historical psychology he emphasizes the application of critical thinking to students' own experiences. His personal multicultural and multiethnic background allows him to bring an international perspective to critical theory. Website: http://www.yorku.ca/tteo

Courte Voorhees is a PhD candidate in the Community Research and Action programme at Peabody College, Vanderbilt University; he received his MA from Peabody College in 2008. Raised and educated in the high desert of northern New Mexico, Voorhees developed and practised an interdisciplinary and ecological perspective that continues to inform his work today. His research and practice centre on the intersection of poverty, class, and the environment – both built and natural. He also teaches critical research methods and community psychology at Peabody College and is a member of the Society for Community Research and Action.

Michael J. Zyphur received his PhD in industrial/organizational psychology (I/O) from Tulane University in 2006. Before and after this time, he has maintained an active interest in being critical of accepted I/O doctrine regarding the relationship between and among organizations and the human beings they employ. Although Michael's research interests are broad, including statistical and other research methods as well as the biological underpinnings of organizational behaviour, his critical interests have resulted in an acceptance of a plurality of views on institutions and the individuals that populate them.

Preface to the Second Edition

When the first edition of *Critical Psychology: An Introduction* appeared in 1997, books about critical psychology weren't all that common. Students and others new to critical ideas rarely stumbled across the topic in a bookstore or on the newly created World Wide Web. Critical psychology courses, journals, and conferences were rare. Blogs had yet to appear.

Today critical psychology is taught in many countries and languages. It remains distant from mainstream psychology's core, but it's a little easier to find. New books, along with new journals and websites, have exposed more professors and students to critical psychology's varying approaches. We are glad that this book's first edition has been part of that expansion, helping to connect critical authors and readers around the world – even in its Greek and Indonesian translations! Connecting with kindred spirits is invigorating, and often essential for intellectual and political survival when exploring ideas that are critical of mainstream institutions.

Another way to connect with critical psychology is through Internet networks, discussion groups, blogs, and other websites. Excerpts from the first edition have been posted online for more than a decade (www.dennisfox.net/critpsy/). Also online is the Radical Psychology Network, co-founded by Dennis Fox and Isaac Prilleltensky and described in the preface to the first edition. RadPsyNet reached more than 500 members in three dozen countries (including several contributors to this book) before moving from a membership organization to an online network. The group maintains an active listserv and an online journal, *Radical Psychology* (radpsynet.org). Other websites by and for critical psychologists are noted throughout this book.

If you compare this edition of *Critical Psychology* to the first, you will see some similarities as well as many important differences. Instead of a simple update, this second edition is fully revised, reconfigured, and expanded. More than half of the 23 chapters are appearing for the first time, and all but one of the remainder have been completely re-written. This new edition takes a fresh look at critical psychology's core concepts and concerns and offers chapter-length treatments of some of psychology's key subdisciplines.

Contributors highlight the distinctions between critical psychology and mainstream psychology and introduce readers to a range of critical perspectives, this time with a greater emphasis on the major theoretical, political, and practical dilemmas that critical psychologists face in their research and practice. New sections assess critical psychology's relevance to central issues of social justice as well as giving practical advice for theorists, researchers, therapists, and social change advocates.

One thing you will notice is that critical psychologists are more likely to acknowledge the subjective nature of their efforts than their mainstream peers. You will see how critical psychology theory and practice relate to the authors' values. This contrasts with more traditional texts in which academics have hidden the impact of their values, as well as of their political and professional allegiances, on the choices they must make and the positions they present. Critical psychology, in contrast, aims to demonstrate that choices such as these are never entirely objective or free from values, assumptions, and biases. By acknowledging how our own values and experiences affect us, we expose our work to a kind of scrutiny that mainstream work hopes to avoid.

Our own work, of course, also reflects our past experiences of growing up in three different countries in different decades and taking different paths after that. Isaac grew up in Argentina during a period of intense political repression; Dennis, a decade older, was influenced by the 1960s' antiwar movement and counterculture in the United States; Stephanie, a former student of Isaac's and a couple of decades younger still, grew up in predominantly English-speaking Canada as part of a Francophone minority. Isaac and Dennis are descendants of European Jews who left the lands of their birth to escape life-threatening repression; as teenagers we each came in contact with the Israeli kibbutz system, settlements based on communalism, economic collectivism, and a search for social justice. Stephanie was greatly influenced by her mother – a feisty Francophone single mother who worked as an academic in a department with very few women. In this environment, Stephanie learned how rewarding it could be to use her white, middle-class, straight-girl privilege to promote equity and social justice, leading her to become involved in community development work internationally as well as in Canada.

No doubt our histories have much to do with our critique of modern society. Those who occupy marginal or minority positions will frequently confront mainstream injustices that members of the majority will more often overlook. Similarly, our experiences in a movement reinventing social institutions have affected our vision of what kind of society is possible – and have also introduced us to the ambiguities of conflicting claims to justice and differing views of history. But our critiques, our vision, and our effort to sort out ambiguities are not unique; they are similar to those of many others who are also of our time, and from very different backgrounds, but who have come to more or less the same place: a commitment to resist institutions – especially those institutions that we ourselves are part of or benefit from – that choose to protect the powerful by oppressing the powerless.

We thank Michael Carmichael at Sage for persuading us to produce this second edition. Dennis and Isaac, who had each acquired other priorities and commitments over the years, hadn't been planning a sequel. Michael's enthusiastic encouragement eventually wore us down. Also instrumental was Stephanie's willingness to become a third co-editor. Aside from sharing the work, we knew that her familiarity with other literatures and perspectives would make the book even better.

One of our central goals was to create a book that students would find interesting and understandable even if they were not familiar with other critical work. We're happy to report that the chapter authors routinely responded to our endless rewrite requests with much more amiability than we had any right to expect. We respect them enormously and thank them for participating in this project.

If we've succeeded, *Critical Psychology: An Introduction* will help you contribute to the important struggle to make psychology a tool for emancipation and social justice. We'd love to hear your reports about how it's going.

Dennis Fox
Isaac Prilleltensky
Stephanie Austin

June 2008

Preface to the First Edition

The two of us met a few years ago after discovering each other's published articles, which presented overlapping and complementary critiques of psychology and of society. Like many of the authors in this book, we each had written criticisms of psychology for supporting social institutions that perpetuate injustice and promote selfishness. Although we had varied a bit in our emphases, the way we approached our work had something in common beyond the substance of our parallel critiques. Rather than writing only in obscure political journals primarily for people who already agreed with us, we did most of our writing for mainstream psychology journals. We hoped to stimulate critical reflection by psychologists who didn't usually read journals that were critical of the field's basic assumptions and norms. We saw this reflection as crucial if psychology was to outgrow its political innocence and become a more enlightened and responsible participant in public life. Our goal was not just to grumble on the sidelines but to change the status quo.

Another thing the two of us had in common was that we generally cited the work of older, more established critical psychologists who had demonstrated how societal institutions hindered social justice. Although certainly not a universal trend, there even seemed to be a tradition of long-time leaders of organized psychology reflecting on their careers and concluding that the norms they had followed for most of their lives could not bring about social change. Thus, because we were not starting from scratch, we could always resurrect and build on earlier critiques.

Once we noticed the similarity in our approaches, we began to wonder if we could do more than present older arguments to the same mainstream audiences who had rejected them the first time around. Grumbling from within had its advantages, but it didn't seem quite enough. The minor tradition of respected mainstream psychologists criticizing the mainstream was matched by another tradition, this one followed by the majority: listening politely to the critics and even publishing their critiques and giving them awards, but still going about their business as usual. We wondered how we could actually change things, not just write about the need for change.

Our musings led us to arrange a meeting at the 1993 convention of the American Psychological Association, a discussion session called 'Will Psychology Pay Attention to its Own Radical Critics?' The two dozen psychologists who attended – many of them graduate students – founded the **Radical Psychology Network** (RadPsyNet), which the two of us have coordinated since then. The group remains small, a hundred or so members around the world. We have a newsletter, and an Internet discussion group and World Wide Web site (www.radpsynet.org). The group enables like-minded critics of psychology's mainstream norms to meet one another, share their concerns, and stimulate projects for members to work on together.

It became clear as RadPsyNet developed that our student members in particular had a strong interest in figuring out how to meld their political values with their interest in being psychologists. Many had hoped psychology would enable them to make a difference in the world, but were frustrated by the traditional demands of their professors, supervisors, and potential employers. Some said they wished RadPsyNet had existed when they had begun their studies, to help them pick a subspecialty or graduate school with more of a social change focus, or to expose them to the critical literatures that their coursework had omitted.

The two of us realized that critical psychologists needed to try harder to reach students, as well as other psychologists who were not yet established in mainstream careers. Although we had written for mainstream audiences, we realized we had not done enough to get critical perspectives into the hands of students and those others who don't read journals. *Critical Psychology: An Introduction* is an outgrowth of this realization. As Chapter 1 explains in more detail, the book presents an overview of critical psychology for readers with little exposure to critical perspectives. We have tried to produce a book that graduate students and many undergraduates can comprehend. This is the kind of book we wish we could have read when we began our own studies in psychology many years ago.

In addition to students, we think two other audiences will find the book useful as well: working psychologists who wonder about the relevance of critical psychology to their own work, and those who already see themselves as critical psychologists and want to find out what critics are up to in other areas of psychology. By covering a broad range of areas and issues, the book points out connections and common themes that otherwise might be missed in more narrowly targeted (and more complexly written) academic articles.

A point we emphasize in Chapter 1 is that personal values, assumptions, interests, and backgrounds affect the decisions psychologists make about how to go about their work. This is certainly true in our own cases. We each bring a passion and a history to the cause of critical psychology.

For me (*Dennis*), growing up relatively privileged in working-class and middle-class Brooklyn neighbourhoods, I was embarrassingly unaware for many years of social justice issues. When very young I merely accepted the 'fact' that being white, Jewish, and middle-class was better than being black or Hispanic and poor – the only categories of people I encountered with any frequency – just as I knew that being an American and a male was better than being anything else. As I grew a little older, my acceptance of this common-sense knowledge slowly turned to suspicion. I remember John F. Kennedy's call to young people to think beyond themselves, the fear of annihilation as we practised nuclear survival techniques in school, the murders of early civil rights workers. As a teenager, I embraced the call of socialist Zionists trying to create collective settlements in Israel based on humanistic, egalitarian principles while seeking to avoid oppressing Palestinians. Over time my Zionism faded, but I remained forever aware of how difficult it is to sort out conflicting values and interests. I also remained influenced by my experiences on Israeli kibbutzim. The kibbutz system's utopian vision – the commitment to working toward a fundamentally better world even while knowing the effort can never fully succeed – inspired my later efforts in an array of social movements opposing varying forms of elite power. It directed much of my writing and teaching in psychology and, more recently, in interdisciplinary legal studies. And it led me to suggest to Isaac that we organize the Radical Psychology Network. Today, I struggle in my different roles of activist, professor, father, and husband to avoid the complacency all too common in middle age, like Isaac trying to resolve issues about my own power and hypocrisy despite my inevitably limited vision, capabilities, and sensitivities.

For me (*Isaac*), wanting to be a critical psychologist has also a lot to do with personal background. Argentina is a good place to develop a social conscience. Israel, in turn, is a wonderful place to feel torn between values of self-determination and justice. That's where I grew up, worlds apart. Canada, on the other hand, is a great place to experience privilege. That's where I'm growing old. Places and personal history fuse to propel ideals and projects. Dictatorships and disappearances in Argentina made injustice and impunity very palpable, whereas living in Israel forced me to struggle with dual national identities: oppressed and oppressor. Settling in Canada sharpened the contrast between 'first' and 'third' worlds – galaxies apart. As a Jewish child in Argentina, others made sure I wouldn't feel welcome there for too long, while as an immigrant in Canada I could sympathize with other immigrants who, like me, were not always welcome. But the sensitizing effect of these experiences is sometimes forgotten amidst instances of privilege. I am aware of the privileges I have by virtue of my education. As a professor, I am aware of the power I have over students. As a father, I am aware of the control I have over my son. As a community psychologist, I realize the influence I have in community settings. But much as I would like this awareness to prevent me from abusing power, I don't always reach the level of integrity I expect of myself and others, a realization that humbles me every time I have the courage to face it. But there is no escape from questioning my own morality, a painful exercise at the best of times. I believe in disclosing hypocrisy. Professionals and governments who profess honorable values but act in oppressive ways are dangerous because they hide their own interests under a veil of self-righteousness. I see my work in critical psychology as helping to unveil hypocrisy in relationships, in the profession, in public life – and in myself.

Our backgrounds and values are reflected in the choices we made in organizing and editing this book, choices we describe in Chapter 1. When we first discussed editing a book, others warned us about a variety of potential pitfalls. It would stretch the imagination too far to claim we never encountered any. Anyone who has ever edited a book will know that not every deadline was met and not every request for revisions was warmly received. But we did avoid serious complications. And despite the inevitable hassles of editing (and while learning a few things we might do differently next time!), we are pleased that this book serves the purpose we initially proposed: to expose the unholy alliance between psychology and social norms that benefit the powerful and harm the powerless, and to offer emancipatory alternatives. We are especially pleased that our own friendship has not only withstood our occasional disagreements and differing styles but has actually deepened throughout the process of working together.

We could not produce the book we wanted without the help of many others. We owe the most to the authors who wrote the individual chapters, not only for what they wrote but also for their enthusiastic response to our original proposal and for their continued cooperation and suggestions. Most of the authors have written or edited their own books, and we especially appreciate their tolerance of our sometimes clumsy efforts to keep things on track. All the authors wrote two or more drafts of their own chapters, taking into account our picky requests for revisions with almost universal good grace. We thank even the ones who gave us a hard time.

Ziyad Marar's enthusiasm was the primary factor that led us to choose Sage as our publisher. His instant agreement that such a book was needed confirmed our own somewhat-biased assessment and led to a congenial working arrangement. The assistance of Lucy Robinson, Kiren Shoman, and Jackie Griffin at Sage made working with a publisher an ocean away much less of a problem than it might have been. At Wilfrid Laurier University in Canada, we'd like to thank Linda Potter, Administrative Assistant at the Department of Psychology, for her help with manuscript preparation.

We acknowledge the financial support of the University of Illinois at Springfield, which (when it was still called Sangamon State University) allowed Dennis the time to work with Isaac on the book proposal. More crucially, the university provided a sabbatical leave that allowed Dennis to work on the book full-time for a full academic year.

To ensure that the book would be understandable, we asked several students to read the individual chapters and identify material that was unclear, repetitious, or in other ways in need of revision. Stephanie Campbell, Milo Fox, and James Taylor gave us excellent feedback, which we incorporated in the revisions we asked the chapter authors to make. We especially admire the students' willingness to tell us when they didn't understand something we ourselves had written, forcing us to look at our words anew. That some portions of this book remain difficult to read is a result of our not always following their suggestions.

We are also indebted to our spouses, Elizabeth Caddick and Ora Prilleltensky, for reading and commenting on never-ending chapter drafts and other material. Most of all, we thank them for allowing us to share with them the pains and excitements associated with this project. It's not possible to focus intently on an undertaking of this magnitude without inconveniencing families in many ways. So we are grateful that our partners were willing to put up with our schedules, our obsessions, and our lives in front of the computer screen – and grateful that they sometimes made us stop.

This book seeks a better world. We dedicate it to our children, who could use a better world. Observing the older ones already out in the world, Avram Safran Fox and Milo Safran Fox, reminds us that we have not yet found the solutions we were already seeking when they were young. Interacting daily with the young ones at home, Emily June Fox Caddick and Matan Prilleltensky, renews our commitment to keep on trying.

Dennis Fox
Isaac Prilleltensky

1996

Part 1

Critical Overviews

1

Critical Psychology for Social Justice: Concerns and Dilemmas

Dennis Fox, Isaac Prilleltensky,
and Stephanie Austin

Critical Psychology: An Introduction presents an array of approaches that challenge mainstream psychology in fundamental ways. By **mainstream psychology** we mean the psychology that universities most often teach and that clinicians, researchers, and consultants most often practise. It is the psychology you probably studied in your introductory course, presented as a science whose researchers use objective methods to understand human behaviour and whose practitioners help individuals cope with distress. Building on their research findings, mainstream psychologists who recognize the societal sources of that distress sometimes propose institutional reforms to help people function more effectively. In short, most psychologists expect to do good. And often they do. Critical psychologists, in contrast, see things very differently. We believe that mainstream psychology has institutionalized a narrow view of the field's ethical mandate to promote human welfare. That narrowness leads to many negative consequences, as this book elaborates in some detail.

As we see it, the minor reforms to smooth out society's rough edges that mainstream psychologists most often endorse simply don't go far enough. Dominant cultural, economic, and political institutions exhibit two fundamental problems especially relevant to psychology: they misdirect efforts to live a fulfilling life and they foster inequality and oppression. What concerns us as psychologists is that these institutions routinely use psychological knowledge and techniques to maintain an unacceptable status quo. Instead of exposing and opposing this use, however, mainstream psychology strengthens it. Its prevailing conceptions of human needs and values and its image of scientific objectivity too readily accommodate harmful institutional power. Furthermore, as a powerful institution in its own right, psychology generates its own harmful consequences that fall particularly hard on those who are oppressed and vulnerable. Instead of tinkering with the edges, thus, critical psychologists from a variety of critical traditions advocate not just minor reform but fundamentally different social structures more likely to lead to social justice and human wellbeing. We imagine and explore alternatives. We think psychology can do better.

We also know firsthand how uncomfortable it can be to read criticism of values, assumptions, and practices that we think are basically sound. Mainstream psychology courses typically do not scrutinize in any serious way the social, moral, and political implications of research, theory, and practice. Partly because **critical psychology** rejects the underlying perspectives taught in those courses, our critique might strike you as 'too political' or 'ideological'. Unfortunately, psychology's fragmentation and overspecialization reduce exposure to fields such as political theory, sociology, and anthropology that more often explore critiques of the status quo. Students planning to work as psychologists and psychologists already in practice may misinterpret as a personal attack our critique of the system. As critical psychologists see it, however, justifications for our own roles within that system sometimes reflect political or ideological values too often left unexamined.

You will discover in the chapters ahead that, despite our overlapping analyses, suspicions, generalizations, and conclusions, critical psychologists do not know all the answers. You will also discover that most of us occupy traditional professional roles as therapists, researchers, evaluators, consultants, teachers, students, or advocates. What makes us different, or so we like to think, is our effort to raise questions about what we and others are doing. We want to be agents of social change, not agents of social control. We move ahead despite knowing that we cannot always succeed, or be entirely consistent, or even always know for sure what success might look like.

Reflecting our varied backgrounds and interests, critical psychology's intersecting approaches differ from one another in philosophical justification, methodological preference, political strategy, favoured terminology, and ultimate priority. It would not be too far off the mark to talk about a range of critical psychologies rather than a single approach. To make this even more confusing, many critical psychologists do not even use the term critical psychology, and sometimes psychologists do important work that advances progressive aims despite being steeped in mainstream assumptions and methods. That's why, when inviting colleagues to contribute to this second edition of *Critical Psychology: An Introduction*, we did not insist upon a single perspective. We focused instead on central themes that are common to a variety of critical traditions: pursuing social justice, promoting the welfare of communities in general and oppressed groups in particular, and transforming the status quo of both society and psychology.

In the remainder of this chapter, we first introduce core concepts related to critical psychology's central concerns and internal dilemmas. We then explain how the rest of the book explores these concerns and dilemmas in greater depth.

central concerns and relevant core concepts

We have already touched on three interrelated concerns drawing significant critical psychology attention, which we can summarize loosely as follows:

1 by focusing on the individual rather than the group and larger society, mainstream psychology overemphasizes individualistic values, hinders the attainment of mutuality and community, and strengthens unjust institutions;

2 mainstream psychology's underlying assumptions and institutional allegiances disproportionately hurt members of powerless and marginalized groups by facilitating inequality and oppression; and

3 these unacceptable outcomes occur regardless of psychologists' individual or collective intentions to the contrary.

In this section we describe these concerns in more organized fashion. In the process, we explain the relevance of three central concepts: mainstream psychology's restricted **level of analysis**; the role of **ideology** in strengthening the status quo; and psychology's false claim to *scientific objectivity and political neutrality*. Although these are not the only relevant concepts, they are the ones you will encounter throughout this book.

individualism and meaninglessness: the level of analysis

In every society, economic, educational, religious, and other institutions inculcate into their members preferred views of human nature and social order. Those views, and the institutions they support, vary from society to society much more widely than we often realize. The enormous normative diversity among the world's thousands of historical and currently existing cultures often astonishes people who grew up assuming their own beliefs and preferences represented 'normality'. In contrast to anthropologists, whose field most directly studies the world's diverse behaviours, institutions, and power arrangements, psychologists too often forget that many of the behaviours they and others around them engage in every day reflect culture and history rather than universal inevitability. Thomas Teo notes in Chapter 3 that mainstream psychology shows little awareness of psychological perspectives from other cultural traditions, or that Western psychology itself is a 'local psychology' – or, as Ingrid Huygens puts it in her discussion of colonization, an 'indigenous psychology' (Chapter 16). 'No culture has all the answers', Tod Sloan adds, 'but our theories ... should at least not universalize the values of the culture from which they arise' (Chapter 19).

Despite globalization's expansion and corporate efforts to homogenize human experience, it is important to keep in mind that traditional Eastern cultures do not share the West's dominant individualistic underpinnings, and that colonizers trumpeting individualist, nationalist, Christian, and capitalist values have routinely dominated and decimated indigenous cultures. Knowing that our values reflect our own cultural assumptions, critical psychologists pay particular attention to dominant institutions in Westernized societies – the societies within which most psychologists live and work and mainstream psychology developed. From childrearing advice and school curricula, to work and consumption, to media coverage and political decision making, these institutions encourage people to seek identity and meaning through individual and competitive pursuits instead of through collaborative or community endeavours. Watching television and surfing the Internet, advancing in careers, keeping the lawn green, and shopping for fun are only some of the things many people do that divert attention and energy from constructing more meaningful friendships, participating in community life, or recognizing and working to end injustice. It is no coincidence that a self-focused mindset offers more benefits to those who control corporate capitalism and other members of relatively privileged groups than to the vast numbers who congregate in shopping malls and football stadiums or search for anonymous on-line community.

That mainstream psychology's Westernized, individualistic worldview accepts and even endorses isolating, self-focused endeavours has not gone unnoticed. A surprisingly large literature explores the serious consequences (for a sampling of perspectives in the psychological literature, see Bakan, 1966; I. Prilleltensky, 1994; Sarason, 1981; Teo, 2005). Of particular concern is that an individualistic worldview hinders mutuality, connectedness, and a psychological sense of community, partly by leading people to believe that these are either unattainable or unimportant (Fox, 1985; Sarason, 1974). It also blinds people to the impact of their actions and lifestyles on others who remain oppressed, on the environment, and even on families and friends. Overall, psychologists fit too comfortably within a capitalist democratic system that gives lip service to both individual freedom and political equality but in practice prefers political apathy and the freedom of the market over participatory democracy and distributive justice (Baritz, 1974; Fox, 1985, 1996; Pilgrim, 1992).

Psychology's embeddedness in capitalism, Teo suggests (Chapter 3), conflicts with its potential as an emancipatory science. Capitalism is not the only destructive force at play in the world, but its assumptions are perhaps the most dependent on an individualistic worldview that sees economic class as a natural rather than constructed state of affairs (see Heather Bullock and Wendy Limbert's Chapter 13). Of course, mainstream psychologists defend their field's individualistic orientation by defining psychology as the study of individuals, contrasting it with disciplines such as sociology and anthropology that examine larger groups. Although this explanation seems reasonable, it oversimplifies. Psychologists trying to make sense of why an individual behaves in a certain manner, holds certain views, or seeks certain goals inevitably confront the direct and indirect impact of other people. But even mainstream social psychology, the traditional discipline most likely to address interaction and social context, has become increasingly individualistic, as Frances Cherry recounts in Chapter 6.

Imagine a therapist whose client suffers from the kind of 'work stress' Jeanne Marecek and Rachel Hare-Mustin describe in their critical discussion of clinical psychology (Chapter 5). Should the clinician investigate the client's long-term psychological difficulties? Teach stress-management techniques? Try to change the stressful job situation or advise the client to get a new job? The psychologist offering therapy (or teaching students about this topic, or conducting research on it) might consider a number of factors, one of which – an important one – is the therapeutic setting's constraints. Is the psychologist in private practice helping an upper-management professional cope with subordinates? Does she or he work at a clinic, providing therapy for an overloaded working-class secretary with relatively few options? Or at a factory, hired by corporate management to make sure workers keep up the pace?

Different roles lead to different interpretations of the problem and, as Scot Evans and Colleen Loomis emphasize in Chapter 22, different problem interpretations lead to different kinds of solutions. Evans and Loomis pay particular attention to the relevant level of analysis, as do Bullock and Limbert in their discussion of social class (Chapter 13). Thus, in the case of our stressed-out client, a critical therapist might step back from the client's individual personality and habits (the *individual level of analysis*) and even from the specific work setting (the *situational or interpersonal level*) to consider the *societal level of analysis*. Gazi Islam and Michael Zyphur point out in their discussion of industrial/organizational psychology (Chapter 7) that treating work stress as a medical problem means solutions focus on individual rather than systems change. Learning to relax or finding a less-stressful job, even when successful, does nothing to change the system generating so much stress to begin with. Individual therapy may still be warranted; Isaac Prilleltensky, Ora Prilleltensky, and Courte Voorhees describe in Chapter 21 how critically minded therapists can adopt approaches less restricted by mainstream assumptions. But the critical psychologist simultaneously aims higher, at the level of community change Evans and Loomis describe and at broader political efforts such as those which Vicky Steinitz and Elliot Mishler describe (Chapter 23), among others.

George Albee (1990) pointed out the absurdity of defining as 'individual' any problem that confronts thousands and even millions of people. Beyond the absurdity lies 'blame-the-victim' politics (Ryan, 1971). Blaming individuals for their widely shared problems and legitimizing only individual solutions such as therapy, education, or stress-management training makes people less likely to advocate social change. Psychology's reconfiguration of social problems into psychic maladies thus reinforces the conservative notion that there's no need to change the system when you can change the person instead (Fox, 1985; I. Prilleltensky, 1994; Teo, 2005).

Because it is so far-reaching, the implications of psychology's individualistic worldview are especially relevant to some of the field's subdisciplines; so are other concerns and concepts introduced in this chapter such as ideology and the appropriate level of analysis. Some of this book's contributors, thus, describe how mainstream and critical psychologists bring different assumptions and methods to particular areas of interest. These include personality theories (Tod Sloan, Chapter 4); clinical psychology (Jeanne Marecek and Rachel Hare-Mustin, Chapter 5); social psychology (Frances Cherry, Chapter 6); industrial–organizational psychology (Gazi Islam and Michael Zyphur, Chapter 7); community psychology (Isaac Prilleltensky and Geoffrey Nelson, Chapter 8); health psychology (Kerry Chamberlain and Michael Murray, Chapter 9); and psychology and the law (Bruce Arrigo and Dennis Fox, Chapter 10). Unfortunately, there was not enough room to include other disciplines that appeared in the first edition (Fox and Prilleltensky, 1997): developmental psychology, intelligence testing, crosscultural psychology, political psychology, lesbian and gay psychology, and ethics in psychology.

inequality and oppression: the role of ideology

Critical psychologists understand that overemphasizing values related to individualism and competitiveness disproportionately hurts members of relatively powerless groups. Equally damaging is the assumption that what's good for the Westernized world is best for everyone, a point Huygens emphasizes in discussing representative democracy's oppressive impact on indigenous cultures (Chapter 16). Modern nation-states, especially those describing themselves as democracies, formally guarantee political and legal equality, but political, legal, and economic power are not equally divided. Thus, critical psychologists explore mainstream psychology's participation in maintaining disadvantage and oppression on the basis of obvious categories such as race (Kevin Durrheim, Derek Hook, and Damien Riggs, Chapter 12); social class (Heather Bullock and Wendy Limbert, Chapter 13); gender (Victoria Clarke and Virginia Braun, Chapter 14); and disability (Ora Prilleltensky, Chapter 15). They also increasingly explore psychology's role in a world shifting from colonization to globalization (Ingrid Huygens, Chapter 16) and in communities emerging from war where mainstream trauma efforts fail to incorporate a focus on human rights and social justice (Brinton Lykes and Erzulie Coquillon, Chapter 17). And as Michael McCubbin explains (Chapter 18), critical psychologists have also begun to examine oppression inside the mental health system that employs so many psychologists.

Sometimes inequality and oppression are obvious, making these forms of injustice relatively easy to identify and (at least for those at a safe distance) to oppose (see, e.g., Huygens' description of colonizers' imposition of capitalist land ownership on indigenous peoples). Other times they are institutionalized in subtle ways, making it harder both to understand their operation and to combat their presence; that's what happens, for example, when legal systems follow procedurally correct rules that mask substantive injustice (see Arrigo and Fox, in Chapter 10). In either case, dominant individuals and groups maintain their power at the expense of others even when they think their actions are merely 'normal' and 'traditional' rather than unfair or oppressive (I. Prilleltensky, 2008). This normalization assumption complicates efforts to sort our way through complex global issues using our own (culturally derived) sense of universal principles of social justice (e.g., Fox, 2008a; Fox & Prilleltensky, 2002).

Maintaining an unequal social order requires ideological persuasion. *Ideology* has different meanings in different contexts (Prilleltensky & Fox, 2007). Most critical psychologists use the term generally in its traditional Marxist sense, referring to widely disseminated beliefs that political elites call upon to justify an unfair society and thus blunt criticism of the status quo – or, as Sloan puts it in discussing personality theories (Chapter 4), 'ideas or images that sustain unjust social relations'. Some ideological beliefs eventually fade away; today it is hard to imagine ordinary people accepting the notion that kings rule by divine right. Other beliefs persist, however, and new ones come into play. For example, institutional power still relies upon widespread ideological assumptions that are often social psychological in nature – for example, that people generally get what they deserve and thus people are poor because they don't work hard; that a capitalist economic system is best because human beings are inherently selfish and competitive; and that the government always goes to war for good reasons. While not universal, agreement with the dominant ideology's institutionalized beliefs represents what many critics consider *false consciousness*, a Marxist term referring to widespread acceptance of inaccurate ideological beliefs (see Chapter 4). By teaching that the source of most oppression and inequality is individual or interpersonal rather than societal and political – 'bad apples' rather than a 'bad system' – institutions such as schools, religious bodies, courts, political parties, and the media deflect movements for social change. Most authors in this book emphasize the role of ideology in this sense.

Some writers use the term more broadly. Over time, ideology became associated in public discourse with any statement having critical political overtones, ironically allowing those defending the status quo to dismiss as 'ideological' challenges from the left end of the political spectrum. Mainstream social psychologists and other social scientists broadened the meaning even further to refer to any system of beliefs and values as a synonym for a general worldview. This even-handed, depoliticized usage, according to which everyone 'has' an ideology, can make any strong beliefs seem somewhat suspect, thus reinforcing the notion that only those in the conventional middle see things clearly (Fox, 2008a). Of course, making claims such as these frequently brings accusations from mainstream psychologists that our criticisms are ideological, and thus somehow suspect and illegitimate. In our view, the mainstream's focus on individualism is itself ideological. Indeed, the emergence at the end of the twentieth century of a 'positive psychology' that completely disregards critiques of individualizing social problems illustrates the dominant ideology's continuing strength (Pawelski & Prilleltensky, 2005).

A primary goal of critical psychology, accordingly, is to identify and reveal ideological messages and related practices that direct our attention away from the sources of elite power and privilege. According to Michel Foucault (1980), whose influential work many of this book's contributors cite, we need to understand power relations to determine morality. And because power does not reside in social structures alone, we must also explore more fluid non-institutional forms of power. The capitalist's power over the labourer is but one form. Power also resides in interpersonal exchanges, in daily acts of resistance, and in the very language we use, including how we draw a line between personal and social phenomena (see Hepburn and Jackson's discussion of discursive psychology in Chapter 11). Throughout this book, thus, you will see contributors discuss various methods of consciousness raising, often referring to the work of Brazilian educator Paulo Freire (1970). Freire's emphasis on developing *critical consciousness* has had an enormous impact in helping the oppressed break through the ideological defenses of the status quo and identify the source of their oppression.

_____ *intention and consequence: the trap of neutrality* _____

Many psychologists are motivated by positive values and political commitments to study psychology in the first place. True, some knowingly use their professional skills and status to help elite segments of society retain control. Steinitz and Mishler (Chapter 23) describe one such instance: psychologists' participation in interrogation techniques using torture. But, as Ben Harris especially emphasizes (Chapter 2), even though psychology has been used repressively, many psychologists have embraced its liberatory potential. The problem, as noted above, is that too many psychologists identify their task in overly narrow terms: helping clients on an individual basis or increasing scientific knowledge about traditionally framed topics using traditional research practices. Many support relatively minor reforms they consider 'responsible' and 'practical', while their professional associations increasingly enter the political arena to advocate particular public policies (Herman, 1995), generally consistent with liberal-to-moderate political reform (Fox, 1993b).

Bullock and Limbert point out that mainstream psychologists have not yet embraced *reflexivity*, a conscious exploration of how our own values and assumptions affect our theoretical and methodological goals, activities, and interpretations. Instead, they conform to professional norms portraying psychology as an objective science, neutral in values and politics. Psychology's main policy job, according to those norms, is to provide impartial scientific knowledge for a rock-no-boats, data-hungry public. This emphasis on data rather than on values and power (itself a value preference, as Teo points out) leads in conventional rather than system-challenging directions. Professional status and job demands, narrow preferences of granting agencies, external political pressures and commitments, and the hope that policy makers will actually pay attention to our research channel psychologists away from topics and conclusions that might shake things up.

Psychology shares this establishment orientation with professions such as education, law, and medicine. Norms typically reflect the values, assumptions, and interests of older middle- and upper-class professionals, particularly (still) those who are white and male. As in any professional field, advanced training transforms would-be do-gooders into cautious professionals who internalize the field's substantive, social, and political limits (Schmidt, 2000). Teaching what is legitimate and what is not, it restricts more far-reaching ideals. It directs students toward easily manageable research projects consisting all too often of trivial variations of past work unlikely to advance either significant scientific knowledge or transformative social justice. And so, as we shift the gaze from intentions to more important consequences, we ask a number of questions: Does a mainstream stance mislead people – both psychologists and the general public – into identifying systemic problems as purely individual? Does restricting interventions to those that are manageable – and fundable – within professionally convenient timeframes hinder more significant possibilities? Does failing to pursue more fundamental solutions discourage work toward more transformative change and thus become a self-fulfilling prophecy?

In comparison with fields such as anthropology, sociology, history, and even law, psychology is especially resistant to acknowledging that social science is neither neutral nor value free (Rein, 1976). By reshaping their account of psychology's history, Harris tells us (Chapter 2), mainstream courses make it seem as if psychological questions are always answered purely logically. But we know that personal, professional, and political biases affect which research questions we ask, which methodology we use, which conclusions we reach, and which policy recommendations we advocate (see Wendy Stainton Rogers' methodology discussion in Chapter 20). Hiding those choices to match an objective and neutral pose rather than acknowledging them leads to political timidity. The pro forma phrase researchers commonly append to published articles – 'more research needs to be done' – implies that no question can ever be resolved. After all, we don't yet have enough data! And we never will!

central dilemmas

The world of critical psychology is larger and more diversified than it was a dozen years ago when this book's first edition appeared. As you might expect given its identity as a critical alternative, that world remains largely distant from mainstream psychology's core. Despite this marginality, though, there is more room today than in the past for critical psychology scholarship, critical psychology education, and even critical psychology practice. New books (including many written by this book's contributors) explore various arenas of the expanding terrain. Other indications of critical psychology's growth range from conferences, journals, and courses to organizations, websites, and blogs. Although most critical psychologists still find themselves relatively isolated within traditional institutions and most psychology students have trouble finding professors who appreciate, or even know about, critical psychology, the field's expansion makes us less lonely on the national, inter-national, and virtual levels. A special issue of the *Annual Review of Critical Psychology* describes developments in many parts of the world (Dafermos, Marvakis & Triliva, 2006).

This expansion also has a practical downside: increased theoretical and methodological diversity makes critical psychology somewhat more confusing than it seemed not so long ago. There are overlapping and competing notions of what critical psychology is about and what it should be about (directly addressed, for example, by Teo in Chapter 3 and Cherry in Chapter 6). Some notions are especially conducive to exploring particular concerns. For example, some of psychology's discriminatory norms are easier to grasp when focusing on issues of sex and gender, making a feminist analysis particularly fitting. At the same time, neo-Marxism is more directly relevant to issues of economic class and power. This book's 35 contributors refer to these and other intellectual traditions: German critical psychology, Latin American liberation psychology, social constructionism, discursive psychology, postmodernism, anarchism, critical race theory, and more. All find a place within critical psychology to the extent that they aim to eliminate oppression and promote social justice. But the multiplicity of approaches and jargons does make it harder to keep track of the terrain.

It also contributes to a number of dilemmas. Today, less often defining our work simply by its departure from traditional norms, critical psychologists more often wrestle with competing positions. From the theoretical and methodological to the political and personal, our choices come into sharper relief. Some of these choices divide psychologists more generally, differing from one another as they do, for example, about whether human beings are primarily rational or irrational. Other dilemmas concern critical psychologists more directly, such as whether – despite our suspicion of psychology's claimed scientific authority – we should use our professional status to boost our credi-bility. For both sorts of dilemmas, no single answer satisfies critical psychology as a whole. As individuals working in critical psychology, as a group of profes-sionals engaged in a discipline, and as members of the flawed societies we are working to change, we each must sort out just what needs to be done.

In trying to get a sense of what brings people to critical psychology, Sloan (2000) asked 20 critical psychologists to reflect on their background as well as on their sense of the field. Among other things, he asked 'What are the big debates in critical psychology? What issues remain to be resolved?' In this section we build on our own answers to that question (Fox, 2000; I. Prilleltensky, 2000) as well as on Austin and Prilleltensky's more systematic (2001) approach and on important work by other scholars (e.g., Hepburn, 2003). We loosely divide our dilemmas into the two overlapping categories noted above: *the nature of human nature*, consisting primarily of choices facing psychologists in general; and *the scope of social change and political action*, a topic particularly important to critical psychologists. Many of this book's contributors address one or more of these dilemmas, sometimes explicitly but other times just beneath the surface.

_____ *the nature of human nature* _____

After describing how critical psychologists 'do theory', Tod Sloan asks this:

> **What sorts of assumptions about psyche and society would best guide critical theorizing? What common assumptions are problematic? What positions on the old questions – such as free will vs. determinism, nature vs. nurture, conscious-ness vs. unconscious forces – are most appropriate for critical psychology? What new questions will need to be addressed? (Chapter 19)**

As you can see, we have questions, but no answers as yet!

One of critical psychology's key distinguishing assumptions is that our subjectivity, our psychological world, is deeply embedded in our culture and social practices. Our wants, needs and desires reflect the norms and expecta-tions we absorb as members of a particular tribe, group or community. Awareness of this embeddedness helps explain why we reject mainstream psychology's exclusive focus on the individual and interpersonal levels of analysis and also raise our sights to the societal level.

This awareness also leads us toward reflexive exploration of our own wants, needs, and desires. Which flow from our inner self, if such a self exists, and from a culture that, strictly speaking, does not exist outside ourselves but that we and other members of society have created? And although we emphasize the individual's socially embedded nature, we also see – and we seek to strengthen – sparks of agency and resistance that allow us to change our personal lives and communities. Critical psychologists struggle to locate themselves within this dialectic between determinism and free will (Teo, 2005).

Again like mainstream psychologists, critical psychologists also manoeuvre between the conflicting legacies of the hyper-rational person resembling a computer and the thoroughly irrational being modelled on Freudian concep-tions. A rational person, at least according to mainstream economic theory and certain psychological perspectives, makes decisions based purely on a logical calculation of the costs and benefits. An irrational person, on the other hand, acts by passion and instinct. Subjectively we know we have both tendencies, but we also know that subjectivity can lead us astray.

As noted in Sloan's discussions of theory and Arrigo and Fox's chapter on psychology's intersection with the law, some critical psychologists use aspects of psychoanalysis to inform our understanding of subjectivity and rationality (e.g., Oliver, 2004; Parker, 1997). The concepts of the conscious and the unconscious can help explain how cultural injunctions traverse the individual-society nexus. And they raise questions: If unconscious forces drive our social, ethical, and political behaviour, do our attempts to be helpful or to advocate social change simply indicate a stratagem to gain praise and recognition or some other unconscious urge? Are our political commitments nothing more than selfish and irrational pursuits? Yet, even if this is so, what is the alternative? Deconstructing the human experience, interpreting it according to abstract models, risks stripping our existence of meaning. It also makes social change less likely.

_____ *the scope of social change and political action* _____

Victoria Clarke and Virginia Braun remind us that social change is not a primary goal of all critical psychologists (Chapter 14). Kerry Chamberlain and Michael Murray, noting disagreement about whether critical health psychology 'should focus on revealing disparity and disadvantage or on changing it' (Chapter 9), point out that narrative and discursive research emphasize the former and action research the latter (Alexa Hepburn and Clare Jackson describe discursive psychology in Chapter 11). Despite this political diversity, we think it fair to say that most critical psychologists believe something is fundamentally wrong with a discipline that not only fails to challenge unjust societal practices but actually reinforces them, and something is foundationally wrong with social systems that exclude, alienate, and oppress masses of people. The internal debate in critical psychology is not so much whether social change is needed but what level of change to seek and how to bring that change about. Positions on this issue reflect a confluence of influences from the political and personal to the professional and pragmatic.

A conscious reflexive stance reminds us that the surrounding environment affects what we do. That environment includes the traditional academic settings that employ most self-defined critical psychologists. Academia offers a number of advantages, not just practical benefits such as professional status, schedule flexibility, and opportunities for travel but also the important norm that intellectual exploration is part of the job. Our generally comfortable and privileged work environment, however, imposes a variety of formal and informal limits, some of which lead to what Huygens refers to as academia's 'political defeatism' (Chapter 16). These limits especially constrain graduate students looking for jobs and untenured faculty hoping to keep the jobs they have. Both know that remaining in academia, especially in mainstream institutions, requires more than just showing up on time and doing good work.

As is true for jobs in hierarchical settings more generally, it also means pleasing administrators and senior professors. That's a difficult enough task for academics who accept institutional norms, particularly in an era when cost-cutting universities hire part-time faculty to replace full-timers. The task is even more difficult for critical scholars whose work criticizes, implicitly and often explicitly, academic norms in general and their own institution in particular. Critical psychologists who challenge the research, values, and politics of those in their departments and in their administration who have the power to hire and fire often put themselves at professional risk. (Dennis Fox addresses some of these concerns in this book's concluding collection of frequently asked questions.)

Constraints such as these contribute to two kinds of interrelated dilemmas, one personal and one political. The personal dilemma is that academics have more career incentives to write the next article or obtain the next grant than to work more directly for social change. As is true much more widely within the larger society, time-consuming and often stressful work – job-hunting, job-advancement, and just doing a good job – does not leave much room for the political activism most critical psychologists endorse. Beyond the time overload is the pressure to demonstrate a professional focus. Senior professors sometimes advise graduate students not to spend much time teaching, which takes time away from more valued career-advancing research and publishing. Some tell younger colleagues that political or community involvement will hurt their job prospects.

Given all this, it can be tempting to decide that our most important contribution is writing books that identify problems for others to solve. Academia's heart, after all, is intellectual, not activist. And as Teo (2005) noted, deconstructing the present state of affairs and offering visions for a better one both fall within the critical tradition. Still, most of us try to find some workable balance between theory and action, between critiquing the world and trying to change it. Teo points out in Chapter 3 that, although increasing knowledge is a legitimate form of action, 'theorizing for the sake of theorizing and research for the sake of research must be considered indulgent practices given that lives and deaths are at stake'.

So we try to merge our critical politics with our professional work, sometimes doing the sorts of politically relevant research and intervention illustrated throughout this book. But adopting a critical methodology as Stainton Rogers describes in Chapter 20 is easier in some subdisciplines than others. For example, the nature of community psychology makes it particularly conducive to approaches such as community-based participatory action research (see, e.g., Chapters 8, 17, and 22).

Contributing to the academic's dilemma is the trap of neutrality we discussed earlier: adapting to mainstream psychology's neutral apolitical persona and believing we need more research before we can advocate significant change. It makes sense to understand the existing system's flaws before we advocate something new. On the other hand, our existing societies have so many flaws we could spend a lifetime dissecting them. As one of us noted elsewhere, 'Awareness is Good, but Action is Better' (Fox, 2003).

The second dilemma, generated partly by our academic environment but also reflecting broader issues of political philosophy and strategy, is determining the level of appropriate action. As Prilleltensky and Nelson note (Chapter 8), and as reflected in many other chapters, there is an important distinction between *ameliorative* practices – for example, those that tend to the wounded, care for the disabled, and treat the infirm – and *transformative* practices that aim instead to change systems that wound and marginalize so many in the first place. Critical psychologists accuse mainstream psychology of being almost exclusively ameliorative, focusing on therapy for the distressed, policy research aimed at minor reform, and similar limited-horizon endeavours. Given these criticisms, should critical psychologists abandon the ameliorative realm and only embrace more far-reaching transformation? In practice, it's not always easy to identify transformative efforts, or to determine what role we might play within them (see Steinitz and Mishler's related discussion of the politics of resistance). We don't always agree among ourselves, for example, whether a particular project is truly transformative or merely ameliorative at a higher level. It does seem clear that, at least in the short-term, amelioration most quickly helps those in need even if that help is more limited than psychology's emancipatory or liberatory potential might envision. Even conditions less dire than the kind Lykes and Coquillon address in communities emerging from war (Chapter 17) demand a practical response.

Describing critical psychology's philosophical terrain, Teo notes that 'in critical thought one can find ethical–political orientations that range from left-liberal progressive to radical' (Chapter 3). A number of this book's authors, falling along different points of this continuum, address the resulting political dilemma. Some describe how traditional research methods firmly embedded in mainstream psychology's **positivist** worldview have helped marginalized or oppressed people in significant ways (e.g., Ora Prilleltensky's chapter on disability, Cherry's on social psychology). Indeed, Ignacio Martín-Baró (1994), whose development of liberation psychology many contributors point to as a model, used traditional survey methods to advance liberation. Can we call these crucial efforts 'critical'? Does critical psychology's focus on 'transformative change' going to 'the root of the problem' place it only at the radical end of the political spectrum, or can political liberals and progressives who seek pragmatic reforms also be 'critical'? If so, how might we distinguish them from their progressive but 'non-critical' peers?

Perhaps there is more distance than we sometimes like to think between a theoretically, methodologically, and politically consistent 'critical psychology' and a messier, more inconsistent 'psychology of social justice'. In Chapter 2, Ben Harris uses perceptions and misperceptions about the history of psychology to remind us that dichotomous thinking can lead even critical psychologists astray. Definitions are tricky. Our dilemmas persist.

Part 1 of *Critical Psychology: An Introduction*, **Critical Overviews**, continues with two more chapters. The first offers pointers on how to read the history of mainstream psychology; the second introduces critical psychology's basic philosophical concepts, many of which return in several guises throughout the book. Part 2, **Critical Disciplines**, describes in some detail the place of critical psychology in eight specific subfields. These chapters highlight varying critiques of the mainstream approaches you may have encountered in traditional courses and alternative approaches appropriate to each subdiscipline. In Part 3, **Critical Social Issues**, seven chapters explore arenas for social action motivating significant work in critical psychology across a range of subdisciplines. The five chapters in Part 4, **Critical Practice**, explore how psychologists go about their daily work as theoreticians, researchers, practitioners, community change agents, and political activists.

The 23 chapters complement one another as they answer our primary question: How can psychology foster emancipation, social justice, and social change? Each presents a different piece of the puzzle or a different way of looking at the whole picture. Some examine broad themes running through psychology as a whole, others a relatively narrow segment. The book's structure enables professors to assign it either as a supplemental text in mainstream courses or as a main text in critical psychology courses. The chapters cover traditional subject areas, so that readers looking for material applicable to specific courses can easily locate relevant information. This organizational system does have a disadvantage, however: it maintains distinctions among different areas of psychology that critical psychologists insist are artificial. Disciplinary boundaries that seem distinct on paper make it difficult to see real connections among different areas, such as between social psychology and clinical psychology, or between methods and theory. That is why you will see different authors address common themes using slightly different lenses.

No chapter can describe all the meaningful critical work that has preceded us. In this new edition, every chapter ends with a short summary, a glossary of important terms, suggested readings and Internet resources, and questions for discussion. The reading suggestions point you to larger literatures, more detailed discussions, and fascinating tangents. You should also keep in mind that there was not enough room to include chapters on every subdiscipline and every issue. To expand this edition's scope to critical social issues and critical practice, we had to leave behind chapter-length coverage of important topics that appeared in the first edition. Some of those topics are addressed elsewhere in this book, but for others we urge you to locate a used first edition (Fox & Prilleltensky, 1997).

We know that delving into new literatures marked by sometimes confusing and unfamiliar language can be intimidating. As scholars working mostly within academic settings, we usually follow academic norms and write for others who expect and even admire academic jargon and styles. Despite our reflexive and critical stance, we develop some bad habits! Still, we have tried throughout this book to limit obscure language, make our sentence structure less imposing, and define key terms. Although we sometimes found it impossible to remove specialized terminology without altering the substance as well, we think you will find this book reasonably accessible.

After a century of manipulating variables in laboratories, the field still has not fundamentally altered the status quo. We need research that can teach us how to transform real societies. We need action. And we need your help.

■ ■ main chapter points ■

1 Critical psychology refers to a number of overlapping approaches that challenge mainstream psychology's implicit and explicit support for an unjust and unsatisfying status quo.

2 Psychology's negative impacts occur despite the good intentions of most psychologists.

3 Central concerns fall into several categories: individualism and meaninglessness; inequality and oppression; and unintended consequences.

4 Central concepts include level of analysis; the role of ideology; and the trap of neutrality.

5 Critical psychologists differ among themselves about a number of dilemmas, which we discuss here in two categories: those facing psychologists in general related to the nature of human nature, and those facing critical psychologists most directly related to the scope of social change.

glossary

- **critical psychology**: a variety of approaches that challenge assumptions, values, and practices within mainstream psychology that help maintain an unjust and unsatisfying status quo.

- **ideology**: generally, a worldview or set of assumptions about how a society works; more strictly, the set of ideas inculcated by dominant sectors of society to justify elite power and the society's established institutions.

- **level of analysis**: the scope of generalization in thinking about relevant behaviours, from the narrowest (individual level) through the middle (interpersonal or situational level) to the broadest (structural or societal level).

- **mainstream psychology**: psychology as practised by the field's dominant professional institutions and its professionals.

- **positivism**: the philosophical position that progress comes only from a logical, objective application of the formal scientific method.

For accounts of critical psychology's development in different countries, see *Critical Psychology in a Changing World*, a special issue of the *Annual Review of Critical Psychology* (Dafermos et al., 2006, online at www.discourseunit.com/arcp/5.htm). Sloan (2000) provides stories by two dozen critical psychologists who relate their personal backgrounds to their perspectives on psychology and social justice. Several introductory texts examine various subfields, e.g. social psychology (Hepburn, 2003; Tuffin, 2004); community psychology (Nelson & Prilleltensky, 2005); health psychology (Murray, 2004). Prilleltensky and Nelson (2002) discuss critical psychology applications to a variety of fields. We also strongly recommend Sampson (1983), Sarason (1981), and Martín-Baró (1994).

; // internet resources /

- **Dennis Fox's Critical Psychology Page** – resources, readings, links, frequently asked questions: dennisfox.net/critpsy/

- **RadPsyNet** – Radical Psychology Network co-founded 1993 by Dennis Fox and Isaac Prilleltensky – includes online *Radical Psychology Journal*: radpsynet.org

 ■ **Questions**

1 How often do mainstream psychology courses address issues raised by critical psychologists? Are most mainstream psychologists familiar with critical psychology?

2 How can psychology help advance social change?

3 Is critical psychology really political activism?

2

What Critical Psychologists Should Know About the History of Psychology

Ben Harris

Chapter Topics

encountering the history of psychology

Most students have two significant encounters with the history of psychology. At the beginning of their studies, students receive a historical introduction. Like a welcoming handshake, teachers use history to usher students into the discipline and convey the seriousness and sincerity of those who work within. Like a quick tour around the lab or shop, a historical overview also marks the field's boundaries and shows which research topics and methods are legitimate and profitable.

Later, those who major in psychology have a second important encounter with history. In a course entitled 'history and systems', students learn about the theoretical disputes that have divided psychologists into warring factions: behaviourists, Gestaltists, phenomenologists, and so on. To study these debates taking place in the nineteenth and early twentieth centuries, students read the no-longer-fashionable writing of figures such as Herman Ebbinghaus, William James, Edward Thorndike, and John Watson. For the critically minded student, exposure to earlier generations' views of psychology has the potential to subvert the ideology of consensus that today's undergraduate courses convey. For the vast majority of students not yet familiar with critical approaches, however, courses in history and systems serve to strengthen, rather than weaken, psychology's dominant paradigm.

For the history of psychology to serve the status quo, it is turned into a narrowly **intellectual history**. Dissociated from national and world events, the history of psychology becomes a history of the intellectual discussions within elite groups such as university professors. Removed from the social world, the discoveries of psychologists are presented as the products of individual inspiration, motivated by a timeless quest for knowledge.

As the traditional history and systems course surveys psychology's roughly 100-year history, students learn how the genius of great psychologists allowed them to design great experiments and construct great theories from the experiments' results (Roback, 1961). When such theories conflict, students are told, the result is a competition for the most scientific accuracy, which is settled on logical rather than ideological or political grounds. If social context is allowed to intrude into this story of psychological discoveries, one or another scientist might be inspired by a social concern to conduct certain experiments. The design and success of those experiments, however, are portrayed as determined by intellectual and logical criteria, rather than by factors such as social class, gender, or politics. There may be reference to a line of research fitting the *Zeitgeist* of the day, but that worldview is said to act through the genius of the individual scientist, in a process resembling telepathy more than social psychology (Schultz, 1969).

_____ *Whiggish history*_____

Implicit in such histories of psychology is the reassuring idea of gradual progress from ignorance to enlightenment. In the language of professional historians, this type of history is 'Whiggish,' 'presentist,' and 'celebratory'. Like political histories written in England when the Whig party was in power, Whiggish histories assume that the current status quo is a preordained result of historical progress. Guided by this false assumption, the Whiggish historian views events according to the values and biases of the present, creating an essentially non-historical, **presentist** view of the past.

Most relevant to critical psychology, Whiggish histories of psychology fail to appreciate the validity of earlier scientific trends if they conflict with today's orthodoxy. Instead of appreciating past versions of psychology by the standards of their time, Whiggish historians categorize them as either helping or hindering the ascendance of currently accepted psychological theories.

The resulting history views the past according to categories that are currently dominant, reinforcing today's orthodoxy and providing its practitioners with a celebratory account of their inevitable rise to power (Samelson, 1974).

Today's cognitive psychologists, for example, may know of Wilhelm Wundt's pioneering research in the late nineteenth century. The real nature of his research is likely to be ignored, however, as the cognitivist focuses on the experiments that seem most familiar or relevant to today. The resulting view ignores Wundt's social psychological and anthropological work, which to him was an essential part of psychology. The resulting, Whiggish perspective is that Wundt was the father of today's cognitivists – robbing him of his wider, more philosophically complex vision (Brock, 1993).

The Whiggish historian also ignores the more egalitarian social relationships in Wundt's laboratory. Unlike today, in the 1880s the roles of designing an experiment and responding to experimental stimuli could be reversed. In those circumstances, treating one class of participant unethically or ignoring their subjectivity – as happens today – would be unthinkable (Danziger, 1990). But today's distinction between subject/participant and experimenter seems so natural that it is projected back into an earlier, and different, era.

Although **Whiggish history** is biased, its authors are usually the last to see this because of their apolitical view of historians and their craft. To them, good historians should avoid developing a viewpoint toward what they study. Instead, they should be able to write an unbiased account – a view from a sort of intellectual heaven.

_____ *Betty Friedan: using history to criticize and create alternatives*____

Despite these conservative historical trends, some students use history to challenge the status quo rather than support it. Such a student was Bettye Goldstein, a psychology major at Smith College in 1938–1942. Later a leading feminist known as Betty Friedan, Goldstein was taught the historical and philosophical underpinnings of various trends in psychology. Her professors were mostly Gestalt psychologists who challenged the mechanistic trends then coming to dominate American psychology. To them, intellectual struggle was normal in young sciences, as different philosophical and methodological approaches vied for supremacy.

Accordingly, Bettye's essays and term papers made heavy use of the history and philosophy of psychology. Consistent with her Marxist political views, she used these to advocate for a more socially informed, socially useful science. In one 33-page paper, she portrayed Lewis Terman and other intelligence testers as methodologically shallow and narrowly hereditarian. Although their work had received much financial support, that did not prove its validity. If this work were not so narrow in its focus, she argued, it would suggest how to improve children's intelligence and it would try to understand the individual child (Goldstein, 1942a).

Turning to clinical psychology in another essay, Goldstein again used history to add a critical viewpoint. Anticipating a theme in *The Feminine Mystique*, she agreed with much of Freudian psychoanalysis. While Freud had great insights, she explained, his ideas were also the product of his era and social setting. The result was a psychology that was overly pessimistic about social change and human fulfillment. As she explained in her term paper:

> **Freud says civilization [and] society conflicts inevitably with man's needs ... I say our society patterns and develops needs which it cannot satisfy and therefore conflict ensues ... ; Our society produces an isolated sharply differentiated ego; our society isolates him, makes him insecure, acquisitive; our society gives him needs that will never be satisfied and gives man a [crippling, unsocialized] super ego ... (Goldstein, 1942b: n.p.)**

Clearly, Bettye Goldstein was not a neutral observer. Consistent with today's critical psychologists, she looked beyond the accepted wisdom of the day. Using an analysis of the past, she was promoting an alternative future. In the words of psychologist Jill Morawski: 'Critical thinking, whether initiated through historical reflection or some other method, enables us to identify what psychological images of human nature are actually perpetuated and marketed, and to contemplate what images are ultimately possible' (1984: 120).

revisionist history of psychology

In her writing about psychoanalysis, Bettye Goldstein was a *revisionist*. That is, she presented a history of Freud and his ideas that *revised* the existing historical viewpoint (e.g., Freud, 1917). To use history to criticize the status quo, one is always a revisionist – challenging the ceremonial history that supports it. Although the US government recently tried to equate 'revisionist' with 'dishonest' or 'disloyal', historians see history as needing constant revision and renewal (McPherson, 2003).

Throughout the twentieth century, psychology books and journals always offered the occasional bit of **revisionist history**, written by advocates of new theories, usually research psychologists. Starting in the Vietnam War era, however, some researchers took up history as a primary activity. Some were historians, others social critics who saw psychology as an oppressive discipline. Most, however, were psychologists disenchanted with their profession. As critics of the status quo they looked to history to offer alternative ways of doing, thinking and viewing the world.

Because the United States contains the vast majority of the world's psychologists and is a highly psychologized society, the development of US psychology has offered much to revisionist historians. Also, academic psychology in North America is an enterprise large enough to support hundreds of amateur historians within its ranks – revisionists included. For these reasons, the history of psychology in the United States has been the intellectual terrain most contested since the 1960s. Similar discussions have taken place about psychology in other countries, however. Reflecting the origins of North American psychology, initially these countries were usually European (Ash & Woodward, 1987; Dehue, 1995). Recently, however, scholars have turned to the developing world to study psychology's historical transformation as it crosses national boundaries and cultures (Brock, 2006; Pols, 2007).

Initially, the enthusiasm of Vietnam-era revisionists produced histories with a simple plot: psychology developed to serve the forces of racism, male chauvinism and class bias. This approach was generally consistent with the worldview of many critical psychologists seeking to advance social justice. Later, however, the stories became more complex and more subtle. What changed was the historians' methodology and social viewpoint. Just as scientists can learn to do better science by studying past missteps, historians learn their craft by seeing old accounts replaced by new. If today's critical psychologists want to see history clearly – and critically – they must keep in mind how today's historical knowledge has evolved. To this end, this chapter emphasizes the work of psychologists who have tried to write a history that challenges conventional accounts while avoiding conspiratorial, simplistic storytelling.

Each successive group in this story has tried to do better than the previous one. You will see celebratory histories challenged by revisionists, whose own excesses were corrected in turn by a movement for a '**new history of psychology**'. The successors to that movement (and some of its veterans) don't call themselves 'new' or 'revisionist.' We just try to write good history, hoping to provide the clearest view of the past to those who want to make changes today.

revisionist critics of IQ and its measurement: Leon Kamin and Stephen J. Gould

The most influential revisionist history to appear in the 1970s was written by Leon Kamin, an experimental psychologist at Princeton University. Typical of scientists who have become self-taught historians, Kamin's primary goal was to discredit a contemporary trend in psychology. The focus of his criticism was the idea that intelligence tests measure the effects of heredity rather than environment. A corollary was that African Americans and the poor were constitutionally less intelligent. Promoted by the psychologists Arthur Jensen (1969) and Richard Herrnstein (1971), these hereditarian ideas seemed to Kamin to be both unsupported by research and socially reactionary.

Having been a political activist as a graduate student in the 1940s, Kamin knew US social history (Harris, 1997). He thus knew that the 1960s debate over intelligence might be linked to debates around the time of World War I – an era of conflict over immigration, politics, race and gender. After reading the psychology literature of that earlier era, Kamin wrote *The Science and Politics of I.Q.* (1974), describing that earlier era to the generation of psychologists born after World War II. In his book, Kamin argued that the pioneers of intelligence testing were motivated by social concerns as much as scientific curiosity.

Reviewing their writings from the period 1915–1935, Kamin showed it to be biased against anyone other than prosperous, white Protestant males whose families had lived in the USA for many generations. Quoting the important psychologists Lewis Terman, Robert Yerkes, and H. H. Goddard, Kamin demonstrated their belief in the genetic inferiority of immigrants, African Americans, Native Americans, Jews, and women.

In Kamin's account, the prejudice of these experts was reflected not only in their academic writings but also in their complicity with inhumane social policies that caused widespread suffering. First were the restrictive immigration laws of the 1920s, justified by psychologists' **nativist** misinterpretation of World War I intelligence tests. Because of these laws, Kamin charged, East European Jews were denied entry to the USA in the 1930s, perishing instead at the hands of the Nazis. Second were involuntary sterilization laws passed by many states to halt the spread of feeblemindedness. These provisions for the mandatory sterilization of the mentally retarded, Kamin revealed, conformed to the eugenic views of Goddard, Yerkes, and the other promoters of intelligence testing. In offering this critical, revisionist history, Kamin was suggesting the potential for social injustice inherent in the new hereditarianism of the 1970s.

In the decade following Kamin's book, the most influential revisionist history of psychology was the aptly titled *The Mismeasure of Man* (1981). Its author was Stephen Jay Gould, a Harvard University paleontologist and science popularizer. Like Kamin, Gould was motivated by a long-standing concern about the political misuses of science; during the Vietnam War he had been a prominent member of the activist group Science for the People.

In *The Mismeasure of Man*, Gould suggested that twentieth century claims that intelligence was inherited were nothing new. Rather, the hereditarianism of the 1920s and 1970s echoed nineteenth century attempts to reduce human personality traits to biology. In his 150-year survey of biological reductionism, Gould showed the logic of Arthur Jensen first appearing in Europe in the period 1830–1900. There, craniometrists measured intelligence by looking at skull shapes and volume, and physiognomists assessed criminality by looking at the face – measuring the angles of noses and foreheads. Anticipating the IQ pioneers of the 1920s, these European experts on human diversity claimed to have found quantitative evidence of the mental inferiority of women, blacks, and non-Western nationalities. By implication, according to Gould, Jensen's racial interpretation of IQ data was no more scientific than craniometry.

Moving to the early twentieth century United States, Gould fleshed out Leon Kamin's history of restrictive immigration policies based on misinterpreted Army intelligence tests. He also showed how such early tests were poorly standardized, resulting in the absurd finding that half the US population was mentally retarded. To Kamin's portrayal of IQ pioneer H. H. Goddard, Gould added the story of Goddard's famous study of an allegedly degenerate, rural New Jersey family that he called the Kallikaks. Consistent with eugenic calls for the sterilization of the unfit, Goddard portrayed generation after generation of Kallikaks as feebleminded, immoral, and criminal. Offended by the social pessimism of Goddard's *The Kallikak Family*, Gould reprinted some of its illustrations and accused Goddard of retouching photos to make his subjects look demented and depraved.

In concluding his history of hereditarian errors Gould disputed the idea that intelligence was a single quality, known as 'g' to its proponents. The primary mid-century advocate of that idea, Gould showed, was the elitist British psychologist Cyril Burt. Not only was Burt dishonest in dealing with those sceptical of his research, but Gould blamed his pessimistic hereditarianism for Britain's two-track educational system, in which the working classes were condemned to vocational schools and second class careers. Although Burt was now dead and discredited, Gould equated his theories to the doctrines of Arthur Jensen, the most prominent hereditarian of the 1970s and 1980s.

_____ *feminist revisions of the history of psychology*_____

In their historical writing, Kamin and Gould were contributing to an important political campaign of the day: debunking hereditarianism and theories of Blacks' inferiority. Simultaneous with that campaign was the rise of the women's movement. Inspired by books like *The Feminine Mystique*, women demanded equal rights with men, just as African Americans had demanded their share of economic and political power.

Within psychology, activists formed the Association for Women Psychologists in 1969 as a feminist caucus (Herman, 1995). Its goal was to win equal rights for women in the field, while correcting the masculine bias of psychological theories. For women who felt excluded from positions of power in their field, it was natural to look to history for support and solace. Scouring the research literature and institutional records, feminist psychologists soon discovered the neglected women of psychology. The rebellious spirit of this quest was well expressed by the title of a pioneering article in the *American Psychologist*: 'The History of Psychology Revisited, or "Up with our Foremothers"' (Bernstein & Russo, 1974).

Soon, scholars retooled themselves from doing experimental psychology to researching the feminist history of psychology, inspired by the women's history movement (Lerner, 1979). One notable result of this effort was the book *Untold Lives* by Elizabeth Scarborough and Laurel Furumoto (1987). Its subject was the first generation of women PhDs in psychology, who were largely missing from textbooks and psychologists' consciousness. In recent years, scholars have added other generations of neglected women psychologists (Harris & Curti, 1999; Johnston & Johnson, 2008; Rutherford, 2006).

For many feminists in the 1960s and 1970s, the neglect of these historical figures paralleled their own experience as graduate students in male dominated departments. This was the case for Laurel Furumoto at Harvard, where E. G. Boring promoted a masculinist style of psychology that was unsympathetic to women's interests and perspectives. Harvard also felt oppressive to Naomi

Weisstein, a graduate of Wellesley College who was patronized and undermined as a graduate researcher in experimental psychology (Herman, 1995). In response, she published a theoretical and historical critique of the psychological literature on women, titled *Kinder, Küche, Kirche as Scientific Law: Psychology Constructs the Female* (Weisstein, 1968). Characteristic of the time, she accused personality and clinical psychologists of ignoring the social context in which women's personalities were embedded.

_____ *uncovering the political history of psychology* _____

While feminists were discovering their foremothers and anti-racists were finding the ethnocentric skeletons in psychology's closet, a third group of psychologists used history to advance a progressive political agenda. Led by Larry Finison, a small group of New Left psychologists began uncovering the history of political activism by psychologists from the 1930s through to the 1950s. Critical of psychology's insipid response to the Vietnam War and the social unrest of the 1960s, these young scholars discovered an activist past that they offered as an alternative for the future. During the Depression of the 1930s, they showed psychologists were active in mass movements against war, militarism, racism and anti-Semitism (Finison, 1976).

Perhaps the best known product of this New Left scholarship was the story of the Society for the Psychological Study of Social Issues (Harris, 1986; Harris & Nicholson, 1998). In the 1930s and 1940s, its members conducted research disproving the idea that Blacks are less intelligent than whites. Next, they studied the self-esteem of African American children. Research conducted most prominently by Mamie and Kenneth Clark became part of the social scientists' brief in the *Brown v. Board of Education* case before the US Supreme Court, resulting in the end of statutory school segregation (Kluger, 2004). Neglected by traditional accounts of the history of psychology (Harris, 1994), parts of this activist past have now been incorporated into American psychology's self-image (Benjamin & Crouse, 2002).

_____ **the new history of psychology** _____

By the 1980s, all subjects in the history of psychology were given makeovers by a generation of young scholars. In the process, amateurs such as Leon Kamin and Steven J. Gould were supplanted by those schooled in the history of science, women's history, and social history. The result was a more mature and sophisticated view of psychology's past. Gradually, the enthusiastic but simple view of the 1970s was discovered to be not just preliminary and incomplete but critically flawed.

In their place, there arose what was called 'the new history of psychology'. As described by one of its leading advocates, this new style of history was 'more contextual, more critical, more archival, more inclusive, and more past-minded' (Furumoto, 1989: 30). In other words, its practitioners focus on non-elite groups in psychology, they look at consumers of psychological information, they use archival records to supplement the field's official literature, and they recreate the social context in which intellectual trends develop.

Looking at the development of intelligence testing, for example, the new historians of psychology realized that psychologists and their tests had played at best a peripheral role in the passage of restrictive immigration laws in the 1920s. Racist politicians, it turns out, had decided long before that period that eastern and southern Europeans were inferior. They didn't need Army IQ tests to tell them so (Samelson, 1975).

Moreover, the racist unanimity Kamin and Gould attributed to psychologists is an illusion. As shown by more thorough studies, figures like Terman, Yerkes, and Goddard disagreed sharply among themselves on questions from the inferiority of immigrants to the relation of IQ to crime and delinquency (Zenderland, 1998). Also, there were many lesser known psychologists who never accepted nativist views of intelligence. Fifty-five years before Gould linked psychological hereditarians with nineteenth century physiognomists, for example, an assistant professor at Smith College named Margaret Curti was writing articles making the same point (e.g., Curti, 1926). By studying only elite psychologists – almost all male – Gould inadvertently overlooked the rank and file opposition to racist notions of intelligence, which tended to be female.

A final corrective that recent scholarship has provided for *The Mismeasure of Man* concerns Gould's claim that Goddard had retouched photos in one of his books to make members of the Kallikak family look stupid. As explained by Raymond Fancher (1988), this is not only a false accusation but one based on an ignorance of Goddard's motives and methods for promoting his brand of psychology. The feebleminded were not always detectable by surface examination, Goddard argued, and thus the services of a psychologist were needed. As a result, Goddard was one of the few people who wanted the Kallikaks to look *normal*, rather than retarded or evil. By understanding that Goddard was more interested in professional expansion than oppressing the underprivileged, one sees his role more clearly. One is also better equipped to see how psychologists have gained the power they exercise *today*: by convincing generations of institutional managers that psychological expertise will make their work more efficient.

For the critical psychologist interested in social justice today, the important point here is the frequent disjunction between motive and outcome (Grob, 1994). The world would be much easier to improve if destructive social forces could be blamed on the malevolence of a scientific elite. In the history of psychology, however, psychologists rarely have a monopoly on ignorance and prejudice. Rather, the social prejudice and blindness of scientists and clinicians is usually no greater than that of politicians, popular writers, or business executives. This is the lesson that the new history draws from the development of the intelligence test.

In addressing the subject of gender, the new history of psychology moved beyond the task of replacing the great men in psychology with forgotten great women ('**compensatory history**'). Instead of just focusing on individual women whose careers were thwarted or who deserve to be added to history texts, the new history looks at the mechanisms by which power is exercised. Those mechanisms include assigning lower status to research areas considered to be 'feminine' (e.g., educational psychology) and equating scientific rigour with traditionally male attributes such as the ability to make decisions in an unemotional style (Nicholson, 2001). The result is a history that focuses on social context and power as much as intellectual discovery and the warring egos of great men.

the romance of American psychology

Perhaps the greatest contribution of the new history of psychology is its refusal to see psychology dichotomously, as either good or evil. Rather, today's scholars see that both liberation and oppression coexist in this discipline and among its practitioners. The best expression of this viewpoint is Ellen Herman's book, *The Romance of American Psychology* (1995). Examining the period 1940–1975, Herman shows psychological experts pursuing political and cultural authority as much as scientific success. They do so by helping those in power to deal with key social issues: war, poverty, race, and gender. One result is a psychological dimension to social and political policy, from the Supreme Court's *Brown v. Board of Education* decision to the CIA's Project Camelot and the Kerner Commission's report on urban violence. Another result is the cooptation of psychologists by the post-World War II political state, silencing their political dissent until the crisis of the Vietnam War.

Unlike the conspiratorial histories of earlier eras, Herman's perspective rejects the dichotomous view of psychology as either manipulative or freedom-enhancing. Rather, she understands that increasing personal freedom and social engineering are not always separable processes. Although we like to make 'distinctions between democratic and antidemocratic uses of [psychology]', Herman notes, 'the line separating them has a great deal more to do with the social context of ideas than with factors intrinsic to knowledge production' (1995: 11). One of her goals as a historian, then, is to show how 'the respective genealogies of "control" and "freedom" are as connected as their political reputations are disconnected' (1995: 11–12).

In looking at the rise of the psychological expert from 1940 to the 1970s, Herman shows psychology to be politically malleable, serving functions that can prove contradictory. 'It has served to ... obscure the exercise of power in recent US history, but it has also legitimized innovative ideas and actions whose aim has been to personalize, and expand the scope of liberty' (1995: 15). The former was the case in Vietnam and Chile, where psychology provided a social science rationalization for political repression.

The latter, more liberatory function can be seen by looking at the creation of domestic social policies toward race relations and poverty. In the case of schools segregated by race, psychology helped outlaw this practice in the 1950s by testifying to the damaged personalities it created. In the 1960s, experts turned to the psychological harm caused by poverty and suggested reforms in the welfare state. They were persuasive, Herman explains, because 'the ugliness of psychological deformation offered a justification for the Great Society that was more durable, or at least fresher, than such tired old abstractions as equality and social justice' (1995: 208).

Herman's point is not that the human sciences are ethically neutral technologies that fit the user's politics. Rather, psychology has been used repressively but contains a liberatory potential. Its repressive functions are related to the authority and power that psychologists have tried to win from social elites. Its liberatory potential comes from psychology's ability to address human, subjective experience. Accordingly, psychological knowledge can add a powerful dimension to political movements, including those on the Left with which many critical psychologists identify.

The women's liberation movement of the 1960s was one such movement. As histories of that era note, a key feature of the second wave of feminism was its criticism of traditional psychology's male bias. Less appreciated are the ways in which the same movement incorporated humanistic psychology into its philosophy and methodology of social change. Feminist 'consciousness raising' groups, for example, assumed a dialectical relation between psychological and political experience, and refused to exclude either. The result, Herman asserts, was a more powerful women's movement.

Ironically, traditional histories of politics and science share with traditional histories of psychology a disdain for the subjective experience of individual actors. By restoring that dimension, Herman improves our historical vision. She also offers a lesson to activists wishing to avoid anti-psychological excesses that have crippled the political left in its sectarian and ultra-left phases (Harris, 1995). Addressing the activists of today, Herman explains, 'If psychological knowledge is to mobilize people for progressive change, rather than equip them to endure new variations on old injustices, the dichotomy between internal and external transformation will have to be rejected as false and useless' (1995: 16).

—————— *Betty Friedan and psychology's two faces* ——————

The life of Betty Friedan, whose early work as Bettye Goldstein is noted above, illustrates psychology's contradictions: it can promise liberation *and* threaten to impose an oppressive, false consciousness. According to Daniel Horowitz's (1998) biography, this pioneering feminist found psychology both empowering and oppressive. Moreover, the mixture of these two qualities changed as Friedan's political life and career evolved. As an undergraduate, psychology seemed unproblematic once its theories were made more socially conscious. Like other radicals in the 1930s, Friedan was optimistic that Marx's programme for social change would prove compatible with a reworked version of psychoanalysis (Bartlett, 1938).

By the mid-1950s, however, things had changed both politically and personally. Abroad, repression in Communist countries was causing Marxists at home to reconsider their collectivist faith. Domestically, McCarthyism was crippling the social movements that Friedan had drawn upon for hope. And personally, Betty needed the help of a psychotherapist to regain her sense of self – suppressed by motherhood, marriage and the suburbs (Horowitz, 1998).

In response, Friedan wrote *The Feminine Mystique* (1963), with its pessimistic but openly conflicted views of psychology. Popular psychoanalysis was misogynist, she asserted in the chapter 'The Sexual Solipsism of Sigmund Freud'. That is understandable, however, since psychoanalysis was the product of a patriarchal era. In today's society, however, neo-Freudian and humanistic psychology could enlighten women to what society denies them: personal fulfilment and an authentic self.

In her text and more openly in her footnotes, Friedan's readers saw this positive message attributed to the writings of Abraham Maslow, with whom she established a cordial correspondence (Friedan, 1959; Maslow, 1963). Her positive view of psychology also reflected her gratitude to her psychotherapist, William Menaker, with whom she later planned to write a book (Friedan, n.d.). It was Menaker whom she quoted rejecting Freud's theory of penis envy. 'If the patient doesn't fit the book,' "he explained, 'throw away the book, and listen to the patient' (Friedan, 1963: 122). Unfortunately, Friedan complained, 'many analysts threw the book *at* their patients' (1963: 122).

Although radical feminists would view 'the psychological' differently than Betty Friedan, her struggle with its role in social change is an illuminating historical event. We see her talking back to some experts while enlisting others in her campaign of women's liberation. Moreover, her changing views of psychology support our argument that historical circumstance changes how psychology is used. As someone who lived in more than one historical period, it was natural for Friedan to revise her opinions of how the psyche relates to society.

how does psychology change?

A final contribution that historians can make to critical psychology is to ask the question: 'How does psychology change?' For example, how did psychology come to abandon its belief that homosexuality was a form of psychopathology in the 1960s and 1970s? I ask this question because some critics of psychology answer it differently than historians. More specifically, some critical psychology accounts downplay the role of empirical research in changing how psychology and psychiatry understood gays and lesbians (Kitzinger, 1997).

In criticizing this neglect of empirical evidence, I speak from experience. In the 1970s and 1980s, I made this error while teaching Abnormal Psychology. Suspicious of psychiatric authority and diagnosis, I was attracted to Thomas Szasz's writings (e.g., Szasz, 1962). To him, the removal of homosexuality from the psychiatric diagnostic manual (the DSM) was a cause for ridicule rather than celebration. It proved, Szasz said, that mental illness was a myth – created and perpetuated by a profession of moralists disguised as scientists.

Echoing Szasz, one of my lectures portrayed the revision of the DSM as caused by social pressure and bureaucratic cowardice rather than scientific research and debate. I spoke out of ignorance, however, because the history of research on sex and sexual orientation had not been written. Also, the gay activists of the Vietnam War era seemed more daring and admirable than middle-aged, middle-class figures from the 1950s like Alfred Kinsey and Evelyn Hooker.

Recently, however, a number of excellent histories have been written of sex research in the mid-twentieth century. While Alfred Kinsey's had long been famous, Henry Minton (2002) and others have now told the story of rank-and-file gay men and lesbians who collaborated with sex researchers such as Kinsey. Believing that good science would lead to enlightenment, these activists supplied the data and life stories to help normalize homosexuality. Also in the 1990s, gay and lesbian psychologists celebrated the life of psychologist Evelyn Hooker, a key figure in overturning the DSM's view of homosexuality (Schmiechen, 1992).

The resulting story may seem too 'empirical' for some critics of psychology, who, as addressed elsewhere in this book, differ among themselves over the role of empirical research in creating social change. But the story shouldn't be ignored since it serves as a reminder of how political commitment and social conscience can motivate scientists to challenge the status quo. In Hooker's case, her anti-fascist political sympathies led her to see the evils of anti-Semitism and fascism in the 1930s and 1940s (Hooker, 1993). She also experienced discrimination as a female academic, and was fired from her only tenure-track job because of her politics (Meyerowitz, 2004). Then, as a lecturer at the UCLA Extension Division she was befriended by a gay student of hers – Sam From – and his social circle, who then led her into the gay subculture of Los Angeles.

Finding her young gay friends different from textbook portrayals, Hooker decided to see whether homosexuals and heterosexuals differed on tests of psychopathology. While the clinical literature found differences, earlier researchers had found their gay subjects in prisons and psychiatric clinics. Hooker, by contrast, aided by a sympathetic group of activists, recruited well-adjusted male homosexuals. She found no differences between gay and straight subjects, and gradually her research became known by psychologists and psychiatrists.

Of course, the gay rights movement deserves credit for creating an atmosphere in which anti-gay prejudices would be questioned. However, psychologists were more likely influenced by Kinsey's and Hooker's normalization of homosexuality than by protests at American Psychological Association meetings

(Chiang, 2007). And within the other APA (American Psychiatric Association), it was research and lobbying by sympathetic colleagues that resulted in homosexuality being removed from the DSM. One such colleague was Judd Marmor, who had embraced Marxism and psychoanalysis as a young man, and whose clinical experience and social contacts with gays had changed his mind about homosexuality (Marcus, 2002; Marmor, 1949; Stone, 1946).

It is ironic that some critics who emphasize the role of outside pressure see themselves as humanists, but rob Evelyn Hooker and fellow scientists of their agency – their human ability to create social change. They also rob students of an appreciation of the real struggles taking place within professions and organizations. The history of those struggles reinforces the positive message that, at least sometimes, groups of collaborators can marshal evidence to change the existing psychological wisdom. This turns out to be a messier story than simple accounts in which APA bureaucrats buckle under assaults by gay activists who are disrupting their meetings (Kitzinger, 1997). But history is often complex. That's what makes it more valuable than the conspiratorial rants of Szasz and his collaborators in the Church of Scientology (e.g., Citizens Commission, 2006).

conclusion: a student's guide to the history of psychology

What are some of the lessons of our brief history of the history of psychology? For the psychology student, the first lesson is that methods of historical inquiry are as important to learn as methods of research. Without them, those eager for social reform are easily drawn to well-intentioned but simplistic histories claiming to be critical. In those histories, psychological ideas primarily exist to serve social inequality (Shields, 2007). Such reductionism, we suggest, is no less dangerous in history than in psychological research. Rather than empowering, it blinds the student to the contested nature of all ideas as well as to past struggles that have changed the field (e.g., Rosenberg, 1982).

Second, from a critical perspective, historical accounts themselves are never value-neutral. The historian always has to choose some method of data collection and organization over another. The historian also has to choose an interpretive framework to present an account of the past that is more than a laundry list of dates, names, and places. Said plainly, history is never a straightforward, unmediated account of the facts of the past. It is always a representation or reconstruction of some aspect of the past perceived through a particular lens and relying on only a portion of the data that could, theoretically, be retrieved. It is impossible to illuminate or reconstruct any but a small portion of the past; any 'comprehensive collection of historical facts' is by definition incomplete. Whose facts these are, and what counts as a fact, are also openings for interrogation and critique.

Furthermore, once any historical account is written, it can then be used to strengthen a particular interpretation of the past and its implications for the present, that is, it may serve a political purpose. Critical histories do less to undergird the 'rightness' of the present than to ask questions of the past that get at *why* and *how* certain theories arose and gained acceptance in lieu of others, and *why* and *how* certain groups of people or movements gained professional authority in given times and places. History is used to analyse the past on its own terms, without necessarily seeking to glorify or justify the present. We also acknowledge that any analysis is shaped by contemporary interests: the historian cannot escape his or her present.

The third lesson of this chapter is that good history can be enjoyed. As exemplified by Herman's *Romance of American Psychology*, it can be compelling reading. Equally encouraging is the fact that good history, like good fiction, challenges one's implicit ways of thinking and makes the world look different afterwards. By reading good examples of the new history of psychology, one can learn to appreciate the frequent disjunction between intent and outcome and the role of irony in history. At the same time, one can see the field from the bottom up and from a socially informed view. The result is an appreciation of the contributions of previously neglected figures, and of the role of sociopolitical forces in shaping the work of psychologists from Asch to Zimbardo.

In the end, the critically minded reader may not find ready-made 'lessons of history' to apply to today's psychological research. But through historical awareness, it will be easier to critically view what is taking place today.

◼ ◼ main chapter points ◼

1   Whiggish History: A traditional history of psychology supports the status quo. It suggests that today's dominant perspectives are the inevitable result of scientific progress.

2   Revisionist History: In the 1960s, anti-racist psychologists rediscovered the ethnocentric history of their field.

3   The New History of Psychology: In the 1970s and 1980s, a new generation of historians corrected the revisionists' accounts. They also included the perspective of groups omitted from traditional history.

4   The best historical writing now shows how psychology has always offered the promise of both liberation and oppression. Historians of psychology must struggle to maintain a critical perspective while avoiding simplistic and conspiratorial accounts.

glossary

• **compensatory history**: the discovery and celebration of individuals (e.g., women, ethnic minorities) neglected by traditional historical accounts.

• **intellectual history**: the history of ideas and how they change over time.

• **nativist**: prejudiced against immigrants and their nationalities.

• **new history of psychology**: a new style of history in the 1970s and 1980s that stressed the social context of psychological ideas and included the perspectives of groups other than prominent psychologists.

- **presentist history**: a distorted view, projecting today's values and concerns onto the past.
- **revisionist history**: a historical account that challenges the accepted perspective on some feature of the past.
- **Whiggish history**: History written from the perspective of a currently dominant group or ideology, conveying the inevitability of the status quo.

▨ ▨ reading suggestions ▨

As emphasized in the chapter, Herman's (1995) look at the development of American psychology is invaluable. The life and writing of Betty Friedan, as re-examined by historians, has significant relevance to an understanding of feminism, labour and the Cold War in the USA (see Horowitz, 1996, 1998, and Meyerowitz, 1993). Also according to this chapter, historians of psychology have begun to study how the gendered nature of psychological theory affects both women *and* men. A good example is Ian Nicholson's (2003) biography of Gordon Allport. For those interested in clinical psychology, Jack Pressman's (1998) history of the lobotomy is a fine example of history that is critical but avoids taking a conspiratorial or Whiggish perspective. Finally, the debate over the Cyril Burt scandal is psychology's longest-running, politically loaded historical argument. See Samelson's authoritative (1992) review essay.

⋮ // internet resources ⌐

Links for further study of Betty Friedan:

- www.h-net.org/~hst203/documents/friedan1.html
- www.marxists.org/reference/subject/philosophy/works/us/friedan.htm

⌒ ▪ Questions ▬▬▬▬▬

1 This chapter connects some authors' social concerns and lives with their scholarly writing. How might this connection contribute to a critical perspective on history? How could it be a distraction? How is this chapter different from traditional texts in the history of psychology?

2 Why might advocates of critical psychology disagree about what is good history? Is it useful to reveal those disagreements to students?

3 How did Betty Friedan's writing and activism help create a social movement? Why have her methods of research and writing come under criticism in recent years? How have the details of her life become the subject of controversy?

3

Philosophical Concerns in Critical Psychology

Thomas Teo

psychology as a problematic science

An academic field of study is problematic when it does not address, let alone resolve, basic issues. This has been the case with psychology, which has excluded or neglected key problems or pretended they do not exist. As described in this chapter, three interconnected issues make psychology problematic: (a) a limited understanding of the complexities of psychology's subject matter and **ontology**; (b) a preference for a selectively narrow **epistemology** and methodology; and (c) a lack of reflection (critical thinking) on psychology's **ethical–political** concerns and praxis.

It would be inaccurate to suggest that these problems reflect only contemporary concerns. Indeed, from its beginning as an institution and independent field of study, psychology has had to cope with ongoing critiques (see Teo, 2005; Woodward & Ash, 1982). One of the most influential critiques in the eighteenth century was developed by Immanuel Kant, who argued that the *study of the soul* – this is what the term *psychology* originally meant – could not be natural-scientific because psychology could not be made into an authentic experimental discipline like physics. Instead, he recommended that the field limit itself to a description of the soul and focus on the notion of moral *agency*, the ability of the person to act intentionally according to moral principles.

In the nineteenth century, psychology was transformed from a philosophical discipline into a natural-scientific discipline. Adopting the principles and methods of the natural sciences meant that mainstream academic psychology shunted aside genuine psychological topics such as *subjectivity* – subjective, personal experiences and the meanings that human beings attribute to these experiences. This transformation had intellectual, but more importantly, sociohistorical origins: when psychology emerged as a discipline and was struggling for academic respect in terms of money, power, and recognition, it seemed more promising to align itself with the highly successful natural sciences rather than with the seemingly ambiguous human sciences such as history (Ward, 2002). Later it was hoped that the natural sciences would appreciate psychology if the discipline committed itself to ostensibly objective topics such as *behaviour* rather than to notions of the *soul* or human *experience*. This sentiment of establishing psychology as a rigorous discipline was so strong that even Sigmund Freud intended psychoanalysis as a natural science (see Habermas, 1968/1972).

This attempt to establish psychology as a natural science like physics led to many critiques and also to what are known as *crisis discussions* within psychology. Indeed, the first systematic book on the crisis of psychology was published by Willy (1899), who challenged the dominant natural-scientific oriented research programmes of his time. He identified speculative theory-building and an inadequate methodology as sources of psychology's crisis. The crisis literature has been on the rise since the 1920–1930s and again since the 1960s and 1970s (for an overview, see Goertzen, 2005). A critique of psychology's lack of ethical–political relevance can also be found in the nineteenth century when Beneke (1845) suggested that psychology could help overcome political, social, and religious tumults. He challenged mainstream psychology's focus on theory rather than practice and he protested that German psychology refused to deal with social reality.

A relevant question in a book on critical psychology is this: Should all approaches that provide a critical evaluation of psychology's mainstream be labelled *critical psychologies*? A *general concept* of critical psychology would include all approaches that critique psychology's subject matter, or methodology, or praxis, or a combination of these elements. A *specific concept* of critical psychology, on the other hand, would include approaches sceptical of the mainstream that give primacy to the ethical–political dimensions of praxis. I use the term *praxis* in contrast to the term *practice* to emphasize the political nature of human activity in any applied area. In addition, it should be mentioned that while some psychologists use the label *critical psychology* to address their own psychological position (see Fox and Prilleltensky, 1997; Hook, 2004; Sloan, 2000; Walkerdine, 2002), others who are critical of the mainstream do not use the term (e.g., some feminist or social-constructionist psychologists).

Very prominent in, but not limited to, critical psychology are cultural–historical (Marxist), feminist, social-constructionist, and more recently, postcolonial critiques. All have fuelled the critical literature on the mainstream's limitations. For example, Marxist approaches could be interested in the role of insurance companies in the development of diagnostic manuals; feminist approaches might question generalizations of developmental models based exclusively on male participants; social-constructionists might look at the role of persuasion in making psychological theories dominant in a culture; and postcolonial experts might question the significance of American and European theories and practices for African contexts. More importantly, these various critiques provide alternative approaches, some of which sometimes contradict one another.

ontological concerns and psychology's subject matter

In philosophy, the term ontology refers to the study of Being (the study of the fundamental characteristics of reality). In psychology, ontological studies address the nature of the psychological 'object': What should psychologists study? What are the specific and defining characteristics of the psychological subject matter? Ontological discussions include the proper definition of psychology, its appropriate subject matter, the models for representing human mental life, metaphors for understanding human subjectivity, theories of the human mind, theories of human nature, the relationship between mind and body, and so on.

It is important to keep the following distinctions in mind: the word *psychology* refers to a subject matter, a field of topics, a discipline, and a profession. In Western history the word *psychology* has been used to refer to the study of the soul, consciousness, mental life, behaviour, human experience, the mind, or the brain, depending on the era and cultural context. *Psychological topics* have been studied in the Western tradition since the classical Greeks, for instance, when Aristotle in his pioneering work *On the Soul* discussed the topic *memory*. However, *psychology as an independent academic discipline* did not exist before the nineteenth century, and *psychology as a profession* became a social reality only in the twentieth century. The term *mainstream psychology* refers to an academic field of study as taught and researched in North American and European institutions such as universities.

A few key issues regarding mainstream psychology's implicit assumptions about its subject matter are discussed here. Some psychologists consider that the most important models in psychology are *technological* ones and that the history of psychology parallels the development of technology. For instance, cognitive psychology's model and metaphors of human mental life are based on the computer, whereas in earlier eras psychology made use of more basic mechanical devices (e.g., clocks, steam engines, and radios). Machine models are embedded within a network of ontological assumptions. One of these assumptions is that a person reacts towards an external stimulus like a mechanism; the machine model excludes notions of agency, the ability to reflect, choose, and act. Other models in psychology include animal metaphors that, from a critical perspective, often neglect an understanding of how human mental life differs from various forms of animal mental life.

Thus, psychology's mainstream operates with a *mechanistic*, and hence an *atomistic* and *reductionistic*, model of human mental life. A *mechanistic* concept of human action is also apparent in biological traditions such as behaviourism. Despite a commitment to an evolutionary perspective by many behaviourists, the machine model is dominant in behaviourism because it is assumed that the individual responds to stimuli. Dividing psychological life into stimulus and response (behaviourism) or into independent and dependent variables (mainstream psychology) is problematic because it neglects subjectivity, agency, and meaningful reflection and action in concrete contexts (Holzkamp, 1992; Tolman and Maiers, 1991).

The selection of variables in the context of focusing on isolated aspects of human mental life (*atomism*) does not do justice to the integration of human mental life in concrete individuals. Instead of looking at the complexity of human life, which is the source of human subjectivity, the mainstream in psychology assumes that it is sufficient to study small parts. For instance, cognition is divided further into attention, thinking, and memory. Memory is divided further into long-term, short-term, etc. It is *reductionistic* to assume that the parts sufficiently explain the complexity of human subjectivity; yet, this is another consequence of the machine-model. In reality human subjectivity is experienced in its totality. From the perspective of the subject, cognition, emotion, and will (to use a Western division of mental life) are usually experienced in their connection in concrete life-situations and not as isolated parts. The idea that studying the parts of a whole is sufficient and that the parts will fit together into a meaningful whole through additive processes is based on a limited worldview. Parts do not just add up when it comes to human mental life. Critics have argued that a psychology that does justice to human subjectivity should begin with the nexus of human experiences in order to understand the parts and not vice versa (Martin, Sugarman, & Thompson, 2003).

The machine-model of human mental life has another consequence: because it conceptualizes the person as individualistic and society as an external variable, the model sees the individual and society as separate (see also Parker & Spears, 1996). Seldom do psychologists realize that they base their theories and research practices regarding the mind on an individualistic concept. Consider the following: the fact that you speak a particular language, let's say English, has become part of your *self*. But of course, if you had been raised in Denmark with Danish parents, your language would be Danish. The passage of time also matters: you can produce unique sentences in English, sentences that have never been expressed before, yet these sentences are only meaningful because they are embedded within a sociohistorical trajectory. Because language changes, a sentence like 'I am reading a chapter on critical psychology that challenges the problematic nature of psychological ideas' would have been incomprehensible to English-speaking persons living 500 years ago. Although language can be unique to an individual, it only makes sense within a larger community to which one has been socialized, a community that shares the linguistic properties of communication. Thus, it is insufficient to conceptualize the sociohistorical reality as a stimulus environment to which one reacts; the individual is not independent of the environment and vice versa. For contemporary psychology to be regarded as a scientific discipline it is crucial to represent human subjectivity as embedded in historical and social contexts.

In terms of alternatives, various forms of critical psychology have moved away from a mechanistic and individualistic concept of human mental life. All critical psychologies promote an understanding of the nature of human beings and of human mental life as active and societal. *Cultural–historical approaches* have argued that the environment, culture, and history are not just other variables. The context is interwoven with the very fabric of personal identity. For instance, Vygotsky (1978) and his followers have challenged psychology's individualistic nature. One of his best-known alternative concepts is the *zone of proximal development*. It is based on the idea that testing an individual in isolation is limited and that it is more important to find out what an individual child can learn under the guidance of, and in collaboration with, peers and adults. For example, Vygotsky would be less interested in your individual performance in a multiple-choice test on research methods than in how you would solve a concrete research problem under the guidance of a mentor or in collaboration with other students.

Holzkamp attempted to develop basic categories for psychology in order to understand the specificities of human subjectivity. For him, subjectivity meant acknowledging the societal nature of human beings. Yet, conceptualizing the person as part of a larger sociohistorical and economic context did not mean that the subject should not be taken seriously. Holzkamp (1984) suggested that subjectivity and a psychology from the *standpoint of the subject*, which he conceived as the only viable psychology, should be understood literally. For example, it is conceivable that for an individual, drinking alcohol is the best option to deal with problems. If psychologists already know the outcome of a certain intervention, independent of the context and the individual, then they already have neglected the *Other's* subjectivity. Of course, this does not imply agreeing with everything that the *Other* suggests and does.

Most feminist approaches recognize the nexus of person and society and emphasize the concept of subjectivity in context. In addition, they have suggested that a focus on the mental life means neglecting the *body* (see also phenomenologists such as Merleau-Ponty, 1945/1962). This means that embodied theories of subjectivity need to be developed, theories that do not exclude the body from psychological theorizing on the subject matter of psychology (Bayer & Malone, 1998). Social-constructionist thinkers have also provided conceptualizations of an individual that are not independent of his or her context but are embedded in society and community (Gergen, 1985).

Some hermeneutic oriented psychologists have emphasized the intentional, dialogical, and active side of a person (Richardson, Rogers, & McCarroll, 1998).

A postcolonial critique begins with the argument that the psychological subject matter is part of a wider historical and cultural context and the theories that try to capture this subject matter are part of Western theorizing. Thus, it must be understood as Western models of human mental life rather than universal ones (Teo & Febbraro, 2003). The question is how concepts developed in Europe and North America can be applied meaningfully to different cultural contexts. The task for psychologists from other countries is to find psychological theories, concepts, and practices that work in their life-worlds rather than importing or exporting American ideas. For instance, Freire (1970), who emphasized that learners should be treated as subjects and not as objects, and Martín-Baró (1994), who applied Freirean ideas to psychology, have developed categories dealing specifically with psychological issues in Latin America.

Wilhelm Dilthey (1976) divided the sciences into *natural* and *human sciences*. Following his lead, there has been increased discussion of the *nature of concepts* to describe humans and human mental life. Danziger (1997), who emphasized the social construction of psychological ideas and practices, addressed whether psychological concepts have a different status from natural-scientific concepts. He called this the difference between *natural kinds* and *human kinds*. *Natural kinds* are physical, chemical and biological objects and events and are arguably different from psychological categories: the study of water or a rock formation is different from the study of IQ, grief, or 'race'.

Psychologists need to understand that concepts in psychology are constructed in a specific cultural context for specific purposes. Mainstream psychologists often pretend that constructed concepts are natural concepts because they have empirical support. But empirical support says nothing about the ontological status of a concept. For instance, the fact that a certain number of individuals identify themselves as *British* does not mean that *being British* is a natural kind variable. Critical investigations emerged from the historical fact that certain psychological concepts have become a reality in social practice but their ontological status is completely problematic (for instance, 'race' or IQ). But these socially constructed concepts have become a central part of our identity: once the concept of IQ has been established and you do well on IQ tests, it becomes a part of your psychological self-understanding. Yet, at the same time psychological concepts such as IQ can also be understood as sources of power and oppression (see Foucault, 1966/1970; Rose, 1996).

Once a concept has become a cultural phenomenon, it is important to challenge the cultural familiarity of a specific concept and the socialization into this concept that makes many psychological ideas seem self-evident when, in fact, they are culturally embedded. The process of social construction is easy to understand when relatively new concepts such as *emotional intelligence* become part of our cultural self-understanding. Critical psychologists also try to analyse whether these culturally embedded concepts used in psychological theories express a certain worldview and are *ideological* (that is, they may serve the interest of power and money). For instance, if we say that a *behaviour is not adaptive* instead of *this person is alienated* we have made a theoretical choice with consequences for specific persons (change the person or the environment). It is through its concepts that psychologists perceive sociopsychological reality.

epistemological concerns and psychology's methodology

In philosophy the term epistemology refers to the study of knowledge. In psychology we are interested in the nature of knowledge, the ways of achieving knowledge, and the meanings of knowledge and truth. Ontology and epistemology, although divided in this chapter for descriptive purposes, are in practice intertwined. Certain ontological assumptions and decisions about what psychologists should study have epistemological as well as methodological consequences. A commitment to a specific conceptualization of the subject matter implies specific methodological commitments and vice versa. For example, a machine-model of human mental life implies a mechanistic methodology, and the results based on this methodology seemingly support, but indeed are implied in, a machine-model (an example from everyday life: if one has a hammer, then one thinks that everything one sees needs to be hammered). This relationship between ontology and epistemology is not acknowledged in mainstream psychology and, thus, it is a problematic issue for the discipline.

From a critical perspective, one would demand that the specificities of an object or event (in psychology it would be mental life or subjectivity in context) demand and necessitate appropriate methodologies. It appears trivial to suggest that if researchers are interested in the biological basis of memory, then they are required to use a biological, natural-scientific methodology; however, if they are interested in studying the subjective meaningful content of memory, then they need a methodology that is able to do justice to this subject matter (for example, *hermeneutic* approaches that emphasize the understanding of meaning). However, the mainstream promotes the idea that a natural-scientific methodology can and must be applied unquestionably to all research areas. This assumption has its intellectual roots in positivism's *physicalism*, developed in the first half of the twentieth century, which suggested that everything in the empirical world could be studied with the concepts and methods of physics.

As taught at most universities in the world and expressed in most textbooks, psychology is committed to a natural-scientific, experimental-statistical or empirical-statistical methodology. It operationalizes most concepts as variables (independent, dependent, moderating, mediating).

Indeed, traditional psychology is a *psychology of variables* (Holzkamp, 1991). From a historical point of view, one can reconstruct a shift from a science that was interested in the *why* of psychological phenomena to the exploration of the *functional relationship* between variables. For instance, psychologists do not study the *why* of unemployment in a person's life, which would include an analysis of the problem as a sociohistorical issue. Instead mainstream psychology looks at the relationship between the variable of unemployment and other variables such as wellbeing, depression, self-esteem, personality, and so on. This functional relationship is understood in psychology, depending on the nature of the research design, as causal or correlational.

Typically, within the logic of mainstream psychological research, it has been suggested that psychologists should formulate hypotheses derived from theories (they are framed and understood within theoretical arguments); the hypotheses should be expressed as law-like statements (if – then); theories and methods should be formalized; hypotheses should be tested using objective, valid, and reliable observations and measurements; and, based on the results of hypothesis testing, psychologists can provide deductive-nomological (law-providing) or statistical models of explanation and prediction. Many mainstream psychologists consider the experiment to be the best or most effective means of gaining knowledge in the discipline. Within a quantitative *methodology*, psychology has developed a variety of *methods* (e.g., analysis of variance, factor analysis, path analysis, etc.).

Yet, as pointed out earlier, psychological topics such as memory can be studied from a natural-scientific perspective as well as from a human-scientific perspective. If one looks at memory's physiological basis, its functions, principles, and divisions, one is not necessarily interested in an individually developed memory in context, the very *content* of memory. As clinical psychologists are well aware, a person's unique memory of past experiences that gives meaning to a person's identity and action is part of a cultural–historical trajectory and as such is the topic for a human-scientific perspective. From a disciplinary perspective one could argue that studying the meaning of memory is as important as researching the physiological basis of memory. Yet, the subjective dimension of human mental life and subjectivity in general have been neglected in psychology and excluded in the mainstream's ontology and thus do not find a way back into methodology. *Qualitative* research that tends to focus on the content of human subjectivity is still very much marginalized in mainstream methodology.

Since Kuhn (1962), historians of science have emphasized the difference between what researchers are supposed to do and what they actually do. Critics such as Koch (1985) target the idea that psychology provides psychological laws by arguing that despite the discipline's natural-scientific orientation for over a hundred years, despite the hundreds of thousands of experiments, and despite the long accumulation of very technical writings, it would be difficult to find statements in psychology that could be counted as *natural law* in the sense of the natural sciences or in the sense of being universally valid. The fact that psychology fails as a law-providing science should give pause for reflection on whether the prevailing methodology does justice to the subject matter.

Yet, as pointed out earlier, certain ontological and methodological commitments cannot be resolved by looking at the discipline's internal shortcomings. Science is also a social enterprise and should be understood in the context of power, money, and prestige. The discipline that struggled with acceptance in academia and by the public would rather associate itself with the use of brass and steel instruments that had mechanical sophistication and were associated with science, adopt the white coats of scientists in labs, and rely on complex machines such as computers and fMRI machines. Of course, it was also important to suggest that psychological measures have the same status as physical measures. Critics of this approach suggest that the use of natural-scientific paraphernalia does not really make psychology a science even though it makes for a good pretence (see also Politzer, 1994).

The focus on methodology rather than on subject matter has led to an epistemological attitude that I call *methodologism* (Teo, 2005). This term refers to a research practice in which the subject matter is secondary but the method has primacy. Others have used similar terms: *methodolatry* (Bakan, 1967), the *cult of empiricism* (Toulmin & Leary, 1985), and the *methodological imperative* (Danziger, 1985). Methodologism means that the experimental-statistical or empirical-statistical methodology is applied to all research questions. Yet, if a methodology prescribes what psychologists can study, research is unnecessarily limited. Critical psychologists such as Holzkamp (1991) even argued that adequacy of the methodology with regard to the subject matter should be a central scientific criterion: as long as the adequacy of a methodology is not known, the scientific value and all other objectification criteria are worthless. To illustrate this point, consider the following: the best thermometer in the world is worthless for measuring speed.

Psychology's methodologism leads to a *methodological theory of knowledge*: instead of asking about the nature of knowledge in psychology, such as whether studies would be valid in a hundred years and valid in all cultures (which they should if we found causal relationships that can be generalized into a natural law), it is assumed that accepting and following the methodological and methodical rules outlined by the discipline, handed down and enhanced by succeeding generations of psychologists, will automatically lead to psychological knowledge. Such a methodological theory of knowledge also prevents critical questions about the purpose of research: What are the personal, social, and political–economic interests involved in executing a certain study? Who benefits from which results? Critical psychologists do not think that methodology is independent from the subject matter and independent from the sociohistorical context from which it emerges.

The methodologism of natural-scientific psychology leads to various sub-problems. From a critical as well as from a human-scientific perspective the experiment in psychology has limited value given the nature of the psychological subject matter, which includes the agency of persons embedded in sociohistorical contexts. Even Wilhelm Wundt, still heralded as the father of modern experimental psychology, was aware of the experiment's limited value. Thus, he called for a psychology that includes the sociohistorical context and uses what we would call qualitative methods (see Danziger, 1990).

An experiment can only capture what goes into the theoretical and methodological framework. For instance, if I stand up as a participant (or 'subject') in an experiment and suggest that the task demanded of me does not make sense to me, I am excluded from the data as an error. Thus, my reaction – based on a legitimate concern – is excluded. The experiment needs the willing and well-behaved participant, but in social reality, humans can stand up and change the world, or at least, their life-worlds. This cannot be captured in an experiment. The experiment uses variables and looks at the functional (causal) relationship of isolated variables, but in the real world, all the factors that had been excluded in the experiment emerge and play a role in human action (Holzkamp, 1972). Thus, psychological studies often do not have practical relevance, let alone *emancipatory* relevance, which is a core issue for many critical psychologies. Emancipatory relevance means that research should contribute to overturning oppressive social situations.

There is a large literature regarding the critique of mainstream psychology's identity as a science that supposedly provides universal laws, explanations, and predictions. In addition, some critics have argued that psychology mistakes reasons for causes and that empirical hypothesis-testing is not a test but an application of good reasons (is your decision to study critical psychology *caused* or do you have *reasons* for it?) and that *if-then-statements* have implicative character (for some of these complex issues, see Smedslund, 1988). The discussion of mistaking reasons of humans for physical causes points to another important issue: psychology's hermeneutic deficit (see Teo, 2008). Because the mainstream excludes hermeneutic methods (methods that emphasize an *understanding* of human subjectivity), psychologists are often unaware of the problems that are related to what assumptions go into the establishment and *interpretation* of data. Interpretations impart meaning to data and make results understandable, for the authors themselves, for peers, and for a general audience and the mass media. Interpretations allow data to be understood better than they present themselves. The mainstream rhetoric of psychological 'facts' suggests that facts speak for themselves even when those 'facts' or 'empirical knowledge' contain data *and* interpretations.

This hermeneutic deficit becomes clear in the context of the interpretation of group differences (e.g., gender or 'race' differences). I suggest that epistemological violence is committed when the interpretation of data (not data themselves) leads to statements that construct marginalized groups as inferior, restrict the opportunities of marginalized groups, and lead to aversive recommendations for marginalized groups. For instance, if a researcher suggests that a gender difference in faculty positions at elite universities is due to the lower ability of women, then this researcher has committed epistemological violence (because the data do not determine this interpretation, because alternative interpretations are available, and because this interpretation has negative consequences for women). Unfortunately, as described in more detail in other chapters, psychology has a long history of *invalid interpretations* of group differences regarding women, ethnic minorities, gays and lesbians, people with disabilities, and people living on low incomes, among others.

In terms of alternatives, critical psychologists continue to use methodologies that strive to do justice to the subject matter, methodologies that capture the active, meaning-oriented, intentional nature of human mental life embedded in sociohistorical contexts. Some critical psychologists have incorporated psychoanalysis, the best-known approach that does not exclude subjectivity from research (see Parker, 2003). Critical researchers also emphasize the transformative potential of research: this means that research not only addresses the status quo but also provides knowledge on how to change it.

Although there exists no consistent methodology in the varieties of critical psychology, one can often find the idea that qualitative methods are more appropriate for understanding human subjectivity than quantitative methods. However, it is evident that certain issues should be addressed from a quantitative point of view, and even more, that quantitative methods can be critical and can challenge the status quo (see Martín-Baró, 1994). For example, if someone makes the argument that men interrupt women more often than vice versa, one can begin with a quantitative method in order to measure the frequency of interruptions by men and by women. Thus, quantitative methods are not inherently problematic because the usage of methods depends on the subject matter, the specific question or the particular issue. The problem is not the usage of quantitative methods; the problem is giving primacy to a natural-scientific methodology without looking at the 'object'. The limitations of a quantitative approach for many psychological issues have become the source of many alternatives.

Feminist researchers have identified the ideology of mainstream scientific methodology as *male biased*. In her classical studies, Keller (1985) explored the association between objectivity and masculinity and defended the thesis that scientific research was based on masculine discourses, ideals, metaphors, and practices. She argued that the emphasis on power and control, widespread in the rhetoric of Western science's history, represented the projection of a male consciousness. The language of science expressed a preoccupation with dominance and an adversarial relationship to nature. She pointed out that science divided reality into two parts, the knower and the known, with an autonomous knower in control, distanced, and separated from the known. According to Keller, the masculine separation of scientist and subject matter opposed the feminine idea of connectedness and at the same time reinforced beliefs about the naturally masculine character of science. Instead, she suggested research that emphasizes a connection with the participant and does not exclude the participant's authentic experiences. Obviously, qualitative methods are preferred within such a framework.

In cultural–historical approaches, when it comes to educational psychology, research on assessment, teaching, and learning has been understood as holistic. For example, in co-teaching models all stakeholders participate in the design of a curriculum as well as in the actual teaching practices (see Roth and Lee, 2007). Such a process provides a grounding of theories in praxis – a method that has been applied to social workers and other professions. According to German critical psychology, research should be able to capture the *standpoint of the subject*. This means, for instance, that in psychotherapy research how psychotherapy shapes a person is less interesting than how a person contributes to his or her own change (Dreier, 2007).

Social-constructionist or postmodern thinkers (the label may be problematic) such as Michel Foucault have inaugurated various methods of *discourse analysis*. Critical discourse analysis, a method that focuses on the analysis of written or spoken language, understands language as a social practice that is infused with biases. This method operates based on the idea that language is often embedded in ideological, oppressive, or exploitative practices. Discourse analysis allows, for example, historical reconstructions of how the multiple personality was made into an object of academic discussion (Hacking, 1995) as well as the analysis of very specific discourses such as racist discourses (Van Dijk, 1993). Foucault (1977) also provided suggestions for an analysis of non-discursive practices: for instance, an analysis of prison architecture allows an insight into the workings of power in the context of human subjectivity and interpersonal relations.

In Martín-Baró's (1994) approach, epistemology is intertwined with critical praxis. He suggests that psychology must base its knowledge production on the liberation needs of the oppressed people of Latin America. This means that knowledge must be generated by learning from the oppressed: research should look at psychosocial processes from the perspective of the dominated; educational psychology should learn from the perspective of the illiterate; industrial psychology should begin with the perspective of the unemployed; clinical psychology should be guided by the perspective of the marginalized. What does mental health mean from the perspective of someone who lives in a town dump? Martín-Baró suggests an epistemological change from the powerful to the oppressed and recommends *participatory action research* (see below). It must be mentioned that feminist, sociohistorical, postmodern and postcolonial ideas can be integrated into a meaningful *methodology of the oppressed* (Sandoval, 2000).

ethical–political concerns and psychology's praxis

Psychological practice is interconnected with epistemology and ontology. If one assumes that humans act like machines, then practice will emphasize control, manipulation, and technologies. If one conceptualizes humans as meaning-making agents embedded in sociopolitical contexts, then practice will call attention to human action and agency. I will focus here on one issue: the emphasis on control and adaptation neglects psychology's *emancipatory* potential. Psychology has been an extremely successful discipline in Europe and North America in terms of academic and professional expansion. However, success does not necessarily imply the ethical–political quality of its practice. Psychological practice has often involved abuses perpetrated by the powerful, from intelligence testing as a means to control immigration into the United States (see Chapter 2 and Gould, 1981) to applying psychological techniques to extract information from suspected terrorists (see Chapter 23).

Although it is difficult to make generalizations and to identify an underlying tenet, mainstream psychologists in the past and present have emphasized that *fact* (what is) and *value* (what ought to be) are two different domains that should be kept apart. The problem is that, in any social science, these two domains are inherently intertwined. Even in natural science, as environmental issues such as global warming show, the effect of human activity on the environment is not just a fact but something that has implications for action. Critical psychologists challenge the mainstream idea that one cannot derive *ought* from *is*, and that science should remain neutral on political issues and concerns. Instead, most ethical–political critical psychologists emphasize that we should derive *ought* from *is*. For instance, if research shows the negative effects of poverty on mental life, then poverty should be targeted and in the end abolished; psychologists should participate in its abolition. In terms of social injustice in general (when it comes to class, ethnicity, gender, sexual orientation, disability, globalization, etc.), critical psychologists take up issues of inequality and make them a practical research concern.

Of course, in practice the mainstream is ambivalent about ethical–political issues because the separation of *is* and *ought* is not really maintained in professional organizations, and the public demands an ethical position on certain issues. The American Psychological Association, the Canadian Psychological Association, and many other professional organizations have adopted codes of ethics to which members submit. Obviously, values come into play when doing psychology (see I. Prilleltensky, 1994). From a Latin American point of view, Martín-Baró (1994) pointed out that an ethical–political stance and objectivity do not conflict with each other. For example, when it comes to torture it would be possible to be ethical (thus rejecting torture) while at the same time maintaining objectivity (understanding the objective consequences of torture on human mental life).

Foucault not only wrote about the prison system but also became active in the prison reform movement. This path relates to Karl Marx's famous notion of the primacy of praxis over theory: intellectual reflection should not be about interpreting the world so much as changing it. For Marx, the final goal of all praxis was changing society's fundamental economic foundations, which he perceived as the source of inequality. A member of the Frankfurt

School of critical theory, Max Horkheimer (1992) also pleaded for an end to the separation of value and research, knowledge and action, and the individual and society. Instead of denying that values guide research and instead of hiding interests, Horkheimer specifically laid out values to guide critical research: an organization of society to meet the needs of the whole community and to end social injustice. Critical social research should be guided by these ethical–political ideas and should generate knowledge that has emancipatory relevance.

Two things should be emphasized: mainstream psychology is also guided by certain values, beginning with the value of value-neutrality; and a lack of reflection on the values that guide one's research maintains the status quo. Critical psychologists have analysed psychology's role in maintaining capitalism, patriarchy, colonialism, and Western ideology (for instance, see Weisstein, 1993). In not challenging the mainstream, psychology reinforces the status quo, which also means performing psychology in the interest of the powerful. This embeddedness of psychology in the market economy has made it difficult to promote psychology as an emancipatory science. Even social psychology, which has a history of contributing to emancipation, has largely been transformed into a field that produces huge amounts of socially irrelevant data.

To make this argument about the mainstream's primarily adaptive praxis more transparent I would like to mention one example from psychotherapy. A psychologist can work in a therapeutic setting with gays and lesbians to make their homosexuality (seemingly) disappear. This was considered adaptive by some people at a particular point in time. On the other hand, working with such individuals on the transformation of personal attitudes *and* societal perspectives, a praxis that may include social action can be considered emancipatory. Rather than *making homosexuality into a problem*, psychotherapy should be about *working on problems that homosexuals encounter* in a particular society. An emancipatory praxis does not silence the needs and concerns of people suffering from societal prejudices.

In terms of alternatives, cultural–historical, Neo-Marxist, and other critical approaches in the West have acknowledged the primacy of praxis but have often remained in the comparably safe environment of academia. Thus, instead of becoming politically active outside the political mainstream, many critical theorists have suggested that research, if not emancipatory itself, should at least have an emancipatory intention (Habermas, 1972). In fact, in critical thought one can find ethical–political orientations that range from left-liberal progressive to radical. Many ivory tower critical psychologists also justify theoretical research as a legitimate option, because the production of knowledge is considered a form of praxis (as is teaching) that is not inferior to concrete community-based interventions in the abolition of social injustice.

Although Marxists, feminists, and social constructionists have developed ideas on the unity of theory and practice, the most obvious consequences of praxis can be seen in economically less developed contexts where theorizing for the sake of theorizing and research for the sake of research must be considered indulgent practices given that lives and deaths are at stake. Again, Martín-Baró (1994) argues that it is insufficient to put ourselves in the shoes of oppressed people. Instead he pleads for a new praxis, which he defines as an activity that transforms social reality and lets us know not only about *what is* but also about *what is not*, and by which we may try to orient ourselves toward *what ought to be*. In consequence, the psychologist is less a traditional clinician and more a resource for the community regarding intervention and support in the fields of disability, mental health, and drug use and also in terms of economic development and anti-poverty programmes.

For Martín-Baró it is not so much that theory defines the problems but rather that the problems demand their own theorization. In consequence, he worked with victims of state oppression, assumed active social roles, and worked with marginalized groups as a collective. This allowed for an understanding of suffering as a shared issue rather than an individualized problem. His *preferential option for the poor* was influential in shaping his political–ethical ideas. The concrete praxis method that he used has been labelled *participatory action research* but he also believed it needed to be accompanied by an analysis of the history and social theory of oppression. Originally, action research was introduced to psychology by Kurt Lewin (1946) who, motivated by the unity of theory and praxis, believed in the transformative power of research in social psychology. This method of praxis allows for studying and changing a problem at the same time.

Certain fields in psychology lend themselves to practical interventions based on progressive ethical–political systems. For example, although not all parts of community psychology are emancipatory, some critical psychologists are associated with community psychology (see Prilleltensky and Nelson, 2002 and Chapters 8 and 22 in this volume). Concrete critical psychological praxis has also been addressed in the context of AIDS in Africa (Hook, 2004) and in Latin America in terms of various forms of liberation psychology (Montero and Christlieb, 2003).

current issues for critical psychology

Critical reflection and recognition that psychology is a problematic science should not be understood as a call to abandon psychology. Instead, it is an argument to transform psychology in a direction that does justice to the complexity of the subject matter, chooses methodologies for the particularities of mental life embedded in contexts, and develops ethically responsible practices and ideas that challenge the status quo. The future of psychology as well as of critical psychology depends on understanding that the world has become more interconnected. Despite the negative consequences of economic globalization for many nations, groups, and individuals, opportunities present themselves for the theory and praxis of the discipline.

This opportunity can be described as *internationalization* (see Brock, 2006). It should be noted that this term connotes two opposing strategies: it could mean the propagation of Americanized psychology around the world; indeed internationalization traditionally meant the world-wide distribution of American psychology (or at best, cross-cultural studies based on a Western ontology and epistemology). But the term could also mean a move away from an American to a genuine global psychology. A global postcolonial psychology involves a process of *assimilation*, by which mainstream psychology incorporates non-Western concepts into the discipline, but more importantly, a process of *accommodation*, by which the very nature of psychology changes based on ideas from around the world. If one assumes that any local psychology (including American psychology) could learn from other local perspectives, then an international postcolonial psychology requires more than a process of incorporation.

The notion of internationalization is based on the idea that Western psychological concepts are neither universally applicable nor superior to concepts from other cultural contexts. In addition, Western psychology should pay attention, for instance, to the classical Indian concept of a *fourth state of consciousness* (reaching a non-dualistic, undivided, and unchanging Self through meditation; see Paranjpe, 1998) or to the concept of *ubuntu* (personhood is understood in relationship with others) in South African psychology (Mkhize, 2004).

Indeed, we all, including psychologists, have limited horizons, restricted psychological perspectives within which we develop our research and practice. Exposure to historically and culturally significant horizons that transcend our own point of view will allow the development of broader, deeper, and more sophisticated perspectives that address the significant problems of the discipline.

▨ ▨ main chapter points ▨

1 The various approaches to critical psychology can be studied along three philosophically distinctive, but in reality integrated, problem complexes: (a) *ontological* discussions include a critique of the *subject matter* of psychology; (b) *epistemological* concerns focus on the *methodology* of psychology; and (c) *ethical–political* frameworks challenge the *practice* of psychology.

2 These three problem areas are analysed in terms of accepted ideas in mainstream psychology, the critique of the mainstream, and alternatives developed in various critical psychologies.

3 Finally, some ideas on the future of critical psychology are presented.

- **epistemology**: the study of knowledge. Psychologists interested in epistemological questions discuss the discipline's adequate *methodology* (a general framework for studying psychological topics), *methods* (specific approaches for studying psychological issues), and their relationship to knowledge.

- **ethical–political concerns**: the dash emphasizes that ethical concerns are also political concerns and vice versa. In psychology those concerns influence the *praxis* of psychology. The term *praxis* is used in order to emphasize the ethical–political nature of all psychological practices.

- **ontology**: the study of *Being* in general. In psychology researchers in this area address the nature of the psychological subject matter (the 'object' of psychology), the nature of human mental life, human nature in general, and the nature of psychological categories.

▉ ▉ reading suggestions ▉

For an introductory overview of the various forms of critical psychology, I recommend the following books: Hook's (2004) textbook provides critical psychological theory and praxis from an African perspective; Tolman (1994) presents a good overview on the history and theory of Holzkamp's German critical psychology, of which not many works have been translated into English; Sloan (2000) includes the personal voices as well as the ideas of critical psychologists; Teo (2005) provides a historical and systematic reconstruction of the various critiques of psychology; Slife, Reber, and Richardson (2005) address critical thinking in psychology and its areas; and Prilleltensky and Nelson (2002) explore critical praxis systematically.

: // internet resources /

- History and Philosophy of Psychology web resources: www.psych.yorku.ca/orgs/resource/

- History and Theory of Psychology Graduate Program – York University, Canada: www.yorku.ca/health/psyc/graduate/ht_more_info.htm

- Illuminations: The Critical Theory Project: www.gseis.ucla.edu/faculty/kellner/illumina%20Folder/

- International Society for Theoretical Psychology (ISTP): psychology.ucalgary.ca/istp/

- Kritische Psychologie – German critical psychology: www.kritische-psychologie.de

- **Marxist Internet Archive**: www.marxists.org/index.htm

- **Philosophy Resources on the Internet**: www.epistemelinks.com

- **Radical Philosophy**: www.radicalphilosophy.com

- **Society for Theoretical and Philosophical Psychology of the American Psychological Association**: soe.indstate.edu/div24/

- **Stanford Encyclopedia of Philosophy**: plato.stanford.edu

Questions

1 What is the proper subject matter of psychology?

2 How would you conceptualize theoretically and practically the relationship between the individual and society?

3 Provide examples and, if possible, personal experiences of methodologism.

4 Discuss how ethical–political values influence psychological research and practices.

5 Discuss how theory and praxis are related.

Part 2

Critical Disciplines

4

Theories of Personality
Tod Sloan

Human nature. Individuality. Experience. Self. Character. Identity. Psyche. Each of these terms overlaps considerably with at least one definition of '**personality**'. Within psychology, few terms encompass so great a scope. Few concepts are as fundamental. Concepts of personality not only shape the thoughts one can have about the phenomena of human existence, but also inform one's views on what life is about and how society should be organized. It is therefore with a certain urgency that we ask in this chapter: How have theories of personality operated in mainstream psychology? What concepts of personality might serve the purposes of critical psychology? How can we theorize about personality in a manner that contributes to the construction of a humane and just society?

In its essence, a *theory of personality* is a set of interrelated concepts for understanding the actions and experiences of human individuals. Most theories of personality attempt to provide a comprehensive and integrated general psychology of motivation, development, individual differences, psychopathology and mental health, as well as an account of more specific phenomena such as dreams, creativity, aggressiveness, or social conformity. In other words, a **personality theory** aims to provide an understanding of individual experience and behaviour at both the general and the particular levels. If a set of concepts happens to fall short of this comprehensiveness, we call it a mini-theory, a model, or simply a theory of motivation or a theory of development. The immense challenge of producing a full-blown personality theory has only been met by a dozen or so individuals. These are the figures whose work was sufficiently original and comprehensive as to merit separate chapters in textbooks on personality theory: Freud, Jung, Adler, Fromm, Horney, Erikson, Murray, Allport, Skinner, Kelly, Maslow, Rogers, Bandura, and a few others. Personality theories, however, are not always the products of single individuals. Several approaches to personality theory have managed to coalesce without being identified with a single theorist, for example, cognitive-behavioural theory or existentialist theory.

Personality theories vary widely in scope, intent, and style. Nevertheless, they all tend to address several enduring questions about human nature and differ primarily according to the positions they adopt on these issues. For example, theories can either be optimistic or pessimistic about the possibility of personality change. Does personality remain roughly the same throughout life or can it change in significant ways? Theories also differ on the issues of determinism, nature vs. nurture, and the degree to which persons should be viewed as unique. Throughout this chapter we will see why theoretical stances on these issues should not be considered merely matters of personal preference.

Despite wide divergence among personality theories on such issues, they share the characteristic of being sets of concepts designed to help us understand or explain human nature. Thus they tend to be lumped together in textbooks designed for the survey course on personality theory, which remains one of the more popular courses in the standard psychology major. Strangely enough, this course generally contains little about how to theorize. Students are only expected to memorize the main points made by various theorists and perhaps to compare their positions. Even in courses in which critical thinking is encouraged, students are usually taught neither how theories should be constructed nor how they should be assessed as theories. Instead, in keeping with general practice in mainstream psychology, future psychologists are taught that the validity of theoretical concepts is to be ascertained by operationalizing them for experimental or correlational studies. In conjunction with this practice, they are trained to describe personality mechanistically with an impoverished vocabulary, reducing the complexity of personal experience to a few quantifiable dimensions or dichotomous categories. Psychologists are thus unable to reflect critically on theory construction and its implications for practice. From this deficit in training stems many of the problems that plague all sorts of applied psychology.

Put simply, mainstream approaches have systematically reduced our capacity to understand personality. Psychologists need to know how to think about personality in order to understand it. The consequences are serious and not only because we end up befuddled. Theorizing about personality or the self within the context of mainstream psychology has generally served to maintain the societal status quo (Venn, 1984). This happens in many ways, two of which are mentioned here to illustrate this point.

First, concepts of personality always reflect a 'historical form of individuality' (Sève, 1978) associated with a particular social order. Mainstream approaches tend to generalize these views to all societies and historical periods. One quickly jumps to the conclusion that since people will always be more or less the way they are now (e.g., greedy, aggressive), one need not bother with improving society.

A second form of status quo maintenance occurs when views of personality present individualistic perspectives on human development. Mainstream personality theories lead their consumers to define problems in living as private matters to be solved by personal growth or self-actualization (Holzkamp-Osterkamp, 1991). This diverts attention away from seeking collective solutions to problems that are actually social, not personal, in origin. Individualistic theories also forget that the luxury and leisure to be concerned with personal growth are available mostly to the privileged classes in modern societies. Massive social change would be necessary before the vast majority of citizens could dedicate themselves to psychological wellbeing in the manner implied by many theories. In short, individualistic perspectives tend to blame individuals for their problems and leave social inequality unchallenged.

To flesh out these and other critical points, I discuss in this chapter the historical development of the field, factors affecting theoretical choices, and the purposes served by personality theories. In the final section, I propose a few guidelines for theorizing about personality in a critical mode.

historical background

A glance at the contents of any textbook of personality theory shows that the field defines itself as having started in Central Europe at the turn of the century with Sigmund Freud and psychoanalysis. Of course, human cultures have always had ways of talking about individual character and notions about why individuals are the way they are, but these were not full-blown theories, nor did they pretend to be scientific. By the time of Freud, there were major theories of psychopathology and even some fairly well developed systems of 'characterology', particularly in France. But before Freud, most thinking about personality was primarily theological, philosophical, and speculative in nature. Freud, like all personality theorists, also had his philosophical and speculative moments, but he also sought to derive his concepts from systematic observations in the consulting room. Over four decades, he energetically elaborated and illustrated dozens of concepts through case studies, wove his notions together, sought new evidence, and revised basic principles. The result was psychoanalytic theory and the practice of psychoanalysis itself, both of which constantly undergo further revision by theorists and practising analysts. Inspired by Freud, Carl Jung also laboured for decades and accomplished roughly the same feat albeit with different objectives and results.

As the standard textbook shows, the centre of gravity in personality theorizing soon shifted from Europe to the United States. This happened in part because important European theorists emigrated before and during World War II, but also because the modern scientific worldview had weakened theological concepts of personhood in the USA just as it had in Europe. Psychologists began turning to secular models of personality for answers to their questions about human nature. The details of the ensuing search fill the pages of personality textbooks.

The main contours of the search derive from various reactions to Freud, who in turn embodied the central contradictions of European modernity. On one hand, Freud's pessimism about change and his questionable scientific methods were not well-received by hard-nosed, down-to-business psychologists in the United States. Behaviourists insisted on concepts that referred to observable and measurable phenomena. As pragmatists, they also wanted to see results; they had little patience for interventions that implied years on an analyst's couch. On the other hand, humanistic psychologists sought visions of human nature that offered more hope for individuals and society than Freudian perspectives (Jacoby, 1975). They also preferred to avoid deterministic approaches that overlooked individual uniqueness, consciousness, and agency (agency refers to a process in which one reflectively determines personal needs and interests and then acts to fulfil them). Most of the major theories proposed since Freud and Jung reflect these behaviourist or humanistic concerns, but recently, in attempts to overcome obvious ethnocentrism, textbook authors have begun to include chapters on the elaborate concepts of self in traditional Hindu and Buddhist thought. Simply put, the history of personality theory is the history of a European and North American debate about the nature of human individuals and the sort of science that would be appropriate for understanding them.

To conclude this necessarily brief history, one might note that roughly a quarter century has passed without seeing the addition of an original major theory to the textbooks. What this means for the field is not exactly clear, but perhaps it indicates that we finally have enough theories and have shifted our attention to evaluating them in research and practice. Since the 1970s, researchers have preferred to work on mini-theories relevant to specific topics and practitioners eclectically seek techniques that work, often with little regard for their theoretical justification.

Mainstream psychology expects theories of personality to synthesize or integrate knowledge produced by the various subdisciplines of psychology such as social, developmental, abnormal, cognitive, and so forth. Although some cross-fertilization occurs between subdisciplines, only personality theorists claim the task of synthesis as their own.

Personality theorists are thus generalists who stand back to get the big picture on human nature. A certain grandiosity may motivate this pretension to omniscience, but the move toward synthesis and integration is problematic for other reasons. As theorists seek concepts or findings to incorporate in their general perspective, they necessarily make assumptions about the nature of human nature and about how it should be studied. Even when a theorist makes these assumptions explicit, a great deal of unnecessary baggage is imported in the process, much of which has the function of sustaining the societal status quo. Chapter 19 addresses this problem of ideology in theory extensively. Among the baggage that sneaks into personality theories as they are developed and employed, one finds (a) choices about how to frame personality, (b) choices about how personality develops, (c) choices related to a worldview, and (d) choices about what counts as knowledge about personality. Each of these deserves further discussion.

choices about how to frame 'personality', the object of inquiry itself _____

Some theorists think of personality in terms of dimensions on which individuals can be said to differ. Most trait theory takes this approach. Others see personality as the stable core of character that produces a person's relatively consistent behaviour. Psychodynamic approaches adopt this definition. Personality can also be construed in terms of uniqueness, temperamental dispositions, social aspects of individual behaviour, qualities of emotional experiences, an ideal to be achieved – the list could go on and on. Thus, in the very first act of theorizing, in decisions about how personality is to be defined, numerous assumptions enter into the construction of the object of inquiry. In other words, to varying degrees, personality theories tend to stack the cards in their favour before the game even starts. For example, a theorist who has things to say about unconscious processes has nothing to lose by defining personality in a manner that highlights unconscious processes. A psychologist who wants to prove that personality is inherited will define it in terms that relate to temperament. Such preferences stem from factors ranging from professional training in a particular school of thought to religious background and personal concerns. Obviously, such initial framing of the object of inquiry directs attention to certain aspects of human behaviour or experience and not to others. This is problematic because personality theories are presented as comprehensive systems. Their advocates rarely suggest that we look elsewhere for understanding. Furthermore, as we saw above, definitions of personality are also likely to reinforce implicitly a model of society that justifies the status quo and the fates of persons within it. In critical social science, this is known as a form of ideology. If we define ideology as ideas or images that sustain unjust social relations, then we must be alert to the probability that concepts of personality are ideological constructions (Sloan, 1994, 1996b).

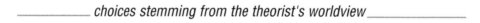

choices about how 'personality' develops

Theorists tend to have biases about whether the behavioural phenomena they observe are due to social learning, inherited temperamental factors, long-term evolutionary processes, aspects of the present situation, a combination of the above, or an individuality that transcends all determinants. As with definitions of personality, these biases can stem from training, sociocultural context, political assumptions, and other influences. Of course, theorists' positions on the question of development direct their attention to specific spheres of behaviour or experience. These positions shape subsequent thinking about the meaning or function of any aspect of personality. Again, the consequence is not only that important aspects of development may be overlooked; ideological functions may be served as well. For example, if personality is viewed as mostly inherited, it follows that changing social institutions to foster healthier personality development would be less important than improving genetic screening for desired or undesired psychological types.

choices stemming from the theorist's worldview

Every psychologist has ideas about the purpose (if any) of life, the goals that people should have, notions about right and wrong behaviours, sociopolitical notions regarding the good society, right government, the nature of history, and so forth. Each of these ideas represents a particular value stance. A few theorists have made serious attempts to link their ideas on personality to values grounded in an overarching worldview – Unger (1984) and Holzkamp (Tolman, 1994; Tolman & Maiers, 1991) come to mind. The majority, however, have insisted that they are value-free scientists describing human reality as it is. Psychologists have been exceptionally slow in catching on that it will never be possible to be value-free in the human sciences (Fox, 1985; Howard, 1985). Yet, our embeddedness in value systems is not necessarily a problem, as many would quickly assume. A meaningful science of personality is still possible. But to be meaningful, a science must adjust to the nature of its object as well as to the nature of the subjects who conduct scientific inquiry. This means making value stances explicit.

Philosophers may never resolve the basic issues about human knowledge. Personality theorists reflect this lack of resolution in the stances they take on how to study personality. At one extreme, one finds theorists who have been content to trust their intuitions, personal experience, or common sense. At the other extreme are a few theorists who prefer to derive their conceptual frameworks exclusively from data gathered in laboratory experiments or correlational studies. These epistemological and methodological preferences may be the product of professional socialization, a personal inclination toward speculative philosophy or empirical science, the requirements for publishing in scientific journals, and developments in the philosophy of social science itself. Many of the ongoing arguments between proponents of different personality theories have little to do with substantive issues; instead, they flow from different choices about what counts for knowledge. For example, to prove the validity of a concept, a Freudian might submit an account of how a patient's dreams changed after hearing an interpretation of her transference reaction. A cognitive theorist might want to see that reaction times to certain stimuli had changed as a result of the interpretation. A phenomenological theorist would probably put a lot of weight on what the patient had to say about the matter.

Despite a vague recognition of these four relatively arbitrary components of any theory of personality, mainstream psychology insists on dealing with theoretical propositions about personality as if they were statements about hypothesized relations between mass and energy or about the functioning of organisms such as frogs or amoebae. As a result, partisans of whatever theory scurry to amass sufficient empirical evidence to prove that their favourite theory is indeed the most accurate, valid, fruitful, practical, insight-laden, all-encompassing, or deserving of research funding. Since choices regarding the criteria and methods for evaluating a theory depend on the litany of factors we visited in the four points above, the entire science of personality gets caught in a vicious cycle. Simple ideas with non-scientific origins become scientific variables used ubiquitously to account for behaviour (e.g., 'self-esteem', Jungian types). Complex ideas that are perhaps very useful in understanding personality but not operationalizable are neglected or rejected as unscientific (e.g., defense mechanisms, individuation). Years are spent to prove that a certain theory is valid only for it to be forgotten by the next generation or displaced by a theory that says roughly the same thing with different terminology.

In general, mainstream psychology imports its criteria for evaluating theories of personality from those used in the natural sciences: empirical validity, verifiability, internal consistency, parsimony, and so on. Criteria such as these have limited relevance for studies in psychology in general. They have been especially irrelevant to the advance of personality theorizing. Critical psychologists must take this irrelevance very seriously. Instead of rushing to find an isolated empirical justification for concepts associated with a particular theoretical framework, we must first engage in extensive critiques of the ideological underpinnings of basic psychological concepts. In part, this implies becoming hyper-aware of how the factors listed above enter into our thinking about personality. The point of doing so will become clear if we back up a few paces and ask why we need theories of personality in the first place.

the purposes of personality theory

Here we will focus not on the motivations of the grand theorists, but on the purposes fulfilled by personality theory in everyday psychological practice. This strategy takes into account the fact that consumers of theories rarely use them as their authors intended. Furthermore, what ends up having a direct impact on individuals and societies is the way ideas are adopted and implemented.

Within mainstream psychology, personality theories are primarily used to guide attempts to change behaviour, to predict future action, or to understand individual lives. Although these purposes overlap somewhat, we will address them separately.

intervention

A personality theory can serve as a source of descriptive concepts or categories to help explain a problematic aspect of an individual's behaviour and guide an intervention to change it. For example, repetitive handwashing might be understood by relating it to the category of obsessive-compulsiveness. Once the category is applied, various treatments would be indicated. Or, a therapist might determine that a student's test anxiety is due to a fear of success linked to his Oedipus complex, and again a specific course of intervention would be specified. In such cases, one assumes that the correct assignment of a category will aid a psychologist in knowing how to change the problematic behaviour. Knowing how a particular behavioural manifestation is linked to a more general feature of the individual's personality guides the intervention toward causes and not just effects. From this perspective, the purpose of a personality theory is to provide concepts that link symptom to syndrome, behaviour to trait, effect to cause, etc. A theory is judged to be a good one if interventions based on these linkages actually work. Note that the main purpose of a theory in this case is to produce successful interventions, that is, to achieve a desired effect at the level of individual behaviour or experience.

prediction based on an assessment of individual differences

A personality theory can also serve as a source of concepts or categories that chart the basic ways in which individuals differ from each other in enduring ways. The practical aim here is to use assessments of an individual's personality to predict future behaviour, as in personnel selection or clinical screening. Subjective human judgments are supplemented or replaced by supposedly objective personality descriptors. The interest in individual differences is also relevant to research in mainstream personality psychology. In that field, debate still continues on the question of which traits are the most central to human personality in general and which traits make the best predictors of future behaviour (Sloan, 1986). The field has also tried to determine the importance of personality relative to situational determinants of behaviour. Eventually these concerns come around again to issues of prediction, since according to the mainstream philosophy of science, one should be able to predict future behaviour if one has explained it correctly in the first place. Note that in this case as well the main purpose served by theory is to suggest a technical intervention to produce a desired outcome.

biographical understanding

The first two purposes of personality theory fall clearly within the general expectations of mainstream psychological science. A good theory is expected to increase our ability to explain, predict, and control behaviour. But psychology is not monolithic (Kimble, 1984). Thus, a third purpose of personality theory meets expectations that come from other quarters, in this case, the educated public and humanists. People want to understand why people, especially famous individuals, do what they do. *Understanding* differs significantly from explanation in terms of cause and effect in order to predict. The aims of understanding are multiple, and on occasion the ability to predict is desired, but even if it were possible, it would have little impact. For example, there would be no point in trying to predict a political leader's or a movie star's future behaviour, but one might attain a certain enlightenment about politics or pop culture through studies of their lives. Biographical understanding requires a mustering of numerous perspectives on a person's life: childhood, family, friendships, contacts, influences, cultural trends, social institutions, historical period, and so forth. One never attains a sense of understanding a person totally, but one does begin to comprehend the struggles, the joys and disappointments, and the 'meaning' of the person's life. Biographical understanding also requires a related empathic identification on the part of the person who seeks understanding. Biographical understanding necessarily involves an interpretive moment based on the subjective expressions of the person being understood (diaries, letters, interviews, creative works, etc.). Thus the issue of how to study lives scientifically is often raised and personality theories are often called upon to support a biographer's argument. An entire subfield known as *the study of lives* has arisen to address such issues and continues to inspire important contributions to our understanding of personality (cf. McAdams & Ochberg, 1988; Rosenwald & Ochberg, 1992).

It is no coincidence that the purposes served by personality theories in mainstream psychology coincide with two of the three primary interests served by knowledge-seeking in general. Following the German social theorist Habermas (1972), we may refer to these as the interest in technical control (typical of the physical and natural sciences) and the interest in interpretive understanding (the hermeneutic interest characteristic of historical and humanistic studies).

In light of this, we may begin to differentiate between the purposes of mainstream theorizing and the interest to be served by critical approaches. Critical psychology seeks knowledge in order to serve a third sort of purpose. Habermas contrasts the interests in technical control and interpretive understanding with an emancipatory interest that motivates critical social science (cf. Fay, 1987; Held, 1980). As prototypes of emancipatory scientific inquiry, Habermas cites psychoanalysis and Marxist social theory. Both modes of inquiry attempt not only to explain and understand, but also seek to enhance human agency in order to modify conditions of systematic suffering. Psychoanalysis invites the patient to move away from neurotic and ideological structures toward awareness, responsibility, and desire. Marxist social theory urges oppressed social classes to be cognisant of their exploitation and to work for social change. In Chapter 19, I expand on the critical functions of these two approaches. Both approaches also focus on identifying the obstacles to effective action in their own interest, in these two examples, unconscious 'resistance' or alienation and false consciousness. As these examples indicate, the emancipatory interest differs from the other two in that it requires the self-reflective involvement of the persons who hope to bring about change in their own situation. In other words, rather than intervening in people's lives as if they were objects to be manipulated toward desired outcomes or simply interpreting lives out of mere curiosity, emancipatory modes of inquiry depend on the conscious participation of individuals and groups in articulating their needs and working toward their fulfilment. The emancipatory interest overlaps considerably with several other terms: liberation and de-**ideologization** (Martín-Baró, 1994); conscientization (Freire, 1981); empowerment (Cowen, 1991; Rappaport, 1981); the enhancement of subjectivity (Rosenwald, 1985, 1988).

Strangely enough, while the emancipatory interest is relatively inoperative in mainstream psychology, it is this interest that the general public expects the field, and personality theory in particular, to serve. When readers go to counsellors and therapists or pick up books by Freud, Rogers, or Skinner, they seek exactly the sort of enlightenment that follows when the emancipatory interest of science is being fulfilled. They have problems in living; they are perplexed, alienated, and confused (Rosenwald, 1985, 1988). They do not seek merely to be fixed by an expert technician. If they were offered the chance, they would want to understand their situations, articulate their needs more concretely, and move forward with a greater sense of agency, autonomy, and meaningful relatedness to others.

How did mainstream psychology happen to deviate so far from this fairly obvious *raison d'être*? As many chapters in this volume insist, the field managed to get so far off track partly because it has been trying so hard to be respected as a science. This meant adopting various methods associated with positivism. But given that psychology's subject matter is people, positivist criteria for scientificity are inappropriate and not even based on a correct understanding of positivism (Phillips, 1987). People do not need to be studied as if they were plants or crystals, unable to communicate about their desires, needs, hopes, and sufferings. People do not need a set of universal principles or laws of behaviour. Instead, people need to be invited by psychologists and other social scientists to participate in an ongoing process of reflection on our personal and collective problems in living meaningfully.

One senses that personality theories could play a very important role in the process of social transformation and human betterment, in particular by showing how personal concerns and social injustice are intertwined. Occasionally, personality theories have painted pretty pictures of what the good life might be like (the fully functioning person, the self-actualizing individual), but they tend to end up simply exhorting us to change without empowering us to do so. Some theorists, such as Fromm (1955) and Skinner (1971), even wrote tracts on how society should be changed. Nevertheless, a theory of personality with well-articulated links to a theory of modern society has yet to appear. Since critical psychologists have their work cut out for them, let us turn to the question of how we might go about the task of theorizing about personality in a different manner.

theorizing critically about personality

To this point, the values that guide my critique of mainstream approaches to personality theory have remained relatively unspecified. In this final section, I will move gradually toward an explicit statement of the criteria that critical theorizing about personality should meet. What I present here is my own formulation and should not be construed as broadly representative of a critical psychological approach. Nevertheless, the particulars of my formulation will show that I am indebted to the influence of various authors who provide key elements for critical theorizing about personality. Georges Politzer (1928), Lucien Sève (Sève, 1978; Sloan, 1987), and Klaus Holzkamp (Tolman, 1994) worked out the core principles of a dialectical-materialist psychology of personality, providing a strong corrective for both the individualism and the asocial character of mainstream psychology (dialectical materialism is the basic philosophy underlying Marxism, which views change as the transcendence of contradictions or oppositions in the material world). Jacoby (1975), Earnest (1992), and Barratt (1993) show how the integration of ideology criticism and psychoanalytic theory can radically subvert mainstream notions of personhood. Sampson (1989) and Broughton (1986) demonstrate how our concepts of self are shaped by historical contexts in ways that serve ideological functions. Marcuse (1955) and Benjamin (1988) critique patterns of socialization and social structure that interfere with our capacities for enjoyment and meaningful relatedness to others.

First, critical psychology needs a definition of personality that guides our attention to the aspects of personhood that have something to do with both systematic suffering and emancipation from it. Instead of thinking of personality as simply a system of enduring dispositions or a set of personal characteristics that make one unique or different from others, we might consider personality as a problem, in the sense that 'character structure' is generally viewed as a problem because it indicates rigidity or a lack of boundaries, impaired awareness, automatic behaviours that increase one's suffering, and so on. We should hasten to add that, seen this way, personality is not only a problem but a social problem with social origins and effects. The aspects of personhood that concern critical psychologists are those that social relations characterized by domination and oppression systematically produce. A critical definition of personality might thus refer to socially produced aspects of identity and affective experience that impede self-reflection, agency, autonomy, mutuality, participation, and other capacities that characterize meaningful living. In this view, personality is something to be transcended. A critical theory of personality would help us individually and collectively to accomplish this transcendence. In moving beyond personality, the capacities toward which we would want to strive could be lumped together under the term *intersubjectivity* (Habermas, 1981). (The term derives in part from a notion of full communication between self-determining subjects.)

Given this rough definition of personality, we need some idea of how personality develops. Here several varieties of psychodynamic theory suggest themselves, because these models focus on ways that early relationships limit our capacities to experience our needs and to reflect on and communicate them adequately to others (Sloan, 1996a). As a consequence of the limitations and power relations associated with early socialization, we each become unable to experience and understand our lives as fully as possible. How we label this deficit (the terms 'neurosis' and 'alienation' work fairly well) is less important than correctly analysing its origins. For this task, standard psychodynamic theory is insufficient because it focuses primarily on intrafamilial factors. The processes that restrict our capacities for meaningful living derive not only from regular interaction patterns peculiar to family members and caretakers, but also from other sociocultural factors operating through the family and other socializing institutions (Münch, 1988). I have in mind factors such as social class, gender, ethnicity, and other social realities that always mediate personality processes throughout the life span (Gregg, 1991).

To the extent that all these factors can combine to restrict capacities for self-reflection and meaningful activity, they may be called ideological processes. Critical approaches define ideology as a system of representations and practices that sustain and reproduce relations of domination within a given social order (Thompson, 1984). In this light, personality can be viewed as a crystallization of ideological processes. Power and powerlessness move not only through social institutions but also through personality and are reflected in high aspirations or a lack of hope, assertiveness or passivity, wellbeing or discontent. We saw earlier that mainstream concepts of personality are ideological to the extent that they are individualistic and asocial in character. Moreover, personality itself, as it is lived, can be understood as an ideological construction. Freud had something like this in mind when he coined the term 'compromise formation' to refer to the symptoms or character structures that form at collision points between nature's impulses and the constraints of civilization in the individual psyche (Marcuse, 1955). Much of the work of the Frankfurt school of critical social theory, in particular that of Adorno and Marcuse (cf. Elliott, 1992; Held, 1980; Sloan, 1996a), makes this basic assumption. More recently, Habermas (1981) and Foucault (Rabinow, 1984), working from different critical angles, have detailed the ways in which capitalist modernization invades the structure of identity, disrupting the possibilities for intersubjectivity and fulfilment.

Keeping in mind the emancipatory interest as the primary impulse for theorizing, we employ a form of non-objectifying epistemology (theory of knowledge) and allow our methods to flow from it. Personality, even as defined here, has objective features that could be described, assessed, explained mechanically, and manipulated. This fact explains the partial success of mainstream psychology in predicting 'some of the behaviour some of the time'. But we need not conclude that the stability of ideologically fixed patterns of experience and action justifies interventions that treat people as mere objects and totally bypass individual capacities for self-reflection and self-determination. Nor must we run to the other extreme, as some phenomenological approaches do, of idealizing personal narratives as avenues to subjective truth when they are in fact also saturated with ideology in both their origins and effects. To the extent that self-reflection and agency are possible, they will occur in a difficult and challenging process of dialogue (in the broadest sense). This is so because personality itself, as defined here, is the product of failed intrapsychic and interpersonal communication (Habermas, 1972). Through dialogue, our identities and experience are reshaped to allow for the construction of fuller meaning. As Barratt (1993) argues, such critical, de-ideologizing activity is exactly the aim of psychoanalysis properly understood. He demonstrates that, unfortunately, much that passes for 'psychoanalysis' and most psychotherapy simply shores up crumbling identities, re-ideologizes, and restores people to correct functioning within oppressive social relations.

In conjunction with dialogue that challenges and undercuts impediments to capacities for meaningful living, I see a great deal of promise in an epistemology known as **negative dialectics** (Adorno, 1973; Held, 1980). Put simply, an approach to personality grounded in negative dialectics would note that our attempts to capture behaviour with models, concepts, and theoretical systems tend to obscure more than reveal the object of study. Any concept necessarily aims to establish an identity or a complete correspondence between itself as a representation and the object it intends to portray. But something is always left out of the concept because of limitations of language, cognitive biases, complexity, and so on. Thus, it can be held that concepts are always false, and especially so when they claim to have fully represented their object.

Now, in the case of concepts of personality, critical psychologists can make enormous progress by simply examining what it is that widely used concepts ignore or exclude as they pretend to capture the essence of a particular phenomenon. For example, one could look at trait theory, which reduces personality to a system of specific enduring behavioural dispositions. It would be fairly simple to show that although two people have identical profiles on a trait inventory, the meanings or intentions typically fulfilled by the actions related to those trait dimensions are so different that to say they have similar personalities would be ridiculous. The aggressiveness of the first person, for example, might be directed toward finding housing for the homeless, while the same trait in the second leads him to get into fights in bars. The supposed comparability of the two people on the trait dimension breaks down as soon as we consider what the concept left out. The objectivism of trait theory turns out to be yet another ideological trap (Sloan, 1986). This conclusion may be reached even before one considers the various questionable uses to which trait inventories are put by psychologists working in administrative settings (for selection and screening in courts, schools, clinics, and corporations).

To illustrate a second negative dialectical move, we could consider how mainstream concepts of personality fail to capture the ways in which personal characteristics are hardly personal at all. The sociality of personality is erased by individualistic concepts that see the person not only as the container but also the origin of enduring characteristics. In a critical view such as the one proposed here, personality is not asocial; instead, it can be viewed as a congealed moment of social process. For example, my 'shyness' and your 'confidence' are manifestations of a complex intertwining of social class, ethnicity, socialization, life experience, identity development, and so forth. What we think of as 'individual' and 'social' are, in the final analysis, the same. An epistemology suitable for critical theorizing about personality would consistently take this into account and attempt to transcend individual/society dualism in a dialectical manner. The point of revealing the social in the individual, the general in the particular, is to denaturalize the phenomena of personhood that are taken ideologically as innate, unchangeable, and only matters for private concern (Sloan, 1996b).

To be fair, I should bring the same negative dialectical strategy to bear on the definition of personality I proposed above. One could ask what would be neglected if we were to view personality as those aspects of a person that interfere with capacities for meaningful living and which can be transcended through critical dialogue? First of all, this view could be faulted for remaining quite individualistic. Individual persons appear to remain the locus of ideological processes, when one could just as well look at obstacles to full communication that exist because of institutional structures. For example, state-sponsored terrorism, union busting tactics, issueless political campaigns, and suburban isolation do just as much to prevent productive communication about human needs as do features of personality. Our concept thus needs a clear anchoring in social structure and institutional arrangements. To some extent, this anchoring comes with a critical use of the term 'ideology' (Earnest, 1992; Thompson, 1984), for it emphasizes not only ideas and images but also concrete practices. Nevertheless, the critique is a valid one that could perhaps be levelled at any position that puts too much weight on features of individuals rather than on sociohistorical conditions that produce phenomena observed at the individual level. The issue deserves the serious attention of critical psychologists.

A second weakness of the definition I have proposed is that it highlights communication processes both in the production of impediments to meaning and in their transcendence. In other words, it interprets the absence of capacities for self-reflection and relatedness that are essential for meaningful social living primarily as a communication problem. Similarly, it characterizes the route toward improved capacities in terms of fuller communication about needs and interests. This emphasis on communication derives in part from the work of Habermas (1981) and is meant as a corrective for mechanical and cognitive views of self-transformation. The latter see growth as a matter of manipulating oneself toward change or of thinking more realistically about oneself without addressing the emotional obstacles to change. But it could be that the interest in communicative competence is still too rationalistic in that it ignores other equally valid modes of expression that also lead beyond ideologized personality structures toward social transformation. I have in mind, for example, certain aesthetic and affective experiences that are clearly important forms of expression but are not well captured in terms of dialogue and democratic consensus formation in groups.

This brief critique demonstrates how the primary dynamic of critical personality theorizing derives from the dialectical play between concepts and experience. This process will never end. There can never be, therefore, a personality theory that will do the trick for any problem it encounters. Yet, personality theories in particular have suffered from a totalizing impulse, a desire to explain everything once and for all. They thus provide maps of human reality that try to indicate all the essential landmarks and connections between them. But they can only be maps. They may indicate that the terrain includes such things as Oedipus complexes, introversion, or self-actualization, but they will never begin to capture the lived essence of your Oedipus complex, your partner's introversion, or your client's process of self-actualization. The totalizing impulse must be resisted in all psychological theorizing as part of a larger political move against the technical control of human subjectivity. The interests in pinning us down, labelling us, locating us on basic trait dimensions – and often in the guise of helping and increasing self-understanding – are part and parcel of contemporary ideological processes related to social administration and the efficient functioning of the market economy. The state and the market now cooperate to distort our own concepts of who we are and what is possible but also to negate our possibilities for becoming something else within a more humane social order (Sloan, 1996a).

In summary, the central task for personality theory is to disengage itself from the outset, in its most basic principles, from any participation in the continuing oppression of humankind by social forces that systematically reduce capacities for meaningful living. This goal implies an intimate engagement with core issues related to the quality of life of diverse groups both at the level of understanding and concerted action. As we move into the twenty-first century, some of the most pressing questions to be taken up by critical psychologists interested in personality are the following:

- How can deep-set societal patterns of gender inequality be addressed at the psychological level? What institutional changes (in couples, families, work settings) will be necessary to bring about true relational equality and mutuality?

- What sorts of processes will help individuals and groups distinguish between real needs and artificial needs manufactured by the culture industry?

- What can psychologists do to support social movements that are likely to eliminate racism and classism and bring about greater social justice?

- What can be done to increase empathy and subsequent action to help people who suffer from poverty, war, natural disasters, and illness? What sorts of prevention can be accomplished without simply reinforcing the status quo?

- How can alienation and ideologization be overcome? What psychological factors interfere with self-reflection, democratic decision making, and sense of community?

- In postmodern social contexts, what are the possibilities for meaningful living? What social arrangements seem to be working for individuals, families, and communities? What constitutes meaningfulness in the first place?

These questions are, of course, just a few of the possible directions critical psychologists might pursue. Nevertheless, they indicate that theorizing about personality in a critical mode may inspire not only changes in psychological practice but a radical transformation of the social order as well. Being a critical psychologist also implies an ongoing willingness to call our own practices into question and to link our own local and global concerns as directly as possible to what we do professionally. This implies taking risks, breaking new ground, and perhaps enduring isolation. There is some consolation, however, in knowing that at least we are not part of the problem. We can also derive sustenance from the knowledge that we are not alone but are in fact participating in a vast collective effort – humanity's historic struggle for social justice.

This is a slightly revised version of the chapter published in the first edition of *Critical Psychology: An Introduction*. I have focused on clarifying my original argument in light of questions from readers over the past decade. In the field of personality itself, the main recent trends have been (a) a further entrenchment of cognitive approaches that see the stability of individual behaviour across situations and life stages as due to engrained patterns of thinking, and (b) genetic and neuroscientific discoveries related to traits, moods, and temperaments. These perspectives are, of course, of interest and remind us of the fact that anything social also has a connection to the brain and body, but I continue to insist that for the most part interest in cognitive neuroscience distracts us from the societal factors responsible for most of humanity's suffering. Promising critical work is being done at the frontiers of transpersonal psychology and ecopsychology as proponents sense the need to address core power structures in postmodern society.

_____ ▓ ▓**main chapter points** ▓ _____

1   Theories of personality address core questions about human nature and individuality.

2   Mainstream theories of personality have reflected Western individualism and therefore locate responsibility at the level of the individual.

3   Scientific approaches to personality can serve different interests, such as prediction and control, interpretive understanding, and emancipation.

4   Critical approaches to the understanding of personality promote participation and agency on the part of individuals to change social relations that systematically produce problems in living.

_____ **glossary** _____

*   **ideologization:** a social process that channels experience and action toward patterns that reproduce systems of domination and oppression, such as sexism or classism.

*   **negative dialectics:** an approach to knowledge, pioneered by Theodor Adorno, that urges attention to the ways in which concepts obscure or misrepresent what they are supposed to explain, and thereby fulfil an ideological function.

*   **personality:** the stable patterns of experience and action that define us as individuals.

*   **personality theory:** a set of interrelated concepts that aims to explain human nature in general as well as individual differences in experience and action.

For early critical approaches to personality, Erich Fromm's *Man for Himself* (1947) offers a good place to start. Herbert Marcuse's *Eros and Civilization* (1955) or Wilhelm Reich's *Character Analysis* (1972) sets up a stronger Marxist reading of personality processes than Fromm develops. Russell Jacoby's *Social Amnesia* (1975) is an essential antidote to individualistic, humanistic theories of personality such as those of Rogers and Maslow. Jessica Benjamin's *Bonds of Love* (1988) kept critical psychoanalytic theory alive at an important moment and helped establish a feminist view of the centrality of mutuality and relationship as a factor in personality development dynamics. Anthony Elliott's many books (e.g., Elliott, 1992) do a wonderful job of making difficult theories about postmodern personality and subjectivity accessible. For a more recent twist on the possibilities of critical personality psychology, see Oullette's fine (2008) overview article.

⁞ // **internet resources** /

- **Social Anarchism Journal** – look for fascinating discussions on the nature of human nature and the possibilities for alternative forms of human community: socialanarchism.org

- **Social and Personality Psychology Compass** – a new space for reflection on personality processes, includes a section on critical perspectives: www.blackwell-compass.com/subject/socialpsychology/

- **Subjectivity Journal** – if the term 'personality' is going out of fashion, as did the concept of 'character' before it, 'subjectivity' is clearly the focus of attention now: www.palgrave-journals.com/sub/

 ▪ **Questions** ▬

1 Reflect on one of your most prominent personality traits and figure out something about its social origins and effects.

2 To what personality theorist do you tend to be drawn? Consider the meaning of this interest by reflecting on the values and principles emphasized by that theorist. Is the view of human nature painted by the theorist one you hope we can achieve or one that depicts humans as they currently are?

3 If personality is viewed, as Sloan argues, as an expression of the larger ideological process that maintains systems of oppression and domination, how can we productively talk about stable aspects of persons that resist oppression and domination? Should they be counted as part of personality, too?

5

Clinical Psychology: The Politics of Madness

Jeanne Marecek and Rachel T. Hare-Mustin

Chapter Topics

More than 100 years ago, a great man fell in love with a young actress. The problem was that he was married and had ten children. His solution was to insist that his wife was mentally ill, take away their children, and put her in an asylum. The man was a famous champion of home and hearth in his day, the author Charles Dickens. In the same era, many women, including several social reformers and writers, were afflicted with a mental disorder called neurasthenia, a condition combining aspects of what today might be labelled chronic fatigue syndrome, premenstrual syndrome (PMS), and depression. *The Yellow Wallpaper*, an autobiographical novella by Charlotte Perkins Gilman (1899/1973), described an acclaimed treatment for female neurasthenia. The treatment involved compulsory bed rest, the forced deprivation of mental stimulation, isolation from adult company, and constant heavy feeding, leading to weight gains of 50 pounds or more. Gilman's heroine, rather than being restored, is made mad and driven to suicide.

From our vantage point today, it is easy to see how the mental health system at the end of the nineteenth century reflected the values of that era. We argue that the present-day mental health system reflects the values of our era. Textbooks in clinical psychology typically applaud our mental health system for its humane values, protection of patients' civil rights, and scientific outlook. In this chapter, we take a closer look at such claims. Actual practices, we suggest, sometimes fall short of the ideal. We pay special attention to the experiences of those who are economically disadvantaged, women, and members of marginalized groups.

the social construction of psychological knowledge

Our approach to critical psychology draws on the framework of **social construction** (Berger & Luckman, 1966). For social constructionists, what is taken to be reality rests largely on a social consensus. Language shapes what we know and what we see, as well as what we can say. The terms that are available highlight certain features of objects, situations, and relationships; in that way, they determine what our experience is. For example, a psychiatric label such as borderline personality disorder profoundly influences what we think about individuals so labelled, how we judge their actions, and how they think about themselves.

Knowledge, including psychological knowledge, is always shaped by its social context. The theories and practices of the mental health profession at the end of the nineteenth century reflected and furthered certain ideologies, as our opening examples showed. Present-day psychology inevitably reflects the dominant themes, ideologies, and preoccupations of our time and place. In our critical examination of clinical psychology, we ask questions like these: Whose ideas and interests shape standards of mental health and illness, treatment practices, and priorities for research? Whose voices are heard? Who can speak authoritatively within the field of clinical psychology and for the field in the public arena? Who decides what will be called truth? The recipients of mental health services, for instance, are seldom regarded as credible judges of their experiences or of the treatments they receive. (See Chapter 18 for a discussion of recipients' responses to this situation.)

The power to determine what is normal and what is pathological contributes to a disciplinary regime (Foucault, 1980). Definitions of normality and optimal mental health serve as ideals of behaviour. Definitions of abnormality identify ways of thinking, feeling, and acting that one should avoid. These authorized meanings of normal and abnormal constrain everyone. Assertions of what is normal and what is abnormal are not matters of science, but judgments based on social, cultural, and ethical standards. At what point does shyness, for example, shift from being a personality trait to a psychiatric condition demanding professional intervention? In North America, more and more forms of human action are coming under the umbrella of psychiatric diagnosis, with behaviours formerly regarded as crimes, sins, or eccentricities regarded as diseases (Kleinman, 1984).

what is critical psychology?

Critical psychology embraces many forms of critique. For us, one element is a commitment to challenge psychology's focus on the individual and instead to view human action in its societal and cultural context. Thus we question the logic of the current diagnostic system, which focuses narrowly on individuals. Related to this is our commitment to attend to culture and cultural differences. For the most part, psychologists presume that their theories pertain to all human beings, irrespective of social group membership, cultural background, or life circumstances. Such universality, we believe, is rare. We worry that clinicians' judgments of normality and abnormality, the way they conduct treatment, and the goals they set for clients may tacitly impose the worldview and values of middle-class white Americans. Not only will this lead to inappropriate treatment, it is also a form of cultural imperialism.

Another element of our critical stance is the value we place on social justice and democratic participation. We are concerned to foster an equitable allocation of social and material resources, as well as equal access to self-determination, opportunities, and bargaining power. Social justice also demands that control over meanings and language be distributed throughout society. When the power to influence meanings is concentrated in pre-eminent social groups, the dominant meanings typically justify the existing power structure; the experiences of subordinate groups are erased (Hare-Mustin & Marecek, 1990).

Another element of our critical psychology concerns the politics of knowledge in the discipline. Psychological knowledge is not a body of pristine facts accumulated through research. All knowledge is inevitably shaped by the social location and political investments of those who produce and disseminate it. Furthermore, psychology (like all disciplines) is not separate from society, but is an institution existing in society and constituted by it. Its questions and answers are shaped by its cultural and historical contexts. It is not that psychological knowledge is untrue, but rather that truths are always partial and always contingent on the social surround.

Both of us came to critical psychology through our engagement with **feminism**. We have been concerned with psychology's knowledge base about gender, including claims about men's and women's supposed 'natures' and their proper roles and obligations. These claims serve to regulate social life and to perpetuate relations of inequality between men and women and among different racial, ethnic, and social class groups. Also, both of us have worked outside the USA. For Rachel, this has included work in Nigeria, Uganda, the Philippines, and China; for Jeanne, it has included work in Sri Lanka and Sweden. These experiences have led us to a strong respect for the centrality of culture and national context in personal experience, worldviews, and social life. For us, bringing culture into the study of psychology is a priority.

The field of clinical psychology encompasses many activities, including diagnosis and assessment, **psychotherapy** and other forms of treatment, research, teaching, and the development of public policy. In this chapter, however, we limit our discussion mainly to diagnosis and treatment.

clinical diagnosis: the invention of reality?

Diagnostic categories are a central feature of the mental health system. They have also become part of our everyday vocabulary for expressing and understanding personal suffering, with terms like depression, post-traumatic stress disorder, and attention deficit disorder part of ordinary talk. Because of their importance in clinical psychology and in everyday life, we discuss diagnostic categories in detail.

the Diagnostic and Statistical Manual of Mental Disorders

The *Diagnostic and Statistical Manual of Mental Disorders* (*DSM*) (American Psychiatric Association, 2000) is the standard compendium of diagnostic categories in the USA and the official *lingua franca* of the mental health establishment (Wylie, 1995). As Lloyd Rogler reminds us, the *DSM* influences not only individual treatment decisions, but also 'judicial deliberations, third-party payments, budgetary allocations by private and governmental bodies, and many other key institutional functions' (1997: 9). The *DSM*, however, is far from a scientific inventory of psychiatric conditions. Rather, it is a patchwork of scientific data, cultural values, political compromises, and material for making insurance claims. First published in 1952, the *DSM* has increased the number of diagnoses in each subsequent revision. The first edition listed 198 categories of disorder; the second, published in 1968, listed 221 categories. The number of diagnostic categories in the 1994 revision was 340. Later we shall ask whether this inflation in psychiatric diagnoses is beneficial or harmful.

The expansion of psychiatric diagnoses is not the only change from edition to edition of the *DSM*. The 1980 edition was a watershed in psychiatry, incorporating a dramatic reorientation in substance, language, and theory. The revised descriptions of psychiatric conditions were revised to emphasize possible biological and heritable aspects. In addition, the style of defining psychiatric conditions by lists of symptoms mimicked the style of biomedical diagnostic categories. This reorientation was part of a larger movement among psychiatrists to medicalize the field (Luhrmann, 2000). This effort to portray psychiatry as a bona fide branch of medicine was undertaken in order to bolster the flagging credibility of the profession and ensure its financial viability (Wilson, 1993).

We shall return to the biomedical reframing of the *DSM*, but for now, let us acknowledge some benefits of a formal and shared system for categorizing and naming psychological difficulties. Categorizing sufferers in diagnostic groups permits the accumulation and synthesis of knowledge and clinical experience, enabling generalizations to be drawn. Moreover, most research on psychological problems – whether on their causes, prognosis, treatments, or distribution across the population – requires some means of identifying a group of similar individuals for study. For example, if we wish to learn about the family environments of adolescents who have suffered a schizophrenic breakdown, we must have a systematic way of deciding which adolescents belong in our research sample. Furthermore, diagnostic categories provide professionals with a common language, enabling them to communicate ideas, clinical experiences, and the results of research.

Psychiatric researchers have put a lot of effort into setting the criteria for disorders. Indeed, the criteria have been continually revised over successive editions of the *DSM*. They typically include clinicians' observations along with sufferers' reports of their thoughts, feelings, and behaviours. Herein lies a crucial point of difference between biomedical diagnoses and psychiatric ones. In biomedicine, diagnoses typically are made on the basis of etiology (that is, underlying causes), not symptoms. For example, a fever and a flushed face (symptoms) would not be regarded as sufficient grounds for a biomedical diagnosis. Instead, a physician would test for various possible causes of those symptoms. Psychiatric diagnoses, however, are usually based on symptoms; underlying causes (if any exist) are rarely known, and seldom can be assessed.

To be useful, a diagnostic system must be reliable. That is, different diagnosticians should arrive at the same diagnosis for the same individual. Have psychiatric diagnoses achieved an adequate degree of reliability? Although there have been extensive efforts to improve the reliability of diagnostic judgments, reliability remains a problem (Kirk & Kutchins, 1992). Sometimes discrepancies are systematic. For example, in the 1960s and 1970s, clinicians in the USA often gave a diagnosis of schizophrenia to the condition that British clinicians diagnosed as manic-depressive illness (now called bipolar disorder), a cross-national difference that no longer exists. However, fads in diagnoses continually emerge and then recede. In the USA, for example, bipolar disorder has shifted from being an unusual diagnosis to an extremely common one. Indeed, there has been a 40-fold increase in the number of children who have been given the diagnosis in less than ten years (Moreno et al., 2007). Could this drastic increase reflect a true increase in the number of children with bipolar disorder? Almost certainly not. Possibly clinicians have acquired a new acumen in recognizing a previously unrecognized problem. Possibly, the formal diagnostic criteria have been changed, so that less extreme behaviour now warrants the diagnosis. It is also possible that clinicians have unwittingly shifted their judgments in response to the aggressive marketing efforts of drug companies.

_____ *the medicalization of suffering* _____

As we noted earlier, one of the crucial changes instituted with the 1980 revision of the *DSM* involved medicalization. The *DSM* – and the mental health professions in general – adopted the language of medicine to describe and understand psychological suffering. This language includes terms like disease, symptom, patient, syndrome, relapse, diagnosis, and prognosis. The fields of clinical psychology and psychiatry are now so saturated with this medical language that it would be difficult for professionals to converse without it. Moreover, when the field of psychiatry re-positioned itself as a 'medical' specialty, research efforts concentrated on searching for biological bases of suffering and pharmaceutical treatments.

As critical psychologists, we take issue with the pervasive adoption of biomedical frameworks for psychological suffering. These frameworks effectively set aside sufferers' personal history, the interpersonal and relational context for distress, and the influences of the larger social, political, and cultural system. An example is post-traumatic stress disorder (PTSD), a category invented to name the debilitating difficulties of some Vietnam War veterans after their return to civilian life. Those who agitated for the recognition of PTSD in the Vietnam War era insisted on connecting horrific experiences (such as witnessing or perpetrating death) to their subsequent psychological suffering. However, as the culture of the mental health professions shifted over the next three decades, researchers set their sights on the possible neurological and genetic substrates of PTSD, the anatomical locus of post-traumatic stress in the brain, and possible childhood precursors of PTSD. These new interests shifted attention away from wartime experiences to long-standing vulnerabilities 'inside' the person. The medicalization of PTSD both de-politicizes the diagnosis and wipes away the troubling moral implications of war.

psychiatric diagnoses are bound up with
_____ *cultural mores and societal values* _____

Ultimately, the decision to regard any set of behaviours or experiences as a psychological disorder – rather than an eccentricity, a criminal act, or a response to oppressive and intolerable circumstances – is not and cannot be a scientific one. It is a political and moral choice and a judgment grounded in a social consensus as to which behaviours are acceptable. Prior to 1980, for example, homosexuality was included in the *DSM* as a category of mental disorder. That categorization served to reaffirm the cultural and moral sanctions against non-heterosexual behaviour that prevailed in the USA in the 1950s and 1960s. In 1973, members of the American Psychiatric Association voted on a proposal to remove homosexuality from the *DSM*. (The idea of a referendum to determine the disease status of homosexuality is surely a clue that psychiatric illness is not equivalent to biomedical disease.) In accord with the outcome of the referendum, homosexuality was removed from the main body of the *DSM* in 1980.

Judgments of normality and abnormality necessarily depend on cultural standards, social norms, and local customs. For example, clinicians in the USA are trained to distinguish between 'normal' bereavement and clinical depression according to the length of time since the death of the loved one. However, the customary period of mourning in many countries (for example, Greece and India) is several months longer than in the USA. Bereaved individuals following the customs of those countries might be wrongly diagnosed as depressed by an unknowing American clinician. Even such seemingly unambiguous symptoms as hallucinations and delusions must be interpreted in light of the cultural background of the individual. In some cultures, for example, newly deceased family members are expected to communicate with their living relatives as they slowly depart from this world. Hearing dead people speak and speaking to them is not unusual and no cause for alarm. For most white Americans, however, hearing voices and conversing with the dead would be taken as strong evidence of mental illness.

To sum up, human behaviour always takes its meaning from its sociocultural surround. We worry that the criteria for mental illness put forward in the *DSM* reflect the values, customs, and norms of white, middle-class North Americans. This risks misjudgments – false positives and false negatives – when clinical encounters span cultural, social, and economic divides. Cultural competence demands not only a knowledge of other cultures, but also what is more challenging: an awareness of one's own.

_____ *psychiatric diagnosis, social power, and social regulation* _____

If we look at times and places other than our own, the relation of psychiatric diagnoses to social power is readily apparent. Before the emancipation of slaves in the United States, for example, the diagnosis of drapetomania was offered as an explanation for slaves' uncontrollable urge to escape from slavery (Stampp, 1956). Another example is the diagnosis of kleptomania, which refers to an irresistible compulsion to shoplift or pilfer. The diagnosis of kleptomania originated in parallel with the invention of large department stores at the turn of the last century. These stores afforded shoppers – who were mainly women – anonymity, an array of tempting merchandise, and the freedom to handle items for sale. This created not only an incentive to purchase, but also the temptation to steal. Shoppers of all social classes stole, but the authorities distinguished between criminal acts of theft and acts purportedly reflecting mental pathology on the basis of social class. To put it bluntly, ordinary women were regarded as thieves, but upper-class women's acts of theft were explained as a consequence of mental illness. The diagnosis of kleptomania not only served to excuse individual women and shield them from criminal prosecution, it also enabled the upper classes to maintain a posture of moral superiority (Camhi, 1993). The saga of the film star Winona Ryder, who was apprehended in 2001 for shoplifting expensive garments, bears a strong resemblance to the vicissitudes of kleptomania. As Ryder's crime was publicized, some mental health professionals proclaimed that she was not a criminal, but the victim of an illness (not included in the *DSM*) called Atypical Theft Offender Disorder, a condition claimed to result from 'emotional stress (cf. Cupchik, 1997). Categories like drapetomania, kleptomania, and Atypical Theft Offender Disorder illustrate how diagnoses may serve to promote the interests of those who are in power or high in status (e.g., slave owners, the upper classes, or celebrities).

We pointed out earlier that the number of categories of mental disorder has swelled in recent times. In addition, the criteria for many diagnoses have become less stringent, so that less severe difficulties are now seen as illnesses in need of professional remedy. As critical psychologists, we see ample reason to resist the reach of psychiatric diagnoses into everyday life. Even if the intent is benign, the proliferation of diagnoses brings increasing scrutiny and the regulation of personal life by the mental health professions. An apt example is sexuality, as Leonore Tiefer (2004) has shown. In recent revisions of the *DSM*, a wide assortment of sexual practices, difficulties, and choices has come to be defined as psychiatric or medical problems requiring intervention (Potts, 2008). Tiefer, Potts, and others ask why it is that pseudo-medical standards should be imposed on intimate pleasure. Moreover, as the slogan 'Sex for our pleasure or their profit?' implies, this reframing of sexual activities as psychiatric or medical conditions plays into the hands of pharmaceutical companies seeking to market their products. Tiefer and her colleagues have organized the 'New View', a public awareness campaign to challenge the medicalization of women's sexuality. (The New View campaign is described further in Chapter 14.)

More generally, the psychiatric regulation of personal life has numerous negative implications. It contributes to what has been called 'the diffusion of deficit', that is, the tendency to label everyday unhappiness, ordinary shortcomings, and personal quirks as pathological. It also entrusts considerable social power to the mental health professions, usurping what had earlier been the province of other social institutions, such as the law, the police, or religion.

Psychiatric regulation is an especially potent form of social control because the public seldom recognizes the mental health profession's control function.

judging and naming: do clinicians make biased diagnoses?

Clients' encounters with the mental health system typically begin with an assessment of their difficulties. This assessment includes a formal diagnosis. Its central element is the standardized name(s) for the client's condition(s), for example, schizophrenia, depression, or post-traumatic stress disorder. Although this formal diagnosis is not of central importance for psychotherapy, diagnostic classifications play an important role in prescribing medications. Moreover, diagnoses have assumed a new importance in the USA because managed care systems use them to determine if clients are entitled to reimbursed mental health treatment and how much and what type of treatment they can receive.

Do clinical practitioners make biased judgments? In asking this question, we are especially concerned for the rights and welfare of those in less privileged positions in society. There are large disparities in the apparent rates of many disorders across gender, racial, ethnic, and social class lines. Of course, such disparities do not in themselves indicate bias. They may reflect genuine differences in the distribution of these disorders in the population, differences stemming from different life experiences or from unequal access to economic and social resources. Nonetheless, many studies have found that clinicians evaluating identical case materials make different diagnostic judgments in response to information about gender, social class, racial identity, or sexual orientation (cf. Becker & Lamb, 1994; Landrine, 1989; Robertson & Fitzgerald, 1990; Strakowski et al., 1995). Moreover, given identical diagnoses and symptom descriptions, clinicians may make different treatment recommendations depending on the social status of a client. For example, if a clinician expects that individuals from lower-class backgrounds or with limited education will not benefit from psychotherapy, he or she might rule out psychotherapy as a treatment option.

Cultural disparities between therapist and client can mar clinical judgments. Not only do these disparities occur between individuals from different regions of the world, they also occur between different social groups, between communities of gay, lesbian, bisexual and transgendered individuals and straight communities, between urban and rural dwellers, and between religious individuals and secular individuals. Cultural differences easily lead to misinterpretations of behaviour and, thus, to misdiagnosing, over-diagnosing, or under-diagnosing. Over-diagnosing may occur when a clinician mistakes experiences and behaviours that are normative for a particular social group as signs of psychological disorder. For example, in the 1970s, the prevailing norms of femininity dictated that women should behave in ways that resembled the symptoms of a disorder then called hysteria (Chesler, 1972). In another instance, related by Gananath Obeyesekere (1984), an American clinical psychologist visiting Sri Lanka observed the sombre outlook that a devout Buddhist businessman had cultivated as part of his meditation practice; the psychologist opined that the man was suffering from clinical depression.

Another kind of over-diagnosing involves misinterpreting an adaptive response to a dangerous situation as pathological. In an account of her work as a rape counsellor, Michelle Fine (1989) described the reactions of a young African American woman 'Altamese' after she was gang-raped by men from her neighbourhood. Altamese refused to press charges, she was not interested in being counselled, and she declined further help from social service agencies. Tempted to label Altamese a 'passive dependent personality' or a victim of 'learned helplessness', Fine came to understand that Altamese's course of action was dictated by the constraints she faced as a low-income woman of colour and an unmarried mother, as well as by the myriad negative consequences she and her family would face if the police were involved.

Under-diagnosing – that is, overlooking or minimizing psychological suffering – is no less a problem than over-diagnosing. Under-diagnosing, of course, deprives sufferers of the treatment they need. For example, depression may be seen as 'just a developmental phase' in an adolescent or as hypochondriacal complaining in an elderly person. Under-diagnosing may also occur in situations in which individuals feel it necessary to conceal their difficulties. The culture of militarism in the United States, for example, labels soldiers who display psychological distress as weak or unmanly. Furthermore, seeking help from a mental health professional may jeopardize any chance for promotion. In consequence, few soldiers seek professional help in times of need (Chappelle & Lumley, 2006).

Can clinical psychologists guard against diagnostic errors and biases? The biases that we point out are neither simple mistakes nor acts of ill will; therefore, individual efforts will not suffice to correct them. The diagnostic system constitutes a system of interpretation that directs attention to some issues and relegates other issues to the periphery. The system must be expanded to take into account an individual's cultural background and relevant aspects of the social environment, such as poverty, racial and ethnic discrimination, urban disarray and violence, economic inequality, and immigration. Improved models of accountability in clinical work settings are also needed. One such model, called Just Therapy, requires clinicians who are members of dominant groups to listen respectfully to the voices and perspectives of team members from marginalized groups (Tamasese & Waldegrave, 1996). Finally, serious discussion of these issues in textbooks and training materials is needed. At present, nearly every textbook of clinical psychology available in the USA is organized around the *DSM*, thereby giving students and trainees no exposure to alternative points of view (cf. Marecek, 1993). In this way, the field of clinical psychology helps to conceal the costs incurred to individuals and society when power and wealth are concentrated among a privileged few.

A teenage girl with a persistent cough and frequent headaches says her father's friend has been making sexual advances to her when she accompanies her father on visits to his household. No one believes her. Her father takes her to a therapist and tells him to bring the girl to her senses. The therapist was Sigmund Freud, the founder of psychoanalysis, and the patient, Dora (Freud, 1905/1963). Her case is one of the most frequently cited in psychoanalytic literature (Hare-Mustin, 1991).

Dora's father often took her to the K. household where he was having an affair with Frau K. The husband, Herr K., had been making sexual advances to Dora since she was 14, apparently encouraged by Dora's father. Dora's mother maintained the standards of housekeeping expected of a Viennese *hausfrau* of her day. Although Freud never met Dora's mother, he did not hesitate to diagnose her as having 'housewife's psychosis', a diagnosis not included among the standard categories. Freud, from his patriarchal perspective, assumed that any young girl would appreciate the attentions of a man like Herr K. and accede to them. Therefore, he regarded Dora's problems as symptoms of hysteria resulting from her aroused and disguised sexual desire. When he tried to press these views on Dora, she quit therapy. This led Freud to label her not only as disturbed, but also as disagreeable, untruthful, and vengeful. The adults involved acknowledged some time later that her claims about Herr K. were true.

Freud's views of Dora, her family situation, and the origin of her difficulties reflect the gender politics of his era, as well as his dogmatic insistence on the accuracy of his theories. He failed to help Dora in part because of his refusal to take seriously Dora's account of her experiences, preferring his interpretations instead. In the discussion below, we trace similar problems with many present-day therapies: a focus on the inner life to the exclusion of the external situation; class, gender, and ethnocentric biases in psychological theories; and the concentration of power in the therapist, including the dominance of the therapist's point of view.

_____ *a focus on the individual* _____

Conventional *psychotherapies* often presume that what is wrong lies within the individual; the external conditions need not be addressed or changed. The focus then is on helping clients adjust to the circumstances rather than on helping them to transform the circumstances that are contributing to the problem. For example, the excessive work hours required by so-called greedy occupations are a source of stress for many workers, as is the 'double shift' of paid work plus family work that many women shoulder. These forms of 'work stress' indicate a need for structural changes in the institutions of work and family. A therapist, however, might construe 'work stress' as an individual problem and suggest remedies such as 'time management' or stress-reduction techniques like relaxation exercises or meditation.

Many therapists who work with couples assume that nothing is wrong with the institution of marriage. When couples come for help, therefore, they presume that something is wrong with the partners in the marriage. In our era, however, the institution of marriage has become burdened by exaggerated visions of romantic fulfilment and self-enhancement (Coontz, 2006). Also, marriage is expected to cushion or compensate for men's frustrations in the public arena, such as lack of economic mobility, a sense of powerlessness, and lack of recognition from the community. The unrealistic expectations placed on marriage contribute to the tension and violence in contemporary marriages, including wife beating and child abuse. Levels of violence in some families in the USA are such that women and children are safer in the streets than in their homes.

culture, class, and gender: seeing from the centre?

Psychotherapists are, by definition, members of the professional class and most have worldviews consonant with those of the middle class. Often, therapy unreflectively incorporates the ideals and norms of white, Euro-American, middle-class culture. Ideals of autonomy, independence, and self-fulfilment through individual achievement and material acquisition are a few such examples (Cushman, 1995). Echoing the historic American preoccupation with success and self-improvement, many psychological theories have posited autonomy and achievement as indicators of maturity and psychological health (Hare-Mustin & Marecek, 1986). However, autonomy and personal achievement are not compatible with the communitarian ethos of many social groups and the norms of interdependence, family solidarity, and mutuality of many cultures across the world. In addition, therapists' ideas about the proper and effective ways of coping with adversity may be based on a presumption that the privileges, social capital, and material resources afforded to members of the middle class are available to all. Moreover, therapists – like members of the middle class more generally – may have a blind belief in societal benevolence, an equality of opportunity, and the fairness of the criminal justice system. For people in marginalized and oppressed groups, such faith would be naïve and dangerous.

the power hour

In psychotherapy, individuals who have been unable to relieve their suffering seek help from culturally sanctioned experts. Therapy is thus inevitably characterized by differences in expertise, authority, and power between therapist and client. This has led some ruefully to label the therapy session 'the power hour' (Green, 1995). Therapists who are sensitive to the power imbalances in therapy have sought ways to share power with clients and to check the tendency to regard the therapist as the authority (Guilfoyle, 2003; Zimmerman & Dickerson, 1996). The feminist therapy movement, which flourished in the 1970s and 1980s, focused particular attention on power in therapy. Feminist therapists worked to heighten their awareness of operations of power in therapy and to encourage clients to recognize and exercise what power and authority they do have. For example, some tried to diminish the social distance between themselves and their clients by making the therapy setting more informal. Some challenged the usual strictures against therapists' personal disclosure by responding to clients' requests for biographical information and by occasionally offering accounts of their own experiences. Some designed ways to re-position clients as informed consumers rather than patients who submit to the doctor's orders (Hare-Mustin, Marecek, Kapan, & Liss-Levenson, 1979). At the institutional level, some feminists organized to exert pressure on professional organizations to revise their ethical codes and training standards to protect clients – especially women – from abuses of power and from sexual exploitation in therapy (Hare-Mustin, 1992).

alternatives to psychotherapy

shifting the therapeutic focus beyond individuals

Historically, it was family therapists who mounted an alternative to the individualism of conventional therapy. Family therapy involved a paradigm shift to an interpersonal perspective that focused on transactional patterns within the family context. The work of Bateson (1972) and Watzlawick, Weakland and Fisch (1974) drew on cybernetics to understand behaviour as part of a mutually influencing social system. More recently, **narrative therapists** such as Michael White (1995) have helped families and individuals to challenge and revise problem-focused narratives and to generate new narratives that open the way toward positive change (Freedman & Combs, 1996). The field of family therapy has also been the site of pioneering efforts to situate the experiences of families, couples, and individuals within the larger contexts of society and culture. For example, feminist family therapists have insisted that therapists take careful account of the prevailing gender inequalities in the workplace, households, and public life and their influence on heterosexual couples and family life (Goodrich, 1991; Hare-Mustin, 1991; McLean, Carey, & White, 1996). The Dulwich Centre in Adelaide, Australia, has further expanded the scope of therapy to include community work with marginalized and racialized groups.

Office-based psychotherapy is not the only kind of assistance that psychologists provide to people in distress. Some psychologists have looked beyond the office to community-based efforts to change the lives of suffering individuals. One example is community psychology, which can trace its roots to the community mental health movement of the 1960s and the progressive politics of US President John F. Kennedy. Community psychologists seek to understand and challenge the sociopolitical causes of psychological suffering, such as urban poverty, economic marginalization, and racial injustice, along with the demoralization, substance abuse, violence, and family chaos that often follow. Chapter 8 discusses community psychology in detail.

Like community psychology, the emerging field of psychosocial work focuses on the human suffering engendered by social and political conditions. The field of psychosocial work was developed by humanitarian aid workers seeking to help people caught up in war, genocide, forced migration, state-sponsored violence, torture, and natural disasters (Miller & Rasco, 2004; Wessells, 2006b; see also Chapter 16). In the field of psychosocial work, suffering and wellbeing are seen to have collective dimensions, as well as personal ones. Thus, for example, workers may help communities to reconstitute and strengthen themselves by sponsoring programmes of reconciliation and conflict resolution, by assisting them in rebuilding civil society organizations, or by strengthening local governance.

the political economy of clinical psychology

Clinical psychology – and the mental health professions in general – are at the centre of political and economic changes that are profoundly altering therapists' work. One such change is the introduction of managed care, a system of rationing treatment to contain costs (and in many instances, to generate profits). As you might expect, managed care organizations promote mental health treatments that are brief, routinized, and cheap. Many discourage the use of therapy entirely, preferring to rely on medication. Treatment goals are often limited to superficial changes that merely suffice to get people back on their feet (Cushman & Gilford, 2000). Problems involving longstanding personality difficulties or complex social and familial situations may be entirely disqualified for reimbursed treatment.

Many therapists have protested that the strictures of managed care organizations violate standards of good care and their professional integrity. Many have complained that working for managed care confronts them with serious ethical dilemmas. Breaches of confidentiality and invasions of privacy are the most commonly reported ethical problems. Other problems are 'gag' rules that limit what therapists are permitted to say to clients about the treatment and demands to offer forms of treatment that the therapist believes are inadequate or ineffective (Cohen, Marecek, & Gillham, 2006). Thus far, therapists who object to the way that managed care distorts their work have had little recourse except to stop working in managed care systems or quit doing therapy. Such individual actions, however, do little to change the system; for that, collective action is needed.

A second change concerns the intrusion of drug companies into the field of mental health. In recent years, the sale of psychiatric medication has mushroomed into a multi-billion-dollar global business. Roughly 10 per cent of women and 4 per cent of men in the USA, for example, take anti-depressant drugs. Between 3 and 5 per cent of American children take Ritalin, just one of the many drugs for Attention Deficit Disorder (Eberstadt, 2008).

The dramatic upsurge in medication use is due in large part to relentless efforts by pharmaceutical companies to market their products. The USA is one of only two countries in the world that permit direct-to-consumer advertising of prescription drugs. Consumer advocates and regulatory agencies have raised numerous objections to many such advertisements, which often give falsely optimistic impressions about the effectiveness and safety of the products they promote. The advertisements encourage people to consider taking medication for minor or transient difficulties. They also promulgate the inaccurate idea that most psychological problems are caused by brain malfunctions or so-called chemical imbalances. Not only do these ads shape popular attitudes about drugs, they also shape attitudes about psychotherapy. For example, ads implying that pills can provide instant improvement may discourage people from investing the effort and time that psychotherapy requires.

As some clinical psychologists seek the authority to prescribe medication, pharmaceutical companies – with sales and profits as their primary motive – are poised to gain entry to the field of clinical psychology. This should sound an alarm for critical psychologists. Critics have pointed out how psychiatry's cosy relationship with the pharmaceutical companies has compromised the field's scientific and ethical integrity (Koocher, 2007; Pacht, Fox, Zimbardo, & Antonuccio, 2007). These companies now have an overwhelming (though covert) presence in nearly every aspect of psychiatry – education, training, funding for research, scientific publications, and professional conferences. Furthermore, Lisa Cosgrove and her colleagues (2006) have documented extensive financial ties between drug companies and the psychiatrists who compiled the *DSM-IV*. Pharmaceutical companies also routinely intrude into the everyday work of psychiatrists, with sales representatives providing gifts, meals, consulting fees, and other incentives to practitioners and their employees. Documenting such conflicts of interest is an urgent task for critical psychologists. Concerted efforts are needed to pressure professional organizations to curb the drug companies' influence on scientific research and clinical practice and to formulate new ethical standards pertaining to psychologists' relationships with pharmaceutical companies.

It is not only pressures from corporate interests that have created crises for the mental health professions. The social and political conservatism of our times has also undermined the ideal of societal responsibility for the welfare of individuals in need. With drastic cuts in federal and state funds for mental health care, the public mental heath system is in crisis. The President's New Freedom Commission on Mental Health (convened by President George W. Bush, hardly a proponent of social welfare) described the system as

> ... fragmented and in disarray ... lead[ing] to unnecessary and costly disability, homelessness, school failure and incarceration ... In many communities, access to quality care is poor, resulting in wasted resources and lost opportunities for recovery. (2003: 11)

As resources for the care of people with severe mental disabilities have dwindled, many of those individuals – particularly those from impoverished backgrounds and racial and ethnic minority groups – have ended up homeless or incarcerated in prisons. Indeed, in the USA today, there are more mentally ill people in prisons than in mental hospitals. Needless to say, as prisoners, they receive little or no mental health care; moreover, prison conditions frequently exacerbate their difficulties (Human Rights Watch, 2003). From a standpoint of human rights and social justice, the state of public mental health care demands urgent redress.

summary and conclusions

Clinical psychologists, as part of the mental health system, provide care for people suffering from psychological disorders. Their work necessarily involves social control as well, a function that is usually disguised. Diagnosis, for example, sanctions certain experiences, emotions, behaviours, and relationships; in this way, it is a form of social regulation. We presented historical examples of diagnostic categories that served the interests of dominant members of society. However, diagnosis and other aspects of the mental health care system serve a regulatory function in the present as well.

We also drew attention to the present trend of medicalizing emotional suffering. We argue that framing psychological suffering as 'disease' and speaking about suffering in biomedical metaphors is a political choice, not a matter of scientific evidence. It places the origins of suffering 'inside' the person and thus downplays the role of those sociopolitical forces that produce deprivation, discrimination, exclusion, oppression, and marginalization.

As authors we are not the first to call attention to the issues raised in this chapter. Critics inside and outside the mental health professions have registered similar concerns for many years (e.g., Albee, 1977; Goffman, 1961; Keniston, 1968; Rosenhan, 1973; Szasz, 1974). These critics questioned the validity of diagnostic judgments; they sought to check therapists' power over clients; they challenged the regulatory function of the helping professions; and they argued against substituting psychotherapy for societal change. However, these issues have gained new urgency today. As flows of people across national borders have escalated, the risk of cultural biases in diagnosis has multiplied. Moreover, corporate interests threaten to seize control over much of the mental health system; profit motives thus threaten to reshape mental health care. This does not mean that mental health professionals can no longer exert social control; it does mean, however, that they must simultaneously struggle against being controlled by corporate interests. What we have called 'the politics of madness' thus takes on a double meaning, further jeopardizing the interests of those whom the system is meant to serve.

▪ ▪ main chapter points ▪

1   What we take to be reality always reflects the perspectives and social location of the knower.

2   Psychiatric diagnoses give the mental health professions power to assert that certain ways of thinking, acting, and feeling are deviant or abnormal. This gives them considerable control over social life and the ability to regulate personal behaviour. Although the *DSM's* authors aspire to scientific validity, its codification of psychiatric diagnoses falls short of this aspiration.

3   Psychotherapy has traditionally promoted such individualistic goals as personal fulfilment and autonomy. Its goals and practices reflect the values and norms of mainstream US culture. Moreover, theories of normality and abnormality reflect the values, ideals, and interests of privileged social groups.

4   As clinical psychology comes under the sway of corporate interests such as insurance companies, managed care organizations, and pharmaceutical companies, the challenges to professional integrity and progressive ideals will multiply.

glossary

- **feminism**: feminism comprises several political, social, and cultural movements, as well as bodies of scholarly knowledge, concerned with gender, gender inequalities, and rights for women. Feminists work to improve women's standing in society so that all women can live safe and satisfying lives.

- **Narrative Therapy**: built upon the ideas of David Epston and Michael White, Narrative Therapy holds that our identities are shaped by the accounts we give of our lives. A key aspect of Narrative Therapy is 'externalizing the problem' – that is, focusing on the effects that a problem has on a client's life, not on the problem as if it were 'inside' the person.

- **psychotherapy:** the general term for a diverse collection of efforts to relieve people's emotional suffering. Psychotherapies draw on a variety of different theories of behaviour, theories of change, and conceptions of mental health.

- **social constructionism:** a theory of knowledge concerned with how social phenomena develop in particular social settings. Research focuses on uncovering how individuals and groups participate in creating what they perceive as social reality.

▪ ▪ reading suggestions ▪

We recommend browsing such journals as *Subjectivities* (formerly *International Journal of Critical Psychology*); *Intervention: International Journal of Mental Health, Psychosocial Work and Counselling in Areas of Armed Conflict*; and *Feminism & Psychology*. We also recommend Luhrmann's *Of Two Minds* (2000), which discusses the 're-medicalization' of the mental health professions, Kirk and Kutchins' *The Selling of the DSM* (1992), Goodrich's *Women and Power* (1991), and Angell's *The Truth About the Drug Companies* (2004).

; // internet resources /

- **Dulwich Centre** – a centre for developing, practising, and disseminating Narrative Therapy: www.dulwichcentre.com.au

- **Freedom Center** – a supportive and activist community run by and for people labelled as having severe 'mental disorders': www.freedom-center.org

- **New View Campaign**: www.fsd-alert.org/manifesto4.asp

- **Psychologists for Social Responsibility (PsySR)** – an independent organization of progressive psychologists committed to peace and social justice: www.PsySR.org

▪ Questions

1 The next revision of the *DSM* is currently underway. Consider what is beneficial and what is detrimental about expanding the number of its diagnostic categories.

2 Compose a critical review of a clinical psychology textbook. Are there gaps in its coverage? Does it discuss social, political, and economic conditions that affect the risk for psychological difficulties? Does it describe the mental health consequences of poverty, war, immigration, rape, and other forms of violence?

3 Consider popular advertising for psychiatric medications. What implicit and explicit ideas do the ads contain about the nature of psychological suffering and wellbeing?

4 How can the wellbeing of all members of society be achieved? What social arrangements would facilitate this? What conditions must prevail if those who are disabled by mental disorders are to have satisfying and productive lives?

6

Social Psychology and Social Change
Frances Cherry

Social psychology, no less than psychology in general, has always found itself in contested space: Is it best understood and practised as a natural science or as a human science (Teo, 2005)? As such, I think of social psychology as a field perpetually under construction because the contested space is about how to portray human nature, what constitutes acceptable scientific knowledge and – most relevant to my concerns in this chapter – what use this knowledge should serve. Social psychology's great potential, or so it seemed when I encountered the field in the 1960s, was its ability to help advance progressive social change not just by illuminating the causes of discrimination, poverty, and other social ills but by suggesting and testing solutions. As Morawski and Bayer point out in their critical history of social psychology, the field arose in the context of twentieth century notions of modernity, a belief in the scientific method and the parallel creation of the psychological subject. Because social psychology is inseparable from the history in which it is embedded, its

evolution must be understood, therefore, as plural, multisited, and morally and politically inspired. Such a historical perspective situates social psychology as one, albeit crucial, project to understand human nature through scientific

method, and ultimately, to apply that scientific knowledge to the enhancement of human welfare. (2003: 224)

For me, the test of social psychology's success, both in its mainstream and in its varying critical alternatives, is whether it enhances human welfare by contributing to social change.

It is worth noting that, in the late nineteenth century and into the first decades of the twentieth, social psychology's understanding of human nature rested on premises of social order and social control by ruling elites. Enhanced human welfare would result from applying scientific expertise in a top-down approach setting experts apart from those for whom solutions were 'engineered'. In the interwar period of the 1920s, older models of social order were contested by models of social conflict. The classic studies of the 'Hawthorne effect' often cited as an example of workers' increased productivity and satisfaction resulting from an attentive workplace have been re-analysed to show that both the original results and subsequent textbook accounts have perpetuated mythical notions of docile factory workers when in fact there was greater resistance to management practices than reported (Bramel & Friend, 1981; Gillespie, 1991).

Particularly in the early part of the twentieth century, psychology departments offered a place for social psychologists to combine behaviourist, quantitative, and laboratory approaches to social phenomena. Yet even as an individualistically oriented social psychology was taking shape, social psychologists did not agree about the nature of the 'social'. For example, in the 1920s and 1930s there was an early contrast about the nature of 'groups' between Floyd Allport and Muzafer Sherif; the former considered 'the group' to be the sum of the behaviour of the group's individual members, while the latter viewed it as something greater than all those comprising it (Gorman, 1981). While the laboratory suited both for demonstrating social phenomena, Allport's social psychology drew on a fairly mechanistic notion of individuals influencing one another whereas Sherif's social psychology drew on the dynamics of Gestalt notions such as frame of reference and group norm formation.

By the 1930s, with the Great Depression underway, many social psychologists turned their attention to poverty, unemployment and the rise of fascism in Europe. In 1936, they founded the Society for the Psychological Study of Social Issues (SPSSI, www.spssi.org) to address the relevance and importance of combining research and advocacy in the face of pressing social problems (Morawski & Bayer, 2003). In this way, they contested the idea that the social psychologist's proper focus is only at the level of individual thoughts, feelings and actions by including the broader economic and political context that brings groups into conflict.

Social psychologists participated directly in World War II, studying issues such as civilian and soldier morale, industrial conflict, and attitudes towards war and international conflict. Generous post-war funding through military and government sources put the field of social psychology on the map (Capshew,

1999; Herman, 1995). In the immediate post-war period and throughout the 1950s, social psychologists, many of whom were inspired by Kurt Lewin's emphasis on group dynamics and action research, developed both a laboratory and a community based social psychology with the idea that each would contribute to the other. Intergroup conflict preoccupied social psychologists in the post-war period, but the anti-communist political climate in America created suspicions around those interested in changing America's racialized status quo. Increasingly, social psychologists moved their work to the laboratory, studying prejudicial attitudes rather than community based discrimination. Those who did retain their desire to bring research to bear directly on societal change were able to contribute to the civil rights movement – for example, Kenneth Clark and others were involved in the United States Supreme Court's 1954 *Brown v Board of Education* ruling on public school desegregation, among other projects for racial inclusion (Cherry & Borshuk, 1998; Jackson, 2001).

While there was substantial methodological diversity among social psychologists in the mid-twentieth century, both in North America and Europe, by the mid-1960s laboratory experimental work had become the dominant paradigm. Even with that, by the end of that decade there were already rumblings about experimenter bias and demand characteristics getting in the way of an objective social psychology. As early as 1966, Gordon Allport, speaking to a Conference on the Teaching of Social Psychology, felt the need to warn students about the dangers of becoming mired in well-conducted but trivial experiments (Cherry, 1995).

Unaware of these 'distant early warnings', I entered an American experimental social psychology doctoral programme in 1970. Shortly thereafter, Ken Gergen gave a guest lecture to the programme, the substance of which was published in 1973 as 'Social Psychology as History'. In Europe, England, Canada and the USA, critical social psychologists' voices were once again audible and by the late 1970s they had reached 'crisis' proportions (Pancer, 1997). Whether this was a crisis of confidence or of disciplinary identity, there was growing concern that no amount of technical rigging could keep the epistemological project of a positivist social psychology afloat. I want to emphasize that 'crisis' is nothing new to psychology. In *The Critique of Psychology*, Thomas Teo (2005) points out that psychology in general has had crises about what kind of science it is going to be since the nineteenth century; a similar continuity is found in social psychology (Teo addresses this history in Chapter 3). Social psychology's critical voices have been a bit like a Greek chorus, sometimes cut off from the unfolding drama but ever ready to interpret the central character(s) even if those characters would rather not hear.

critical and experimental social psychology

Throughout the 1980s, critical social psychologists were unlikely to stay loyal to the disciplinary boundaries drawn by experimental methods. Many parallel tracks developed, less prestigious than the experimental mainstream but nevertheless carving out ways of studying social phenomena with the goal of privileging the 'subject'. *Changing the Subject* (Henriques, Hollway, Urwin, Venn, & Walkerdine, 1984), an important collection of essays, was instrumental in bringing strands of interpretive, politically informed, and postmodern practices together. In these emerging critical social psychologies and their nascent communities of practice, there was an implicit, and often explicit, challenge to the dominance of an overly mechanistic and reductionist natural science framework and an exclusive reliance on experimental methods for establishing knowledge claims about the social world.

Although from the mid-1980s to the present critical social psychologists have varied in their views of the nature of the world (ontology), their differences from one another are very much outweighed by their differences from experimental social psychologists. Experimental social psychologists hold a realist position of the social world where facts lie waiting to be discovered, whereas critical social psychologists reject the position that 'facts' speak for themselves. Multiple critical perspectives vary along a realist–relativist continuum. Where some critical social psychologists draw attention to the material conditions in society as the context for factual discovery, others see facts as part of a narrative telling of the world. Some psychologists for whom social change is key argue that this often-nonjudgmental emphasis on competing stories of what is 'real' reduces rather than strengthens work for social change (Ibáñez & Iniguez, 1997).

While the experimentalist claims to study what is 'out there', as if looking through a pane of glass, the critical social psychologist is more intrigued by how people socially construct 'out there' in the course of their everyday lives. As a result, critical social psychologists are more likely to take as valid knowledge (epistemology) what people say (or do not say) and do as they go about their lives. Very importantly, critical social psychologists explore what is 'social' (language, culture, power relations) and reconceptualize cognitions (attitudes, attributions) as social products. They argue against the possibility of value-free theory and in favour of greater **reflexivity** on the part of scientists who themselves speak from a social location of gender, ethnicity, social class and sexual orientation. Critical social psychologists recognize the contradiction between claiming expertise and a knowledge of others while attempting to close the gap between the scientist and his or her 'subjects' who have their own agency and voice.

Today there are numerous entry points into critical social psychology (e.g., Henriques et al., 1984; Hepburn, 2003; Ibáñez & Iniguez, 1997; Parker, 1989; Stainton Rogers, 2003; Tolman & Brydon-Miller, 2001; Wexler, 1996). Each introduces broad questions: Can the individual be split from society or from the situation? How is knowledge constructed and validated? How does this knowledge engage with progressive social change?

There is no formulaic way to *do* critical social psychology and, in fact, it would be counterproductive to devise a formula. Some critical psychologists remain interested in replicating and extending iconic experiments to better understand their ideological hold on the discipline; see, for example, Reicher and Haslam's (2006) replication and extension of the Stanford Prison Experiment. Some emphasize the importance of narrative in social life, in some cases arguing that language and conversation (talk and texts) are the very essence of social meaning. Discursive practices, which take language and the making of meaning as priorities, explore new ways of understanding society, subjectivity, and social change (see, for example, Wetherell & Potter, 1992, on racism; see also Chapter 11 in this volume). Others have become a part of the broader community of participatory action researchers whose diverse roots span critical pedagogy, international development work, and community and labour organizing, among others (e.g., Tolman & Brydon-Miller, 2001).

It is worth keeping in mind that certain forms of critical social psychology have generated their own critics. Two kinds are most relevant here. The first is mainstream psychologists working with traditional methods and assumptions; given that they are the primary target of critical social psychology's core critique, it is not surprising that they reject it. The second kind reflects a dilemma noted in Chapter 1 of this book and addressed in several other chapters: politically liberal and radical psychologists who use mainstream methods to advance social change and social justice. As an example of the latter, feminist psychologist Sue Wilkinson critically analyses critical social psychology's discursive and constructionist strands. She argues that these approaches incorporate the moral relativity of textual construction and insufficiently attend to the material conditions of women's lives. As a result, Wilkinson says,

> **feminist psychology and critical social psychology are united in that they both offer critiques of the mainstream of the discipline. However, unlike critical social psychology more generally, the motivating force behind the feminist critique of psychology is unashamedly *political*: feminist psychology aims to end the social and political oppression of women. (1997b: 181)**

Michael Billig's expression of 'mixed feelings' is closest to my own sentiments, because it warns against defining critical social psychology in any one fixed way. Commenting on critical psychology's growth in the mid-1980s, Billig remarked:

> **It has been good to see the boundaries between social psychology and other social sciences become increasingly permeable. In my own work, I've tried to cross disciplinary boundaries. On the other hand, every approach that becomes successful carries the potential to become an orthodoxy. Critical social psychology, when established as a discipline to be taught to undergraduates, will be in danger of becoming an uncritical orthodoxy. Then it will be time to return to experiments. After all, Solomon Asch was both a great experimentalist and a great critical social scientist. (Billig, in Hepburn, 2003: 41)**

In the remainder of this chapter, I explore what it might mean to 'return to experiments', not because critical social psychology has become an 'uncritical orthodoxy' but because it is terrain that I believe should not be ceded quite so easily to the mainstream. I think that one important strand of critical social psychology is to (re)search some of the scientific, ethical and practical issues in mainstream social psychology from the vantage point of a now more-established critical social psychology. Drawing from different periods in the field's history as well as my own personal history, I discuss some points of connection and divergence between experimental and critical social psychology and return us to the social, moral and political project that historically has been part of the field.

multiple perspectives and reflexivity

Many of us who began graduate work in social psychology in the 1970s were educated in a paradigm which privileged the laboratory experimenter's authoritative voice in an unproblematic way. It was unnecessary to question what impact one's own identity – gender, racialized, social class, sexual orientation – might have on research. It was equally unnecessary to treat reflexivity – an ability to see oneself as part of the experimental scenario – as an integral part of human science research. Instead, when the experimental situation's demand characteristics or experimenter bias intruded on objectivity, the researcher could handle them technically. This traditional experimental approach was very much at odds with an interpretive sociohistorical approach; the two can seem like mutually exclusive worldviews (Sampson, 1991; Stainton Rogers, 2003).

In graduate school, conversations with research participants in post-experimental debriefing sessions provided several direct challenges to the experimenter's unproblematic point of view. Experimental social psychologists use such debriefing for both educational and ethical purposes. They consider it an opportunity to inform research participants of their study's purpose in greater depth and also to undo any of the negative consequences of the deception, frustration, embarrassment and/or negative evaluations that experimental scenarios often induce. While the first is certainly possible, the second is dubious given empirical research showing the persistence of beliefs, self-perceptions and affect in the face of attempts to invalidate them (e.g., Davies, 1997; Ross, Lepper, & Hubbard, 1975; Sherman & Kim, 2002).

multiple viewpoints

I began to wonder what research participants were thinking early on in my graduate school life. In a laboratory study I conducted about interpersonal aggression (Cherry, Mitchell, & Nelson, 1973), one of my research participants told me during the debriefing session that he gave more (pseudo)shocks because he really wanted to motivate the experiment's 'learner' to do well in remembering his part. He elaborated on this with a sports analogy: when you don't get the ball in the hoop, the coach runs you around the track so you'll be sure to remember and try harder the next time. He saw his situation in helpful terms whereby mild punishment motivated performance, whereas I labelled his behaviour harmful to another person. If we are interested in subjectivity and social change, then it is extremely important to acknowledge the multiple subject positions bearing on the construction of any particular social reality that we're trying to understand. It is equally important to understand the disciplinary and societal factors shaping these subjectivities.

Within every experiment lies multiple subjectivities. In one of my undergraduate social psychology classes this past year, I was teaching a class on the differences in the ways actors and observers see and explain the behaviour of others. The textbook authors wrote that 'people are what our eyes and ears notice' (Aronson, Wilson, Akert, & Fehr, 2007: 114). I chose this textbook, I should add, because of its excellent descriptions of research studies. The classic study, chosen to illustrate the role of perceptual salience in social judgment, was by Taylor and Fiske (1975) and I liked its relatively 'social' nature. In their study, six observers sat surrounding two confederates (secretly working with the experimenter) who were seated face-to-face and engaged in a 'get-acquainted' conversation. Because of their positioning, two observers had a clear view of both conversationalists while the four other observers had only partial views. I thought this was a fairly controlled and elegant way to set up an opportunity to look at point of view and the attributions of causality.

I decided to look up the original study to see what more I could learn from it. Indeed, the textbook had reported the observers' judgments correctly in that 'the person whom they could see the best was the person whom they thought had the most *impact on the conversation*' (Taylor & Fiske, 1975: 114; my italics). However, there was no support for the fundamental attribution error – that is, the observers did not attribute a greater impact on the conversation to the personality attributes of the person they could see best. It is not unusual for textbooks to overstate their claims in the service of narrative continuity, in this case that Taylor and Fiske's study of perceptual salience 'helps explain why the fundamental attribution error is so widespread' (Aronson et al., 2007: 115). I would still maintain it is an elegant demonstration of perceptual salience, and it might also be quite useful to our understanding of how we judge peoples' contributions in any number of small group settings, but it does not do what Aronson et al. claim it does.

I then went on to read the second study in this same article (Taylor & Fiske, 1975). The authors were perplexed by their failure to find the expected pattern of attributions. In the second study they presented research participants with a videotaped version of the two conversationalists. In one condition they covered over one of the conversationalists on the video monitor. They still failed to find their expected results for the fundamental attribution error, but they did find what they deemed a 'confusing' trend that was the opposite of the one they expected. In a rare glimpse of the 'subjects'' perspective, Taylor and Fiske reported this:

> **Spontaneous subject comments and questions during the debriefing helped clarify this confusing trend. Many subjects found the task peculiar, and they were curious about why they were not allowed to see the other participant on their screen. The strange task seemed to endow the unseen participant with a mysterious quality, making the participant who was pictured on the screen seem more at the mercy of situational factors. (1975: 444)**

If one looks at the kind of analyses some critical social psychologists have developed – participatory or collaborative sense-making – then the passage just quoted is very interesting. The standardized experimental setting serves as a starting point for sense-making and engagement in social conversation. The experimental social psychologist is interested in aggregated and primarily quantitative data relationships between and among independent and dependent variables. In contrast, the critical social psychologist is interested in the voices of those producing the data, the multiple and sometimes contradictory construals of the social situation by experimenters, confederates, and participants, and the society in which this small group is embedded.

I like returning to earlier documents of experimental research in this way, and finding within the standardization of procedures those rare instances in which the voices of research participants emerge inadvertently (and still only indirectly through the experimenters' reports). I take pleasure in re-analysing the convergence of experiment, talk and text in a way that reveals multiple viewpoints. It is rare to find this type of convergence in reports conforming to the APA's *Style Manual*; it is typically more abundant in the research reports of the 1950s and 1960s (Cherry, 1995; Chapter 6).

_____ *learning reflexivity* _____

From a critical social psychology perspective, the post-experimental debriefing session is an important part of the experimental scenario and can serve the function of teaching reflexivity. This requires that one does not 'run' people through experiments, but rather that one 'walks' through experiments in conversation with participants.

In my own case, as a graduate student I was involved in a study that included an elaborate deceptive procedure intended to convince participants that we could know their true attitudes through an apparatus falsely presented as a lie detector (the 'bogus pipeline'). The principal experimenter had good intentions; he didn't believe you really had to lie to people at all to determine their attitudes on various questions. However, to test that proposition, we needed to compare straightforward methods to the deceptive method (Cherry, Byrne, & Mitchell, 1976). Much to my horror, I discovered in my role as debriefer that some research participants would not believe the lie detector did not work. I can remember showing one research participant that the machine was not even plugged into the wall. Even though he saw no plug, he remained convinced that lie detectors worked even if this one didn't; he was employed at a local pharmacy which used lie detectors to inhibit shoplifting and was already convinced of their veracity. As a result, I was unable to debrief this participant because he had arrived already a believer and he left believing more strongly that lie detectors are accurate. The benefits of the knowledge gained from this study (that elaborate ruses were not required to find out what people think) were at odds with reinforcing the larger societal problems of growing surveillance and people's overconfidence in technological attitude detection. The 'undebriefable' research participant incorporated me into his scenario. This is a problem worth thinking about, in part because debriefing's general goal is to restore participants to their prior state which, as previously mentioned, may be impossible. In another way, it may only be in debriefing conversations that experimenters encounter their own embeddedness in the ongoing construction of social knowledge.

shifting frameworks

The various strands of critical social psychology generally assume that researchers bring personal and political values to their research and that there is no technical way to prevent this. Researchers can choose to make their values explicit to the best of their ability. In many of the participatory modalities of research, the construction of knowledge is collaborative and includes the perspectives of the populations in the study. It is still the case, however, that experimental social psychology is premised on the neutrality of the researcher's gaze. Fortunately, several challenges to prevailing frameworks cast doubt on this neutrality; here I discuss three of them: the Hawthorne effect (Bramel & Friend, 1981; Gillespie, 1991), the banality of evil hypothesis (Haney, Banks, & Zimbardo, 1973; Milgram, 1974), and the bystander effect (Latané & Darley, 1970). Each of them, as you will see, brings the notion of power into the mix – the researchers' power, in particular – and contests previous frameworks accordingly.

the Hawthorne effect

The notion that workers respond positively to social and emotional management practices – subsequently known as the Hawthorne effect – was established as an unproblematic set of findings through a series of studies in the late 1920s and early 1930s conducted by social/organizational psychologists at the Hawthorne plant of the Western Electric Company. Mayo and Roethlisberger, two Harvard social/organizational psychologists, believed that a more relaxed and humanized management style would enhance cooperation between workers and management in the joint support of industrial capitalism. Even at the time, some saw this human relations framework as naïve and paternalistic. It also ignored the Marxist framework of an inherent conflict of interests between owners and workers and downplayed the importance of workers' resistance to exploitation through their own union organizing efforts (Bramel & Friend, 1981).

Bramel and Friend returned to the published accounts of these studies 50 years later to determine whether, in fact, the original data supported the human relations framework. Accounts generally presented workers as passive and easily transformed into a highly cooperative team; hostility towards management was interpreted as irrational paranoia, based on a misunderstanding or short-lived. Bramel and Friend retrieved a different story from the published reports wherein workers were reprimanded, replaced by other workers and dropped from the experiment when they showed signs of hostility and resistance to management practices. The workers were active participants in the experiments and interview studies; they often modified their output in accordance with their suspicions that management was continuing to exploit them and they spoke rationally about exploitation when they were interviewed. Bramel and Friend write:

> **It is ironic that the Hawthorne effect, which is considered to have given scientific recognition to the psychological, subjective point of view of the factory worker, should be based upon a research project which in its generally accepted conclusions suppressed a major part of that subjectivity: collective resistance to exploitation. (1981: 876)**

These authors go on to show how the Hawthorne effect has persisted in general psychology, social psychology and research methodology textbooks. In these sources, the supposed result – that the mere attention of management and experimenters, without any change in the material conditions of work, increases productivity – vindicates the laboratory method itself and the view that experimenters are the mediators of discovered facts rather than working from value oriented frameworks to construct a picture of the social world. This situation argues strongly for continuous re-assessments of social psychology's classic studies, of the sort described in this section, for tracings of how psychologists present these studies to incoming students and the general public.

_____ *the banality of evil hypothesis* _____

For many years, the Milgram obedience studies as well as Zimbardo's prison simulation have bolstered a view of how it is that 'well-behaved people can be led by situational influences to torment others' (Berkowitz, 1999: 247). In these examples, the importance of immediate, relatively simple, yet powerful situations is key to the findings. Yet, years later, when placed in a contemporary context, a more sophisticated interpretation can change the framework of analysis. The long-held notion of the 'banality of evil' has come under considerable scrutiny (Berkowitz, 1999; Haslam & Reicher, 2007) and so has the **situationist** perspective that bolsters it and runs through much of mainstream social psychology, to the near exclusion of individual differences and structural constraints. Berkowitz argues for a second look at personality differences between those who commit evil acts and those who don't, and for a deeper understanding of what characterizes the prototype of evil. For Haslam and Reicher, **interactionism** is more than the view that 'behaviour is simply the product of two independent factors: person and situation' (2007: 615); the more dynamic and emergent view is that 'both person and situation are transformed through their interplay' (2007: 615). People do not succumb without thinking about the requirements of a given role such as 'prison guard'; instead, they retain agency as they get caught up in institutions offering support for their hyperauthoritarian profile. Becoming emboldened by that support, they can begin to encourage others in tyranny.

Haslam and Reicher see theories which reduce tyranny to pathological persons or situations as unproductive, and argue instead for an intricate process by which evil becomes normative. In their view, it is equally if not more interesting for social psychologists to understand those who oppose the seeming 'banality of evil'. Whether trying to account for the tyranny of the Nazi death camps or the abuse at Abu Ghraib, Reicher and Haslam (2006) contest role theory and the banality of evil as adequate frameworks. In their BBC Prison Experiment, they found that tyranny did not always result and that a power vacuum in failing groups is a more critical consideration. The frameworks expressed in these two prison experiments are at odds and possibly irreconcilable: Reicher and Haslam see agency among all the parties to the experiments; they see groups as a cauldron of possibilities for good and/or evil; and they emphasize as key factors such as social identity, power relations and group processes.

_____ *the bystander effect* _____

The overwhelming emphasis on the power of the situation has not gone uncontested in another of social psychology's classic set of studies. Following the 1964 murder of Kitty Genovese, social psychologists Latané and Darley found in several studies that the more bystanders there were to an emergency situation, the less likely any one bystander would intervene to help the person in need (Latané & Darley, 1970). Eventually, these various instances of inhibition in emergency situations were connected to other situations of social influence to produce a theory of social impact (Latané, 1981). The theory and its resulting psychosocial law relate the strength, immediacy and number of people to a variety of everyday social behaviours: anticipated stage fright, tipping in restaurants, and social loafing, among others. But, to my mind the theory of social impact did not make sense of the murder of Kitty Genovese. In fact, by the time I set to work thinking through the bystander intervention literature that her murder evoked, I saw it quite differently. I argued (Cherry, 1995) that violence against women is responded to differently than attacks on men. And, in fact, when Latané and Nida (1981) acknowledged that bystander research had not led to greater helping, I wondered again whether this was a productive line of inquiry for understanding the solidarity emerging in the women's movement around intervening in the lives of women threatened or harmed by violence. Yet while I shifted the framework from the immediate situation and the diffusion of responsibility among bystanders to the gendered particulars of societal violence, I was still assuming that the facts were valid: 38 witnesses to the murder of Kitty Genovese failed to intervene.

More recently, another layer has emerged to the story of the 38 witnesses, a parable recounted endlessly in introductory social psychology as evidence of the problem with groups. The case's legal documents reveal a different story. British researchers Manning, Levine and Collins (2007) lay out the evidence that the traditional account misrepresents what really happened. The 38 witnesses did not act in the way the psychology literature claims. It turns out that there was evidence that people came to Genovese's assistance. Manning et al. point to a serious consequence of this misrepresentation: the 'message that groups have a negative effect on helping ... has caused psychologists to be slow to look for the ways in which the power of groups can be harnessed to promote intervention' (2007: 556). Once again, as with the BBC Prison Experiment, the possibility that groups are not always dangerous or indifferent is brought to the fore and social identity and power relations re-enter as important considerations. I find this recent reframing of the Genovese murder far more helpful to understanding solidarity movements for social justice as well as the perpetuation of social psychology's ideological frameworks that deter us from looking for solutions to pressing problems of societal violence. Challenges such as these to the frames of reference of some of the field's iconic studies can return us to the study of groups and relations of domination and subordination that once figured more prominently in post-Second World War social psychology.

The power of critical social psychology is in its challenge to prevailing frameworks of studying and understanding social life. It is important to think about the 'critical' part not just as negativity but as a purposeful reframing in order to reveal underlying biases of the type that we have just examined. In social psychology, we are constantly studying aspects of social life that engage deeply held values and moral positions with staggering consequences for the equality and inclusion of those on the margins of society. It is my experience that common ground is often difficult to achieve within diverse frameworks. For example, where is the common ground between those who advocate against and those in favour of psychologists' involvement in interrogations using torture (*Analyses of Social Issues and Public Policy*, 2007; see also

Chapter 23)? Where is the consensus between those who frame same sex marriage as a human rights issue and those who see it as a mental health issue (Kitzinger & Wilkinson, 2004)? Critical social psychology acknowledges the way in which values saturate scientific work. While I don't advocate mean-spirited science, I think the social justice focus of interest to many social psychologists lends itself to perpetual and unavoidable debate.

social change

As mentioned at the start of this chapter, my own criteria for social psycho-logical work has largely to do with whether it enhances human welfare by contributing to social change, but it is not always clear to me what approach is the best route to that end. There are times when I have favoured research in conjunction with top-down legal and policy changes administered by experts in consultation with communities; there are other times when I have favoured research in support of bottom-up grassroots organizing for change. I've observed that both strategies lead to a greater inclusion of marginalized groups so I remain open-minded and pragmatic about the relationship between research and social change.

Lewin wrote this: no research without action; no action without research. I'm in that camp where one develops experimental and other investigative practices with action in mind. I don't oppose responsible experimentation that has a purpose beyond what Allport thought of as 'well-constructed trivia'. And to complicate matters further, interviews and other forms of qualitative research also present ethical dilemmas. No single form of research is problem-free or universally applicable.

One of the important ways critical social psychologists have challenged mainstream social psychology has been to call into question the notion that an objective scientific enterprise requires separating research and action. For some, this was and continues to be a discussion of the possibility of a value-explicit human science, while for others it is a turn towards participatory action research. In my own case, it is a turn towards critical historical schol-arship. My historical projects are intended to reclaim social psychology's scholar/activist tradition and to tell the history of social psychology in a way that examines both continuities and discontinuities with contemporary work by critical social psychologists.

As already mentioned, I have found generally that up to the 1960s, there was greater methodological diversity among social psychologists and greater openness to forging a connection between research and social change. While the received historical view is one of increasing progress through experi-mental method, another possibility is to talk about what has been lost along the way and what might be retrieved. Through disciplinary histories, it is possible to see that the very meaning of the 'social' has been transformed from membership in diverse cultures and groups to the interpersonal and individual levels of meaning. This has occurred largely by adopting specific styles of investigative practice (Danziger, 1992; Greenwood, 2004a). The projects I am drawn to allow me to dig into library and archival records to find a fuller history of social psychological practice and examples of researchers whose work exemplifies the kinds of issues taken up by contemporary critical social psychologists.

Take for example, Kenneth B. Clark, a well known African American social psychologist and leader in the struggle for desegregated schooling in the United States. Clark had a way of understanding his research, I discovered, that would resonate very clearly among contemporary critical social psychologists. For Clark, a viable social psychology was one that attended to differential power relations between real social groups. In his writings about research, he paid particular attention to defining the researcher's difficult role in powerless communities in a way that is resonant with contemporary calls for community empowerment and reflexivity. Conducting research as he did in the Harlem community in which he grew up, he referred to himself as an 'involved observer'. His methods were eclectic: gathering hard statistical data, unstructured small group discussions, questionnaires, interviews, and observations of community activity. He was sympathetic to the view that the data obtained in research are shaped by the type of relationship one has with research participants (Cherry, 2004).

Clark was one of several social psychologists who stressed the importance of connecting research and action, an idea proposed among social psychologists in the 1930s in response to the devastation of the Great Depression. A vibrant activist/scholar tradition developed throughout the 1950s and into the early 1960s as part of the African American civil rights movement, producing an effective argument for changing educational policy at the US Supreme Court level as well as for changing community-based discriminatory practices (Cherry & Borshuk, 1998; Jackson, 2001).

Thus, although social psychology became more heavily invested in the study of individual attitudes and cognitions than of small groups, action research with an emphasis on the participation of those affected by the research has a history in North American social psychology, even if mainstream textbooks rarely fully articulate it. Throughout the 1950s, social psychologists associated with the New York-based Commission on Community Interrelations, among many civic organizations, assisted communities with self-surveys and audits of discriminatory practices. Probably inspired by the civil rights movement's direct action practices, action researchers developed a more systematic practice of auditing racial discrimination in communities. Pairs of researchers – African- and Euro-American – went into restaurants or to rent apartments to uncover discrimination, an investigative practice that continues to this day and continues to yield data on the racialized inequality of treatment (Cherry, 2007). While auditing discrimination began at the grassroots level, it has in the United States become a more bureaucratic activity sponsored by government auditing agencies.

In the early days of action research, social psychologists argued that an iterative process of intervention, an evaluation of outcomes, and the reworking of an intervention could steadily improve the field's contribution to solving social problems (Lewin, 1946, 1947). Lewin framed action research within a liberal democratic model of expertise in the service of social reform. In this regard, several contemporary social psychologists have continued to move research findings into action by informing social and legal policy decisions (see, for example, Crosby, Aarti, Clayton, & Downing, 2003; Fiske, Bersoff, Borgida, Deaux, & Heilman, 1991) in the areas of employment and educational discrimination.

Contemporary participatory action researchers – influenced by Marxist, feminist, anti-racist and postcolonial critiques – are generally more interested in political engagement and empowerment in whole communities. They build into their work the vital role of those the research will directly affect, often by collaborating with community members on the research design, its interpretation and the dissemination of results. Different perspectives still remain concerning the relative effectiveness of grassroots (bottom up) vs. social policy (top down) points of intervention. There is no calculus for deciding what route is most effective, but both concentrate on finding ways to link research and social action.

Not surprisingly, critical social psychologists are willing to debate the merits of different strategies for change. I would argue that in a world as inequitable, and oppressive as ours, we need to encourage our colleagues and our students to bring together whatever approaches they embrace – whether in the lab, using surveys or archives, or more critical alternatives – to enhance social justice.

author's note

I would like to thank the students in my graduate social psychology seminar and my two undergraduate social psychology courses during the 2007–2008 academic year for giving their consideration to some of the ideas expressed in this chapter.

■■ main chapter points ■

1 There is a history of debate about the nature of the 'social' and how best to study social phenomena. Critical social psychology has developed several strands of critique, addressing scientific, ethical and applied issues.

2 Critical social psychologists typically take reflexivity and multiple perspectives as important aspects of the research process.

3   My chapter has stressed re-interpretations of classic studies in the mainstream literature as a way of bringing the voices of research participants and alternative frameworks to the surface.

4   Social psychologists in the mid-twentieth century developed a paradigm for linking research and action; one strand of critical social psychology focuses on more recent developments in participatory action research.

glossary

- **interactionism**: an older static view that persons are independent of their social context and interact mechanically with one another; a newer dynamic view that persons and their context are interdependent and each is transformed by the process of social interaction.

- **reflexivity**: a way of doing social psychology that reflects an awareness that one is part of the research process.

- **situationism**: the tendency for experimental social psychology to interpret research in the immediate experimental surrounding to the exclusion of personality and structural factors.

reading suggestions

Stainton Rogers' (2003) book, *Social Psychology: Experimental and Critical Approaches*, is structured as a counter-text; it contrasts the standard topics found in experimental social psychology textbooks – self, social cognition, attitudes, groups – with critical perspectives. Hepburn (2003), in *An Introduction to Critical Social Psychology*, takes the reader through a variety of critical perspectives (Marxist, feminist, psychoanalytic, postmodern, to name but a few); she explains how each can be linked to a critical social psychology. She includes brief autobiographical notes written by a number of critical social psychologists explaining how they arrived at their self-description, and she emphasizes the way critical social psychology's project aims to transform both society and the discipline of psychology. Ibáñez and Iniguez's (1997) publication is a collection of papers first given in 1993 at a conference in Barcelona on critical social psychology and then published to take into account the debates that each of the papers generated. It provides a wide range of positions in critical social psychology.

: // internet resources /

- **Account of the murder of Catherine 'Kitty' Genovese** from the perspective of Joseph de May, a longtime resident of Kew Gardens where Genovese lived: www.oldkewgardens.com/kitty_genovese-001.html

- **Analyses of Social Issues and Public Policy** (@sap - SPSSI's online journal): www.asap-spssi.org

- **Personal Reflection on Kitty Genovese**, 40 years after her murder, by her partner, Mary Ann Zielonko: www.npr.org/templates/story/story. php?storyId= 1763547

- **Society for the Psychological Study of Social Issues (SPSSI)**: www.spssi.org

- **Stanford Prison Experiment**: www.prisonexp.org

- **University of Exeter's Discussion of the BBC Prison Experiment** has contested the Stanford Prison Experiment: www.psychology.ex.ac.uk/projects/theexp intro.shtml

 ■ **?uestions**

1 What are the main differences between experimental and critical social psychology and among various strands of critical social psychology?

2 Locate any one of the Point/Counterpoint exchanges in the online journal, *Analyses of Social Issues and Public Policy* (@sap). How does the debate present different frameworks for analysis? What are the compatibilities and incompatibilities?

3 Choose a study dated between 1920–1970 that is presented as a classic study in a current social psychology textbook. What was the study's original context? What does the current citation tell you about shifting frameworks? Place this study in another chapter of your textbook and elaborate on why it fits into the chapter you have chosen.

7

Concepts and Directions in Critical Industrial/Organizational Psychology

Gazi Islam and Michael Zyphur

Chapter Topics

From its inception, critical theory has attempted to uncover the ideological underpinnings of everyday actions, beliefs, and interpersonal relations. Horkheimer (1982), a key figure in the Frankfurt School of critical theory, framed this objective as one of liberating human beings from often taken-for-granted social and economic conditions that shape their understandings of who they are and of what they are capable. Thus, from the beginning, critical theory in the social sciences has involved examining the interface between human understanding and the social and economic systems that frame and limit human possibilities.

Stated as such, it would seem that industrial/organizational (IO) psychology should be a natural home for critical theory. IO psychology is commonly defined as the study of human behaviour within organizational systems (e.g.

Katz & Kahn, 1978), and has held that the multilevel nature of its constructs requires theorizing between levels of analysis (e.g., House, Rosseau, & Thomas-Hunt, 1995). One would thus expect that the analysis of the socioeconomic context which frames and conditions human beings' lives, and which, to use Horkheimer's vivid language, forms the 'circumstances that enslave them' (1982: 244), would be a central topic of study in this area of psychology.

To date, however, critical perspectives have remained on the periphery of IO psychology (Islam & Zyphur, 2006). While related areas such as Organization Studies (e.g., Alvesson & Deetz, 1996) and Industrial and Labour Relations (e.g., Edwards, 1992) maintain strong traditions in critical studies as well as quantitative empirical work, the IO literature has remained firmly tied to experimental and quantitative roots. Although this does not necessarily exclude a critical approach, a *uniquely* quantitative approach tends to take for granted pre-existing facts rather than unpack the social relations which led to the establishment of certain orders *as* facts. As an 'applied' science, IO psychology has tended to employ a 'scientist-practitioner model' (e.g., Hayes, Barlow, & Nelson-Gray, 1999) in which scientific research is used to further existing managerial goals and add utility to current managerial procedures, rather than call into question these goals and question managerial capitalism as such (Baritz, 1974). One way to undo a managerial bias, we argue, is to question the politics inherent in the very categories used by IO psychologists.

This combination of a plethora of fertile areas of inquiry and the lack of a firmly established and critical programme of research in the centre of the discipline should be enticing to current and future IO psychology scholars. This chapter is an attempt to demonstrate the potential for critical work throughout the major subfields of IO psychology. While it is impossible to tackle all the areas within the discipline, we have chosen some of the key topics found in most IO textbooks and syllabi, and contrast existing perspectives in current work with future possibilities using a critical perspective.

The chapter is structured as follows: first, we examine individual-level IO psychological theory involving **individual differences** such as cognitive ability, motivation, personality and attitudes, contrasting traditional perspectives with current and potential critical contributions. Next, we address the power implications of key human resources technologies developed and used by IO psychologists, suggesting implications for critical theories of technology and social control. Finally, we examine work–life balance issues, focusing on 'macro' ramifications of psychological theories of the workplace, such as stress and public health, governance, and the changing nature of work. Given the wide purview of this coverage, this review is meant to whet the appetite of IO researchers rather than provide a comprehensive discussion of critical perspectives as applied to IO psychology. As stated above, there is much room for new and interesting debate in this emerging field.

the psychology of individuals in an organizational context

individual differences at work

The study of stable individual differences in IO psychology has been largely based in the attempt to create effective selection systems (e.g., Anderson, 2005) as well as to understand the role of such differences in behaviour at work, such as job performance (e.g., Weiss & Kurek, 2003) or team behaviour (e.g., Stewart, 2003). The first and prototypical example of the study of stable individual differences in work settings concerns the century-old study of intelligence or 'general mental ability' at work (e.g., Thorndike, 1986), but research has also proliferated regarding the roles of stable personality in predicting applied work outcomes such as job performance (e.g., McCrae & John, 1992). These literatures, while not denying change and social influences in affecting individual characteristics (cf., Roberts, Walton, & Viechtbauer, 2006), tend to underplay change and treat change as an intrinsic development of pre-existing potentials (e.g., Costa & MacCrae, 2006). In addition, traditionally, the study of individual differences has tended to emphasize genetic inheritance (e.g. Loehlin, 1992; Jensen & Johnson, 1994) and downplay the role of culture, seeing individual cognition and personality as 'universalizable', if not universal in a more objective sense (e.g., McCrae & Costa, 1997).

Such perspectives are anathema to critical views, which tend to focus on subjective *potentials* rather than the psychological 'individual differences'. What distinguishes potentials from individual differences is that the former do not simply involve observable individual variables. Rather, they refer to a line of thought where an agentic human **subject** grasps at objects in the world through perception and action, and is actively involved in finding his or her own identity. Rather than attempting to pin down the universal features of this subject, which is always essentially undefined but in search for self-definition (e.g. Wittgenstein, 1961), this line of thought defines individuals not by their z-scores on given variables but in the projects and struggles they set for themselves within a given social context. In the words of Foucault, 'What I wanted to try to show was how the subject constituted itself, in one specific form or another … in each case one plays, one establishes a different relation to oneself' (1984: 290). As such, the self is always embedded in a specific, grounded context, but also always reaches beyond that context in the search for itself. A critical view, thus, compared to traditional IO psychology, leaves much more openness in the notion of the individual, which is dynamic and projective, but also locates more explanatory value in social and cultural situations, since it is only through social contexts that the self finds the institutional moorings it needs to ground its projects.

If the mainstream IO view of the structure of human psychology is essentialistic, its view of human motivation is largely utilitarian. That is, human beings, according to traditional IO models, are driven to achieve certain ends in order to satisfy personal demands (cf., Salancik & Pfeffer, 1977). In classic models of motivation, these demands may be extrinsic, as in money or benefits (see Komaki, 1986) or intrinsic, in terms of social value (see Tyler, Degoey, & Smith, 1996), power and achievement (McClelland & Boyatzis, 1982), or more 'existential' demands such as growth (Alderfer, 1969) or **self-actualization** (Maslow, 1943). In many ways, IO psychology has provided a counterpoint to economistic views of human behaviour by showing that the diversity of human motives escapes a purely monetaristic view. However, the traditional IO psychology view is not incompatible with the classical economic view of human beings in that people strive after goals in order to satisfy their personal utility functions (see Schwartz, 1986), an essentially economic vision of human beings. What changes in the psychological version is the diversification of objects of utility and of social and psychological needs and desires, not the basic view of people as utility calculators.

The more starkly economistic variants of IO motivation theory, such as goal setting (e.g., Locke & Latham, 1990), expectancy theory (e.g., Vroom, 1964) or behaviour modification (Komaki, 1986), are the easiest to submit to a critical approach, because they view human motivation in simple means–ends terms that might be as much the *outcome* of socialization into an economistic view than the proof of the validity of this view (e.g., Ferraro, Pfeffer, & Sutton, 2005), that is, people may learn their means–ends mentalities from the theories themselves. An ideological critique of such approaches would, at a minimum, point to their framing of human nature in ways that conveniently fit into a modern consumer capitalist system, and leave out human potentials which might not be realizable in such a system.

While more humanistic variants of motivational models attempt to capture a richer picture of human motivation through concepts such as self-actualization, the basic picture of utilities as something that an individual *has* obscures a richer picture of human action as establishing who one *is* (Fromm, 1976). To place self-actualization as a need in a hierarchy of other needs (Maslow, 1943) is to turn self-actualization into a utility among others, drawing critiques from critical theorists that the pyramid of needs looks more like a pyramid of post-war American values (Cooke, Mills, & Kelly, 2005). Thus, rather than conceptualize self-actualization as a drive or a need of the self, a critical perspective might attempt to break free of such a utilitarian anchor and view growth needs as possibilities for radical self-transcendence.

Although the academic literature on leadership is increasingly varied and multidisciplinary, much of mainstream thought on leadership still relies on the concept of a leader as a singular, charismatic, and courageous individual who emerges at the head of an organization through personal merit and enterprise (Meindl, Ehrlich, & Dukerich, 1985). Contemporaneous to and following Meindl et al's well-known exploration of the 'romantic' conception of leadership as an important organizational sense-making process, and similar treatments exploring the primarily symbolic function of leadership (e.g., Pfeffer, 1981), many studies have moved away from only looking at the individual leader, to also examining, for example, leader-subordinate relationships (e.g., Graen & Scandura, 1987) and follower cognitive processes (e.g. Lord & Maher, 1991).

These works have theoretically decentred the leader as the locus for understanding leadership, but have rarely directly called into question the entrenched system-reinforcing powers inherent in the modern concept of leadership in general (Meindl et al., 1985). For example, in a historical exploration of leadership, Pears (1992) traced the roots of the individualistic notion of the great leader to nineteenth-century Europe, where this picture of leadership allowed the ruling elite to maintain power in the newly consolidating European states and avoid popular revolution. Trait-based conceptions of leadership provide an ideological buttress to dominant power systems by giving the impression to organizational members that they are less competent to make decisions, that if they contributed more to the organization then they might achieve upward mobility, and that all important successes of the organization are attributable to power-holders (Haslam et al., 2001). As such, a critical perspective would start from Haslam et al's observation, and attempt to explore how beliefs about leadership contribute to a psychology of subordination, while on the other hand providing important meaning-giving resources for organizational members (Pfeffer, 1981).

inside the organization:
human resources technologies

In the section above, we dealt with issues in IO that are focused around individuals. Since critical theories view individuals as embedded in social contexts marked by unequal power relations, and maintain that human liberation requires an analysis of these relations, a major criticism of individualistic perspectives is their neglect of such expositions. With regards to IO treatments of human resources technologies, which occur at the collective level of the organization, the key critique shifts from ignoring contextual factors to misframing the social effects of these techniques. While personnel psychology purports to be about administrative efficiency, critical perspectives would attempt to unearth where power relations and elite interests lie behind claims to efficiency.

job analysis

Job analysis was developed from scientific management principles to systematically divide and organize job-related behaviours in organizations (Harvey, 1991). It consists of defining performance behaviours, required knowledge, skills, and abilities, and eventually job categories to best meet productivity needs. The control of job characteristics extends even to the physical movements of workers when, for example, jobs are broken down into their requisite physical movements. As such, in minutely analysed tasks, each worker movement may be considered an administrative target. At the organizational level, job categories often form the basis of departmental divisions that structure communication and can create distinctive departmental cultures.

Townley (1993) describes Human Resource Management techniques such as job analysis according to a Foucaultian view (e.g., Foucault, 1966/1970), such that the technical–scientific process of 'partitioning' takes place where managers identify a sphere of analysis and break up this sphere into relevant units to arrange and rearrange. From a Foucaultian perspective, power is not simply a coercive force, but lies in the ability to impose definitions and modes of interpretation on the situations people use to structure their lives. In this view, job analysis gains its power from its ability to pre-define people's actions from morning to evening on each day of their careers.

Relatedly, many jobs in the upper echelons of organizations are difficult to submit to strict scientific management principles such as job analysis. This is because top management performance is notoriously difficult to define or measure (see Longenecker & Gioia, 1992). Thus, the very control systems justified by efficiency rather than social control are most frequently employed in particularly those segments of the organization marked by low power rather than those leadership positions which presumably are the drivers of firm success. Such an observation may reinforce the view that job analytic techniques are often used to maintain power as much as to ensure firm effectiveness.

Alternatives to the strict delimitation of job aspects have appeared in the literature, including job revision (Wrzesniewski & Dutton, 2001), task revision (Staw & Boettger, 1990) and role innovation (Van Maanen & Schein, 1979). Such treatments involve participation by employees in remaking their jobs and cite worker needs for control and intrinsic motivation as key factors. In line with this stream of research, critical theory could be employed in exploring the political as well as the operational implications of such a reworking. This added dimension might explain why such programmes have been slow to take off in the marketplace, or demonstrate the conditions under which such programmes could be used by employees seeking empowerment.

If job analysis techniques are essentially geared toward providing stability and order within a hierarchical system by imposing definitions on tasks and occupational categories, selection procedures complement this process by matching these categories with potential actors in the job market, searching for an ideal 'fit' (Chatman, 1991) between organizational culture and individual traits. This process not only assumes but depends inherently on the idea that individuals are 'observable, measurable and quantifiable' (Townley, 1993: 529). The above described picture of human nature lends itself easily to organizational selection processes. In fact, the histories of the study of individual differences and that of selection procedures are highly interdependent, with early intelligence testing, for example, being used in immigration control (Richardson, 2003) and university admissions (National Commission on Excellence in Education, 1983). The racial and ethnic discrimination that accompanied early selection initiatives is also well-documented (see Sternberg, 2005). However, at a deeper level, the view of human nature as individual difference variables has itself an ideological patina, a theoretical choice that is understandable only in light of the social structures to which such knowledge was and still is applied.

With regards to group bias in testing, it is certainly true that IO psychology has produced many studies attempting to counter inequality in the workplace through improving selection tests and increasing non-discriminatory selection criteria (e.g. Maxwell & Arvey, 1993). In addition, many studies have attempted to show the benefits of diversity on individual and team functioning (e.g., Dovidio, Gaertner, & Validzic, 1998) – although diversity is often shown to have a deleterious impact on such outcomes (e.g., Tsui & O'Reilly, 1989). Such research claims a progressive political agenda in attempting to undo the negative effects of gender, racial, and other group-based prejudice in selection contexts. However, similar to the literatures described above on job redesign, rethinking individualistic leadership, non-monetary motivation, and change in individual differences, such studies do not question the basic structure of managerial **ideology** in the workplace, but rather work to mitigate the social harms brought about *given* the status quo system of work employment. In the selection context, studies questioning the validity of selection tests seldom question the notion of management-based selection as a method of social organizing or draw out the political ramifications of this nearly ubiquitous practice.

Following Townley (1993), selection systems follow closely the Foucaultian 'ranking' function that is comprised of the evaluation, testing, and placement within a hierarchy of people within the managerial purview. Managerial control is in large measure based on these hierarchies, and although such control is not specifically spellt out in the 'objective' selection test procedures, this very objectivity is what justifies managerial authority, as it provides a gloss of disinterestedness that hides power interests. Thus, debates about the content, construct and predictive validity of selection measures hide the fact that observation and quantification themselves – explicitly aimed at judging and ranking people as qualified or disqualified for resource linked social roles – are elements that are taken for granted in organizational life.

training and socialization

In a way, the training and socialization literatures form a counterpoint to selection and individual differences approaches, in that they do not take individuals to be relatively stable entities to be selected for or against, but rather, acknowledge the malleability of organizationally relevant aspects of human beings. The training and socialization literatures are joined together here because both involve the changing of individuals' attitudes, beliefs, values, or behaviours in order to bring these in alignment with organizational norms, demands and/or culture (e.g., Kolb & Frey, 1975). In the socialization literature, the focus tends to be on the automatic social processes that bring newcomers into alignment with the organization, usually early in their tenure (Chatman, 1991), through norms, rituals, stories, and other informal mechanisms (Trice & Beyer, 1984). The training literature, on the other hand, tends to focus on the specific formalized procedures used to change employee cognition and behaviour (Arthur, Bennett, Edens, & Bell, 2003).

While both literatures focus on change in individuals based on social contextual variables, they do so in quite different ways. For example, the training literature tends to use more of an educational model (see Huddock, 1994), focusing on processes of individual cognitive change rather than the content that organizational members learn (e.g., Bandura, 1986; Salas & Cannon-Bowers, 2001). Thus, outcomes in the training literature take the form of memory and retention and the application of learned material (e.g., Hacker, 2003; Kolb & Frey, 1975). On the other hand, the socialization literature tends to be more self-conscious about the links between training and ideology, emphasizing much more often the negative influences of acculturation in terms of legitimizing unethical behaviour in organizations (e.g., Ashforth & Kreiner, 1999), the alienation and rejection of external groups by the organization (e.g., Pratt, 2000), and socialization into cultures of brutality or violence (e.g., Van Maanan, 1973).

Perhaps the difference in focus between training and socialization literatures may be explained by the tendency of socialization researchers to take a dynamic, interdisciplinary view of culture, mixing psychological theories of cognitive change with an anthropological sensitivity to social systems as wholes (Schein, 2006). In contrast, the training literature tends to draw more on individual-level educational psychology theory (e.g., Bandura, 1986) rather than look critically on the training systems themselves as parts of social systems. This interdisciplinary tendency in organizational socialization aligns it much more closely with critical theory, which integrates macro-level political perspectives, interpersonal, meso-level communicative practices, and individual psychological tendencies (e.g., Fromm, 1976; Marcuse, 1964).

A critical overview of the discipline would be incomplete without a treatment of the growing importance of work–environment issues. The emergence of such interest has grown from the recognition that business practices do not exist in an entirely separate sphere from other life spaces, but are highly influential in the way that, among others, familial, cultural, political, and environmental institutions are affected by the meanings of work and the terms under which people labour (e.g., Ciulla, 2000). To give a flavour of how critical theory can inform further discussions about the interface of work and society, we review a small sample of the social spheres affected by the terms and understandings of labour.

_____ *organizational stress* _____

The notion of stress is to some extent a quintessential case of a dense work–society mixture with multiple nuanced facets. On the one hand, stress is often viewed as a medical condition and treated in terms of its negative biological effects, such as an increased risk of heart disease and lowered immunity (e.g., Cooper & Marshall, 1976). However, stress is also often analysed in terms of individual cognitions and emotions (e.g., Bhagat, 1983), thus creating an interface between biological and psychological theory. Simultaneously, stressful working conditions are also examined as precursors of experienced stress, adding a public health/occupational safety dimension to the mix (e.g., Parker & DeCotiis, 1983). Finally, some recent treatments of stress have highlighted the sociocultural aspects of stress as a discourse (Barley & Knight, 1992; Meyerson, 1994), an addition which greatly increases the potential for studying stress under a critical lens.

Prior to Barley and Knight's (1992) discussion of stress as a social symbol, there was a dominant tendency to treat the stress phenomenon using a 'medical model'. According to this model, stress could be discussed as a disease, whose etiological factors fell into one of two categories, (a) environmental stressors such as workload, family problems, or economic distress, and (b) personal dispositional factors, such as personality traits, attitudes and values. The interaction of personal proclivities with environmental factors gave rise to the 'presence' of stress, with its concomitant social, psychological, and biological effects.

The 'critical turn' in the early 1990s (e.g., Barley & Knight, 1992; Meyerson, 1994) challenged this view by treating stress not as an objective disease that appears or disappears given the right conditions, but as a 'dominant cultural metaphor' that can be used to encode various cultural contradictions. While within the disease model culture still entered the picture, it did so only as a cause of individual beliefs and attitudes, or because it structured the environment in stress-producing ways; in other words, culture existed as a cause of stress, but stress was not itself cultural. By contrast, in Barley and Knight's view, the use of the stress concept enabled the expression of various cultural tensions, such as that of the relation between individual utility and organizational performance and the relation between the mind and the body. Playing the stress card offered a justification for individuals requesting organizational resources and offered an avenue for legitimate escape, as disease is considered a justifiable external cause for poor performance. On the other hand, medicalizing stress allowed organizations to implement 'stress management programmes', implicitly transferring responsibility onto the worker for managing his/her own stress and avoiding radical system change. It should be clear how this type of analysis is fundamentally different from an analysis which seeks to measure and reduce stress-related problems at work. The latter approach takes for granted a certain problem, and attempts to solve it, while the former seeks to explain the discursive construction of the problem in the first place, and relies much more on historical and interpretive paradigms.

_____ *the changing nature of careers* _____

While a critical approach to stress focuses more on the construction of individual experience, the study of careers takes as its focus more macro institutions such as the nature of occupations. In some cases, such as academic careers (e.g., Meyer, Ramirez, Frank, & Schofer, 2006), these institutions may be thousands of years old, whereas in other cases, such as project managers or software developers, they may be nascent or transitory categories. The traditional approach to the psychological study of careers is a type of matching exercise between pre-set occupational categories and individual profiles; tests, interviews, and other psychometric tools are used to ensure that people follow career paths that 'fit' their sets of knowledge, skills and abilities in order to improve both their personal wellbeing and their performance at work (e.g., Kristoff, 1996). In our view, critical perspectives can inform this traditional view on two important and related fronts.

First, rather than viewing career trajectories as existing 'natural' categories in which people have varying aptitudes, a critical perspective would attempt to unpack systems of power and ideology underlying these trajectories. As discussed above, views of the human being that are based in typological profiles undercut the sense of human freedom and agency that is critical to a liberated view of human beings; in a parallel fashion, views of occupations as stable categories overlook the potentials for social change and reify existing social structures (e.g., Lukacs, 1923/1967). Rather than viewing careers as taken-for-granted categories, a critical IO psychology would view career categories as reflective of who gets to define what work is to be done and to impose methods of ensuring newcomers are socialized into these definitions. Such perspectives with regards to the making of doctors (e.g., Islam & Zyphur,

2007), executives (e.g., Ferraro et al., 2005) and public workers (e.g., Van Maanen, 1973), among others, have demonstrated that the establishment of career role identities is fraught with hard socialization and 'strong' situations (Mitchell, 1974), that is, those that impose social structures through training and occupational norms.

Second, a more prolific literature has examined society-level changes in the structure of work relationships, reflecting widespread concerns about fundamental changes in the way people work (e.g., Howard, 1995). Several parallel phenomena are worth noting here: changes in work relationships based on technological developments in the workplace (e.g., Griffith & Neale, 2001), increases in the variety of careers over the lifespan and shortening times spent in careers (e.g., Mainiero & Sullivan, 2006), the globalization of markets and concomitant issues of off-shoring labour (cf., Harrison & MacMillan, 2006), child labour (e.g., Cigno, Rosati, & Tzannatos, 2001), the diminishing power of local labour organizers (Goldfield, 1987), and the 'flexibilization' of labour and the increase in spot contracts and part-time work among adults (e.g., Askenazy, 2004). All have led to a difficulty in using traditional career categories to describe the world of work. In all these phenomena, critical scholars should be paying attention to how career categories are remade by powerful actors and how local workers react to a new and confusing workplace.

_____ organization and culture _____

Although organizational culture (and culture in general [see Kroeber & Kluckhohn, 1952]) has long groped for a consensus in definition, a general way to describe the phenomenon would be as a set of basic assumptions about roles and practices that develops in an organization, is taught to new members, and influences how people think, feel, and behave with regards to organizationally relevant issues (Schein, 1990). The organizational culture literature is varied and interdisciplinary (Schein, 2006); however, it is worth noting that this literature became increasingly popular in the late 1970s and 1980s, when culture theorists attempted to explain the high efficiency of Japanese management as a consequence of 'cultural' factors that led to increased worker productivity (e.g., Ouichi, 1981). The use of culture as an explanation for efficiency and its subsequent treatment as a management technique has led to criticisms that the management literature pulled anthropological and sociological facets of cultural studies out of context, and inappropriately used the concept of culture in a purely functional sense (e.g., Meek, 1988).

The ways in which organizational culture would appropriately use critical theory to further its already interdisciplinary views on practices and belief structures could be divided into two broad levels of analysis. The first would look within the organization's culture, and would take the form of a micro-analysis of organizational politics and symbolic actions (e.g., Pfeffer, 1981). The second would be to link organizational culture with wider cultural dynamics, attempting to map the relationships between ideologies and practices originating in organizational cultures and those prevalent in society at large, in order to formulate a cultural theory of organization, and explain the cultural functions of organizations in terms beyond mere efficiency explanations.

The first of these two approaches has been described as a **microsociological** approach (e.g., Goffman, 1983), and most often has drawn on interpretive anthropology and ethnography (e.g., Geertz, 1973), ethnomethodology (e.g., Garfinkel, 1967), and micro-analyses of events such as rituals (e.g., Trice & Beyer, 1984) or speech acts (e.g., Austin, 1962). Based on the above perspectives, the researcher would begin at the level of everyday practices, routines or habits, and attempt to infer 'hidden meanings' that reveal organizational ideologies. From there, the critical scholar could attempt to demonstrate how these ideologies reinforce elite power structures or maintain a hegemonic status quo, or else demonstrate spaces in everyday practices where resistance to such structures occurs.

The second, macro approach would look at larger institutions, such as managerialism, organizational forms or relationships between national and organizational cultures. For example, a critical culture study at this level might examine where organizational cultures reflect and reinforce national level cultural beliefs or values or where organizational cultures might signal a challenge to dominant country-level social structures (cf., Bucheli, 2006; Grieder, 1997). In this case, organizational culture would be thought of as a mode of being that competes with others for expression in a social space, and individual workers' socialization into a particular organizational culture might be thought of as a political conversion into a specific clan. Venturing into institutional levels of analysis could provide alternate explanations of norms and selection systems from a social standpoint.

implications and recommendations

In contrasting mainstream IO psychological views with critical alternatives, it is important to note that we have provided a necessarily broad and caricatured view of mainstream IO psychology. In reality, IO psychologists often temper their views with considerations of socioeconomic context and are aware of the ideological undergirding of the theories they use. Conversely, critical theorists often fall victim to many of the mainstream presuppositions that they attempt to problematize. What are provided here, then, are prototypes of the mainstream and critical views, the function of which is to highlight major points of distinction between the two approaches.

Complicating the situation, the 'industrial' side of IO is often discussed separately from the 'organizational', where the former regards more personnel-related topics such as selection and testing, and the latter, more 'humanistic' topics such as motivation and attitudes. In this case, the current critique regards the former side more than the latter, although several points are applicable to both. Further complicating the picture still, the field of Organizational Studies, which is distinct from, but in many ways parallel to, IO psychology, has a rich and growing critical and postmodern tradition that encapsulates some of the points made here, but has been more strongly represented in business schools and in sociology departments than in IO psychology departments. Thus, even separating out IO psychology as an independent field of study involves some premises that are difficult to hold. It may be, for example, that IO psychology has been able to focus on quantitative, psychometric approaches at the expense of critical theory precisely because other related fields have more thoroughly explored critical alternatives – allowing critical studies in allied fields to serve a kind of relief-valve function for any critical motives within IO psychology itself. If this is the case, then critiquing mainstream IO approaches may be somewhat misplaced.

To a large extent, promoting a critical IO psychology is not a call for a radically changed set of objects of study. We believe that critical theory is more of a posture taken with respect to the object of study than a specific set of variables under study. To some extent, this involves an awareness of how the results of one's study are to be used in a social context. Will a certain theory of intelligence be used against marginalized groups? Will motivational techniques be used to exploit workers? Whatever the answer to such questions, it is important to note that the critical posture goes beyond a simple usage of empirical data, and asks why certain things are studied in the first place, whose idea it was to study such things, and what individual and social interests may have been secured or compromised through such a study. For example, in a criticism of the use of IQ testing to establish racial differences, Sternberg states, 'Deciding to show that one group is genetically inferior on an index is a value judgment as to what is worth showing. These decisions, among others, indicate that there is no value-free science. Few of us can hear our own accents when we speak – only other people have accents!' (2005: 295). Although Robert Sternberg is a mainstream psychologist not normally associated with the critical theory paradigm, the critical recognition of what psychologists are doing, and why we are doing it, is clear from such statements. Thus, promoting critical IO psychology can take place through a sensitizing of scholars to the effects of their work, and does not require that IO psychologists immerse themselves in nineteenth-century German or postmodern philosophy.

That said, an important point to be stressed is that while critical theory entails a multi-level approach, integrating cultural, political, interpersonal, and psychological phenomena into a holistic worldview, simply bringing social effects into the picture as *variables* – for example as a moderator or boundary condition – is not sufficient to do justice to the critical view. In many of the cases cited above, researchers (rightly) brought social context into their discussion of psychological effects, without taking on a critical viewpoint. For example, intelligence researchers have searched for bias in testing conditions, motivational researchers have stressed the role of social values in creating utilities, leadership researchers have studied followership, stress researchers have looked at context in the etiology of stress, and many other examples of examining context are readily available. However, looking at context in this way misses a fundamental point stressed by critical theory. For instance, a critical theorist might not stop at asking how culture affects peoples' preferences, but rather might look at how the notions of motivation and preference help make sense of the world in the first place, and at the same time, hold in place institutional structures. So, for example, a stress researcher who studies how harsh labour conditions augment stress might be doing important research, but is not really critical in orientation because nothing essential is being problematized. Barley and Knight's (1992) theory of stress, however, could be considered critical, because it doesn't take for granted the object under study, but asks how such an object is constituted within a social-discursive nexus.

As a final note, we stress that we are not suggesting that critical scholarship replace quantitatively oriented, 'objective' science, a worry that some organizational psychologists have voiced when viewing this peripheral scholarship from the centre of mainstream organization studies (e.g., Donaldson, 1992; Locke, 2002). While some scholars feel that analysing the social construction of commonly held ideas, particularly intimate psychological constructs such as selves, emotions, or values, can cause scholars to lose their grounding and fall into academic nihilism (e.g., Crosby, 1988), we feel that the danger is greater for scholars *not* to examine the social premises and origins of their theories and applications. While the promotion of self-reflection can cause vertigo, it also provides a basis for the scholarly quest for evermore coherent discourses (Habermas, 1981). While such discourses may not provide the bedrock of absolute truth that some scholars unrealistically demand (e.g., Locke, 2002), there is no indication that ignoring self-criticism can do any better, although such a posture certainly increases subjective certainty. If scientific progress depends on the right mix of humility, perspicacity, and drive, then we believe that no better recipe for such a mix is at present available than the cycle of disciplinary self-questioning that defines critical studies in the social sciences, and has the potential to define an emerging field of critical IO psychology.

▨ ▨ main chapter points ▨

1 Often, mainstream IO psychology builds theory around unspoken managerial assumptions about human behaviour and social order.

2 Critical approaches analyse psychological theory and workplace techniques from the point of view of power dynamics and ideologies.

3 At the level of individuals, mainstream approaches see persons in terms of objective traits, whereas critical approaches view people in terms of subjective potentials.

4   At the level of human resources techniques, mainstream approaches view such techniques as pragmatic, whereas critical approaches view these techniques as power-reinforcing.

5   Critical perspectives on work–environment issues question social categories such as careers, work related stress, and organizational culture, reframing these categories as power-relevant.

glossary

- **ideology**: a collection of organized ideas. In critical theory, refers to where ideas are used to further dominant social or economic orders.

- **individual differences**: any variable (e.g. psychological, demographic) on which people differ from one another.

- **microsociology**: the study of social structure in terms of patterns of interactions between individuals, often in small groups.

- **self-actualization**: in humanistic psychology, the process by which people realize their potentials for full selfhood.

- **subject**: in the context of critical theory, refers to thinking and acting agents, with particularistic points of view and life projects.

reading suggestions

Alvesson and Deetz (1996) offer a good introduction to critical perspectives applied to organizational settings. Barley and Knight (1992) show how occupational stress entered workplace discourse and became a dominant cultural trope among organizational thinkers. Pratt's (2000) study of identification among Amway workers shows how organizational identity is manipulated to fit managerial objectives, and the sometimes negative results of organizational socialization on members' wellbeing. Pfeffer's (1981) treatment of management as a symbolic activity is an overview of the ways in which socially shared symbolic meanings are politically leveraged by managers. Finally, Townley's (1993) review of Foucault in the HR literature provides a link between this key thinker and the practices of organizational selection and surveillance.

internet resources

- Ephemera Journal: www.ephemeraweb.org

- European Group for Organizational Studies: www.egosnet.org/index.shtml

- Stanford Encyclopedia of Philosophy: Critical Theory: plato.stanford.edu/entries/critical-theory/

Questions

1 What are the main assumptions about human nature that managers hold? Under what circumstances should these assumptions be questioned or challenged?

2 Are acts of defining job roles politically neutral, or are they necessarily based on ideological premises? Are some managerial actions more political than others, and if so, which ones?

3 Should organizations concerned with the bottom line take into account worker wellbeing even where wellbeing is not linked to profits? If so, are such concerns sustainable in a competitive marketplace?

8

Community Psychology: Advancing Social Justice

Isaac Prilleltensky and Geoffrey Nelson

To what extent has **community psychology** fulfilled its promise of advancing individual, relational, and collective wellbeing? To what extent can a critical community psychology help? These are the two key questions that concern us in this chapter. After comparing and contrasting mainstream and critical community psychology's assumptions and practices, we discuss key elements of a critical community psychology. We argue that social justice should be the overarching value of critical community psychology for the promotion of wellbeing at multiple levels of analysis.

community psychology: where we are and where we're going

where we are

Both of us worked for the Child Guidance Clinic of Winnipeg (Canada) during the late 1970s and 1980s. In our work as clinicians, we discovered we were often expected to provide individual solutions to problems that were essentially social and communal. For example, native children living in inner-city Winnipeg, under inauspicious conditions, were failing at school. We also discovered that the system's traditional diagnostic process resulted in pathological portrayals of children and parents. What's more, we were regarded as experts who knew the answers to the families' struggles. Despite paying lip service to collaborating with other agencies and professionals, we carried out most of our work in isolation, behind an intelligence test or a desk.

Enter community psychology. Much to our relief, we both discovered this discipline that emphasized an ecological, value-laden, community-based, strengths-oriented, collaborative approach (see the second column of Table 8.1). Community psychology made immediate sense to us because we knew, theoretically but also experientially, that the **ecology** of the child was crucial in her or his academic, social, and behavioural outcomes. We also knew that values mattered. We saw first hand the impact of social injustice and could not pretend that we were value-neutral professionals or that it was up to somebody else to fix the ills of the past. We also found ways to build on children's assets and strengths. In short, we felt hugely gratified to find a professional home in community psychology. The traditional psychology we had been taught did not sit well with us. In contrast, community psychology felt very progressive.

Unfortunately, whereas in the 1960s community psychology was indeed socially progressive especially in comparison to clinical psychology, we believe it lost its progressive edge and became a part of the conservative mainstream. It would not be the first time a profession's or social movement's radical impulses have waned (Chavis & Wolff, 1993), but it is disappointing nonetheless. We, of course, are not immune to this trend, so we find ourselves in the uncomfortable but humbling position to critique our field and ourselves. In this chapter we will reflect on what happened to the field, and what happened to us, including our struggle to remain engaged in community psychology and to remain critical. We are, after all, part of the field.

To understand where community psychology has fallen short, first we need to review some of its basic tenets. Table 8.1 offers an overview of five domains that guide the work of community psychologists. To begin with, community psychology is explicitly guided by a multi-level, ecological perspective introduced by Jim Kelly in the 1960s (Kelly, 1966). In their analysis of human problems and wellbeing, community psychologists often focus on risk and protective factors that operate at multiple ecological levels of analysis. However, while community psychology has developed a more contextualized approach than clinical psychology and has focused on setting-level concepts and interventions, it often ignores the collective level of analysis, which, as we shall see, turns out to be its Achilles heel.

Since Rappaport (1977) underscored the importance of 'values, research, and action' (the subtitle of his text), values have been a part of community psychology's discourse. However, values often take a back seat to research in community psychology. Since values are present but often not front and centre in community psychology research and action, we believe that community

Table 8.1 Assumptions and practices of mainstream community psychology and critical community psychology

Dimension	Mainstream community psychology	Critical community psychology
Explanatory framework	Ecological (person, micro, meso, macro, but macro is in the background), focus on risk/protective factors, contextualized but depoliticized	Oppression, liberation, wellbeing (multi-level, ecological analysis), contextualized and politicized
Place of values and ethics	Value-laden (the influence of multiple values is noted), increased attention to ethics at the community level	Value-driven, social ethics
Research	Community-based, primarily post-positivist, relatively minor emphasis on constructivism	Critical constructivist and post-positivist, participatory, action-oriented, and community-based
Focus of intervention	Focus on competence and strengths, prevention of problems in living for populations	Focus on liberation and wellbeing for individuals, organizations, and societies
Relationship between disadvantaged community members and CP professional	Collaborative model with multiple community stakeholders	Accompaniment, solidarity between professionals and disadvantaged community members in their struggle for liberation and wellbeing through praxis

psychology is value-*laden* rather than value-*driven*. Community psychology research is community-based, and community psychologists work collaboratively with community groups to conduct research in ways that are participatory, meaningful, and empowering to the community (Jason et al., 2004). For example, in the early 1990s, I, Isaac, joined the community psychology programme at Wilfrid Laurier University, where Geoff was already a professor. Soon after my arrival, Ed Bennett, a senior community psychologist in the programme, introduced me to the Sand Hills community, a housing project inhabited mostly by immigrants from Central and South America. Being also an immigrant from that part of the world, I resonated with the community's struggles. Together, the community and I established a partnership and created an organization called the Latin American Educational Group (Prilleltensky, 1993; Prilleltensky, Nelson, & Sanchez, 2000). It was a very reciprocal collaboration through which we created academic, advocacy, and social programmes for children and families. Parents and children conducted focus groups and interviews and helped to analyse the data. The results informed our work related to smoking prevention and advocacy. To my mind, this project was representative of a community psychology approach to the wellbeing of immigrant families.

The field has also seen an increase in the number of qualitative research articles based on a constructivist paradigm published in community psychology journals (e.g., Martin, Lounsbury, & Davidson, 2004). However, on the whole, community psychology research remains rooted in a positivist philosophy of science that is 'scientistic' in its emulation of the natural sciences (Nelson & Prilleltensky, 2005).

With respect to interventions, community psychology focuses on the promotion of competence and wellbeing and the prevention of problems in living. The Better Beginnings, Better Futures (BBBF) project in Ontario, Canada, is representative of such an approach. I, Geoff, have been involved with the project since the early 1990s. In the project, we worked with the Highfield community in Toronto to improve the behavioural, cognitive and social health of children. Among other things, we implemented a social skills training programme in the school to help children resolve conflict (Nelson, Pancer, Hayward, & Peters, 2005). Although the skill building approach is useful and necessary, much of community psychology intervention, especially prevention, is individualistic or micro-centred, focusing on teaching life skills to individuals or building social support among small groups of individuals (Cowen, 1985). While community psychologists who work from a community development perspective have focused more than prevention scientists on systems change, the community psychology literature on systems change has been slow to develop. Few examples exist of systems change at the collective level of analysis (Foster-Fishman, Nowell, & Yang, 2007). Our own BBBF project strives to blend individual improvement with community change through school reform and advocacy.

Mainstream community psychology places a strong emphasis on collaboration with many different community stakeholders (Trickett & Ryerson Espino, 2004). However, it is not clear in many community interventions that community psychology's primary allegiance is to the most disadvantaged community members and their agenda for social change (Nelson, Prilleltensky, & MacGillivary, 2001). Sometimes, community psychologists work with gatekeepers or other professionals (e.g., school teachers, mental health professionals), with disadvantaged community members having only token participation or only playing the role of consumers of services. This is how most clinicians operated at the Child Guidance Clinic.

_____ *where we're going* _____

Our aim in this chapter is to forge an integration between community psychology and critical psychology. We envision a critical community psychology that is contextual *(ecological)* and political (focusing on social injustice and **power**), value-driven (emphasizing social justice), and critical in its ontological, epistemological, and methodological underpinnings (see Chapter 3 by Thomas Teo). Furthermore, it utilizes a praxis approach in which professionals work in solidarity with disadvantaged communities to enhance liberation and wellbeing by changing social systems (see the third column of Table 8.1). We realize this is a mouthful, but all these components are important. Carolyn Kagan and Mark Burton's definition of community psychology captures well what we mean by critical community psychology:

> Community psychology offers a framework for working with those marginalized by the social system that leads to self-aware social change with an emphasis on value-based participatory work and the forging of alliances. It is a way of working that is pragmatic and reflexive, whilst not wedded to any particular orthodoxy of method. As such community psychology is one alternative to the dominant individualistic psychology typically taught and practiced in the higher income countries. It is *community* psychology because it emphasizes a level of analysis and intervention other than the individual and their immediate inter-personal context. It is community *psychology* because it is nevertheless concerned with how people feel, think, experience, and act as they work together, resisting oppression and struggling to create a better world. (Burton, Boyle, Harris, & Kagan, 2007: 219)

As clarified in Table 8.1, the explanatory framework of critical community psychology replaces depoliticized language and concepts (e.g., risk, protection) with more sociopolitical ideas (e.g., social injustice, liberation). From the perspective of critical community psychology, moving from a state of oppression to one of wellbeing is a multi-level, ecological process that involves the self in the context of relationships embedded in community and society. For example, the feminist movement, as discussed in this book's chapters on gender and history, exemplifies a social change process where women acted at the personal, interpersonal, family, community and political levels to effect lasting changes in their private and collective lives.

We have defined *oppression* as '... a state of domination where the oppressed suffer the consequences of deprivation, exclusion, discrimination, exploitation, control of culture, and sometimes even violence' (Prilleltensky & Nelson, 2002: 12); *liberation*, in turn, refers to the process of overcoming oppression; and *wellbeing* is a positive state of affairs experienced at different ecological levels: individual (e.g., perceptions of control), relational (e.g., participatory structures), and collective (e.g., community support settings and policies) (Prilleltensky & Prilleltensky, 2006). The value of this framework is that it draws particular attention to the role of social justice and power in conceptualizing human problems (I. Prilleltensky, 2008). Once again, the women's movement is an apt illustration of a meaningful segment of society resisting oppression and striving towards emancipation through social change. Consciousness raising groups afforded many women opportunities to establish bonds of solidarity that helped them challenge unjust social structures. Community psychology was again not immune to the male-centric approaches it was fighting in the external world. In the United States, for example, women struggled to increase their visibility in the American Psychological Association's Division of Community Psychology (Angelique & Culley, 2007). The creation of a women's interest group helped their cause greatly.

As noted in the second column of Table 8.1, critical community psychology is explicitly values-driven and concerned with social ethics. Individual, relational, and collective values guide the work of community psychologists (I. Prilleltensky, 2001). I, Isaac, have been concerned with the social ethics of psychology since working on my dissertation in the 1980s. In order to overcome the individualistic tendencies in professional ethics, I have been trying to expand the scope of the discussion ever since, urging the field to move beyond ethics as an exchange occurring between psychologist and client.

The third domain of Table 8.1 refers to research. Critical community psychology is based on a critical paradigm of knowing and uses methods that are community-based, involve the participation of disadvantaged people in all phases of the research, and are oriented towards social action (Nelson & Prilleltensky, 2005). Borrowing a concept from Aristotle, Flyvbjerg (2001) has argued for a *phronetic* social science, which is concerned with how values and power play out in social change processes in various contexts. Flyvbjerg argues that a phronetic approach is most appropriate for a human social science because it combines the search for wellbeing with power and interests, a most pragmatic pursuit. Thus, in the Sand Hills project, the community, children included, organized to petition the city council against the advertising of cigarettes to minors. The children delivered petitions to city hall in a memorable presentation. In the BBBF project, the community often mobilized itself to maintain levels of provincial funding. However modest, in both instances research participants were active in social change efforts.

Critical community psychology intervention strives to overcome social injustice and to promote liberation and wellbeing at the personal, relational, and collective levels. The role of the professional in critical community psychology is one of accompaniment and solidarity with disadvantaged community members. Together, community psychologists and disadvantaged people struggle for liberation and wellbeing through praxis, a continuous 'reflection and action upon the world to transform it' (Freire, 1970: 33). An example of this is community psychologists partnering with mental health consumers/survivors to help establish the value of consumer-controlled housing (Sylvestre, Nelson, Durbin, George, Aubry, & Ollenberg, 2006) and consumer-run organizations that engage in both peer support and systems change (Janzen, Nelson, Hausfather, & Ochocka, 2007). I, Geoff, along with a grassroots community coalition, have been involved in policy work to improve housing conditions for people with serious psychiatric problems (Nelson, 1994).

critical community psychology: values, social justice, and praxis

By now, you should get a feeling for what we value in critical community psychology, as outlined in Table 8.2. For us, critical community psychology is:

- Ecological in nature, recognizing the need to concentrate simultaneously on individuals, relationships, and communities.

Table 8.2 Key dimensions of critical community psychology

Ecological spheres	Wellbeing	Values	Oppression and social injustice	Praxis
Individual	Absence of disorder Positive subjective wellbeing Positive psychological and social functioning	Health	Unequal distribution of health problems (SES gradient) and exposure to risk factors for disease	Health promotion and prevention
	Voice, choice, control Perceptions of control, self-efficacy, and mastery Independence Skills Citizen participation	Self-determination and participation (empowerment)	Disempowerment and internalized oppression	Conscientization, recognizing sources of injustice, situating personal struggles in the larger context of oppression Citizen participation in the creation and/or transformation of settings
Relational	Positive social relationships Social support Social inclusion	Caring and compassion	Social exclusion, marginalization, abuse and neglect	Emphasis on informal support and self-help Advocacy for inclusion
	Positive identity, pride Alternative settings and transformed mainstream settings Elimination of stigma in settings and communities	Diversity	Racism, sexism, heterosexism, ableism	Celebration of strengths and diversity Confronting racism, sexism, heterosexism, ableism
Collective	Strong social programmes that are readily accessible and available High levels of social capital and sense of community	Support for community structures	Barriers to health care, education, housing, employment, social services for marginalized people Low levels of social capital and sense of community	Advocacy for universal supports and services Community capacity building
	Elimination of poverty and reduction of economic inequality	Distributive justice	Extreme economic inequality	Advocacy for changes in social and economic policy Investment in human development and community economic development

- Values-driven.

- Guided by the central value of social justice.

- Praxis-oriented in its efforts to overcome social injustice through social action in partnership with disadvantaged people.

_____ *values* _____

Following Baier (1973), we define values as principles and practices that confer benefits to individuals, relationships, and the collective. Thus, values should guide the enhancement of human wellbeing (Prilleltensky & Prilleltensky, 2006).

individual values   An important value at the individual level is *health*, which can be defined not just as the absence of illness, but also as

> **the capacity of the individual, the group and the environment to interact with one another in ways that promote subjective wellbeing, the optimal development and use of mental abilities (cognitive, affective, and relational), the achievement of individual and collective goals consistent with justice and the attainment and preservation of conditions of fundamental equality. (Epp, 1988: 7)**

This definition places the health of individuals in the context of the environment and underscores the importance for health of justice and equality (Hofrichter, 2003). Another important individual-level value is *self-determination and participation* or *empowerment*, which can be defined as '… enhancing the possibilities of people to take control of their own lives' (Rappaport, 1981: 15). A subsequent elaboration of empowerment has suggested that it is both a process and an outcome that exists at multiple levels of analysis (Zimmerman, 2000). Critical community psychology emphasizes the political nature of power and views power as something that: (a) permeates every aspect of social life; (b) is relational and involves resistance as well as domination; (c) can be blatantly coercive or subtle and difficult to 'see'; and (d) can be used to either oppress ('power over') or liberate people ('power with') (Martín-Baró, 1994; I. Prilleltensky, 2003).

relational values   It is hard to fathom the relevance of other moral values in the absence of *caring and compassion*, for they provide the basic motivation to look after someone else's wellbeing. Community psychology has historically been concerned with social support, mutual aid, neighbourhood helping, and a psychological sense of community for the wellbeing of all community members (Perkins, Hughey, & Speer, 2002).

The value of *human diversity* holds that differences among people should not be viewed as deficits or used to marginalize or exclude people from opportunities, participation, or resources by virtue of their differences (Rappaport, 1977). Watts (1992) has made a distinction between multicultural and anti-racist approaches to diversity. The former focuses on culture and celebrates and supports cultural differences and strengths through public education and the creation of cultural organizations, while the latter focuses on racism and power and strives to transform institutions to achieve equity.

collective values Support for community structures is an important collective value. 'Human beings cannot flourish in isolation, nor can they develop without access to communal goods such as health care, housing, high-quality education, and a clean environment' (Prilleltensky & Prilleltensky, 2006: 62). In many developed nations (e.g., Canada, the United Kingdom, the United States), progressive social policies that support community structures have been under attack by governments beholden to the corporate agenda of tax cuts (Barry, 2005; Korten, 2001), resulting in a diminished capacity of state-supported community structures to promote wellbeing. Critical community psychology is concerned both with community structures and the policies that support them.

Distributive justice refers to the fair and equitable allocation of bargaining power, resources, and burdens in society (Brighouse, 2004; Miller, 1978; Rawls, 1972). While community psychology has been concerned with the unjust allocation of resources and power, it has not had a profound grasp of this central concept. As a result, discussions of injustice tend to be superficial. To counteract this shortcoming, we offer an extended definition of distributive justice below.

_____ *social justice* _____

Distributive justice is especially important because it is crucial for the attainment of all the other values. All values are goods subject to fair and equitable principles of distribution. For example, how we allocate resources to minorities, a corollary of the value of diversity, depends on the definition of justice. Similarly, how we care for the infirm, is also a matter of justice. When there is an unjust allocation of resources, negative consequences ensue.

definition and questions for social justice The classic conception of justice is *to each his or her due* (Miller, 1978, 1999). While useful, this definition begs four key questions: first, who or what is *each*? Second, how do we decide what is his, her, its or their *due*? Third, *who* or *what* will be responsible for the distribution? And fourth, how do we decide what is due *from* each person or entity? Only after answering these four questions will we be able to devise a more useful definition.

first question: who or what is each? The *each* in *to each his or her due*, has been traditionally conceptualized as an individual (Brighouse, 2004; Kraut,

2007). This is a valid but insufficient answer, for the *each* can also be a family, a group, a community, or public institutions entrusted with providing services to the population. Families are entitled to certain benefits and resources, such as child care, health insurance, special education, privacy, and other privileges. Families are units that have been defined operationally and socially as separate entities. Communities are also deserving of special dispensation, such as affirmative action, Medicare, or discounts for seniors. It is possible, therefore, to expand the definition of *each* to families, communities, and public institutions.

second question: how do we decide what is due a person, family, or group?
How do we determine what is the right amount of reward for a person? How do we figure out a fair allocation of resources to a family or community? Some moral philosophers argue that *needs* and *work* are the main criteria (Facione, Scherer, & Attig, 1978); whereas others include *rights* in the distribution formula (Miller, 1999). Assuming we accept these three criteria, the question becomes when to apply each, and which one should take precedence. The answer depends on the context.

Facione et al. (1978) propose two useful criteria for distributing resources: *work* and *need*. If I have a limited resource that several people claim, I will distribute it first among those whose basic needs have not yet been met. If I still have some left after I fulfil the basic needs of a person or a group, I should proceed to distribute it on another basis, like work or merit. While reasonable, this logic is limited, because it does not take into account power differentials, which are a key element of context. A person might have abilities and the willingness to exert considerable effort, but due to lack of power, she/he is deprived of opportunities. Hence, power counts.

Therefore, we propose six criteria for the distribution of resources and obligations: *needs, ability, effort, rights, opportunity* and *power*.

third question: who or what is responsible for distributing resources and obligations? The third question relates to the entity responsible for distributing resources, burdens, pains and gains. This question complements the first. Instead of *to*, we now say *from* each his, her, their, or its due. Who or what is the *each* in this case? In our view, the *each* in this case can be the same as the each in *to each his or her due: individuals, families, communities, or public institutions*. These four entities are responsible for dispensing justice in different forums: individuals in relationships, families among their members, communities among groups, and public institutions such as housing authorities, hospitals, libraries and schools among their constituencies (Nelson & Prilleltensky, 2005).

fourth question: how do we decide what is due from a person, family, group, or institution? We suggest that the criteria of needs, ability and opportunity expressed for the receiver of justice apply equally to the provider of it. Three criteria vary however. These are duties (instead of rights), obligation (instead of effort), and privilege (instead of power). A person or entity entrusted with allocating resources ought to do so in light of their own needs, abilities, and opportunities, and in accordance with their civic duties, moral obligations, and degree of privilege (Nussbaum, 1999, 2006). The more privilege there is, the higher the obligation. These six criteria are interdependent. A person may have an opportunity to contribute to the wellbeing of others, and she/he may even have a civic duty to do so, but if her own needs are not satisfied, her ability to deliver justice will be diminished.

working definition of social justice   Having answered the four foundational questions of justice, we are now in a better position to formulate a working definition. Justice, then, consists of two complementary statements:

1   To each (individual, family, community, or public institution) according to her or his needs, ability, effort, opportunities, rights and power, and

2   From each (individual, family, community, or public institution) according to her or his needs, ability, obligation, duties, opportunity and privilege.

the consequences of social injustice   When there is not a fair and equitable allocation of resources, there are dire consequences for individuals, their social relationships, and the broader society, as Barry (2005) recently documented in *Why Social Justice Matters*. These interrelated impacts can be conceptualized in terms of the core values of critical community psychology (see the third column of Table 8.2) and are felt in the health, education, housing, transportation, and social capital domains, among others (Barry, 2005).

Health is unevenly distributed within and across nations. As a result, individual health suffers. There is a well-documented gradient between health problems and socioeconomic status (SES) (Marmot, 2004). Explanations for how SES impacts on health include differential exposure to environmental risk factors, differential perceptions of relative inequality, and differential occupational control (Barry, 2005; Evans & Kantrowitz, 2002; Marmot, 2004). Disadvantaged people are also disempowered with little voice, choice, or control over their lives. In individualistic societies, disadvantaged people often internalize the dominant cultural narratives, which hold individuals responsible for the problems they experience (Moane, 2003), leading to self-blame and self-denigration.

Second, in their relationships, disadvantaged people are often marginalized, stigmatized, and excluded. For example, people with disabilities and mental health problems have historically been institutionalized, where they were subject to abuse and neglect and were 'out of sight and out of mind' (Lord & Hutchison, 2007). Even today with the shift to community living, many people with disabilities have impoverished social networks and are excluded from participation in the mainstream of community life. By virtue of being 'different', women, minorities, gays and lesbians, and people with disabilities continue to be subject to prejudice, stigmatization, and systemic discrimination (i.e., sexism, racism, heterosexism, and ableism) (see Part V of Nelson & Prilleltensky, 2005). As Oliver noted, 'sexism, racism, and homophobia are covered over and denied within dominant culture through the double movement of the colonization of psychic space, which operates first as a form of social abjection and exclusion and second as a form of silencing' (2004: 88).

Finally, the unequal allocation of resources has adverse social consequences for the collective. In the USA, the most wealthy and powerful nation in the world, poor and disenfranchised people experience numerous obstacles to accessing health care, quality education, decent and affordable housing, meaningful and well-paid employment, and empowering social services (Levy & Sidel, 2006). As well, declining social capital and sense of community (Putnam, 2000) are further indications of the erosion of the collective in the USA. But marginalized collectives suffer not only from material deprivation but also from the psychological exclusion and silencing that Oliver alluded to above. Adding insult to injury, excluded collectives are not supposed to complain because they are reminded that it is, after all, their own fault that they live in misery.

In community psychology, we struggle to advocate for social justice. I, Isaac, am presently involved in policy work to advocate for universal early childhood education in Florida, where I now live. Lack of access to quality child care and pre-kindergarten education are justice issues. Children of well-to-do families have access to high-quality centres, whereas poor families cannot afford services offering a stimulating and nurturing environment. To convince legislators of the need to have poor children (the *each* in our definition of social justice) receive high-quality child care and education (the *due* in the definition of social justice), I have made several presentations describing the social, human, and economic return on such an investment (Belfield & Levin, 2007; Kirp, 2007; Lynch, 2007), both in Florida's capital and in Congress in the US capital.

The research demonstrates that good early childhood education programmes can prevent school dropout, welfare dependency, criminal behaviour, and health problems, among other positive social outcomes. I am struggling to make a policy impact. To do so, I travelled to Tallahassee, Florida's capital, to meet with legislators and with the Commissioner of Education. I have also met with members of the Miami Chamber of Commerce, and have held at the University of Miami a 300-person conference on the topic. Guests included researchers, advocates, politicians, educators, community organizations, and business people. My goal is to increase state investment in early childhood education. My approach, so far, has been to use mainstream channels of advocacy and public education.

Some might argue that a critical community psychologist should demonstrate in front of the legislature or engage in other forms of political activism instead of sitting with politicians inside their comfortable offices. Others might object to my willingness to use the economic term *return on investment* for something that can be regarded as a human right. As we have argued elsewhere (Nelson & Prilleltensky, 2005), both insider and outsider approaches to social change have benefits and limitations. In my own way, I am trying to bring more resources to a particular underprivileged population from a powerful source (the government), and I am willing to use my position of academic power to do so. Whatever strategy is utilized, I know that issues of justice are at stake. And I do believe research can help procure more resources for poor children (Kirp, 2007).

_____ *praxis* _____

Our construal of critical community psychology is predicated on comple-mentary building blocks: ecological conceptions of wellbeing and values, multilevel understandings of oppression and social injustice, and a praxis orientation. Our critical praxis approach includes four components: (a) vision and values; (b) context; (c) needs, and (d) action. This approach is a continuous, reflexive cycle (I. Prilleltensky, 2001; Prilleltensky & Nelson, 2002). Vision and values point to the ideals of change; attention to context provides an understanding of how social injustice is currently manifested and what opportunities present a potential for change; and needs refer to how the injustice is perceived and experienced by disadvantaged people.

Critical praxis is transformative rather than ameliorative in nature. First-order change, or change within a system, is ameliorative because it strives to improve the existing system without questioning its underlying values and assumptions or its inequities in power and resource allocation (Watzlawick, Weakland, & Fisch, 1974). Critical community psychology is more concerned with second-order change, or a change of the system's values, structures, and power arrangements. This type of change is transformative because it entails a fundamental alteration in how the system operates and allocates resources (Nelson & Prilleltensky, 2005).

In our view, critical praxis must address the individual, relational, and collective levels (see the fourth column of Table 8.2). Community psychol-ogy still focuses much of its intervention at the individual level, including the promotion of health and the prevention of health problems. While this important work is necessary, it is insufficient. George Albee (1986) reminded us that by neglecting to act on social injustice we fail to reduce the 'causes of the causes'. In its focus on resilience, helping individuals overcome adverse conditions (Luthar, Cicchetti, & Becker 2000), preventive intervention inadvertently reinforces an ideology of rugged individualism through which individuals can presumably rise above and conquer social injustice (Albee, 1986). In a recent review of the effects of positive youth development programmes on systems change, Durlak et al. (2007) found that the majority of interventions targeted family-level and school-level change. Community-level changes were confined to connecting youth to adults in the community (i.e., mentors). None of the programmes directly addressed social injustice or the collective level of analysis. In contrast, Julie Morsillo, a community psychologist in Australia, worked with me, Isaac, to develop a series of social action workshops with teenagers in schools. Following months of preparation, the youth organized demonstrations against racism, sexism, and homophobia. In addition, they planned environmental actions that drew the local community. All were involved, in a small way, in social action. The project was meant to raise not just consciousness but also action (Morsillo & Prilleltensky, 2007).

At the individual level, prevention must be accompanied by empowerment. Rappaport (1981) argued that community psychology should be guided by empowerment, which is based on a *rights model* emphasizing citizen participation and control, rather than prevention, which is based on a *needs model* emphasizing the professional as expert. We believe it is important to engage disadvantaged people in a mutual process of *conscientization*, in which the struggles of disadvantaged people are situated in the larger context of social injustice (Freire, 1970). This process often moves in stages from a growing awareness, to linking with others, to participation and social action (Lord & Hutchison, 1993; Watts, Griffith, & Abdul-Adil, 1999). Social action might involve the transformation of existing settings or the creation of new settings. Potts (2003) provides an excellent example of an empowering, preventive intervention for African American students in a middle school in Connecticut. The goals of the school-wide programme were for the students to develop an understanding of their roots and a positive racial identity and to become social change agents. Preliminary evaluation suggested that there were positive impacts compared with African American students from other schools lacking this type of programme. The students in the intervention engaged in *decolonization*, the process whereby targets of cultural diminution resist the negative ascriptions attributed to them by the dominant culture (Oliver, 2004). Combining a personal project of positive identity formation with a collective project of decolonization is the prototypical critical community psychology intervention that is so sorely lacking in the present landscape of depoliticized health improvements.

At the relational level, strategies are needed to promote relationships and the social inclusion of disadvantaged people. The hallmark of a critical community psychology intervention is the amalgam of personal wellness and social critique. It is the social critique mounted by the disenfranchised that acts as a buffer against the devaluation of personal dignity which Oliver (2004) calls the colonization of psychic space. Without social critique, the sources of suffering continue to be defined in intrapsychic terms that blame the oppressed for their misfortune (Barry, 2005). For example, people with disabilities have been instrumental in creating or advocating for the transformation of settings so that they emphasize informal support and self-help (Lord & Hutchison, 2007). Such transformative work is needed to prevent the often impoverished social networks of people with disabilities, who often live or work in segregated settings such as group homes and sheltered workshops and count their caseworker as their best friend.

Praxis intervention is also needed both to celebrate the strengths of people from diverse backgrounds and to confront racism, sexism, heterosexism, and ableism. A good example of confronting colonization and racism can be found in the work of Huygens in New Zealand (Glover, Dudgeon & Huygens, 2005; see also this volume). Her work entails institutional change in government and places of employment to enact the rights and entitlements promised to Maori people in the Treaty of Waitangi in the middle of the nineteenth century. The outcomes are not defined in terms of individuals but rather in terms of rights and the vindication of legal documents guaranteeing the status of indigenous communities. She used the term 'depowerment' to put the onus of a redistribution of resources on society's powerful and not on the powerless.

Praxis intervention at the collective level is indeed sorely lacking and needed in community psychology. For example, in a review of values and research on housing for people with mental illness, Sylvestre, Nelson, Sabloff and Peddle (2007) found that while the citizenship values of access, affordability, accountability, rights, and security of tenure (i.e., those that focus more on social justice) were apparent in a review of mental health policy documents, they received little research attention compared to the therapeutic values of choice, control, quality, and community integration. Community psychologists and other researchers concentrate on evaluating the processes and outcomes of housing programmes (therapeutic values), rather than concentrating on research and social action to improve housing policy and access to housing for people with mental health problems (citizenship values). Community psychology has to devote much more energy to research and advocacy for universal services and supports. This work is needed to complement the community capacity-building work that community psychologists are undertaking to promote social capital and a sense of community (e.g., Foster-Fishman et al., 2007; Perkins et al., 2002).

Also at the collective level, community psychologists need to work actively to reduce poverty and economic inequality both within and across nations (Carr & Sloan, 2003; I. Prilleltensky, 2003). Counter to the assertions of free market capitalists, Nobel prize winning economist Amartya Sen (1999) has shown that investments in community infrastructures (health, education, social services) in some Asian countries have improved rather than detracted from the economic development of these countries. The state of Kerala in India is an excellent example of how such an approach not only benefits the economy but also improves the wellbeing of individuals and the collective (Sen, 1999). The Grameen Bank in Bangladesh, started by

Nobel prize winner Muhammad Yunus, is one example of how poverty can be reduced through community economic development. Micro-credit loans, which mainstream banks refused to provide, enabled low-income people to operate small businesses and become more economically sustainable. These are the types of interventions in which community psychologists need to partner with economists and scholars from other disciplines to address poverty and injustice.

conclusion

Community psychologists operate in a world of competing demands and possibilities. Decisions must be made as to how best to invest time and resources. Given the multiple and salubrious ripple effects of achieving justice, we vote for concentrating our efforts on a fair and equitable distribution of resources that takes into account power differentials and privilege. That is the call of critical community psychology.

We also know that many mainstream community psychologists do aspire to change society. That much can be seen from the mission statement of the Society for Community Research and Action: Division 27 of the American Psychological Association, from publications and policy statements of the European Community Psychology Association, and from a review of community psychology around the world (Reich, Riemer, Prilleltensky, & Montero, 2007). The issue is not one of declarative intent, however, but rather of effectiveness and outcomes. By linking its fate to mainstream funders (e.g., public health departments in governments), traditional community psychology walks a fine line between influencing mainstream institutions and being swallowed by them. Critical community psychology, on the other hand, runs the risk of being more radical at the cost of becoming more marginalized.

As critical community psychologists, we search for the sweet spot where we can advocate transformative social change without being relegated to marginality. Whether the master's tools can dismantle the master's house is an open question for critical community psychologists who wish to be part of community psychology and critique it at the same time. The lure of grants, prestige, and social respectability is not insignificant. That's the bittersweet spot many of us inhabit.

■ ■ main chapter points ■

1 While community psychology promotes an ecological analysis of problems and wellbeing, it falls short of identifying the power dynamics and the ideological underpinnings of social injustice.

2   Similarly, while community psychology is value-explicit, in its practices it does not sufficiently enact the value of social justice. We argue that social justice should be the centrepiece of critical community psychology.

3   We present a value-based approach to praxis that is designed to overcome social injustice and promote individual, relational, and collective wellbeing.

glossary

- **community psychology**: the subdiscipline of psychology that is concerned with understanding people in the context of their communities, the prevention of problems in living, the celebration of human diversity, and the pursuit of social justice through social action.

- **depowerment**: the process whereby people who are privileged share power with people who are disadvantaged.

- **ecology**: a metaphor used in community psychology to understand the interrelationships of people with various eco-systems, from small systems to large social systems.

- **power**: the capacity and opportunity to influence the course of events in one's personal life or in the life of others in the community.

reading suggestions

Two edited books offer international perspectives on community psychology. Our book *Community Psychology: In Pursuit of Liberation and Well-being* (Nelson & Prilleltensky, 2005) covers many topics of concern to critical psychologists. *International Community Psychology* (Reich et al., 2007) discusses the emergence of the discipline in 36 countries.

: // internet resources /

- Community Psychology Network: www.cmmtypsych.net

- European Network of Community Psychologists: userpage.fu-berlin.de/~cpbergol/

- Psychologists Acting with Conscience Together: www.psyact.org

- Society for Community Research and Action: www.apa.org/divisions/div27/

■ Questions

1 Critical community psychologists are concerned with fairness and justice. How is justice defined in the media? When you read magazines such as *Time* or *Newsweek*, what are the implied notions of justice expressed in their pages? What is the scope of justice in our culture?

2 Critical community psychologists link the personal with the political. Have you ever experienced oppression as a result of your background, interests or ideology? What were some of the reasons for this oppression? Who got to benefit from marginalizing you?

3 We live in power laden environments. Think back to a situation in which you may have abused your power and privilege. What were some of the personal, relational, and societal reasons for your abuse of power? Who suffered because of your abuse of power?

9

Critical Health Psychology

Kerry Chamberlain and Michael Murray

health psychology: development and context

The field of health psychology was formally established when a group of psychologists met in the late 1970s to discuss the relevance of psychological theory, research and practice to physical health and illness. That meeting, which took place in the United States, resulted in the formation of the American Psychological Association's Health Psychology Division.

Health psychology, of course, did not arise independent of other developments occurring around it. Connections between medicine and psychology have been suggested and examined for centuries, and these became more explicit as the disciplines of biomedicine and psychology developed. Psychosomatic medicine, which considered particular health problems such as ulcers, asthma, migraine and arthritis to have psychological causes, developed in the 1930s and was strongly influenced by psychoanalytic theory. Behavioural medicine developed as an interdisciplinary approach to health issues in the 1970s, drawing from the strong interest in psychology at that time in behaviourism and the experimental analysis of behaviour. Health psychology has its roots in these developments, but differs from them in having a more strongly psychological, rather than interdisciplinary, focus, and also in encompassing a broader range of issues within its research and theorizing (Sarafino, 2005). Liaison psychiatry, a specialized subdiscipline of psychiatry concerned with psychiatric problems experienced by patients in medical settings, also developed alongside health psychology. Again, health psychology is arguably differentiated from this approach by its broader remit of research and theory (Kaptein & Weinman, 2004).

A definition of health psychology was developed for the new APA Division of Health Psychology in 1979. This definition, unsurprisingly, reflected the current *zeitgeist*, and essentially defined health psychology as the contribution of all the educational, scientific and professional aspects of contemporary psychology to any and all areas of physical health, specifically including *health promotion and maintenance, illness treatment and prevention*, and *the role of psychological factors in health and illness* (Matarazzo, 1980). Later, the definition was extended to include the remaining aspects of health by identifying a role for health psychology in *improving health care services and policies* (Matarazzo, 1982). This definition of health psychology, with its four 'core elements' (Kaptein & Weinman, 2004: 6) or 'goals of health psychology' (Sarafino, 2005: 14), remains commonly in use today, although the degree to which health psychologists take up the challenges of policy development and improving health care services is rather limited.

Health psychology, then, developed within the sphere of psychology at large and took on its dominant assumptions and methods: a psychology that saw itself as a science applying an agreed scientific method to the study of individuals and their psychological processes. Inevitably, given this genealogy, health psychology was, and largely remains, subject to the same general criticisms that critical psychologists have levelled against the discipline, as rehearsed throughout this text. Hence it is no surprise to find health psychology focused on the rational individual, placing an emphasis on measurement and statistics, adopting the use of various narrowly defined psychological models with limited theorization, and largely ignoring the social aspects of health and illness.

More recently, some alternative approaches have developed. One common distinction is that proposed between 'mainstream' health psychology and critical health psychology (e.g., Crossley, 2000; Murray & Chamberlain, 1999a), a distinction based upon the differing values, epistemologies and research methodologies favoured by each. Mainstream health psychology takes the conventional 'scientific' approach to the field, and assumes that knowledge can be uncovered through traditional scientific research processes, and that it is fixed and independent of the context in which it is found and the methods used to reveal it. It focuses on measuring, predicting and changing health and illness behaviours, and seeks to discover the 'truth' about the relationship between psychological factors and health. The approach draws on the biopsychosocial model, and has developed a variety of social cognition models of health behaviour. It focuses strongly on the individual, and assumes that people behave in rational, thoughtful, and predictable ways. These assumptions and the use of traditional scientific methods serve to legitimate mainstream health psychology as a professional adjunct to biomedicine and a specialist partner with medicine in research into, and the treatment of, illness (Murray & Chamberlain, 1999a). This is the dominant approach presented in most health psychology textbooks, the basis for most research in health psychology and for most health psychology interventions.

Critical health psychology, in contrast, challenges many of mainstream health psychology's assumptions and practices. The critical approach argues that people are complex, changing and multi-faceted, rather than fixed 'objects' that can be studied 'scientifically'. It generally takes a social constructionist position, assuming that knowledge is variable and changing and always a product of the historical, social and cultural context in which it is located. Critical health psychology seeks understanding and insight into, rather than the prediction of, human conditions and practices, and frequently employs qualitative interpretative research methods, although is not restricted to these. More fundamentally, critical health psychology seeks to challenge assumptions, including its own, and to identify how forms of knowledge and practice can empower or enfranchise people.

Marks (2002) proposes an alternative classification of health psychologies with differing values, assumptions, objectives and research practices. He argues that, alongside *clinical health psychology* (the practice of mainstream health psychology), three other approaches can be identified – *public health psychology*, *community health psychology*, and *critical health psychology*. *Public health psychology* adopts a public health agenda, emphasizing the structural and social determinants of health and illness and engaging in multidisciplinary activities focused on epidemiological research and community health promotion interventions (see Marks, 2002; Hepworth, 2004). This changes the focus for the causes of ill health from medicalized pathogens to social problems (Young, 2006). *Community health psychology* posits that social context is crucial in shaping opportunities for health, and considers social change fundamental to practice. It argues for a praxis that promotes community participation and creates community-level action for enabling and sustaining health-enhancing activities (see Campbell & Murray, 2004). Because both public health psychology and community health psychology can adopt (or not) a critical approach to practice, there can be considerable overlap between a critical approach and these other two (although this is more strongly marked in community than in public health psychology). Because our focus here is on the critical approach, we will continue with the mainstream/critical distinction, and illustrate critical work in the field drawing from public and community health psychology where applicable. However, we should also note that a critical approach is not readily defined or agreed on within the field, an issue that we discuss below. Further, a critical approach can also be applied at the clinical level, although this rarely occurs (see Chapter 5 in this volume).

some limitations for a mainstream health psychology

There are serious concerns, from a critical psychology perspective, about how mainstream health psychology conducts its research and practice. We comment on several below, noting that this is neither an exhaustive set nor an extensive discussion of any single issue.

First, mainstream health psychology takes a highly individualistic approach to its research and practice. Given that health psychology is built substantially on theories and approaches drawn from social psychology, this may appear surprising. However, as Greenwood (2004b) has demonstrated, social psychology itself adopted this individualistic approach to its endeavours around the middle of the twentieth century (see also Chapter 6). As we see below, this focus severely limits the way in which research and practice can be both understood and integrated into the social context.

Health psychology has widely adopted the biopsychosocial model (Engel, 1977) as a framework. This model proposes that health and illness arise from the interplay of biological, psychological and social factors. Although this proposal seems reasonable on the surface, it has been the object of substantial criticism. Spicer and Chamberlain (1996) argue that adoption of this model fails to solve the fundamental problem of how to integrate theorizing across the three domains it incorporates. Other critics have argued that the model retains an essentially biomedical perspective (e.g., Armstrong, 1987) and that its function within health psychology, which has been largely rhetorical rather than theoretical (Ogden, 1997), serves mainly to sustain health psychology as a partner in the medical agenda (e.g., Suls & Rothman, 2004). Stam, arguing that the model is neither explicit theory nor formal model, proposed that it is merely 'a clever neologism masquerading as a model and its naïve distribution to undergraduates ought to lead us to urge publishers to place a warning label on textbooks indicating that they are a danger to the health of one's theoretical education' (2000: 276).

One of the major areas of health psychology research and intervention involves an ongoing attempt to explain and predict health behaviours. This goal is important since there is considerable evidence that many people engage in 'unhealthy' behaviours such as smoking, eating poorly or engaging in 'unsafe' sexual activities. This work comprises a substantial component of health psychology research activity, and frequently utilizes social cognition models such as the Health Belief Model, Protection-Motivation Theory, the Theory of Planned Behaviour, and the Determinants of Behaviour model. These models typically involve a set of individualized cognitions, attitudes and beliefs, combined into predictive pathways.

However, illustrating a more general problem highlighted in Chapter 19, this process reduces theorizing to model building. This 'pathology of flow-charting' (Spicer & Chamberlain, 1996) encloses key variables within boxes and connects them with causal arrows, places major emphasis on the variables included and largely ignores any conceptualization or theorization of the causal processes involved. In spite of substantial research involving such models, outcomes so far have been extremely limited. Mielewczyk and Willig (2007), in a highly critical review of this field, conclude that this approach is not only ineffective but, more fundamentally, inappropriate. They also identify the limited explanatory power of these models and their failure to perform any better when enhanced in various ways, such as by limiting prediction to intention rather than behaviour (thereby losing the major intent), or by adding further variables or using different mixes of variables (thereby destroying the theoretical significance of the 'theories' in the first place).

Mielewczyk and Willig (2007) conclude that the theoretical, methodological and performance-based limitations of social cognition models mean these models should be replaced by research approaches that can examine the specificity of particular health behaviours in naturally occurring contexts. As Mielewczyk and Willig point out, there is probably no such thing as a 'health behaviour' (in the abstracted sense that it is used in this research). Rather, social practices involving behaviours with implications for health (such as smoking) are necessarily embedded in context; they need to be studied in context to understand their meaning and the logics of their enactment. For example, Laurier, McKie, and Goodwin (2000) illustrate how the act of smoking a cigarette varies across the day; how the meanings of the first cigarette in the morning, the last cigarette of the day, the social cigarette in the bar and the snatched smoke during work are all fundamentally different. Furthermore, as Mielewczyk and Willig (2007) note, changing the focus of our research has implications beyond how we do our research. It extends to how we might practise health psychology to reduce the threat and burden of illness. As they argue, social practices determine not only how we should, can, and do (or do not) *behave*, but equally constitute who we should, can (or cannot) *be*, and how we can be.

An inattention to context extends far beyond personal behaviours; there is an equal inattention to the wider social issues that affect health and illness. Many years ago, Crawford (1980) noted a concern with 'healthism' – how contemporary societies, and the citizens that constitute them, are preoccupied with health as an agenda, as a project, and as an integral part of everyday living. Crawford (2006) argues that this concern has not receded but has increased in intensity and that the pursuit of health has become 'one of the more salient practices of contemporary life, commanding enormous social resources, infusing every major institutional field and generating an expansive professionalization and commercialization, along with attendant goods, services and knowledge' (2006: 404). He also argues that this 'new health consciousness' is strongly connected to the ways medicine extends its control and power over everyday life activities, a process labeled **medicalization** (Conrad, 2007), and to ideologies of consumption and personal control, so that 'personal responsibility for health is widely considered the *sine qua non* of individual autonomy and good citizenship' (Crawford, 2006: 402).

Medicalization is pervasive, producing a range of new disorders. These are highly gendered, mostly target women, and are largely identified as mental health 'problems' (see Chapter 5). However, many relate to physical health 'problems' such as excessive sleepiness (for which there is a drug treatment), andropause (declining testosterone levels in older men, treated with testosterone replacement drug therapy), obesity (treated with surgery or drugs), bodily enhancement such as breast enhancement (treated with surgery), with other forms developing as pharmaceutical and genetic technologies advance (see Conrad, 2007). **Pharmaceuticalization** is equally pervasive, raising concerns about the role of large international pharmaceutical companies in creating illness (Applbaum, 2006; Busfield, 2006) and in turning healthy people into patients (Moynihan & Cassels, 2005) and 'neurochemical selves' (Rose, 2004, 2007). Many health psychologists, oblivious to the concerns of biopower and control (Rose, 2006) raised by medicalization, pharmaceuticalization and health **consumerism**, are unwittingly implicated in the production of these new forms of disorder and their treatments.

We could continue with further limitations. For example, adherence to medication is a prominent agenda in mainstream health psychology because it is generally agreed that only about 50 per cent of medications are taken as directed. A review of mainstream research covering three decades concluded that, in spite of more than 200 studied variables, none consistently predicted adherence (Vermeire, Hearnshaw, Van Royen, & Denekens, 2001). A more critical view suggests that, rather than being assessed as a static or fixed phenomenon, adherence is better considered as a fluctuating choice made in the social contexts of everyday life (e.g., Wilson, Hutchinson, & Holzemer, 2002). Another limitation concerns the body's centrality in health and illness and associated issues of **embodiment** – having and being a body – materially, socially and symbolically. Mainstream health psychology has given scant attention to bodies and embodiment, and its biomedical view of the body is inappropriate for addressing concerns with suffering and healing (Radley, 2000). These are just some of mainstream health psychology's limitations that a critical perspective reveals, limitations that shape and inform possibilities for a critical health psychology.

possibilities for a critical psychology of health

One of the original drivers of the critical turn within health psychology was the growing interest in language and discourse within critical social science. This led critical health psychologists to use various qualitative research methods to give voice to the experience of health and illness (Chamberlain, Stephens, & Lyons, 1997; Murray & Chamberlain, 1998, 1999b). Although this linguistic turn provided insights into the experience of the 'other', several critiques (e.g. Murray & Campbell, 2003) raised concerns about the new approach: it was largely limited to individual interviews, still treated research participants as passive subjects, still failed to capture broader social contexts adequately, and gave limited consideration to how research could contribute to a social and personal transformation. These criticisms led to a wider array of more innovative qualitative and participatory methodologies that could not only provide greater insight into the experience of participants but could also contribute to transformation and change. Several critical researchers have turned for inspiration to action research (e.g., Jacobs, 2006) and to the arts (e.g., Camic, 2008; Murray & Gray, 2008), opening up a new array of approaches that are still being developed. We next consider examples of these to illustrate possible new directions for a critical health psychology.

Our understandings of health and illness are constructed and reconstructed in our everyday social interactions within the broader societal context that exists in a world of inequality, conflict and pain. Within any society certain discourses and social representations attain hegemonic power (Arribas-Ayllon & Walkerdine, 2008; Howarth, 2006) and inhibit, oppress and marginalize individuals, groups and larger collectives. However, the power and truth status of such representations can be challenged. For example, Freire's work on critical literacy discussed how dialogue and debate can allow people to develop critical consciousness and learn to 'perceive social, political and economic contradictions and to take action against oppressive elements of reality' (1970: 17). Freire's pedagogy emphasized working with people to develop this critical consciousness, so that the poor and disenfranchised can begin to reassess themselves and the nature of their social reality. Critical health psychologists can play an active role in this process.

This work by Freire (1970) and other critical theorists (e.g., Martín-Baró, 1994) led to the development of participatory action research. Brydon-Miller describes this as 'a collaborative process in which the researcher works with community members to identify an area of concern to that community, generate knowledge about the issue, and plan and carry out actions meant to address the issue in some substantive way' (2004: 188). Rather than acting as expert, the researcher is positioned as a co-learner, with community participants acting as co-researchers; together they engage in a joint project to identify, challenge and change the sources of oppression in their lives. In the health arena, this approach has been used in community settings, particularly with disadvantaged communities, as in Cornish's (2006) collaborative project with sex workers in India. Her research was embedded within a wider project based upon '*respect* for sex workers and their profession, *recognizing* their profession and their rights, and *reliance* on their understanding and capability' (Jana & Banerjee, 1999: 11). Cornish drew upon Freire's (1973) concept of problematization, the process by which learners begin to question the established social order and consider alternatives. In this setting, a fatalistic acceptance of the nature of sex work was challenged through making workers aware of their rights, comparing them with other groups of workers, and gaining evidence of sex workers' success. The success of this and similar projects (e.g., Lubek et al., 2002) shows the potential for this approach in promoting health and the importance of attention to the psychological processes that underlie its practice.

Historically, the arts have been used for a variety of purposes, to entertain, distract, excite, or build collective bonds (see Dissanayake, 2007). Within a critical perspective, the arts can reveal sources of discomfort and energize communities to take action to transform those situations. Used in this way, the arts become enjoined with action research (Murray & Gray, 2008). We consider some examples that illustrate these exciting possibilities.

Photography, painting, and other visual arts have become popular within health care as a form of adjunct therapy, but more recently critical health psychologists have explored these as forms of research and intervention. Perhaps the most prominent technique is **photovoice** (Wang, 2003), which involves people using cameras to capture their everyday experiences and then using the resulting photographs not only to explore their experiences but to campaign against disadvantage. The technique, used originally with Chinese peasant women (Wang, Burris, & Xiang, 1996), has since been adopted widely and used successfully across a range of settings (see Baker & Wang, 2006; Hodgetts, Chamberlain, & Radley, 2007). The approach is related to Freire's (1970) notions of critical consciousness and aligns with perspectives on empowerment drawn from feminist and community development theory.

Another example of arts-based participatory intervention is that of Washington and Moxley (2008), who worked with a group of older African American homeless women to develop strategies for combating homelessness, a significant health issue (Hodgetts, Radley, Chamberlain, & Hodgetts, 2007). These women provided narrative accounts and photographic representations of their experiences. The project culminated in a public exhibition that included their photographs and extracts from their accounts, together with other artifacts of their homeless experience such as poems they had written, scrapbooks they had made, and material artifacts they had collected from the streets. The project was designed to draw attention to the issue of homelessness in the community and also to empower the women to campaign for change in housing provision and improvements in health.

Visual research methods have been extended further in participatory action research through placing video recorders, rather than cameras, in the hands of participants. For example, Stewart, Riecken, Scott, Tanaka, and Riecken (2008) worked with a group of Canadian indigenous youth in a collective action about health concerns to produce short videos about issues such as drug and alcohol use, diabetes and depression. The youth were involved in all stages of the project from identification of the key health issues and development of the script to camera work, video editing and the presentation of the video. Through this process the youth grew in understanding their community, their culture, and the meaning of local health issues and also developed competencies to change health outcomes.

Performance, including music, dance and drama, is another art form used in therapy that has potential for critical research and practice, particularly when used to engage critically with oppression. Denzin (2003) proposed performance ethnography and argued for a renewed social science, an oppositional **performative social science** to challenge oppression and injustice through performance. Some critical health psychologists have taken this up. Gray and Sinding (2002) began their project by collecting stories from cancer patients. With the assistance of a professional playwright, they transformed those stories into a dramatic work that was performed by actors and cancer patients in hospitals, communities, and on radio. The performances were a resounding success, helping audience members understand the implications of cancer and helping cancer sufferers learn positive ways to live with the condition. Murray and Tilley (2006) collected stories of fish harvesters about accidents and risk-taking, and then worked with a songwriter to transform the stories into a song that was widely played in different settings, including union meetings and concerts, and on radio and television. Murray and Tilley also worked with residents of fishing communities to develop a series of artistic products including paintings, writings, plays and concerts. This research provided powerful evidence that the arts can provide an effective means of engaging communities and promoting community awareness of health and safety issues.

Sullivan, Petronella, Brooks, Murillo, Primeau, and Ward (2008) used another performative technique, Theatre of the Oppressed (Boal, 1992), to engage marginalized communities in taking action to transform their living conditions and promote their health. This approach involves developing a dramatic performance, culminating in a public presentation where the audience is encouraged to participate in a dramatic dialogue, transforming them from spectators to spect-actors (Boal, 1992). Sullivan and his colleagues collaborated with Hispanic workers living in a highly polluted neighbourhood to develop a variety of forum theatre performances. The core group of actors researched the environmental health hazards of their neighbourhood and developed the performances. The impacts of this forum theatre included 'community empowerment and organizing, teaching concepts, building issue awareness, connecting citizens with movements and widening coalitions' (Sullivan et al., 2008: 168). Forum theatre is becoming a widely used technique for community engagement, collective empowerment and social transformation.

We have concentrated here on recent innovative arts-based practices, but critical health psychologists have also continued with language-based narrative and discursive research to provide insights into sociostructural changes and accompanying issues of power and disenfranchisement. For example, Willig (1998) uses critical discourse analysis to examine how sexual activity is variously constructed and considers the implications of these constructions for sexual practices. Madison (2005) describes how critical ethnographic approaches can be used to examine issues as diverse as the functions of Non-Government Organizations in a developing country, gay identity, and community theatre. Hodgetts and Chamberlain (2006), in considering how media are deeply implicated in the construction of shared understandings of health, discuss how health psychologists can utilize critical approaches to media research.

New media forms have also attracted attention, although so far more has come from social scientists in other disciplines than from health psychologists. For example, Seale (2005) discusses new directions for critical Internet health studies, using representations of cancer experience on the web as an illustration. Gillett (2003) considers media activism played out in Internet use by people with HIV/AIDS. Health psychologists have had only limited involvement in critical analyses of key social processes that are transforming the health arena, such as **health consumerism**, medicalization and pharmaceuticalization. For example, health psychologists have not been prominent in the critical emerging debates around the moral panic of the 'obesity epidemic' and the construction of obesity as a disease (see Campos, Saguy, Ernsberger, Oliver, & Gaesser, 2006; Jutel, 2006; Pieterman, 2007). They have had some presence in the critical debate about new drug technologies like Viagra (e.g., Potts & Tiefer, 2006), and a more limited presence in the debate around processes of **disease mongering** and the role of 'big Pharma' in creating and fostering new diseases (e.g., Moynihan & Henry, 2006; Tiefer, 2006).

These issues are starting to attract more attention within critical health psychology as researchers deconstruct dominant meanings of health, illness and health care, work with participants to further understand health and illness experience, and seek to achieve change and transformation in an increasing range of ways. However, possibilities for a critical health psychology do give rise to some problems of their own.

problematics for a critical psychology of health

One important issue arises from the meaning of 'being critical'. For many mainstream health psychologists, this merely involves being self-critical within their existing framework (e.g., Owens, 2001; Vinck & Meganck, 2004). However, as Hepworth (2006b) and others have argued, a critical approach involves a more extensive and wide-ranging critique that seeks to challenge the very bases of practice at theoretical and epistemological levels as well as at the more practical level of method. Criticality must involve unencumbered critique, and this requires a critical examination of the assumptions, values and practices of critical health psychology itself. As McVittie (2006) comments, the notions of fairness and justice underpinning the critical agenda must be critiqued for their function in context, rather than serve as broad all-encompassing value directions. Hence, calls to action (e.g., Campbell & Murray, 2004; Marks, 2004), calls for a critical health psychology that is 'not content with describing reality, but rather seeks to transform reality' (Murray & Poland, 2006: 383), raise a dilemma for critical health psychologists (and equally for other critical psychologists, as noted elsewhere in this book). When we espouse a need for our research and practice to inform and emancipate the disadvantaged and oppressed, we also need to reflect on what this means for others who may not be included amongst those we consider, or who do not consider themselves, disadvantaged and oppressed (see also Hepworth, 2006a; McVittie, 2006).

We also need to be aware that emphases within critical psychology are constantly changing and developing. A critical approach is neither fixed nor stable. Hepworth (2006a) suggests that there have been three phases of critical health psychology: the rejection of reification (critiquing and rejecting the existence of 'facts' and 'objects' of health); the rise of consensuality and subjectivism (the expansion and pluralism of theories and methods); and calls for justice and fairness (an emphasis on action and equality). While we agree that these phases can be identified, we suggest they are more interrelated and integrated than this stage-based argument suggests. However, they do background a debate about directions for research practice: whether critical health psychology should focus on revealing disparity and disadvantage or on changing it. At one level this is essentially a debate around methodologies, with discursive and narrative research directed largely towards revealing issues of power and control and action-oriented methods directed to changing the status quo. We propose that both have benefit, and in practice are interconnected in any critical engagement. In the examples above, we can see that action-oriented research produces knowledge at several levels, revealing concerns and circumstances, constructing new knowledge, empowering and changing participants, and changing communities. These different types of projects vary in terms of what they can accomplish, but each can contribute to the critical agenda.

Another debate relates to the division between qualitative and quantitative approaches. For some, a critical approach should be qualitative, based on social constructionist epistemology and interpretative methodology. However, we agree with Parker (2007) that, although critical psychologists have been suspicious of the move to quantify everything, there is value in knowing how much of something is occurring as well as how it is experienced. Knowing both can be important in supporting an action orientation to change. Thus, a critical approach does not require qualitative methodologies, although, as our examples above illustrate, 'there is a sound rationale for why qualitative methods are at the forefront of critical approaches' (Hepworth, 2006b: 405).

Finally, critical psychologists need to be aware that almost all forms of social action have been subject to critique, which can lead to justifications for a lack of action. We side with Hepworth (2006a, 2006b) about the need for action, and for research and practice designed to produce insight and change rather than merely describe why change is needed. We turn away from 'the same old neutral observer, rational scientist bullshit' (Murray & Gray, 2008: 149). In a world of widespread pain and suffering, we join with others in promoting social change to bring about a healthier world.

the future of critical perspectives in health and health psychology

Critical health psychology maintains an ongoing critique of mainstream health psychology but this should not condemn it to the sidelines forever, to being always 'on the edge of the mainstream looking in' (Marks, 2002: 16). We can recognize changes. One relates to the increasing acceptance of qualitative research methods, demonstrated in several ways: the British Psychological Society's (BPS) requirement that undergraduate and graduate health psychology curricula include qualitative research; the rapid growth of the new BPS Qualitative Psychology Section and the pressure to develop a similar division within the American Psychological Association; the increasing acceptance and use of qualitative research by mainstream health psychology researchers; and the emergence of qualitative research articles in mainstream journals such as *Health Psychology*. Further, as we can see in other chapters of this text, similar critiques and developments are occurring within other areas of applied and professional psychology. Moreover, we noted earlier that health psychology is heavily influenced by its master discipline, medicine, which faces similar pressures. These have led to a growing acceptance of narrative medicine and medical humanities, more detailed engagements with the lifeworlds of the sick, and the development of a more critical public health. All these moves will undoubtedly influence the practice of health psychology over the next few decades.

These changes also mean that critical health psychology research has increasingly begun to ask different questions – questions that focus more on experience, that give voice to the ill and disadvantaged, and that bring to the fore issues of inequality more in tune with critical approaches. These new questions reveal problematic issues for mainstream health psychology arising from its focus on the specific problems of the particular case. This focus should, but does not, extend to the experience of the person in a broader social context and to the role of helping in that person's lifeworld. However, the nature of mainstream health psychology research sets the agenda for, and drives the forms of, practice, so that, as with medicine, assessment, diagnosis and treatment prioritize the problem rather than the person. The turn to qualitative, interpretative, and emergent research coming from critical health psychology has the potential to change the drivers for treatment and care and bring the person back into view. Certainly the reflexive engagement promoted within critical approaches can facilitate this result.

Through such processes, as critical health psychology moves to accomplish its agenda of social change and action, it may become more mainstream. Such progress would not obviate the need for any critical approach to always question its own values, assumptions, practices and outcomes. However, because the near future is likely to see an expanding medicalization of everyday life, an increasingly technologized health care, and an ongoing ideology of neo-liberalism and consumption with health remaining highly valued, critical health psychology's 'mainstreaming' does not appear imminent. An ongoing, but changing, social justice agenda will remain, as will an explicit need for critical approaches that hold this agenda in focus at the forefront for health care. A critical approach will always remain necessary.

We agree also with Hepworth's argument for a 'need to work across disciplines to further strengthen critical approaches to health' (2006b: 407). We can learn from other critical disciplines. For instance, critical gerontology raises similar challenges for mainstream gerontology and geriatrics. Phillipson and Walker suggested critical gerontology should aim to develop 'a more value-committed approach to social gerontology – a commitment not just to understand the social construction of ageing but to change it' (1987: 12). Bernard and Scharf (2007) emphasized the need to bring back into discussions of ageing considerations of context, values, and a commitment to change. Similar debates occuring in other disciplines relevant to health, such as geography, sociology and anthropology, can be informative for critical health psychology.

Stam contends that arguments against the mainstream also serve 'to affirm the ground of the contest' (2006: 388). These arguments have now penetrated health psychology, establishing the critical agenda to reduce inequality. While we see evidence of work in this direction, advancing that agenda remains the ultimate challenge for critical health psychologists.

■ ■main chapter points ■

1 Health psychology is concerned with the application of psychological knowledge to issues of physical health and illness. It arose from a series of related developments concerned with body–mind connections and physical health.

2 The chapter distinguishes between mainstream and critical approaches, and comments on the assumptions, theories and practices underlying each.

3 Limitations of the mainstream approach involve the assumptions, theories and models of health behaviour, the research methods employed, and the lack of attention to social processes that shape health and illness.

4 A critical psychology of health focuses on research seeking transformation and change, using participatory action research and performance-based arts approaches. Other forms of research seek insight into the sociostructural processes and power relations that sustain disadvantage.

5 Problematic issues for a critical psychology of health include the meanings of criticality and debates around methodology.

6 The changing nature of psychology and related disciplines suggests that critical perspectives in health and health psychology will advance, although a critical reflexive approach will always be required.

glossary

- **consumerism**: the organized practices of consumers involving the consumption of services (including health care); the ways in which services have become commodified for delivery or sale to consumers.

- **disease mongering**: the creation or promotion of relatively minor conditions or diseases by pharmaceutical companies with the aim of increasing sales of medications.

- **embodiment**: the experience of both being and having a body.

- **health consumer**: a model of the patient as an informed and empowered person actively involved in his or her own health care, treatment and decision-making.

- **medicalization**: the expansion of medicine into everyday life; the processes through which problems become defined and treated as medical concerns, as illnesses, syndromes or disorders.

- **performative social science**: a form of social science that actualizes the performative in everyday life and uses various art forms to engage the audience, provide insight and motivate action for change.

- **pharmaceuticalization**: the increasing use of drugs to manage the problems of everyday life and the promotion of drug-based solutions to such problems; similar to medicalization.

- **photovoice**: an approach to research using various forms of camerawork to engage participants and audiences and provide deeper understandings of issues.

▪ ▪ reading suggestions ▪

Crossley (2000) and Murray (2004) discuss relevant issues for critical health psychology. Lyons and Chamberlain (2006) is a general text emphasizing a critical approach to health psychology. Radley (1994) provides important coverage of health and illness in a social world. Aboud (1998) provides a global perspective. Moss and Teghtsoonian (2008) provide critical discussions around contestation, power and illness. Murray and Chamberlain (1999b) cover qualitative methodologies and related research issues. The *Journal of Health Psychology* regularly contains articles from a critical perspective – see especially Special Issues on reconstructing health psychology (Volume 5, Issue 3), Community Health Psychology (Volume 9, Issue 2), Public Health Psychology (Volume 9, Issue 1), Health Psychology and the Arts (Volume 13, Issue 2), the Prilleltenskys' (2003) article and following commentaries, Hepworth's (2006a) article and ensuing commentaries on critical health psychology. See also Crossley's (2001) article in *Psychology, Health & Medicine* and the subsequent commentaries. Other journals that carry critical health psychology articles include *Health, Social Science & Medicine, Critical Public Health*, and *Sociology of Health and Illness*.

﹕// internet resources /

- **Global Forum for Health Research** – Promoting the potential of research and innovation to address the health problems of the poor: www.globalforumhealth.org

- **ISCHP** (International Society for Critical Health Psychology): www.unil.ch/ischp09/

- **New View Campaign** – Challenging the medicalization of sex (Leonore Tiefer): www.newviewcampaign.org

- **Photovoice.com** – Caroline Wang's site on the photovoice method for research: www.photovoice.com

- **PhotoVoice.org** – International charity to bring about positive social change for marginalized communities: www.photovoice.org

- **SiRCHESI** (Siem Reap Citizens for Health, Educational and Social Issues) – Grassroots health promotion (Ian Lubek): www.psychology.uoguelph.ca/research/lubek/cambodia/

- Many local websites relevant to health and illness can be located through Internet searches. These are often organized around or connected to a specific illness. Such sites can offer support and resistance but many also support biomedical power and imperialism.

 Questions

1 Consider a serious life-threatening illness, such as cancer or renal disease, or a chronic on-going illness, such as diabetes or epilepsy. Discuss the differences in how your chosen illness is understood by mainstream clinical health psychology and by critical health psychology. Consider these differences from an experiential perspective (by the person with the illness) and from a treatment perspective (by the health professional).

2 Consider a disputed illness, like ME (myalgic encephalitis), OOS (occupational over-use syndrome) or SAD (seasonal affective disorder). Discuss the ideology and politics of their presentation and treatment.

3 Locate a set of Internet websites that relate to an illness (e.g., cancer information) or a health issue (e.g., obesity, breast augmentation) and discuss their content from a critical perspective. How do they function to sustain or resist a biomedical imperative? How is the illness or health issue constructed by those experiencing it? By those providing services in relation to it?

4 In what way can social psychological theory inform participatory action research for understanding and enhancing health?

10

Psychology and the Law: The Crime of Policy and the Search for Justice

Bruce Arrigo and Dennis Fox

―| **Chapter Topics** |―

Three things about 'psychology and law' were already clear when this book's first edition appeared: the relatively new field sought to influence legal practice and policy; despite appeals by some institutional leaders, most psychology-law researchers had abandoned the field's initiating focus on justice, and critical perspectives had had little impact (Fox, 1997). More than a decade later, critical work is more evident, but the mainstream retains its status quo-friendly assumptions and priorities.

Psychologists have addressed the legal and criminal justice systems for more than a century. Cattell's (1895) research on response accuracy and confidence levels paved the way for studies of eyewitness testimony. Binet's intelligence-testing work eventually led to forensic assessment tools (Bartol & Bartol, 2006). Munsterberg's *On the Witness Stand* (1908/1981) suggested links between psychology and criminal law. Although these efforts had little immediate influence on legal institutions (Ogloff, Tomkins, & Bersoff, 1996), their legacy was transformed in the 1970s into the formal subspecialty of psychology and law. Just as organized psychology sought to influence public policy more generally (Herman, 1995), the new subfield helped justify the law's use of social science evidence (Monahan & Walker, 1991). Psychologists identified empirically inaccurate legislative and judicial assumptions about human behaviour, evaluated policy options, and suggested how the legal system might work better.

By conventional measures, the field is healthy. The American Psychology-Law Society, the European Association of Psychology and Law, and similar organizations, often working through psychology guilds such as the American Psychological Association and public interest groups such as Physicians for Human Rights and the Innocence Project, emphasize psychology's legal relevance. 'Psycholegal' journals such as *Law and Human Behaviour; Psychology, Public Policy, and the Law;* and *Psychology, Crime, and Law* address theory, research, treatment, and programming. There is a steady stream of new models of education and training (Arrigo, 2001), collections of course syllabi (American Psychology-Law Society, 2007), textbooks (Costanzo, 2004), edited volumes (Brewer & Williams, 2005), handbooks and encyclopedias (Barnes, 2006; Weiner & Hess, 2006), assessment practices and testing instruments (Grisso, 2005), career resources (Kuther, 2004), and international and comparative research (Arena & Arrigo, 2006; Kocsis, 2007). The field even penetrates the mass media when television and movie plots fictionalize and even glamorize the work of jury specialists and forensic psychologists.

Unfortunately, all this activity blurs the field's critical origins (Fox, 1999; Williams & Arrigo, 2002). The anti-establishment turmoil of the 1960s and 1970s brought many students and young professors into psychology who were determined to seek systemic rather than individual solutions to serious human problems. Hoping to 'challenge and transform a prevailing "judicial common sense" that had been used to keep the disenfranchised down so long' (Haney, 1993: 375), psychology and law assumed that 'the union of social science and law promotes justice' (Tapp & Levine, 1977: xi). Very quickly, though, Haney was emphasizing a dilemma: '[P]sychologists have been slow to decide whether they want to stand outside the [legal] system to study, critique, and change it, or to embrace and be employed by it' (1980: 152). He later lamented 'a sense of the waning of collective effort, a loss of common goals, and an abandoning of a sense of mission – the mission of legal change' (Haney, 1993: 378–379).

This chapter addresses a fundamental question: Does current practice at the law-psychology interface reduce individual and group harm and advance the good society, collective wellbeing, and citizen justice, or does it instead foster marginalization, disenfranchisement, and oppression? The first section briefly reviews the strengths and limitations of the three primary approaches to mainstream psychology and law: **forensic psychology**, **legal psychology**, and **psychological jurisprudence**. The second delineates several critical frameworks originating outside the field: feminism, **postmodernism**, **anarchism**, and **chaos theory**. These approaches focus in varying ways on the law's questionable legitimacy, science's circumscribed claims to knowledge, psychology's continued inability to develop alternative views on identity, and society's misplaced emphasis on control, prediction, and order. The final section briefly suggests alternative initiatives in psycholegal research, policy, and education.

doing psychology and law

Education and training in psychology and law generally follows one of three overlapping approaches: *clinical*, emphasizing research and practice in *forensic psychology*; *law and social science*, stressing evidence-based *legal psychology*; and *law, psychology, and justice*, promoting social change and action through theory-sensitive *psychological jurisprudence*.

forensic psychology: the clinician as expert witness

The majority of professionals working in psychology and law identify themselves as forensic/clinical psychologists. They typically assist the police, the courts, and correctional institutions through psychotherapeutic testing, diagnosis, treatment, and programming. In court, they often provide expert testimony. Judges often assume that clinicians can effectively respond to legal and justice system concerns, given the therapist's role in resolving various forensic disputes (Weiner & Hess, 2006).

Some practitioners are trained in interdisciplinary law and psychology graduate programmes, but most pursue traditional clinical instruction. Organizations such as the American Academy of Forensic Psychology provide advanced training and certification. Although clinical education and training is useful for a forensic psychology career, critics doubt it is sufficient (Perlin, 1991). Narrowly trained forensic clinicians, lacking exposure to the law, sociology, criminology, and other relevant fields, too often have little understanding of the real-world institutional dynamics facing officers, inmates, juvenile delinquents, and other system participants (Arrigo, 2001).

legal psychology: applied empirical research

Unlike forensic psychology's clinical focus, legal psychology originates in social psychology and other experimental fields such as developmental psychology, neuropsychology, perception and memory. Legal psychologists function as 'legally informed clinicians' (Bersoff et al., 1997: 1305), integrating psychology's knowledge and values with questions of law and legal decision making. Most legally trained psychologists investigate non-clinical topics such as jury behaviour and eyewitness accuracy while others focus more closely on clinical areas such as child and family law (e.g., child custody) and mental health law (e.g., civil commitment). Many hope to influence legal policy making.

Being an insider (or believing that one is an insider) directs attention towards the minutia of the law – technicalities, rules, procedures – rather than towards the structural forces underpinning injustice and oppression. This narrowed focus strengthens researchers' self-serving but unproven belief that government and justice system personnel will actually use the data they generate (Williams, 2004). As a result, they fail to recognize that important social problems persist because of conflicting group values and competing political and economic interests, not because the authorities lack accurate information (Fox, 1991; Williams & Arrigo, 2002). Focusing on the immediate setting rather than on the broader context, as is common in social psychology more generally, limits mainstream psycholegal work to minor tinkering with current legal procedures when more expansive change is necessary. Thus, for example, psycholegal research designed to reduce illegal corporate behaviour generally fails to challenge the notion of corporate 'personhood' that renders corporations relatively immune from democratic control (Fox, 1996).

_____ *psychological jurisprudence: from theory to public policy* _____

Psychological jurisprudence refers to 'theories that describe, explain, and predict law by reference to human behavior' (Small, 1993: 11). Whereas legal psychologists study how judges and other legal system actors make decisions, theories of psychological jurisprudence tell judges and legislators how they *should* make decisions: guided by psychological data and psychologically preferred values that suggest not just what the law is, but what it ought to be. Admittedly, legal psychology and psychological jurisprudence are interdependent, and empirical work sometimes exposes oppressive legal practices. However, psychological jurisprudence holds the most promise for stimulating a critical psychology of the law aimed at transformative policy reform and social change. Regrettably, this promise remains unfulfilled. Although the three primary forms of psychological jurisprudence differ from one another in tone and objective, their mainstream orientations are hardly radical (Arrigo, 2004a; Fox, 1993b).

Dignity-focused psychological jurisprudence, the earliest approach, was the most promising. Advocates suggested legal decision makers should choose actions likely to enhance psychologically desirable values related to human dignity, such as personhood, privacy, community, equality, and justice (Melton, 1990; Melton & Saks, 1986). However, because this liberal-progressive orientation assumed the law's goal was to promote human welfare rather than implement social control for the benefit of elites (Melton, 1992), its adherents rejected more radical critiques. This approach has since been eclipsed by two newer frameworks even further removed from a critical psychology of law.

Therapeutic jurisprudence essentially seeks to transform the law into a therapeutic agent (Wexler, 1993). Its advocates urge psychologists to evaluate how legal rules, procedures, and participants 'may be viewed as social forces that sometimes produce therapeutic or antitherapeutic consequences' (Wexler, 1993: 21). Therapeutic jurisprudence assumes, thus, that clinical advice can and should help judges and legislators make decisions (Winick & Wexler, 2003), that this input will not produce the feared *therapeutic state* typified by paternalism and coercion (Wexler & Winick, 1996), and that justice is best served when courts act as mental health professionals (Stolle, 2000). These assumptions lead to a status quo agenda, which may help explain the approach's current popularity (Arrigo, 2004b). Advocates of therapeutic jurisprudence regularly examine potential applications such as ethical dilemmas in sex offender treatment programmes and re-entry initiatives for former incarcerates.

Cognitive science underlies psychological jurisprudence's third approach (e.g., Gazzaniga, 2005; Tancredi, 2005). Especially influential are developments in neuroscience such as the use of functional magnetic resonance imaging technology (fMRI) (i.e., brain imaging) to assist with legal-system tasks such as lie detection, counterterrorism surveillance, and punishment decisions. The fast-spreading notion that the 'rules of the physical world' (Gazzaniga, 2005: 88) can provide solutions to every aspect of human functioning, so that determining criminal responsibility requires little more than applying biological laws, violates the law's traditional assumptions about free will and personal responsibility. It also strengthens the medicalization of psychotherapy, which reduces every problem to a diagnostic category amenable to scientific remedy (see Chapter 5). Most regressively, cognitivism encourages 'adjust[ing] the mind, and not society, in order to promote well-being' (I. Prilleltensky, 1994: 93; see also Arrigo, 2007).

_____ **critical perspectives in psychology and the law** _____

Fortunately, critical approaches to psychological jurisprudence do exist that challenge mainstream psychology and the law's business as usual. Building on insights from more radical political and philosophical movements originating outside of both psychology and the law, their adherents ask fundamental questions about why the law exists and what purposes it serves. The four approaches described here – *feminism, postmodernism, anarchism,* and *chaos theory* – differ among themselves in important ways, but what they have in common is important: unlike the mainstream approaches noted above, they reject traditional assumptions about the nature of the law and the workings of legal institutions that hinder the pursuit of justice and social change. Significant critical attention has focused on family law, the mental health and criminal justice systems, and other arenas of particular interest to psychologists of the law.

Critiques of the law, and by implication of mainstream psychology's role in strengthening legal institutions, are neither new nor surprising. Many ordinary people resent legal authorities whose decisions seem unfair and lacking in common sense. All those jokes about lawyers, many of which turn out to be ancient, point to widespread discomfort with the rule of law. Sharing that discomfort were early psychology/law scholars who understood that a legal system's legitimacy requires the population to hold inaccurate beliefs about human behaviour (Tapp, 1974). In other words, we often believe that people behave justly and responsibly only because the law requires it – that we cannot be good unless we are forced to be good (Lerner, 1982). This belief allows legal authorities to proceed with policies we might otherwise reject.

The modern field of psychology and the law developed in concert with **critical legal studies**, a movement by legal scholars to cut through the law's self-serving justifications (Kennedy, 1973; Tushnet, 1986) to reveal the politics of the law (Kairys, 1998). Critical legal studies generated a wide-ranging literature that proved useful to scholars from other critical traditions. Two kinds of critiques are particularly relevant. To oversimplify a bit, the first is primarily political. It emphasizes how legal rules, traditions, and institutions disproportionately serve the interests of favoured groups or societal elites. The law accomplishes this in many ways, often using specialized language to mask institutionalized biases. Thus, work in this tradition often aims to help the powerless confront the powerful. Feminist scholars, for example, might dissect a specific legal opinion to identify the underlying principles such as that of the 'reasonable person', who used to be called, and still resembles, a traditional view of the 'reasonable man'.

The second kind of criticism adds a social psychological component by addressing the law's inherent consequences quite apart from the important political question of whose interests those consequences serve. Indeed, it would apply even more strongly if the law really was independent of external influence, as its traditional proponents imagine it to be. In this critical view, the law's primary purpose is to impose a rationalized, centralized order, despite older norms, changing circumstances, and individual and cultural differences. As anarchists especially maintain, 'legalism' would displace justice even in some future society marked by true equality because even 'good law' categorizes, rationalizes, and bureaucratizes human relationships by prioritizing order and rationality over interaction, collaboration, and spontaneity.

The remaining part of this section describes selected highlights of the four critical traditions that apply to psychology and the law. All have extensive literatures we can only hint at here.

_____ feminism _____

Feminism's critique of traditional sex roles, power imbalances, and other components of institutional sexism, described in other contexts elsewhere in this volume, extends to the legal system as well. Maintaining that fundamental assumptions of conventional legal theory and logic inadequately account for women's experiences, radical feminists challenge the prevailing view of science and, by implication, of mainstream psychology-and-law's quantitative evidence-based research.

The critique of knowledge   The maxim *the personal is empirical* (McDermott, 1992: 237) summarizes the liberal feminist approach to knowledge. Women's experiences can be retrieved, recorded, and counted; the resulting statistical variables can be used, among other things, to describe and explain any gender differences (Frazier & Hunt, 1998). However, the more radical converse is also important: *the empirical is personal*. Indeed, the empirical is a form of power that subordinates those who experience things differently (Arrigo, 1995). Thus, for example, radical **feminist jurisprudence** questions values embedded within quantitative law and social science inquiry that strengthen a system so male-dominated that 'any issue brought before the court that substantially deviates from this body of knowledge is less likely to attain a hearing and a favorable resolution' (Milovanovic, 2003: 139). Unlike those who suggest explanatory rationales should be based on 'the values that make up conventional knowledge of the community of scientific psychology' (Wiener, Watts, & Stolle, 1993: 93), radical feminists do not consider an unsatisfactory status quo the appropriate standard.

Much is at stake when the prevailing legal logic reflects masculine reasoning and sensibility, as shown by such notions as burdens of *proof,* a demand for *factual evidence, actual* legal intent, *expert* testimony, and *causes* of crime (Arrigo, 1995). Consider Bartlett and Kennedy's (1991) position on the difficulties of putting forward a defense based on battered women's syndrome. As Milovanovic (2003) explains, rather than making the preferred argument – that a woman's killing of her abuser is reasonable under the circumstances – defense attorneys ordinarily use a 'diminished capacity' argument that fits better into standard legal categories that ignore the psychology of abuse and power. This strategic decision, thus, hides the context that disempowers women.

A wide range of studies describes how to embody the unique experiences of women in legal reasoning (Arrigo, 1992), in the articulation of sexualized violence (Coker, 2001), and in psycholegal theories integrating feminism, epistemology and science (Anderson, 2002). Despite the growing literature, however, it would be fair to say that feminism's liberal wing has had more impact than more radical feminism on mainstream psychology and law's values and practices. Liberal feminism's attempt to equalize the legal system's treatment of women and men is more conducive to moderate reform than is radical feminism's broader challenge. By reframing our understanding of women in juridical thought and, consequently, in legal practice, radical feminism aims to reimagine social interaction and the communities that both women and men inhabit.

_____ *postmodernism* _____

Modernism is a broad-ranging movement that assumes in part that rationalism, science, and other optimistic, energetic facets of modern life are inevitable routes to progress. Postmodernism, on the other hand, is suspicious of claims to certainty and absolute truth. Postmodernists, thus, reject the law's traditional self-description as 'legal science', an out-of-fashion term traditionally used by those who proclaimed the law to be a purely logical endeavour. For postmodernists, as for other critics, legal decision making has less to do with logic than we often assume. For many, language is the key.

For example, many postmodernist investigators dissect (or 'deconstruct') legal texts to expose implicit values and hidden assumptions that legitimize existing practices. This language-sensitive strategy challenges the imagery and logic of conventional legal reasoning's claims to truth, progress, reason, and knowledge. More specifically, postmodern legal scholars demonstrate how the ideology embedded in law is a function of language (i.e., words, phrases, codes). Language choice is powerful. It channels various interpretations of a case, statute or decision into tightly controlled meanings, often consistent with status quo interests (Arrigo, Milovanovic, & Schehr, 2005; Sarat & Kearns, 1992).

the critique of subjectivity and discourse   Flourishing in the 1990s (Best & Kellner, 1997), postmodernism has taken a psychoanalytic turn. One of the principal luminaries has been Jacques Lacan (1977, 1985, 1991). In reworking Freud's (1900/1965) views of the unconscious, Lacan recognized that the subject (the self) was inexorably connected to discourse (to language). He considered the modernist notion of a purposeful, active, and fully autonomous individual – the law's 'rational person' – nothing more than a fiction. Throughout his career Lacan emphasized identifying the voice (language) and way of knowing (desire) that spoke for, and on behalf of, the subject (the self).

As is the case for postmodernism more generally, Lacanian terminology is highly abstract. Postmodernists defend this abstraction on the grounds that reducing thoughts to their most elemental level eliminates nuance. Such simplification makes the meaningful meaningless, homogenizes identities, and renders individuals powerless to resist the powerful. Lacan's observations represent a political response to the oppressive and unconscious normalization of identity that constantly takes place through everyday language use. For Lacan, language 'speaks the subject's identity' (Arrigo & Schehr, 1998: 632–633) and is a 'stand-in' for the subject's unique being.

Whose identity speaks for the subject through the system of communication in use? Is it actually the person who speaks or writes? Or is it the voice (and the way of knowing) of someone else, perhaps reflecting an ideological inculcation of society's dominant values? For Lacan, the voice conveyed through language typically represents the interests of the 'Other' (with a capital O to signify the unconscious). Further, for Lacan, this 'Other' quashes alternative ways of knowing, being, and living. To the extent that these alternative ways of speaking are silenced, 'violence' in speech manifests itself.

Consider the person threatened with involuntary civil commitment to a mental hospital. To avoid confinement, the person must rely on a style of speech that conveys 'wellness' or 'normalcy' or the absence of 'mental illness'. Consider, too, the person who represents him or herself in a court of law. The law requires that the person adopt its system of communication ('legalese') in order to be understood. Absent this, opposing counsel will object, arguing that the person's communication is 'prejudicial', 'immaterial', 'irrelevant'. Of course, in these examples, if the individual appropriates the language of 'wellness' or 'legalese', the person has sacrificed the self (identity) in order to convey acceptable, status quo, mundane meaning (the voice of the 'Other').

Using Lacanian psychoanalysis, several investigators have directed attention to law-related speech's capacity to obscure the subject's internal being. For example, Shon (2000) explained how police officers' embrace of 'cop talk' hinders peaceful interactions with citizen-suspects. Shon and Arrigo (2006) described how television shows like *COPS* or *America's Most Wanted* use language that reduces persons with mental illness either to objects of humour or sources of fear, further pathologizing or criminalizing the image of mental illness. Stacey examined how the gendered and raced dimensions of juridical language deprive indigenous women in South Australia of their legal identities, wherein 'the orthodox, modernist legal narrative [could] not transcribe, [did] not have the words to write of, women, race, and identity' (1996: 287).

The association between subjectivity and discourse is especially noteworthy in psychological jurisprudence. Echoing critical legal studies and feminist critiques, Lacanian psychoanalysis suggests that the taken-for-granted language of law and psychology reflects certain assumptions about the individuals and agencies constituting the mental health and justice systems (e.g., Arrigo, 2002; Schroeder, 1998). By unconsciously valuing certain ways of talking about, experiencing, and interpreting people and their behaviour, these assumptions dramatically affect the decision-making process. Words or phrases such as 'sexually violent predator', 'psychotic killer', 'incompetent to stand trial', and 'poses an imminent danger to self and/or others' are freighted with meaning. The law reduces these meanings to system-maintaining values that, intentionally or otherwise, make it impossible to articulate and legitimize alternative constructions. The task of a critical psychology of the law following Lacanaian insights is to ascertain how the prevailing discourse can be rearticulated to advance wellbeing and social change.

_____ *anarchism* _____

Despite its reputation, anarchism does not condemn institutionalized authority for the sake of negation or chaos alone. Anarchists have in mind not society's destruction but its reconstruction along lines better suited to human needs and values. Two of its fundamental assumptions are directly relevant to the law: change, ambiguity, and difference warrant celebration rather than routinization, and social life requires mutual aid, shared responsibility, and cooperation. These assumptions re-frame the law-human behaviour relationship, suggesting an entirely different set of questions relevant to the social psychology of the law, social organization, and the centralized state (Fox, 1993a, 2001a). The anarchist rejection of the law is based in part on an awareness that so-called 'primitive' groups resolved disputes and maintained order without legal systems for most of human history (Barclay, 1982), thus making the law a relatively recent invention.

celebrating change, ambiguity, and difference   Classical anarchists argued that the 'creative source of life' is rooted in a 'passion for destruction' of existing constraints (Bakunin, 1974: 58). Dynamic transformations produce life-affirming opportunities that enhance both individual freedom and communal consciousness. In the philosophy of anarchism, ambiguity and difference maximize prospects for change because the new ideas and identities they generate help resist pressures toward hierarchy and uniformity (Ferrell, 1999).

From an anarchist perspective, mainstream psychology and the law hold assumptions that weaken ambiguity and difference and thus harden rather than disrupt status quo routines. These include an emphasis on procedural rather than substantive justice, an acceptance of the 'rule of law's' application of general principles despite unfair results in actual cases, and an endorsement of policies that enhance rather than challenge the law's homogenizing, bureaucratizing legitimacy (Fox, 1993b, 1999). Not only does the mainstream logic foster people's experience of injustice, its legalistic core dismisses as irrelevant the ambiguities, inconsistencies, anomalies, and differences that make individual identities unique and that allow different communities to develop in different directions. Among many other beneficial possibilities, an acceptance of difference would help free people from the constraints of powerful regulatory and disciplinary regimes such as the mental health and criminal justice systems that typically extend their reach more broadly than is justified (Arrigo, 2000).

mutual aid   The different personal identities that anarchism nurtures increases mutual awareness, which in turn makes community sustainable (Williams & Arrigo, 2001). Because living with others depends on ensuring both a sense of individuality and a sense of community (Fox, 1985), members of anarchist communities are 'more free to be themselves, and at the same time, [are] more directly responsible for themselves and others, than they are in situations regulated by external authority' (Ferrell, 1999: 97). The community that anarchists seek, thus, could not exist without *mutual aid*, which 'grants the best chance of survival to those who best support each other in the struggle for life' (Kropotkin, 1902: 115). Effective mutual aid implies localism, regionalism, or decentralization wherein people participate in community actively and directly (Moreland, 1997).

Anarchist-influenced psychologists have demonstrated how state institutions and policies erode social justice and thwart human needs and values despite any transient gains (Fox, 1991, 1993a; Sarason, 1976). For example, Williams showed how mental illness determinations, risk and dangerousness assessments, and civil commitment practices – extensions of institutional and governmental regulation – limit 'more natural forms of order' that would free people to become 'fully human' (2004: 40; see also Williams & Arrigo, 2001).

Fox (1993b) urged psychologists of the law to pay attention to three areas that seemingly reflect popular suspicion about legal control: the formal distinction between the law and equity (in other words, between legalism and basic fairness); jury nullification (the criminal jury's ability to evade the law's harshness by rejecting rigid judicial instructions); and the Ninth Amendment to the US Constitution (designed to protect individual rights beyond those specified elsewhere, making commonsense notions of rights particularly important). Not surprisingly, legal and political authorities have attacked each of these endorsements of autonomous and community decision making as relics of old values that are incompatible with the rule of law. An anarchist perspective directs attention to the disparity between legal system assumptions and the commonsense or everyday conceptions held by ordinary people about just how much power they want the law to have.

Although some anarchists have contemplated variations of law-like modes of social order (Holterman & van Meerseveen, 1984), anarchism more generally challenges psychologists of the law to consider how societies can achieve social order and stability without legal institutions. Whether anarchist societies of the past and anarchist modes of organization in current political struggles (e.g., in the anti-globalization movement) can be adapted to larger societies adds an empirical component to the anarchist critique, reflecting Paul Goodman's approving description of the 'anarchist principle' as a 'social-psychological hypothesis with obvious political implications' (1966/1979: 176).

_____ *chaos theory* _____

Chaos theory, or *chaology*, emerged in the natural sciences, especially within physics and mathematics where it is also termed *nonlinear dynamical systems theory* or *complex systems science*. Chaology rejects the notion that researchers can reliably forecast the behaviour of complex adaptive systems: those which behave in unpredictable, discontinuous, unstable, or anomalous ways (Barton, 1994). For example, in a simple linear system, knowledge of the causal factors allows a prediction of the result. In complex systems, however, the process is 'nonlinear' because the contributing causal factors do not lead to a single predictable result. That is why we cannot predict with certainty the exact pattern of waves washing up against a particular shoreline.

Social science – and, more specifically, a critical psychology of the law that appropriates these insights – argues that people, too, are complex adaptive systems. In other words, they behave in 'orderly disordered' ways (e.g., rationally *and* emotionally; objectively *and* subjectively). Believing that both aspects of our humanity possess inherent value, chaos theory advocates allowing natural or organic processes to unfold rather than overly constraining or regulating them, which is typically the legal (and psycholegal) system's response. Thus, chaos theory's assumptions about human interaction and social conduct challenge approaches that seek predictability and control. Despite the best plans of their creators, complex systems tend toward unpredictable patterns, often at odds with the intended or stated goal.

the critique of order within chaos　Chaology assumes that order lurks within supposed randomness. Among the most significant principles is the **attractor**. Attractors 'are patterns of stability that a system settles into over time' (Goerner, 1994: 39). As their name suggests, attractors 'exert a "magnetic" appeal for a system, seemingly pulling the system toward it' (Briggs & Peat, 1989: 36). This attraction or pull produces order and stability in an otherwise disorderly, complex system. Alternatively, a 'strange' attractor can encourage systems to settle into apparently disorganized patterns such that the system's activity never traces the same path twice, revealing order within apparent randomness. The strange attractor is 'the epitome of contradiction, never repeating, yet always resembling, itself: infinitely recognizable, never predictable' (Van Eenwyk, 1991: 7).

In other words, what appears to be random and unexplainable, even in the workings of legal institutions, may actually reflect patterns that, while unpredicted, can be discovered. For chaos theory scholars, the uncertainty accompanying systems left unregulated is preferable to over-reaching a regulation that prematurely channels behaviour down some paths at the cost of making others unreachable. In contrast to anarchism, which generally envisions a socially constructed order free of centralized control, chaos theory rejects the notion that any complex system will actually work as planned.

In keeping with this approach, critical scholars have examined how the system of law behaves as an attractor. In certain instances, the magnetic pull of the formal and informal justice system harnesses individual behaviour, restricting it to established interaction patterns with fixed, settled, and predictable legal identities. For example, Brion (1993) explains how legal processes and institutions facilitate overreactions to false reports of child sexual abuse. The legal apparatus relies on its limited system of communication (legalese) to ascertain facts, filters these facts through the narrow prism of a court or other legal tribunal, restricts the dispute's focus (i.e., what happened, was there harm?), and declares these judgments the final source of truth and justice. This constrained approach makes hysteria more likely. Because the legal system is attracted to order, control, equilibrium, and predictability, best expressed through its language, it restricts its capacity to discover more about the behaviour in question (child sexual abuse) and, simultaneously, makes exaggerated responses to inaccurately reported incidents more likely.

Similarly, Arrigo and Schehr critiqued the victim-offender restorative-justice dialogue in juvenile cases. Young offenders have trouble making sense of these ritualized dialogues where the setting's rules, though unspoken, 'are unconsciously organized to produce limited outcomes consistent with the ... language of restoration and reconciliation' (1998: 647). The mediator's job is to reach certain goals, not to allow the unexpected to intervene. Lost in the process are opportunities for sense-making and understanding beyond those that the setting – the legal point attractor – imposes upon its subjects. In this instance, the restorative dialogue, as regulated and facilitated by the mediator, is pulled toward finite methods of communicating and interacting, reducing possible outcomes to those the dialogue will permit.

Following the related principle of *order out of chaos*, radical scholars have demonstrated how a variety of systems function as instruments of social control by impeding or denying natural adaptation and spontaneous order. In looking at the mental health system, for example, Butz (1994) explained how the use of psychotropic medication to facilitate prediction and control (as Michael McCubbin describes in Chapter 18) is antithetical to the logic of self-organization. Extending this reasoning to treatment refusal, Williams and Arrigo (2002) argue that 'pushing through' chaos (Chamberlain, 1994: 48) to restore order relegates people to the status of machines that need fixing. Studies of other law-related systems have reached similar conclusions (Arrigo & Barrett, 2008; Milovanovic, 1997; Sobell, Ellingstad, & Sobell, 2000; Williams & Arrigo, 2007).

A critical psychology of law sympathetic to chaos theory would reevaluate all forms of psychotherapeutic intervention and state-sponsored social control because of a fundamental insight: systems that discipline the human subject quash the potential for self-healing and personal growth. As proponents of chaos theory see it, treatment protocols, surveillance practices, and regulatory schemes prevent human beings from exercising their complex adaptive capacities to self-organize (Butz, 1997; Milovanovic, 1997, 2002). The benefits of self-organization, in this view, far outweigh the current system.

the crime of policy and the search for justice

The four perspectives described in this chapter bring to psychology and the law disparate philosophical assumptions, levels of abstraction, and political goals. Despite their different emphases and even contradictions, however, they share a suspicion that law as we know it – and perhaps any conceivable legal system – is at least as likely to reinforce inequality and injustice as to combat them. Each suggests in its own way how psychologists of law might reevaluate their values, assumptions, and practices so that the field can help either to transform the legal system or bypass it.

Unfortunately, and despite intentions to the contrary, policy work at the mainstream law-psychology divide is as apt to reproduce harm as prevent it. In part that's because psychologists use their science to justify only narrowly conceived tinkering with an unsatisfactory status quo. This approach might be termed 'criminal' if the standard were justice rather than legal technicality. Can psychology contribute instead to justice-focused policy making? Several issues come to mind as we imagine a critical psychology of law. It remains the case, however, that psychologists and psychology students seeking to understand and make use of critical perspectives will have to find their own way around mainstream barriers.

education and training Graduate psycholegal training should expose students to philosophy, political economy, cultural studies, anthropology, and other subjects, including of course critical perspectives within those fields. Narrowly focused education cannot generate either holistic appraisals of the status quo or the imaginative explorations needed to expand the bounds of any given system. Focusing education on transformative policy making would require a substantial openness to change for students and teachers as well as for the communities to which both are connected. Curricula must be reconstituted to better reflect cross-disciplinary instruction. Faculty members with interdisciplinary experience and skills must be hired to enable more robust theoretical, methodological, and practice-based instruction. Internship settings and practicum placements must be reconfigured to connect integrative classroom instruction and fieldwork with an expanding range of service needs, including advocacy for social change at community, state, national and international levels. A primary goal should be the injection of legal control into institutions such as courts, psychiatric hospitals, prisons, and social welfare agencies, together with new ways of thinking about mental illness diagnosis and treatment, offenders and victims, power and justice. Although changes like these do not seem imminent in traditional psychology/law programmes, there may be more room for cross-disciplinary input and community applications in subfields such as community psychology where legal institutions have already received some attention.

theoretical integration/unification in critical psychological jurisprudence The conceptual approaches described in this chapter overlap with one another and with other critical alternatives despite differing terminologies and emphases. Concerns for identity, knowledge, agency, power, shared responsibility, being, and becoming are all, to some extent, integral features of a critical psychology of law. Efforts to synthesize points of convergence across these orientations, while certainly daunting, are an important step in developing a psychological jurisprudence that mobilizes divergent strains of theory into transformative policy.

race, gender, and class Avowedly neutral and objective research on issues relevant to race, gender, class, and other identity categories must be complemented by psycholegal theories and methodologies reflecting the experiences, ways of knowing, and identities of those in less favoured positions.

Research reflecting traditional legal and psychological assumptions about 'the reasonable man', 'rational thought', 'choice', 'responsibility', 'wellness', 'illness', 'facts', 'truth', and so on helps marginalize those who have had little input into legal and policy-making assumptions. Research designs sensitive to these differences require theory that explains the lived, evolving identities of those who depart from dominant norms: women, people of colour, the poor and working class, people with disabilities, gays and lesbians, and other marginalized groups. In addition, the kind of research suggested here involves the development of 'testable' conceptual models that can lead to assessments and evaluation protocols whose reliability and validity may very well be steeped in alternative logics, languages, measurements, and meanings.

advocacy and rights-claiming   Rather than getting bogged down in technical and procedural matters based on quantification, statistical analyses, and data sets, psycholegal work must look beyond procedures to outcomes. We should challenge unjust systems, not legitimize them using whatever methods elite decision makers deem acceptable. To rely on existing methods as a basis for evaluation represents nothing more than a 'reaction-negation' dynamic (Nietzsche, 1966). In other words, critics who dissect mainstream values, norms, and assumptions are typically challenged and then negated from within prevailing theoretical and/or methodological paradigms. Those paradigms do not seriously contemplate anything intrinsically new or different (Arrigo, 2003).

Our challenge is to foster within psychology and the law a profound reconsideration of values related to individuality and communality consistent with a psychological sense of community (Fox, 1985, 1993a, 2001a) and a sociological sense of individuality (Arrigo, 2003). Central to this undertaking is commitment to a care ethic steeped in relationships and connectivity, situated knowledge and standpoints, the celebration of being and becoming that enables self-growth, and resistance to hierarchal systems that reduce difference to sameness. The mainstream values of the law and psychology – saturated in the discourses of science, objectivity, and impartiality – represent the unspoken platform through which psycholegal decisions mask their political assumptions. Resisting such political normalization is crucial, especially when it denies alternative expressions of identity, agency, justice, and humanity.

▪ ▪main chapter points ▪

1 The field of 'psychology and the law' seeks to influence legal systems and public policy.

2 Psychology and the law consist of three overlapping approaches: forensic psychology, legal psychology, and psychological jurisprudence.

3 Mainstream assumptions and goals hinder more radical transformative possibilities.

4 Critical psycholegal approaches applying external political and philosophical perspectives include feminism, postmodernism, anarchism, and chaos theory.

5 Making the field more critical requires altering education and training, the theoretical integration of varied critical perspectives, the inclusion of less powerful groups, and looking beyond fair procedures to justice-based outcomes.

glossary

- **anarchism**: the philosophy that societies should be organized non-hierarchically, without coordination through the law, government, and other centralized state institutions.

- **attractor**: in chaos theory, the point/location into which a complex system settles over time.

- **chaos theory**: the view that traditional linear efforts to understand behaviour cannot sufficiently account for the behaviour of complex systems.

- **critical legal studies**: a movement that considers the law to be inherently political rather than independent or purely logical.

- **feminist jurisprudence**: an approach, broadly consistent with critical legal studies, that assesses the impact of legal principles and institutions on women.

- **forensic psychology**: the psycholegal approach emphasizing the use of clinical expertise on civil commitment to mental hospitals, child custody evaluations, and similar topics.

- **legal psychology**: the psycholegal approach emphasizing research on legally relevant behaviour such as that of jurors, eyewitnesses, and police.

- **postmodernism**: in contrast to earlier modernist conceptions emphasizing rationalism, scientific optimism, and similar routes to inevitable progress, postmodernism refers to a variety of positional, relational, and provisional approaches that emphasize the lack of absolute certainty and truth.

- **psychological jurisprudence**: the psycholegal approach that advocates restructuring legal principles and institutions to better achieve psychologically desirable goals.

reading suggestions

Arrigo (2004a) presents a more detailed overview of critical approaches to psychological jurisprudence. Fox (1999) assesses the role of psychology and the law in maintaining inaccurate assumptions about justice. Kairys (1998) collects a variety of readings on the politics of the law from positions that are consistent with critical legal studies and a critical psychology of the law. Herman (1995) recounts mainstream US psychology's efforts to influence public policy.

- **Dennis Fox's website** – essays on psychology/the law/justice and critical psychology, course syllabi, links to other resources: dennisfox.net
- **Division on Critical Criminology of the American Society of Criminology** – includes course syllabi, blogs, activist essays, and links: critcrim.org

 **Questions**

1 Why might critical psychologists consider the law a source of injustice and inequality?

2 What are some of the conceptual commonalities and differences found across feminism, anarchism, postmodernism, and chaos theory? How might each address a particular psychology and law issue?

3 Does human nature require the law? If not the law, what?

11

Rethinking Subjectivity: A Discursive Psychological Approach to Cognition and Emotion

Alexa Hepburn and Clare Jackson

The landscape of human thought over the last two millennia has often considered the world discoverable through an understanding of its timeless defining features. In psychology this developed into a dominant focus on the individual's inner life of thoughts and memories, faculties for information processing, and an evolutionary heritage of hot emotions and cool reasoning. This internalized or '**cognitivist**' focus has become one of the unquestioned premises for most forms of psychology. Mainstream psychology, then, often takes personhood to be constructed through supposed fundamental internal features and processes such as personality, gender, cognition and emotion. Treating these features as natural, discoverable and measurable warrants psychology's claim to be a science, with all the associated characteristics of an objective, apolitical and benign scientific endeavour. As emphasized throughout this book, psychology's individualistic notion of personhood and mind leads to individualizing explanations of human conduct that can undermine the potential for social change and social justice. By locating 'causes' of behaviour inside people, psychologists often miss the deeply situated, social, political and cultural contexts in which human behaviour is produced.

However, over the past few decades there has been a steadily growing but often unnoticed (within mainstream psychology) revolt. Originally pioneered by Edwards and Potter (1992), this research has developed into a new and radically critical force in psychology – **discursive psychology** (occasionally DP). Rather than working with predefined notions of personhood and mind, discursive psychologists are interested in how these things actually appear, and how they are managed between people in talk-in-interaction. Fundamentally, people *do* things in talk. Interaction is the 'primordial site for sociality'. Whoever we are to each other – relations, lovers, friends, colleagues – and whatever the nature or purpose of our interactions – requesting, inviting, seeking medical treatment, interrogating suspects, complaining about ill-treatment – talk-in-interaction is *the* key (though admittedly not the only) medium through which these relationships and actions are realized. DP opens up new possibilities for exploring the discursive accomplishment of inequalities, discrimination, and power, and how these are actually enacted in social contexts (see Hepburn and Wiggins, 2007 for a contemporary overview of the different possibilities).

We argue in this chapter that discursive psychology provides a powerful resource for critical psychology. Our aim is to emphasize some of contemporary discursive psychology's exciting and radical features. We first document DP analyses that flesh out a new vision of psychology. We show how DP understands 'individuals' and their various 'inner states' such as 'memory' as interactionally produced – 'DP in Practice'. We then show a discursive approach to social justice – 'DP in Principle' – and finally we take emotion and illustrate the discursive psychological approach to crying, drawing contrasts with the way more traditional approaches have treated this topic – 'DP in Action'.

what is discursive psychology?

Discursive psychology developed originally through applying notions from **discourse analysis** and **rhetoric** to psychological issues (Billig, 1991; Edwards, 1997; Edwards & Potter, 1992; Potter, 1996; Potter & Wetherell, 1987). As an approach to science, discursive psychology does not accept that the traditional methods of psychology can reach inner worlds – thoughts, emotions, memories. This is not to claim that these processes do not exist, or are not important, but that they are not discoverable through experiments, surveys or interviews. Although the upshot of this may lead to questioning psychology's very basis as a discipline, discursive psychologists seek to re-specify psychology rather than diminish it.

Discursive psychology treats the objects of traditional psychological research as products of discourse – as appearing in interaction between people. They are external rather than internal. Discursive psychology works with the *displayed* perspectives of participants in interaction, perspectives embodied in people's constructions and orientations, both visual and verbal. As such, and as we show in this chapter, discursive psychology counters the traditional social psychological view of the individual as part of a matrix of abstract social processes that are driven by individuals' thoughts and feelings, and replaces it with a focus on people's everyday practices in various settings. The notion of *situated practice* is key here. It serves, amongst other things, to distinguish DP from other qualitative methods in psychology, for example Interpretative Phenomenological Analysis, or more psychoanalytic app-roaches, which treat talk as more or less revealing of inner states (thereby leaving intact the 'objective' and individualistic notion of personhood). DP entails an important change in analytic focus. Rather than whether, or how accurately, participants' talk reflects inner and outer events, DP investigates how 'psychology' and 'reality' are produced, dealt with and made relevant by participants in and through interaction. Discursive psychologists work closely with naturalistic data (that is, everyday conversations that would have occurred whether or not the researcher was there to record them). They focus on *orientation to action* – the things people *do* in talk – and the *resources* (metaphors, categories, commonplaces) from which actions are constructed. This rather specific treatment of language contrasts with psychology's mainly cognitivist approach, which treats language as an intentional mode of trans-mitting inner thoughts and emotions (Edwards, 2004).

discursive psychology in practice: memory

So, people formulate the world as they speak. Let's look at an example: US President Bill Clinton's claim that he forgot. This claim is a flexible resource to manage responsibility and accountability. In the following extract, the psychological construct – memory – is not treated as a taken-for-granted property of an individual nor as an expression of some 'real' inner state, but as *being made relevant* in the data as part of some on-going social action. (Readers unfamiliar with transcription symbols may first refer to the key at the end of the chapter.)

One of the features of US political life is the regular occurrence of high-profile judicial hearings. President Clinton's grand jury inquisition involved being questioned about lying and inappropriate sexual relationships. Michael Lynch and David Bogen (1996) were particularly interested in the way notions of remembering were used in these hearings. The 'don't remember' response has the virtue of defeating trouble. While a 'yes' can implicate guilt, a denial can suggest dissembling when contradictory evidence is produced. Not remember-ing is neither agreement nor denial. Let us explore this with an example from President Clinton's grand jury testimony, taken from Hepburn (2003).

Clinton has been asked about a phone call with his 'lover' Monica Lewinsky on a particular day. The issue at stake (although it is not spelt out here) is her reported anger and its possible causes. Could it be because Clinton had asked her to lie in an impending court case that was to involve both of them? This is how Clinton replies, after 12 seconds of silence:

Extract 1

Clinton: Mister Wisenberg ((C raises an index finger at
Q)) I remember that she came in to visit that
day, (0.5) I remember that she was very upset.
(2.5)
I don't recall whether I talked to her on the
phone before she came in to visit, (.) but I
may well have.= I'm no- not denying that I did.
I just don't recall that.

Note how Clinton manages the contentious phone call. He does not *recall* talking to Lewinsky, but he *might* have. This usefully evades various dangerous alternatives. If he were to accept that he had talked to her on the phone the interrogator might have come back directly with a question about what was said in the call, presenting yet another possibility for incrimination. If he were to deny talking to her he may be contradicted by a public record or testimony. Clinton is able to avoid both dangerous options by his claim, and display, of not recalling.

This seems a fairly simple illustration, but note the far-reaching implications. First, remembering and non-remembering are practices done as a matter of public display in discourse. Second, remembering is evaluated not through comparing input with output as in a traditional cognitive psychological memory experiment, but via normative criteria that are brought into play locally, managed rhetorically, and open to contest, as Clinton's most certainly were. Third, there is no simple objective record against which a remembering or failure to recall can be compared. Outside the world of the laboratory where researchers can use their unlimited definitional authority to specify the nature of the input, there are only versions that can be more or less telling or open to doubt (Edwards & Potter, 1992). All of this is *not* to say that nothing is going on in Clinton's head; the point is that *the practice of remembering and forgetting is always a public and social one*. If we want to understand that practice, we need to understand the interaction in which it plays its part.

Psychology has been dominated by the traditional cognitive approach that compares input with output. This has offered some interesting observations about capacities and competences. However, its relation to memory as a social practice in interactional settings such as courts, relationship disputes and school classrooms is complex and, as yet, not well understood. Discursive psychology takes a very different approach. It considers how memory, remembering, failures to recall and so on appear in practical settings. It considers the way versions are built up as plausible versions of the past, or dismissed as mistakes.

It follows that participants' discursive practices do not represent 'mind' (the attempt to understand what people are 'really' thinking, knowing, feeling) or 'reality' (the attempt to understand what 'really' happened). Rather, they are, first and foremost, resources in dialogue – which also makes them a useful resource for the analyst. The aim is to explicate participants' displayed deployment of psychological resources. In a Foucauldian move that turns traditional approaches in psychology on their heads, subjectivity and inner life are seen as the *outcome* of interaction. We believe that this interactional focus is vital for understanding how matters of social justice (e.g. inequality, prejudice, and power) are made live – how they are actually done – between people in talk in the everyday contexts of their lives. Indeed, social justice is a central concern of DP, and by way of illustration, we next present a discursive psychological approach to inequality.

discursive psychology in principle: inequality

Let us take a short example to illustrate what a discursive psychological approach to inequality would look like. The example comes from a project that is studying the work of the child protection helpline of the UK National Society for the Prevention of Cruelty to Children (NSPCC) (see Hepburn, 2005, 2006; Hepburn & Potter, 2003). The helpline provides information, advice and counselling to anyone concerned about a child's safety. Child Protection Officers (CPOs) with three years' social work experience take more than a quarter of a million calls each year. One of their principal roles is to refer information about abuse to the relevant social services departments.

The following extract occurs about a minute into a call to a child protection helpline. The caller is complaining to the child protection officer about her neighbour's treatment of her children:

```
01  Caller:  But (0.2) to me what they're fed is:
02           (0.3) is all wrong.
03  CPO:     Right.=what've you see 'er buy:in then.
04  Caller:  WELL ER:m:: (.) a pack of eight sausages.
05  CPO:     Mm[ : ,]
06  Caller:     [An a] bag of fro:zen chips.
07           (0.3)
08  CPO:     Mm:,
09           (0.4)
10  Caller:  Ye know.
11           (0.4)
12  Caller:  Er::m an a loafa bread >an a mean she<
13           shops daily.
14  CPO:     Mm. N-w- some people do do: that.=don't
15           they.=>a [m'n< i-]i- ye know is she on
16  Caller:           [ Yeh. ]
17  CPO:     benefi:ts.=cos that-that's not unusual
18           if [somebody's on benefits yeah ]
19  Caller:     [ye:s, she's on benefits, but] er::
20           (0.5) she's got somebody else livin
21           with her?
22  CPO:     Ri:ght. (.) [Right.]
```

Let us offer a series of illustrative observations about this brief extract.

1 *It is naturalistic* In contrast to the vast majority of work in psychology, it uses material that is taken from an actual social setting. It would have occurred in more or less this way if the researcher had not been recording the material. We have called it naturali*stic* (rather than natural) in recognition of the potential for 'reactivity' in such records. Nevertheless, this situation is not flooded by categories introduced by the social researcher; nor are the participants speaking on the basis of identities pre-defined by the researcher (Potter & Hepburn, 2005).

2 *It uses transcript to capture features of speech delivery* In contrast to the majority of interview-based research and ethnographic work the transcript uses conventions (developed by Gail Jefferson, 2004) that are designed to capture features of speech delivery that are consequential for interaction. Overlap, delay, emphasis and various intonational contours are part of what give talk its meaning – they are crucial to participants and so are potentially important aids to analysis.

3 *There are potential inequalities between the speakers* We can study inequalities between the Caller and CPO. There are a range of possibilities here – the Caller is probably doing something unusual, the CPO is doing something they do all day every day; the Caller treats the CPO as knowing about child protection; the CPO treats the caller as knowing about this specific case. The nature and consequences of these things are a topic of study.

4 *Speakers construct and invoke inequalities in their talk* We will focus on the CPO's observations about 'benefits' on lines 15–18. To suggest that someone is 'on benefits' suggests that they are a recipient of state aid and therefore poor. In the abstract, then, it is a categorization for a range of disadvantaged groups in UK society. However, our discursive construction approach encourages us to look at the *specifics* of how this description is assembled and what it is doing.

   Note that the CPO's turn from 14–18 is constructed from a series of elements. For example, her construction presents what 'some people' do as scripted or standardized – in Edwards (1997) terms it is a *script formulation*. Edwards notes the way that script formulations present actions as normal, standard or expected, and are often contrasted with dispositional formulations which present actions as a product of the features of individuals (their personality, views or moral shortcomings).

5 *Constructions of inequality are part of actions* The CPO then asks the Caller if the person she is calling about is on benefits (line 17), offering this as an account for the behaviour of the person being called about. This offers the Caller a way of seeing this problem as normal or standard for people in that social category. This can be seen as part of the CPO testing the information in the call to establish whether it is appropriate for a referral (with the work that it will involve for social services).

   Although the CPO cannot (easily) say that the Caller's neighbour's children look healthy enough she constructs her potentially counter version using scripts and common knowledge. She deploys what 'everybody' knows about, for example, what poor people on benefits are like. This provides a basis for testing out the claims made by the Caller in preparation for a possible referral to social services.

6   *Inequality is an interactional object*   What we have tried to do here, briefly and schematically, is to indicate some of the ways in which inequality can be understood as a participant's issue. We have considered the way inequality talk is constructed, situated and oriented to action. A similar argument could be made of course for notions such as equality, domination, exploitation and superiority. We have particularly tried to highlight how taking seriously the study of these notions as members' concerns also requires us to take seriously the situated practices that they are embedded within.

7   *What this gives us and what it leaves out*   Taking this approach to inequality does not assume prior to our analysis that we know what inequality is, and 'join in' with the participants. For example it does not take the CPO's side by condemning the Caller for trying to report a woman struggling to feed her children on a low income, nor does it take the Caller's side and condemn the CPO for being inactive about a case of possible child neglect. This approach does however sensitize us to the actions that references to social inequalities might be involved in for speakers in talk. There may be social inequalities that are important for our participants, but these are something that we have no understanding of as yet. Assuming we know in advance what they are and how to tackle them might serve to replicate rather than eradicate them. This type of approach therefore moves us towards a deeper understanding of the way something like inequalities becomes a live issue for participants. As such it can provide useful tools for critical approaches.

discursive psychology in action: emotion in interaction

emotion and counselling

Emotion is a theoretically interesting topic for discursive research as it is something of a 'hard case'. Mainstream psychologists often treat it as something close to biology, something lying underneath language and maybe even culture. Often social psychologists treat emotion as a causal variable that exerts a distorting effect on cognition. Psychology curricula endlessly talk of the sympathetic nervous system's ability to generate a surge of neurotransmitters and hormones that trigger the famous fight–flight response, which people experience internally as 'emotion'. This is a highly abstract, individualistic and conservative view. It is conservative in the sense that it maintains the status quo by seeing individuals and their psychological states as explanatory resources. However, a number of researchers have started to work up a very different image. This image does not take emotion as something underlying discourse, and separate from discourse, but as something that is first and foremost managed and made accountable in discourse. Emotion is invoked, described, and displayed for the purposes of social actions. Rom Harré (1986) and Richard Buttny (1993) have made important contributions to this area of research, but we will begin with a look at more recent developments by Derek Edwards (1997, 1999, 2007).

Edwards has two rhetorical targets. On the one hand, there is the ethological, universalist idea of people, whatever their culture, sharing the same basic set of emotions. Although this notion dates back at least to Darwin, it has been more recently popularized by the work of Paul Ekman (1982). On the other hand, there is a cognitive psychology of emotions, developed by researchers such as Anna Wierzbicka (1999). This considers emotions in terms of abstract models that build on 'universal' concepts such as 'good' and 'bad', 'happy' and 'sad'.

Edwards (in common with many other critics of Ekman's style of work) raises a major concern with various styles of cross-cultural research on emotions. Their problem is that rather than being open to cultural variation they invariably start with Western categories of emotions. That is, if you have been trained and have lived in the West and you are doing cross-cultural work on emotions, it is very difficult to avoid looking through Westernized lenses for anger, sadness and so on. This means that typical Western emotion terms are treated as the kind of thing that emotion *is*, and the problem is to look for *it* – emotion – cross-culturally. This privileging of Western academic ways of looking at the world is one way in which traditional psychology reproduces rather than challenges its own hegemony.

Edwards proposes an approach that considers the way emotions enter into actual practices through being described, avowed, and displayed. Here he is starting from the fundamental discursive psychological idea that *words, categories and so on are there for what you do with them*. To understand emotion, the thing to do is not to consider it in the abstract as a reified entity, as something separate from interaction, but instead to look at emotion in its home environment – in everyday situated practices of interaction. This approach to emotions leaves aside any consideration of the truth or motives of a situation – as Locke and Edwards suggest, we should 'leave those notions for the participants to deal with' (2003: 253). In DP a central concern is with how emotion and other psychological constructs are invoked in discourse and what interactional conse-quences they have. It is through looking at these psychological resources as they appear in these practical situations that we can start to understand their role and the way they can provide particular rhetorical oppositions. It captures just the stuff that is missed from the abstract cognitive modelling and cross-cultural studies of the 'perception' of emotions in faces.

We can see the situated use of emotion discourse to manage blame and responsibility in another example taken from Bill Clinton's cross-examination testimony. Many commentators had come to see his relationship with Monica Lewinsky as exploitative, and an abuse of his powerful position (Locke and Edwards, 2003). Building on Edwards's (1997, 1999) proposal that emotional states are invoked in opposition to rational thought and function to make sense of social actions, Locke and Edwards (2003) show

how, in the following extract, Clinton presents Lewinsky as irrational and needy and himself as responsible and caring in order to account for her apparent continued attachment to him after their 'affair' had reportedly ended. Immediately before this extract starts, Clinton has been asked why Lewinsky was sending him romantic cards and letters at a time when he claims they were no longer involved in 'inappropriate contact'. Note that in asking the question, Lewinsky's conduct, for which there is documentary evidence, is already seen as setting up something surprising or contradictory for which an account is warranted. Perhaps the relationship had not actually ended. Here is Clinton's response.

Extract 2

```
 1  C:  Well my recollection is that she um (4.0) that
 2       (.) maybe because of changed circumstances in her
 3       own life, (0.7) in nineteen ninety seven= after
 4       there was no: (2.0) more inappropriate contact
 5       that she sent me more things in the mail.
 6       (1.0)
 7       And that there was sort of a disconnect sometimes
 8       between what she was saying, (0.5) and the plain
 9       facts of our relationship.
10       (0.7)
11       A:nd I don't know what caused that, (0.8) but it
12       may have bee:n (1.5) dissatisfaction with the rest
13       of her life I don't know- I- you know it- (1.0) uh
14       (0.5) she had from the time I first met her talked
15       to me about- (1.0) the rest of her personal life,
16       and uh (1.0) it may be that- that- there was (.)
17       some reason for that= it may be that (0.2) when I
18       (0.2) did the right thi:ng and made it stick that
19       (4.0) in a way she felt (.) a need to cling more
20       closely or try to get closer to me even though
21       she knew nothing (.) improper was happening, or was
22       going to happen.= I don't know the answer to that.
```

Clinton's response counters the (implicit) suggestion that his sexual relationship with Lewinsky had extended beyond the period he had previously specified by appealing to various vulnerabilities in Lewinsky's character and circumstances. She continued with romantic gestures due to vaguely stated 'changed circumstances in her *own* life' (lines 2–3) and her apparent psychological inability to connect what she did with the reality, or 'plain facts' (lines 8–9) of the situation. The rhetorical work of 'systematic vagueness' is explored by Edwards and Potter (1992), and here we may see an example of it working to pre-empt independent investigation/verification by not detailing any of the purported changes Lewinsky went through in 1997. The stress on these changes occurring in Lewinsky's 'own life' downgrades any responsibility Clinton had for her, by placing these events outside their shared lives. The fact that these 'changes' are referred to first in an account of her sending him romantic material constructs it as something of a coping mechanism – her way of coping, that has nothing to do with him. Added to this, the description of Lewinsky's 'disconnection' between reality and her actions is built as part of her character – particularly through the use of 'sometimes' (line 7); it is not something that she displayed on this one occasion, but with 'sometimes' she is presented as having these 'disconnects' more frequently, perhaps even repeatedly. Later (lines 14–15), Clinton dates Lewinsky's personal problems to a time before they met, problems which she shared with him and he'd tried to make sense of – 'it may be that...' (line 17). Clinton construes himself as rational throughout this extract – he was in touch with the 'plain facts' and in fact had instigated them; as an honourable man he had done 'the right thing' and had been able to carry his decision through to make 'it stick' (line 18). In contrast, Lewinsky is seen to live a life that she is dissatisfied with and that causes her to behave irrationally by clinging to a relationship despite knowing that it's over.

Edwards (1997) has suggested that the boundaries and contrasts of what makes up 'emotion' are different across cultures and settings. Indeed the category of 'emotion' is itself a feature of a particular modern and Western idea of the person. Edwards has used ideas from **conversation analysis**, cultural anthropology and constructionism as the basis for a respecification that focuses research on: (a) the use of 'emotion' categories; (b) orientations to objects and actions as 'emotional' and (c) displays of 'emotion'. Some of these features appear in a further development of the first author's child protection project where callers' crying and Child Protection Officers' responses to crying are the topic of analysis (Hepburn, 2004).

_____ *crying and empathy* _____

It seems incredible that psychology, which seeks to empirically and objectively understand human behaviour, has completely failed to study crying as it occurs *in situ*, let alone examine the interactional features of something so central to human behaviour. However, prior to Hepburn (2004) there was no work that provided either situated descriptions of crying or any analysis of its different interactional features.

Psychologists who adopt more traditional approaches have conducted numerous studies of crying, especially crying in infancy (see Barr, Hopkins & Green, 2000). This work typically deals with crying as a dependent variable, interesting for its communication of psychological distress. Research has typically used an instrument known as the Crying Patterns Questionnaire (CPQ) developed by St. James-Roberts (1988). This involves mothers (and note the gender-stereotypical choice of participant here!) offering reports on the amount of crying, where it occurs, whether it was 'upsetting' to the mother, and what her response was. No attempt is made to represent the nature or interactional organization of crying.

There is less research on adult crying. What has been done has conceptualized it in terms of various factors that may influence its occurrence. For example, Nelson (2000) coded different 'types' of crying – 'healthy crying', 'crying for no reason', 'prolonged or frequent crying' – and tested how strongly these types of crying are associated with depression or different physiological disorders.

From a similar perspective, Peter, Vingerhoets, and Van Heck (2001) conducted a questionnaire-based study of gender differences in crying, associating basic personality traits with self-reported indices of crying. Discursive psychologists are suspicious of 'differences' research (here we have gender, but our concerns apply equally to other categories of presumed difference) on a number of grounds: What is its agenda? Is gender really such an unproblematic always-and-forever relevant variable? Perhaps unsurprisingly, given the research question's already problematic and sexist basis, Peter et al. found that 'crying frequency' and 'crying proneness' were reported more frequently in women, and high scores on these indices were associated with emotional instability. What should we make of this research? The 'science' behind it makes the investigators dispassionate observers, presenting the 'facts' in a disinterested way. This is bad science in two ways. First, in terms of the process – rather than conducting an analysis of people actually crying, the research relied on people's self-reports. Crying is again taken as the easily described measure, something arising from a person's internal emotional state, to be linked to other 'factors' such as gender and emotional stability. Second, it is bad science in terms of outcome and the potential harm it does to whole sections of human society.

In developing this approach to crying, I (Alexa) decided that rather than assuming I knew what crying was, I should look closely at the kind of things participants themselves treated as signs of upset. As with 'inequality' and 'memory', a discursive psychology approach asks more basic research questions such as 'what is crying?' as opposed to more traditional psychological research questions such as 'how is crying related to gender and depression?'. DP thereby avoids (as much as possible) importing the analysts' own understandings about what these things are. To represent these signs of upset in the transcript, I drew upon the work of conversation analysts such as Gail Jefferson (1979). Jefferson notes that if we assume that laughter, like crying, is an uncontrolled bodily function – a 'flooding out' that is therefore not part of the ongoing vocal interaction – we will be tempted to merely note that it occurred, rather than transcribe it in detail. Jefferson takes an example where laughter was originally presented in a transcript as 'bubbling through' the talk, and shows that with a more detailed transcript the laughter was only present in that part of the talk that involved 'the saying of an obscenity' (Jefferson, 1979: 30). As a 'complex and interactionally delicate' task, at least in this context, the saying of an obscenity is 'distorted' by laughter. A more developed transcript is therefore vital to any understanding of the variety of interactional features of laughter in different contexts. This chapter develops a similar case for the analysis of the interactional properties of crying.

One of the early research tasks was to develop an extension to the Jeffersonian transcription scheme to represent crying's different interactional features such as sobs, whispers, wet sniffs and tremulous voice, as well as the usual features of delivery (e.g., silences, emphasis, pitch changes) that conversation analysts have shown to be crucial to speakers' actions in talk (see chapter appendix for details). This fine-grained description of crying, which provides a way of seeing how the different activities in crying and crying recipiency are organized together, obviously makes the transcript more of a challenge for the uninitiated reader. The thing to stress about this detail is that, as analysis shows, it represents noises and patterns of delivery that are crucial to the participants themselves (see Hepburn, 2004; Hepburn & Potter, 2007).

In the following extract, again from the NSPCC child protection helpline corpus, various characteristic elements of crying on the helpline are highlighted in the right hand column, e.g. CPO uptake such as 'right-thing' descriptions (RT), 'take-your-times' (TYT) and 'empathic receipts' (ER). These characterizations of action are grounded in the interaction, not pre-defined codings. The caller has phoned to report an attack on his son. He has become upset over the course of the report of abuse.

Extract 3 JK distraught dad

```
 1   Caller:   >.Hhih .hhihhh<
 2   CPO:      D'you want- d'y'wann'ave [a break for a    ] moment.=          ←TYT
 3   Caller:                            [Hhuhh >.hihh<]
 4             =>hhuhh hhuhh<
 5             (0.6)
 6   Caller:   .shih
 7             (0.3)
 8   Caller:   °°k(hh)ay°°
 9             (1.8)
10   Caller:   .shih >hhuh hhuh[h]<
11   CPO:                      [S]'very har:d when                            ←ER
12             they're not there with you isn't it.=                          ←ER
13             and [you're-] (.) you're tal:kin about it.                     ←ER
14   Caller:       [>.hhih<]
15             (0.8)
16   Caller:   >.Hhuh .HHuh<
17             (2.1)
18   Caller:   .shih
19             (0.2)
20   Caller:   °.shih? (.) °° (Need) hhelp(h) °°
21             (2.5)
22   Caller:   .HHhihh?hh?
23             (0.5)
24   Caller:   HHhuhh >.hih .hih<
25             (0.7)
26   CPO:      .Htk.hh Well you're doing what you can now to                  ←RT
27             actually offer them protection and help though                ←RT
28             are:n't you.                                                   ←RT
```

```
29  Caller:   .Skuh (.) Huhhhh
30            (0.5)
31  Caller:   °°I:'m not the(hehheh)re. Hh °°
32            (3.2)
33  Caller:   .Shih
34            (0.4)
```

Once we have a description that allows this level of detail to be revealed we can start to observe a range of interesting features about the way the extract develops – we will try to give a flavour of the style of analysis here. First, note the way the take-your-time in line 2 is occasioned by both the caller's sobbing that starts in line 1 and continues through to line 4, as well as his long silences prior to the start of this extract. In a previous study, Hepburn and Potter (2007) noted the way 'take-your-times' are typically offered by CPOs where callers are attempting, but failing, to articulate talk. They suggested that they offer both a licence for the late delivery of talk, and a formulation of, and account for, the time already taken. The caller's whispered response on 8 is delayed and preceded and followed by sobs and a sniff – all common features that constitute crying on this helpline (Hepburn, 2004).

The CPO's turn on lines 11–13 is the type of turn that we have elsewhere (Hepburn, 2004; Hepburn and Potter, 2007) called an 'empathic receipt', a recurrent object in calls which contain crying, but extremely rare in non-crying NSPCC calls. Empathic receipts are made up of two key elements:

1   a formulation of the crying party's mental/emotional state;

2   a marker of the contingency or source of that formulation.

They can also provide an account for the caller's crying, especially in ways that draw upon known-in-common features of the world.

This turn fits the pattern, in that it indexes the caller's difficulties in dealing with the current situation: '[S]'very har:d,' in combination with generalized features of the world 'when they're not there with you'. Note the scripted (Edwards, 1994) quality of 'they're' and 'you,' indexing things known in common about parents and children, and things any parent would feel in this situation. This turn thus offers an account for the caller's crying episode, and is combined with a marker of contingency – the tag question 'isn't it?' –which treats the caller as having the primary access to his own feelings about how hard it is.

Following a further delay, and sobbing and sniffing noises (lines 14–19), we continue with the caller's response on line 20 offering what sounds like a whispered formulation of the needs of his sons, which itself may be offering further elaboration and accounting for what makes his situation 'very hard' and therefore upsetting – he is some distance away and his sons need his help. It therefore has elements of self-flagellation, in which the caller is blaming himself for his inability to help. This is followed by further long delays and sobs prior to the CPO's further turn on lines 26–28 – 'Well you're doing what you can now to actually offer them protection and help though aren't you.' Another simplified description of these types of turns is a 'right thing description' (Hepburn, 2004). These appear commonly in crying receipts on the helpline, and typically entail descriptions constructed from information provided by the caller, in which the caller is described as having done the right thing in some way.

The CPO's 'right thing' turn here contains a number of features that build it as contrastive to the caller's prior (somewhat self-deprecating) response to what is making his situation seem 'very hard' – that his sons need his help, and he's not there. First, it is 'well' prefaced, a common contrastive move in talk. Second it emphasizes what the caller is 'doing now'. Third, the formulation of the caller's 'protection and help' is marked by 'actually' (line 27), another feature that picks out the offering of protection and help as contrastive, and fourth, the whole description is finished with 'though', yet another contrastive element. Hence the whole of the CPO's turn here is designed to counter the caller's assessment of his 'very hard' situation as something that arises from his own impotence or negligence with regard to his sons – it is therefore an aligning and supportive description. This whole turn shows up the wonderful subtlety of the CPO's talk and her enormous practical sensitivity to the different features of the caller's barely audible whispered turn in line 20.

More generally, although emotion is often thought of as something that is beyond the purchase of a discursive approach such as DP ('isn't it all just about talk?' is a common complaint!), studies of this kind show the way that issues and actions which we understand as emotional can be tractable to interaction analysis. DP offers the possibility of understanding the various phenomena loosely glossed as emotion by the more 'scientific' approaches in psychology, in terms of what they are doing and where they appear in peoples' lives. It also starts to unpack what we might loosely understand as 'empathy' in a more specified way.

In terms of critical psychology, the problem with ethological and cognitive notions of emotion is that they encourage a static determinist notion of human action. They make emotion seem very resistant to change, and thereby encourage a conservative approach to understanding people. These more traditional constructions of emotion also imply that explanations for action need to consider the *features of individuals*, as do programmes for change, rather than seeing actions in relation to broader social and political arrangements.

Just as with the notion of memory, a very different perspective than that of the traditional 'factors and variables' approach in psychology comes from taking *practices* rather than *emotions* as primary. We move away from seeing emotions as inner objects that influence behaviour and are perceived by looking inwards, to seeing them instead as public, social entities that have a role in getting things done. Moreover, by focusing on practices as discursive psychology does we can get away from the abstract, technical concerns of psychologists and start to consider issues that arise as important for people in the settings of their everyday lives.

This research therefore starts with the orientations of the participants – it begins with what the participants themselves treat as crying. It is not attempting to improve on the understanding that is embedded in these practices; rather it is trying to make that understanding explicit and track its organization. Tracking these different elements of crying shows us just how subtle Child Protection Officers can be in identifying and responding to 'emotional turbulence'. Once we have explicated these orientations we can start to make more refined observations. For example Hepburn (2004) showed that a lack of attention to, and acknowledgment of, crying in calls to the helpline was present in more problematic calls, where callers terminated the call before giving crucial details about abuse.

social justice: implications and applications

Social justice is a central concern of discursive psychology. DP has at least three major areas of contribution to the promotion of social justice.

First, the classic work in discursive psychology was concerned with issues such as racism and sexism. The particular focus of Wetherell and Potter (1992), for example, was on the way inequalities could be discursively legitimated through people's flexible use of a range of interpretative repertoires and rhetorical commonplaces. The key point here was to highlight the way the repertoires and commonplaces functioned to undermine movements toward social justice by minority groups such as New Zealand Maori.

Second, one achievement of the classic work was to highlight the way notions of social justice were themselves mobilized against minority and less powerful groups. One of the features of the 'new racism' for example was its mobilization of notions of justice and fairness (Augoustinos, Tuffin, & Every, 2005). Thus DP provides an analytic approach that can consider critically the way social justice is mobilized in practice.

Third, recent discursive psychology has focused on providing a more socially and institutionally situated alternative to traditional cognitive, neurocognitive and individualistic psychology. DP has inspired doubts about the ability of traditional psychology to address issues of social justice because of its failure to theorize the interactional and institutionally situated nature of human action. The NSPCC helpline work, for example, situates emotion as something relational and institutionally situated. It offers simultaneously a critique and alternative to traditional individually reductive approaches to emotion and new pathways to application. Specifically it works with the NSPCC in support of their provision of social justice for abused children.

In terms of the 'utility' and 'engagement' of this research with the NSPCC, CPOs report the feedback from this research as providing them with valuable aids to appreciating and reconsidering their own practices. The research can be seen as an attempt to turn practices into strategies (Hepburn, 2006), where the kinds of embodied, untheorized, practices that people do in a highly occasioned and finessed way are explicated by the researcher. This allows those identified practices to be turned into strategies, for example of successful practice or increased reflexivity, to prevent a communication breakdown with vulnerable groups.

■ ■ main chapter points ■

1 Discursive psychology positions itself as countering the individualistic, cognitivist and conservative approaches that dominate contemporary mainstream psychology.

2 Discursive psychologists have rejected presuppositions that 'expressions of emotion' are straightforward traces of underlying psychological states. By contrast, they have shown the way emotion avowals and emotion displays can be parts of particular activities, for example, managing issues of blame and responsibility. Such work suggests both that we should be cautious about taking emotion avowals and displays as immediate evidence of underlying emotional states, and that they may be involved in other activities.

3 Like conversation analysts, DP practitioners have also expressed caution about how far people's abstract judgments and claims about their actions can capture what goes on in practice.

4 The form of constructionism here is distinct from some other varieties. It is focused on the constructions of participants in their talk and texts. The focus is therefore on specific descriptions or conversations, and what they are being used to do. It appreciates the enormous sophistication of people as world constructors, and the elaborate set of resources that they have available for building constructions, as well as the further set of resources that can be used to tear them down.

5 We hope to have demonstrated that taking *interactional practices* rather than *cognition* and *emotion* as our primary explanatory resource we can start to consider issues that are displayed as important for people in the settings in which they live their lives.

glossary

- **cognitivism:** the idea that human action must be explained by reference to underlying cognitive processes and entities.

- **conversation analysis:** an analytic perspective that reveals the normative organization of action in interaction.

- **discourse analysis:** the study of language use and its role in social and psychological life. It highlights the practical and constructive use of language, and the way versions of the world are used in actions such as blaming and accounts.

- **discursive psychology:** an approach to psychology that understands it as an object in and for interaction.

- **rhetoric:** a focus on the way talk and texts are organized to counter alternatives. It emphasizes the way even apparently individual assertions such as attitudes and beliefs are often rhetorically organized.

▪ ▪reading suggestions ▪

Edwards (1997) provides a high level overview of how a discursive psychological perspective transforms notions such as scripts categories, knowledge and emotion, which have hitherto been understood as cognitive or internal phenomena. Edwards and Potter (1992) provide the foundational statement of the discursive psychological approach illustrated by a reworking of classic studies in memory and attribution and exploring a set of political controversies. Hepburn and Wiggins (2007) is the first book to collect together a wide set of discursive psychological research. Potter (1996) develops a discursive psychological rewriting of the perspective of constructionism, focusing on the way versions of the world are produced and made solid and objective.

: // internet resources /

- **Online resources** including transcription tutorial, audio and video resources and a number of online publications: www.lboro.ac.uk/departments/ss/centres/darg/dargindex.htm

 ■ **Questions**

1   Consider the following conclusions from Edwards:

The conceptual repertoire of emotions provides for an extraordinary flexibility in how actions, reactions, dispositions, motives and other psychological characteristics can be assembled in narratives and explanations of human conduct. (1999: 288)

Consider the way that Edwards's conclusions about the operation of emotion discourse can be exemplified by the data fragment below. You can then compare your suggestions with Edwards's (1999: 277) analysis.

1   *Mary:*   (. . .) so that's when I decided to (.) you know to tell him. (1.0) U::m (1.0)

2   and then::, (.) obviously you went through your a:ngry stage, didn't you?

3   (.)

4   Ve:ry upset obviously, .hh an:d uh, (0.6) we: started ar:guing a lot, an:d

5   (0.6) just drifted awa:y.

2   What are the implications of a non-cognitivist approach

   (a) for psychology as a discipline?

   (b) in terms of fitting a critical agenda?

3   In what ways can the close study of interaction make connections with personal,
    social, political and cultural understandings of people and their institutions?

appendix – transcription notation

The transcription notation is most fully described in Jefferson (2004). Hepburn
(2004) has developed symbols specifically for dealing with features of crying.

general transcription notion

[ ]	Square brackets mark the start and end of overlapping speech.
↑	Vertical arrows precede marked pitch movement, over and above normal rhythms of speech. They are for marked, hearably significant shifts. The aim is to capture interactionally significant features, that are hearable as such to an ordinary listener.
→	Side arrows are not transcription features, but draw analytic attention to particular lines of text.
Underlining	signals vocal emphasis; the extent of underlining within individual words locates emphasis, but also indicates how heavy it is.
CAPITALS	mark speech that is obviously louder than surrounding speech.
°↑I know it,°	Degree signs enclose obviously quieter speech (i.e., hearably produced as quieter, not just someone who is distant).
that's r*ight.	Asterisks precede a 'squeaky' vocal delivery.
(0.4)	Numbers in round brackets measure pauses in seconds (in this case, four tenths of a second).
(.)	A micropause, hearable but too short to easily measure.
((text))	Additional comments from the transcriber, e.g. context or intonation.
she wa::nted	Colons show degrees of elongation of the prior sound; the more colons, the more elongation.
hhh	Aspiration (out-breaths); proportionally as for colons.
.hhh	Inspiration (in-breaths) – note the full stop to differentiate from out breaths; proportionally as for colons.
Yeh,	The comma marks continuing intonation, that the speaker has not finished; marked by fall-rise or weak rising intonation, as when enunciating lists.

y'know?	Question marks signal a stronger, 'questioning' intonation, that is irrespective of grammar.
Yeh.	Periods (full stops) mark falling, stopping intonation ('final contour'), that is irrespective of grammar.
bu-u-	Hyphens mark a cut-off of the preceding sound.
>he said<	'Greater than' and 'lesser than' signs enclose speeded-up talk.
solid.=	'Equals' signs mark the immediate 'latching' of successive talk, whether of one or more speakers, with no interval.
heh heh	Voiced laughter. Can have other symbols added, such as underlinings, pitch movement, extra aspiration, etc.
sto(h)p i(h)t	Laughter particles within speech signalled by h's in round brackets.

_____ *features of crying* _____

°°help°°	Whispering or mouthing – enclosed by double degree signs.
.shih	Wet sniff.
~grandson~	Tremulous voice – enclosed by tildes.
↑Sorry	High pitch – represented by one or more upward arrows.
k(hh)ay	Aspiration in speech – an 'h' represents aspiration: in parenthesis this indicates a sharper more plosive sound.
hhhelp	Outside parenthesis indicates a softer more breathy sound.
Huhh .hhih	Sobbing – combinations of 'hhs', some with full stops before them to indicate
Hhuyuhh	Inhaled rather than exhaled, many have voiced vowels, some have voiced
>hhuh<	Consonants. If sharply inhaled or exhaled – enclosed in the 'greater than/less' SYMBOLS (><)

Part 3

Critical Social Issues

12

Race and Racism

Kevin Durrheim, Derek Hook,
and Damien W. Riggs

Chapter Topics

Research on racial prejudice and discrimination within the discipline of psychology has traditionally sought to understand why individual people engage in behaviours defined as 'racist'. This large body of research has also examined how racism affects people's lives. As such, psychological research has demonstrated not only the existence of racism but also its negative effects.

This body of research, however, has a number of limitations that arise from how it conceptualizes the category of race itself. First, its starting point is typically an individualised understanding of racism as the product of individual beliefs or cognitions. Second, this research has largely focused on racism as it occurs in interpersonal relations, thus again restricting its interest to individual enactments of or responses to prejudice. And third, this research has often relied upon a notion of race that presumes that racial categories reflect actual differences between groups of people.

(How) Can We Talk/Write About Race?

'Race' is a social construction. The idea that people are divided into groups designated as races is the outcome of historical, locally prescribed ways of seeing, thinking and talking which have their roots in the racist history of colonialism, slavery, and apartheid. For this reason even use of such race labels is considered offensive in many contexts. Many critical writers have thus adopted the convention of placing the word 'race' as well as references to supposedly racial categories – e.g., 'black', 'white' – in quotes. This practice interrupts an easy commonsense reading of race, and signals the constructed nature of such categories.

On the other hand, as we also argue in this chapter, 'race' is also very real in many material and political ways. The legacy of racism has entrenched massive inequalities between groups of people designated as races – e.g., in terms such as health, wealth, and land ownership. And these differences continue to be perpetuated by ongoing practices of segregation and exclusion which means that power continues to be concentrated in the hands of groups that have benefited from an explicitly racist past. In such contexts there are good political reasons for wanting to emphasize the reality and not the constructedness of race. In South Africa, for example, many critical scholars argue that it is very convenient for white writers to argue that race is nothing but a social construction at a time when government is designing programmes of affirmative action and land redistribution which aim to address the material legacy of colonialism and apartheid. And so there are critical writers who argue against the use of scare quotes in talk and writing.

In contemporary Australia the explicit naming of white privilege is often undertaken as a political move aimed at challenging racialised power. To place 'white' in quotes in this context would thus potentially let white Australians 'off the hook', downplaying the realness of their privilege. In addition, not using scare quotes allows for the recognition of ways of knowing held by Indigenous people: Indigenous understandings of place and belonging retain a distinct and unique sense of meanings which should not be simply 'translated' into the terms of white people. As such it is important to acknowledge such terms as holding their own legitimacy as descriptors of the world.

What this shows is that race and race categorizing are troubling in different ways in different contexts. As we argue in this chapter, race is socially constructed and yet takes very real material forms; it is often the basis for a sense of identity and a terrain for contesting power. There are many different identity-related and political effects of either putting 'racial' categorizations under question – e.g. by the use of scare quotes – or of not doing so. It all depends on the context: Who is doing the representing, to what ends, in what historical and political context?

After much deliberation, we have decided not to use scare quotes in this chapter. Instead, we invite the reader to think about which racial designations in this chapter they feel should (and should not) be in quotes, and to reflect on why they think so.

By contrast, the rapidly growing body of critical psychological research on racism starts out with a focus on power relations. Racism is understood primarily as the product of particular historical relationships between groups of people in which some people have unjustly asserted claims to dominance over others. In this sense, 'race' refers to a form of categorization that reflects particular power relations between groups rather than reflecting actual group attributes (physical or behavioural). Racism, then, is thinking and behaviour that seek to preserve race hierarchy.

In applying this understanding of race and racism to research, critical psychologists have asked questions that differ considerably from those of psychologists working from more traditional perspectives. Instead of focusing primarily on beliefs or cognitions, critical psychologists have examined how individuals and groups are located in broader historical and social relations and how their identities emerge from these relations. They also study how race categories are deployed in commonplace ways, and how this serves to maintain the belief that races are real or natural. While questioning the reality of race, critical psychologists have also examined the very real effects of racism. They have attempted to show how racism shapes the lives of people who are both privileged and oppressed by the operations of racism, marginalized and dominant social groups.

In this chapter we (a) outline two traditional approaches to psychological research on racism (and their critical impulses and limitations), (b) introduce the dominant critical psychological approach to understanding racism (and its limitations), and (c) provide an account of racism through the lens of critical psychology that encompasses both individual interactions and their location within particular social and material contexts. We suggest that racism must be understood in terms of both institutionalized inequality and socialized patterns of talk, interaction, representation and behaviour that reiterate and extend these institutionalized relations. In this respect we propose studying beliefs and feelings about race in terms of collective psychology, as a feature of what we term **distributed mind**. Race is part of a collective knowledge that allows people to coordinate social interaction in racist terms while explicitly denying racism. In our social interactions, in talk and embodied practices, we reproduce not only explicit beliefs of race but also implicit beliefs that constitute the **background** to what we say and do in everyday situations of social encounters, conversations and interactions.

traditional approaches

Traditional approaches to the psychological study of racism have been important for naming racism and for attempting to understand why it persists. Indeed, as we discuss below, two major theories in psychology – personality and cognition – have been used critically to challenge racism.

personality

One of the most important early social psychological understandings of racism emerged in the aftermath of the Second World War. Both the hatred and the intensive intergroup conflict of world war, epitomized in this instance by the Holocaust, raised urgent questions about the source of prejudice even in supposedly civilized and developed societies. Such excesses of violence and bigotry – evident in the spread of anti-Semitism and fascist ideology – suggested that a psychological pathology may lie at the root of racism. This idea was formalized in theories of authoritarianism (Adorno, Frenkel-Brunswik, Levinson, & Sanford, 1950; Fromm, 1941) that described the personality type susceptible to fascist and racist ideologies. Racism and out-group intolerance were understood as character traits that were anchored in a personality syndrome, a stable organization of psychological and unconscious needs and desires that determined the attitudes and actions of authoritarian individuals. Such psychoanalytic explanations focused on irrational aspects of the personality, on basic emotional needs, indeed, on 'the most primitive wishes and fears' (Adorno et al., 1950: 10) which could be manipulated by propaganda and the efforts of political leaders. The origin of authoritarianism was traced to early childhood development. Several factors were considered to be of primary importance: rigid discipline at home, an emphasis on strictly prescribed roles and duties, interrelationships of dominance and submission, and conditional affection (Adorno et al., 1950).

The Freudian influence behind this theory is evident in the idea that punitive childrearing practices produce in children hostility and aggression toward their parents. Since this cannot be expressed – for fear of punishment – it is repressed, producing individuals who, on the surface, idealize and are submissive to their parents. Later, this repressed aggression is displaced onto those deemed inferior in society, and is manifest as racial prejudice. An authoritarian personality is thus based on a sado-masochistic personality structure which finds comfort in submission to authority whilst displacing aggression onto out-groups who are made blameworthy for society's ills. Authoritarians glorify authority figures, stress obedience to law and order, maintain a conventional and conservative outlook on life, and hate minorities and out-groups (Altemeyer, 1988).

Importantly, the theory of authoritarianism acknowledges that racism at the individual level must be connected to a broader system of power. Fascism, say Adorno et al., 'is imposed on the people' (1950: 480) and it must be understood in conjunction with a variety of structural features of society such as the breakdown of traditional belief systems and the confusion and uncertainty arising from industrialization and modernization. Authoritarianism was accordingly understood as a historically specific personality syndrome linked to the fear of freedom that was produced by modernization (Fromm, 1941). This was a radical theory that attempted to understand how social structures (the industrialized capitalist state) were supported by a particular psychological substrate. Unfortunately, the radical impulse of this theory was lost as later theorists focused their attention on early childhood relationships and longstanding patterns of family interaction and much of the research became concerned with how best to measure authoritarianism.

The strength of this personality-based theory lies in its ability to account for such extremes of hatred. It attempts to understand the emotional factors underlying racism; it argues that there may be a degree of pleasure in racism, that the racist affirms his or her identity by denigrating others (Hook, 2006, 2008). As such, personality theorists were able to appreciate not only racism's resistance to change, but also the fact that it so often erupts into violence and hatred. However, this strength of the personality approach coincides with its weakness. While these theorists hoped that racist irrationality could be dispelled – through rational critique – the theory implies that challenging racism requires, first, the changing of individual personalities. A prerequisite of social change would, presumably, be the undoing of childhood upbringing. By continual reference to a depth psychology that locates racism predominantly in the unconscious mental processes of individuals, personality accounts leave themselves open to claims that they ignore situational influences and the ongoing interaction between subjects and their environment (Billig, 1976). Systemic change thus seems almost impossible: once we understand racism in terms of personality, as a learned character trait or unconscious emotional dynamic, how, other than by long-term psychotherapy, might it be eradicated? This approach offers us little by way of a theory of progressive social change. By emphasizing individual *pathology*, the theory neglects the fact that racism may emerge in a variety of social situations and institutions without any evident pathology and without maladjusted individuals.

cognition

The cognitive tradition in psychology explains racism in terms of mental processes that, it argues, operate behind what we do and say, and which prestructure our perceptions of the world. This approach suggests that a cognitive 'perceptual readiness' is apparent at the moment of perception, which is already an interpretation of the world (Bruner, 1957). We perceive 'things' in the world in terms of the categories of our culture: for example, we see 'chairs' and 'tables', 'men' and 'women', 'blacks', 'whites', 'Asians' and 'Muslims'. All of these categories, group differences and their meanings are socially constructed and yet we tend to see the world in these terms. Thus, the groundwork for racism is already laid at the moment of perception.

Underlying mental processes do more than partition the world into stable social categories. They also operate behind the scenes to render these categories fully meaningful. Association, the linking of one set of meanings with another, is of fundamental importance for cognitive theory because it allows people to 'go beyond the information given' (Bruner, 1973). We stereotype by associating certain sets of features and attributes with the categories of people we encounter, thus allowing us to know more about them than we can see.

Like the theory of authoritarianism, cognitive accounts of racism were developed to understand and criticize a particular sociohistorical system of inequality and discrimination, namely, the Jim Crow racism of the American South in the first half of the twentieth century. This was a social system that maintained race-based power differentials by means of segregation in which black children were bussed away from their neighbourhoods to black-designated schools where they received an inferior education. The legality of this racist practice came under scrutiny in the landmark *Brown vs. Board of Education* Supreme Court case in 1954. A team of psychologists led by Kenneth Clark (see Clark, 1953) provided an academic statement of the psychological damage that segregation perpetuated. They also argued that desegregation could proceed smoothly even in the face of the virulent racism of many whites who believed that blacks had less ability to learn.

Clark's latter argument was directly informed by cognitive theory. In the words of Allport, 'the 1954 decision said in effect personality is irrelevant. A social change can ... be wrought without a prior effort to alter individual feelings' (1962: 121). Rather than being fixed in personality, racism could be addressed by changing social practices. The network of mental categories, associations and beliefs that individuals carried around with them could be realigned by changing the way they interacted with others. According to the contact hypothesis (Allport, 1954), desegregation would bring blacks and whites together where they would establish friendly relationships and have their stereotypes disconfirmed. This would spark a whole realignment of beliefs and feelings about the other group; a psychological balance would be achieved by eliminating contradictions between positive and negative beliefs or emotions toward the same groups.

However, the cognitive tradition has been criticized for naturalizing racism by explaining it as the outcome of universal mental processes of categorization and stereotypical association (Hopkins, Reicher, & Levine, 1997). It often ignores the ways in which group differences are a social product, the outcome of historical patterns of exploitation and representation, and are reliant upon ongoing power relations that position people in the specific racial terms relevant to the particular social context in which they are developed. Instead, race categories are taken as reflecting natural points of group difference. In theorizing prejudice as the natural outcome of individual cognition, there is a considerable risk of reifying points of difference as a priori, rather than conceiving of race in terms of social factors, as constructed points of difference. This shifts attention away from historically forged networks of power relations that construct particular groups as mattering more than others.

critical psychological approaches

Critical psychological research on racism has sought to show that racial categories continue to matter not only because of their location within ongoing histories of discrimination and privilege, but also because we continue to ascribe value to them as ways of understanding or interpreting the world. Discourse analytic research, in particular, has revealed how racism can be perpetuated in everyday talk by people who perceive themselves to be anti-racist.

<hr>

discourse and race talk

The discursive approach focuses on the analysis of text. Written transcriptions of spoken interaction have been of primary concern. This approach has allowed discursive psychologists to focus squarely on how expressions of racism are developed in social interaction and how they are justified, criticized and defended. This tradition provides us with rich descriptions about how talk of race is done and how it is accounted for.

The starting point for this work is the idea that race is a social construction. In describing the social world, speakers construct different versions of given social groups, or others. These constructions – which typically entail stereotypes and generalizations about what such 'others' are like – are motivated by certain types of benefit, and can be used in a variety of ways. For example, based on a series of interviews conducted with Pakeha (white) New Zealanders, Wetherell and Potter (1992) identified several key ways in which Pakehas spoke about Maori people. Their findings highlighted the variable and often contradictory character of these representations. For example, the Maori people were portrayed both as a group defined by traditional culture and as a group who had lost their culture through modernization. Such findings suggested that Pakeha stereotypes and beliefs about the Maori were not part of a consistent psychological attitude or underlying prejudice. Rather, these beliefs were part of a collectively shared racist background to New Zealand social life, which Potter and Wetherell argued could be studied by identifying **interpretative repertoires**, which are 'recurrently used systems of terms used for characterizing and evaluating actions, events and other phenomena ... organized around specific metaphors and figures of speech (tropes)' (1987: 149). Interpretative repertoires are collective routines of language use which order perceptions and interactions. In these terms we can understand racial stereotypes and beliefs not as individual mental representations but as social representations that have been developed historically to justify racist practices and hierarchies.

In addition to providing content (metaphors) about race, the collectively shared racist background also provides strategies for talking about race. The idea that prejudice is irrational is part of common sense, and thus speakers avoid being seen to be prejudiced as this would undermine their credibility. Accordingly, race talk takes the narrative form of the disclaimer, 'I'm not prejudiced, but ...' (Billig, 1988). This allows speakers to articulate racist views at the same time as denying racism. In his study of the European press and parliamentary discourse, van Dijk (1992) identified a number of rhetorical strategies by which racism was denied, including disclaimers, euphemisms, excuses and justification. Speakers framed racial interaction in non-racist terms (e.g., 'I did not threaten him, but gave him friendly advice'). They gave extenuating circumstances and justifications for actions and, ultimately, reversed the accusation of racism, redirecting it at others.

Discursive research also studies the distributed nature of race talk as 'joint action'. Not only is racism perpetrated in social interaction, by speakers drawing on resources of content and strategy that are informed by the background of social life, it is also perpetrated collaboratively as speakers excuse, justify or deny racism on behalf of others. For example, Condor, Figgou, Abell, Gibson, and Stevenson (2006) show how, in an informal discussion about race and neighbourhood, one speaker's expressions are worked up through the support of her interlocutors, who reinforce her comments by markers of agreement and interest and through displays of intersubjectivity echo her comments. Race talk, as well as definitions and denials of racism, are collaborative accomplishments.

The implication of this is that hearers, and not only speakers, are involved in the reproduction of racism. In his analysis of stereotyping by implication, Durrheim (under review) extends this line of analysis by showing how speakers carefully avoid expressing explicit race stereotypes, which can leave them open to censure and criticism. Instead, knowing that culturally competent listeners have access to a background knowledge of unutterable racist stereotypes, speakers can simply use forms of talk that gesture in regulated ways to invoke background knowledge and thus help hearers to get the full but unstated sense of race talk. Such 'stereotyping by implication' allows people to be explicitly non racist at the same time as reproducing racism in the background of social life. At the same time hearers are involved in doing part of the work of stereotyping, by attending to, making sense of and getting the full meaning of the race talk.

The theories and methods of discursive psychology have played a very important role in the development of critical psychology. Nonetheless, there are also limits to their value. Most importantly, the discursive approach has focused on language to the exclusion of other kinds of collective action and forms of social interaction. This elision is no mere coincidence. The strident constructionism and anti-realism of much discursive psychology has led to a suspicion of description, including people's descriptions of their social interactions. Correctly, descriptions are treated as occasioned and interested constructions of the world which perform a host of rhetorical functions. For example, the description of some race groups as intellectually inferior (a claim that regularly resurfaces in psychology, see Richards, 1997) serves to explain and justify unequal education outcomes, excuse school authorities, and put the blame for social inequality on the victims themselves. As a consequence of the constructive nature of descriptions, discursive psychologists restrict their interest to the use of language, showing how such descriptions are put together and defended in contexts of social interaction; and they remain agnostic about the reality or truth of the things described.

Notwithstanding these cautions about the constructed nature of description, a critical psychology must also focus on practices outside of language (Brown, 2001). This is because race categories are not only constructed in language, but also in other kinds of located and embodied interactions. Racial segregation, for example, is a material practice in which embodied and spatially located persons live, work and attend school in different places. Similarly, racial profiling involves recognizing people as members of a race category and discriminating against them in various ways, such as by a police search and arrest. In fact, the system of racial inequality which critical psychology seeks to challenge is constituted from an array of such racial practices, ranging from rude gestures, or being followed around in stores while shopping, to being denied employment and accommodation, and even to being shot at or threatened with violence (Feagin, 1991). Although such acts are often accompanied by talk, they need not be. As we highlight in the following section, racism may more productively be understood as the product of collective understandings of racial categories – or a 'distributed mind' – that plays out in both verbal and nonverbal interactions.

racism as a feature of 'distributed mind'

Social life depends on our ability to coordinate our activity with others in multiple and complex ways. For a conversation to proceed smoothly, for example, two people need to take turns speaking, start and stop speaking at the right time, and say the appropriate thing when it is their turn to speak, in an appropriate way, accompanied by gestures and facial expressions. Our ability to coordinate our activity in this way depends on the existence of shared implicit knowledge which culturally competent members have access to. To interact successfully, we need to have a shared cultural knowledge about the rules, norms and conventions of action, as well as a mutual knowledge about what others in interaction know (Edwards, 1997). These two kinds of shared knowledge form the background to social life because our interactions depend on (are grounded in) them even though they are not consciously part of them.

What is the nature of this shared 'background' knowledge? Because it is implicit and action oriented, it is not what we would conventionally call knowledge, that is, information stored in our head. Rather, it is practical knowledge, a knowing *how*, not a knowing *what*. It is a knowledge that comes from the practice of *doing*, much like skills in sports such as tennis become embodied capacities. Tennis players know the rules of the game and the strategies that regulate play. They can predict where the ball might bounce, how their opponent might return a shot and so on. In short, they have a good implicit sense of the game, which is the result of an experience of playing. This is a kind of knowing that is embodied and developed in practice, not from reading manuals on the rules and strategies of tennis (although these may help).

A theory of this bodily knowledge of how to do things has been developed by Pierre Bourdieu through his notion of the **habitus**. Bourdieu (1988) directs our attention to the orientation of bodies in space, to aspects of demeanour and posture, to cadences of voice, movement and poise that remain grounded in the routines of a particular place or cultural location – that of the habitus. Bourdieu gives us a sense of how we pick up certain bodily dispositions, modes of relating, types of response – patterns of avoidance or of physical proximity, styles of reverence or aloofness – which become habits, automatic actions ingrained through the repetitions of everyday social practice, even though we have (perhaps) never explicitly learnt them. We are dealing here with a repertoire of appropriate types of being, ingrained styles of interaction and comportment, an etiquette of conduct which functions in a pre-reflexive and intuitive manner. The habitus is the tacit 'knowledge' that is apparent when people act in routine but accomplished ways. Not only is it the 'know-how' of successfully performed social acts in specific locations, it is also the appropriateness of how our actions, bodily comportment and demeanour suit certain situations and reflect a series of unstated social values. One might think, for example, of the poses, the movements, the spatial and embodied routines of activity, performance and dress that suit a typical beach holiday. This theory draws attention to the importance of 'how we hold ourselves' in social contexts, and to the role of such dispositions, behaviours and styles of interacting for sustaining particular forms of social life, including racist ones. We have thus a far wider range – of bodily, behavioural and interactional styles – within which to understand how people might *enact* racist presumptions. These non-verbal enactments – which cannot be caught in types of analysis that focus on language – may function to underpin and extend racism at an institutional level.

If action-oriented and implicit shared knowledge forms the background to social life, then our public actions, our conduct, constitute the **foreground**. The things we say and do, our routines of speech and action, are forms of conduct that are located in social contexts. These are the foreground of social life, subject to constraints of accountability that issue from the background. Our conduct is interpreted and judged by ourselves and others, and part of the work we have to do in conducting ourselves in social life is to account for our actions. All this work of accountability is done with reference to the background, the shared knowledge of the rules, norms and conventions of action in terms of which we justify ourselves and criticize other possible modes of conduct. In acting and in justifying and defending our actions, we show commitment to both our conduct and to the background. In this sense, our social conduct manifests an investment in a way of life. This investment is not some deep psychological attachment, but a series of commitments that are set in motion by action, by participating in social life.

The relation between foreground and background is dialectical as there is both agreement and contradiction between these two modalities of activity. Agreement between foreground and background is a social accomplishment that is effected when social actors communicate the background to their actions either explicitly or by nuance, implication, innuendo, and suggestion, and when this agreement is recognized by others. Disagreement, in contrast, is manifest when the flow in interaction is disrupted by challenges and calls to account.

The relationship between foreground and background, explicit and implicit knowledge, performance and habitus constitutes a 'distributed mind' – a set of rules and relationships that are commonly held by members of a particular culture. This concept of a distributed mind is particularly important when we examine racism, as it allows us to read not only the explicit, but also the background or shared knowledge that shapes the behaviours and language of racism. Distributed mind is a product of human interaction, the coordinated activity of people who conduct themselves in ways for which they are accountable. A special feature of distributed mind is that it has both an explicit and an implicit dimension which we have called the background and foreground to social life.

_____ racism as embodied and discursive practice _____

In this section we provide two examples of the aforementioned distributed mind in action. The first highlights the ways in which people can manage their lives, bodies and spaces in racial terms even when the rules governing this management are typically unmentioned. In the second example, the background of racial privilege is shown to be evident within talk even when it is not explicitly a topic of conversation.

Segregation on the beach Durrheim and Dixon (2005a) studied racial segregation on a beach in post-apartheid South Africa. They were interested in the 'micro-ecology' of segregation (see http://www.contactecology.com/), the ways in which people interact and use space so as to reduce intergroup contact. Although the beach was officially integrated, they observed high levels of segregation as different groups sat in different places on the beach and used the beach at different times. Most notably, white beachgoers arrived early and left as black people started arriving. Even without speaking, the beachgoers conducted themselves in a way in which race was highlighted and counted as meaningful. Segregation was not the explicit intention of the beachgoers – they came to the beach to relax. However, in doing so, they were also implicitly orienting to race. In all the ways in which they arrived at the beach – who they came with, when, where they sat, and when they left – individuals and groups of beachgoers were acting in such a way as to bring about collective patterns of racial segregation. Norms and expectations about race formed the background to their beach conduct.

Dixon's (2006) analysis of the Schelling simulation illustrates how collective racial phenomena such as segregation emerge from the coordinated practices of a collective of individuals who are not necessarily acting in a racist or race conscious manner. (Schelling segregation simulation demonstration software can be downloaded from http://www.econ.iastate.edu/tesfatsi/demos/schelling/schellhp.htm.) Using a spatial matrix much like a chess board, with individuals moving from square to square, Schelling shows how quickly a completely integrated space becomes almost completely segregated when each individual moves in such a way as to ensure that just a few of their neighbours are the same race as them. It is startling that none of the individuals want total segregation. However, by making lots of small choices for a little segregation, they produce at a collective level the kind of totally segregated space that none of them want. These simulations illustrate a number of important features of the distributed nature of racial thinking and practice. First, they show how the practices of many individuals who exercise small race-based preferences may result in collective outcomes that none of them intended. Second, once these unintended outcomes materialize, for example, in racial segregation, they produce a new reality that then feeds back into their preferences, choices and racial beliefs. Because of the existence of segregation, people develop race-based preferences for living among some people of their own race group.

Although Schelling's simulations are instructive, they ignore the role that talk plays in shaping people's preferences and in regulating the exercise of their choices. The beachgoers in Durrheim and Dixon's (2005a) study were not silent. They described what was going on, and they accounted for, justified and explained their own preferences in a series of interviews. Black beachgoers described how, under apartheid, they had been excluded from the beach; and they complained that now that they were allowed onto the beach they saw whites 'running away' from them, an act they interpreted as continuing white racism. Whites described the interaction in their own terms as blacks taking over and pushing them off the beach. In both these accounts we can discern implicit stereotypes that each group has of the other. Blacks believe that whites are racist and this is why they run away; and whites believe that blacks are aggressive and spiteful and this is why they push them out. From the background, as it were, these implicit stereotypes shape ongoing day-to-day interaction without necessarily being articulated or spelled out.

Both the talk about segregation and contact and the embodied practices of contact and division were socially coordinated forms of interaction, and in fact they were coordinated with each other. They were connected to each other by relations of possibility and constraint. For example, both black and white beachgoers pointed to practices of segregation and division on the beach to 'prove' the point that the other group was either running away from them or pushing them out. The reality of segregation was the condition which made the utterances about whites running away from blacks and blacks pushing whites out 'true'. The talk about segregation and the embodied practices of segregation were arranged in 'mutually reinforcing relations, each acting as the condition of possibility and constraint for the other' (Durrheim & Dixon, 2005b: 456).

Seeing race privilege in talk In Australia, continuing forms of colonization have resulted in dramatic disparities between the health and wellbeing outcomes of Indigenous and white Australians. Corollary to the disadvantages experienced by Indigenous people are the privileges accorded to white people. Understanding how racial privilege functions today is thus an important aspect of challenging racism (Riggs & Augoustinos, 2004, 2005).

Racial privilege is enacted in the everyday talk of white Australians when they a) assert the belief that Indigenous people, but not white people, belong to a racial group, b) assume that a white model of subjectivity is appropriate for understanding the experiences of all people, and c) reinforce stereotypes of Indigenous people and cultures that legitimate colonization. These three examples (amongst many others) serve to normalize white hegemony by pathologizing Indigenous people and thereby explaining away social and material inequality.

The extract below provides an example of how talk about welfare makes visible such hidden assumptions about white privilege in Australia. It also shows how this serves to justify social exclusion and inequality, blaming Indigenous people for their poor health, housing and other outcomes.

Extract 1

Andrew: There is a fine line between them being compensated and them taking advantage of their position as it is felt to be. A lot of Anglo-Australians would umm are sort of are concerned about, they feel they are taking advantage; they're given much more than they need …

In this extract constructions of 'us and them' are used to highlight the differences between groups referred to by the speaker as 'Anglo-Australians' and 'Aboriginals' in ways that render indigeneity the problematic category. Thus 'Anglo-Australians' are depicted as being upset because Indigenous people are 'taking advantage' and that 'they're given much more than they need'. Such accounts position Indigenous people stereotypically as being greedy and unappreciative rather than as being justly compensated for the impact of colonization.

Interestingly, despite the explicit focus on Indigenous people 'taking advantage' of the welfare system, we can also read these accounts for what they do not mention. The talk in Extract 1 betrays the tacit assumption that indeed, white Australians are privileged. Andrew notes that Indigenous people are 'given' things, denoting at the very least a group of people who are in the position to 'give'. The implication of this is not only that this particular group has the power and indeed privilege through which to give, but also that there must be a reason for such giving (i.e., colonization). So, there is an implicit recognition of privilege and historical injustice in the very act of arguing against welfare. Talk in this extract shows some of the ways in which the advantages that white people hold simply by being white are ignored, and instead Indigenous people are depicted as unjustly and ungratefully receiving handouts.

Extract 2 is about land rights claims:

Mark: Something the media failed to bring out – the sort of aid – you've been given all this chunk of land and that it was sort of 'save the backyards' kind of mentality and a lot of people got scared ... the truth of the matter was that unless they had continual contact with their land they didn't have a claim under that decision so I think that people failed to realise that *and* that scared a lot of people.

Andrew: Umm and I was surprised 'cos I guess you read about ... some group that was about to make a claim on Adelaide and it really freaked me out.

Mark introduces the topic of land rights by portraying sovereignty rights as 'aid'. Such a depiction fails to acknowledge ongoing histories of colonization by constructing the white Australian nation as generously giving aid or assistance to Indigenous people, rather than land rights following from the fact that the title to land was never ceded by Indigenous people. Constructing land rights as 'aid' allows Mark and other Australians to ignore perplexing questions about the colonial history by which land came to be in white hands and so remains an ongoing basis of white privilege in Australia. This historical amnesia of ongoing white privilege is shored up by expressions of incredulity at the land claims: 'I was surprised', 'it really freaked me out', 'scared a lot of people'. The very fact that the participants can appear so surprised by claims to a native title is a result of the ways in which white Australians are often able to ignore their own privilege.

The two extracts above show the subtle ways in which the background to social life in Australia, shared commonsense assumptions about 'race privilege' and inequality, shape the everyday interactions of white Australians. These routines and ways of talking are the product of what we refer to as distributed mind. They are collective and conventional ways of interacting that serve to reproduce race relations and the operations of race privilege. In these examples, as in the foregoing discussion of segregation on South African beaches, we need to pay careful attention not only to the uses of talk, but also to the practices, assumptions and conventions which ensure that such physical traces as bodily health, housing, and land ownership continue to reflect the racial injustices of the past.

conclusions: critical psychological challenges to racism

How then might we think about responding to racism, particularly when, as the above examples show, racism persists in a variety of socially interacted forms against a backdrop of implicit understandings? Harold Garfinkel's writings on ethnomethodology help us to develop a view of distributed, collective psychology at the supra-individual level of analysis, locating the agency in the background of social life. For Garfinkel, settings are self-organizing because they frame the rules, norms and conventions of actions in the meaningful ways we use to account for our conduct in them. It is this background, not individual intentions alone, that animates individual people:

'Any setting organizes its activities to make its properties as an organized environment of practical activities detectable, countable, recordable, reportable, tell-a-story-aboutable, analysable, in short accountable' (1967: 33).

This self-organizing accountability of settings means that our talk about race and our practices and material arrangements are 'articulated' with or connected to each other. The articulation between talk and embodied practice can be explicitly stated, as when the white beachgoers that Durrheim and Dixon spoke to explained that they left the beach because they were being pushed out. However, even when race talk and other material and embodied products of racism are not explicitly linked, they are still 'articulated' with each other because they both have their source in the self-organizing accountability of settings. Thus, the talk of white Australians is organized in the broader context of colonization, dispossession and privilege that always already determines how differing groups relate to one another. A first task for a critical psychology of racism is to try to understand how the domains of talk and embodied routines of practice work together, are jointly articulated, and thus come to exceed the effects of either on its own.

A second task for a critical psychology of racism is to disrupt the conventional organization of race. Garfinkel's work is useful here too because he provides a framework for thinking about how to challenge the background: 'For these background expectancies to come into view one must either be a stranger to the 'life as usual' character of everyday scenes, or become estranged from them' (1967: 37). He gives a number of examples of how this estrangement from everyday life can be accomplished. For example, Garfinkel instructed his students to ask 'What do you mean?' about mundane features of ordinary conversations. In response to the report that an acquaintance had a flat tyre, one student asked, 'What do you mean you had a flat tyre'? This strategy of disrupting the routines of everyday life is called **Garfinkeling**. It produces confusion; it disrupts ongoing social interaction; and it is often read as being impolite. It also has critical potential because it can force the tacit background of life into the foreground if the comfortable but tacit routines of conduct are spelled out, and made explicit.

Garfinkeling thus provides a platform for developing a practical anti-racism. We can challenge racism by interrupting the routine action – both of talk and embodied practices – through which the racist background of social life is reproduced. There are two basic classes of strategy for doing this. The first involves 'saying the unsayable': speaking out on what cannot be said, that is, the background racist presumptions which are effective because they are implicit in unfolding social situations. For example, we can show how talk that is not explicitly racist nonetheless enacts racial privilege. Critical psychological research can make explicit the hidden presumptions about race that inform many discussions about crime, immigration, welfare, national identity (or other social problems).

There is a related strategy for interrupting the implicit routines of racism. Rather than speaking out what otherwise remains implicit, one might act as though one 'doesn't get' the background social assumptions being re-enacted. This can force others to make them explicit. Like Garfinkel's students, we can interrupt racist routines through staged ignorance. As a broader form of social or discursive analysis, this would amount to a demonstration that a variety of everyday assumptions about where to live, who deserves safety, power, and so on, often rely precisely on unarticulated racist notions that can be made more overt.

The concept of distributed mind highlights the subtle and mundane ways in which racial discrimination and privilege are perpetuated. Rather than being authored by explicitly racist individuals, racism is the production of the tacit and collective knowledge, know-how and assumptions that inform our interactions in everyday life. By conducting analyses of distributed mind, critical psychologists can design education programmes to highlight the subtle operation of racism in institutions and increase awareness of how ordinary talk is implicated in ongoing racism. Rather than apportioning blame, such interventions would show how histories of oppression continue to be played out in concrete ways in everyday life.

These strategies of disruption can be applied in many different ways and at different levels of analysis. They needn't involve talk, but can be undertaken by interrupting routines of activity. For example, people who live in segregated worlds have routines of commuting and visitation – places they go to and places they avoid – that maintain segregation. Breaking these can be personally challenging because they help people to confront their fears and concerns. These strategies can also be targeted at collective rather than individual levels of analysis. Policies and laws that target society as a whole can be very effective in disrupting racist routines. The desegregation rulings, affirmative action and other policies such as bussing that have been applied in the USA, South Africa and elsewhere typically encounter fierce resistance from whites precisely because they challenge taken for granted racist assumptions about what is fair, just and right.

Finally, a caveat. The success of such strategies is not guaranteed. There are no foolproof strategies for social change. All that disrupting routine can do is to set in motion new forms of accounting and activity. The outcome of such activity, its trajectory and anti-racist potential, depends on what social actors make of that situation.

▮ ▮ main chapter points ▮

1 Although racism must be understood as a socialized pattern of talk, it cannot be reduced to language; it must also be viewed in reference to embodied practices which extend institutionalized forms of inequality.

2 Such practices can be grasped with reference to the relationship between everyday talk/behaviour and the social context against which such behaviours become

intelligible. This relationship constitutes a 'distributed mind', a set of rules and relationships commonly held by members of a particular group.

3 We can read not only the explicit, but also the implicit background or shared knowledge that shapes the behaviours and language of racism.

glossary

- **background:** the implicit knowledge and shared assumptions that a given community takes as given, as not needing to be overtly stated. The background is the frame within which social interaction occurs and in terms of which it is intelligible.

- **distributed mind:** the relationship between foreground and background, explicit and implicit knowledge, constitutes a 'distributed mind', a set of rules and relationships commonly held by members of a particular culture.

- **foreground:** the details of everyday social interaction, our opinions and routines of speech and action, our ordinary instances of conduct and behaviour, which need be contextualized in a background if they are to be adequately understood.

- **Garfinkeling:** a means of making explicit the normally unstated rules, norms and conventions which frame everyday behaviour by constantly questioning what appears to be obvious.

- **habitus:** the bodily dispositions, behaviours and modes of relating, including a wide variety of non-verbal expressions (posture, demeanour, interactional style), that are grounded in the routines of a particular cultural location that reflect its social values.

- **interpretative repertoires:** flexible strategies of talk and representation which utilize routine types of argument, persuasion and description as a means of making sense of, evaluating, and actively constructing the social world.

reading suggestions

Wetherell and Potter's (1992) *Mapping the Language of Racism* was a groundbreaking analysis of racial discourse which replaced the psychologism of prejudice studies with a focus on ideology, representation, power and identity. On the basis of interviews with Pakeha New Zealanders, the authors show how racism can be expressed in non-blatant ways and how lay accounts of racism overlap with academic accounts. Durrheim and Dixon (2005a) also report research on racial discourse, but they were also interested in the material, spatial and embodied features of racial interaction. In addition to interview data, they gathered ethnographic, observational and spatial data to study the unfolding dynamics of racial encounters and segregation on a South African beach. They argue that a critical psychology can benefit from studying racism as an articulation of talk and embodied practices.

⠆ // internet resources /

- **Australian Critical Race and Whiteness Studies Association:** www.acrawsa. org.au
- **Contact Ecology:** www.contactecology.com
- **Darkmatter Journal: Independent Post-colonial Writing Machine:** www.darkmatter101.org/site/
- **Institute of Postcolonial Studies:** www.ipcs.org.au
- **Racism Review:** www.racismreview.com/blog/
- **Social Psychology Research into Racism and Multiculture:** www.psych.lse.ac. uk/socialpsychology/research/racism/sprram/
- **Symposia on Gender, Race, and Philosophy:** web.mac.com/shaslang/SGRP/ Welcome.html

 ■ **Questions**

1 The perspectives of traditional personality and cognitive psychology conceptualize racism very differently from critical psychology. Discuss, paying particular attention to how critical psychology aims to improve the limitations of these traditional approaches.

2 By focusing on language, discursive approaches avoided the problem of overly internalising racism. This focus however led to problems of its own, including the exclusion of a great variety of other forms of social interaction. Discuss.

3 The notion of distributed mind might be understood as a relation between foreground and background. Introduce each of these concepts – foreground, background, distributed mind – with reference to an example of racism drawn from your own experience. Why are these concepts important to a critical psychological understanding of racism?

13

Class

Heather E. Bullock and Wendy M. Limbert

| Chapter Topics |

Psychologists and social scientists are often part of the machinery of control (e.g., schools, universities, and mass media) created and maintained by the ruling elite, and their job is to perceive and conceptualize the realities as defined by the interests of the dominant political system.

Mehyrar, 1984: 166

Social class shapes every aspect of human life. This point is tragically illustrated by the death of Deamonte Driver, a 12-year old US boy who passed away in 2007 when an infection from an abscessed tooth spread to his brain. A routine $80 extraction could have saved Deamonte's life but his family, struggling with poverty and homelessness, could not find a dentist willing to accept Medicaid. When they lost their medical coverage altogether because of an administrative error, even the most basic health care services were out of reach (Otto, 2007). The Drivers' experiences contrast sharply with those of professional middle-class families in the USA, who increasingly pay 'retainer fees' on top of insurance premiums to purchase 'concierge' medical care, thereby ensuring round-the-clock access to physicians. Compared to Germany, France, Canada, and other countries with universal health care policies, class disparities such as this are common in the USA, the wealthiest industrialized country without a universal health care system.

Alternative conceptualizations of social class yield very different understandings of differential access to resources such as health care and even whether class-based inequality is a problem that needs to be addressed. In many Western capitalist societies, most notably the USA, most people understand class inequality and class status as a matter of fact, a 'natural' consequence of economic markets that reward those who work hard. Differential access, thus, reflects individual 'choices', 'lifestyle', and 'merit'. Critical perspectives reject such individual-focused understandings of class and instead attribute the lack of medical care among families like the Drivers and the purchase of specialized, high quality services by the professional middle class to systemic class-based power differences.

As you will see, mainstream psychology too often ignores the impact of social class on human behaviour. As Ostrove and Cole observe, 'At a time when psychology as a discipline has increasingly defined itself as interested in the ways race, class, and gender critically shape our psychological experiences, it seems that class is the least explored of these three' (2003: 679). A study by Ostrove and Long (2007) offers just one example of the far-reaching impact of class and its centrality to psychology. They found that class was strongly related to college students' sense of belonging, and that belonging, in turn, predicted social and academic adjustment, quality of college experience, and academic performance. These findings call for us to look as closely at the 'class climate' of classrooms and workplaces as we do at racial and gender climates. For critical psychologists this also means situating class differences in educational attainment and achievement within structural power differences.

In this chapter, we provide an overview of conceptual differences between mainstream and critical frameworks for studying and theorizing about social class. We deconstruct assumptions underlying the social construction of class to illustrate how a dominant ideology and hierarchical power relations reinforce each other. We especially emphasize how critical conceptualizations of social class and class inequality can lead psychologists to ask new research questions and develop alternative understandings. Our goals are twofold: (a) to highlight mainstream psychology's role in legitimizing hierarchical class relations and (b) to provide a contextualized, critical understanding of social class. Although class is a meaningful social construct around the world, many of our examples are drawn from the USA, where steep class inequality and strained interclass relations serve as particularly powerful illustrations of how class works and of its impact. We also consider intersections of class with race, ethnicity and gender.

defining social class and classism

What social class do you belong to? This seemingly simple question is far more complex than it appears at first glance. In contrast with European countries and other parts of the world, most people in the USA, particularly Whites, self-identify as 'middle class'. This tendency is well documented, but analysis of demographic data challenges the accuracy of such judgments. The stigma associated with the poor and working classes may lead many people to identify as 'middle class' despite not fitting the demographic criteria.

Social class refers to 'a group of individuals or families who occupy a similar position in the economic system of production, distribution, and consumption of goods and services in industrial societies' (Rothman, 2005: 6). Class scholars, particularly sociologists, debate how to define and measure social class and even whether contemporary class groupings are relevant. Here we provide a brief overview of how social class is conceptualized and measured in the psychological literature.

_____ *class as a composite of socioeconomic indicators* _____

Class status is frequently measured using formulas based on combinations of income, education, and occupation and to a lesser degree other markers such as neighbourhood and home ownership. Researchers use these indicators to classify individuals into hierarchical class groupings. Although overt and quantifiable, socioeconomic indicators are also symbolic markers of broader social power and prestige (e.g., access to resources such as safe, reliable housing and health care). Many frameworks based on socioeconomic markers exist but all position those with greater income, education, and occupational status higher than those without. The term 'class', unlike socioeconomic status (SES), makes these power relations overt by making clear the hierarchical nature of class groups (Saegert, Adler, Bullock, Cauce, Liu, & Wyche, 2007). For this reason, we prefer the term class to SES. Throughout this chapter, we use the class designations widely used by researchers in industrialized countries: the elite; the professional or 'upper' middle class; the middle class; the working class; and the poor (Rothman, 2005).

Elites control major institutions and hold the vast majority of wealth. This very small group derives their status and power from ownership of property, businesses, and stock, or from high-level government and corporate leadership positions (Rothman, 2005).

Statistics on income and wealth inequality provide insight into the great resources elites hold. Worldwide, income inequality is highest in Latin America and lowest in European countries (Regional Income Distribution, 2008); however, the trend toward greater inequality is nearly universal (For Whosoever Hath, 2007). The distribution of wealth is even more skewed than income. The top 1 per cent of the world's population holds approximately 40 per cent of the world's total net worth, while the bottom half of the population owns 1.1 per cent of the globe's wealth (Porter, 2006). In the USA during the early 2000s, the wealthiest 1 per cent of families held one-third of the total wealth and the next wealthiest 9 per cent controlled another third, leaving only one-third of the country's wealth for the remaining 90 per cent of the population (Neckerman & Torche, 2007).

While elite power comes from the ownership and control of resources, in the *upper middle class* (sometimes referred to as the *professional middle class*) status is based on professional expertise (e.g., professors, doctors, lawyers, high level managers). Increasingly a graduate degree is needed to enter this class. The *middle class* includes computer specialists, public school teachers and lower-level managers. A college, but not necessarily a graduate, degree is typically needed. Unlike elites, the middle class depends on earned income from work rather than income from stocks and dividends.

Working class describes people who are employed in service positions in restaurants and stores or perform physical labour in factories, construction, and agriculture (Rothman, 2005). Working-class positions typically do not require a baccalaureate degree; however, extensive technical training is needed in some fields (e.g., mechanics).

The poor hold the least status within the class hierarchy. Different measures and definitions are used in different countries, but poverty is usually assessed in relation to an income standard (e.g., distance from the median income). In the USA, poverty is determined by an individual or family's relationship to federally set poverty thresholds. In 2006, a family of three was officially considered 'poor' if their income was below $16,242 (US Census Bureau, 2007). Children, the elderly, unemployed adults, and part-time and full-time workers in low-wage service jobs comprise this diverse group. Families of colour, particularly those headed by women, are overrepresented among the poor. In 2006, 39.1 per cent of Black, 36.9 per cent of Hispanic, and 22.5 per cent of White female-headed households lived in poverty. High rates of poverty are also found throughout Native communities (Webster & Bishaw, 2007). These same patterns are found worldwide: women and indigenous peoples are more likely to be poor and more likely to live in extreme poverty (Buvinic, 1997; Patrinos, Skoufias, & Lunde, 2007). Intersections of class with gender, race, and ethnicity and the unequal distribution of power and opportunity are evident in the overrepresentation of people of colour, indigenous groups, and mothers among the poor, and the overrepresentation of Whites among elites and the professional middle class.

class as social and cultural capital

In addition to defining social class based on quantifiable socioeconomic indicators, some scholars emphasize the importance of social and cultural capital by focusing on social networks and the role of dominant cultural understandings in creating and reproducing class groupings. *Social capital* refers to 'the ability of actors to secure benefits by virtue of their membership in social networks or other social structures' (Portes, 1998: 6); *cultural capital* refers to knowledge of, and familiarity with, the practices of the dominant culture (Bourdieu, 1986). This perspective is prominent in research examining the impact of social and cultural capital on educational attainment in low-income groups and communities of colour. Collectively, this research highlights how a lack of cultural or social resources (e.g., unfamiliarity with higher education, scholarship programmes) among low-income groups and people of colour contributes to the reproduction of social class and how dominant systems value the cultural and social capital of dominant White, middle-class groups (Hoades, 2007).

class as subjective assessment

Subjective conceptualizations focus on *perceived* class status. Feminist psychologists emphasize the need for more subjective and holistic approaches (e.g., Walkerdine, 1996). Traditional work-based definitions, for example, do not speak to the experiences of caregivers (usually women) who work inside the home. By using qualitative research methods to study personal experiences of class stigma and class **privilege**, feminist psychologists deepen our understanding of what class membership 'feels' like and how class influences everyday experiences (Reay, 1999, 2005). Reay's (1999) study illustrates how class position shapes British mothers' aspirations for their children. Working-class mothers described wanting their children to do 'better than' or 'different from' what they themselves had accomplished, whereas middle-class mothers perceived their own lives as normative and wanted their children to replicate their 'success'. Middle-class mothers' relatively uncomplicated goals for their children illustrate the privileges of being a member of a dominant group.

The most widely used subjective measure of class asks participants to position themselves on a ladder upon which the top rungs represent people with the most money, education, and respected jobs and the lowest rungs represent those who are the worst off (Adler, Epel, Castellazzo, & Ickovics, 2000). Collectively, these studies find that individuals' self-rankings correspond reliably to objective measures of socioeconomic status (Saegert et al., 2007) as well as to mental and physical health (Schnittker & McLeod, 2005).

class as power

Power is at the core of all conceptualizations of social class. Critical perspectives make these relationships overt by treating class as a form of social, economic, and political dominance that permits elites and other privileged classes to prosper at the expense of workers and those with less privilege (Saegert et al., 2007). Prilleltensky describes class-based power as the 'power to fulfill basic needs, to restrict access to basic resources, and resist forces of destitution' (2003: 21). From this vantage point, class inequality is not only a matter of 'differential access to resources but also the structural re-creation of privilege and the fusion of wealth and power, particularly in capitalist societies' (Saegert et al., 2007: 6–7; see also Lui, Robles, Leondar-Wright, Brewer, & Adamson, 2006; Marx & Engels, 1848/2001).

Power-based conceptualizations are commonly found in psychological research examining classism. **Classism** is the composite of attitudes, beliefs, behaviours, and institutional practices that sustain and legitimize class-based power differences that privilege middle- and high-income groups at the expense of the poor and working classes (Bullock, 1995). Classist discrimination, which can range from subtle to blatant, occurs at both the interpersonal level (e.g., face-to-face behaviours that distance or devalue the poor and working classes) and the institutional level (e.g., limited access to legal representation, high-quality health care, and employment in the primary labour market).

societal representations and understandings of social class

Varying conceptualizations of social class are not merely academic distinctions. Because they frame discussions of class and socioeconomic status, much of our everyday understanding about class comes from the daily messages we receive from the broader society. For example, put-downs such as 'he's got no class' or the compliment 'that car is the money' reveal the value judgments undergirding common understandings. As with other socially constructed categories such as race and gender, beliefs about social class are culturally transmitted through messages from family members, peers, and the media. Understanding popular representations of poverty and wealth is crucial because it is the media that teach 'ordinary citizens how to think about and understand complex policy problems' (Nelson & Kinder, 1996: 1058).

By depicting poverty as a personal failing and wealth as a personal achievement, US news media and popular programming reinforce the belief that class is an earned rather than ascribed status (Kendall, 2005; Lott & Bullock, 2007). Dominant media representations stereotype the wealthy as enviable and self-made, the middle class as normative, the working class as industrious but crass, and the poor as dangerous, lazy, or suffering (Kendall, 2005; Mantsios, 1998). The media frequently conflate race with class by disproportionately featuring African Americans in news stories about poverty (Clawson & Trice, 2000; Gilens, 1996).

Reinforcing the powerful myth that most people in the USA are middle class, both television and print media operate in an unexamined middle-class or upper-middle class context (Mantsios, 1998; Webb, 2004). While the media pay relatively little attention to poverty (Entman, 1995), they present issues directly affecting elites and the professional middle class as though they are relevant to all viewers. One example is the round-the-clock tracking of the stock market. Although the wealthiest 20 per cent of households hold over 90 per cent of all stock value (Economic Policy Institute, 2006), market indicators are reported as reflecting the economic health of everyone in the USA. Other indicators, such as the value of the minimum wage (which in 2006 reached its lowest level since 1955) or the purchasing power of the median family income, receive less attention (Bagdikian, 1997; Center on Budget and Policy Priorities, 2006). By obscuring the fact that economic interests are not universally shared, the media contribute to the misperception that the USA is a classless society (Mantsios, 1998). The news media in other countries share these biases; constant tracking of world financial markets is common worldwide.

Discussing the power of dominant media representations, Kendall observes that 'framing is an important way in which the media emphasize some ideological perspectives over others and manipulate salience by directing people's attention to some ideas while ignoring others' (2005: 5). This framing is certainly true of idealized representations of individualism and meritocracy, two of the most cherished ideals in US society. *Individualism* refers to a cluster of beliefs emphasizing personal autonomy, independence, and individual responsibility for achievement. **Meritocracy** is the belief that anyone – regardless of family of origin, class, race, or gender – can rise to the top of the class hierarchy through hard work and perseverance (Hochschild, 1995).

These themes are easily identifiable in 'rags-to-riches' stories about the economic success of individuals who overcome obstacles to become wealthy, famous, or politically influential. In reality, upward mobility is increasingly difficult, especially for those who start with the fewest resources. Only about one-third of young adults in the USA are 'upwardly mobile' relative to their parents (Isaacs, n.d.(a)) and children in the USA are less likely than their counterparts in Canada and numerous European countries to obtain higher economic status than their parents (Isaacs, n.d.(b)). Nevertheless, more people in the USA today than 20 years ago believe in the possibility of upward mobility (cf. Scott & Leonhardt, 2005). In Britain, on the other hand, poll data show that a majority of residents expect that they and their children will remain in their social class of birth (Class, 2006).

Individualism and a belief in meritocracy blunt critical analyses of structural inequality by creating unfounded hope among the poor and working classes about their prospects for upward mobility (Armstrong, 1996; Langston, 1998). Among the middle class and elites, the myth of an open class system contributes to the perception that their privilege is the deserved outcome of hard work and individual effort rather than structural advantage (hooks, 2000; Langston 1998; Wise, 2005). Approximately 72 per cent of US federal spending to promote upward mobility is geared toward middle- and higher-income households through employer-provided work subsidies, aids in asset accumulation, and savings incentives; only 28 per cent is channelled toward lower- to moderate-income groups (Carasso, Reynolds, & Steurle, n.d.). Such figures rarely make the headlines, and deep-rooted beliefs about meritocracy ensure that challenges to class privilege are met with defensiveness (hooks,

2000; Smith, 2007). In this way, critical public dialogue is stifled, with little acknowledgment that government policies block asset building among the poor and people of colour and promote wealth accumulation among White elites (Lui et al., 2006).

_____ social class in mainstream psychology _____

Mainstream psychology's treatment of social class largely parallels that of the broader society. For the most part, it is invisible or inconsistently conceptualized, with empirical studies only sporadically reporting participants' social class. In Liu, Ali, Soleck, Hopps, Dunston and Pickett's (2004) content analysis of 3,915 articles published in three counselling psychology journals between 1981 and 2000, only 98 studies included social class as a core variable. Class fares no better in intersectional analyses of race, class, and gender. Reimers' (2007) content analysis of two mainstream counselling journals found that articles published between 1996 and 2006 were more likely to treat race and gender comprehensively (i.e., assessing, analysing, and discussing them) than class, which they mentioned only superficially. Only 15 of the 998 reviewed articles focused on the intersections of class, race, and gender at a primary or deep level.

Such findings are consistent with other problematic tendencies, such as equating ethnic minorities with lower socioeconomic status and neglecting gender inequities in class-based analyses. Collectively, these oversights lead to skewed conclusions and limited understandings of important social problems. For instance, the class status of respondents frequently goes unreported in studies of workplace harassment, or respondents with middle-class occupations are overrepresented. Yet class is likely to shape responses to workplace harassment (e.g., whether and to whom harassment is reported) and how it is experienced. A food service worker is unlikely to have the same 'options' and resources to respond to harassment as a midlevel executive.

The majority of participants in psychological research are college students. Researchers frequently acknowledge this bias but rarely discuss it in the context of over-representing middle-class participants and viewpoints. Researchers are more likely to overtly identify the poor, which makes middle-class status normative and reinforces poor and working-class status as 'other' in psychological research.

Consistent with mainstream psychology's focus on the individual rather than on the structural level of analysis, its approaches to poverty are largely based on deficit models of human behaviour. From this vantage point, poverty reflects deficient cultural values, norms, and behaviours that deviate from assumed middle-class values. Poverty is a problem to 'fix' through individual rather than structural change. For example, deficit philosophies guide interventions to reduce poverty by teaching low-income women to value two-parent families and hard work. This same thinking underlies health promotion studies that focus exclusively on the behavioural shortcomings of low-income communities, or that compare the health-related behaviours of poor and middle-class communities without taking into account the structural factors that contribute to potential differences (e.g., safe spaces for outdoor exercise, affordability and access to fresh produce).

Even when the mainstream psychology literature has a direct application for understanding class-based inequality, it is generally apolitical and decontextualized. This point is illustrated by research on the attributions for poverty (see Harper, 2003). Two of the most prominent attributions are individualistic explanations which focus on the role of poor people themselves in causing their poverty (e.g., laziness, lack of talent) and structural explanations which emphasize the role of societal factors (e.g. low wages, discrimination). People with greater power (e.g., Whites, men) tend to endorse individualistic attributions, whereas those with less power (e.g., African Americans, women, low-income groups) tend to support structural explanations (Cozzarelli, Wilkinson & Tagler, 2001; Kluegel & Smith, 1986).

The potential impact of these intergroup differences is heightened when we regard attributions for poverty as one dimension of a broader network of hierarchy-legitimizing beliefs. For example, strong endorsement of the Protestant work ethic (i.e., hard work as a moral imperative) is associated with individualistic attributions for poverty. Moreover, individualistic attributions correlate with support for punitive welfare policies, while structural attributions correlate with supporting generous welfare policies (Bullock, Williams, & Limbert, 2003). Collectively, these findings provide an important foundation for understanding public attitudes. However, mainstream researchers often present them without discussing 'real-world' implications and study them in ways that strip these beliefs of an intergroup context. They do not focus on whose interests dominant attributional patterns serve, how political discourse influences public opinion about poverty, or how these attributions influence day-to-day interclass relations (Harper, 2003).

social class as a critical social justice issue

Class inequality is among the oldest social problems, leading Marx and Engels to observe 'The history of all hitherto existing struggles is the history of class struggles' (1848/2001: 8). Worldwide, the current widening gap between elites and the rest of the population underscores class inequity as a growing crisis and critical social justice issue. In 2006, CEOs of large US companies averaged $10.8 million in total annual compensation, over 364 times the pay of the average US worker (Anderson, Cavanagh, Collins, Pizzigati, & Lapham, 2007). In Canada the highest paid CEOs earn in approximately 13 hours what a full-time, minimum wage worker earns annually (Monsebraaten, 2008).

It isn't only the poor and working classes who are falling further behind. The middle class and professional middle class are also losing ground. Debt has increased and savings have declined among US families in the middle 60 per cent of the income distribution (Weller & Staub, 2006). More than half of middle-class families have zero or negative net worth (assets minus debts; Wheary, Shapiro, & Draut, 2007). Families of colour are particularly vulnerable, with one in three African American families and two in five Latino families at high risk for slipping out of the middle class, compared to one in five White families (Wheary et al., 2007).

These inequalities come at a high cost. Class shapes every aspect of human welfare – physical and mental health, educational attainment, political representation, and access to safe housing. With diminished life chances and opportunities in all these areas, the poor and the working classes undoubtedly bear the brunt of class inequality, but inequality is not only the problem of the poor. Residents of egalitarian societies have longer life expectancies than residents of the wealthiest industrialized societies (Belle & Doucet, 2003), leading some researchers to regard income inequality as a form of 'social pollution' that affects wellbeing across the class spectrum (Subramanian & Kawachi, 2006). In their analysis of the impact of USA state-level income inequality on health, Subramanian and Kawachi (2006) found negative health profiles for both economically advantaged and disadvantaged residents of unequal states. Such findings point to the importance of carefully examining the social and health consequences of inequality such as the 'stresses of life in a winner-take-all economy' and the accompanying 'losses in social cohesion and trust' (Belle & Doucet, 2003: 105).

Treating class as a social justice issue demands that we work to reduce both poverty and class inequality. It also means questioning society's dominant values. Should people come before profits? Should equality be valued over personal gain? What price do we pay for individualism?

approaching social class through a critical psychology lens

Adopting a critical perspective involves more than just class-focused research, practice, and advocacy. It is important to start with ourselves and develop greater reflexivity regarding our own class background. Class informs every stage of our work, from the research questions we ask, to our interpretation of research findings, to which data we choose to highlight or discard (Lott & Bullock, 2007). Reflexivity is the 'continual consideration of the ways in which the researcher's own social identity and values affect the data gathered and the picture of the social world produced' (Reay, 1996a: 60).

Reflexivity is a tool for understanding 'the effects we have within the context of the knowledge that we are co-constructing' (Lykes, 2000: 387). Its power is highlighted by first-hand accounts of scholars working across participant/researcher differences in class, race, and gender (Langhout, 2006; Reay, 1996b). Now a common feature of feminist scholarship, community psychology, and ethnographic research, reflexivity has yet to be embraced by mainstream psychology. The absence of critical reflexivity, particularly by experimentalists, perpetuates the myth of objectivity and reinforces the dominant power relations critical psychologists seek to expose.

One of critical psychology's fundamental features is the level at which social issues are analysed. Critical psychologists approach social concerns broadly, focusing on individuals and groups in the context of larger social structures. For the study of social class, this means identifying how economic conditions shape individual and group behaviour. It also means grounding research questions in the context of class-based power relations. Such an approach requires a paradigm shift from mainstream conceptualizations deficient in several ways: they ignore class (e.g., not reporting class status when participants are middle class), treat it as a simple descriptor or demographic characteristic (e.g., survey research that portrays class as an apolitical construct), or pathologize it (e.g., using deficit models when participants are low-income).

The benefits of the paradigm shift we are calling for are illustrated by contrasting the different levels of analysis that characterize research on 'barriers' to economic 'self-sufficiency' and the impact of US 'welfare reform' on low-income families. Individual-level perspectives emphasize moving individuals out of poverty, for example through job training or education programmes. This perspective assumes individual behaviour change will bring upward mobility through developing better work habits, improving parenting skills, and adopting so-called 'middle-class' values (e.g., valuing work). Mainstream welfare-reform researchers typically go beyond individual levels of analysis to identify the immediate structural barriers that poor families face, such as lack of high-quality affordable childcare, unreliable transportation, and inadequate educational opportunities. Critical psychologists delve even deeper by examining welfare recipients' position in the broader economic system, the root causes of inequality, and the beneficiaries of this inequality. Who benefits from restrictive welfare policies and the erosion of safety net programmes in the USA, Great Britain, and other industrialized countries? How do welfare policies maintain or challenge the class structure and other social hierarchies? How do cultural values about work, achievement, and individualism shape social policies?

Shifting the focus to long-standing structural forces draws attention to previously hidden relationships. For example, US welfare recipients are required to work for their benefits. This policy ensures a steady supply of workers for undesirable, low-wage jobs. The real benefit goes to the large corporations who administer and prosper from these programmes, not the families living on an income that barely assures their survival.

_____ *research* _____

Fully examining the impact of social class on individual and group experience requires diverse participants, methods, and theories.

participants   The common practice of using 'convenience samples' of middle-class college students is problematic when findings are assumed to apply across the class spectrum. A study by Stephens, Markus, and Townsend (2007) examining US students' personal choices found that students from working-class backgrounds tended to prefer being similar to their peers, whereas students from middle-class backgrounds preferred to differentiate themselves. These findings call into question previous assumptions of a universal need to distinguish oneself from others – perhaps the drive for uniqueness is especially pronounced among the middle class. Additionally, perhaps because psychologists tend to be middle class themselves, 'independent thinking' may be judged more positively than assimilating to others' behaviour.

For many years, feminist researchers have studied the lived experiences of low-income women and their families, providing significant insight into stigma, oppression, and critical resistance. Far less attention has focused on the lives of upper-income families or the psychological processes associated with economic privilege. For example, little is known about how those with economic power justify class privilege on a daily basis, or about the strategies they use to maintain status. More importantly, by focusing class-based research almost exclusively on low-income groups and neglecting those with high incomes, researchers define poverty rather than inequality as a problem to be solved. Access to elites and other power holders is inherently difficult by virtue of their status, but critical psychologists can narrow this gap in the literature by focusing on inequality, by questioning whose interests problematizing poverty rather than wealth serves, and by examining how this emphasis reproduces class disparities.

methods   Critical psychologists oppose so-called 'drive by' social science research in which researchers 'mine' low-income groups and communities of colour for information but offer little if any follow-up. Calling for an end to these exploitive relationships, critical psychologists advocate methods that minimize power differences and increase the relevance and external validity of psychological research (see Chapter 20). The OCAP principles, developed by First Nation communities in Canada, provide an example of research standards consistent with critical approaches. OCAP stands for Ownership (the community owns information or data collectively); Control (communities have the right to control all aspects of the research process); Access (communities have the right to access data about themselves, and to determine outsiders' access to community data); and Possession (communities have the right to literal possession of community data) (Schnarch, 2004). These principles help to empower low-income groups and ensure that research benefits everyone involved.

Participatory action research (PAR) is another strategy for moving beyond superficial participant/researcher relationships and the reproduction of decontextualized, culturally dominant discourses. Core PAR tenets include (a) an explicit focus on generating information for action and meaningful social change; (b) the belief that community members and local 'knowers' are important sources of knowledge; (c) an emphasis on conducting research *with* people rather than *on* people; and (d) the belief that knowledge should be developed collaboratively through a dynamic process of analysis, reflection, and action (Savin-Baden & Wimpenny, 2007).

Research based on the OCAP and PAR principles can advance theories that strengthen psychological, social, and ideological understandings of class while also helping us question and disrupt its reproduction. Yet, no method is a panacea. Researchers work within the same group dynamics and social structures that they seek to challenge and run the risk of replicating the same dynamics of class privilege (Saegert et al., 2007). PAR, for example, has been criticized for being too focused on community problems rather than on strengths and successes (Boyd & Bright, 2007). Critical researchers encourage alternative, non-hierarchical thinking and social change by acknowledging these limitations (Fine & Torre, 2004).

theory   Class disadvantage has received far more attention in the psychological literature than class advantage. Recognizing that poverty does not exist in the absence of wealth, a critical psychology embraces inquiry and theory development across the full socioeconomic spectrum. This means addressing questions related to class privilege: How does class privilege parallel or diverge from race and gender privilege? Under what conditions do individuals identify their own class privilege? How are unearned privileges justified? How do middle-class attributions for wealth and beliefs about inequality influence support for safety-net programmes and policies that benefit elites?

Critical approaches encourage conceptualizations of class that are fluid and contextualized rather than static and decontextualized. A growing body of literature explores subjective experiences of moving from working-class to middle-class status (e.g., the experiences of first-generation college students), illuminating upward mobility as a process that is not without difficulties and psychological consequences. By challenging popular understandings of upward mobility as unproblematic (Reay, 1999; Walkerdine, 2003), this body of work draws attention to the need for critical theories of both upward and downward mobility, as well as of class stability.

A critical psychology positions power and oppression at the forefront of theories of class. One important next step is the development of theories that explain how ideology functions to neutralize class inequities and perpetuate oppressive interclass relations. This requires moving beyond documenting the prevalence of individualism in dominant beliefs about wealth, poverty, and social class to studying the perpetuation of these ideologies. How is class privilege reproduced institutionally and interpersonally and made to seem 'natural' and acceptable? How can classist attitudes be reduced? What role does media framing play in generating popular support for policies that primarily benefit elites?

Equally crucial is greater theoretical attention to critical resistance – movements that challenge dominant constructions of class and meritocracy, foster the development of alternative critical perspectives, and construct counter-frames. Changing the individualistic and meritocratic beliefs that support class inequality is no easy task. Critical research on framing can identify how ideology is used to promote the status quo and how alternative 'equality' and 'fairness' frames can foster cross-class alliances and justice-oriented understandings of class.

<hr>

practice

While practitioners recognize gender, race, ethnicity, and sexuality as important dimensions of human diversity, social class is largely overlooked as a significant factor affecting diagnosis and treatment. Diagnostic and therapeutic models are still based on the assumption that clients are White, college-educated, middle-class professionals with the time and resources to pursue therapy (Hill & Rothblum, 1996). 'Blind spots, classist stereotyping, and feeling overwhelmed' by the hardships that accompany poverty likely inform how therapists interact with their clients and the (lack of) treatment that they provide to low-income clients (Smith, 2005: 601).

Multicultural competency training must fully integrate social class, class privilege, and classism into psychological practice and interventions. Practitioners need to consider how their social class affects their own attitudes and perceptions, how class influences their clients' histories and life experiences, and how class shapes both groups' experiences and perceptions of therapy (Liu et al., 2004; Saegert et al., 2007). To sustain action on behalf of social and economic justice, critical psychologists go a step further: they self-reflexively analyse class biases, explore new ways to decrease inequality, and provide pro bono services to clients who cannot afford counselling or treatment (Saegert et al., 2007).

Critical psychologists also call for clinical practitioners to raise their sights higher and consider structural levels of analysis. As the modern economy results in ever more fractured career paths, workers are constantly pressured to reinvent themselves while frequent job-related moves that weaken family and community ties exacerbate the strain of doing so. As Walkerdine (2003) points out, an exclusive focus on service delivery bolsters the same individualistic ideologies that inhibit widespread social change. A critical perspective calls on practitioners to strike a balance between helping individuals and addressing inequities at the root of widespread mental health needs.

Practitioner training must provide the tools needed to work effectively with clients from diverse class backgrounds. These include learning how to recognize subtle and overt forms of classism and the impact of classism on individual wellbeing. One important step is heightened awareness of norms that idealize and normalize middle-class status and generate feelings of inadequacy among those with limited resources (Reay, 1999). A critical class perspective moves practitioners from deficit- to strength-based understandings of human behaviour. Rather than defining marginalized individuals and groups by their hardships, it recognizes the assets and strengths (e.g., perseverance, intelligence) of economically disadvantaged people. Such a shift represents a significant departure from mainstream perspectives in psychology.

advocacy

Critical psychologists regard advocacy as integral to their work. This perspective, which blurs mainstream distinctions between 'science' and 'politics', is not shared universally. Conflict surrounding psychologists' role as advocates is illustrated by the passage of US 'welfare reform' regulations in 1996 and the subsequent evaluation opportunities that the new policies generated. Some evaluators defined their task as identifying 'who can succeed under this new system' (Kalil, 2001: 184). Critical psychologists challenged this perspective by focusing instead on the very soundness of the new policies. Rather than accepting the changes at face value, critical psychologists questioned their guiding assumptions. Does 'welfare reform' reduce poverty or does it just reduce the welfare rolls? Are low-income families measurably better off as a result of 'welfare reform'? Do poor women benefit from these new programmes as much as the middle-class administrators and large corporations paid to design and run them? By taking this perspective, critical psychologists draw attention to how social policies and power holders, including psychologists, contribute to class disparities. (Chapter 23 describes working with welfare rights groups to oppose these policies.)

Critiquing how privileged groups benefit from unjust social policies may discomfort those who are unaccustomed to overtly political research or practice models. Critical approaches to social class might seem to require a belief that policymakers and others are classist and knowingly craft policies to benefit the wealthy. But critical psychologists are concerned with outcomes, not intentions. Moreover, the alternative – unexamined acceptance of dominant ideology or issue frames – is not a 'neutral' stance because it helps reproduce class inequality. A critical perspective requires conscious awareness of which views we choose to represent in our work and which we reject.

Advocacy – working on behalf of social change – may also feel uncomfortably 'political'. But advocacy is far from unfamiliar to psychologists or to our professional associations. Lobbying for policy changes or standards that directly affect our research (e.g., increased government funding) or practice (e.g., better mental health coverage) is commonplace. As a profession, we must move beyond 'guild' issues and concentrate on attacking the roots of inequality and class oppression and promoting social justice. Doing so requires overturning narrow conceptualizations of psychology's constituents and concerns, taking a political stand as a profession on a wide range of disparity-enhancing economic policies, and questioning our individual and collective contributions to both the reproduction of structural inequality and social change.

1 Critical psychologists conceptualize class as a form of social and political dominance whereby groups with greater resources profit at the expense of those with fewer resources.

2 Dominant societal representations of social class in the USA bolster individualistic and meritocratic ideologies and reinforce middle-class standards as 'normal' and 'desirable'.

3 Social class in mainstream psychology is often invisible and usually stripped of context and 'real-world' power relations.

4 Social class touches nearly every aspect of people's lives through its influence on access to resources such as education, health care, and housing. As inequality continues to rise, only elites benefit; younger generations cannot take upward mobility for granted.

5 Approaching class through a critical lens means grounding research and practice in the context of class-based power relations and advocating for economic justice when the status quo is harmful for those with less power and fewer resources.

————— **glossary** —————————————

• **classism**: the composite of attitudes, assumptions, beliefs, behaviours, and institutional practices that maintain and legitimize class-based power differences.

• **meritocracy**: the belief that anyone, regardless of family of origin, class, race, or gender, can rise to the top of the class hierarchy through hard work and perseverance.

• **privilege**: benefits that result from membership of a normative or dominant group.

• **social class**: a group of individuals or families who occupy a similar position, distribution, and consumption of goods and services in industrial societies.

————— ▪ ▪ **reading suggestions** ▪

Schiller's (2003) text is a good starting place for learning about poverty and economic discrimination. Carr and Sloan's edited (2003) volume provides an excellent international overview of key issues related to poverty and psychology. Try Lott (2002) and Lott and Bullock (2007) for critical analyses of mainstream psychological research and practice. For an insightful discussion of how race and racism influence US welfare policy, see Schram et al. (2003). Read Fine and Weis's

(1998) ethnographic study of US poor and working class young adults for a deeper understanding of how social location shapes our understandings of power, access to resources, and lived experience.

// internet resources

- **American Psychological Association Office on Socioeconomic Status**: www.apa.org/pi/ses/homepage.html
- **Class Action**: www.classism.org
- **The Economic Mobility Project**: economicmobility.org
- **United for a Fair Economy**: www.ufe.org
- **Unnatural Causes: Is Inequality Making Us Sick?** www.unnaturalcauses.org

Questions

1 What social class do you belong to? What do you base this assessment on?

2 What class privileges do you have? What disadvantages?

3 Identify a class-related media story. What ideological assumptions does the report make? Who benefits from the framing of the story, and who is disadvantaged?

4 Think about a psychology topic you've studied recently. How might class play a role in the research or theorizing of that topic? How would taking a critical perspective change the focus of the study or how the findings are interpreted?

5 Identify a specific area of class inequality (e.g. housing). How do race, gender, sexuality, or ability intersect with class to influence the differential treatment of diverse groups?

|14|

Gender

Victoria Clarke and Virginia Braun

Chapter Topics

> Gender is the backcloth against which our daily lives are played out. It suffuses our existence so that, like breathing, it becomes invisible to us because of its familiarity.
>
> Burr, 1998: 2

Imagine the following scenario: you are a man walking down the street wearing lipstick, heels and a skirt. People look at you – some casting sidelong glances, others openly staring – attempting to make sense of the 'social aberration' they see before them. They may well decide that you are (a) a transgender person who (perhaps deliberately) didn't get it quite 'right'; (b) a gay man heading for a drag club; or (c) a straight man in fancy dress for a stag night. **Gender** limits how we view the world and people in it and what we can do with our lives. It is not considered 'normal' for men to routinely wear what are perceived as 'women's' clothing or makeup – there has to be some sort of explanation for it. In order to acceptably engage in such 'gender-bending' behaviour, you are seen as either a special category of person (e.g., gay, transgender) or in an exceptional context which allows or demands deviations from 'the norm' (e.g., a stag night).

This chapter introduces a critical psychology of gender. We aim to provide you with tools for critically analysing the construction of gender in mainstream psychology and in everyday life. First we demonstrate why gender is a critical social issue and discuss what we mean by gender. Next we illustrate some of the core assumptions underpinning mainstream psychological approaches, using the example of Victoria's research on lesbian-mother families. We then consider assumptions about gender in the wider culture, using the example of Virginia's research on dictionary definitions of female and male genitalia. Finally, we outline features of a critical psychology of gender. However, we do not want to suggest simply that 'critical is good, mainstream is bad'. Some mainstream psychological work has been very important. More to the point, few examples of critical psychological work on gender have made practical contributions to social change. We end by considering whether critical psychologists *can* make effective interventions into our two-sexed, two-gendered world, and describe one positive example.

gender as a critical social issue

Gender is a hugely important, influential and complex categorization system which has profound consequences on the lives of everyone – those who always notice it, because they do not fit within its remits, and those who virtually never notice it, because they do. Think back to the last time you completed a form asking for personal details (e.g., for medical reasons or insurance). Chances are you were expected to mark either 'male' *or* 'female'. Many of you, like us, marked one box without any thought. In contrast, some of you may have agonized over which box to tick, perhaps wishing for another option, as neither option allowed you to be true to how you see yourself. The forced choice was yet another instance reminding you that you do not 'fit' within this either/or categorization system.

Gender is a critical social issue because it is associated with various social inequalities, exclusions, and the experience of abuse. Ideas about *gender-appropriate* behaviour structure people's most mundane practices, such as whether you use public toilets with urinals or without, whether you bare your chest or not at the local swimming pool, whether you buy perfume or aftershave, and whether you button your shirts from the left or right. Gender is a strong indicator of how your behaviour is judged, and how much your time and work are valued. In the Western world, despite legislative reforms, gender-based pay inequality remains. Women in **heterosexual** families still overwhelmingly perform the majority of domestic and parenting work. Although some men participate more in domestic labour and childcare, these men typically see themselves, and are seen by others, as 'helping out'. In most cases, even when women and men perform equal amounts of domestic labour, women retain the overall responsibility for deciding what tasks need to be performed (Dryden, 1999). The point is that although there has been significant social change in the last 30 years, and despite protests that 'things are equal now', women's and men's lives continue to be shaped by rather different expectations and opportunities.

Another example of gender's influence is that our sex/gender is crucial in determining the likelihood that we will enact, or experience, violence. Women are far more likely than men to be subject to sexual violence, and to physical violence within the context of heterosexual relationships. While many men experience physical and sexual violence, it results typically from other men. People who transgress gender norms, such as people who are transgender, are also highly likely to experience a wide range of victimization, ranging from harassment on the street to sexual assault (Hill & Willoughby, 2005). However, gender norms don't simply marginalize certain groups (e.g., women; people who are transgendered); they also privilege certain groups (e.g., men; people who conform to gender norms).

These gender dimensions of privilege and marginalization intersect with other dimensions of privilege. Gender influences, and is shaped by, other social categories associated with inequality and exclusion, such as race, culture, class, and sexuality. Within this framework (referred to as *intersectionality*), the experience and impact of gender are mediated by these (and vice versa), but the effects are not simply additive. The intersectional dimensions work more like the ingredients that make bread than the different layers of a ham, cheese and relish sandwich. It is not possible to remove one ingredient from bread dough and still successfully make the bread. Neither is it possible to point to the effect of just one ingredient and say 'there, right there, that's the yeast' or 'there's the salt'. If one component is removed, the resulting bread is fundamentally different. In contrast, if one component of a sandwich filling is removed (ham, cheese, or relish), the others remain the same, unaffected, but the overall filling of the sandwich would be less. This demonstrates that gender + race + sexuality does not simply equal more oppression than just gender + sexuality; and you cannot easily point to, or remove, the effect of one from the overall experience. Multiple social categories work in concert (and sometimes in opposition) to shape each other, and how we can live in, and experience, the world.

For example, let's look at gender and *sexuality*. We use the term sexuality in this chapter instead of a more traditional concept like sexual orientation or sexual identity because it fits with a critical psychology that acknowledges several things: sexuality is broader than just *who* one has sex with; it is socially shaped and produced (it doesn't just reside within individuals); and it is characterized often by fluidity and change. Gender and sexuality are closely associated categories. Lesbian women who defy **normative** expectations about sexuality are often seen as gender 'inverts', as butch or masculine. Early sexuality theorists portrayed lesbians as male souls trapped in female bodies and wrote of lesbians' fondness for male clothing and traditionally masculine activities (Clarke, 2008). More broadly, a gendered ideology of passivity and activity pervades Western societies' notions of sex and sexuality: men, masculinity, and male sexuality embody activity; women, femininity, and female sexuality embody passivity. The point we emphasize is that for the individual, gender is never independent of other social identities.

what is gender?

At this point, you may be asking 'what do they mean by gender'? This is the million dollar question! There are multiple ways of theorizing gender in psychology, many of them contradictory. Most psychological research is concerned with gender on two interrelated levels. First, at the social level, gender is a social categorization system, which simultaneously informs individuals about the importance of gender and its origin and provides us with information about appropriate ways to live as gendered people. Second, at the individual level, there is the personal experience and expression of gender – people's sense of themselves as gendered beings, the way they enact their lives in a gendered fashion. Cutting across these different levels are three main models of the origin and meaning of gender. We outline these models here, and then discuss some in more detail in subsequent sections.

gender as nature   Here, gender is used to refer to the *sex* of our body and/or to masculine/feminine personality traits. This is a biologically based explanation, where our personalities, desires, needs, abilities, beliefs and so on result from hormones, genes or some other biological factor. Prior to the 1970s, this was the dominant framework for thinking about gender, but it still frequently appears in various guises, especially in the field of evolutionary psychology. In complete contradiction to its initial meaning, the term 'gender' has come to be used as a stand-in for the term 'sex', to refer to the biological body – as in the question 'which gender are you, male or female?' This is an *essentialist* view of gender, meaning that gender is a fixed and stable feature of the person or their personality – their nature – from birth to death, and does not change depending on context or situation. Gender is *what you are*.

gender as nurture   Here, gender typically refers to masculine or feminine (or androgynous) personality traits. Gender is a cultural overlay of sex – what culture adds to a biological bedrock. Gender is seen as something individuals learn at an early age, from the social environments we grow up in and from the ideas about gender available in our culture. Children learn the range of culturally appropriate and inappropriate desires, practices, beliefs and feelings to match their sexed body, which then become internalized as a stable part of that person. It is impossible not to have gender. This use of gender was first theorized in the 1970s, and was a radical idea at the time, because it separated *gender* (socially learned) from *sex* (biology), and demonstrated no necessary relationship between the two. It is still the dominant model of gender in **feminist psychology**, and some mainstream and critical psychology. Again, this is an *essentialist* view of gender, as learned gender is seen to be stable and relatively impervious to the influence of immediate context. Gender is *what you have.*

gender as social construct This is the most challenging way gender is theorized, and the basis of much of the critical psychology work around gender we discuss further below. It refers to a complex set of ideas about gender which question the core assumptions of both nature and nurture frameworks. The social constructionist approach moves away from any idea of gender as a natural phenomenon. Instead, gender is seen to be a social construction, particular to a specific sociocultural historical period, a result of shared cultural knowledge and language use (Bohan, 1997) rather than of internal psychological or biological processes. Two key components of social constructionist accounts of gender are worth noting: *anti-essentialism* and *social categorization.* Anti-essentialism means that gender is not seen as a stable, permanent feature of individuals, as something that resides *within* individuals as part of either biology or personality. Instead, gender is theorized as an *unnatural* social categorization system, which prioritizes, and emphasizes, gender difference. Categories of masculinity and femininity are not seen as naturally resulting from biological difference between 'male' and 'female' bodies, but as social products, resulting from society. Some social constructionists see the idea that there are two types of sexed bodies, and two types of gendered people who are different from each other, as a powerful ideology that shapes reality rather than one that simply reflects reality. In this sense, we believe there are two sexes because the world around us continually reflects this idea and tells us it is so (and we in turn participate in reproducing this idea). Within this approach, gender is *what you do*, rather than something you *have* or *are.* Individuals *do* – 'act out' – gender in our lives and interactions. However, we still 'perceive ourselves as *intrinsically* gendered because gender so thoroughly infuses our experience' (Bohan, 1997: 40, emphasis added) through the power of social norms.

Importantly, regardless of your framework, gender is something that *all* people experience. However, women are most frequently seen to have or embody gender – men just 'are'. This reflects a long history in psychology where men are presented as normal and women as 'different' from men, and their difference is in need of an explanation (Tavris, 1993). The term gender can be used as more acceptable shorthand for 'women' – e.g., 'gender issues' studied within a university are typically 'women's issues'. From the social constructionist viewpoint, men and women are just as 'gendered' as each other, because the social categorization system affects us all. Even if we resist it and do gender differently (e.g., we become what Kate Bornstein [1994] refers to as a 'gender outlaw'), we are still engaged in 'doing gender'. Thus, while men as a group are often privileged over women as a group by gendered constructions and practices, individual men are just as constrained by constructions of gender as women are. For example, traditional constructions of masculinity around rationality, individualism and aggressiveness (and femininity around emotionality, relationality and submissiveness) have reinforced strongly gendered divisions of labour where top-paying jobs 'requiring' 'masculine' qualities are seen as unsuited to women – thus privileging men as a group. However, at the same time, these constructions of masculinity can be bad for men individually. For example, they can result in a 'stoicism' which sees men not seeking help for health problems.

gender in feminist psychology

In mainstream psychological research, gender is a hugely important category, even if it is not a focus of research. Psychological researchers will nearly always report the sex of their participants, assuming this to be relevant, regardless of whether gender is a key theoretical consideration. More explicitly, the broad framework of 'sex differences' is pervasive in psychology. Psychologists have searched for evidence of sex differences in everything from mathematical ability, to olfactory perception, to spatial abilities, to brain organization, to … the list goes on (e.g., Geary, 1998)! But this framework is highly contentious, and has been questioned right from the start (Thompson Woolley, 1910).

Within feminist psychology – which has been defined as 'psychological theory and practice which is explicitly informed by the political goals of the feminist movement' (Wilkinson, 1997a: 247) – there are different perspectives on a sex-difference approach. Although many contemporary feminist psychologists view sex differences research as meaningful and useful, others have critiqued it, and questioned whether psychologists *should* study sex differences (e.g., Kitzinger, 1994). Ideas about gender also shape which topics and methods psychologists see as important. Mainstream psychology has been referred to as 'malestream' psychology because it ignored women, failed to address topics of relevance to women's lives, and offered an androcentric (male-centred) perspective on psychological life. In the late 1960s, Naomi Weisstein damned psychology's analysis of women, declaring that 'psychology has nothing to say about what women are really like, what they need and what they want … because psychology does not know' (1993: 197).

Feminist psychologists swept into the discipline with a radical, new agenda, re-examining classic psychological models to demonstrate gender bias (such as Kohlberg's moral development scale – see Gilligan, 1982), and studying topics that had been previously ignored. It wasn't until feminists started researching topics like rape and sexual assault that these topics were taken seriously as an important focus for research. There is still relatively little non-feminist psychological research on topics such as emotion, marriage and motherhood because these are seen as 'women's issues' (Dryden, 1999). Similarly, feminist researchers were instrumental in developing the use of qualitative methods in (and beyond) psychology, methods that some mainstream psychologists still devalue as unscientific and subjective.

gender in mainstream psychology: the psychosexual development of children in lesbian-mother families

In this section, we identify and explore problematic assumptions underpinning mainstream psychological approaches to gender, using Victoria's research on lesbian-mother families (Clarke, 2007). Research on lesbian mothers, which began in the early 1970s, falls under the banner of lesbian, gay, bisexual, trans and **queer (LGBTQ) psychology**, often considered part of the broad domain of critical psychology (see Clarke & Peel, 2007). LGBTQ psychology initially emerged as a protest against the privileging of heterosexuality (sometimes referred to as **heterosexism** or **heteronormativity**) in mainstream psychology. It is focused on understanding the lives of LGBTQ people and LGBTQ sexualities and genders, and on countering prejudice and discrimination against LGBTQ people. It is both a scholarly enterprise and a practical, politically oriented project.

The early 1970s, a time of significant social change, witnessed the emergence of the women's and the gay liberation movements. These political movements had a profound impact on many people and were a key factor in some people exploring their sexuality and 'coming out' as lesbian or gay. Many of the women who came out as lesbian were heterosexually married and had children. In custody cases involving lesbian mothers, judges reversed their usual practice (based on gendered assumptions) of placing the child with the mother, and tended to give custody to the father (Harne & the Rights of Women, 1997). They often placed severe restrictions on lesbian mothers' contact with their children: some were instructed not to discuss their lesbianism with the child or to allow a woman partner *any* contact. Judges and others had significant concerns about how children would develop in lesbian households, specifically about children's gender and sexual identities. Judges were clearly influenced both by psychological constructions of lesbianism, which had pathologized it, and by popular nurture theories of gender, which theorized two appropriately gendered, and opposite sexed, parents as necessary role models for 'normal' gender and sexual identity development.

Supported by activists, 'radical' psychologists worked to intervene positively into the lesbian-mother custody crisis. Their approach was to scientifically test the assumptions held by judges and others. Using quasi-experimental models, psychologists compared children of lesbian mothers to children of divorced heterosexual mothers as the control group. Most research focused on comparisons of children's gender and sexual identity development. A good outcome consisted of children in lesbian-mother families appearing to be no different from children in heterosexual-mother families and of children conforming to normative expectations about gender and sexuality. Let's consider a classic example of this sort of research.

The highly regarded developmental psychologist Susan Golombok conducted one of the first and most influential comparative studies of children in lesbian-mother and single heterosexual-mother families (Golombok, Spencer, & Rutter, 1983). A key assumption was that children possess a fixed and internal gender identity that directs their gender-role behaviour. Golombok et al. constructed two gender-role scales that measured the frequency with which children engaged in a selection of 'traditionally masculine and feminine activities' (1983: 555) (e.g., playing imaginary games such as cops and robbers or tea parties, and playing with mechanical toys or dolls). They treated gender-role behaviour as something that could be measured directly (e.g., through observing children playing). Gender identity was regarded as a psychological construct, inside children's minds, and so not directly measurable. Instead, it was measured indirectly, using observations of sex-role behaviour, and through asking questions about gender identity.

Golombok et al. reported no evidence of inappropriate gender identity for any of the children, that all were glad to be the sex that they were, and none preferred to be the 'opposite' sex. They also reported that in both types of families, boys showed gender-role behaviour 'that would ordinarily be regarded as characteristically masculine, and the girls behaviour of a feminine type' (1983: 562). Finally, they reported that most pre-pubertal children conformed to the 'typical' pattern of having friends of their own sex; the pattern of romantic crushes and friendships in the pubertal and post-pubertal adolescents was also regarded as typical (heterosexual or no interests 'in either direction').

Before we examine some of the problematic assumptions about gender that underpin these examples (you may have an idea already of what some of these might be), it is important to acknowledge the major contributions made by these and other studies to changing the political context in which lesbian mothers sought custody of their children. In Britain and other Western countries, the courts' attitude to lesbian mothers has changed significantly since the early 1970s, and there is much greater acceptance of lesbian families. Lesbian mothers are now highly unlikely to lose custody of their children purely because of their lesbianism.

We highlight three overlapping problems with this type of research (Golombok et al's 1983 study was not unique in the approach it took!) from a feminist and a **queer critical psychology** standpoint, and discuss critical psychology approaches to these issues: (1) the binary construction of sex/gender, with sex belonging to the biological realm and gender the psychological and cultural realm; (2) the reification of gender – the treatment of an idea as a real or living thing; and (3) the regulatory role of psychology in upholding normative conceptions of gender and gendered beings. Here, we are defining a feminist critical psychology approach as one in which assumptions, categories and implications of gender are interrogated within psychology and the wider society. A queer critical psychology goes further – it seeks not just to interrogate or reveal but to dismantle the normative gender and sexuality categories within, and beyond, the discipline.

The first problem is that this research assumes sex and gender occupy different (complementary) realms, with a clear and appropriate mapping of gender
to sex. Sex is treated as a natural (biological) fact, as is the notion that there
are (only) two sexes (Garfinkel, 1967). Gender is psychological, but develops within certain cultural parameters. It is similarly dichotomized, and
appropriately associated with only one sexed body. The assumption in
Golombok et al's (1983) and other early lesbian parenting research – which
was radical at the time – is that when children are born, they are (or should
be) male or female. Gender (identity and role-behaviour) develops shortly
thereafter, with sexuality emerging later. All are binaries: male *or* female;
masculine *or* feminine; heterosexual *or* homosexual. Ideally, sex and gender
match up, and heterosexuality follows. If this matching does not occur, the
assumption is that there is something 'wrong' with the child, the environment, or the mother – but not with the model.

This structure is problematic for anyone who is perceived as not fitting the
model, such as lesbian mothers. Their gender role behaviour (and sexuality)
is viewed as suspect, and likely to adversely impact the gender or sexuality of
their children (i.e., they might be lesbian or gay, or not appropriately masculine or feminine). Hopefully one of the key points you will take away from
this chapter is that people who attempt to resist or to refuse the either/or
possibilities of sex/gender and sexuality and become 'outlaws' from hierarchical binary constructions, or who occupy the female, feminine, homosexual side of the binary, are subjected to often-severe social marginalization.

_____ *the reification of gender* _____

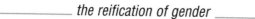

Reification means treating something that is essentially abstract as a living
or real thing. What we know as gender is *abstract*. It is a construct that
psychologists use to theorize and explain patterned differences and experiences, which they then treat as real, reflecting some underlying thing. This
'thing' gender is treated as a thing that exists inside us, something we possess
that shapes our actions and interactions with others and our identity.
Gender is also treated as something that can be measured through behaviours and practices (such as playing cops and robbers, or playing tea parties);
these are taken to be outward 'expressions' of our inner gender identity,
which should match our sex.

The social constructionist model of gender as *something that we do*,
outlined earlier, is the preferred model of many critical psychologists,
ourselves included, and within that model, gender is not reified. The
cultural/queer theorist Judith Butler has famously argued that gender is
performative: 'there is no gender identity behind the expressions of gender...
identity is performatively constituted by the very "expressions" that are said

to be its results' (1990: 25). In simple terms, this means that practices like mainly girls playing tea parties, or mainly boys playing cops and robbers, create the reality of gender. By engaging in these practices moment-by-moment, day after day, we produce and reproduce a *gendered reality* and, along with it, the illusion of a stable inner gender identity (which is reified in research like that conducted by Golombok et al., 1983). Butler uses the notion of performativity rather than performance because the latter suggests that there is an inner *gendered* being directing the outward enactment of gender. In Butler's model, the gendered subject is produced in and through the performativity of gender, and there is no inner essence of gender.

But this does not mean that gender can be anything we want it to be! When teaching social constructionism, students often ask us some version of the following question: 'If things are socially constructed does that mean they are not real?' This is an interesting and important question. Our socially constructed realities are intensely powerful. The effects of language can feel as real as the sun on our skin or the wind in our hair. Our gender enactments are regulated by powerful social norms that are reinforced every time gender is done in a normative fashion; there are sanctions for not doing gender in normative ways: from stares (recall the example that we started the chapter with) to violence; from psychiatric diagnoses and treatment to unemployment and poverty. We have already mentioned the violence done to people who are transgendered as an instance of the policing of gender norms. Some feminist theorists have argued that the social construction of the category 'lesbian' by early male theorists of sexuality was an integral part of attempts to police women's gender behaviour at a time when there was a strong feminist movement. The image of the doomed, barren and mannish lesbian was used to encourage female conformity to heterosexual gender norms, meaning heterosexuality, marriage, and motherhood (Clarke, 2008).

We almost all live our lives as if gender were 'real'. Even fully paid-up members of the social constructionist club like ourselves both do gender in relatively normative ways. It is very difficult to resist or refuse gender. Attempts to do gender differently may not be read in the way they are intended precisely because of what the sociologist Garfinkel (1967) called the 'natural attitude' to gender – a set of social facts (shared beliefs) about gender, including the 'fact' that there are two and only two genders. People's perception of the world is filtered through this natural attitude. And gender infuses our language completely. Try telling a friend about your last night out without using any gender pronouns to describe the people you were with – it's very difficult! 'Gender outlaws' have developed words such as 'hir' and 'ze' to make it easier to talk about people who attempt to live outside of a binary sex/gender system (e.g., Bornstein, 1998). Others, like Bornstein, often pass as female (or male), even if not identifying as such.

Butler's (1990) theory of gender performativity also challenges the notion that gender flows from sex (see our first point of critique) by highlighting discontinuities between sex, gender and sexuality and arguing that *sex* is just as socially constructed as gender – there is no naturally *sexed* body. This is a radical idea! Butler argues that gender does not flow from a *natural* sex difference in biological bodies, but, because gender is such a pervasive framework, we read the body as sexed (see also Laqueur [1990] for an interesting account of 'making' sexed bodies). In these accounts, gender is conceptually prior to sex. Some feminist theorists use the concept of 'sex/gender' to signal that both concepts are socially constructed (rather than biologically or socially derived facts) and that, in some models of gender at least, it is not possible to conceptually separate 'sex' and 'gender': each is implicated in the construction of the other (Kessler & McKenna, 1985).

psychology's regulatory role

Finally, mainstream psychology has played a regulatory role, policing normative conceptions of sex, gender and sexuality, through research such as Golombok et al's (1983). Golombok et al. define gender-role behaviours as those *regarded by the culture* as masculine or feminine. Although they acknowledge the existence of cultural norms around gender, they do not offer any critique of these norms. They do not question the many assumptions implicit in concerns about children's psychosexual development in lesbian families: that heterosexuality is the norm; that (most) heterosexual people are appropriately gendered; and that lesbians' gender identities and sexualities are potentially suspect. Rather, by investigating the concerns that arise from these and other assumptions, they treat such assumptions as legitimate. This implicitly reinforces the framework that leads to the perceived problems. So although their research is beneficial in that it shows 'good' psychological development within these frameworks, on another level it is problematic. It participates in the policing of damaging gender norms and of a binary model of sex/gender, where sex is treated as a natural fact and gender as a psychological/cultural one.

So, even mainstream psychological research that is critically engaged and politically motivated, that seeks to challenge problematic practices in relation to gender and sexuality (such as the denial of child custody to lesbian mothers purely on the basis of their lesbianism), and which can and does lead to social change, also comes at a cost. In this instance, the cost is the reinforcement of problematic assumptions about gender and the perpetuation of a binary sex/gender system – the very conditions which lead to the suggestion that lesbian mothers might not be 'fit' parents. How would a critical psychology approach be different? As an academic and political project, critical psychology should be engaged in the task of working outside, and critiquing, the normative frameworks of gender (and sexuality) which make these debates and practices seem reasonable and sensible, which make them *possible*, as we have done briefly here.

gender in the wider culture: dictionary
definitions of genital parts

In this section we use Virginia's analysis of English language and medical dictionary definitions of female and male genital terms (see Braun & Kitzinger, 2001) to illustrate the ways in which supposedly neutral cultural texts like dictionaries, as well as the supposedly acultural biological body, are permeated with gendered discourses. We use this as a starting point to further outline features of a critical psychology of gender which draws on social constructionist ideas (e.g., Burr, 2003; Davis & Gergen, 1997). The questions constructionists ask relate to what the effects of different gendered constructions are and whose interests they serve.

Dictionaries are not value-neutral. As an authoritative source on words and meaning they lend authority to the values they reflect. Genital definitions, thus, provide a particular version of what genitals are and what they are used for. For example, the *Oxford English Dictionary* (*OED*; online) defines *clitoris*, *penis* and *vagina* like this:

- Clitoris: A homologue of the male penis, present, as a rudimentary organ, in the females of many of the higher vertebrata.

- Penis: Anat. and Zool. The male genital organ used (usually) for copulation and for the emission or dispersal of sperm, in mammals containing erectile tissue and serving also for the elimination of urine.

- Vagina: 1. Anat. and Med. a. The membranous canal leading from the vulva to the uterus in women and female mammals. (*OED* Online, accessed 2 November 2007)

These definitions do not provide a neutral factual account of anatomy. Instead, they are infused with gendered sexual assumptions:

- Only male genitals are used in sex. If you looked up 'copulation', you would discover this only refers to *heterosexual* sex (and only sex intended for procreation); the *OED* defines it, zoologically, as 'the union of the sexes in the act of generation'.

- Only male genitals have any sort of 'function' in the body – female genitals are just there.

- The clitoris is like a much lesser version of the penis – rudimentary, according to the *OED*, means 'undeveloped, immature, imperfect'. This does not sound good!

- The vagina's location is the most important thing about it, but the location isn't relevant for penis or clitoris.

- The vagina is an (open) space for other things to pass through – but the passage is directed *inward*. With a leap, this suggests penile penetration is the vagina's purpose.

- The penis is, the clitoris is sort of, but the vagina is not, an organ. What is an organ? It is 'a part of an animal … that serves a particular physiological function' (*OED*). Hmmm.

What gendered assumptions are evident here? First, the penis appears as the primary referent, about which we learn the most, and in relation to which the clitoris is defined (as inferior). This illustrates the longstanding tradition of viewing the male body as the norm, a point which ties back to the idea that people often equate gender with women. Second, gendered assumptions of masculine sexual *activity* and female sexual *passivity* are also evident in a sexualizing of the male body and a de-sexualizing of the female. This is particularly notable in relation to the clitoris definition; as the only organ whose sole function is sexual pleasure, the failure to mention this seems astounding! Is it that this function is obvious? That argument does not hold when we consider the penis definition, however, or, for instance, the definition of 'anus', which includes the 'ejection' of 'the excrements' (*OED*). Passivity is also encoded in the definition of vagina – a 'canal' is a passive space through which things pass, rather than an active organ that allows or inhibits passage. These tell us that female bodies are not coded as sexual bodies. Dictionary definitions appear still to 'encode the dominant ideology of gender' (Willinsky, 1987: 147), with masculinity and femininity written on to anatomy. This illustrates Judith Butler's (1990) argument, discussed earlier, that gender is conceptually primary and shapes how we see the sexed body.

This discussion illustrates a key social constructionist argument: language is not neutral, but ideological, filled with assumptions. It does not reflect the truth, but rather constructs truths. The traditional view of language in most mainstream psychology (also our commonsense one) is that language is a neutral vehicle for transmitting ideas and information. The contrasting view, often related to the Sapir-Whorf Hypothesis (the theory that language precedes cognition/thought rather than following it), is that language *enables* thought. The theory that language does not simply *reflect* reality, but is involved in the *creation* of reality, is fundamental to social constructionism. The idea is this: we know what we know, we think what we think, and we see and experience the world in the ways we do, because the communities we exist within share linguistic traditions and practices (Davis & Gergen, 1997). Within linguistic communities, there is a *patterned*, rather than random, nature to language and thought (e.g., masculinity active, femininity passive); some social constructionists use the term *discourse* to refer to this patterning. Discourse here refers to a linguistic organizing framework for giving *particular* meaning to an object or concept (Gavey, 1989), which then precludes other possible meanings. Language and discourse make available to us certain ways of understanding the world (truths); we reproduce those ideas when we speak or otherwise express them. Truth is not fixed and stable; truth can change (such as the idea that lesbian mothers were pathological).

No account is neutral. Language constructs the objects to which it refers in ways which foreground certain meanings and hide or deny others. Particular constructions of gender (e.g., gender difference, and gender as linked to sexed bodies) support the view of men's and women's genitalia *as different* (and as a key sign of who we are, as gendered people). This view of genitalia as different, and linked to identity, similarly reinforces the binary construction of gender based around a 'two-sex' model (Laqueur, 1990).

Why does this matter? The theory is that language, discourse and representation have effects: real material effects; personal, experiential effects. Gendered discourse about genitalia provides a context in which individuals whose genitals and gendered identities do not match up are especially likely to experience distress and discrimination. This context also makes practices to change genitals to fit gendered identities seem necessary and desired (e.g., gender reassignment surgery for transgender people or surgery on the genitalia of 'intersex' people who are born with genitalia that do not conform to social norms for 'male' or 'female' bodies). So language and discourse are intimately bound up with personal, social and institutional practices – they enable and constrain certain gendered identities, certain desires and practices. As another example, in the domain of heterosexual sex, the gendered constructions of passivity (female) and agency (male) make it difficult for women to instigate, or even insist on, condom use (Gavey & McPhillips, 1999).

can critical psychology help us to change the 'two-sexed, two-gendered' world?

We hope we have challenged the growing assumption that mainstream psychology is *only* associated with shoring up inequalities and critical psychology is *only* associated with reducing inequalities and creating social change. It is more complicated: both gender and sexuality are domains in which mainstream psychology has the potential to make a difference. Sue Wilkinson (1997a) and Celia Kitzinger (1997) pointed out in the first edition of this book that many feminist and LGBTQ psychologists have been reluctant to wholeheartedly embrace critical psychology because of a concern that critical psychologists cannot (and do not) make meaningful contributions to social change. Thus, feminist and LGBTQ psychologists who prioritize social change over allegiances to particular theoretical or methodological approaches have advocated 'using the master's tools to dismantle the master's house' (Unger, 1996).

While critical psychology challenges frameworks which help construct gender, it does not inevitably or easily lead to meaningful social change. The 'high theory' focus of work that deconstructs gender and sexuality categories often makes it inaccessible to a wide audience and lacks obvious application to the issues facing people in the real world. Indeed, the problems that critical psychologists often identify and challenge are not typically the problems everyday people identify, or are not couched in the same terms. So *if* social change is a goal (and it is not a goal for all critical psychologists), then the challenge is twofold: (a) How do you make claims about problematic constructions of gender while not reinforcing the idea of gender as essential and inherent? And (b) how do you make ideas which so profoundly challenge the commonsense accessible and appealing? We continue to grapple with these questions.

However, the task is not impossible! We end with an example of how critical psychology ideas have produced meaningful social change. The *New View Campaign* (www.newviewcampaign.org) aims to challenge the medicalization of sex and associated practices like 'disease-mongering' – 'creating' new diseases, with accompanying pharmaceutical 'treatments' (see Moynihan & Cassels, 2005). Formed in 2000 by Leonore Tiefer, a leading feminist social constructionist scholar of human sexuality (e.g., Tiefer, 2004), and others, the *New View* emerged in response to an increasingly popular medical model of sexuality and the escalating influence of the pharmaceutical industry in sexuality research, education and treatment. The medical model is problematic because it locates the origin of sexual expression and sexual 'problems' in biological bodies, ignoring the influence of the socially gendered constructions of sexuality. This domination of biologically based sex theorizing fits within the 'gender as nature' model discussed earlier.

Using a social constructionist view of sexuality (Tiefer, 2004), the *New View* argues that the meaning and experience of sexuality and gender are constantly being created and contested. It aims to challenge what it sees as particularly problematic constructions around women's (and by extension men's) sexuality, which pathologize women's bodies and sexualities. Gender constructions not only infuse how we can think about and experience sex, things work the other way as well. Discourse around sexual 'dysfunction' constructs gendered, sexual bodies and subjects – you can see this in relation to Viagra and masculinity (Marshall, 2002). This flips on its head the usual understanding, which is that gender flows from sex; it reiterates Butler's (1990) point about gender as the primary, most important, conceptual framework.

Importantly, the *New View Campaign* emphasizes both critique and alternatives. Interventions utilize the media, education, activism and academic work. The campaign has developed sexuality curriculum resources (Kaschak & Tiefer, 2001; Tiefer, Brick, & Kaplan, 2003) and online continuing education courses for medical professionals (http://www.medscape.com/viewprogram/4705; http://www.medscape.com/viewprogram/5737). Members testified at the 2004 US Food and Drug Administration hearings around Intrinsa, a testosterone patch to treat 'low sexual desire' in women, which is often thought of as a 'symptom'/outcome of menopause. They opposed approving the drug and critiqued the notion that menopause is a *medical* condition, characterized by hormone deficiency. They questioned the idea (implicit in the diagnostic category 'low sexual desire') that we can assess sexual 'dysfunction' as the simple result of hormonal deficiencies, and highlighted the importance of social and contextual/relationship influences in sexuality. The *New View* approach suggests assessing if, in what ways, and why, 'low sexual desire' is experienced as problematic by a woman, rather than treating it as a dysfunction inherent in her. And if it is problematic, exploring ways to change that (see Kaschak & Tiefer, 2002). Intrinsa was not approved.

This successful campaign demonstrates the ongoing, and sometimes rapidly changing, construction of the 'truth' of sexuality, but it does not rely on essentialist gender or sexuality categories, or on a supposed biological truth of genitalia or sexed bodies. Instead, it focuses on how pharmaceutical interventions, which claim to *uncover* a true, inner sexuality, are actually involved in the *construction* of that sexuality, and demonstrates how they are informed by particular societal constructions that we often see as normal and natural. Crucially, the *New View* demonstrates how the links between knowledge and power work in the interest of certain groups (here, big pharmaceutical companies) at the expense of others. In this way, it is a critical psychology of gender and sexuality in action.

■ ■ main chapter points ■

1 Highlights the 'social fact' that we live in a world saturated by gender.

2 Outlines three theories about the origins and meanings of gender: gender as nature, as nurture and as social construct.

3 Critiques mainstream psychological assumptions about gender.

4 Outlines key features of feminist and queer social constructionist theories of gender.

5 Challenges the assumption that mainstream psychology is only associated with shoring up inequalities, and critical psychology is only associated with social change.

6 Provides an example of a critical psychology of gender in action.

glossary

- **feminist psychology/feminist critical psychology:** informed by the goals of the feminist movement, feminist psychology interrogates the assumptions, categories and implications of gender within psychology and the wider society. Feminist critical psychology marries the political goals of the feminist movement with the particular theoretical and methodological interests of critical psychology.

- **gender:** at the social level, gender is a social categorization system, dividing humanity into 'male' and 'female'. At the individual level, gender is the experience and expression of oneself as 'female' or 'male' (or neither of these).

- **heteronormativity:** from queer theory, heteronormativity describes the social privileging of heterosexuality and the assumption that heterosexuality is the only natural and normal sexuality.

- **heterosexual**: people whose sole or primary sexual and emotional attachments are to people of 'the other' sex. Many critical psychologists seek to challenge the taken-for-granted status of heterosexuality – that's why we're including it in this glossary!

- **heterosexism**: the pervasive assumption of heterosexuality as the normative (or only) sexuality, evident in social institutions and everyday interactions.

- **LGBTQ psychology**: a branch of psychology affirmative of LGBTQ identities, it focuses on providing psychological perspectives on the lives and experiences of LGBTQ people, and on challenging both prejudice and discrimination against LGBTQ people and the societal and psychological privileging of heterosexuality.

- **normative**: preferred to the term 'normal', which implies a moral judgment, critical psychologists often use 'normative' and 'non-normative' to highlight what is constructed as 'normal' and 'abnormal' or 'different' within dominant social values.

- **queer**: used in the past as a derogatory term for homosexuals, queer is now used both as a generic term for LGBTQ people and for a particular body of critical theory ('queer theory') that questions the usefulness of identity categories such as 'lesbian' and 'gay'. People who identify as queer often want to signal their allegiance to values associated with queer theory and queer activism.

- **queer critical psychology**: seeks to interrogate and dismantle the normative gender and sexuality categories within, and beyond, the discipline of psychology.

▪ ▪ reading suggestions ▪

Tavris (1993) provides a compelling critique of psychology's gender bias against women and is a good place to get a historical sense of feminist critique within the discipline. Hare-Mustin and Marecek (1998) provided a groundbreaking critique of the basic gender-difference framework dominating psychology. For an overview of different theoretical frameworks around gender, try Bohan (1997), and see Burr (2003) for an introduction to social constructionism. Bornstein (1998) provides an entertaining (non-academic) read which challenges basic assumptions about gender identity; for a more theoretical take, and an accessible introduction to Judith Butler and queer theory, try Sullivan (2003).

: // internet resources /

- **American Psychological Association Division 44** (Society for the Psychological Study of Lesbian, Gay and Bisexual Issues): www.apadivision 44.org

- **Press for Change** – campaigning for respect and equality for all trans people: www.pfc.org.uk

- The Intersex Society of North America: www.isna.org

- Vagina Vérité – diverse conversation forum and resource site: www.vaginaverite.com

- XY: Men, Masculinities, and Gender Politics: www.xyonline.net

 ■ Questions

1   Find a recent example of comparative research on lesbian mother and hetero-sexual families (e.g., Fulcher, Sutfin, & Patterson, 2008) and consider the follow-ing questions: Is the study guided by heterosexist assumptions? Does the study reinforce social norms around sex/gender and sexuality?

2   List all the terms and associations you can think of for 'lesbian', 'gay', and 'hetero-sexual' (e.g., slang terms, stereotypes, famous people, behaviours or practices). What do the terms and associations reveal about cultural attitudes?

3   List the ways gender shapes your daily life. What are some positive and negative aspects of this? Is your experience of gender shaped by your membership of other social categories?

4   How could you challenge gender norms either individually in your daily life or in the form of a group action? What are some of the barriers to success?

15

Critical Psychology and Disability Studies: Critiquing the Mainstream, Critiquing the Critique

Ora Prilleltensky

Chapter Topics

When the first edition of *Critical Psychology* was in the works, I was invited to write a chapter on critical psychology and disability. I declined. At the time, I was busy working on my doctoral research on a topic close to my heart and personal experience: women with physical disabilities and motherhood. In the process of doing so, I was exposed, for the first time, to literature from a **disability studies** perspective. I resonated with this literature that offered a critical lens for examining both the construct of disability and, more importantly for me, the lives of disabled individuals. I was intrigued by what I was reading and by the impact that this literature had on me as a woman living with a progressive neuromuscular disorder. As a then-doctoral student in counselling psychology, I also saw the potential benefit of a disability studies framework for enhancing the wellbeing of individuals with disabilities. Furthermore, I believed the synergy between the newly emerging fields of disability studies and critical psychology held much promise.

This new edition of *Critical Psychology* provides a second opportunity. My own ideas have been enriched by recent publications that have explored possible alliances between psychology and disability studies and their potential for enhancing wellbeing for persons with disabilities (PWD) (e.g. Goodley & Lawthom, 2006; Olkin, 1999; Olkin & Pledger, 2003). However, I must admit that the excitement I feel as I embark on this chapter is mingled with some hesitation and trepidation. My perspective has changed somewhat over the past dozen years and this chapter is not the one I would have written for the first edition. Still, I believe today, as I did then, that critical psychology is well positioned to advance the needs of PWD. Writings from a critical psychology perspective have urged the discipline to highlight social justice and diversity and work to change community conditions antithetical to wellbeing. Critical psychology, thus, is closely aligned with a foundational assumption of disability studies that barriers to full inclusion and the participation of people with disabilities are largely rooted in unaccommodating structures and social arrangements.

Disability studies refers to the interdisciplinary investigation of how social, political, and economic factors interact to construct the phenomenon of disability. Emerging within the last two decades, this new academic discipline critically analyses the construct of disability. Disability studies scholars highlight the importance of infusing throughout the entire academic curriculum a critical understanding of disability. According to Olkin and Pledger (2003), the field focuses on issues of power, oppression, and civil rights; is committed to the empowerment and self-determination of people with disabilities; and regards disability as a basic human condition that must be studied as part of the diverse fabric of human experience. Disability studies is closely linked to the social and minority model of disability which highlights oppression and discrimination as primary barriers in the lives of a distinct minority group: people with disabilities.

I resonate with this conception and thus espouse a disability studies and disability rights framework. Nonetheless, I believe that the critical lens through which we view mainstream approaches should not evade criticism. This caution is akin to Rappaport and Stewart's (1997) insiders' call for 'a critical look at critical psychology', the title of the final chapter of the first edition of this book. In this chapter, thus, I critique both traditional views of disability in mainstream psychology and some critical perspectives as well.

disabling structures, attitudes, and professional practices

> **There would be no privacy screens or anything ... they'd have us literally running around in our underwear ... at ages 9, 10, 11, 12, you know, when you become painfully aware of your body and you're becoming aware of the opposite sex as well ... they weren't sensitive at all to how it would make you feel and how it would impact on you later on ... I really see this as a sort of systemic abuse. (O. Prilleltensky, 2004: 115)**

This quote, from a participant in my research on the lived experience of women with physical disabilities, provides a glimpse into some of the oppressive practices that PWD were historically subjected to. The participant, in her late thirties at the time of the interview, was reflecting on her physiotherapy sessions at a school for children with disabilities in Canada in the late 1960s. As a mature and reflective adult, she was able to name this practice for what it was: a form of systemic abuse by the very individuals charged with meeting the physical, educational, and psychological needs of the youngsters in their care. Sadly, such stories are not rare. Experiences such as these, entrenched in the equation of disability with organic pathology, reflected a professional focus on remediation and rehabilitation and resulted in a host of psychologically iatrogenic practices. The **medical model**, with its focus on bodily abnormality, called for medically driven solutions. A host of professionals designed, implemented and evaluated treatment with little input from disabled individuals (Barnes, Mercer, & Shakespeare, 1999; Oliver, 1996). What could not be cured had to be rehabilitated, and what could not be rehabilitated had to be accepted. People with disabilities were largely regarded as helpless, dependent victims in need of professional assistance and care. Many spent their lives in institutions with limited contact with the wider community. Their daily routine was primarily determined by professional attempts to maximize institutional efficiency. The very identity of PWD became inextricably bound with their perceived incapacity (Barton, 1998; Brisenden, 1998).

The medical model (also referred to as the *personal tragedy model*) was not exempt from psychological research and practice. The mental health field's traditional perception of impairment as an inevitable cause of distress and probable cause of psychological maladjustment is illustrated by this 1977 comment:

> **Patients must be allowed to come to terms, they must grieve and mourn for their lost limbs, lost abilities, or lost looks and be helped to adjust to their lost body image. Personally, I doubt if anyone who has not experienced the onset of irreversible disability can fully understand the horror of the situation. (Dickinson, in Abberly, 1993: 108)**

This quote, more than three decades old, is particularly extreme in its depiction of disability as a tragedy of immeasurable proportions. I expect that we would be hard-pressed to find similar comments in more current publications, and perhaps it was atypical at the time it was published. Still, terms such as 'adaptation', 'adjustment', 'acceptance' and 'coming to terms' were ubiquitous in traditional psychosocial literature on disability. These terms reflect the deficit-oriented and pathologizing approach that dominated psychological research in general, and practice with people with disabilities in particular. Vestiges of that approach are still found in what Linton (1998) called the 'adjustment literature' in mainstream psychology.

>r many years, psychological literature on disability postulated stages that
>'iduals go through as they come to terms with their impairments.

Current phase models (Livneh, 2001; Livneh & Antonak, 2005) continue to support the notion of an orderly process of adaptation to chronic illness and disability (CID), while acknowledging that phases may reverse, overlap, or be altogether omitted, depending on a host of contextual factors. For example, in a recent publication in a counselling journal, Livneh and Antonak (2005) describe 'anger/hostility' sandwiched between 'depression' and 'adjustment' and further subdivided into 'internalized anger' and 'externalized hostility'. In contrast with internalized anger,

externally oriented attributions of responsibility tend to place blame for the CID onset or unsuccessful treatment efforts on other people (e.g. medical staff, family members) or aspects of the external environment (e.g. inaccessible facilities, attitudinal barriers). Behaviours commonly observed during this time include aggressive acts, abusive accusations, antagonism, and passive-aggressive modes of obstructing treatment. (2005: 14)

While the authors do acknowledge the mitigating role played by external factors, it is curious that they ignore the possibility that 'externalized hostility' may be a legitimate reaction to condescending and paternalistic attitudes, preventable barriers to needed resources, and a systemic exclusion from a full participation in society.

It is important to note that stage models of adjustment are increasingly described as antiquated and untested, not only by psychologists such as Rhoda Olkin (1999; see also Olkin & Pledger, 2003) and Carol Gill (2001), who clearly espouse a minority model of disability, but also by leading rehabilitation psychologists such as Timothy Elliot and Ann Marie Warren (2007).

the healing effects of a social understanding of disability

Empowerment of marginalized groups does not happen as a result of spontaneous majority-group enlightenment. It was women rather than men who illuminated oppressive factors that constricted women's lives, just as members of ethno-cultural minority groups challenged white privilege. In the same vein, it was the bold and tireless work of disabled activists that began to challenge public perspectives on disability.

The 1960s and 1970s were historic years for people with disabilities as disabled activists collectively fought to eradicate barriers. Their work, most notably in Britain and the United States, shifted the focus from disabled minds and bodies to oppression and discrimination. These activists brought to light the poverty, the lack of affordable and accessible housing, low employment rates, and the poor education that characterized the lives of individuals with disabilities. They insisted that these conditions emanated not from biology but from socially constructed barriers that systematically excluded people with disabilities from full social participation. For example, the historical neglect of the educational needs of children with disabilities is well known. Consequently, many youngsters were further disadvantaged by inadequate preparation for the job market or for further education, as exemplified by a research participant in my own study who referred to the special school she attended in Canada in the 1960s as a 'huge playground'.

The goal of disability rights activists was to expose socially created barriers and work toward changing unaccommodating social structures that prevented PWD from fully participating in society and realizing their potential. In the USA, the formation of the Independent Living Movement in the 1960s and 70s resulted in greater individual autonomy, while the work of grassroots coalitions and organizations, including mass protests, contributed to important legal gains such as the Rehabilitation Act in 1973 and the Americans with Disabilities Act in 1990 (Olkin, 1999). In Britain, the Union of the Physically Impaired Against Segregation (UPIAS) was one of a number of groups formed by disabled activists in the early 1970s after years of power-lessness and subjugation caused mounting outrage and militancy:

> **We reject the whole idea of 'experts' and professionals holding forth on how we should accept our disabilities, or giving learned lectures about the psychology of impairment. We already know what it feels like to be poor, isolated, segregated, done good to, stared at, and talked down to – far better than any able-bodied expert. We as a union are not interested in descriptions of how awful it is to be disabled. What we are interested in is the ways of changing the conditions of life, and thus overcoming the disabilities which are imposed on top of our physical impairments by the way this society is organized to exclude us ... We look forward to the day when the army of 'experts' on our social and psychological problems can find more productive work to do. (UPIAS, 1976: 4–5, as cited in Barnes, 1998: 68)**

These activists believed that any effort to change individuals rather than the oppressive conditions of their lives meant colluding with the subjugation and pacification of people with disabilities and thus diminishing their wellbeing rather than promoting it.

Of course, psychologists have always been aware that environmental factors play a role in shaping individuals' psychological reality. As early as 1935 Kurt Lewin highlighted the critical interaction between the individual and his or her environment. As a field, rehabilitation psychology has long acknowledged the impact of environmental and attitudinal barriers on the lives of people with disabilities. Nonetheless, as Dunn has noted, 'empirical efforts are rarely contextual; that is, investigations are Lewinian in spirit but rarely in practice ... the focus is on people with disabilities and not on the environmental constraints that they encounter' (2000: 573). Furthermore, according to some theorists, psychosocial research on disability seemed to backtrack from a greater focus on sociopolitical context in the 1960s (see Wright, 1960) toward an impairment-centred approach that amplified individual coping with impairment effects (Gill, 2001). This, according to Gill, was taking place in the 1970s just as disability rights activism was gaining visibility.

This historical analysis provides a context for the strong se𝚛. expressed by UPIAS leaders and founders. As Donna Reeve has note𝚍 appears to have been an avoidance of engaging with *anything* psycho within disability studies lest the individual tragedy model be re-in through suggesting that disabled people need some form of psycholᵧᵧₐₗ help' (2006: 94). Given mainstream psychology's dual focus on intra-psychic factors and deviance, it is understandable why those who dedicated their lives to fighting disability oppression were weary of any discourse on the psychology of disability. As long as social change was perceived to be outside the purview of psychological theory, research and practice, focusing on the lived experience of life with a disability ran the risk of diluting the urgent push for societal transformation.

Nonetheless, as Thomas (1999) notes, barriers that hinder participation can be present not only on the outside, but also on the inside. These psycho-emotional dimensions of disability can also restrict activity, albeit indirectly, when a person decides not to attend a social gathering in order to avoid others' stares and reactions to her body. Thus, the need to address psychosocial issues in disability studies is undeniable. A cautionary body of literature highlights the psychological risks inherent in being defined totally in terms of one's impairment and incapacity; being treated as needy, dependent, and fundamentally different from the non-disabled majority; being perceived as unattractive, asexual, and incapable of attracting a partner; being told or made to feel that one should not strive for partnering, parenting, or other fully reciprocal relationships; being discouraged from associating with other disabled individuals; and the list goes on (Gill, 2001; Olkin, 1999; Reeve, 2002, 2006; Thomas, 1999).

Such analyses are necessary as they portray honest, if at times painful, accounts of lived experience. More importantly, they consistently emphasize that, like the structural barriers to access and participation, many psychosocial barriers are neither inherent in the impairment itself nor an inevitable, unchangeable component of the disability experience. Rather than a simple rehashing of early preoccupations with disability stigma, critical social-contextual literature celebrates disability culture and highlights the strength inherent in collective efforts to counteract exclusion, marginalization, and other psychologically damaging practices. It portrays people with disabilities not as passive victims of such practices and attitudes, but as active agents of change who lead meaningful and fulfilling lives, resist oppressive narratives and structures, and work toward enhancing the wellbeing of future generations. It tells the story of a disability community whose members have discovered the joy and affirmation of associating with one another and working toward social change. It reveals the determination and feistiness of a people who increasingly perceive themselves as worthy and whole and demand to be accepted as such. Increasingly, people with disabilities from various backgrounds are learning to think about disability as a social justice issue rather than as a category of individual deficiency (Gill, 2001).

disability and wellbeing: empowering theories, studies, and practices

Blind psychologist and philosopher Adrian Asch asserts that medically oriented understandings of impairment are typically based on two erroneous assumptions. The first is that life with a disability is an unremitting tragedy, 'forever disrupted, as one's life can be temporarily disrupted by the flu or a back spasm' (2001: 300). The second is that 'if a disabled person experiences isolation, powerlessness, poverty, unemployment, or low social status, these are inevitable consequences of biological limitations' (2001: 300). Inasmuch as oppressive societal structures and iatrogenic practices are based on these erroneous assumptions, they have been consistently challenged in disability studies and are increasingly and actively discounted in more mainstream literature. The debunking of these assumptions denotes a promising beginning, and turning them on their head contributes to empowering, health-enhancing practices. In the following sections, I use the antithesis of these faulty assumptions as an organizing framework for theories, studies and practices that can empower and enhance wellbeing for people with disabilities. Although these assumptions and their antitheses are separated for organizational purposes, such separation is inevitably artificial as they operate in tandem.

disability and wellbeing are not mutually exclusive

Earlier in the chapter I criticized psychological literature that portrays disability as inextricably linked with tragedy and mourning and antithetical to wellbeing. Not only is this totalizing and inaccurate portrayal contrary to how most people with disabilities describe their own lives, its 'awfulizing', pity-invoking account impedes wellbeing. It is thus important to emphasize a significant disconnect between how people with disabilities evaluate their own quality of life and how this life is evaluated and imagined by those without disabilities. In fact, it has long been established that people with disabilities rate their lives as far more satisfying and fulfilling than their non-disabled counterparts imagine. Studies comparing life satisfaction and subjective wellbeing among those with and without disabilities have generally found that while disability is associated with a reduction in subjective wellbeing, this difference is relatively small and diminishes further as people learn to live with their disability (Dijkers, 1999; Dunn, 2000; Putzke, Richards, Hicken, & DeVivo, 2002). Most of the research on life satisfaction has studied individuals with spinal cord injuries. Comparative studies have found that people with such injuries have life satisfaction scores not much lower than those without injuries (Dijkers, 1999). This finding is contrary to the belief of most individuals, including health-care professionals, that sustaining such an injury is 'among the greatest calamities that might befall them' (Dijkers, 1999: 867). In a similar vein the relationship between severity of impairment and life satisfaction is mediated by a host of attitudinal and environmental factors and highly dependent on the perceived ability to carry out valued life roles, activities, and social interactions.

Researchers have conducted studies and proposed theoretical explanations to account for this commonly replicated 'happiness gap' (Ubel, Lowenstein, & Jepson, 2005: 111). For example, Ubel et al. (2005) examined the disconnect between the positive emotional adaptation made by most people who sustain an injury and the negative prediction of non-disabled research participants regarding what life would be like should they themselves sustain such an injury. They found that not only do individuals fail to predict the extent to which they would adapt to changed life circumstances, but asking them to think about how they have adapted to past adversities changed their estimate of how disability might affect their quality of life.

The insider–outsider distinction and actor–observer difference are helpful constructs in accounting for the discrepant views of non-disabled observers, on the one hand, and insiders' view of life with a disability, on the other. The salience of disability contributes to the oft erroneous assumption by 'outsiders' regarding 'insiders'' preoccupation with their physical state and the former's belief that it invariably permeates every aspect of the latter's life. Insiders, on the other hand, know what disability is like, have found ways to minimize its impact, and thus regard their situation as far more favourable than outsiders imagine (Dunn, 2000; Dunn & Dougherty, 2005; Dunn & Elliot, 2005).

A number of rehabilitation researchers have critiqued the rehabilitation field for its historical focus on pathology, distress, and negative emotional reactions to disability, along with a neglect of health, positive coping, and psychological growth (e.g., Dunn, 2000; Dunn & Doherty, 2005; Elliot, Kurylo, & Rivera, 2002). Traditional rehabilitation assessments defined and measured wellbeing as an absence of distress and other negative emotional reactions.

Unfortunately, this work does not increase our understanding of how people can experience positive growth and meaning following disability. Indeed, psychological models in which people with a disability are portrayed as recipients of care or victims of misfortune preoccupied with matters of health cannot inform us about positive growth following disability. (Elliot et al., 2002: 688)

Psychologists and other helping professionals are not immune from the tendency to view disability as anything but tragic (Dunn & Elliott, 2005). This is not surprising given the historical absence of conceptualizations of health in the context of disability. Furthermore, as outsiders, many psychologists have been wary of accepting insiders' perspectives that are inconsistent with stereotypic expectations of preoccupation with physical states (Dunn & Elliott, 2005). Alternatively, 'models of thriving are more elusive but would afford a fresh perspective on the generativity and wellbeing that are as much the birthright of PWD as they are of nondisabled individuals' (Mona, Cameron, & Fuentes, 2006: 88).

The past three decades have seen dramatic progress in the conceptualization of disability. In 2003, a special issue of *American Psychologist* was devoted to disability issues (Pledger, 2003). The articles covered such diverse topics as future directions for disability and rehabilitation research (Tate & Pledger, 2003), possible alliances between disability studies and psychology (Olkin & Pledger, 2003) and disability policy's implications for psychology (Gill, Kewman, & Brannon, 2003). Common to all the articles was their '*new paradigm*' orientation, a term popularized by the National Institute of Disability and Rehabilitation (NIDRR) and adopted by a wide range of researchers and practitioners. Distinguished from the '*old paradigm*' which focused on the biological condition and defined disability as a deficit within the individual (Pledger, 2003), the 'new paradigm' regarded disability as 'a product of the intersection of individual characteristics (e.g. conditions or impairments, functional status, or personal or socioeconomic qualities) and characteristics of the natural, built, cultural, and social environment' (NIDRR, cited in Pledger, 2003: 282). During the same period, the World Health Organization came up with a renewed definition of impairment and disability (The International Classification of Functioning, or ICF) which places a much greater emphasis on the physical, social, and attitudinal environment in shaping the disability experience (Whiteneck, Meade, Dijkers, Tate, Bushnik, & Forchheimer, 2004).

The increased emphasis on life satisfaction and subjective wellbeing, along with a growing recognition of the role of the environment, are important steps in disability research and practice. The ethos of the new paradigm gave rise to such measures as the Craig Hospital Inventory of Environmental Factors (CHIEF), which quantifies perceived environmental barriers as well as the frequency with which such barriers are encountered, their magnitude, and the impact they have on the life of people with disabilities (Whiteneck et al., 2004). Studies which measure life satisfaction and wellbeing in conjunction with the impact of perceived environmental barriers represent a refreshing trend that can enhance our understanding of life with a disability. For example, a study which incorporated the above constructs supported previous research that life satisfaction has more to do with social participation than with level of impairment and that environmental factors are significant correlates of life satisfaction. Contrary to expectations, environmental barriers were not found to significantly limit participation, although their presence was related to life satisfaction. The researchers concluded that while this finding may reflect limitations of the study, it is also plausible that people go to great lengths to overcome barriers, but at the price of reduced satisfaction (Whiteneck et al., 2004).

This new work has also contributed to a more holistic and nuanced understanding of health and wellbeing. Whereas traditional definitions of health focused on an absence of illness, such definitions have been recently expanded to include physical, mental, and social wellbeing and such diverse constructs as meaningful occupation, fulfilling roles, self-actualization, and optimal environmental functioning (Becker, 2006; Harrison, 2006). These expanded definitions have been an important impetus in shifting the focus from simply preventing disability (and thus excluding people with disabilities) to promoting health and wellbeing for all citizens, irrespective of disability status.

The focus on health promotion means exploring the subjective experience of health and wellbeing as well as the factors that impede or facilitate it. According to a recent literature review, the importance of functioning as an aspect of health was common to many of the studies reviewed, as was the importance of performing chosen roles; having reciprocal relationships that allow people to both be cared for and care for others; and being able to take part in desirable activities (Harrison, 2006). The ability to exercise self-determination, feel in control of one's life, and live unencumbered by pain are other common correlates of health (Becker, 2006; Putnam, Greenen, Powers, Saxton, Finney, & Dautel, 2003). These correlates were noted in a recent qualitative study of 99 individuals with mobility impairments (Putnam et al., 2003). Furthermore, most study participants perceived health and wellness as distinct from their disability and not precluded by it. Most importantly, perhaps, this study focused on participants' perceptions regarding the barriers and facilitators to health and wellness for themselves and for people with disabilities in general. Based on a thematic analysis of 19 focus groups, participants' perceptions of barriers and facilitators fell into three main levels: personal, community, and societal, with some responses cutting across categories. The main themes were emotional wellbeing, personal attitudes and health behaviour at the personal level and social support and health care providers at the community level. Two main themes were identified at the systems level: one pertaining to access and accommodation and the other to institutions, regulations, and financing (Putnam et al., 2003). The latter category entailed such things as financial worries related to assistive devices and the generally high cost of living with a disability, coupled with the lack of societal recognition of such costs. Thus, a direct link was made between financial status and the promotion of wellness.

Studies such as these are essential. They highlight the multidimensional nature of disability and the imperative of recognizing and addressing needs at their respective levels. This seems to be stating the obvious, but too often professional efforts continue to focus on personal change despite a changed ethos and stated recognition that disability is often more a social problem than a personal problem. Indeed, Smith, Langa, Kabeto, and Ubel (2005) found that despite the relatively weak correlation between financial status and subjective wellbeing, financial resources enhance subjective wellbeing after disability onset.

The functioning of persons with disabilities is affected by the entire network of biological, psychological, social, environmental, economic, legal, policy, and

political factors. However, disability research in psychology has been limited primarily to the first three factors. Psychology needs to go beyond an emphasis on the person with the disability to a broader-based approach that includes the family as well as the political and societal realms. (Olkin & Pledger, 2003: 298)

dealing with impairment effects: an inconvenient truth

The salutary effects of a sociopolitical understanding of disability are undeniable. Liz Crow, a British disability rights activist, has written a compelling account of the transformative impact such an understanding had on her wellbeing:

> My life has two phases: before the social model of disability, and after it. Discovering this way of thinking about my experiences was the proverbial raft in stormy seas ... For years now this social model has enabled me to confront, survive, and even surmount countless situations of exclusion and discrimination ... It has played a central role in promoting disabled people's individual self-worth, collective identity, and political organization. I don't think it is an exaggeration to say that the social model has saved lives. (Crow, 1996: 206–207)

Whereas all social-contextual approaches to disability highlight social barriers, British disability activists and scholars went the farthest in their definition of disability as social oppression. In what became known as the British **social model of disability**, there is a conceptual separation of *impairment*, the actual condition, from *disability*, the social oppression that people with impairments are subjected to. According to this definition disability is not a condition that exists in individuals, but a social ailment whose eradication can result in a disability-free society. Although impairment effects are not necessarily denied, their explication is not perceived as useful in eliminating disability.

The conceptual separation between disability and impairment is appealing in its simplicity and makes a strong case for focusing on socially created barriers. Nonetheless, as noted by critics from within and outside the social model, this same simplicity makes it an easy target for critique. For one thing, defining impairment as purely biological does not account for the fact that it is often caused and/or exacerbated by social structures. Examples abound of impairments caused by war or exacerbated by such social conditions as poverty. By the same token, defining disability strictly in social terms risks minimizing the potentially distressing effects of physical impairments, effects that removing social barriers cannot always alleviate (Shakespeare, 2006; Thomas, 1999). This can be as invalidating of the personal experience of disability as the suggestion that impairment effects are the main culprits of distress. Crow (1996), who credited the social model with saving lives, also contends that its exclusive focus on oppressive attitudes and practices has silenced bodily struggles:

> The experience of impairment is not always irrelevant, neutral, or positive ... many of us remain frustrated and disheartened by pain, fatigue, depression and

chronic illness ... many of us fear for our futures with progressive or additional impairments ... Yet our silence about impairment has made many of these things taboo and created a whole new series of constraints on our self-expression. (Crow, 1996: 209–210)

The acknowledgment that impairments may entail suffering not caused by social barriers or easily alleviated by their removal is risky and fraught with challenges. In multiple studies and personal narratives, people with disabilities describe their struggles to correct erroneous assumptions about their quality of life and dispel myths about the tragedy of disability. They often go to great and exhausting lengths to accentuate their similarity with the non-disabled majority who often perceive them as so different and far removed from themselves that any social relation feels strained and artificial. In an outstanding chapter titled 'Divided Understandings: The Social Experience of Disability', disabled psychologist and disability studies scholar Carol Gill (2001) describes efforts to bridge the divide felt by many people with disabilities. Energy which is already in short supply is often spent on responding graciously to intrusive questions and behaviours, attempting to reduce awkwardness and put other people at ease, and deliberately acting to smooth over social relations (Gill, 2001).

Despite the difficulties inherent in explicating impairment effects, they cannot and must not be absent from psychological discourse on disability lest they become the proverbial elephant in the room. Impairment effects can be an important part of the disability experience, depending on their nature, severity, static versus progressive nature, and so on. As Shakespeare noted,

[i]mpairment affects individuals in different ways. Some people are comparatively unaffected by impairment, or else the main consequences of impairment arise from other people's attitudes. For others, impairment limits the experiences and opportunities they can experience. In some cases, impairment causes progressive degeneration and premature death. These features of impairment can cause distress to many disabled people, and any adequate account of disability has to give space to the difficulties which many impairments cause. (Shakespeare, 2006: 92–93; see also French, 1993; O. Prilleltensky, 2004; Thomas, 1999)

While the impairment/disability divide has been debated within disability studies and a number of theorists have raised the need to address both, its implications for therapeutic interventions remain unclear. For example, Donna Reeve's (2002, 2006) excellent work on the psychoemotional dimensions of disability includes important implications for therapeutic work designed to counteract socially engendered barriers. Impairment effects are also acknowledged, but their implications for counselling interventions are unaddressed. Similarly, impairment effects are not even mentioned in a chapter titled 'Counselling with the Social Model: Challenging Therapy's Pathologies' (Swain, Griffiths, & French, 2006). Thus, it seems that impairment effects are an inconvenient truth the field has yet to fully reconcile with.

Impairment is indeed an inconvenient truth because its mere acknowledgment risks a throwback to the deficit era and to a professional focus on the individual instead of the societal. Yet, attention to impairment does not have to devolve into a person-centred, out-of-context, asocial orientation. Glossing over the physicality of the impairment runs another risk: ignoring or neglecting lived experience. I agree that psychology should not be preoccupied with impairment effects and that 'there is an urgent need for therapy to undo a widely held assumption that pathologises people simply on the basis of impairment' (Goodley & Lawthom, 2006: 1999). However, I also believe that psychologists cannot ignore impairment effects, lest we give the message that real struggles with real bodies are superfluous to this discourse and of little relevance to therapeutic interventions. As Shakespeare has argued (2006), giving space to impairment effects is not contingent upon perceiving impairment as only and always negative, or adhering to simplistic notions that impairment equals distress. At the same time, ignoring or downplaying the potentially problematic reality of biological limitations is not the path to enhancing wellbeing for people with disabilities. In some cases, social barriers do not account for the totality of lived experience. Dichotomizing impairment and disability does not take into account the fact that they are often experienced in tandem and do not lend themselves to simplistic separation.

conclusions

Psychological research and practice with people with disabilities is both personal and political. Magnifying the former at the expense of the latter is not only ineffective, but potentially harmful (Olkin, 1999; Olkin & Pledger, 2003). Isaac Prilleltensky (2008) has coined the term *psychopolitical validity* to denote the inseparable nature of psychological and political dynamics and the need to attend to both. This framework is highly relevant to psychological discourse on disability.

As researchers and practitioners, critical psychologists who espouse a disability studies orientation are well positioned to enhance the wellbeing of people with disabilities. Goodley and Lawthom (2006), for example, make very explicit the connection between critical psychology and disability studies. Others, such as Gill (2001) and Olkin (1999), embrace a critical psychology paradigm without necessarily invoking critical psychology's terminology. Their critical perspective and awareness of the role that social arrangements and access to resources play in subjective wellbeing are invaluable. Their willingness to pose tough questions, even when such questions disturb the status quo and make some people uncomfortable, serves an important function.

- Why, despite new-paradigm thinking, do researchers and practitioners continue to focus on the person and his or her immediate environment and rarely enter into the larger social-political dialogue?

- Why, despite significant advances in anti-discrimination laws, assistive technology, and rehabilitation practices, do people with disabilities continue to be disproportionately unemployed, underemployed, and on the bottom rung of the socioeconomic ladder?

- What are the values and assumptions that guide our research questions?

- Who gets to do the asking, and why do people with disabilities continue to be significantly underrepresented as psychological researchers and practitioners?

- Why is research on individuals with disabilities who have satisfying careers, a loving partner, children they nurture, and the ability to balance their multiple roles still scant?

- What environmental supports would allow more people to thrive in the context of disability?

These are but some of the relentless questions critical researchers and practitioners pose (Gill, 2001; Olkin, 1999; Olkin & Pledger, 2003; Schriner, 2001). Additionally, critical theorists, researchers and practitioners are making meaningful contributions and providing roadmaps for doing empowering work with people with disabilities.

The importance of critical perspectives notwithstanding, it is important to balance the personal and the political, the structural and the physiological. In what at times seems like an uphill battle to put macro-level and structural barriers at the centre of the debate, critical researchers and practitioners run the risk of minimizing or paying lip-service to impairment effects that are not easily rectified by changes in social arrangements. Perhaps downplaying impairment effects was the inevitable consequence in the struggle to balance the pathologizing impairment-focused tendencies that have historically dominated psychological approaches to disability. Nonetheless, the binary distinction between bodily struggles and socially engendered barriers is neither representative of the lives of many people with disabilities, nor helpful to advancing their psychological wellbeing (Prilleltensky & Prilleltensky, 2006; Schriner, 2001; Shakespeare, 2006).

As an academic and a counselling psychology professional who also lives with a progressive impairment, I resonate with and applaud critical perspectives and am inherently suspicious of non-critical conceptions of psychosocial aspects of disability. At the same time, I'm increasingly convinced that work situated within disability studies and critical psychology must acknowledge and attend to impairment's role in the lives of some individuals. Its social-political dimensions notwithstanding, disability is an embodied experience that cannot always be perceived as desirable or even neutral. Indeed, impairment effects, especially those associated with progressive and increasingly more debilitating conditions, can certainly pose a challenge to life satisfaction and wellbeing. Psychology and other helping professions cannot afford to shy away from exploring those, and other impacts, on the lives of affected individuals. Professional or political ambivalence about impairment effects can result in subtle and not-so-subtle messages that this part of one's experience is not acceptable and that personal, impairment-related struggles should be kept private.

Just as it is possible to have both negative and positive emotions that are not simply opposite ends of the same continuum, it is possible to experience frustration, sadness, and loss over bodily functions, and at the same time (given the right contextual factors) to lead a life that is satisfying, rewarding, and deeply meaningful. While this is a simple message, I believe it has important implications for people with disabilities, the non-disabled family and friends with whom they have meaningful relationships, and the health professionals who sometime work with them. People with disabilities need multiple avenues to form positive identities and reject devalued images of themselves and others like them, even if they do not see their disability as desirable or neutral, although some do; even if they believe that their life would be easier and more satisfying if they were not disabled, although some do not believe that. Importantly, such beliefs do not preclude a positive identity, high self-esteem, or a satisfying and rewarding life. Neither are they incongruent with thriving, positive growth, and finding meaning in life with a disability.

Given the prevalence of 'stereotypical identity ascription' (Gill, 2001: 353) by those they interact with, many people with disabilities have become experts at managing other people's reactions to their impairment, enhancing the latter's comfort level, and emphasizing the many commonalities they share with their non-disabled counterparts. While this allows them to manage social relations and is thus adaptive at some level, there is little doubt that it can come at a price. Just like messages that one must be forever positive and cheerful (or be seen as a tragic victim) are antithetical to wellbeing, so are messages and beliefs that sadness, loss, and other negative emotions must be completely disavowed; only experienced as private but not shared; or over-defined as resulting from structural barriers. It is imperative that this schism must not be reenacted in the therapeutic relationship.

Persons with disabilities seeking counselling would not be helped by therapists who ignore personal accounts of impairment, just as they would not be helped by therapists who neglect oppressive societal conditions. Talking about impairment is not tantamount to tragedy-laden narratives. Biasing the conversation in favour of external or internal limitations may signal that only certain issues are justified and legitimate for counselling. Although slogans are easy to coin and even easier to follow, therapeutic and social interventions demand a level of complexity that is hard to attain. The achievement of political goals through a focus on oppressive social policies can advance social transformation and personal liberation at the same time. This, however, does not translate into an automatic elimination of personal struggles related to structural barriers, socially engendered stressors, or impairment effects. Every situation is different and endless permutations of the balance between factors exist. The helper's tool kit should include implements to dismantle societal oppression and amplifiers to hear lived experience in all its complexity.

1 Historically, psychological research and practice with people with disabilities has focused on helping individuals adapt to their disabilities, with little attention paid to systemic barriers.

2 Disabled activists and academics challenged public perceptions of disability and worked toward identifying and eradicating socially created barriers. This was an empowering process that led to important changes.

3 People with disabilities rate their quality of life and subjective wellbeing much higher than those without disabilities imagine. Additionally, many disability-related barriers are not inherent in the impairment itself, but are socially created and can thus be removed.

4 At the same time, impairment effects can be troublesome to some people and may need to be addressed in a therapeutic setting. Psychologists should address structural barriers, but also attend to possible impairment effects that are not easily amenable to social change.

glossary

- **disability studies**: A multidisciplinary field which examines disability as a social, cultural, and political phenomenon and is committed to the empowerment and self-determination of people with disabilities.

- **medical model of disability (old paradigm):** Disability is reduced to a medical condition which highlights pathology and deficit within the individual, with little attention to the role of the environment.

- **social model of disability (new paradigm):** A person–environment approach which considers the complex interplay of individual differences and social environments. According to this model, many of the barriers encountered by people with disabilities result from environments that fail to accommodate them and from negative attitudes towards them.

Two sources, *Handbook of Disability Studies* (Albrecht, Seelman, & Bury, 2001) and a special issue of the *American Psychologist* dedicated to disability issues

(Pledger, 2003) offer a good overview of the field, with some specific applications to psychology. For practitioners looking for guidelines for working with people with disabilities, Olkin (1999) is a must read.

// internet resources

- **List of disability studies programmes in North America**: isc.temple.edu/neighbour/ds/dsprogrammes.htm

- **Open Directory Disability Studies** – database of various related websites: www.dmoz.org/Society/Disabled/Disability_Studies/

- **Society for Disability Studies**: www.disstudies.org

Questions

1 When asked what they think is the most difficult thing about being disabled, people *without* disabilities usually mention limitations caused by the impairment itself. Conversely, people *with* disabilities often point to misconceptions about disability and structural and attitudinal barriers. What do you think accounts for this difference, and how can the disability experience be better understood?

2 Professionals working in the field are increasingly accepting the idea that people with disabilities are primarily hindered by unaccommodating structures and social arrangements. Nonetheless, professional intervention often limits the focus to personal change. How can psychologists' training be expanded to include strategies for working toward social change at the individual, organizational, and societal levels?

3 This chapter emphasizes the importance of focusing on strengths and enhancing wellbeing for people with disabilities and on identifying and alleviating barriers. At the same time, impairment effects may present challenges that social change cannot alleviate. How can psychologists provide a safe place that allows clients to explore these dynamics, without misconstruing and pathologizing their experience?

16

From Colonization to Globalization: Continuities in Colonial 'Common Sense'

Ingrid Huygens

Chapter Topics

For me, oppression is the greatest calamity of humanity. It diverts and pollutes the best energies of man – of oppressed and oppressor alike. For if colonization destroys the colonized, it also rots the colonizer.

Memmi, 1965: xvii

Modern Western psychology emerged and developed in the context of European conquest, exploitation and domination. That historical link is no accident. Indeed, it can help us understand how psychological concerns may be approached more critically in our increasingly globalized world. Thus, American community psychologist Tod Sloan, in his useful introduction to globalization, poverty and social justice, asks a largely psychological question: why, in light of what the world has experienced through exploitation built into capitalist economics, do so many people believe capitalism is a good system? His answer – 'the curious phenomenon associated with ideology' (2005: 319) – is a central theme of this chapter.

I present first a brief critical history of colonial relations to help link cultural and psychological phenomena such as ideology with 'the entangled web' of global economic and political processes in which human survival and wellbeing are now embedded (Marsella, cited in Sloan, 2005). I focus throughout on the relationship between *colonizer* and **indigenous peoples**. The term 'indigenous peoples' emerged in the 1970s from the struggles of the American Indian Movement (AIM) in the United States and the Canadian Indian Brotherhood as a way to internationalize the experiences and issues of some of the world's colonized peoples (Smith, 1999). I also attempt to internationalize the issues, in this case for some of the world's **colonizer peoples**, by using an approach consistent with a critical psychology. In this chapter I consider globalization as a form of ongoing **colonialism**, open to the same criticism that it relies on an instrumental racism and European cultural supremacy as ideological supports. These ideologies are the building blocks for a contemporary version of a colonial 'commonsense' that colonizer groups in modern societies draw upon for everyday decisions. Such 'common sense' continues to see indigenous people as an enemy and assertions of their collective rights as primitive impediments to a world-wide capitalism.

A single case story woven throughout the chapter illustrates a situation in New Zealand in which I was involved as an activist Pakeha psychologist. The story provides an example of how racism and cultural supremacy are 'lived ideologies' (Billig, Condor, Edwards, Gane, Middleton, & Radley, 1989) in contemporary Western societies. These ideologies underpin a pervasive 'common sense' with which colonizer groups support, or at least acquiesce in, modern-day confiscations and suppressions of indigenous peoples. The impact of such a 'colonial common sense' on indigenous peoples in New Zealand has particular application to other former British colonies such as Australia, Canada and the United States of America where non-indigenous groups are now the numerical majority.

> In Aotearoa New Zealand, we love our beaches. We consider the coastline and marine resources 'ours', and feel privileged. For the indigenous Maori, or First Nation people of these islands, the coastal and marine resources were, and are, an integral and treasured element of life. The incoming white settlers, called Pakeha, quickly used the beaches and abundant sea food for sustenance, and for commerce and recreation. Nowadays, more recent immigrants from Asia and Africa enthusiastically swim, walk and gather seafood all around the coastline. Visitors from overseas admire our coastline too, and in increasing numbers those with currencies valued more highly in global finances than our own buy coastal properties and offshore islands. So who do we believe 'our beaches' belong to? And who is entitled to make decisions about such treasured resources?

colonization and globalization

Colonization may be seen uncritically as a process of people settling in an area distant from their homeland, thereby creating a colony (*Collins English*

Dictionary, 1994). People in colonies often exploit the environmental and human resources in these new territories for the benefit of the homeland. Such exploitative colonization has often been viewed as an inevitable outgrowth of European industrial capitalism. In such an economics-focused approach, the efficiency of industrial production drives a search for more raw materials to be used in the homeland to produce manufactured goods which are then sold back to the colony. In this uncritical view, the economic 'success' of European capitalism justifies European and American expansion over the past 500 years.

However, colonization may also be understood in more critical terms that articulate human agency, values and the exploitative use of power. The term colonialism, for instance, has been defined as the 'forcible, long-term occupation by a metropolitan country of territory outside Europe or the USA' (Kiernan, 1993: 294). The European colonial project undertaken from the 1500s differed in its scale and scope from earlier forms of territorial domination. By the beginning of World War II, Europe and the United States held most of the earth's surface in some sort of colonial subjugation. Critical indigenous writer Smith (1999) describes this colonialism as an expression or method of **imperialism**, facilitating Europe's economic and cultural expansion by ensuring European control over distant colonies. Such large-scale domination of overseas territory depended on sustaining a huge disparity in power and required securing and subjugating the indigenous populations.

Similarly, advocates of globalization uncritically promote it as bringing 'the benefits of science, democracy, free trade, communications systems and corporation-controlled capitalism to the entire world' through transnational, transcultural and transborder processes (Sloan, 2005: 314). Critical writers, however, describe globalization as a form of continuing colonialism or imperialism, calling it 're-colonization' or 'neo-colonialism', because the pattern of present-day global relationships follows that of the former European colonial empires.

Although most colonies gained independence after World War II, they had to borrow heavily to finance modernization because the colonial powers had extracted raw materials and labour without investing in local development. The former colonial powers' lending institutions, such as the World Bank and the International Monetary Fund, set harsh conditions on those loans, for example, reducing government spending on health and education and removing barriers to foreign investment. Most former colonies became encumbered with such astronomical debts to Europe and the United States that they had to reorder their societies to increase the efficiency of capitalist production. As a result, the powerful classes in many of these developing countries have accumulated wealth and adopted Westernized lifestyles while the rest of the population lives in extreme poverty (Sloan, 2005).

Internal inequities as a consequence of colonization are not restricted to so-called Third World nations. A stream of theorizing in the USA during the 1970s identified sixteenth-century European colonization as the source of present-day inequality in the Americas and elsewhere. Initially established by force, European appropriation of land from Native Americans and labour from African Americans, and later from Mexican Americans, was institutionalized through racism to create a structured 'internal colonialism' (Feagin & Feagin, 1978). Exacerbated by economic underdevelopment and social injustice in former colonies, the contemporary flow of goods and capital in most countries thus retains the colonial pattern both globally and domestically. The entire globe can be considered to have developed colonial relationships between economies, peoples and cultural groups.

Approximately 300 million indigenous people live in 70 countries in the Americas, Africa, India, South Asia, Australia and the Pacific. These First Nations of colonial First, Second and Third World lands are sometimes described as the Fourth World (Nikora, Levy, Masters, & Waitoki, 2006). As many of them see it, globalization simply extends colonization (Smith, 1999). Colonizer groups first took control of indigenous land, law, spirituality, language, education, health and family structures, and finally culture itself. They exploited the physical, intellectual and genetic property of indigenous peoples through land seizures, language suppression and the repackaging of indigenous culture as an exotic commodity to be sold (Nairn, 1990). Today, contemporary vehicles for such exploitation include confiscatory legislation, commodifying indigenous cultural forms, and biomedical projects appropriating genetic material for profit (Glover et al., 2005).

Considering the nature of the colonial relationship, Memmi, a Tunisian Jew writing of his experience in the French colonies in North Africa, noted that 'the deprivations of the colonized are the almost direct result of the advantages secured to the colonizer' (1965: xii). For this reason, international conflict mediator Adam Curle described colonial relationships as 'unpeaceful' because they cause 'damage to one or more of the parties concerned, through physical violence, or in economic, social, or psychological ways' (Curle, 1971: 1). Australian anthropologist Stevenson views the so-called 'encounter' between Europeans and indigenous peoples as so all-encompassing and systematic that it can only be described as a war: '[T]he central endeavour was, and still is, to lay waste a people and destroy their culture in order to undermine the integrity of their existence and appropriate their riches' (1992: 27).

Considering the social and psychological mechanisms of colonization, Irish psychologist Moane describes the colonial relationship as one of domination and control which becomes over generations 'more pervasive and more subtle' (1999: 32). The colonizer's control of economic, political and symbolic systems becomes institutionalized and obscured by ideologies which justify exploitative uses of power and naturalize the superiority of the colonizer and inferiority of the colonized. Stevenson (1992) argues that imperialism was thereby embedded in language. A language of total war against indigenous peoples provided the colonizers with the 'psychological momentum and confidence to determine the fates and identities of masses of human beings' (1992: 28). He compares the language used to support North

American colonization to the language supporting globalization today, and concludes that such psycho-linguistic processes help the group that covets the lands and resources of others by expressly masking predatory action and intention – for instance, by asserting that exploitation is really just tough-minded economic action.

British psychologist Howitt and Ghanian psychologist Owusu-Bempah consider that the discipline of psychology continues to play its part in the European colonial project along with the mass media and other Western institutions. Citing Masson's view of the power underpinning a 'psychological imperialism', they argue that military forces, police, weapons, prisons, abuse, instructions, laws, rituals and such like are simply the tools by which one definition of reality can be made to prevail over others. They suggest that psychologists, compared with members of other disciplines, have been particularly prone 'to make the European definition of reality prevail over those of the rest of the world' (Howitt & Owusu-Bempah, 1994: 118). Even where psychologists intend to ameliorate the effects of impoverishment and underdevelopment, their interventions generally do little more than help individual people adjust to capitalist modernization and assimilate European cultural forms.

Indigenous psychologist Levy (2007) uses Moghaddam's approach to a power structure among global psychological communities to analyse their differing capacity for producing and disseminating psychological knowledge, and, as a consequence, for shaping and defining what the discipline considers mainstream, conventional or normal. In Moghaddam's framework, the 'First World' (the United States), by virtue of its position as the major producer and exporter of psychological knowledge, holds a dominant and unchallenged position. The 'Second World', including Britain, Canada and India, although each produces its own knowledge, is heavily influenced by the First, reinforc-ing the legitimacy of First World psychological knowledge. The Third World, including countries such as Bangladesh, Cuba and Nigeria, solely imports knowledge from the First and Second Worlds. In Moghaddam's view, the primary gap between psychological communities lies in the capacity to produce psychological knowledge, including psychologists able to create the knowledge bases and publishing outlets which disseminate that knowledge. Levy concludes that through processes of exporting and importing, the disci-pline of psychology promotes a mono-cultural Western tradition which 'seeks and accepts universals while invalidating other systems of knowledge and dissemination' (2007: 37). Howitt and Owusu-Bempah similarly conclude that because psychology is exported from the First World in a 'one-way stream' (1994: 118), it contributes to European and American cultural imperialism.

While psychologists from indigenous and oppressed groups have been working, in Memmi's words at the beginning of this chapter, to resist colonization's tendency to 'destroy the colonized', psychologists from dominant and elite groups have been slower to examine how colonization also 'rots the colonizer'. The remainder of the chapter explores ways in which the psychology of colonizer groups and individuals sustains imperialism and colonialism, and then suggests how critical psychology can contribute to a new agenda: **decolonization**.

racism and cultural supremacy

From 1840 to 1860, Maori commercial enterprise in the global economy of the day was highly successful. The indigenous, intensive horticultural methods using collective labour and collectively owned machinery and mills were far more efficient than individually owned European farms worked by single families. Maori were quickly able to transport and sell their produce to the new Pakeha settlements and to export to Australian and American markets. However, the settlers pressured Britian's colonial office to allow them to set up a local settler government, and began passing legislation to destroy the Maori advantage. The Native Land Court Acts (1862/65) established a system to pass collectively held Maori land into individual European title, and thence into Pakeha ownership (Williams, 1999). Similarly, the 1866 Oyster Fisheries Act prevented Maori commercial oyster fishing and leased Maori oyster beds to non-Maori commercial interests.

While in part intended as a conservation measure, the Oyster Fisheries Act was enacted without consulting tribes in whose regions lay some of the finest oysteries in the world. Maori commercial fishing enterprises went broke and tribes had to sell land to the settlers to meet their debts. Maori commercial success did not fit with the European settler concept of a 'civilized society' in which Maori would serve as a labouring underclass (Barrington & Beaglehole, 1974). The colonizers thus institutionalized their view of society by using legislation and their growing numerical majority to speed land acquisition and give themselves an advantage in a new capitalist economy.

Critical theorists have explored the place of cultural ideologies, or systems of ideas, in creating and sustaining colonization and globalization. The late Edward Said, a Palestinian critical theorist living in the USA, argued that political ideas of domination and colonization find their strength and justification in the production of cultural knowledge. In his view, European cultural ideas revolving around an 'unrelenting Eurocentrism' formed a 'vital, informing, and invigorating counterpoint to the economic and political machinery' to maintain colonial domination (Said, 1988: 294).

Two specific ideologies developed to naturalize European colonial expansion were colonial racism and European cultural supremacy. Spring (1998) explains that memories of the Roman empire infused Westerners with a bold and grandiose vision of their role in creating a global culture and economy. Concepts of empire encouraged a focus on the imperial metropolitan centre as the source of all culture and civilization; those outside the empire were considered irrational barbarians or natural slaves: 'The Roman Imperium was viewed as both a political expression and a source of knowledge... Rome contained the perfect *civitas*, or civilised political order... [which] could be exported to the empire' (Spring, 1998: 9). Concepts of barbarian and natural servitude, which appeared often in European justifications of empire, were reinforced by the advent of Christianity's missionizing motive.

Memmi (1965) argued that racism was an integral part of colonialism's development. Some writers contend that before colonialism there was no European ideology of instrumentalist racism – that is, a racism holding that a particular group of human beings was naturally inferior, or destined for ill-treatment or poverty. According to Davison (1992) and Stevenson (1992), before the development of colonial capitalism neither the Portuguese, the Spanish, nor the English could be considered a racist people. For example, it is reported that the first auction of African captives imported into Portugal in the 1440s was interrupted by the common folk, who were enraged at seeing the separation of families of slaves (Saunders, 1982, in Davison, 1992). However, such conscientious reactions were soothed by an 'ideological balm' quickly developed and applied (Davison, 1992: 22). An instrumental racism developed to justify land seizures, and slave-trading for profit. Theological arguments underwent a transformation to proclaim the benign project of civilizing the primitive, converting the heathen and utilizing the land as God decreed in Genesis. Since greed was traditionally considered a sin, a new 'Protestant ethic' developed that proclaimed the religious value of hard work and the accumulation of wealth so that 'those who gained wealth were considered blessed by God' (Spring, 1998: 32). Particularly important for the economic development of the United States and Great Britain, the pursuit of private wealth became an essential part of capitalist ideology and has continued to serve as a key ingredient in the global economy.

Stevenson points out that England's colonization of Ireland was reinforced by replacing the old view of the Irish as socially inferior with the novel idea that they were culturally inferior and lagging far behind the English on a 'ladder of development' (1992: 39). On such a ladder of development towards civilization, the English defined the Irish as 'a lower order of humanity who "live like beastes, voide of law and all good order"' (1992: 39). These definitions provided the English with the justification for their colonial policies in Ireland, and were later used with little modification by settlers in newly colonized societies to dispossess the indigenous peoples. For instance, in the USA the General Allotment Act of 1887 authorized the president to 'divide an "Indian" reservation into individual holdings, assign a parcel of land to each man, woman and child, and to declare all remaining land surplus to the needs of the "Indians"' (Stevenson, 1992: 33). The Irish Suppression of Rebellion Act (1799) legitimated 'confiscation' of the land of indigenous people who rebelled or fought against the imposition of colonial rule and this was subsequently adopted by settler governments in Canada, the USA, Australia and New Zealand.

A century and a half later, in 2004, the New Zealand Court of Appeal ruled that the nature and extent of Maori customary rights and title in the foreshore and seabed areas could be considered by the Maori Land Court as they had never been legally extinguished. The government responded by drafting legislation to block this right. The Ministry of Justice begins their explanation of the Foreshore and Seabed Act (2004): 'The Act creates public access rights in, on, over and across the public foreshore and seabed to enable its continued use and enjoyment by all New Zealanders' (Ministry of Justice, 2008). There is an implication that the Act protects something (use and enjoyment by all New Zealanders) that was under threat from someone (indigenous claims of ownership). Using the media, the government gained public support for such a drastic measure. Many Pakeha people were easily persuaded to fear that Maori would use any control they gained to limit access to beaches.

Critical voices pointed out that the beaches currently barred to the New Zealand public were either in the hands of private owners (usually foreign, mostly US and Australian) owners, or in institutional hands such as the conservation and port authorities. Maori had not used their title in the coastline areas in the past to limit access (Jackson, 2003) and indeed now proposed covenants of access and non-saleability. The high-level Waitangi Tribunal made an urgent recommendation that the government should go back to the drawing board and support Maori calls for a 'longer conversation' and proper negotiations between Maori and non-Maori New Zealanders about the control of coastal and marine resources (Waitangi Tribunal, 2004).

Significantly in the context of global capitalism, the new legislation meant that the New Zealand government would be unimpeded by having to consult indigenous owners before approving commercial exploitation of our marine resources by local and foreign companies. Global free trade agreements, including the General Agreement on Trades and Tariffs (GATT), list indigenous authority over resources as 'impediments' to free trade. Indeed, the government's first actions subsequent to passing the Act were to give leases – for instance for iron-sand and seabed mining (Kiwis Against Seabed Mining – http://www.blacksands.org.nz) and licences for shellfish farming – to transnational and local non-Maori companies. In the future, Pakeha are likely to find their access to beaches and marine resources increasingly restricted by private ownership and private commercial activity.

Why did so many Pakeha support this modern-day confiscation of Maori rights? How does maintaining colonial dominance become part of a colonizer group's everyday common sense, even when such a position may not be in the group's best interests?

Italian critical thinker Gramsci's concept of **hegemony** links specific ideologies with general culture and what people perceive as common sense at any particular phase of history. In Gramsci's view, cultural ideas are maintained by mutual consent and informal education within the concrete relations of civil and political society, rather than enforced by formal authority (Gramsci, 1971). His concept of cultural hegemony positions every person in every strata of society as a participant in reproducing ideologies such as colonial racism and cultural supremacy. As an illustration, Nehru describes how a sense of the imperial relationship with India spread among all strata of the British people, to become a cultural hegemony:

even the worker and the farmer were influenced by it and felt, in spite of their subordinate position in their own country, the pride of possession and empire ... For a hundred years this ideology permeated all sections of the British people, and became, as it were, a national heritage ... and imperceptibly affected even their domestic outlook. (1946: 66)

Adamson (1980) explains that hegemonic common sense is influenced by all previous ideological currents, both oppressive and humanitarian, so that an individual's personality develops amid assumptions about the world which he or she cannot initially identify. It is in the sense of a normalized cultural hegemony continually reproduced by its citizens that Memmi is able to say of the colonizer:

He cannot help but approve discrimination and the codification of injustice ... and if the need arises, will become convinced of the necessity of massacres. The mechanism is practically constant. The colonial situation manufactures colonialists just as it manufactures the colonized. (1965: 55, 56)

Memmi's suggestion that ideologies of cultural supremacy and colonial racism can convince the colonizer of the 'necessity of massacres' brings to mind our case study, which shows that Pakeha were easily convinced of the necessity of a confiscation of the Maori title to the marine resources. The concept of a cultural hegemony of colonialism, shaped by centuries-long traditions of European colonial racism and cultural supremacy and maintained by citizen consent, explains how even modern democratic societies can consistently produce oppressive colonial outcomes. Such an everyday colonialism, reproducing ideologies that serve to maintain white supremacy in contemporary global processes, is what I would term a 'common sense colonialism'. In this I am following Billig's (1995) notion of 'banal nationalism' and Essed's (1990) concept of an 'everyday' or 'daily' racism to describe similar hegemonic systems of ideas. A 'common sense' colonialism conveys the Western mindset, reflected in the media, in educational settings and in conversations, that treats capitalist modernization and commercial exploitation as a natural and inevitable world order. As with Billig's banal nationalism, such a hegemonic colonial common sense can be called upon at short notice whenever the status quo is threatened by indigenous assertions and claims.

The New Zealand government relied on a 'common sense' colonialism about who should appropriately control resources on behalf of 'all New Zealanders', just as earlier colonialists drew upon accepted notions of the correct place for native people on a 'ladder of development' rather than as owners of fine fisheries. For instance, in the debate about Maori being granted a limited allocation of marine licences, a journalist was able to say 'This means that Maori interests ... will effectively be handed the equivalent sea space for 240 new marine farms – for nothing' (Dohoghue, 2004: 1–2). He drew upon a colonial common sense that the (settler) government naturally owned the country's resources, and that in claiming their share as of right, the indigenous people were receiving unfair privileges. Later in the article, the journalist was able to reassure his readers that 'The government is currently legislating away this right' and that future legislation 'at least gives marine farmers the certainty they can run their businesses without the threat of Maori claims' (Dohoghue, 2004: 1–2). His reassurances rely on the colonial common sense that indigenous claims to resources threaten the colonizer, and that suppressing indigenous rights is healthy for Western business as usual.

Critical psychologists have analysed the psychological ways in which Eurocentric ideologies become a naturalized colonizer 'common sense' in Western countries. Using discourse analysis, Wetherell and Potter (1992) and Nairn and McCreanor (1991) have shown that dismissals of pro-Maori positions rely implicitly on common sense notions held by Pakeha. McCreanor (1997) has explored the historical antecedents of common sense justifications for European colonization. He concludes that contradictions in the position of the 'noble savage' on the 'ladder of development' allow, in contemporary discourse, a division of Maori into good and bad, according to those who cooperate with colonization and those who do not. 'Bad' Maori and 'stirrers' are those who adopt critical stances and protest against Pakeha assumptions of control and supremacy. In their common sense, Pakeha thus use psychological and linguistic resources such as dividing Maori into 'good' and 'bad' as they fit/do not fit settler designs and a notion of unreasonable, privileged Maori claims to rights and resources that should not prevail over those of other citizens in a democratic society. For instance, a Television New Zealand Colmar Brunton poll of 750 voters found that 43 per cent of respondents thought Maori were the most privileged group in the country, while only 32 per cent thought that Europeans were (New Zealand Press Association, 2008). The work of these critical psychologists suggests that the psychology of the colonizer makes use of ideologies to sustain particular outcomes, such as dispossession and the cultural suppression of indigenous peoples (Wetherell & Potter, 1992).

A global example of racism and cultural supremacy producing common sense colonialism is the English language's global dominance. Spring (1998) contends that the current language (and structure) of the global economy is in part a result of past variations in colonial education policies. In Africa and Asia, the British educated a small native elite to serve in their empire's administration. This elite learned the English language and culture and attached their cultural loyalties to England. The result was an English-speaking leadership who played an important role in introducing to their countries the commercial values of the global economy.

Relying upon a colonial common sense among his listeners, former British Prime Minister Tony Blair praised the fruits of the United States' and Britain's colonial language policies: 'the priceless asset of the English language – the language of international politics, of international business, of professional and scientific exchange, of travel and – now – of the Internet' (cited in Spring, 1998: 7). As Spring points out, the global use of English now ensures world access to American and British science, culture, entertainment, and most important, economic and political ideas, and thereby continues to fulfil the European imperialist agenda. Obscuring the linguistic and cultural imperialism involved, Blair used the competitive economic metaphor to conclude that the international use of English 'is a huge potential advantage for Britain' (cited in Spring, 1998: 7). In challenge and critique, Anatoly Voronov, the head of the Russian Internet provider Glasnet, claimed that the Internet represented 'the ultimate act of intellectual colonialism'. Whereas it was 'supposed to open the world to hundreds and millions of people', knowledge of English now divides the world 'into new sorts of haves and have nots' (Spring, 1998: 30). In summary, it is through cultural, psychological and linguistic means that Eurocentric ideologies of racism and cultural supremacy become a naturalized colonizer common sense.

It is worth concluding with a final observation from Memmi, one of the few decolonization theorists to deal specifically with the psychology of the colonizer. Memmi suggests that the misfortune of the colonized (such as not speaking English) seems scandalous to the colonizer, who in response seeks reassurance by conceiving of him or herself as custodian of the values of civilization and history, one who brings light to the colonized darkness. As Memmi puts it, the colonizer can now 'relax and live benevolently, allowed to be both master and innocent' (Memmi, 1965: 76).

tools for decolonization

Many New Zealanders attempted to use the mechanisms of democracy to halt the confiscatory legislation. Morris (2004) describes how democracy was thwarted by cynical 'consultation'. Four thousand submissions were made about the proposed legislation, almost all opposed to it, including many from Pakeha individuals and organizations such as churches and activist pro-indigenous groups. The parliamentary committee granted a hearing to only 250 people whose views were not included in their report. The media presented the opposition as racially based and coming only from Maori, but I joined many other Pakeha in one of the country's largest marches upon Parliament. The Bill was passed under urgency with members of Parliament required to read and vote on 67 pages of amendments within two days. A leading Maori politician who voted against her own governing Labour party was instantly dismissed. She responded by forming a new Maori political party.

Maori representatives laid a complaint with the United Nations Committee on the Elimination of Racial Discrimination (CERD), which found that the government had, by passing the legislation, failed to meet its obligations to prevent racial discrimination and exploited racial tensions for political advantage. The UN Special Rapporteur on the human rights of indigenous peoples was also invited to visit New Zealand. He recommended that the Act should be repealed, that the

(Cont'd)

inherent Maori right to the foreshore and seabed should be recognized and that full public access to the country's beaches and coastal areas should be established without discrimination of any kind (Stavenhagen, 2006). The government, however, dismissed both UN reports as 'biased'. A bill repealing the legislation has been proposed, but is unlikely to receive support from either of the largest political parties.

The case study illustrates that institutionalized democratic processes cannot undo colonial patterns of control and dominance. Small indigenous political parties have difficulty changing majoritarian policy. A more far-reaching decolonization process is needed which deals directly with the colonizer's ideologies and common sense. Smith defines decolonization as a 'long-term process involving the bureaucratic, cultural, linguistic and psychological divesting of colonial power' (1999: 98). Using such a social and psychological orientation, decolonization requires participation and action by the colonizer group itself in divesting colonial power. Just as psychologists Martín-Baró (1994) and Watts and Serrano-Garcia (2003) have advanced a psychology of liberation from oppression focused on the colonized, so do critical psychologists who need to develop a psychology of decolonization for colonizer groups.

developing indigenous psychologies

Native Americans, Africans, Asians, Latin Americans and other colonized peoples found in Said's (1978) *Orientalism* a method to challenge the West's denial, suppression and distortion of their cultures and histories. They created the academic field known as postcolonial studies (Bayoumi & Rubin, 2000) with an agenda for 'decolonizing methodologies', as Smith (1999) entitled her work. Indigenous psychologists consider psychology's continuing European hegemony damaging to colonized groups because Eurocentric thought has colonized non-European psychologists; because the lack of alternatives to hegemonic knowledge leaves the discipline impoverished; and because the dominance of Eurocentric psychology helps legitimize worldwide inequality (Joseph et al., 1990, in Howitt & Owusu-Bempah, 1994). Levy considers that psychological concepts of universalism and individualism have worked to 'actively exclude the perspectives of indigenous communities, in some cases causing harm' (2007: 38).

As part of the decolonization of knowledge undertaken in a postcolonial agenda, indigenous psychologies have developed in many countries. Reviewing these newly developed bodies of knowledge, Levy observes that indigenous psychology scholars do not reject the concept of a universal psychology so much as the assumption that Western psychology in isolation constitutes that universal psychology (2007). She notes that a number of authors conceptualize Western psychology as an indigenous psychology itself, in that it is 'culturally dependent and locally originated' (2007: 37). This point is in keeping with critical psychology's critique of mainstream psychology for failing to explore its own culturally biased assumptions. Supporting the development and dissemination of indigenous psychologies is one way that critical psychologists can contribute to the cultural, psychological and bureaucratic divesting of colonial power.

adopting an ecological metaphor

Psychologists have tended to treat macro-level phenomena such as colonization and globalization as though they were natural and inevitable processes. However, some authors suggest that colonial (and now global) relationships of dominance form a crucial macro-context for relationships between cultural groups which must be made explicit (Feagin & Feagin, 1978; Moane, 1999). Sloan (2005) argues that psychology has made itself irrelevant to debates in economics and politics because it has failed to include broad socioeconomic concepts in the education of psychology professionals. Taking up his challenge, critical psychologists need to become familiar with key critical theorists of colonization and decolonization internationally and locally. A useful critical tool is to critique the links between globalization's economic and cultural 'mission'. Critically exploring the history of particular political and social environments helps to place injustice in structural and cultural contexts. Overall, to remedy psychologists' traditionally uncritical stance will require making an 'epistemological break' (Kagan and Burton, 2001: 7), as community psychology has done with its interdisciplinary ecological metaphor, whole systems perspective, and dialectic of people and system (Seidman, 1988).

analysing 'colonial common sense'

Some critical psychologists from colonizer groups have been working to decolonize psychological knowledge by attending to the ideological and linguistic construction of colonial relationships. Using a social constructionist epistemology, critical psychologists such as Wetherell and Potter (1992) and Nairn and McCreanor (1991; McCreanor, 1993) have looked not only at how colonial ideologies were constructed historically, but also at how the hegemonic common sense prevailing in Western countries *continues* to reproduce colonial relationships between Europeans and other cultural groups. For instance, using historical documents, formal submissions and contemporary media samples, McCreanor (2005) concluded that there is a strong continuity between the historical and more contemporary usages of common sense themes, such as the 'obvious' inferiority of Maori culture to that of Pakeha and its unsuitability for competition in a modern world. Now, as then, racial tensions are considered the result of divisive Maori claims to rights and resources. Maoris who are hypersensitive about their culture and make inflated claims to a 'Maori inheritance' are constructed as the contemporary equivalent of the 'bad' Maori who declined to cooperate with colonization. The common sense argument for New Zealanders as 'one people' implies that unless Maori drop their sectarian interests in favour of national unity as New Zealanders, racial tension will continue to grow. Other projects have looked critically at how the media present Maori in a negative light and as responsible for their current plight (Moewaka-Barnes, Gregory, McCreanor, Nairn, Pega, & Rankine, 2005). Critically deconstructing such common sense sentiments about the colonial relationship contributes to the cultural and linguistic divesting of colonial power.

_____ critical consciousness raising for colonizer groups _____

Memmi warned that while the well-meaning colonizer may dream of a tomorrow in which the colonized cease to be colonized, the colonizer typically does not conceive of a deep transformation of their own situation and personality, believing that 'he [sic] will go on being what he is, with his language intact and his cultural traditions dominating' (1965: 40). However, Freire (1970, 1975) provided a theory of mutual conscientization in which both the colonized and the colonizer are transformed as they work 'co-intentionally' to create a new social reality (Huygens, 2006). Some critical psychologists are beginning to focus explicitly on how colonizer peoples experience the psychological and cultural transformations that becoming critically aware of colonial oppression puts into motion. Moane (1999), for example, has looked at the social and psychological processes involved in liberation from colonial and gender oppression, with a focus on Ireland. Working with Pakeha anti-racism workers, Huygens (2007) has examined the social and psychological processes a colonizer group experiences through conscientizing education about colonization. Black has looked at how a colonizer group may bring to critical awareness aspects of their culture which maintain colonial dominance and applied this analysis to psychology (Black & Huygens, 2007).

_____ supporting social movements for change _____

Kagan and Burton (2001) recommend that psychologists undertaking change in social settings align themselves with social movements to challenge the status quo. In response to globalizing trends such as commercialization and the privatization of public and community space, they suggest possibilities for resistance, local education and an association with wider emancipatory struggles. They recommend forming strategic alliances to build a 'counter-hegemonic bloc' which challenges the prevailing dominant ideologies (2001: 15; see also Chapter 22 in this volume). As well as recommending participation in wider social movements, Kagan and Burton encourage forming coalitions with other progressive movements within psychology, and between psychology and other disciplines (2001: 20).

It has been pointed out that hegemony is never total, since there are always multiple contexts of legitimation for any social order (Adamson, 1980). Therefore, a key tool for decolonization is to create alternative contexts in which non-colonial relationships may be envisaged and practised. Social movements are important contexts for creating alternative social orders, because they achieve ideological change as well as economic and political change. Movements involved with indigenous revival, decolonization, anti-imperialist, environmental or other work have been described as crucibles of counter-hegemonic knowledge and practices (Eyerman & Jamison, 1991; Huygens, 2007). The protests at Seattle, Washington, Prague and Quebec against global financial and trade organizations such as the International Monetary Fund, World Bank and World Trade Organization are expressions of social movements that aim to construct a non-colonial political and economic order (Sloan, 2005).

As a psychologist working within a decolonization agenda negotiated locally with indigenous activists I would stress that involvement in social movements and strategic alliances for decolonization may not be achieved in one meeting, one academic year, or even one decade. Movements for decolonization and against European colonialism and imperialism have centuries-long histories. Dialogues about decolonization may take many years to develop and involve multi-generational communities working for change. My own study of the relatively recent Pakeha response to 170 years of Maori activism confirms that a 'longer conversation' is essential to develop appropriate local strategies for decolonization (Huygens, 2006). Fortunately, the developing ethics of participatory action research encourage researchers to negotiate projects that are useful to the agendas of social movements.

cautions

While taking up critical tools to advance decolonization it is worth considering several cautions. First, the neo-liberal approach to globalization that accepts a world where poverty must inevitably coexist with opulence leads to psychological consequences such as fatalism and hopelessness (Macedo in Freire, 1998: ix). Academics have joined in political defeatism, and in particular have used postmodern theory to justify their 'flight from a politics holding out a prospect of radical change' (Gordon, 2001: 30).

In contrast, adopting a decolonization agenda requires a belief that exploitative globalization is not a given. Freire (1998) warns against treating cynically the critical hope inspired by personal conscientization and enacted in political activism and social movements enact. He considers legitimate anger and critical hope essential components of ideological transformation: 'I have a right to be angry, to show it and to use it as a motivational foundation for my struggle' (1998: 69). He insists that an open-minded person who is upset by injustice and hurt by discrimination should be full of critical hope that the struggle to diminish the causes of hopelessness and immobilization can succeed.

Second, much critical writing on colonization and globalization proffers a conventional solution: democracy. However, as the case story demonstrates, we must critically view Western-style democracy. What is generally called 'majoritarian' democracy denies minority groups the power to develop laws or policy that supports their interests and aspirations. Majoritarian democracy ensures the continuing dominance of a majority settler group in Canada, the United States, Australia, New Zealand and elsewhere. Adding to the problem, by the end of the nineteenth century the doctrine of consent in Western politics had long since been modified by the principle of representation – the delegated few speaking for the many. Representation made it easy for special interest groups to manipulate public affairs (Dickason, 1999). In other words, public policy became identified with special interests, usually related to business, rather than primarily with people. In such a 'special interest' democracy the media assume a key role in what Herman and Chomsky (1988) call 'manufacturing consent'. Dickason points out that many indigenous societies still develop policy by consent or consensus (1999). A critical decolonizing psychology would avoid reproducing the prevailing ideology, based on cultural supremacy, that Western-style representative democracy is a universal solution because it is naturally superior to indigenous models of policy making.

Finally, colonized peoples have looked to the United Nations and international law for support, for instance by developing in 1982 a Declaration for the Rights of Indigenous Peoples. However, the agonizingly slow progress of the Declaration, and the fact that the governments of New Zealand, Australia, the United States and Canada were the only four states to vote against its final passage by the United Nations in 2007, demonstrate that Western states use these international forums to maintain colonial positions.

In conclusion, the passage of New Zealand's Foreshore and Seabed Act 2004 and the surrounding public ferment illustrate how the combination of colonial ideologies and Westernized democratic processes led to a contemporary confiscation of resources from an indigenous people. A century and a half after the British colonized New Zealand, the new Act repeated the injustice of the 1866 Oyster Fisheries Act by seizing an indigenous property right from Maori as the enemy. Pakeha were persuaded that the government were acting on behalf of 'the public' even when the legislation facilitated commercial and foreign access to marine resources and thus led to a loss of public control. Contemporary 'colonial common sense' maintained the injustices of colonization towards indigenous peoples.

Ending the exploitative colonization and globalization of the 500-year European colonial project will require more than political solutions such as representative democracy. A profound decolonization agenda is required for both colonized and colonizer peoples. Given the psychological, linguistic and cultural components of this agenda, critical psychology has an opportunity to make a significant contribution.

1 Contemporary patterns of globalization may be critically viewed as an extension of the European colonial project undertaken in the 1500s.

2 European colonialism has been sustained by cultural ideologies such as Western cultural supremacy and racism.

3 Racism and cultural supremacy support a naturalized common sense about the inevitable, indeed benign, nature of the ongoing dispossession of indigenous peoples in deference to global capitalism.

4 This 'colonial common sense' operates as a cultural hegemony in Western countries, so that majoritarian democratic processes are insufficient to disturb it.

5 More psychologically oriented decolonization processes may help to change hegemonic common sense. It is here that critical psychologists may make a significant contribution.

6 Recommended critical tools are developing indigenous psychologies, analysing colonial 'common sense', and participating in counter-hegemonic social movements.

glossary

- **colonialism:** the policies and practices of the forcible occupation of lands outside Europe and the USA.

- **colonizer peoples:** newer settlers in these lands.

- **decolonization:** the process of undoing colonial relationships, both politically and psychologically.

- **hegemony:** a pervasive cultural consensus supporting a society's current social and political order.

- **imperialism:** the extension of authority, influence or power over others to create an empire.

- **indigenous peoples:** the original inhabitants of lands and continents, also called First Nations.

■ ■ reading suggestions ■

In *Decolonizing Methodologies: Research and Indigenous Peoples*, Linda Smith (1999) describes how research has been implicated in European imperialism and gives recommendations to researchers committed to decolonization. Two issues of *Race and Class*, a journal for Black and Third World liberation, contain useful introductions to critical writing on colonization (*The Curse of Columbus*) and globalization (*The New Conquistadores*). I recommend Albert Memmi's account in *The Colonizer and the Colonized* (1965) about how a colonial system shapes and reproduces the psychology of the colonizer. Finally, I encourage all Anglophone psychologists to peruse two classic collections documenting responses and resistance to colonization by North American First Nations – Dee Brown's *Bury My Heart at Wounded Knee* (1970), and Howard Zinn's *A People's History of the United States* (1980). These volumes provide material for a journey of critical conscientization about the accepted history of North America.

: // internet resources /

- **Peace Movement Aotearoa Website** – useful documents and links about decolonization efforts in Aotearoa, Australia and parts of the Pacific, with particular reference to the Declaration of the Rights of Indigenous Peoples: www.converge.org.nz/pma/

- **Women's International League for Peace and Freedom** – the oldest and largest peace organization in the world carries news, documents and links relevant to globalization and decolonization: international website at www.wilpf.int.ch and country websites include www.wilpf.org.au, www.wilpf.org.uk and www.wilpf.org for the USA.

- **Race Relations in New Zealand** – article by political scientist Chris Ford on Maori-Pakeha relations: homepages.ihug.co.nz/~sai/racernz.html

 ■ **Questions**

1 How does the language used about people in the Third World and Fourth World continue to recreate a Western colonial 'common sense'?

2 What might some of the psychological and linguistic themes be in your country's colonial common sense?

3 What might 'a longer conversation' about control of your region's treasured resources cover? Who do you consider ought to be involved?

4 How might a critical history of the English language's global dominance differ from an uncritical one? How might the Internet be used, and software be designed, in ways that avoid sustaining Anglophone imperialism?

5 How might you go about developing a decolonization agenda for psychology 'co-intentionally' with indigenous and oppressed groups in your region?

17

Psychosocial Trauma, Poverty, and Human Rights in Communities Emerging from War

M. Brinton Lykes and Erzulie D. Coquillon

Chapter Topics

In a marked shift from the nature of warfare just 60 years ago, the majority of victims of modern conflict are non-combatants. In another shift, modern warfare also increasingly occurs in contexts of extreme poverty. Many who survive suffer profound psychological problems and disrupted social functioning. In this chapter we discuss these impacts of war, and argue that structural poverty, war, and organized violence undermine social, economic, cultural, and political rights, such as the right to development, self-determination, and a sustainable environment. Thus, psychologists working with survivors in contexts of extreme poverty where there have been or continue to be gross violations of human rights should respond from within a human rights framework.

Drawing upon critical and **liberation psychology** theory and practice, we expand the dominant approach to **psychosocial** work in communities emerging from war from a singular focus on the mental health problems confronting victims to a broader, contextualized focus on the human rights of survivors. This analysis recognizes the importance of foregrounding culture and of focusing a critical lens on how gender and race have been mobilized to marginalize poor communities during and emerging from war. It thus also recognizes the need for an anti-racist and gender-critical lens in designing psychosocial projects and the need for a focus on both economic survival and activism for structural economic change. In so doing, we urge critical psychologists to draw upon their unique social analytical stance in collaboration with local survivors and community leaders to design anti-racist and gender-critical programmes that reflect a defence of human rights as well as access for survivors to the tools for economic generativity.

Our discussion of the contributions of critical and liberation psychology is exemplified in community-based development practices that engage psycho-social interventions aimed at reestablishing social networks and developing survivors' capabilities and sense of self-efficacy while also building local economic sufficiency. We suggest that such programmes can help survivors to unlock their human potential and to recognize structures of violence, while supporting grass-roots efforts to rethread community relations and the social fabric. We conclude by examining the challenges that face those who seek to do this work.

psychosocial trauma and transitions from war in conditions of poverty: setting the context

Since the end of the Second World War and the establishment of the Universal Declaration of Human Rights, more than 20 million people have been killed in armed conflicts, most of them civilians; 84 per cent of all casualties have been civilians (A Fairer World, 2008). In Iraq alone, estimates of civilian casualties range from more than 80,000 to 100,000 from 2003 to early 2008 (Iraq Body Count, 2008). UNICEF (2005) estimates that 90 per cent of those killed in war and 80 per cent of refugees from conflict are women and children. Whereas warfare was once primarily characterized by interstate conflict, now most violence is intrastate, often targeting civilian populations for economic, strategic, and political purposes.

It is complicated to determine the precise *material costs of war*, due to both practical considerations and the fact that the byproducts of war (e.g., a failure of the state infrastructure and resultant disease, the lack of access to medical care) contribute to many deaths that may or may not be counted as 'civilian deaths'. The costs of war affect the basic infrastructure, agriculture, and educational and health systems (see, among others, Brahm, 2004). The losses due to war and poverty intersect, compounding one another when unchecked; for example, the disruption of agriculture can create food shortages, and prolonged hunger among children can result in a range of problems, including deficits in cognitive development, behavioural problems, and mental illness (Agerbak, 1991; see also Desjarlais, Eisenberg, Good, & Kleinman, 1995). Because many modern conflicts occur in what Greitens (2001) calls debilitating or collapsing states, the process of reconstructing societies after war is often not only one of short-term recovery but also of long-term development.

The *social costs of war* are equally complex. Conflict can displace populations, separate families, and create the constant threat of physical violence including sexual violations and death, all of which may undermine the social cohesion and community life that are crucial for individual strength, meaning, and identity (Agerbak, 1991; Martín-Baró, 1994). Those who intervene on any level in societies emerging from war should thus pay attention to the complex individual and social traumas that have become the legacy of armed conflict and structural poverty.

_____ *human rights and human capabilities* _____

The year 2008 marked the sixtieth anniversary of the United Nations General Assembly's adoption of the Universal Declaration of Human Rights (UDHR). When it was written, the world still shuddered from the horrors of the Holocaust. The document represented a hope that all societies would respond to those atrocities with the words 'never again'. Yet since then genocide has occurred in Rwanda, Cambodia, the former Yugoslavia and the Darfur region of Sudan. Human rights violations of other forms have continued apace throughout the world (see, e.g., Human Rights Watch, www.hrw.org). Although the promulgation of the UDHR has not halted mass violence, it and its progeny provide both a framework within which activists, aid workers, and the oppressed call for an end to immediate violence and a resource for advocating for the cessation of rights violations (Lykes, 2001; Messer, 1995).

Human rights scholars and social scientists have extended the understanding of civil rights, the most common referent for rights discourse in the United States. To capture the historical and deeply political development of formulated rights, they describe multiple 'generations of rights' (*No Hiding Place: Human Rights – A World Report*, 1998; Messer, 1995). Within this understanding, the original Universal Declaration of Human Rights (1948) embodied both first generation rights (civil-political rights) and second generation rights (social, economic and cultural rights). The Conventions on Civil and Political Rights and on Economic, Social and Cultural Rights, both approved by the United Nations in 1966, made these rights legally binding. Subsequently articulated were third generation rights (solidarity rights, including the right to development, self-determination, peace and a clean environment) and fourth generation rights (the rights of **indigenous** peoples). The United Nations only recently endorsed these latter rights; ratification by some member states is still under consideration. The human rights framework, broadly defined across these four generations, has created a shared political discourse and internationally agreed-upon covenants that can sustain actions supporting economic equality, health, gender and racial equity, and other important physical and social needs.

Of course, upholding rights requires providing the means to act upon them. According to the philosopher Martha Nussbaum, ' ... liberty is not just a matter of having rights on paper, it requires being in a material position to exercise those rights' (2002: 54). As significantly, translating statements of universal guarantees into local outcomes is deeply challenging (see, e.g., Merry, 2006, on women's human rights). This translation must be a primary goal of psychosocial interventions in communities emerging from war.

economic inequalities, sustainable development, and societies emerging from war

Economic and human development work informed by a human rights frame-work (see, e.g., Uvin, 2004; Weiss & Collins, 2000) seeks to ensure individuals' access to adequate health care, work, education, and political and civil freedoms, among others. Since the mid-1990s, researchers have identified correlations between armed conflict and income inequality or growing resource scarcity (Birdsall & Sabott, 1994; World Resources Institute, 1998). As noted above, structural oppression and poverty compound the trauma of warfare. Extreme poverty, having little control over one's work or destiny, and being poor relative to others have been found to negatively affect physical and mental health (Desjarlais et al., 1995; Dohwenrend, 1998; Wainer & Chesters, 2000).

Thus, poverty, violence, social discord, and trauma exist in complex relationships that require nuanced and context-relevant intervention strategies – sustainable social, economic, and human development – to redress the effects and address the root causes. Those strategies should engage an ecological approach that weaves the unlocking of human potential, the recognition of 'cultures of violence' that have weakened social systems, and the support of grassroots efforts to rethread local community relations and the social fabric (Nordstrom, 1997; Martín-Baró, 1994; Spence, 1999). As each of these interlocking processes requires the involvement of the local population to sustain it, developing human capabilities is crucial (see, e.g., Brohman, 1996; Remenyi, 2004; Spence, 1999). Or, as economist Amartya Sen has observed, the 'enhancement of human freedom is both the object and the primary means of development' (Sen, 1999: 53).

responding to the psychosocial effects of war and structural poverty: theoretical considerations drawn from critical psychology and development

Social systems during war are often in chaos. The myriad of needs may press psychologists and other aid workers to address immediate crises without thoroughly considering the underlying problems (Greitens, 2001; Spence, 1999). In contrast, interventions informed by critical and liberation psychology focus on the socioeconomic environment and examine the influence of race, class, and gender (Prince, 2004). As Prilleltensky and Nelson (this volume) argue, intervention at the community level should be contextual (ecological), political (focusing on social injustice and power), and value-driven (emphasizing social justice). Critical psychological responses to the traumas of war that engage marginalized communities to enhance liberation and wellbeing are still developing. In this section we describe psychologists' responses to war and an alternative perspective from critical and liberation psychology.

_____ *historical and theoretical perspectives on psychological trauma* __

Contemporary psychologists, psychiatrists, and mental health workers typically focus on the effects of war upon individual survivors, describing their psychological symptoms and observed behaviours. This focus, which first emerged in the study of soldier's responses to warfare, has a long tradition. Some researchers trace its origins to soldiers' 'irritable heart' in the wake of the United States Civil War (e.g., Starcevic & Durdic, 1993). There is consensus that characterizations of the First World War's 'shell shock' or 'war neurosis' and of the Second World War's 'survivor syndrome', 'combat exhaustion', or 'battle fatigue' are clinical antecedents of the modern diagnosis of **post-traumatic stress** disorder' (PTSD) (see Bracken, Giller, & Summerfield, 1995; Kleinman, 1995; see also Chapter 5 in this volume). Other antecedents include Erich Lindemann's discussion of the psychological sequelae of surviving a 1940s Boston nightclub fire (see *American Journal of Community Psychology*, 1984; Satin, 1982).

In introducing the term post-traumatic stress disorder in the *Diagnostic and Statistical Manual III* in 1980, the American Psychiatric Association subsumed under one diagnostic category those outcomes described above, stressors related to bombings and natural disasters, as well as post-torture syndrome and rape trauma syndrome. Thus, this apparently contemporary illness discourse for survivors of political violence is neither altogether new nor recent. What is perhaps 'new' is the widespread and growing involvement of psychologists, psychiatrists and other mental health workers in the diagnosis and treatment of survivors in programmes designed for rapid and long-term responses to war, natural disasters, catastrophes, and other 'exceptionally difficult circumstances'.

Specifically, most contemporary explanations of trauma caused by war are embedded in medical conceptions of illness wherein selected symptoms and behavioural indices provide evidence of post-traumatic stress or other diseases. Although this is not necessarily a 'bad' or problematic approach, attributing the effects of war, state-sponsored violence, and structural oppression primarily or exclusively to biomedical factors constrains medical and social scientific understandings of survivors' deeper distress. Survivors' pain or 'social suffering' (see, among others, Kleinman, 1995) embodies political, economic, cultural as well as psychological phenomena. Bracken et al. (1995) argue that the PTSD disease model, by situating an individual at the centre, and as the source, of meaning and morality, presumes that all forms and content of mental disorder are similar in each individual in each context. However, as the medical anthropologist Arthur Kleinman (1988) observed, identifying a similar phenomenon in different situations does not mean it is universal.

We argue here that psychologists can understand and respond to the psychosocial sequelae of war and postwar through a critical reading of the sociopolitical, historical, and cultural context and through focusing on survivors as historical agents with human rights. Many anthropologists, cultural psychologists, social and community psychologists, and indigenous healers stress a more descriptive, contextualized approach to trauma, one that draws on survivors' narratives and testimonies as resources for understanding the psychosocial experiences of atrocities and other forms of violence (see examples from Jenkins, 1991; Kleinman, 1995). Within this orientation, rather than focus on a general pathology within a single individual, researchers and practitioners press to understand the singularity and particularity of each participant, that is, the survivor's story, within a social, historical, and cultural context. We discuss below some psychologists' attempts to work in this way.

_____ *gendering and racializing theories of psychosocial trauma* _____

Culture, community, gender, race, and social class are core dimensions for critical perspectives that conceptualize trauma and its wake not in terms of a universal syndrome of symptoms but rather within specific contexts. Women, including young girls, are all too frequently the victims of incest, rape, pornography, battering, harassment, and sexual slavery. Violence against women and gender inequalities in war are extreme manifestations of the discrimination and gender violence prevalent under conditions of peace. For example, members of military and paramilitary forces frequently rape women as part of war's booty (Swiss & Giller, 1993) or, as human rights observers in the former Yugoslavia suggest, as part of a strategy of ethnic cleansing (Ecumenical Women's Team Visit, 1992; Mazowiecki, 1993).

Race and ethnicity are similarly complex realities in the contexts of war and extreme poverty. Institutionalized racism and ethnic strife can combine with poverty and political forces as underlying causes of armed conflict, as in Rwanda (Gourevitch, 1998) and the former Yugoslavia (Giles, de Alwis, Klein, & Silva, 2003). The official report of the UN-sponsored Commission for Historical Clarification (CEH, 1999) in Guatemala identified a history of racism against the indigenous population and 'acute socioeconomic inequalities' as direct causes of the country's 36 years of civil war (Seider, 2001: 192).

Understanding particular cultural experiences and forms of institutionalized racism and sexism suggests a range of creative responses for psychologists working with individuals and communities emerging from war. Longstanding cultural practices and traditional beliefs, for example, have served as resources for indigenous survival for centuries, including in recent conflict and postconflict situations (see e.g., Chicuecue, 1997, in Mozambique; Eagle, 1990, in South Africa; and Wessells & Monteira, 2000, in Angola). Cockburn (1998), for example, discusses how gender and ethnicity have been mobilized by women as resources for resistance and survival in and beyond nationalist or ethnic conflict in Northern Ireland, Israel, and Bosnia-Herzegovina. Similarly, Lykes and Mersky (2006) present a framework which foregrounds history and culture to situate psychosocial work in the context of reparations processes in countries emerging from war. However, these and other authors note that many traditional beliefs and cultural practices have been deeply fractured by war or intentionally targeted by the military to limit resistance (see Carmack, 1988, and Falla, 1994, in Guatemala).

community-based approaches to psychosocial trauma in societies emerging from war

As described above, economic and social systems in societies whose social fabric has been sundered by war are often in chaos. Reinstating these systems from which individuals draw meaning and identity is a fundamental part of reconstruction and healing (Martín-Baró, 1994). The psychosocial approach 'suggests that although people are affected in many ways, three areas in particular are affected: human capacity (i.e. skills, knowledge, and capabilities), social ecology (social connectedness and networks), and culture and values' (Mollica, Lopes Cardozo, Osofsky, Raphael, Ager, & Salama, 2004: 2058; see also Psychosocial Working Group, 2003). Collaborative and interdisciplinary teams responding to these factors in contexts of war and extreme poverty speak frequently about both the empowerment of local populations and the development of human capital. Community psychologists, development practitioners, and participatory and action researchers have come to concern themselves more explicitly with the role of empowerment in community development projects, including citizen engagement initiatives, participatory rural appraisal, economic development projects, health assessment and education programmes both in the USA and abroad, and in societies emerging from war (see, e.g., de Koning & Martin, 1996; McTaggart, 1997; Papineau, 1996). Researchers and applied psychologists understand empowerment as encompassing four areas: perception of self-efficacy and competence; acquired knowledge, skills, and access to resources; the development of a critical consciousness; and participation in concerted action (see Zimmerman, 2000, for an overview). Community development workers often use it to discuss how participants in a given intervention, through participation with outside collaborators, can use their participation to gain greater levels of self-confidence and self-sufficiency to carry into other aspects of their lives as agents of change (Jana, Basu, Rotheram-Borus, & Newman, 2004; see also Ayres et al., 1990).

However, as Andrea Cornwall observes, '[t]alk of "empowering women" turns "power" into a transferable commodity rather than a structural relation' (2007). Feminists and other critical scholars, thus, continue to interrogate and re-negotiate empowerment as a term or goal. The Institute of Development Studies (IDS) at the University of Sussex in the UK, for example, maintains a 'Pathways of Women's Empowerment' project that examines the uses and abuses of the concept (see www.pathwaysofwomensempowerment.org). Participants in a recent conference on the subject observed that the 'shifting and fuzzy meanings of empowerment make it a difficult word to use' and that 'some kinds of empowerment are missing from today's mainstream versions: cultural empowerment, collective empowerment, liberating empowerment, pleasurable empowerment, empowerment in the corporate sector, [and] empowerment in trade unions' (Eyben, 2008).

In societies transitioning from conflict and war, 'critical empowerment' is exemplified by survivors' organization of and participation in community projects in, for example, Central American refugee camps in El Salvador and Mexico and civil society in Eritrea and South Africa (Spence, 1999). Similarly, in Guatemala, one community's process of selecting and erecting a monument to those killed in the country's protracted civil war served to 'reactivate community decision-making mechanisms that were distorted during the violence, and power structure[s that] can be renegotiated as the community examines its collective memory and identity' (Roberts & Gidley, 2000).

A sense of efficacy plays an important role in recovering from traumatic experiences (Herman, 1992). According to International Medical Corps physician Melin Vranesic, 'the ultimate goal of every psychosocial program should be to empower [the] community to take care of itself (capacity-building, resource development, skills training, income generating activities, micro-finance, or rural banking)' (2003). Similarly, the International Rescue Committee's Post-conflict Development Initiative observes that 'effort must focus on rebuilding the social welfare and economic development capacity of conflict-impacted communities' (International Rescue Committee, 2003). Such projects can build skills, raise self-esteem, encourage teamwork and shared decision making, and generate local economic activity and sustainability. Local economic development initiatives with a psychosocial perspective may also play a key role in assuring that human rights to health, education, and wellbeing are not mere aspirations but material outcomes.

critical and liberation psychology as resources: two examples from the field

Liberation and critical psychology (see Lykes & Mallona, 2008; Martín-Baró, 1994) offer resources for psychologists who seek to collaborate with survivors and their communities in restoration and transformation (see also *War-Torn Societies Project*, Johannsen, 2003). In Latin America this work continues to be strongly influenced by Paulo Freire's (1970) liberatory pedagogy and theories of critical consciousness (noted in other chapters in this volume, especially 3 and 23). Similar approaches which assume that knowledge generates power and that people's knowledge is central to social change also emerged in Asia (Fals-Borda & Rahman, 1991) and Africa (see, e.g., Hope & Timmel, 1984–2000).

Participatory approaches framed in the liberation perspective emphasize the full and active participation of people historically marginalized from power, decision making, and knowledge-construction. They stress the ideological, political, gender-based, racialized, and economic dimensions of social relations in and through which all knowledge is generated. They also frequently involve international collaborations wherein external catalysts engage with local community members (e.g., Debbink & Ornelas, 1997) or cooperatives (e.g., Arratia & de la Maza, 1997) to improve the quality of life for residents through participatory processes designed to generate change.

Some of these participatory and action strategies have been extended to include humanitarian aid and economic interventions with the survivors of war and state-sponsored violence, to inform collaborative approaches to rethreading social life in the context of structural poverty and in the wake of violence (Lykes & Coquillon, 2006). For example, in a participatory action project in rural Guatemala, Lykes, in collaboration with 20 Maya women in Chajul, addressed challenges related to the country's civil war and ongoing ethnic-and gender-based discrimination (Lykes et al., 1999; Women of PhotoVoice/ADMI & Lykes, 2000). Together they developed a process of story-telling, reflection, and photography to construct a narrative of the community's shared history – stories of the war and its effects, and stories of the women's efforts to re-establish their lives after the war ended and create alternatives for their children. The endeavour emerged from, and was embedded in, the work of a local women's organization that fostered cultural awareness (through the recovery of cultural and religious practices suppressed during the war), economic development (through several animal husbandry projects and a revolving loan fund), education (through a community after-school programme for children and a community library), leadership development, and psychosocial healing (Lykes et al., 1999). The project culminated in the production of a bi-lingual photoessay, *Voices and Images: Mayan Ixil Women of Chajul* (Women of PhotoVoice/ADMI & Lykes, 2000). To complete the project, the co-researchers from Chajul spoke with other women in surrounding villages, thus deepening their understanding of the diverse consequences of the 36-year war. These and other participatory processes offered spaces within which the women could engage in self-discovery and critical analysis. They also facilitated a process of breaking silences to speak the truth in a context of ongoing impunity for those who had committed atrocities against them.

Similarly, psychologist Mike Wessells and the Christian Children's Fund team leader Davidson Jonah (Wessells & Jonah, 2005) describe a coordinated economic and psychosocial participatory community initiative in Sierra

Leone, the Support for Skills Training and Employment Generation project (STEG). Developed by the local players in collaboration with the Christian Children's Fund, STEG aimed to help former child soldiers reintegrate into their communities. During Sierra Leone's more than ten-year civil war, opposition forces, including the Revolutionary United Front (RUF), systematically brutalized Sierra Leoneans and abducted children to serve in their army. The RUF took actions specifically aimed at disconnecting the children from their communities and at violating traditional values, such as raping girls in front of neighbours and family members, killing family members of abductees, and forcing abductees to kill or mutilate family members or neighbours. The RUF also used violence within the army as a means of control. As a result, the reintegration of former RUF soldiers posed myriad psychosocial challenges.

According to Wessells and Jonah (2005), reintegration required several things: (a) reconciliation between former RUF soldiers and communities; (b) addressing poverty, because without meeting basic needs former child soldiers were more likely to use violence to provide for themselves; (c) constructing within former child soldiers a non-military identity; (d) developing for former soldiers positive roles in civilian life through education and job training; and . (e) the spiritual purification of former soldiers through the recovery of cultural practices, including rituals performed by community members. In addition to conflict resolution and reconciliation between and among civilians and ex-combatants, STEG gave the youths a small stipend to support themselves, training in 'locally sustainable skills', and access to a microcredit scheme that provided small loans to develop ongoing, sustainable economic activities.

Project evaluation revealed that the process had a 'humanizing' effect for former child soldiers, who reported that community members were less likely to call them 'rebels' and more likely to apply to them 'traditional processes of remorse, forgiveness, and reconciliation' (Wessells & Jonah, 2005: 21). The opportunities for income generation, however, had the most profound effects. As Wessells and Jonah observed:

> **Many [ex-combatants] said that without the stipends, they would have felt marginalized and uncared for ... Some reported that having clothes and less hunger had helped to rehabilitate them as members of the community since they did not seem to be a drain on community resources. They spoke repeatedly of how having a bit of money and the ability to meet basic needs was necessary for putting the war behind them. In many respects, some of the greatest wounds of the war had been not physical but the isolation, marginalization, and shame they felt on arrival in the community without shoes, clothing, or the ability to feed themselves. (2005: 22)**

Female child soldiers, who were especially stigmatized and ostracized upon their return because of the many sexual violations to which the RUF subjected them, found that 'having an income conferred not only purchasing power but also prestige and a powerful boost in self-esteem' (2005: 16). Wessells and Jonah opined that '[i]f [ritualized spiritual] cleansing enabled them to reenter the social arena, having cash gave them status and a positive place in their villages' (2005: 16).

Building upon those observations, Wessells (2006a) observed that having a 'livelihood', a context-appropriate social role that provides income, can help survivors reconstruct their identities in positive ways. Soldiers re-envision themselves as civilians, and rape victims can re-inscribe themselves as survivors, mothers, and contributing members of the community. The process works in the reverse as well; reconnecting people to their communities can support their abilities to be productive in new social and economic roles.

These two projects exemplify community-based participatory interventions in two of the many communities in Latin America and Africa emerging from decades of armed conflict. They reflect gender and culturally aware approaches to crafting programmes in dialogue with local actors. Although not specifically discussed as 'empowerment projects', the programmes were designed to develop human capabilities, raise self-esteem, and, to varying degrees, rethread the social and cultural fabric of the community. Thus they are grounded both in the discourse of human rights – advocating, through the design and outcomes of their programmes, for survivors' economic, political, and cultural rights – and in the language of 'empowerment', through a programmatic focus on the development of social capital.

Yet these approaches are significantly more complex when taking into consideration the concomitant arrangements of social power based upon gender, race, and class. For example, the project facilitated by Lykes and her colleagues in Chajul did not attend to the myriad and complex effects of the PhotoVoice intervention on men, including but not limited to those who were partners of the youngest women participants. Power shifted within families and in the wider community as women assumed, in their own words, activities that had heretofore been restricted to men.

As significantly, in terms of the project in Sierra Leone, Cornwall astutely critiques the limits of economic interventions that distribute money without a critical analysis of wider forces:

> **Claims to be 'empowering women' through engaging them in the market conflate power with money, and imbue the acquisition of money with almost magical powers – as if once women had their own money, they could wave a wand and wish away overnight the social norms, institutions and relationships that are part of their lives. Empowerment-lite promises this, and more: a chain of causalities culminating in development's holy grail [sic], poverty reduction. (2007)**

Finally, both projects focused on addressing the specific needs of local participants in local communities. Neither was yoked to broader social movements that might have extended their local community focus to the wider societal level. Contemporary activist scholars, while continuing to collaborate with community-based groups, aim to connect similar efforts to broader social movements, a strategy that enhances the possibilities for systemic change and social transformation (see Hale, 2008, for examples).

Thus activist scholars as well as the *Pathways to Women's Empowerment* project discussed above offer important resources for thinking more deeply about these challenging subjects.

concluding thoughts: the challenges of going forward

The work of critical and liberation psychologists, activist scholars, and development workers committed to human rights suggests that psychosocial healing and community development require an integrated, interdisciplinary approach that works with survivors to defend their human rights and develop their capacities as change agents. Such work is not without its challenges (see Lykes & Mersky, 2006, for an earlier articulation of the limits of psychosocial work). First, without a critical lens and a set of transparent social commitments, initiatives brought from the outside into communities emerging from war run the risk of plugging local people into the structures of foreign enterprises rather than building change from the 'ground up'. Such initiatives thereby may fail to strengthen community-level decision making and development and affirm local or indigenous practices. Additionally, those who are implementing participatory initiatives must be mindful of the potential for even well-intentioned approaches to recapitulate hierarchical power structures or otherwise fail adequately to support independence (see Cooke & Kothari, 2001). In Wessells and Jonah's work, for example, the provision of monetary stipends for participation in a localized project 'although valuable initially, created excessive emphasis on money and dependence on external sources of income' (2005: 24).

Second, long-term health and mental health care and development must integrate local concerns and value systems. The failure to do so has drawn criticism among those who advocate sustainable, culturally sensitive intervention models (Carr, McAuliffe, & MacLachlan, 1998; Pupavac, 2000). Furthermore, even interventions that are culturally imbued run the risk of failing to challenge institutionalized racism and sexism and failing to develop explicit anti-racist and gender-critical programming based on systemic analysis of structural equalities.

Third, much of the work reported here has only been descriptively evaluated, if at all. Conditions of war and its aftermath, extreme poverty, and humanitarian crisis are challenging sites for intervention – and even more challenging for evaluation. Although participatory evaluation and other community-based strategies are yielding some data, most findings to date are testimonial or anecdotal.

Fourth is a concern about an unexamined assumption underlying much psychosocial work: that the expected outcomes are 'recovery and healing'. As critical psychologists and human rights activists, we should consider the multiple meanings of words like recovery, healing, reparation, and reconciliation. Critical psychological work with the survivors of human rights violations stemming from war and other forms of violence implicates questions of justice and truth. Thus the psychological language of 'recovery', as commonly used, is insufficient to encompass the search for justice with truth. Moreover, if justice is 'pending' in most if not all communities emerging from war, what are the possible consequences of psychosocial interventions in its absence?

A fifth concern is that psychosocial programmes not embedded in development projects that engage entire communities frequently focus exclusively on those directly affected by violence. Well intentioned though this may be, it carries possible risks. For example, victim-survivors may experience re-stigmatization by being 'selected out' for special services or resources, or removed from supportive relationships with others in their communities. Moreover, diagnostic categories may objectify sufferers rather than engage them as active collaborators in a healing process (that is, as 'the PTSD patient', rather than as the person who has had a traumatic exposure to violence, among other experiences over a lifetime). Alternatively, victims may become 'stuck in victimhood', that is, they may repeat their story of traumatization so frequently that they become the story; they may 'no longer exist' outside the testimony of survival. Feminists working in development projects that target women's participation to the exclusion of men have identified a similar concern. Cornwall (2000), for example, has argued that outsiders have mistakenly presumed gender solidarity among women who actually identify more strongly with men from their communities than with women of other racial, ethnic, or socioeconomic groups.

A final persistent concern in these programmes and processes has to do with time limits. Beyond the question of whether it is possible to heal politically generated traumas, survivors may only recognize their pain or loss years after the violation and therefore not seek help when it is offered. Psychosocial processes are long term and often intergenerational. This reality challenges those negotiating current psychosocial interventions to plan for the possibility of inter- or multiple-generational efforts. As a minimum programme developers must recognize and acknowledge these diversities and constraints.

In raising each of these concerns and complexities we are reminded that the moral positioning of psychosocial and development workers is central. Critical and liberation psychology call for a nuanced, multilayered analysis of the factors contributing to the environment in which one works. They call for an active advocacy of economic, social, and legal justice, as embodied in a human rights framework, to promote healing and social cohesion. We share activist scholars' and human rights activists' conviction that psychosocial interventions must be consonant with and integrated into wider sociopolitical work for justice and against impunity in the struggle for social transformation (see, for example, Hale, 2008; Sveaass & Lavick, 2000). Finally, as critical psychologists and activist scholars we are challenged to act boldly while humbly recognizing the limits of any effort to redress structural injustice and transform social inequalities.

1 Psychosocial trauma in the wake of war and extreme poverty is complex and multidimensional, implicating race, class, gender, and culture. Critical and liberation psychology-informed interventions in communities emerging from war call for a critical analysis of the influences of race, class, and gender on peoples' lived experiences.

2 Structural poverty, war, and organized violence can undermine the social, economic, cultural, and political rights of survivors as well as their psychological wellbeing. Critical and liberation psychology-informed interventions in communities emerging from war should be grounded in a human rights framework and supportive of the rethreading of community and the transformation of social structures at the root of extreme poverty and violence.

3 Psychosocial interventions in communities emerging from war can integrate community-based economic development practices in ways that help to develop survivors' capabilities, sense of self-efficacy, and critical empowerment in order to build the community's economic, social, and cultural sufficiency.

glossary

- **indigenous**: that which has originated in a given environment; local; people who trace their origins to a specific geographic space.

- **liberation psychology**: a perspective within psychology drawing from liberation theology, particularly the 'preferential option for the poor'. Seeks to work in solidarity with the poor, recognizing their unique and particular contributions to the struggle for social justice and equality and to take into consideration the wider social context in the analysis of psychological processes.

- **post-traumatic stress**: socioemotional distress caused by exposure to violence or other extreme threats of physical harm.

- **psychosocial**: psychological processes and development in the context of one's social, economic, and political environment.

▨ ▨ reading suggestions ▨

Judith Herman's (1992) *Trauma and Recovery,* an early foundational text for any reading on post-traumatic stress disorder, places the concept within political and historical contexts. Similarly foundational writings by Ignacio Martín-Baró, a primary thinker at the nexus of liberation psychology and psychosocial trauma, can be found in English translation (Martín-Baró, 1994). Martín-Baró's work has strongly influenced psychologists' work in societies ravaged by armed conflict including, among others, that of Basque physician and social psychologist Carlos Martín Beristain (2006), whose most recent book, *Humanitarian Aid Work: A Critical Approach*, provides an overview of the needs and challenges of psychological work in these contexts. Stuart Carr and Tod S. Sloan (2003) also comment upon both psychosocial work in contexts of structural poverty and the effects of poverty on wellbeing. *World Mental Health* (Desjarlais et al., 1995) provides an important look at the challenges to mental health globally.

: // internet resources /

- **Ignacio Martín-Baró Fund for Mental Health and Human Rights**: www.martinbarofund.org
- **Institute of Development Studies Participation Group**: www.ids.ac.uk/ids/particip/
- **Psychosocial Working Group**: www.forcedmigration.org/psychosocial/
- **Psychologists for Social Responsibility**: www.psysr.org
- **Society for Community Research and Action**: www.scra27.org

 Questions

1 The critical and liberation psychology as well as the participatory methodologies that inform the two examples described in this chapter emphasize personal reflection on the part of all participants in combination with action ('reflexivity'). How might your personal history, race, nationality, gender, and socioeconomic status influence your approach to working in poor communities emerging from war?

2 Consider current or recent conflicts in different parts of the world. To what extent did poverty, social and economic inequality, sexism, or racism contribute to the generation of violence? How might human rights discourse inform how you would engage these issues in an intervention in a context emerging from war?

3 Psychosocial interventions in societies emerging from war require sustained commitment and engagement over time. What kind(s) of professional preparation are desirable for those thinking of responding to such situations? How might you best develop your understanding of critical and liberation psychology?

18

Oppression and Empowerment: The Genesis of a Critical Analysis of Mental Health

Michael McCubbin

Chapter Topics

This chapter does not try to convey an objective, scientific understanding of the psychological distress known as 'mental illness'. Rather, in keeping with critical psychology's more general approach, it explores the social response to what is conceived of as mental illness and provides guideposts for more appropriate responses when the experience of psychological distress is understood to be a socially embedded phenomenon. The chapter's historical perspective shows how a changing society and changing patterns of thinking affect how people understand mental illness – i.e., the 'social representations' of mental illness – and consequently how these changed perspectives alter the policies and practices designed to treat, control, or help persons suffering psychological distress.

A very particular tool is used to approach these questions: *power*. While explicit and systematic use of the power concept is little used outside political science, issues of power have become well established in public health, social psychology and community psychology practice. In these fields we find prominent use of power-related concepts such as **empowerment**, sense of control, feelings of efficacy, and capacity building. All these are dimensions of power, which can be understood as the ability to intentionally change one's self or one's environment. It can mean 'self-improvement', influence among peers, obtaining wanted goods and resources, or helping to make the world a better place.

A primary purpose of this chapter is to suggest that critical psychology can be an agent for positive social change by recognizing the harmful effects of power's opposite – oppression. Oppression is a factor in the appearance of psychological distress, in its exacerbation, in causing greater suffering among those already vulnerable, and in rendering inevitable the 'chronicity' associated with mental illness. Once these roles of oppression are recognized, critical psychologists can help in several ways: they can try to help remove barriers and oppressors; they can work with clients to expand their capacities and their confidence to advocate change; and they can work with social institutions such as governments, community groups, and corporations to encourage the empowerment of psychologically distressed persons and reduce the incidence of mental illnesses. Whereas mainstream psychologists work all too comfortably within institutions that control mentally distressed persons, critical psychologists can bring more challenging perspectives along with their useful skills and professional status.

Psychological distress cannot be directly observed: it is not like a lesion on skin. Rather, it is experiential to the sufferer, but what others observe is not the experience directly but the behaviours and speech of the sufferer. Labels applied to what people understand of mental illness are social constructions that usually tell far more about the persons using them than about the object or phenomenon to which they are supposed to apply. These labels, which reflect the attitudes of the person or group using them, have frequently been shaped by prejudice, mythology, self-interest, and fear. Alternatively, and ideally, a social construction and associated label could reflect hope, compassion, caring, and love. Such an understanding is much more consistent with the view of this chapter: that we should discard negative, self-interested stereotypes of psychological distress and 'the mentally ill' in favour of understandings that let us advance conditions for the empowerment and hence greater wellbeing of the psychologically distressed.

A word about terminology. This chapter variously uses terms such as 'insane', 'mad', 'mentally ill' and so on. Each term has been used to convey different understandings of psychological distress or of people thought to be distressed. The meaning of such terms can change over time, and varies depending upon who uses them. For example, 'madness' was coined centuries ago when severe psychological distress was little understood, and is often considered derogatory. On the other hand, many contemporary user advocacy groups have reappropriated the term as a means of opening up efforts to understand the person behind a condition of 'madness'. Since the expression 'persons suffering psychological distress' is lengthy, this chapter uses the other terms in part to simplify things. Such use should not be interpreted as having any derogatory intent.

Mainstream psychology has for many years more or less objectified persons seeking help, and psychological practice can be infantilizing. These impacts can remain substantially the same even though psychological techniques have changed – evolved, if you wish. Freudian psychoanalysis can be disempowering if it does not foster enablement, if it listens only to dreams and not the actual aspirations of those seeking help. Behavioural therapy can ignore people's volition by treating them as machines to be 'adjusted'. Many practising psychologists today do little or no actual counselling and spend their time administering and scoring tests that aim to 'measure' aspects of human behaviour or feeling without seeking to understand the *whole person*. Cognitive therapy and the psychological neurosciences are becoming dominant. But can the human spirit and consciousness be reduced to the study of neurons and hormones?

This chapter argues that a *critical* approach rejects objectification of the person and works on behalf of clients and groups according to those persons' actual aspirations. Critical psychologists do not substitute their own idea of what is good for the person. Recognizing that psychology should be working *with* and *for* the client is consistent with understanding the whole person. Not only can that person not be reduced to the workings of the brain, but the wholeness of a person has much to do with his or her social environment, which alternatively could be oppressive or empowering.

the power of the unknown in traditional societies: social integration of the 'different'

The historian-philosopher Foucault (2006) vividly described pre-modern societies' attempts to understand mental illness. Insanity in traditional societies was considered beyond human understanding; indeed, the mad were often seen as not entirely of this world. This view was entirely consistent with pre-modern thinking, which did not always require 'rational' earth-bound explanations of phenomena acting upon individuals and community. Birth, death, sickness, light and dark were all felt to stem from acts of powerful and mysterious gods, who might be loving but who might also be vengeful. Even obvious earth-bound 'causes' had little or no explanatory impact. For example, take someone brain damaged as a result of falling from a tree: Did the spirits decide the outcome? Did the spirits shake the person out of the tree in the first place?

As described by historians like Foucault, 'madness' was a term used to describe people with bizarre behaviour, weird experiences like hearing voices, or antisocial behaviours that were hard to attribute to greed, love, lust, hate and the other common emotions and desires. In this respect, nothing has changed in our day: 'mental illness' today is widely seen as the psychological condition that leads to inexplicable behaviours, experiences and feelings; we still can't 'see' the brain malfunctions that we think are behind mental illness. This is in enormous contrast to modern psychiatry, which, as a biomedical profession, believes that mental illness is due to a *brain* disorder, which then translates into thought, cognition or personality disorders.

Traditional peoples did not seek a biological explanation of mental illness, nor did they think like psychiatry today that there must be one to look for. If anyone was seen as having special insight into the meaning and sources of madness, it was the priests and other spiritual seekers (leading several writers, e.g. Thomas Szasz, 1974, to suggest that psychiatry has come to partly supplant the priesthood in terms of the faith of the masses). Hence, since traditional peoples did not assume biological causes, or any 'rational' cause, they did not try to 'treat' mental illness. One could argue that in some ways the traditional approach to the mad was more humane than many modern approaches: as Foucault noted, the mad were not excluded from families and villages. As also noted by ethnoanthropologists describing contemporary traditional societies, they were seen as 'different', but they had a place. Since the mad were thought to be straddling earth and the great beyond, they were respected and given roles as medicine men or women, as seers, as prophets, as priests, or simply as symbols of the gods' power. They were thought to have gifts that the gods gave to few mortal women and men.

Traditional societies were entirely different from modern societies. The primary social organizations were villages, not more anonymous larger structures like corporations, states, churches, and so on. The economies – hunting, gathering, fishing, and, gradually, rudimentary farming and artisanal manufacturing – changed little over thousands of years. Social roles like occupation were often predetermined, passed down through the generations. Except for the interventions of the gods, which they accepted stoically, people felt they had control over their own little parts of the cosmos. Such sense of control and assured social roles probably resulted in fewer mental illnesses than in today's complex, competitive societies. And importantly, although undoubtedly this is a somewhat over-romantic view, mental illness would not be made worse by attempts to 'treat' it, as discussed later in this chapter.

oppression, madness and segregation as a consequence of the industrial revolution

Of course, 'civilization' changed everything. The market economies emerging over the past millennia, and especially since the Middle Ages, punished those who were not sufficiently productive. As Karl Marx (1906) described, fewer people produced for themselves the food, clothing, housing, and so on that they consumed. They sold their labour in the market-place and in return received money which might – or might not – be adequate to meet their basic needs. As Marx said, the peasants and workers 'lost the means of production'. To make a living, they now often had to move from place to place and job to job. If no jobs were available it was next to impossible to feed themselves by going back to the traditional way of life: the land was now 'property', often owned by a very rich man far away who didn't even know the people living on it, but charged them rent, or sold it to whoever had enough money.

In market societies with little social stability, thus, including our own and those emerging in the Industrial Revolution, people no longer had traditional roles to give their lives meaning. And so the mad, having lost the role of being 'in touch with the gods', were increasingly viewed as a burden. As several medical historians with a critical bent suggest, rates of mental illness rose dramatically (e.g., R. Fox, 1978, described California's growing mental illness epidemic). The increasing fragility and uncertainty of modern life, and the necessity of fitting into rather unnatural market-imposed social roles, diminished any sense of control and coherence. This was bad for the public's mental wellbeing: as Antonovsky (1987) surmised (studying the psychological fate of Holocaust survivors), this 'sense of coherence', the feeling that life is meaningful, is essential to good mental health.

Societies with no place or purpose for the growing numbers of mentally ill people increasingly excluded them. Foucault's account of early market societies' handling of mental illness – perhaps over-imaginative but still capturing the essence of the phenomenon – paints a picture of bands of the mentally ill and other deviants, only partly of this world, wandering the countryside and forests. When they made forays into towns, they were either ignored as if invisible or chased out. At this period in history, post-traditional but pre-modern, therefore, oppression of the psychologically distressed can be attributed to the societies that tried to push them out rather than to unknowable powers beyond.

Foucault's (2006) history of psychology describes this as the first stage in the alienation not only of the mentally ill, but also of *mental illness*. In so doing, Foucault (1987) said that the 'sane' world lost whatever hope it might have had of understanding the 'others' and what mental illness is about. The irony is that, under the logical positivism of modern thinking, the thing we are trying to understand must be 'objectified', which requires separating it from the observer. However, mental illness is intrinsically a part of *us*. Separating *it* from *us* renders it meaningless and unknowable.

control of the mentally ill: institutionalization of the alienated in modern capitalist society

As the market economy expanded to replace almost all forms of traditional life and production and turn all land and labour into commodities, the era of the mentally ill as 'ghosts' either inside or outside society inevitably came to an end. The mentally ill could find fewer and fewer places discreetly beyond the view of society at large. Their increased presence coincided with the widespread rejection of superstition and the supernatural as explanations of mental illness. However, with nothing to replace these explanations, mental illness could be even more disturbing to the mentally well than to the mentally ill. Representing the 'dark side' of the human psyche, it could happen to us or to loved ones (although we don't want to admit it). Because insanity is about who we are, as a matter of identity, it can be even scarier than a disease like cancer, which ravages the body but not ordinarily the mind.

The solution was to herd the little-understood 'ghosts' into pens: the great institutionalization of the mentally ill began. As Foucault (2006) describes, at first they were confined in jails, itself a modern invention. Into the same jails were ejected all the other human flotsam of society, the criminals, debtors, 'wicked women' (prostitutes, single mothers), the poor, the physically handi-capped, and the enemies of the powerful. These other 'social deviants' or undesirables were relatively manageable: they could feed and dress themselves, and more or less get along peacefully, or at least predictably, with other inmates and the jailors. The most disturbed mentally ill, however, were often far more disturbing to other inmates and the jailors than even the worst murderers and rapists. They might scream, cry, speak in gibberish, lash out blindly at others, hurt themselves; sometimes they wouldn't eat or maintain their hygiene even at the very minimal levels early jails permitted. So the really disturbing mentally ill were not only alienated by society through incarceration, they were further alienated within the prisons by shackling and isolation. This, of course, was not '**treatment**'. It was *control* by others, certainly not control of themselves.

It became, then, generally accepted that mental illness is forever incurable, and that the mentally ill are defined by their mental illness and should be managed accordingly rather than viewed and treated as persons. It is not surprising, therefore, that the mental disturbances of the insane would not only fail to disappear with time, but would get far worse.

The French physician Philippe Pinel is widely viewed as the first 'reformer' of society's management of the mentally ill. At the dawn of the nineteenth century he advocated placing mentally ill persons in separate institutions. If we were to be charitable, we could surmise that he hoped the application of science in a specialized facility would lead to cures, and perhaps that the mentally ill would be treated more humanely than prisoners and other deviants. In response to his advocacy, France created the first '*asylum*', a term invoking rest, respite from the pressures of society, and perhaps for some the appropriate conditions for **recovery**. Despite Pinel's possible motives, however, it is quite likely that he succeeded not because of outrage at the treatment of the mentally ill but because of concern for the other prisoners. In any event, in most cases the **asylums** spreading throughout the Western world became little more than warehouses. Typically they became enormously overcrowded as societal conditions created the epidemic of mental illness noted above (or of people characterized as mentally ill because they didn't fit in). Overcrowding and poor conditions caused diseases of the body, but physicians were rare. For example, in Maryland, even past the mid-twentieth century there were fewer doctors per inmate than the rate in the surrounding population, and even fewer than in the notorious Sing-Sing prison (Birnbaum, 1969, 1974).

In general, throughout the modern period right up to a few decades ago, the asylums became more crowded and less humane. Nevertheless, there was some movement toward re-evaluating treatment of the mentally ill, primarily for two reasons: the 'moral treatment' movement and the emergence of psychiatry as a medical specialization.

the moral treatment movement: prayers for the souls of the afflicted

Nineteenth-century reformers in the United States and England, motivated by religious faith and by outrage at the inhuman treatment of the mentally ill, organized an activist moral treatment movement. Their advocacy led to the adoption of moral treatment principles – in some asylums. The overcrowded public asylums, dependent upon the state, paid lip service at best. Asylums led by religious orders fared better, but it was above all private retreats with paying customers that instituted the fundamental reforms.

Moral treatment advocates believed that prayer and activity would stimulate people's ability to shake off the worst of their symptoms and perhaps lead to some recovery. Concretely, an asylum run according to moral treatment principles would be a spacious, peaceful, clean, and happy place in which people engaged together in a variety of activities (prayer, needlepoint and basket weaving, gardening, singing, etc.). Unfortunately, society wasn't ready for this potentially positive but expensive development. For the most part, only the well-off could receive such treatment. We will see below, however, that such ideas have endured to the present, converging with the contemporary 'recovery movement' and the emergence of some earlier forms of critical psychology: humanistic psychology, which tried to focus on the whole person in that person's social environment, and radical or liberation psychology, which challenged the power structures of the status quo.

the cult of biomedical psychiatry: objectification and oppression

What did spread in a significant way was the biomedical approach to mental illness, emerging from the nascent profession of psychiatry. Ostensibly this was a radical departure from earlier approaches characterized by neglect, separation, and oppression. Psychiatry brought the modern idea that medical science could treat mental illness. (It should be noted that treating an illness is not the same as helping the ill; the former might help if it works, but the mentally ill need much more help than treatment alone could provide. Treatment is focused on a disease or syndrome and not on the person.) Hence 'asylums' evolved into 'psychiatric hospitals' based on several assumptions: that different mental illnesses can be distinguished from one another, and hence diagnosed; that each type of mental illness has distinct medical causes; and, thus, that each mental illness should receive a specific biological treatment.

A number of psychiatry's critics have largely rejected these assumptions, including even some psychiatrists like Thomas Szasz (1974) and Peter Breggin (1991). I agree with their view that these biological 'treatments' don't effect 'cures'. Indeed, it's quite possible that these treatments aim less at a cure than at control of the patient and the suppression of disruptive symptoms. Aimed at the patient's brain, as a physical organ, rather than at the patient as a thinking, feeling human, they render the patient not so much cured as docile. Indeed, it is not too much a stretch to point out that such docility is achieved via the same means applied to prisoners of war when human rights conventions are ignored: cruel and unusual punishment. Psychiatry's early so-called treatments consisted of baths in ice water (and even something similar to waterboarding), constraints (e.g., straightjackets, being tied down to a bed), and isolation (placement in padded cells with few or no clothes or furniture, no social interaction, no books or entertainment of any kind).

Later, 'new and improved' treatments came along to help solidify the status of some alienists, those who ran the asylums, as, indeed, physicians and not just as lowly jailers and caretakers. Most notable were shock (via insulin injection or electricity to create convulsions) and lobotomy. Convulsions indeed do induce docility for a time; they also, according to studies in the medical literature (see Breggin, 1991), produce brain damage. Critics say that it is precisely this brain damage that creates the docility. In other words, the treatment makes the patient less of what he or she was (a sad reminder of the old joke 'the treatment was a success, but the patient died'). Lobotomy causes brain damage even more directly: it cuts out from the brain a supposed 'problem area', ordinarily in a frontal lobe, which is responsible for the person's intellect, emotions and volition (will). The metaphor 'turning the patient into a vegetable' in critiquing shock and lobotomy practices is, unfortunately, all too often an accurate description.

Finally, in the middle of the last century, psychiatry obtained its holy grail: pharmaceutical drugs. On the whole, the vast majority of psychiatrists and the public accept the use of these **psychotropics** (psychiatric drugs); any concerns generally relate to overdosage and inappropriate prescriptions (the wrong drugs, or bad combinations of drugs). However, a growing number of observers (including this writer) are becoming alarmed about their widespread use. According to the most extreme critical views, in the end psychotropics accomplish the same things as shock and lobotomy: they suppress symptoms without treating causes, and they do so by rendering the patient docile: less alert, less physically mobile, less able to feel and express emotions, and more passive.

Under these conditions, the sufferer of a mental illness is defined not as a person but as a patient. The social role of *patient* is precisely that of accepting blindly the authority and power of treating professionals; the patient has no role in working toward recovery. This is a process of *infantilization*: in effect, it turns the patient into a helpless child. The incapacities induced by modern treatments, as well as other secondary effects like drooling, facial tics and jerky body movements, are a form of illness called *iatrogenesis*: illness *caused* by the treatment. Certainly, psychotropics can sometimes help facilitate recovery. This is likely to be the case, however, only if the patient holds the reins of the treatment plan and if drug treatment is viewed as one of several means, along with others, of achieving better mental health, and not the end in itself.

Everybody has heard about the 'stigma of mental illness'. Who hasn't come across a clearly disturbed person on the street, with disturbing and bothersome behaviours? We should remember this question: How much of this disturbing behaviour is really caused by the *treatment*? How does misattributing what we see to mental illness rather than to the treatment affect our attitudes and beliefs about mental illness and the mentally ill – our 'social representations' (see Cohen & McCubbin, 1990)?

The story of the treatment of mental illness in modern times has been all about one thing: one *finalité*, to use the fine term of French sociology which embraces process, purpose and results. That one thing is *suppressing* the expression of mental illness by *oppressing* the patient.

early deinstitutionalization: control in the community

The famous 'deinstitutionalization movement', begun in the late 1950s, had several causes. Perhaps most obviously, the enormous growth of large public asylums became an increasingly onerous financial burden. As conditions deteriorated even further, the straw on the camel's back was early empowerment efforts by psychiatrized people themselves as well as growing advocacy by others shocked at the neglect and oppression the new mass media were beginning to reveal. Small numbers of a wide range of persons – welfare reformers, religious groups, reporters, family members and, above all in the United States, a smattering of civil rights lawyers – demanded better conditions. The few lawyers, paid not by moneyless public psychiatric patients but by civil rights organizations, took on a number of individual cases. These test cases, often over the 'right to treatment' (McCubbin & Weisstub, 2001), challenged the abuse and neglect in publicly financed institutions. The resulting court orders forced hospitals to renovate facilities and improve treatment and care. This proved impossible, however, primarily for two reasons: the huge size of the hospitals' population made meeting the new rules financially impossible, and too few psychiatrists wanted to work in those hospitals, preferring instead better paid and more prestigious clinics and the 'real' general medical hospitals within communities. Insane asylums were simply not glamorous enough for these practitioners.

It became clear that the psychiatric hospital population had to be drastically reduced. With the arrival of psychotropic drugs psychiatrists cried 'Eureka!' Not only could they now prescribe drugs like other physicians, but the drugs meant they could release large numbers of patients into the community. Why? Because they could *control* patients' behaviours, dulling their perceptions, emotions and will and even rendering their body movements sluggish (Breggin, 1991). This was particularly the case for the 'antipsychotics' (neuroleptics) forced upon persons diagnosed with schizophrenia, one of the most severe mental illnesses. These drugs did the job of padded cells and shackles, permitting the transfer of large numbers of patients to less structured environments like group homes and supervised apartments. Here it should be noted that to some degree the visible, tangible oppression of institutional control and neglect had been replaced by a much more subtle but equally powerful oppression: by handicapping not just a person's body but also that person's very psyche, that person's humanity.

However, despite formally approved policies, for many decades alternative care in the community was minimal to nonexistent. As it turned out, the psychotropics were so powerful that often the authorities simply ejected patients from the hospitals. As long as released patients stayed on the drugs, the authorities could wash their hands of them without providing any non-drug care or treatment (McCubbin, 1994). Indeed, most mentally ill people ejected from asylums were invisible to their communities. Avoiding the gaze of others, they made few waves. Many lived in crowded, filthy, and oppressive rooming houses where landlords often appropriated their welfare cheques (we could say, then, that there was a growth of 'institutionalization in the community').

Nevertheless, public opinion, led by inflammatory news exposés, came to misperceive the large numbers of homeless people on the streets – often the victims of unceasing economic upheavals and, in the United States, damaged Vietnam War veterans – as mentally ill, inflicted upon the community by the downsizing psychiatric hospitals. With little evidence of violence other than a few sensational cases that generally had little to do with mental illness, and building upon fears and myths that had endured since time immemorial, the public increasingly equated mental illness with dangerousness. According to the common circular logic, unexplained violence was taken as proof of mental illness, and hence mental illness could then be seen as raising the spectre of dangerousness (Dallaire, McCubbin, Morin, & Cohen 2000).

Since returning thousands of deinstitutionalized patients to psychiatric hospitals was no longer an option, other solutions were needed. One seemingly simple solution still applies today: forcing the mentally ill to take 'their' drugs. One method was via 'community outpatient treatment orders' authorizing the state to force drugs upon non-hospitalized persons. This was sometimes reinforced by PACT (Programmes for Assertive Community Treatment), started in the 1980s in the United States. Under PACT, a team of practitioners led by a psychiatrist and always including a nurse (and hopefully people like social workers, educators, or community workers) would follow the patient in the community and provide an intervention programme – but the key, and sometimes only, element was the forced administration of psychotropics. If psychologists were involved at all it was in the technical capacity of measuring deficits rather than 'talk therapy' and social intervention.

The story up to now is not a very happy one. The oppression of the psychiatrized followed them from the asylums into the community. The treatment they received had little to do with helping them recover and adapt to a relatively normal life. And the belief seemed to be, more than ever, that serious mental illness was for life: all that remained was control and, above all, suppressing the symptoms and signs of mental illness without any hope of a cure. The result was massive numbers of socially dysfunctional people who, rather than living in the community, suffered in the community.

Fortunately, there is some light on the horizon – a story of consciously addressing the role of power in both oppression and liberation.

the recovery movement: retaking power and fighting oppression

While most deinstitutionalized patients remained lost to the community despite 'living in the community', a margin of liberty arose for those who could escape community institutionalization and overmedicalization. Some returned to their families and some, despite poverty, managed to achieve a semblance of socially integrated normalcy – some kind of job, even if part-time, a room or apartment not under the control of someone abusing them psychologically and financially. They may have received the minimal community services available. Some developed an awareness of, and anger at, the oppression they and other mental patients suffered. These patients and ex-patients, working to carve themselves a reasonable life in society, came to call themselves *survivors* – survivors not just of their illness but, importantly, *survivors of psychiatric oppression*.

It is notable that at that time, in the late 1960s and 1970s, new types of community workers emerged – grassroots organizers, the socially conscious, and radical professionals including some community psychologists, a smattering of dissident psychiatrists, and leftist social workers – who did not see their roles as agents of social control, but instead viewed their mission as advocating for marginalized and vulnerable people and groups. Many were inspired by social movements advancing the liberation of blacks and women in Western societies and the radical ideologies that accompanied these movements – most importantly perhaps the *social conscientization* of South

American educator Paulo Freire (1970) who worked with the poorest of the poor (e.g., see Chapter 23). These activists helped develop the emerging concept of empowerment.

The term empowerment, unfortunately, has since become largely co-opted by an establishment of mainstream health and social service workers and probably well-meaning but nevertheless paternalistic family members. Today the term is so empty that it extends to the notion that patients can pull themselves up by their own bootstraps – but only if they are helped by heavy psychoactive drugs and the guidance of those who think they know better. In the hands of radical activists, however, empowerment was the logical antidote to oppression. In the mental health arena, it involved recognizing the oppression, control and paternalism that society and its medical and social welfare agents imposed upon persons whose psychological distress already made them excessively vulnerable. Instead of 'guiding' the oppressed, these activists tried to work *with* them – supporting survivors in their fight against oppression. Together they began to demand the basic human rights the non-psychiatrized take for granted: the right to treatment and support in the community; the right to self-determination and autonomy; freedom from 'cruel and unusual punishment'; the right to housing, food, clothing, income, and other basics necessary for human dignity; and, highly contested then as now by the medical establishment and the emerging family lobby groups, the right to *refuse* treatment (usually meaning the refusal of psychiatric drugs that the patient perceives as handicapping).

Among the survivors emerged leaders, such as David Oaks and his Support Coalition International (http://www.mindfreedom.org), Irit Shimrat, Judy Chamberlin, and Don Weitz (see the Antipsychiatry Coalition at http://www.antipsychiatry.org). They organized their own lobby groups as well as survivor peer support networks to help one another's struggle for survival and (as described below) recovery. Many of them recognized the systemic nature of the oppression that many sectors of society forced upon mental patients. Each sector had its own interests: the medical profession, the pharmaceutical industry, politicians responding to irrational public fears of 'crazy people', the press using myths about 'dangerous' mental patients to sell papers, family lobby groups deflecting blame from themselves toward genetic explanations of mental 'disease', and social control agents such as government welfare workers and the police seeking to render mental patients docile and invisible.

Survivor organizers understood that overcoming systemic oppression required not just empowering individuals – hard to do given the powerful forces bearing down upon them – but *collective action*. Working as groups, they fought in political arenas to change not just government policies but also how societal institutions dealt with mental illness. With the help of radical lawyers, often from legal aid societies, they fought in court to overturn abuse and coercion. With the help of radical writers like Thomas Szasz and Peter Breggin and activist organizations that had coalesced into networks like the Radical Psychology Network (http://www.radpsynet.org/) and the International Centre for the Study of Psychiatry and Psychology (http://www.icspp.org/), they challenged the longstanding orthodoxy that mental illness is entirely a medical problem situated in the brain and treatable with drugs, a view that gained strength with the arrival of physicians (who would become psychiatrists) in the domain of mental health treatment. Activists, including humanistic psychologists and the more radical community psychologists, strongly objected to the 'medical model' paradigm of mental illness (Conrad, 1992). Consistent with the modern, rational view of linear causality more or less void of human volition, the medical model posits a simplistic view that the complex phenomenon of psychological distress (particularly the most severe conditions) has a very limited set of biological causes. This is not surprising since all so-called 'physical' illnesses seemed attributable to such causes, such as toxins, trauma, gene defects, and so on.

Ironically, a number of scientists, and prominent among them research psychologists, simultaneously began innovative work that would challenge the medical model not only with respect to mental illnesses but also with respect to physical illnesses. They discovered that 'bad' stress (we now know there can be healthy stress) often plays a greater role than physical causes in explaining a variety of diseases like cardiovascular illness. Subsequently, research narrowed in on *lack of control* – in effect, a lack of power – as probably the key factor behind bad stress (Marmot, Basma, Hemingway, Brunner, & Stansfeld, 1997). Such stress then affects both the body and the brain (particularly through the central nervous system and hormones) and also encourages unhealthy physical behaviour such as smoking and other substance abuse, poor diet, and a lack of exercise. The evidence for this is now strong in many areas of physical health, and yet in mental health, where we would expect the impact of stress to be even greater, the widespread social representations of mental illness and mental health care practice implicitly, and often explicitly, consider the medical model of mental illness unquestionable (see McCubbin & Labonte, 2002).

The activist community workers who began the critique of the medical model in mental health asserted that mental illness must be understood as psychological distress experienced by an individual in the context of his or her surrounding world. In other words, mental illness, like other phenomena addressed throughout this book, is *socially embedded* rather than something taking place entirely within the individual. This is so because it is primarily the interaction of the individual with others in that person's family, community, and larger society which provides experience, and hence helps to shape that person's feelings and actions. Radical and critical psychologists aware of the mainstream's overreliance on individualistic explanations have developed this view of mental illness's social embeddedness since at least the 1970s.

Indeed, some of the psychologists active in this area are survivors themselves. Achieving careers in psychology and mental health after being both psychologically distressed and subjected to oppressive treatment, they seek to change how psychologists think of mental illness and to better help the sufferers of psychological distress recover. They also hope, sometimes by making their personal histories known, to reduce the stigma that the label 'ex-mental patient' so often creates (e.g., Bassman, 2007). Their work as part of psychology's activist, humanistic, radical vanguard is consistent with much of what is called critical psychology today.

These varied battles of the survivors did not fall entirely upon deaf ears. Realizing that resuming massive hospitalization was impossible and that controlling mental patients in the community via medical treatment (what I refer to as the *treatment and control in the community model* as opposed to a **community care and support** *model*) often made things worse, as noted above, sectors of the establishment began to find it convenient to listen. The deinstitutionalized, further victimized by a mental health system that failed to intervene appropriately, had become a burden upon the judicial and penal systems, partly because large numbers of ex-patients who were unable to make ends meet landed themselves in jail for minor infractions or simply because other people thought their behaviour bizarre; upon the social welfare system, since the treatments rendered them unable to even think about working; and upon the medical system, since ex-patients frequently ended up in general hospitals. These costs concentrated the minds of government officials wonderfully, who started to put meat on the bones of the long-standing pious words about 'community care'.

True community care and support is what the survivor activists and radical community workers had advocated for years. Such support views the person not as a 'patient' but as a whole person needing help, not just for the brain (if that) but also to achieve what all people need: a sense of meaning, fulfilment in life, and social roles that go with work, family, a home, income, and so on. It recognizes that psychiatrized persons have been oppressed not only by their illness but also by their treatments and by the control, coercion and paternalism operating upon them from all directions.

Although still fairly rare, and despite their pretensions, advanced and progressive community care systems do exist (for exemplars of successful efforts, see the community-based participatory research of the critical psychologists Nelson, Lord & Ochocka, 2001). Using empowerment principles to counter oppression, these systems seek recovery by advancing **social inclusion**. Recovery is a new paradigm – a new way of thinking – that breaks with the biomedical model's search for mental illness in one organ alone, the brain. Instead of viewing mental illness as a brain disease, recovery views it as a socially embedded psychological handicap – that is, its nature, expression and severity are largely a function of the person's place in a social milieu. Hence, recovery is facilitated by changing the social milieu. This includes activities such as accompanying the person in going about basic social functions like shopping, getting from place to place, doing fun or creative things with others, living with others, doing a job, and so on. We must remember above all that, at least for the most severely and long-term chronically distressed, and even more so for those who have lived for many years in institutions, their largest handicap is psychosocial rather than medical. They need help to return to, and to live in, society so that they, like others, can seek to fulfil their aspirations.

It seems to me that it is just common sense to view a mentally ill person as a whole person, to recognize the oppression they feel and 'interiorize'. Interiorization of oppression has been described by the critical psychologist Isaac Prilleltensky as the transmission of oppressive social experience into negative thoughts and feelings which, consequently, can lead to passivity: in other words, the person does not exercise power that may still potentially exist (Prilleltensky & Gonick, 1996). The appropriate response is empowering that person and empowering the mentally ill as a group. To seek their recovery is to embark upon a road where that person is socially included and allowed to work toward her or his aspirations. For me, it is hard to see how such views are 'radical' or 'critical'. And yet they are, because they directly challenge powerful sectors of society and because, despite the progress made here and there to establish community care and support systems, those systems are vastly underfunded and still rely far too much on medical and other forms of control and oppression.

Being a critical psychologist means looking beyond established truths and questioning the interests they serve. Are they self-serving? Do they perpetuate a myth that oppresses others? As the mind works in mysterious ways, so does society. A critical psychologist at least tries to investigate how both interact, going well beyond the superficial. This means advancing a critical psychology whose practitioners respond to what the client actually thinks, feels and says, who pays special attention to that client's aspirations, and works *with the client* to overcome barriers to those aspirations. Any psychologist who thinks barriers are all in the client's head and ignores family, social, economic and cultural structures is not a *critical* psychologist at all.

▪ ▪ main chapter points ▪

1 Understanding 'mental health systems' requires understanding their political, economic, and cultural contexts.

2 The role of *power* is highlighted.

3 Traditional societies viewed mental illness as reflecting the powers of the gods. Civilization and industrialization brought social and institutional exclusion and oppression of the mentally ill, with little hope of recovery.

4 In the twentieth century, humanitarian concerns were advanced by activists, including community and radical psychologists.

5 Advocacy groups led by users, allied with activists and some scientists, began developing new paradigms for understanding and responding to mental illness. Mentally distressed persons need support to appropriate the power – empowerment – to bring social inclusion and recovery.

6 A 'community care and support' model of intervention and services should replace the oppressive 'treatment and control in the community' model.

glossary

- **asylums**: large buildings where the mentally ill were kept, prior to the advent of psychiatric hospitals.

- **community care and support**: a variety of programmes and interventions involving helping professionals but also incorporating the active participation of users and family members, designed to facilitate empowerment, social inclusion and recovery.

- **empowerment**: a process of increasing power on personal, psychological levels, and on social levels (abilities to achieve desired ends by working with or influencing others).

- **psychotropics**: psychiatric drugs.

- **recovery:** recovery in the context of mental illness is a process, a struggle toward greater wellbeing and greater social inclusion. It may imply a reduction of symptoms and suffering and adapting to or coming to terms with a mental illness, but it has everything to do with the person and not the illness alone.

- **social inclusion**: a process leading to the fulfilment of desired social roles and activites, such as working, community living, activities with friends, parenting and other family relationships, political and community activities.

- **treatment**: a medical or clinical intervention aimed at a disease or a symptom; not to be confused with the help or support of a person as a whole.

reading suggestions

An extremely interesting and intellectually challenging view of the history up to the nineteenth century is provided by Michel Foucault (2006). The 'antipsychiatrist' Thomas Szasz (1974), himself a psychiatrist, was first to raise the 'myths' of mental illness and remains a prolific author, situating society's response to mental illness within social power structures. The psychiatrist Peter Breggin (1991), in thoroughly scientific studies, has exposed the dangers and futility of many psychiatric treatments like drugs and electroshock, and has emphasized how appropriate care and treatment should be developed and conducted. Organizations like Critical Psychology, the Radical Psychology Network, and especially the International Centre for the Study of Psychiatry and Psychology have a wealth of information and links on their web pages which are of interest to scientists, helping professionals, users, family members, and anyone interested in advancing humanitarian and libertarian causes. A wide variety of well-organized user-led advocacy groups link on their web pages to user stories and opinions, as well as to analyses of what hurts and what helps in mental health practice; Support Coalition International would be a good starting point for all kinds of Internet resources.

 **:// internet resources /**

- The International Centre for the Study of Psychiatry and Psychology: www.icspp.org

- Support Coalition International: www.mindfreedom.org

- Thomas Szasz: www.szasz.com

⊃ ■ ?uestions

1 How are the mentally ill different from 'normal' people? Do they have the same interest in things like family, friends, work, money, a nice place to live, and respect?

2 When a psychologist or another professional 'treats' a psychologically distressed person, when does it help and when does it hurt? Does a psychologist's expert knowledge tell him or her 'what is good for the patient'? Does a particular diagnosis always mean a particular treatment, or does it depend on the patient and what that patient wants?

3 How might a person be 'oppressed' by society and by professional practices like psychology? What do you think the experience of oppression does to a person's thinking, feelings, and attitudes? What if that person already has a mental illness?

Part 4

Critical Practice

19

Doing Theory

Tod Sloan

Theories do not float in the air like clouds disconnected from the earth. This chapter's purpose is to bring the often-intimidating activity of theorizing back down to the ground, where it can contribute to social transformation. *Doing theory* does not just mean theorizing as an essential part of research and professional practice. It also means taking into account both the complex forms in which power serves dominant groups and the way theorizing itself can unwittingly be part of this process. Attending to this *ideological* dimension of theory, research, and practice is the core of what is known as critical theory.

theory in dominant psychology

Although psychology courses often discuss psychological theories, textbooks are usually relatively silent about *how* to theorize. When theorizing does get attention, it is presented as a sort of self-generating first step a researcher takes to help organize diverse observations, make sense of them with the simplest model possible, and guide subsequent systematic observations. New observations are then made in order to validate, elaborate, or discredit the theory. This process, psychologists traditionally assume, leads to a clearer picture of reality (what we call knowledge) that others can rely upon to solve human problems through practical applications of knowledge, that is, technology.

After rushing through such accounts of theory's role, courses and textbooks take pains to show that psychology's claim to being a science rather than a branch of philosophy depends on careful hypothesis-testing, experimental methods, and statistics. These procedures can establish that observed relationships between variables, or between causes and effects, are unlikely to arise by chance – that they are real. In the realm of 'scientific' psychology, any sets of ideas or concepts that have not been subjected to this sort of *empirical verification* might be written off as mere speculation, journalism, philosophy, or **ideology**. Critical psychologists describe this perspective as a mainstream or traditional view of theory and question whether such procedures or methods can claim to be scientific when the 'object of understanding' is the subjective aspects of our experience and activity.

For an approach to be scientific in relation to the psyche and human action, it would have to engage our capacities to reflect on ourselves, to give accounts of what we are doing (whether they are complete accounts or not), and to participate in the construction (and critique) of fuller accounts. The distinction between mainstream views of theory and critical theory was articulated powerfully by Horkheimer (1982), a founder of the Institute for Social Research in Frankfurt in the 1930s.

In passing, it is worth noting that the area of personality theory is an exception to this inattention to theory. Perhaps that's because much of it arose in clinical rather than research contexts, where the aim is to relieve suffering as much as to make truth claims. Personality theories, such as those developed by Freud, Jung, and Rogers, are essentially worldviews presented as scientific statements about human nature. Given the breadth of a worldview, it would be very difficult to pin down through systematic observations the relations between all the concepts associated with a personality theory. For example, Jung's theory presents specific definitions for concepts such as the Self, archetypes, the persona, the shadow, individuation, introversion–extraversion, and complexes, and elaborates extensively on the relations between the phenomena to which these concepts refer. Nevertheless, in nods to the importance of science, textbooks on the major personality theories usually contain sections presenting some of the empirical evidence marshalled to support each theory. To support Jung's theory, for example, texts often present research on psychological types using the Myers-Briggs Type Indicator. Most personality theories, however, are quite problematic when viewed from the point of view of critical theory. They tend to assume that society cannot be changed and that human nature is fixed. And they fail to recognize the societal roots of personality traits. My perspective on theorizing critically about personality and its ideological (system-maintaining) function is available in Chapter 4 in this volume.

theory in the human sciences (praxis)

Outside scientific psychology, the interpretive human sciences generally view the function or role of theory quite differently. This is particularly so in the politically progressive sectors of fields such as anthropology, sociology, political economy, literary studies, cultural studies, and linguistics. In general, critical psychologists share this different perspective, although they are usually playing catch-up because before discovering these alternative approaches they have to work their way through mainstream psychology (for example, lots of courses on measurement and statistics). The term *critical social theory* is often used to demarcate this body of work. Practitioners of critical theory often refer to 'social theory', or just 'theory', when they mean the broad expanse of conceptual work that has deep roots in the ideas of figures such as Hegel, Nietzsche, Marx, Freud, Heidegger, Sartre, and, later, Foucault, Deleuze and Guattari, Fanon, Giddens, Habermas, and Judith Butler. Currently, a vast and complex field of intertwined work links contemporary poststructuralism, social constructionism, postcolonial theory, phenomenological hermeneutics, feminist psychoanalysis, critical race theory, multiculturalism, and so on. The roots are in fact so deep and the branches so wide that no scholar can master all of critical theory, although some brave souls attempt this – for example, the Slovenian philosopher Slavoj Žižek (Myers, 2003).

What these critical theorists and philosophers have in common is an emphasis on understanding how human beings construct 'reality' through a complex interaction of consciousness, language, power, and embodied social living. They emphasize how little we know about what is going on, similar to the clueless humans in machine-controlled cocoons in the film *The Matrix*, rather than how much we know and understand. Mainstream psychological scientists view this outlook as subversive since it runs counter to common sense and natural scientific epistemologies (see Chapter 3) and because it urges radical enlightenment and resistance to exploitative and oppressive systems. Since most of these thinkers build on previous thinkers, it is important to be familiar with at least the basics of what each contributed (Elliott, 1992).

Critical theorists (and activists, for that matter) are fond of saying that theory and practice stand in dialectical relation to each other. Here, practice can mean either professional activity such as therapy, assessment or consultation, or it can mean simply what people do in various settings, such as schools, street corners, slums, corporate offices, and so on. Theorists use the term **praxis** to refer to this ideal synthesis in which theory informs practice and vice versa. Usually, the idea arises in contexts where theory is divorced from practice as a suggestion that theorists take up a more politically engaged form of intellectual work. Marx, for example, wrote in 1845, 'The philosophers have only *interpreted* the world in various ways; the point is to *change* it' (Marx, 1970: 123).

The idea of praxis contrasts with the primary operative modes of dominant psychology. Three points of focus are relevant: theory, research data (measurement, assessment, observation), and professional practice. A discipline or a profession can develop links in three ways: between theory and research data, between theory and professional practice, and between professional practice and research data. Within dominant psychology's academic sector, the relation between theory and professional practice has been much less delineated than the relation between theory and research data. The point of concentrating on this link is to prove that one's theories or concepts reflect reality, but this focus misses the connection between our theories and our practices.

Practitioners do not necessarily revise their concepts in light of practice if our focus is on the theory/data link. Over the past few decades, largely in response to demands from the health insurance industry to fund only 'empirically validated treatments', researchers have begun to scrutinize data regarding practice outcomes. This focus on the data/practice link leaves intact the gap between practice and theory because the data gathered to evaluate practices must only attend to the observable dimensions of practice process or outcomes. The relation of theory to practice may enter briefly in considering what processes or outcomes to measure, but much is lost in the process. For example, think about the difference between the concept of self-actualization and a 20-item scale measuring self-esteem. The profession thus bypasses the critical moments in which one might ask questions about the practice's underlying theoretical assumptions, questions the insurance companies do not ask: Does the practice respect and foster the human capacity for self-determination within cultural meaning systems? What models of wellbeing do researchers import into assessments of outcomes (e.g., middle-class consumerist functioning)? Thus the ethics and social functions of psychological interventions are left unexamined.

These considerations about theory's relation to practice and the possibility that some practices are part of the problem beg the question of what it means for theorizing to be critical in the first place.

what is critical about critical theory?

Let's start with an exploration of what makes a theory a critical theory. Some theories are essentially verbal accounts of the way things appear to be. Because of this they often strike people as simply a fancy version of common sense. The famous theories in social psychology (e.g., cognitive dissonance, conformity, obedience) often seem commonsensical because they are based on studies that document what most people do, even if it seems irrational for them to do so. As noted in chapters 6 and 23, some of these studies were made by psychologists with progressive political motives, such as to reduce groupthink. Their theorizing, however, tended to stay at the level of developing concepts to describe observed behaviour. It did not, for example, call into question psychologists' ability to know what actions mean without involving research subjects in the interpretation. It did not concern itself with how the findings might be used by the advertising industry.

Many theories of psychological development provide another example of theorizing that is not critical. These theories (for example, those of Piaget or Erikson) often state that as children become adults they tend to pass through stages that can be defined according to the person's changing cognitive or social abilities. Such stage theories usually posit that movement from one stage to the next depends on responding to accumulated experience at higher levels of complexity or integration. The child's ability to respond at higher levels emerges from the interaction of the child with its social or natural environment. New psychological structures that result from these interactions are applied to new situations. There is nothing especially problematic about this way of seeing development, at least not until one begins to theorize critically. Critical approaches to development address concerns such as the following:

- What does it mean to think of earlier or late stages as inferior to others? Whose perspective does this evaluation privilege? Who gains power over whom? Failure to consider these issues can sustain adult power over children or block the development of cultural forms in resistance to unjust authority.

- What is the social scenario in which development takes place? Don't we tend to imagine an individual child learning in interaction with an adult or a school task? Aren't there a lot of other things going on in children's lives? What does this narrowing of perspective imply? For example, narrow, 'productivist' views of what forms of development are important can lead to the curtailment of time for play or social life.

- When a theory defines specific stages or issues as built into the nature of social existence (such as Erikson's second stage, Autonomy versus Shame and Doubt), does it impose a specific cultural frame on humanity in general? Individualistic cultures emphasize autonomy, initiative, and identity, while other cultures focus on the ability to connect, a concern for the group, and self-denial. No culture has all the answers, but our theories of development should at least not universalize the values of the culture from which they arise.

- How can we reconcile a developmental perspective that points to increasing abilities as one matures with the idea that in modern societies we become increasingly alienated from nature and ourselves as we become socialized? Most models of development assume that 'normal' development leads to an ability to participate in society as an adult. Critical perspectives (Elliott, 1992) and emerging ecopsychological theories (Fisher, 2002) argue that the lifestyles of 'normal' adults in postmodern consumer society are highly problematic, both for individuals and for the planet.

- What do institutions do to children or adults who do not move through the designated stages in 'normal' ways? How do schools, workplaces, and families treat such children? Do stage models have unanticipated practical implications in the lives of the people to which they apply? When crudely implemented, developmental models can lead to labelling, stigmatizing, and exclusion that have little to do with supporting people with difficulties in learning or living.

These are just a few of the concerns that critical theorizing might raise about mainstream development theories (Morss, 1996). These concerns have several features in common, each of which is elaborated in the rest of this section since they are key to doing theory critically.

Doing theory critically means exposing and being suspicious of the assumptions that fuel a theory, especially when these assumptions reflect power relations and social processes that foster oppression or exclusion. What values are being sneaked, perhaps unwittingly, into the theory and whose interests does this move serve? Is a certain concept of intelligence unwittingly a form of ethnocentrism in the guise of science? Is a view about human nature held by a dominant social class (for example, an individual responsibility for achievement) being imposed on everyone? Beyond exposing hidden assumptions in others' theorizing, being as clear as possible about one's own assumptions, privileges, and values is obviously also part of doing theory critically.

Doing theory critically means questioning the analytic move that isolates individuals from their life contexts in order to explain their behaviour solely in terms of internal or immediate situational factors. Instead, we must remember that we cannot begin to have a clue about what is happening if we do not understand quite a bit about how particular cultural, historical, economic, familial, institutional, and local processes constitute the meanings of psychological experience. This understanding requires involvement in all sorts of interdisciplinary studies and in research methods and professional practices that privilege the voices and perspectives of research participants, clients, and community members. Again, the fields known as the 'human sciences' and 'cultural studies' attend seriously to these matters.

Doing theory critically means looking hard for what has been hidden by or left out of concepts that purport to explain a certain phenomenon. It means attending to modes of understanding that the theory's main mode of approach systematically excludes. Consider, for example, how extensively psychological theorizing has ignored *embodiment*, the fact that our subjective experience, even abstract cognition, is always felt and mediated by our bodies in relation to our worlds. It has taken decades of feminist theoretical work to expose and address this. But how do we know what has been left out of a concept? Where do we look if we don't know what is hidden or what is missing?

These questions are at the heart of critical theory. In general, our critical work begins when we detect what a theory or concept leaves out or covers up as it purports to have captured the essence of something. We notice contradictions and traces related to what is suppressed or ignored. Here Freud's psychoanalytic theory is a prototype example. Freud held that we cannot understand the meanings of conscious experience if we attend to the explicit content of consciousness alone. He saw the effects of forces impinging on consciousness – unresolved traumatic memories, for example – in dream symbols, slips of the tongue, and neurotic symptoms. His theory of the repressed unconscious is a critical theory in the sense that it tells us what is left out of models of the mind that focus only on the cognitive or the 'rational' aspects of experience and informs us about the power relations that trigger repression in the first place (Habermas, 1972). An extension of this critical theory can be found in my theoretical work and qualitative research on personal life choices (Sloan, 1996b), in which I show how people tend to present their big decisions as autonomous acts when their choices are actually heavily determined by multiple contextual and life-historical factors.

A similar prototype of critical theorizing is provided by Marx's theory of commodity fetishism, introduced in the first chapter of *Capital*. Actors in the capitalist market look at relations between commodities and money as objective and independent from the labour required to produce commodities. Value is believed to inhere in products because they can be exchanged for money, and not because they can be used or because humans worked to produce them. The market erases the specific uses of commodities and evaluates them only by what they can be sold for. In the process, commodities and money are talked about as if they have all sorts of magical powers, that is, they are *fetishized*. The humans who produce, sell and buy them are forgotten, and in the process, exploitative relations between wage-workers and the owner class are obscured. Simultaneously, commodity fetishism reflects how alienation occurs as the role of human creative activity in production is forgotten and itself becomes a commodity traded as labour power in the marketplace. This exemplifies how critical theorists notice the contradictions that arise in the way 'common sense' or dominant discourses present social reality, examine how language mystifies the actual state of things, and then expose alienation and exploitation that some would prefer to mask.

Finally, doing theory critically means evaluating not just the adequacy or accuracy of a theory in relation to the objects or processes it explains, but the social effects of the theory itself as it is implemented. Intelligence and personality are complex phenomena that can be understood in various ways, but governments and bureaucracies have often used so-called objective, theory-based methods for measuring intelligence or personality traits to discriminate against certain groups by drugging or imprisoning them rather than educating or treating them. Theories seem to be autonomous and disconnected from the things we can explain or understand through using them. But theories shape both the definitions of problems and the practices we design to solve them. So if welfare bureaucrats, for example, attribute joblessness to individual behaviour deficits, they will design psychosocial practices to boost self-esteem and train in social skills rather than address the economic processes and employment practices that fuel unemployment.

To conclude this section on critical theorizing, it is relevant to note Culler's (1997) comments about the parallel field of literary theory. Culler concludes that theory is interdisciplinary, speculative, critical of common sense, and concerned with thinking about how we think. He sums up as follows: 'The nature of theory is to undo, through a contesting of premises and postulates, what you thought you knew, so the effects of theory are not predictable' (1997: 16). We next turn to these unpredictable effects of theory and consider what theory is supposed to accomplish, and, more specifically, how we can connect theorizing to critical psychology's role in global and local movements for social justice.

Critical theorists insist on maintaining an intimate and direct multidirectional relation among theory, research, and practice. This is actually quite difficult. Many clinical interventions, for example, were originally based on a theoretical model of some sort, but clinicians who apply the model only rarely develop or elaborate it in relation to everyday practice. This is not to say that they do not gain experience and gradually refine the model that guides their work. They may even talk to a colleague once in a while about how they are beginning to understand a concept a bit differently in light of work with a particular client. But what we do not see in the field, even in training settings, is a commitment to the rigorous crosschecking of theory and practice. Similarly, most research intends to contribute to wellbeing in some manner, but few researchers bother to trace the various ways their findings are understood or applied in practice.

My thinking about a long-term project in which I am engaged illustrates my effort to tease out some of the complexities of doing theory critically in relation to both research and practice. The project, still in its early phases, involves the theory and practice of dialogue. It is linked to my theoretical work over the last 20 years. I have been trying to provide psychologists with a clear framework for understanding the impact of societal modernity on personality structures and psychological wellbeing (Sloan, 1996a). Following the general principles of critical theory, I gradually came to understand that psychological problems that appear as depression or anxiety, for example, stem from a deficit of authentic participation in community, friendships, and intimacy. Dialogue caught my attention as a natural antidote to isolation and the decline of participation in the public sphere. Many others were on the dialogue track for related reasons. In North America, beginning in the 1990s, dissatisfaction with the state of political discourse and decision making sparked an interest in dialogue methods. Democratic forms of government based on electing representatives who, pressured by special interests, do not really *represent* their constituents have obvious shortcomings. Few are the spaces where citizens gather to address the problems of living in contemporary society, reflect on their deepest needs, share their hopes, and work toward solutions. As a result, numerous projects have emerged to find ways for people to have a more direct and effective role in decisions that affect them. Calls for such 'deep democracy' are becoming more insistent. (Many of these projects are listed by the National Council on Dialogue and Deliberation at www.thataway.org and the Canadian Council on Dialogue and Deliberation at www.c2d2.ca.)

In the United States and Canada, dialogue practitioners organize conversation salons and other forms of facilitated dialogue to enhance authenticity, meaning construction, intimacy and personal growth. Along the continuum between deep conversation and deep democracy, non-profit organizations have been sponsoring community dialogues on difficult and divisive topics in neighbourhoods and cities. Using formal dialogue methods, they have effectively confronted issues such as immigration, racism, political polarization, and abortion (cf. www.studycircles.org and www.publicconversations.org).

Although most dialogue practitioners are interested in the practice itself, some have elaborated concepts and theoretical models of what occurs as people participate in dialogue (Bohm, 1996). Here the work on group dynamics and group therapy processes conducted by the Tavistock Institute and other psychoanalytically oriented practitioners is noteworthy, but somewhat different in scope and intent. Meanwhile, extensive theoretical work has, of course, been done from several major philosophical perspectives on language, communication, identity, meaning and understanding. Much of this work points to the difficulties we encounter in communicating and understanding (Habermas, 1981). The factors that impede communication, imagination, and mutual understanding include differences of several kinds: of status and perceived power, language styles, access to rhetorical forms, degrees of investment in the issue at hand, levels of authenticity or sincerity, understandings about the purposes and possibilities of the dialogue, and so on.

The dialogue movement provides a good example of how direct links between theory, research and practice could be forged. Much recent dialogue work is conducted with a certain optimism or idealism about dialogue's possibilities. My sense is that what I see as unfounded optimism would be better grounded by extended practice-based theoretical work. Theory and practice must go hand in hand to maximize dialogue's potential contribution to progressive social change. Dialogue practitioners assume that many social problems exist because people affected by policies or structures have little or no voice in their formation or continuation. If dialogue fulfils its potential all those who have a stake in a situation would be able to reflect on their experience, share their concerns, and really be heard by others. Ideally, this would lead to less suffering and reduced inequity. But, it is also possible that participants in such dialogues merely reiterate dominant discourses and reinforce existing power relations. How would we know which is which? This is where healthy doses of critical theorizing would come in handy to help dialogue practices deepen democracy. How might such theory-informed research proceed? We take a look now at how the theory-research-practice links could be developed in this sphere.

We might first speculate briefly about how a dominant psychology approach might progress. A researcher interested in dialogue would organize or find a dialogue group to study. She or he would have in mind certain dimensions of the process or outcome to measure and would get permission from the participants to give them questionnaires or interview them about these dimensions. The researcher would then analyse the results and try to publish them in a journal. The participants in the research would probably never see the findings.

To be true to their principles, in contrast, critical psychologists, like myself, who take on this project would need to keep several things in mind. As a first step, they would ally themselves with existing dialogue projects that address fundamental issues in social living or policy. They would make this decision after analysing how dialogical practice might respond to the various ways in which certain voices are suppressed in the setting in question (be it a classroom, a neighbourhood, a town hall meeting, or a workplace). The researchers would help organize and/or accompany people in dialogue spaces that might transform the existing power relations. They might enter the setting by explaining to stakeholders the potential of participatory action research to enhance the dialogue project's effectiveness. Once an agreement is reached, the researchers would thoroughly explain their project to participants in the setting and invite them (perhaps individually) to reflect deeply on their experiences there. For example, they might ask participants to examine features of the dialogue experience that either facilitated or constrained their capacity to understand through engagement with others. The researcher would gradually develop or apply generalized concepts that could help capture these constraints and facilitating moments and articulate these to the participants (a form of group process interpretation) and would then continue to accompany the project through subsequent stages, documenting and reflecting on the process all along. Eventually, if the work is successful, the theorist could elaborate a general model of how dialogue is constrained or facilitated by certain factors that can be addressed in subsequent dialogical projects by modifying their design, purpose, or process.

In my initial work in the area of dialogue theory, I have become convinced of the utility of two concepts that are frequently employed in critical theorizing. The first is ideology. Ideology refers to systems of institutional, systemic and intrapsychic processes that sustain relations of domination (Thompson, 1984). What is known as ideology criticism, or the critique of ideology, requires not only an analysis of institutional and cultural factors that reproduce sexism, racism, or classism, for example, but also of the forces that induce individuals to 'buy in' emotionally to related discourses and practices.

Intersubjectivity is a counterpoint to ideology in that it indicates psychosocial accomplishments such as empathy and mutual understanding that provide the basis for deep democracy and solidarity (Bennett, 2005). The term can refer to the process and product of critical self-reflection and dialogue, especially in their capacity to foster authentic self-expression, compassion for the experience of the other, and an appreciation for what we have in common as well as our differences.

In the example of dialogue theory, research, and practice, we have seen how these three activities can proceed hand in hand, enhancing dialogue's contribution to empowerment and social transformation. I am intentionally leaving unspecified the sorts of theoretical perspectives that might enlighten the theorist about what to look for in analysing the group process, for two reasons. First, what is most important is the development of concepts in relation to the lived experience of the participants and in forms that they will recognize when the theorist invites them to reflect. Elaborate theoretical models can get in the way of learning from participant observation and lead to a reliance on jargon and pseudo-expertise. The second reason, articulated in the next section, is that endless battles about which theories are best distract us from doing theory in ways that can more directly help empower communities working for social justice.

theoretical orientations and living life

Not surprisingly, there is little agreement among critical psychologists about which theoretical orientations we should prefer. Although my own thoughts on doing theory stem from a loose synthesis of my favourite compelling orientations, I am refraining in this chapter from making evaluative statements about particular orientations. Excellent overviews of the main bodies of theory that inform critical psychology can be found in Hepburn's (2003) *An Introduction to Critical Social Psychology* and Hook's (2004) *Critical Psychology*.

The variety of theoretical orientations among us has led to plenty of arguing. For example, behaviourism inspires Behaviourists for Social Responsibility (www.bfsr.org). Poststructuralism informed the ground-breaking 1970s British journal *Ideology and Consciousness* and the subsequent compilation *Changing the Subject* (Henriques et al., 1984). Behaviourism and poststructuralism have very little in common except, perhaps, a lack of interest in individuality. We each have our favourites, which reflect our temperament, social position, identity, and interests in ways that are worth reflecting on, questioning, and revising over time. But as someone who has spun his wheels a lot in the realm of theory, I want to share a few thoughts on the personal dimension of theorizing before considering the ground of theorizing, the array of social realities we are up against.

Given dominant psychology's bias against extensive theorizing, it is important to be well-prepared personally to defend the insights and contributions that flow from one's favourite critical theoretical perspectives. This means knowing more than a theory's basic assumptions, and including their historical roots, how the assumptions connect with one another, and how they are mobilized to illuminate various phenomena in ways that other perspectives ignore. It is not really fair to have to do work that adherents of dominant psychology do not require of themselves. However, it is important to understand which aspects of our chosen perspective's theory of knowledge (epistemology) and associated methodology mainstream perspectives would find problematic.

One of the reasons for being very familiar with an orientation's underlying assumptions is to understand why certain perspectives are difficult to integrate with one another. Students of theory can often find themselves agreeing with parts of different theories and may therefore claim to be eclectic. It may be possible to arrive at a form of reasoned eclecticism through a great deal of hard work, but eclecticism should not be used to avoid the contradictory assumptions associated with appealing but conflicting perspectives.

Doing theory well can take a long time. In fact, it can be a lifelong project, but this does not mean one must wait before engaging with change and theorizing in relation to it. I often feel like I haven't 'done all my homework' as new books and articles pile up in my office. The work of theory is ongoing no matter how well prepared we feel, because others are continually articulating perspectives that deserve to be evaluated. We can try out ideas in conversations and dialogues about important issues, for example: 'What if we looked at this from another perspective? How would we say this differently if the people we're trying to help were in the room? What assumptions are you making about people's capacities to act differently?' Furthermore, mentors will generally advise professors in the early phases of their career to focus on empirical research and to avoid trying to publish theoretical work. From the standpoint of critical psychology, however, many important moments of research and action are essentially theoretical in form (for example, critical reviews of literature on a topic) and are easily as justifiable as empirical studies at any stage of one's professional work.

Some people seem to know how to live, or at least they do not spend much time pausing to think about how to live or worrying about what it means to live. Others, however, have the curse of having to theorize. I am one of them. On the other hand, it may be inaccurate to call it a curse because theorizing can be a source of pleasure, in much the way that an obsession produces enjoyment even while it is a mode of suffering. Theorizing about life and other people's actions can make one an outsider, feeling estranged. It is also probable that this is an old feeling, not simply due to theorizing so much. The tendency to theorize is sometimes motivated by a prior sense of separateness that goes back to childhood and adolescence. Other critical psychologists developed their ideas in response to being marginalized by mainstream attitudes and practices in the profession (Sloan, 2000). In short, it may be fruitful to reflect on the personal motives and needs that theorizing seeks to address.

From another angle, we can note that one doesn't stop to theorize if one is fully engaged in what is going on in a setting, and sometimes theorizing even emerges as a defensive means of avoiding the intense fullness of engagement and relationship. There must be an entire 'politics' of this theory-versus-experience dialectic – there is so much to theorize about! I, of course, hope more people will engage in the modes of reflection necessary to develop critical theory in connection with psychological inquiry, but I raise this issue of how theorizing can be connected to alienation or marginalization precisely to urge those who lean toward theory to reflect on the function of this tendency in relation to how we connect to life and action. It may make all the difference to both our enjoyment of the work and its impact in the spheres in which we hope to make a contribution.

grounding critical theory

Since it is easy to get lost in the exciting intricacies of concepts, models, critiques, and debates, critical psychologists must keep in mind a big picture of what is going on in global society and how their theorizing connects with that picture. This is a crucial step if we are to fulfil what Habermas (1972) calls the emancipatory interest that informs knowledge-seeking.

How can we paint a big picture of the social ground from which contemporary critical theory can start? There are many other ways of saying all this and most critical theorists would jump into the fray to question the beginning, middle and end of such statements, but we have to start somewhere. I suggest the following overview as one that reflects emerging perspectives (see Hawken, 2007; Klein, 2007).

Since the mid-twentieth century, in societies around the world, a small group of extremely wealthy persons and the corporations and financial institutions that represent their interests has increasingly come to dominate economic, political, and social life. These individuals' and institutions' fundamental interests are to accumulate wealth and to protect their current and future ability to do so. They mobilize governments and their associated military forces – especially the United States and its industrialized allies – to support this project under the banners of 'democracy' and 'free trade'. They have converted middle-class citizens of the leading Westernized nations into consumers who are living at unprecedented high material levels. Meanwhile, unfair trade agreements and the extraction of natural and human labour resources exploit and impoverish the peoples of previously colonized regions of Africa, Latin America and Asia. As a result of the inequitable distribution of goods, a third of humanity suffers from poverty, hunger, and ill health. The corporately-controlled mass media keep citizens relatively uninformed about this suffering and its causes by producing entertainment and shifting attention to the few challenges to the global corporate empire – terrorists and rogue states. The media and governments stir up fear based on ethnocentrism and racism to justify massive expenditures on the military and security forces, effectively shifting resources away from poverty alleviation, education, and the health services.

Now, a major task of critical theory is to figure out not just how all this is sustained at the psychosocial level but what it would take to change the situation. That means developing and disseminating the following through action research and critical theorizing:

- Understandings of how power and privilege work among global elites and the institutions that serve them, exposing their vulnerabilities and supporting social responsibility on the part of corporations, governments and non-profits.

- Insights into the psychosocial processes that maintain or resist militarism, consumerism, racism, sexism, and classism, as well as those that build the foundations for critical consciousness, solidarity, and hope.

- Forms of advocacy and activism that effectively subvert the power of the mass media and government propaganda in the context of corporate consumerist globalization.

- Examples of successful alternatives to life in the ideological 'matrix' and the processes that support their development.

How does this agenda differ from the political work that can be done by any citizen? While political activists and others are likely to focus on the economic or structural forces at play, critical psychologists and their allies can theorize the relations between individuals and society in ways that include the psychological. People with psychological training would better understand this 'subjective' pole of the individual-society dialectic if it were not for the near-total depoliticization of our professional roles and the decontextualization of the individuals we work with. Because of this, when pointing to the ways in which major social, cultural, economic or political factors impinge on individuals, even critical psychologists tend to get caught up in, and forget to think through, how such factors achieve their effects at the level of the psyche. Sociologists do not usually address this task, given the goals of their field, but critical psychologists need to answer questions such as these: Why do some individuals and groups often continue to do things that are not in their best interest even when they acknowledge that this is so? What sort of psychological process is involved in overcoming the effects of oppression or discrimination? Why do some individuals and groups submit to illegitimate authority while others do not? Why do some people care about future generations and others not? The answers to these questions are directly relevant to designing strategies for social transformation.

These considerations point to a major task for critical theorists in the domain of psychology. Answers to these questions will usually not involve readily available psychological concepts because most existing ones tend to *psychologize* the issues (that is, to explain them only at the psychological level). We need more *bridge concepts* that simultaneously refer to the interpenetration of the psyche and society. For example, the concept of *ideology* bridges the psyche and social relations; *intersubjectivity* is another bridging concept.

Critical theorists tend to resist conclusions, but they do nevertheless have to take positions and articulate how they see things. So, in this spirit, I will conclude by saying how I see the purpose of doing theory critically in the context of critical psychology: the point of doing theory critically is to generate and disseminate ways of thinking and forms of action that undermine ideology and foster intersubjectivity. Let's get down to it.

author's note

Dennis Fox and Teresa McDowell gave invaluable suggestions in response to a draft of this chapter. I also want to thank all the hard-working theory people I have learned from over the years and wish I could have cited all their work here.

▓ ▓ main chapter points ▓

1 Theorizing in mainstream psychology tends to focus on its relation to data and does not reflect on how its assumptions might be complicit with forces of domination, oppression, or social exclusion.

2   In the interdisciplinary human sciences, critical social theory stands out for its emphasis on the relation between how we think and what we do.

3   Critical theorizing addresses the social functions of ideas as well as the effects of practices by attending to the ways in which power works in society.

4   Critical psychologists work with others who are working for social justice to develop theory that is in direct relation to social action.

5   Doing theory is a highly complex challenge that can enliven our life projects, focus our efforts, and foster solidarity as we address the major forms of injustice and suffering of our times.

glossary

- **ideology**: a system of concepts and practices that sustains and reproduces social relations that are characterized by domination and oppression.

- **intersubjectivity**: processes of communication and interaction that foster mutual understanding and solidarity.

- **praxis**: the active synthesis of theory and action, in which both inform each other and thereby become more effective in attaining goals.

reading suggestions

The exciting work in critical theory usually first appears in journals. Check out *Theory & Psychology*, the official publication of the International Society for Theoretical Psychology; the *Annual Review of Critical Psychology*; *Subjectivity* (related to the former *International Journal of Critical Psychology*); the *Journal for Social Action in Counseling and Psychology*. These can all be found through internet searches and many of the articles are online. Handy lists of links to secondary discussions of leading theorists can be found by internet searching for *critical theory resources*. Morrow and Brown (1984) provide a solid introduction to issues connecting theory and method. Hepburn (2003) and Hook (2004) present clear overviews of key theoretical approaches in critical psychology.

internet resources

- **Critical Theory and Critical Theorists**: stephen.macek.faculty. noctrl.edu/critical_theory_.htm

- **Critical Theory Resources**: pegasus.cc.ucf.edu/~janzb/crittheory/

 **Questions**

1   Articulate your own view of how individuals and society are connected. Try to discover some assumptions that inform your view and examine their consequences for your ideas about what actions might lead to change.

2   This chapter lays out a big picture of the global social and political realities that critical psychology can address. What is missing from this picture? How would it have to be modified to mobilize you and the people you know to work harder for change?

3   What sorts of assumptions about the psyche and society would best guide critical theorizing? What common assumptions are problematic? What positions on the old questions – such as free will vs. determinism, nature vs. nurture, consciousness vs. unconscious forces – are most appropriate for critical psychology? What new questions will need to be addressed?

Research Methodology

Wendy Stainton Rogers

Although they are often used interchangeably, the terms **methodology** and method are defined differently: methodology as a general approach to answering research questions, *method* as a specific research technique. In this chapter I mainly concentrate on a critical methodology for psychology (suggested readings about the different methods of data capture and interpretation are listed at the end). The chapter asks several questions: What kind of methodology should critical psychologists adopt? What are we trying to achieve? Where do we want to get? And how are we going to get there?

To do this, I explore the factors shaping (and continuing to shape) the development of a critical research methodology. Four drivers provide a framework for the chapter:

1   Serving particular logics of inquiry – that is, a methodology that can tackle the range and kinds of research questions that critical psychologists pose.

2   Promoting one of critical psychology's main goals of promoting social justice and serving (rather than exploiting) the individuals, groups and communities that the research is 'about'.

3   Making research adventurous – enabling critical psychologists to explore the new places, new questions and new people that critical appraisal and new technology have opened up and areas that the mainstream has previously avoided or ignored.

4   Doing research that 'walks the walk' rather than just 'talking the talk' – that is, research that doesn't just say that social justice is something to strive for, but actually does make a difference, both in the way it is done and, crucially, in what it achieves.

After addressing each driver in turn, I look briefly at the specific ethical issues raised by such a methodology.

critical 'logics of inquiry'

I have adopted the term **'logics of inquiry'** from Blaikie (2000) as a neat way to talk about the underlying philosophical ideas that determine the different ways of carrying out empirical research. The logic of an inquiry of critical psychology research needs to be appropriate to its assumptions about epistemology and ontology, which are different from those of the mainstream, as Thomas Teo describes in some detail in Chapter 3.

a different ontology

Teo notes that, in psychology, ontology has to do with the nature of the world that psychologists study, and with their assumptions about the being-in-the-world of people as individuals, collectives and in relationships. This is not an easy idea to understand in the abstract, so let's look at some metaphors.

Mainstream psychologists see people's being-in-the-world as rather like fish swimming in the sea. Fish are creatures that are independent of and separate from the sea, the environment in which they live. For mainstream psychologists, the social world that we humans inhabit is also 'out there' in nature, separate from us and our understanding of it. It is an objective world, a world of real things (like neighbourhoods), events (like football matches) and institutions (like schools). And, because they *are* objectively real, they can all be objectively evaluated (good/bad neighbourhoods), counted (goals or injury time) and measured (well-performing or under-achieving). It is also, crucially, a world in which questions can be meaningfully asked and answered about how discrete and observable social events and phenomena may be lawfully related. For example, a psychologist may hypothesize that pupils from good neighbourhoods get higher grades and better qualifications than do those from bad neighbourhoods *because* the quality of the neighbourhood in which a child grows up offers better resources (such as libraries and places to play). Another psychologist may disagree, more convinced that 'neighbourhood' is no more than a marker of economic advantage or disadvantage. And yet another may say the real reason is the quality of parenting, with better parents choosing to live in better neighbourhoods. But for all their disagreement, they all agree on one thing: systematically causal relationships operate within the social world, and this lawfulness can be established through rigorous research that tests competing hypotheses against one another.

Critical psychologists work from an entirely different ontology that sees the relationship between people and their social world much more like music-making. Music is a product of human effort, desire, pleasure, emotion, skill, value and meaning. And it only *gains* its meaning and value and so on in respect to the 'sense' people make out of it and their appreciation of it. There is no *law of nature*, independent of human concerns, which specifies whether music is good or bad, makes you happy or sad, is clever or clumsy in its performance. Only human judgment can tell us these things, and human judgment varies from person to person, place to place, time to time, context to context. Indeed, music only *exists* because people make it or represent it or interpret it. Only sentient beings like humans can hear the music in birdsong.

From this standpoint, the social world has no natural laws governing it. Rather its lawfulness and predictability arise from the ways in which human societies and communities and institutions *make* and *operate* the rules: through customs, codes of conduct, social expectations, cultural traditions and religious commandments. Thus critical psychologists do not seek to 'discover' the natural laws determining people's actions and experiences. Rather they seek to gain insight into how rule-systems are made, deployed, enforced, resisted and so on. Crucially, they want to know about who it is that gets to make the rules, and who is expected to conform to them, and what the consequences are.

These ontological differences require a radically different logic of inquiry for research. When critical psychologists seek to explore why, say, so many young women in countries where food is plentiful desperately want to be thin, they start from the position that the mainstream's experiments, surveys and content-analysed observations will not do the job. Other methods and other forms of analysis are required which are more suited to studying meaning and significance (such as that of 'being thin') and how power is exercised (such as via the regulation of young women's aspirations). Once you stop seeing it as 'only natural' that a young woman will strive to 'look nice' and, instead, ask 'who stands to gain and who to lose by such behaviour?' you need new ways to answer these sorts of research questions.

_____ *a different epistemology* _____

Teo (Chapter 3) also points out that a field's ontology and its epistemology (approach to knowledge) are entwined. The different ontological orientation of critical psychology demands a different epistemological foundation too. Here it is positivism and rationalism that will not do, with their assumption that our knowledge of human behaviour and experience can be based on a reality that is 'out there' in nature waiting for us to discover it. This is sometimes called the 'death and furniture' argument (see Edwards, Ashmore, & Potter, 1993) where people, for instance, slap their hands on a table, saying 'Don't tell me this isn't *real*, look for yourself!' Instead, critical psychologists see knowledge *itself* as a human product. Put in a rather more ugly (but expressive) manner, the things and events that make up our experiences and our life-worlds are not real in-and-of-themselves – they are 'knowledged into being' (Curt, 1994) through human agency and ingenuity. Simply, knowledge is something people *make*, not discover.

As such, from a critical perspective, the search for what something 'really' means is a wild goose chase. Things that we may assume are psychological phenomena – such as 'intelligence', 'personality', 'mental health' and 'masculinity' – are not real in any absolute sense. Their reality is being constantly recreated by people (including psychologists), and so cleverly that we become convinced they *are* real. But they are not. They are conjured-up illusions. They cannot be 'measured' or 'demonstrated' in any objective way, only in terms of their definitions. And definitions are slippery, dependent on who does the defining. The difference between 'innocent people slaughtered by the Evil Empire' and 'collateral damage in a just war' is a matter of which side you are on. So too are the meanings and significance of concepts like 'intelligence' and 'personality'.

But, as others have also argued in this book, critical psychologists don't challenge the 'neutrality' claimed by the mainstream just because their epistemology is wrong, but because of what it can be used for. Dismissing underachieving children as 'lacking in intelligence' rather than acknowledging the educational system may have failed them is a powerful way to blame children for their own misfortunes and absolve educators and politicians from responsibility. From a critical perspective, thus, knowledge-making and knowledge-mongering are practices that raise our suspicions and our hackles. We need to expose them to scrutiny, and, methodologically speaking, we need an approach and the tools to do so.

Critical psychology's different ontological and epistemological foundations require a different methodology, better able than mainstream methodology to address something fundamental: the massive levels of complexity in how people operate within a world which is constantly being knowledged-into-being for them and also by them. Mainstream psychology deals with this complexity by creating highly constrained conditions to test hypotheses. Researchers will select just a few variables for study – and often just one. Under experimental conditions, only these are varied, and researchers will take rigorous care to keep all the other factors constant. The goal of this hypothesis-testing approach is to explain, in 'cause and effect' terms, how various psychological processes and phenomena 'work'.

The goal of *explanation* is to be able to predict outcomes and, ultimately, manipulate behaviour. The word 'explain' is derived from the idea of *smoothing out*. Where they can, scientists looking for explanations will do so by excluding interfering variables. Where they cannot, they will ignore any irritating 'noise' in the system (like research participants refusing to do the task set) and simply leave such events out of their data. In this way they can concentrate on what is universal, regular, predictable – and hence lawful. A simple, plausible story, applicable in all contexts, historical periods and places, can then be told about what causes what.

Critical psychologists seek, instead, to *explicate*. This is not just a clever way of saying 'explain'. **Explication** is not about cause and effect, but 'unfolding' – taking little peeks at 'what is going on' as you might do with an origami figure. You would not understand it if you got rid of the folds, because the folds make it work. Explication is about gaining insight and understanding. Complexity, in this approach, is not managed by ignoring complexity or smoothing it out. Complexity is reduced, in part, by asking much more specific questions – what is 'going on' *here*, in *this* situation, to *these* people? It is also managed through a different logic of inquiry – **abduction** – that ignores the expected, the predictable and the lawful and focuses, instead, on the surprising and unexpected.

_____ *abductory research* _____

As an approach to research, the word abduction was introduced by the philosopher Charles Sanders Peirce, who defined it as 'the process of forming explanatory hypotheses' (Peirce, 1940: 42). Peirce contrasted abduction against the usual deductive process that *tests* hypotheses. By 'forming explanatory hypotheses' he meant a process of identifying specific occurrences that stand out in some way – that are unexpected, contrary, don't fit or are puzzling – and then working out the most plausible explanation for them.

Abduction is a frequent means by which people make sense of things that puzzle them – and this includes scientists. A good example is the way that Alexander Fleming 'discovered' penicillin. He was doing experiments on bacteria, and was growing them on agar gel in lidded glass dishes. He came into the lab one day and saw that, in some of the dishes, the gel was ruined because it had gone mouldy. He was about to throw them away when he noticed that there was a clear ring around the mould. What could this ring mean? What could explain it? The hypothesis he formulated from his questioning – that maybe some moulds produce antibiotic substances – was a discovery of immense importance that has saved many lives.

Thomas Kuhn, another philosopher, has written eloquently about the role of such abductive reasoning in science (though he did not call it that). While what he called 'normal science' is usually 'a highly cumulative enterprise, eminently successful in its aim, the steady extension of the scope and precision of scientific knowledge' (1970: 52), this, he said, is not the only way. Sometimes scientists (like Fleming) come across things that surprise them. When this happens, Kuhn says, they have to shift from testing hypotheses to creating them: 'New and unsuspected phenomena are … repeatedly uncovered by scientific research, and radical new theories have again and again been invented by scientists' (1970: 53). Kuhn is famous for drawing attention to this and, in particular, for the name he gave to the consequences – *paradigm shift*.

One of the most enthusiastic advocates of abductive research in psychology is Gary Shank (1998). He says that psychologists should give up producing ever more fine-tuned models and theories and, instead, develop the craft skills and techniques that make it possible to understand how meaning is made and knowledge is deployed. And abductive methodology, Shank suggests, is the way to go.

In an abductive methodology, methods are chosen and/or designed that do one of two things. Either they provide data in a form where it is easy to home in on the puzzling and surprising (which is what many forms of discourse and, particularly, conversational analysis do). Or they actively generate data which are puzzling (an example here is Q methodology). Furthermore, the analysis must be capable of generating provisional, 'what-if?' kinds of explications, where alternative readings of what may be 'going on' can be tried out and explored in terms of their plausibility, their operation and their consequences.

Used together with the more stakeholder-participatory research strategies described in the next section, an abductive methodology does, I believe, offer a basis for a critical psychology methodology in which the goal is to uncover 'the largely tacit, mutual knowledge, the symbolic meanings, motives and rules, which provide the organization for their actions' (Blaikie, 2000: 15).

_____ *critical research methods*_____

For the critical agenda, though, there are bigger questions about consequences. Critical research questions are about the exercise of power and resistance to it.

Who gains and who loses by these 'goings on'? The tools for the job – research methods – are ones that make it possible to explicate and gain insight into the 'goings on' behind the events and experiences that make up people's life-worlds and experiences. Specifically they must allow us to tease out how power is being exercised, by whom, and to what purpose. But they have to go further and lead to socially just, practical outcomes, telling us how the misuse of power can be resisted, and/or how relatively powerless individuals and groups can become more powerful in pursuit of their own wellbeing and liberation.

As noted at the beginning of this section, this chapter cannot offer a detailed overview of the range of methods used by critical psychologists (for such an overview, see Willig & Stainton Rogers, 2008). It is, however, worth making a couple of general points.

First, it is often assumed that because critical psychologists reject positivist epistemology and naturalist ontology, they will also reject quantitative methods and use qualitative ones instead. But, as Parker and Burman (1993) among others have pointed out, and as has been described in several chapters in this book, quantitative data can be used as a potent tool in social justice arguments about discrimination and exclusion. A good example is the massive amount of quantitative data, world-wide and local, that bring to our attention the ways in which disadvantaged people have seriously worse health than those who are part of a privileged group. Conversely, qualitative methods are not used only for critical purposes. Commercial interests (in the form of market research) have always played a strong role in the development of focus groups and various other qualitative methods, simply because they are effective. In general, though, qualitative methods offer the craft tools for critical psychology research, and demand the craft skills for interpretative analysis.

Secondly, as Willig (2001) points out, methods involve both data collection and data interpretation and analysis. In the main, critical psychologists are less concerned about how they get hold of their data (so long as it is ethical and convenient) than they are about the form of analysis they use. Often critical psychologists mark this by referring to their *analytics* in much the same way as the mainstream talk about their methods. Analysis is absolutely crucial and essential to critical psychology research. To be taken seriously, critical research must do a lot more than offer banal *descriptions* or a means of 'giving a voice' to an individual or group. It must always include a clear, careful and theoretically informed interpretation and a well-articulated and systematically informed argument for the conclusions reached. These are what give critical research its rigour and provenance, and allow critical psychologists to present their research outputs as valid and useful.

research to foster social justice

As this book highlights, many (possibly most) critical psychologists are inspired by a social justice agenda – one designed to address the issues and concerns that mainstream psychologists ignore. As Fox puts it, 'our ultimate political goal is to help bring about a radically better society' (2000: 21). Indeed, by now you should be all too aware that this agenda permeates critical psychology.

So – what are the implications for critical psychology's research methodology? Given that pursuing social justice is about increasing wellbeing for both individuals and for communities, research from a critical standpoint needs to do a number of things:

- provide practical outcomes that directly promote social justice;

- contribute to more equitable and sustainable relationships – ones where there is mutual support rather than exploitation and oppression (see Kagan, Burton, & Siddiquee, 2008, for a fuller description);

- offer analyses and insights to inform the arguments we can make for social justice; and

- develop specific systems, strategies and interventions that can reach these goals.

Probably the best known argument for the social justice agenda was expressed by the Brazilian educationalist Paulo Freire (see Steinitz and Mishler, Chapter 23 in this volume, for a further discussion of Freire's work). His concept of 'the pedagogy of the oppressed' (Freire, 1970, 1995) has inspired many critical psychologists, especially those operating in community and postcolonial psychology and those doing action research. I examine its operation in each of these areas in the remainder of this section.

_____ *action research* _____

From action research we can draw a useful definition of how the social justice agenda can be applied to research – requiring it to be 'a participatory, democratic process concerned with developing a practical knowing in the pursuit of worthwhile human purposes' (Reason & Bradbury, 2001: 1). The main purpose of research, Reason and Bradbury argue, is to produce *practical* knowledge that is useful to people in the everyday conduct of their lives by increasing the wellbeing of people and communities, contributing to more equitable access to resources and power, and developing a more sustainable ecology in terms of both natural and human resources. Reason and Bradbury stress that these practical outcomes must include gaining a greater understanding of, and insight into, the barriers to wellbeing, equity and sustainability, so we can see how to overcome them.

Also writing about action research, more recently Carol Kagan and her colleagues have provided a useful summary of what is needed:

- research questions that focus on practical issues and problems – ones that, if tackled, can bring some or all of the benefits described above;

- an awareness of and sensitivity to the politics involved in the research questions, the research process and its outcomes and potential implications;

- researchers who deal reflexively with their own practices, power and influence;

- an active commitment to the participation and involvement of stakeholders in the research process as a whole;

- outcomes that will bring benefits to these stakeholders; and

- the careful and respectful sharing of findings with stakeholders and the dissemination of the knowledge gained. (Modified from Kagan et al., 2008: 32–33)

community psychology

Community psychologists also have a strong social justice agenda. They choose to work mainly with excluded and marginalized communities and groups to 'understand and promote shared values of empowerment and self-determination; collaboration and democratic participation; health, wellness and prevention; and social justice' (Hanlin et al., 2008: 527). Community psychologists see their research as directly contributing to the empowerment of the groups and communities with which they work, through two main means: by directly providing 'a means for marginalized people's voices and narratives to be heard'; and, more vicariously, through the researcher becoming 'the steward of stories, experiences and constructed knowledge of the respondents, rather than just a recipient of the data' (Hanlin et al., 2008: 526). (See Chapter 8 in this volume for a critical discussion of community psychology.)

postcolonial psychology

It is the postcolonial critique of psychology (Macleod & Bhatia, 2008) that makes the most determined challenge to systems that 'create and sustain power relations of domination' (Foster, 1993: 56). Postcolonial theory specifically focuses on the impact colonialism has had (and continues to have) on the individuals, communities and populations subjected to colonial power. Examples include the black and 'coloured' (as defined under apartheid) populations of South Africa, Maori in New Zealand and the indigenous peoples of Canada, South America and the USA.

Don Foster is well known for opposing the way psychology was being used within South Africa to serve apartheid. Subsequent to its overthrow, large numbers of South African psychologists have 'gone critical' in their research into the lives and experiences of poor and oppressed people there. They take a very strong line – for example, Catriona Macleod has claimed that research in critical psychology *must* have 'an explicit focus on power-relations and undermining exclusionary and discriminatory practices' (2004: 524–5). It must, in other words, *always* seek to expose, oppose – and, ultimately depose – elites that mistreat, marginalize and exploit others.

Postcolonial theorists have been highly critical of some aspects of mainstream community psychology's approach. They explicitly condemn any claim to act as the 'steward of stories, experiences and constructed knowledge of the respondents' (Hanlin et al., 2008: 526). Macleod and Bhatia say this creates 'vantage points from which to colonize or objectify the subjects of research' (2008: 576). From a different continent, Linda Tuhiwai Smith, a postcolonial theorist from Aotearoa/New Zealand, has pointed out that, among Maori, the word 'research' is 'probably one of the dirtiest words in the indigenous world's vocabulary' (Tuhiwai Smith, 1999: 1).

The criticality here is much sharper. Tuhiwai Smith talks of the problems of 'research through imperial eyes' (1999: 4). Her work is very cynical about what she sees as some researchers' 'do-goodism', given the history of exploitation and discrimination by colonial forces. Postcolonial approaches are especially sceptical about the *kind* of reflexivity that can be observed in well-meaning but ultimately patronizing research, that can all too easily descend into 'the banality of leftist intellectuals' lists of self-knowing' (Spivak, 1988: 70). It fails, she says, to understand (let alone recognize) that researching with deprived and oppressed people cannot help but 'capture' them. (See Chapter 16 in this volume for a related discussion.)

A postcolonial critical psychology claims that a social justice agenda cannot just be bolted on as some desirable 'added extra'. Critical psychologists must fundamentally change what we do in our research, how we do it, and, most crucially, the nature of the relationships we create between ourselves as researchers and the people we 'do' research upon. This is not about getting better at representing the researched Other. Rather, critical psychologists need new research strategies altogether.

- **New aims** that identify and challenge the distortions of colonial and imperial imperatives (such as linguistic imperialism) and embrace liberatory goals (i.e. ones designed to liberate).

- **New relationships** that are serious about sharing power in all aspects of the research process.

- **New topics** including the impacts of colonialism itself – such as economic exploitation, migration and civil war.

- **New locations** in the borderline spaces where class, gender, religious and 'racial' relationships and identities have been disrupted.

liberatory research

At the core of all this is a commitment to adopt and devise research methods that empower rather than disempower the people whose experiences and circumstances are the subject of study. If we take this as a starting point and draw upon the broader social justice agenda and the work of those who promote it, then I think we can begin to devise a form of *liberatory* research that can take critical psychology forward. Indeed, the concept of being 'liberatory' is what Freire was actually talking about in the original term he used – *pedagogia de libertação*.

Building upon the work of others, I suggest here how we might accomplish such liberatory research:

- by creating conditions where the people we intend to benefit are identified as the main *stakeholders* in the research;
- by committing to identifying and pursuing a common cause with these stakeholders;
- by actively ensuring these stakeholders have a meaningful role in the whole research process and real influence over it (or, indeed, are themselves actively involved as researchers);
- by adopting strategies and methods that enable participants to give accounts that reflect both their own interests, meanings and concerns and those of the community or group they share a common cause with;
- by respecting and treating these accounts as authentic and worthwhile in their own right, and not simply the 'lay views' of individuals;
- by making the research process welcoming, accessible and user-friendly, and reporting its findings in ways that are meaningful to and useful for stakeholders and their communities;
- by acknowledging any antipathy and suspicion arising from the research, respecting their origins and negotiating how to address them; and
- by seeking opportunities to build trust and, hopefully, celebrate shared success.

A growing number of research groups around the world are already pursuing liberatory research. A good example is that carried out by Whariki, a Maori health research group based at Massey University. Their research is based on Maori values and concepts of health, together with a principle that, 'in order for doors and windows to be opened we must tread gently. We cannot ask for information without respecting those who chose to share and without understanding our responsibilities and accountabilities' (Whariki website, http:/www.aphru.ac.nz/whariki/info/index.htm, accessed 3 April 2008). You can get further information from their website.

adventurous research

Critical research is also about having the courage to open up 'cans of worms' – deliberately venturing into edgy, even perilous, places where what is 'going on' needs to be rooted out, opened up, challenged and changed. In this section I look specifically at how and why critical psychologists seek out these troubled, troubling and contested spaces and issues – what we may romantically call 'adventurous research'. These include going beyond the ethnocentric boundaries of the 'Western world', exploring the virtual worlds and social spaces made possible by the Internet, and rediscovering the lost territories that mainstream psychology has abandoned, such as the unconscious.

journeying to exotic places

When visiting Aotearoa/New Zealand it was a bit of a shock to have oak trees pointed out to me and then be told, disparagingly, that they are *'exotics'* and really have no business being there. It made me intensely aware just how much I am, however hard I try to resist, a captive of my own **'habitus'** that makes my own familiarities 'normal' and the familiarities of others **'exotic'**.

Mainstream psychology is intensely parochial in this way, operating almost exclusively in a strange monocultural world of 'people-like-us' where anything different is seen as alien and exotic. It is built upon a profound misunderstanding: that experiments conducted *by* people from a particular worldview *on* people who share the *same* worldview can somehow tell us anything about universal human qualities.

In response to this inward-looking insularity, critical psychologists often deliberately go to places (geographical and metaphorical) that will help them break away from mainstream psychology's narrow-minded worldview. Sometimes they do this by moving out of their own discipline-cultural comfort zone – for example, by adopting an ethnographic approach taken from anthropology. Other times they research as an 'insider' of a 'deviant' group, opening up contrary practices and alternative regimes of power and influence to more respectful understanding. Both involve looking in 'different' (i.e. non-normative) places and require research strategies and techniques that are different from the mainstream's. Some of these have been covered already in the previous section, especially the recommendations coming from the postcolonial standpoint that is critical of psychologists who, they say, can act like tourists visiting 'outlandish places'.

Ethical research 'tourism' demands respect for the inhabitants of the lands and cultures visited and an active determination not to exploit, patronize or insult your hosts. Insight is much more likely if you treat people as the experts of their own culture and of what is 'going on' within it. And, like good tourists, you need to prepare carefully before you go, so you can engage meaningfully and honourably with the locals. Above all you must always remember you are a guest and seek to be a courteous one.

But there is a bigger question: Is it possible to legitimately and ethically research outside your own zone of cultural competence? Among critical psychologists this is actually a highly contested question. Some argue that only those who have cultural authority in a particular setting or community are competent to conduct research within it – that is, say, only gay men can legitimately study the sexual mores of gay men; only women can study the impact of becoming a mother. Whariki tend to take this view – that research on Maori should be by Maori and for Maori. Others say collaboration is the way to go, and yet others raise concerns about 'tokenism'. For example, many of the psychologists who have promoted critical psychology in South Africa are members of groups who were, historically, the colonizers, perhaps because they see themselves as having a duty to dismantle the psychology that supported apartheid. Whatever stance is taken, it is important to acknowledge the ethical and epistemological issues at stake, and therefore the need for caution and reflexivity.

entering virtual worlds

Globally our world is one of rapidly expanding and evolving innovations in information and communication technologies. Social networking sites, blogs and so on are creating an explosion of talk and texts (in terms of volume and diversity). The development and relative lowering costs of mobile phones, disposable cameras and webcams and the proliferation of reality TV are opening up the lived experiences of ordinary (and extraordinary) people. For critical psychologists, less interested in data collection than interpretation, this provides all manner of 'data' that are plentifully available and that can be easily captured for analysis.

Indeed, the change is more fundamental: for those with access to new technology, social worlds are themselves changing. Conversations of various kinds have become easy and everyday across large distances: between intimates parted by relocation; between strangers worlds apart in distance but sharing a common cause or interests. Conversational negotiation and the management of meaning are happening in unprecedented ways. Consequently the ways in which people live and experience their lives are undergoing rapid and dramatic change. From seeking friends, lovers and sexual partners to selling or exchanging goods, from political and religious proselytizing to organizing rebellion and resistance, from medical consultation to online counselling, people are doing things differently, as individuals and as collectives of different kinds. Psychologists now have a whole new landscape to explore that either did not exist before or was hidden.

So what? Quite possibly, it is too soon to tell. But, for all the opportunities opening up, critical psychologists need also to be cautious about the ethical issues raised by the various forms of virtual (but potentially invasive) voyeurism that technological advances make possible. As researchers more interested in data interpretation than its source, we must resist being so beguiled by the ease of snooping that we undermine the very social justice agenda we are so proud to claim. Ease of access also raises the risk of a deluge of papers that appear to be 'good' (especially in a world over-impressed by data quantity rather than data quality) but lack any serious interpretation or theoretical analysis.

Within critical psychology a strong strand has developed which is bringing back psychoanalytic ideas into psychological theorizing, and, in particular, into data collection, analysis and interpretative techniques. Psychoanalysis offers critical psychologists an additional interpretative language – for instance, about the role of emotional investment in operations like subject positioning or role taking. It offers access to potentially new interpretative insights – that, for example, an account may be provided less as an explanation or mere 'telling it like it is' than as a form of psychological defense.

> [P]sychoanalysis conceptualises discourse as a site where the internal world of psychic reality is expressed and revealed. ... A psychoanalytic reading goes 'behind' the text as the positions that individuals construct through their talk are taken to be indicative of anxieties, defences and particular ways of relating (Frosh & Young, 2008: 109).

What is critical about this approach is that it does not regard psychic processes and phenomena (like 'repression') as properties of individual minds, but as socially and culturally produced and mediated 'technologies of the self' (Foucault, 1978). The version of psychoanalytic theory being used in critical psychology owes more, say, to Film Theory than to Freud. It also distances itself from mainstream clinical psychoanalysis, where it is assumed that the analyst has insight about what is 'really' going on in ways that the person being analysed does not. Rather a critical psychoanalytic approach is a form of textual analysis that seeks 'to anchor psychoanalytic ideas in the texture of the research relationship and a close reading of the text' (Frosh & Young, 2008: 109) – that is, that pursues explication (as described above) rather than explanation.

There is not enough room here to do any more than note that psychoanalytic (sometimes called, confusingly, psychosocial) approaches are becoming increasingly common in critical psychology, sometimes combined in interesting ways with others (such as Memory Work, see Stephenson & Kippax, 2008).

_____ **walking the walk** _____

Critical psychologists believe it is important to locate their research *within* the concerns that critical psychology seeks to address, so that the research output can make a real contribution to goals like promoting social justice. The argument is that criticality should not simply be a theoretical position – to espouse it, you also need to 'do' it. Hence critical psychology's methodology has to be moved out of the so-called laboratory into the practicalities of the 'real world'.

I have already examined in some detail the way that critical psychologists go about promoting social justice by the research they do and who they do it with and for. In this section I outline two other ways critical psychologists can 'make a difference': influencing service provision and delivery, professional practice and social policy; and speaking to broader audiences to challenge prejudice and preconception.

influencing policy and practice

In the English-speaking world at least, mainstream psychology has been very successful at convincing government policy makers and the managers of public services that it offers a sound and reliable technology for administering and regulating staff performance and productivity. In particular it has been active in creating and maintaining what is sometimes called the 'audit culture', where systems are put in place that:

- define measures of 'good', 'best' or 'effective' practice, ostensibly based on the 'best research evidence available';

- use these measures to set 'quality standards' and 'targets' that staff (individually and collectively) must achieve; and

- reward achievement as defined by these targets (for example, by financial bonuses) and penalize underachievement (for example, by reducing future budgets).

A telling example is the system currently in place in England and Wales designed to deliver Youth Justice services (i.e., services for children aged 8–18 who are in trouble with the law, or 'at risk' of being so, to prevent them from offending or re-offending). The service as a whole is based upon identifying the 'risk factors' associated with individual children, and then taking action to reduce these risks. Based on mainstream psychology research evidence, these risk factors include impaired personality (such as hyperactivity and restlessness); poor school performance; low intelligence; poor quality and inconsistent parenting; parental disharmony, separation and divorce; low socioeconomic status; delinquent friends; and living in poor neighbourhoods (Farrington, 1996). These are considered markers of 'criminogenic needs' that *require* intervention (to meet those needs) including placing the child in custody, where she or he may be legally subjected to forms of restraint that can lead to injury and even death.

Critical criminologists (for example, Smith, 2005) are already active in disputing the research evidence for this kind of treatment. Given that it is psychologists like Farrington who have generated the data on which the idea of 'criminogenic need' is based and provide the rationale for putting children in prison, in my view critical psychologists have a duty to get involved. Three things need to happen. First, critical psychologists should use work like that of Smith to bring to a psychological audience the limitations of the 'evidence' upon which such 'risk factors' and 'needs' are based. Second, they must educate policy makers about the slippery arguments used to justify intervention. And third, critical research must offer an alternative way of understanding 'criminality', especially among the young, so that we can support our arguments for more just and humane ways of responding to children in trouble with the law.

I have used this example as it is so stark an illustration of the consequences of mainstream psychology's claim to offer politically neutral research evidence to inform policy and practice. But the reach of the audit culture is much wider, ranging into health services (especially their rationing and allocation), education, policing, social care and housing. There is, as they say, plenty of work to do.

broadening audiences

Critical psychologists are already active in devising new ways to disseminate their work, but, as yet, have had little impact upon the mainstream media. The media are saturated with messages promoting mainstream psychology's worldview: highly plausible stories about men coming from Mars and how women can gain self-esteem and life opportunities through breast enhancement surgery. More sinister are the portrayals of obese people, whose troubles can so easily be fixed by a team of experts. This 'edutainment', relentlessly presented on 'reality' TV, convinces us that their problems are their own fault – caused by their own stupidity, lack of self-control and irresponsibility.

Such a blame-the-victim worldview is hard to challenge, but it can be done. In 1966, BBC television broadcast a drama called *Cathy Come Home*. It told the story of a couple – Cathy and Reg – who, through a series of misfortunes, end up destitute, homeless and with their child taken from them. On its first viewing (in the days when there were only three British TV channels) this drama was watched by 12 million people – about one in four of the British population. It had a very dramatic effect, leading to the setting up of a major pressure group (SHELTER, still very active both politically and practically) and a major shift in the way people in Britain saw homelessness. After more than 40 years, people still remember this programme and its impact upon them.

If critical psychologists are to do more than make token inroads into exploitation and prejudice, then we need to become better at not just doing research but also publicizing its aims, approaches and outcomes.

ethics in critical psychology research

Writing about qualitative research in psychology more generally but still applicable to critical psychology, Brinkmann and Kvale assert that it 'is saturated with ethical issues' ... which are 'an intrinsic part of the research process from the initial formulation of the research question to ... when the publications of the study reach readers inside and outside the scientific community' (2008: 263).

Inherently, critical psychology research involves some degree of paparazzi-like capturing of people's private lives and experiences in order to expose them to public scrutiny. The nifty segue from 'private' to 'public' that typifies research in critical psychology not only raises the usual concerns about informed consent and confidentiality (though they may well be sharper, given the extreme intimacy of so many of the topics studied). It also goes well beyond the power gap between researchers and the people who are the subjects of their research. In settings where, for example, therapeutic talk is used as source data for research, then conflicts between what is 'good' for the client and what is 'good' for the research become particularly tricky. The same is true where the researchers position themselves in an alliance with participants in the study – or are so positioned by them. What are the ethical issues when a foster caregiver interviews other foster caregivers – and are these different from when a transsexual researcher interviews other transsexuals? To what extent will an assumed alliance lull research participants into revealing more than they would otherwise feel comfortable to disclose?

Not only is critical research concerned with outcomes (who gains and who loses through the practices or circumstances being studied). It must also consider who gains and who loses from the research itself. Put simply: How can we make sure no individual or group is harmed? This is much more important than the usual question: How can I get approval for my study from the ethics committee? All too often critical psychologists complain about the trouble they have with ethics committees, seeing themselves in a better position to judge than people who neither understand nor respect their methodology or their logics of inquiry. The point is this: How do they (or we) know their/our research is ethical?

Critical researchers must expose their motives and practices to especially critical scrutiny, given how much we claim access to the moral 'high ground'. The goodness we attribute to our intentions can make it easy to rationalize practices we might criticize in others as self-serving. Answer this: How much is researching in *San Serif* justified by the needs of *San Serifians* to be 'empowered', and how much is it just that much more boast-worthy than working in our own more ordinary backyard? To what extent is 'building rapport' merely faking friendship to get better data?

Brinkman and Kvale are clear that there needs to be more to research ethics than following a set of ethical guidelines. Because there are no clear-cut solutions, ethical judgments operate in '*fields of uncertainty*... – problem areas that should continually be addressed and reflected upon' (2008: 265; their emphases). They offer very useful advice about how to go about this which, when adapted and applied to critical psychology, will include the following ways of 'learning to be ethical':

- adopt a *communitarian* standpoint which is less concerned with individual rights and more concerned about our common responsibilities to each other;

- learn (among other ways, by observing researchers you respect) to see through self-serving justifications, to recognize ethical conflicts and to judge appropriate ways to tackle them;

- be alert to power – to who is exercising it and why they are able to do so, who is subject to it, and the resources needed to resist it;

- pay attention to the context of what 'is going on' – its time and history, its place within the tectonics of other events 'going on' around it;

- focus on the *particular* – on narratives, cases and examples, which are easier to make ethical judgments about than abstractions; and

- consult the *community of practice* – don't try to go it alone, but share your ethical considerations with the other stakeholders in the study. (Modified from Brinkmann and Kvale, 2008: 276–278)

conclusions

Researching as a critical psychologist is a very different enterprise from doing mainstream psychological research. It is based on different epistemological and ontological premises, seeks different outcomes, gets done in different ways and places and demands different kinds of ethical scrutiny and probity. And before this all gets too serious, it's also worth saying that when it's done properly, it's a lot more fun, more interesting and more practically useful. This chapter is only a very brief introduction to the excitement of doing research that is positively insight-giving and informative, to the satisfaction that comes from research that is respectful and sensitive, and to the sheer thrill of the challenge to make research productive and ethical. I very much hope that it leaves you enthused and inspired to find out more – and to go and 'walk the walk' in research of your own!

author's note

In writing this chapter I have drawn heavily on my work on *The Sage Handbook of Qualitative Methods in Psychology* with Carla Willig, its lead editor. She has inspired much of what is here, and I am grateful.

■ ■ main chapter points ■

1 Critical psychology is based on a different epistemology and ontology from the mainstream, and hence needs a different research methodology.

2 Research in critical psychology seeks to explicate 'what is going on' rather than explain cause and effect, and deals with complexity through abduction – the generation (rather than the testing) of hypotheses.

3 Critical research pursues socially just outcomes, intended to bring about practical benefits.

4 Research often needs to be adventurous – venturing into 'dodgy' places and opening up 'cans of worms'.

5 Critical researchers must avoid particular ethical pitfalls, and ethical reflexivity must be built into all aspects and stages of their research.

6 Critical research needs passion – to 'make a difference' and 'make trouble'.

glossary

- **abduction**: a 'logic of inquiry' based on generating explanatory hypotheses ('what-if?' propositions) rather than testing them.

- **exotic**: meaning, literally, 'outside' and hence denoting a place or thing that is outside of its usual familiar place.

- **explication**: an analytic that seeks to 'unfold' or 'tease out' complexity, aimed at gaining understanding and insight.

- **habitus**: the dense network of a culture and/or society's 'taken for granted' knowledge, practices, institutions and codes of conduct.

- **logic of inquiry**: the ontological, epistemological and theoretical foundations for a research methodology.

- **methodology**: an overall approach to research rather than a specific method.

reading suggestions

A good place to explore critical methods is the *Sage Handbook of Qualitative Research in Psychology* (Willig and Stainton Rogers, 2008). You already have some specific references to chapters but there are plenty more to get you started. Another good resource to help you plan and conduct critical research is Terre Blanche and Durrheim's (1999) textbook *Critical Research in Practice*. Its stark contrast – in images as well as words – to the traditional US research methods textbook is highly informative. Their material on research methodology is challenging but accessibly written. Finally, Beryl Curt's (1994) chapter entitled 'Crafty Dodges: The Questioning of Method' is still highly relevant and definitely amusing.

- **Critical Methods Conferences** – a site run by a loose grouping of lecturers and students at South African universities, but with an international focus. It archives papers on critical methods and provides a collaborative learning environments sourcebook: www.criticalmethods.org/mains.htm

- **More information about the Maori Research group Whariki**: www.aphru.ac. nz/whariki/info/

 ■ **Questions** ■■■■■■■■■■■■■■■■■■■■■■■■■■■■■■■■■■■

1 How and why is critical psychology's methodology different from that of mainstream psychology's?

2 What must critical psychologists do to make sure their research is ethical?

3 How can critical psychologists do research that 'makes a difference'?

4 How would you answer this question posed in the chapter: Is it possible to legitimately and ethically research outside of your own zone of cultural competence?

5 Identify a research question concerned with promoting social justice, and outline how you would go about investigating it.

21

Psychopolitical Validity in Counselling and Therapy

Isaac Prilleltensky, Ora Prilleltensky,
and Courte Voorhees

Chapter Topics

If you want to become a therapist, reading this book may create some anxiety. Critical psychologists suspect that mainstream therapists focus too much on individual circumstances and not enough on social circumstances. They maintain that changing individuals is not enough to promote mental health because poverty, unemployment, racism and discrimination continue to provoke stress. Indeed, they are very concerned that therapists may cause harm by focusing exclusively on individual pathology instead of social stressors.

By now, you might be wondering what the point of therapy is if we cannot improve mental health for those who suffer from poverty, oppression and discrimination. If critical psychology is concerned primarily with those who are oppressed, therapy might not be something critical psychologists do.

We would like to assure you that therapy does have a place in critical psychology (Smith, 2005). Therapists can help community members understand the role injustice plays in the difficulties they experience (Waldegrave, 2003). They can identify external sources of oppression that need change (Aldarondo, 2007). They can partner with citizens to transform adverse conditions (Pare & Larner, 2004). And – this is the hardest job – they can try to integrate therapeutic roles and social change roles (Prilleltensky & Nelson, 2002; Toporek, Gerstein, Fouad, Roysircar-Sodowsky, & Israel, 2006).

If we accept this book's premise that psychological and political dynamics are intertwined, our interventions cannot focus exclusively on the psychological or even the organizational to the neglect of the political.

> **Given the impact of the environment on the well-being of clients, counselors need to influence educational, corporate industrial, social, and political systems. They can do this by raising the general awareness of the problems common to their clients, gaining support from policy makers, and encouraging positive community action. (Lewis, Lewis, Daniels, & D'Andrea, 2003: 34)**

This might seem a daunting task for many of us in the helping professions who feel that we lack the time and expertise to affect macro-level forces. Social change and systems advocacy are typically not part of the toolbox we assembled over the course of our training. Fortunately, this is changing. In the field of counselling at least, training programmes are increasingly supplementing interventions for personal change with advocacy skills aimed at systems change.

Critical psychologists who become therapists need to consider several potential biases affecting their jobs. For example, the role of power is paramount in mental health. Although having little power over your life is a grave risk (Marmot, 2004), mainstream therapeutic orientations have a definite bias to neglect power and status differentials. Focusing on pathology instead of assets is another prevalent bias. Promoting the myth that everyone who works hard 'can make it' is yet another bias. In this chapter we uncover some of these biases and formulate critical therapeutic alternatives. We, of course, are not the first to do so. We build on feminist and narrative modalities that make 'the personal political' and on other liberation practices that make justice as important as compassion (e.g., Aldarondo, 2007; Brown, 1994; Cohen & Timimi, 2008; I. Prilleltensky, 1994; Teo, 2005; Toporek et al., 2006; Waldegrave, 2003).

If you were a therapist trying to help an abused woman, you would have to consider her lack of power not only in the family but in society as well. Her personal struggles are also political struggles, because they are experienced not only by her but by a large group of women who suffer abuse and injustice. Thus, it is insufficient to enhance women's control of their lives on an individual basis because therapy doesn't change social norms. Norms change through political action. Critical therapy focuses on both levels at the same time.

To attend to political and psychological power simultaneously, we have developed the concept of **psychopolitical validity**. Following an introduction of the construct and its rationale, we articulate its implications for case conceptualization and for counselling and therapy. In this chapter we use the terms *counselling* and *therapy* interchangeably. Both counselling psychologists and clinical psychologists work with individuals to alleviate emotional and behavioural problems and to promote mental health and wellbeing.

psychopolitical validity

As Oliver has noted,

We cannot explain the development of individuality or subjectivity apart from its social context. But neither can we formulate a social theory to explain the dynamics of oppression without considering its psychic dimension. We need a theory that operates between the psyche and the social. (Oliver, 2004: xiv)

We use the term *psychopolitical* to refer to the inseparable nature of psychological and political dynamics that Oliver and many others have addressed. Psychopolitical validity is a criterion to measure how well a particular practice or theory purporting to explain suffering and wellbeing takes into account the role of power (I. Prilleltensky, 2008). Affective, behavioural and cognitive experiences cannot be detached from power dynamics at the personal, relational, and collective levels of analysis. Similarly, we cannot understand political contexts without appreciating the subjective, ideological, and cultural forces that shape power relations.

Power is a central construct in wellbeing. The psychological literature deals with power through a variety of proxies – sense of control, locus of control, empowerment, self-determination, self-efficacy, feelings of inferiority, authoritarian personality, and more. In most cases, however, these proxies *individualize, subjectivize,* and *decontextualize* power. Respectively, this means that they treat power as an attribute of individuals rather than of interactions; they regard it as a phenomenological perception rather than something with tangible consequences, and they interpret it regardless of the surrounding circumstances. By bringing to light power's collective dynamics, its objective sources, and its contextual variables, we can better understand experiences of oppression, struggles for liberation, and wellbeing.

Oppression is a negative condition caused by an abuse of physical, psychological, social, cultural, economic or political power. *Liberation* is a process whereby individuals and collectives resist oppression through empowerment and political action. Liberation refers to the removal of obstacles pressing down on people, whereas empowerment refers to the acquisition of more power to pursue self-determination and social justice. *Wellbeing*, in turn, is a positive state of affairs brought about by satisfying personal, interpersonal, and collective needs. Mental health is a part of wellbeing. The latter consists of subjective and objective dimensions that go beyond mental health.

In therapy, as in social change, critical psychologists try to partner with community members to move from a state of oppression to wellbeing, through a process of liberation. Thus, the more we understand how power influences oppression, liberation, and wellbeing at various levels of analysis – from the personal to the relational to the collective – the more effectively we can help individuals, families, groups, communities, and societies.

We achieve psychopolitical validity when our understandings of these experiences at the various levels of analysis take power fully into account. When we apply this analysis to research, we refer to **epistemic psychopolitical validity**. When we apply it to interventions – including the daily work of therapists – we refer to *transformational* psychopolitical validity (I. Prilleltensky, 2008).

_____ *epistemic psychopolitical validity*_____

Research and action in psychology that incorporate a knowledge of oppression have epistemic validity. Interventions should show an awareness of power dynamics operating at both psychological and political levels, guided by questions such as the following:

1   Is there an understanding of how global and local political and economic forces affect wife abuse, depression in unemployed workers due to plant relocation, or trauma due to exposure to violence?

2   Is there an understanding of how the cognitions, behaviours, experiences, feelings, and perceptions of individuals, groups, and entire communities perpetuate or transform violence, depression, and trauma?

3   Is there an appreciation of how interactions between political and psychological power at the personal, relational, and collective levels affect spousal abuse, depression, and addictions?

_____ *transformative psychopolitical validity*_____

Whereas epistemic validity refers to our *understanding* of the psychopolitical dynamics of oppression, transformative validity demands *changes* towards liberation at personal, interpersonal, and structural levels. The following questions are relevant:

1   Do interventions promote participant understanding of how power dynamics perpetuate oppression?

2   Do interventions educate participants on the timing, components, targets and dynamics of the best strategic actions to overcome oppression?

3 Do interventions empower participants to take action to address political inequities and social injustice within their relationships, settings, communities, states, and at the international level?

4 Do interventions promote solidarity and strategic alliances and coalitions with groups facing similar issues?

5 Do interventions account for the subjectivity and psychological limitations of the agents of change?

Transformative validity reminds us that therapeutic interventions must include both an awareness of political and social stressors and efforts towards social change. Critical psychologists seek not only to ameliorate social conditions but also to alter configurations of power that deprive citizens of opportunities in life due to inequality (Prilleltensky & Nelson, 2002).

_____ *power defined* _____

Defining psychopolitical validity more precisely requires a definition of power. According to Prilleltensky (2008) and Prilleltensky and Nelson (2002), ten important postulates define power:

1 Power refers to the capacity and opportunity to fulfil or obstruct personal, relational, or collective needs.

2 Power has psychological and political sources, manifestations, and consequences.

3 We can distinguish among power to strive for wellness, the power to oppress, and the power to resist oppression and strive for liberation.

4 Power can be overt or covert, subtle or blatant, hidden or exposed.

5 The exercise of power can apply to the self, others, and collectives.

6 Power affords people multiple identities as individuals seeking wellness, engaging in oppression, or resisting domination.

7 Whereas people may be oppressed in one context, at a particular time and place, they may act as oppressors at another time and place.

8 Due to structural factors such as social class, gender, ability, and race, people may enjoy differential levels of power.

9 Degrees of power are also affected by personal and social constructs such as beauty, intelligence, and assertiveness – constructs that enjoy a variable status within different cultures.

10 The exercise of power can reflect varying degrees of awareness with respect to the impact of one's actions.

Psychopolitical validity addresses three aspects of wellbeing. First, it examines the state of oppression in which many people find themselves. Second, it addresses the process of liberation. And third, it concerns itself with wellbeing outcomes. This tripartite focus occurs at multiple levels of analysis. The *macro* level entails collective, structural and community domains. The *meso* or middle level encompasses the organizational, group, and relational fields. The *micro* level, in turn, covers the individual, psychological, behavioural, emotional, and spiritual domains. We use this framework to formulate actions for case conceptualization and therapy.

how psychopolitical validity informs case conceptualization

In this section we apply psychopolitical validity and the constructs of oppression, liberation, and wellbeing to the lives of clients who seek counselling and psychotherapy. We highlight some key problems with traditional approaches to client assessment and case conceptualization and provide an alternative framework consistent with empowerment and wellbeing.

The majority of helping professionals usually receive solid training in assessment and case conceptualization. Most professionals would agree that setting goals and developing an appropriate intervention plan require thoroughly exploring the lives of clients. Once a client tells her or his story and explains the reason for seeking therapy, exploring the problem sets the stage for intervention. This typically includes understanding overt behaviours, affective components, cognitions and beliefs associated with the client's concerns. Case conceptualization from a cognitive-behavioural framework also includes an exploration of the frequency, intensity, and duration of the problem as well as its antecedents, consequences, and pattern of contributing variables (Cormier & Cormier, 1997; Hackney & Cormier, 2005).

pathology driven

Case conceptualization requires supplementing problem analysis with the client's strengths, assets, and resources. However, in most intake interviews, case conceptualization notes, and psychological and psychiatric reports, there is a stark imbalance between the wealth of information denoting problem areas and the dearth of information denoting strengths and resources. 'Being problem-oriented, the clinician easily concentrates on pathology, dysfunction, and troubles, to the neglect of discovering those important assets in the person and resources in the environment that must be drawn upon in the best problem-solving efforts' (Wright & Lopez, 2002: 36).

Psychiatry, as a field, has focused on diagnosing and treating mental ill and, as such, has concentrated on the pathological and abnormal components human functioning. Clinical psychology has followed in psychiatry's footstep leading to a much greater focus on assessing pathology and mental illness tha on identifying and amplifying wellbeing (Maddux, 2002; Seligman, 2002a). Seligman (2002b) quips that the National Institute of Mental Health (NIMH) may well have been called the National Institute of Mental Illness, given its almost exclusive focus on mental disorders and its neglect of mental health.

A case conceptualization largely based on explicating an individual's deficiencies misses the mark on several fronts. It overlooks not just personal strengths and assets but also, as Wright and Lopez (2002) note (drawing upon research on information processing, perception and social psychology), it minimizes the environment's role in mental health. By definition, environ-ment is in the background while individuals are in the foreground, 'active, moving in space, commanding attention by their behavior' (2002: 32). Furthermore, 'where the primary mission of a treatment center is to change the person, assessment procedures will be directed toward describing and labeling person attributes. The danger is that the environment scarcely enters the equation in understanding behavior' (2002: 35). To this we would add that environment is not a single construct. Thus, therapists who do take environment into consideration often focus on the immediate contexts and relationships rather than on the organizational and systemic structures that affect wellbeing. Meso-level organizational structures like good schools and affordable childcare centres and macro-level systemic barriers such as racism and unemployment rarely find their way into assessment and diagnosis.

Case conceptualization that highlights personal deficiencies, ignores personal strengths, and minimizes environmental barriers is disempowering, oppressive, and detrimental to mental health and wellbeing. This is particu-larly the case for people in marginalized populations who contend on a daily basis with a host of structural and systemic barriers such as discrimination, a lack of access to health care or high-quality education, and poor housing and employment opportunities. Ecological theory emphasizes that environment extends far beyond the person's immediate settings. It includes relationships between arenas and the influences of larger settings in which the person may not directly participate, as well as the culture at large (Lemme, 2006). Thus, daily exposure to an unhealthy and oppressive work environment often spills over into the home, just as a board's decision to close down an unprofitable plant leads to dire consequences for particular individuals and families. Factors such as these, however, are rarely taken into consideration when Johnny's parents are summoned to a school conference to discuss his problem behaviour or when a married couple experiences increased marital discord. In the words of social scientist Ellen Berscheid, sayings such as 'love conquers all' are based on romantic beliefs that 'close, committed, and loving relationships are impermeable and unsinkable vessels that can sail through any environmental storm with impunity' (Berscheid, 2004: 31).

Psychological and political dynamics are intertwined. For example, society's unequal resource distribution affects individual wellbeing in multiple ways. Moving from a problem-saturated, person-centred and thus oppressive assessment process toward one that is broad-based, affirming, and liberating requires a paradigm shift.

We support an assessment process that integrates individual-relational, organizational, and systemic factors that affect wellbeing. These factors correspond to the micro, meso, and macro levels of analysis, respectively. Given therapists' narrow focus on case conceptualization, the micro (personal-relational) level is the easiest to understand. We suggest, for example, that an empowering assessment process should directly explore client strengths, assets, and examples of thriving and wellbeing. Some recent proponents of human flourishing have called for a search of virtues. Rather than simply diagnosing the absence or presence of pathology, healthcare professionals can search for indications of mental health and help their clients move in that direction (Keyes & Haidt, 2003).

Moving up to the meso or organizational level, a liberating and empowering assessment process highlights the abuses of power and organizational constraints that interfere with wellbeing (e.g., bullying at school; a top-down, hierarchical work environment) and explores ways of effecting change. Such an assessment process, if properly conducted, results in clear guidelines for interventions, not only at the individual and interpersonal level but at the organizational level as well. We cannot help a child who is the victim of bullying without dealing with the bullies and the system that allows the behaviour to take place.

A liberating assessment process acknowledges the insidious, almost invisible relationship between, on the one hand, cultural norms, power imbalances, and the unjust allocation of societal resources and, on the other hand, the distress and maladaptive functioning present at the personal, interpersonal, and familial levels. Thus, an atmosphere of xenophobia and collective anger toward undocumented workers 'who are taking our jobs' is likely to permeate the work environment and the school climate and potentially infect marital and family relationships. Undocumented workers who suffer from powerlessness on the job may nonetheless abuse power within their families. Internalizing oppression is also a risk, whereby one comes to believe that he or she is not worthy or deserving of more resources or more control over his or her life.

how psychopolitical validity informs
_____ ## counselling and therapy _____

Grounding an assessment in client deficiencies and problem areas invariably results in a treatment plan designed to *fix* the individual in question. Fortunately, a number of therapy approaches have already taken broader contexts into account.

Feminist therapy (Brown, 1994; Watson & Williams, 1992), narrative therapy (Morgan, 2000; White & Epston, 1990), critical psychology (I. Prilleltensky, 1997; Prilleltensky & Nelson, 2002), community counselling (Lewis et al., 2003; Toporek et al., 2006), and multicultural counselling and therapy (Aldarondo, 2007; Ivey, D'Andrea, Ivey, & Simek-Morgan, 2002; Smith, 2005) all represent critical therapeutic approaches that directly address discrimination, oppression, and other systemic barriers. As such, they achieve psychopolitical validity and are consistent with liberation, empowerment, and wellbeing. In addition to addressing personal and interpersonal sources of distress as well as their extra-personal correlates, these approaches focus on harnessing client strengths and helping clients explore ways to resist oppressive forces.

For example, contextualizing personal experience is central to feminism and feminist therapy:

> **Although we view people as active agents in their own lives and as such, constructors of their social worlds, we do not see that activity as isolated ... rather, we locate individual experience in society and history, embedded within a set of social relations which produce both the possibilities and limitations for that experience. (Acker, Barry, & Esseveld, 1991: 135)**

The political analysis of psychological distress is feminist therapy's heart. One of its core principles – *the personal is political*– is highly consistent with the construct of psychopolitical validity. One of feminist therapy's major goals is empowering women who struggle with sexual and other forms of inequality (Brown, 1994; Watson & Williams, 1992). Nonetheless, its principles and strategies are applicable to multiple sources of inequality and oppression and to therapeutic interventions with men as well as women.

Narrative therapists believe people make meaning through the stories they tell about their lives. Life stories that individuals experience as oppressive and diminishing are often based on narratives that others in positions of power and authority make about them. Once these stories take hold, there is a tendency to gather evidence that supports the problem-saturated narrative (Morgan, 2000; White & Epston, 1990). Narrative therapists help their clients develop alternative stories to live their lives by. 'Just as various "thin descriptions" and conclusions can support and sustain problems, alternative stories can reduce the influence of problems and create new opportunities for living' (Morgan, 2000: 14). This is particularly important because some dominant cultural stories about marginalized groups are oppressive and diminishing. Rather than making meaning through these stories, clients can create new stories of resistance, empowerment, and liberation. For new narratives to stick, they have to be supported and reinforced by friends, relatives, and, ultimately, society at large. Empowering and liberating counter-narratives need new story tellers.

Creating new narratives, nurturing optimism and hope, building social skills and emotional intelligence, and enhancing self-efficacy and environmental mastery are examples of positive interventions designed to enhance wellbeing rather than simply ameliorate dysfunction (Lewis et al., 2003; Seligman, 2002a). Therapeutic work can include teaching clients communication, influencing, and problem-solving skills to better negotiate systems and become stronger self-advocates. This is particularly important given the shrinking social safety net and fierce competition for dwindling resources.

As effective as they may be, though, micro-level interventions with individual clients and families are not enough. Interventions should also target the sources of dysfunction in the systems with which clients interact. For example, in Ora Prilleltensky's research on disability, a number of participants described the poor quality of their education in special schools and the lack of emphasis on academic achievement:

> **There was such an emphasis on students doing things like physiotherapy and so kids would be pulled out of class to go to therapy ... the level of the school was not the same as it was in the integrated programs ... it was also like this huge playground ... there weren't the expectations that you do your homework or that you have any movement toward adult responsibilities or any kind of responsibilities. (2004: 110)**

In this case, changing the school is as important as physiotherapy. Mental health professionals can use their effective communication skills and privileged status to intervene with power brokers who can authorize wellness-enhancing services (Kiselica & Robinson, 2001; Lewis, Arnold, House, & Toporek, 2006). A growing body of literature offers a roadmap on how this can be accomplished (Kiselica & Robinson, 2001; Lewis et al., 2003; Prilleltensky & Nelson, 2002). Lewis et al. (2006) have generated an extensive list of advocacy competencies, much like the multicultural competencies that have become widely accepted by counselling professionals (Sue, Arredondo, & McDavis, 1992). The key to implementing these competencies is to accept the need for **role reconciliation** between therapist as healer of the individual and therapist as agent of social change.

_____ *role reconciliation* _____

If counsellors and therapists respond to critical psychology's call for action, they are bound to face a challenge: how to reconcile their various roles as professional helpers on the one hand and as critical agents of social change on the other. Our challenge is to find ways of reconciling the two sets of skills and aims. From the perspective of the professional helper, the critical psychologist must answer three important questions:

1   How does our special *knowledge* of wellness inform our social justice work?

2   How does our ameliorative *practice* inform our transformative practice?

3   How does our insider *role* of wellness promoter in the helping system inform our outsider role as social critic?

From the perspective of the social change agent, the critical counsellor or therapist must address the following:

1   How does our *knowledge* of inequality and injustice inform our counselling work?

2   How does our transformative *practice* in society inform our ameliorative work in the helping system?

3   How does our outsider *role* as social critic inform or relate to our insider role?

Reconciling these diverse roles promotes the dual goals of wellbeing and liberation – the former the primary domain of the professional helper, the latter the main concern of the critical change agent. Ora's work on women with disabilities and motherhood (O. Prilleltensky, 2004) provides practical examples of this role reconciliation. For example, the professional helper informed by a critical perspective can encourage girls and young women with disabilities to explore the impact of negative societal messages about sexuality and disability. This process of consciousness raising can result in de-blaming and may also lay the foundation for taking a stand against oppression. At the same time, transformative work in the community can aim to change restrictive and oppressive concepts of female sexuality and motherhood. Narrow conceptions of motherhood limit the scope of available resources; different types of mothering require different resources.

Wellness and liberation exist in a dialectical relationship. Without liberation many oppressed people cannot experience wellness. And without wellness there is no overarching goal for liberation, for liberation is a means to an outcome: freedom and wellbeing. Our objective is to blend the two so that our various roles and skills attend to emancipation and quality of life at the same time. If we stayed at the level of individual wellbeing alone and didn't consider the impact of inequality, disadvantage, and oppression – if we left these political domains to others – we could not be as effective in our individual work because we would be ignoring the role of power in mental health.

With respect to practice, we need to articulate how the various roles manifest themselves in the day-to-day work of counsellors and therapists. Elsewhere we have proposed ways to blend the transformative role with the ameliorative task (Nelson & Prilleltensky, 2005; Prilleltensky & Nelson, 2002). For us, transformation refers to system change whereas amelioration refers to individual or reformist change that leaves the sources of the problem intact. There are many ways to advance the transformative impulse and critical knowledge in the helping professions (Prilleltensky & Prilleltensky, 2006). Potential avenues include:

*   Creating awareness among colleagues about how power differentials are enacted in interactions with clients;

*   Forming research and action groups in the therapist's workplace to explore how practices might be more empowering;

- Increasing the political literacy of community members to enable them to scrutinize the practices of helping professionals;

- Establishing practices that enable the participation of clients, patients and community members in managing human services;

- Partnering with poor and otherwise marginalized communities to raise the level of public health, advocate for more resources, protest tobacco advertising, boycott sexist advertising, and so on.

As insiders within the health and helping system, counselling and clinical psychologists face many barriers and limitations. While they may be aware of many oppressive policies and practices, their ability to act may be constrained. Outside critics who point to the mental health system's short-comings, in turn, may not have an inside knowledge of how the system works, or of why some practices that seem unnecessary from the outside may be well justified from the inside.

Whereas the therapist's training is mostly for amelioration, the social change agent's impulse is for transformation, liberation, and the disruption of unjust practices. For critical professional praxis to emerge, these two roles need to exist in tension and synergy, not in opposition. If wellness and liber-ation are to emerge, we need psychological knowledge as much as political knowledge, ameliorative therapies as much as social change, and people working inside the system as much as people confronting it. This is a difficult balancing act. Many critically minded professionals are frustrated with systems that discriminate against marginalized groups and refuse to change. Quitting, though appealing, is not always the most effective way to transform systems. And yet, acquiescing to the system is not adequate either.

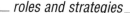 *roles and strategies*

In this section we describe eight roles for interacting with clients and institu-tional structures that can simultaneously promote personal healing and social transformation. The eight roles and concomitant strategies are reflected in the acronym I VALUE IT: Inclusive host, Visionary, Asset seeker, Listener, Unique solution finder, Evaluator, Implementer, and Trendsetter (Prilleltensky & Prilleltensky, 2006). These roles integrate many effective techniques used in mainstream psychotherapy (Brooks-Harris, 2008) with the insights of therapists (Waldegrave, 2003) and activists working from a critical perspective (Nelson & Prilleltensky, 2005). We discuss each role's potential for personal and collective work.

inclusive host Community members often come to therapy to resolve issues that interfere with their mental health and wellbeing. Unless they feel accepted, valued, respected, and appreciated, they will not freely share with the therapist their worries and aspirations. To achieve trust and safety, critical psychologists assume the role of inclusive host, one who accepts people without prejudice and who offers an opportunity to explore the sources and dynamics of external and internal oppression. An inclusive host makes people feel at home, builds a therapeutic alliance, and expresses caring and compassion towards the client. To achieve the highest level of inclusiveness, we should monitor our behaviour, our reactions, our feelings, and our demeanour in front of people who may come from backgrounds very different from ours. How do we react to a different accent? To people from other cultures? What non-verbal signals do we transmit? Psychotherapists, as Smith (2005) pointed out, are not immune to biases such as classism or racism.

If you, as a therapist, engage with colleagues to change organizational structures and practices, you might also use the role of inclusive host in group work. You cannot challenge systems very effectively by yourself. You need to collaborate with others. Chapter 22 of this book contains multiple strategies for engaging in organizational and community change that supplement our ideas here.

The inclusive host's key task is to make sure that experiences of minimization, devaluation, and silencing are not reproduced in interaction with clients, and that self-determination is given full expression. This tenet applies to individual, organizational, and community work. At the start of every change process, a climate of tolerance, acceptance, and genuine interest in others' opinions lays the foundation for meaningful personal and systemic transformation. Such a climate encourages the client to share his or her concerns and visions for a better future.

visionary The role of visionary is crucial. People coming to therapy seek a better future. A critical psychologist helps clients imagine better and fulfilling relationships and better and more just societies. Visioning a future without domestic violence and without racial discrimination, for example, is motivating and energizing. To fight learned helplessness, small wins have to be achieved, because change often seems beyond reach and a vision of harmonious relationships unattainable. This is why nurturing small successes can lead to bigger achievements in personal and collective wellness: it increases hope, a key ingredient in successful therapeutic encounters (Brooks-Harris, 2008).

For many, the route to personal wellbeing goes through collective action. I, Isaac, had a student who experienced an eating disorder. Part of her coping was creating a group of young women who went from high school to high school fostering awareness of the toxic media effects on body image. Her political struggle was personally healing.

asset seeker One consequence of oppression is diminished self-confidence and self-efficacy. Yet, despite exposure to oppression and trauma, many people develop effective resilience and coping mechanisms. Some children learn how to deal with parental rage and some women learn how to cope with abusive husbands. In difficult contexts, many people survive. In non-threatening contexts, people thrive in multiple and creative ways. A critical psychologist would explore assets, strengths, and resilience by asking clients simple questions about what things they are proud of or how they cope with difficult circumstances.

Youth in poor neighbourhoods are used to being treated as 'problem kids'. After a while, they internalize the labels their schools apply to them and become oblivious to their own assets. A culture that construes a population as undesirable and problematic stigmatizes entire groups. Thus, a search for assets is often the beginning of undoing oppressive narratives' negative ascriptions. Asset seeking is very much in line with narrative methodologies and brief therapy approaches that build on strengths and solution-focused interventions (Waldegrave, 2003).

Outside the consulting room, the therapist can use his or her skills to engage youth in community projects that build on their assets and foster social activism. In a project called SAY, Social Action with Youth, Morsillo partnered with young people to mount a play on homophobia, to undertake environmental projects such as an aboriginal community garden, and to engage in fun activities such as a drug-free underage party and entertainment for children in a cultural festival for refugees. The process linked personal passions with community concerns. Participating in youth-led and youth-designed projects built personal confidence and activism at the same time. At the individual level, the projects aimed to develop sociopolitical awareness through group discussions. At the group level, they fostered organizational skills and solidarity. At the community level, the participants created a community awareness of youth issues such as sexuality and drug use. Though not all activities were transformational, some, such as the play on sexuality, inspired much discussion about the intersection of political and psychological issues laden with power (Morsillo & Prilleltensky, 2007).

listener and sense maker People often come to therapy because they feel ignored, minimized, and misunderstood. These seemingly personal experiences have societal sources. Overweight people are subject to demeaning cultural depictions. Immigrants fight stereotypes. Gays and lesbians struggle against discrimination. Often, these people experience isolation and manage their pain by themselves. When they dare speak, they encounter judgment and intolerance. Coming to a therapist might be a first step in liberating themselves from oppressive relationships and cultural mores. This is why being a good listener is probably the defining feature of a therapeutic experience. After deep listening and uninterrupted discourse, a clinician might venture tentative explanations that help to make sense of life's circumstances. Linking psychological difficulties with power differentials in the family, relationships, work and society is an aspect of wellbeing that critical psychologists pay particular attention to.

It can be enormously helpful for an abused woman to hear that she is not at fault for her husband's rage. People subjected to abuse and oppression often blame themselves. Identifying the external source of the problem can be liberating and empowering.

unique solution finder Intrinsic to critical psychology is an appreciation of the diverse ways to achieve fulfilment in life. Our culture extols monetary success and material pursuits instead of alternatives such as spiritual development, creativity, and solidarity. To be helpful, we need to purge ourselves and our clients of cultural prescriptions leading to meaninglessness and alienation. Each client is a unique individual with single histories and private narratives that demand individualized solutions.

Therapy cannot solve all problems. As noted earlier, spousal abuse is not just a personal but a societal and political problem. A poor education is not just a family's problem, but a community's problem. No amount of tutoring will displace the need for better schools. No self-defense training will eliminate violence in the city. Each problem requires a customized solution, and blending therapy with social change is often the best way forward (Toporek et al., 2006).

Applying prefabricated solutions to personal, organizational, or community problems ignores each situation's unique context. Wishful thinking leads to futile searches for *the* solution. Lessons learned from other successful personal or social transformation efforts need to be contextualized and adapted to local realities, as Tod Sloan reminds us in Chapter 19.

evaluator Being an evaluator means developing a critical attitude towards society, towards professional practices, and towards oneself. Nurturing a healthy scepticism in self and clients can prevent adherence to unhelpful and possibly oppressive practices. It is helpful to ask questions, for example, about whether the current plan is working or what kind of evidence shows a proposed approach will work.

Evaluating processes is as important as evaluating outcomes. Both in personal healing and social transformation we have to remember that the ends don't justify all means. We should not sacrifice the values of collaboration and participation to achieve our goals, however 'just' and 'transformative' they might be.

Linda Stout (1969) experienced first-hand what it is like to work for justice when your partners in the cause silence you. She founded the Piedmont Peace Project in North Carolina and worked on many political campaigns, including voter registration, literacy projects, nuclear disarmament, workers' rights, welfare issues and others. Stout grew up poor and could not get the education she always wanted. Among activists, she was different. She didn't speak like them; she didn't have the middle-class manners other activists had. She knew that fighting oppression would not be easy. She encountered opposition from local government, police, and angry citizens. What she wasn't prepared for was the discrimination she would face within progressive social movements:

> **Because we are all products of the world we live in, it is understandable that oppression is also a problem within progressive movements. Most people involved in progressive organizations see themselves as fighting oppression that is 'outside', in the larger society. We all agree that our goal is to end oppression in the world. However, what we have found is that very often it is oppression**

on the inside that keeps us from achieving our goals. Progressive people from the oppressor group carry into their organizations all the things they've been taught about the group they serve and oppressive ways of behaving toward the 'other'. Usually without intending it or seeing it, middle-class progressive people behave in ways that disempower low-income and working-class folks; whites do the same to people of color, men to women, and heterosexuals to gay, lesbian and bisexual folks. (Stout, 1996: 89)

implementer After you and the client explore internal and external sources of suffering, psychological and political dynamics, power dynamics, and visions of a better future, it is time to implement some changes. Multiple theories of readiness for change exist. Common elements include awareness, preparation, action and maintenance (Prilleltensky & Prilleltensky, 2006). The focus of such action might be practising new behaviours or joining a social support or political advocacy group. In all cases, attention should be paid to sufficient preparation for the new behaviour, support for continuing it, and the maintenance of desirable patterns.

If you are working with a group to promote some change, critical *conscious-ness* is an important precursor of action. However, while understanding the role of power and oppression in personal wellbeing is crucial, in itself it is insufficient. Critical *experiences* are also important: first-hand instances in which your client felt discriminated against or marginalized, as in Linda Stout's case. These critical experiences complement critical consciousness in propelling people to critical *action* (Mustakova-Possardt, 2003).

trendsetter After implementation is sustainability. It is not enough to try a new behaviour once or twice or thrice. We need to help clients establish new patterns and set new trends. If your client belongs to a marginalized or powerless group, how can you help her or him start a support group? Support groups may not exist in the neighbourhood for women who come from India or for adults who were abused as kids. Perhaps there are no groups lobbying for universal access to health care or child care. Can you help a client become an activist if this seems helpful to him or her?

I VALUE IT roles embody key therapeutic practices such as creating a therapeutic alliance, empathic listening, solution-focused approaches, and stages of change (Brooks-Harris, 2008). In critical psychology, we emphasize the psychological and political sources and solutions to problems. Even the realization that not all problems can be resolved in therapy is therapeutic in itself if it leads to social action for social change.

_____ **conclusion** _____

As described throughout this book, psychology has absorbed the *zeitgeist* of the last century and concentrated on individual remedies for social maladies.

As a result, the field's mainstream neglects social justice and support for marginalized communities.

The helping professions have traditionally concerned themselves with wellness, health, and wellbeing. Influenced by the hegemonic medical model, disciplines such as psychology, psychiatry, and counselling conceptualized problems in living in intra-psychic terms. Mental health, wellness, and most recently positive psychology became choice metaphors. They all conjure images of people enjoying life, worry free and healthy. This is a most worthy goal, which we fully support. But as with any single value, wellness cannot stand on its own. Unless wellness is supported by justice, fairness and equality, it is bound to fall. An extensive body of research documents the ill effects of inequality and disempowerment on health and wellness (Kawachi, Kennedy, & Wilkinson, 1999; Marmot, 1999, 2004). Poverty, marginalization, exclusion, exploitation and injustice are just as deleterious to the body as they are to the soul. To heal the soul, we need to heal the community. To heal the community, we need to change it.

author's note

Portions of this chapter, reproduced with permission from Cambridge University Press, first appeared in Prilleltensky, Prilleltensky, and Voorhees, 'Psychopolitical Validity in the Helping Professions: Applications to Research, Interventions, Case Conceptualization, and Therapy,' in C. Cohen and S. Timimi (Eds.), *Liberatory Psychiatry* (2008, Cambridge University Press).

main chapter points

1 To be liberating and empowering, both counselling and therapy should strive to achieve high levels of psychopolitical validity.

2 Psychopolitical validity refers to the degree to which power differentials are taken into account in understanding and changing the political and psychological dynamics affecting wellbeing.

3 Although counselling and therapy are directed to individuals, professional helpers must at the same time take into account factors operating at the micro, meso, and macro levels.

4 Therapists should strive to achieve role reconciliation between their roles as healers and agents of social change.

- **epistemic psychopolitical validity:** the degree to which power issues are taken into account when *interpreting* social and human phenomena.

- **psychopolitical validity:** the attention paid to issues of power in understanding and changing the political and psychological dynamics affecting wellbeing.

- **role reconciliation**: the effort to incorporate practices that heal individuals and change societies at the same time.

- **transformative psychopolitical validity:** the degree to which power issues are taken into account when changing the human and social conditions affecting the wellbeing of individuals and communities.

▮ ▮ reading suggestions ▮

The *Handbook for Social Justice in Counseling Psychology: Leadership, Vision, and Action* (Toporek et al., 2006) addresses in detail the topics covered here. A second book very relevant to this discussion is *Advancing Social Justice Through Clinical Practice* (Aldarondo, 2007). For similar struggles in psychiatry, see *Liberatory Psychiatry* (Cohen & Timimi, 2008).

∶ // internet resources ⌐

- **Dulwich Centre for narrative therapy and community work**: www.dulwich centre.com.au

- **Multicultural Centre at Antioch University**: www.multiculturalcenter.org/social_justice.cfm

- **The Family Centre in Wellington Aotearoa New Zealand** - founded Just Therapy: www.familycentre.org.nz

▰ Questions

1 What are some of the barriers in reconciling the roles of agent of wellness and agent of social change?

2 Is infusing social justice in therapy ethical?

3 If you had a need to consult with a mental health practitioner, what attributes would you like the therapist to have?

22

Organizational and Community Change

Scot D. Evans and Colleen Loomis

This chapter focuses on planned **transformative change** – change at the systems level – in both organizations and communities. Intentionally or unintentionally, many organizations within communities provide programmes, supports and services that maintain inequitable, unjust, or other undesirable community patterns. Many community members desiring change do not know how to connect with or mobilize others who would also like to work for change. How community-based organizations can transform themselves to fulfil a 'change agent' role and how organizations can engage other organizations and community members to change community conditions are this chapter's central concerns. We link organizational and community change because most efforts to improve communities involve organizations. Community organizations that function effectively enhance community wellbeing, and new organizations or alternative settings arise to alter existing arrangements.

Change happens because people come together to make it happen. Their organizing may take the form of human services, neighbourhood organizing groups, coalitions, citizen advocacy groups, or other non-governmental organizations. Organizations often possess the social and material capital – the power – to get things done. Unfortunately, these resources are often misdirected. For example, providing anger management classes for troubled teenagers as a way to reduce community violence does little to reduce the structural violence of poverty that generates the real stress for young people and their families. Worse, these traditional practices perpetuate the belief that community violence is a problem *within* young people that requires management and control.

definitions of organization, community, and change

Although many of the ideas presented here apply to change more generally, we focus on non-profit non-governmental organizations that exist in local communities to serve people with various needs. Our particular focus is organizations wishing to get beyond traditional programmes and services.

Communities can be geographical, relational, or political. Geographical communities are place-based and often comprised of a neighbourhood, town, or city. Relational communities are groups of individuals with shared interests such as occupation, religion, or sports; they do not ordinarily engage in change activities. Political communities are relational but have an additional quality, advancing a group's interest or working for a specific cause; by definition, they are engaged in change. In this chapter, *community* refers to either a geographical or political community.

It is important to clarify what we mean by *change*. Change can happen incrementally – in small ways as organizations and communities develop and adjust to their contexts. Or it can happen more transformatively, radically and strategically. The field of organizational sciences offers a typology to help understand two different forms of change (Watzlawick et al., 1974). *First-order change* is change within a given system that itself remains unchanged. The focus is on incremental or ameliorative change within an existing framework or set of operating assumptions. In human service organizations, for example, making small, incremental changes within existing modes of practice – attempting to improve counselling outcomes by instituting a computer-based system for assisting with case management – is **first-order change**. In community settings, first-order change is exemplified by popular approaches to the problem of homelessness: food banks, shelters, training programmes, addictions counselling, and job training. These are first-order changes because targeting individual or institutional deficits as the source of the problem leaves intact the problem's underlying root causes: a lack of affordable housing, low wages, limited access to higher education, and economic inequality.

Alternatively, **second-order change** means altering the fundamental system. Also referred to as transformative or radical change, second-order change requires a more complex *understanding* of the underlying causes of system behaviours and *action* targeting change in these 'root causes'. In community-based human service organizations this means examining deeply held assumptions about individual and community problems and efforts to change shared organizational values, beliefs, and practices. In communities, it can mean recognizing that a lack of resident voices in community decisions results in policies that marginalize and oppress. Action for change involves organizing residents to advocate for fair and equitable procedures and meaningful shifts in power relations. Creating just communities and empowered community organizations requires radical, second-order change targeting the root causes.

In this chapter we focus on what we call *planned transformative change*: a deliberate, conscious decision to improve the system in a deep, fundamental way. We consider the *what* and *how* of this kind of change. In any change attempt, we must understand the specific targets of our change effort – the *what* – as well as the best way to make change happen – the *how*.

transforming organizations and communities

Consider for a moment a situation in your life that you might want to change. For example, maybe you want to quit smoking or lose a few pounds. Whatever the situation, you identify a problem that you wish to change. Now, how would you go about making this change? You'd likely make some sort of plan that starts with thinking about the problem and trying to understand why it exists. With the losing weight example, you might consider how you've not been exercising as much as you used to. You'd bear in mind how your new work schedule has changed your routine and sapped most of your energy. Your new apartment is not as close to the gym as your old one and there's no convenient bus line. This is all part of 'exploding the issue' to fully understand why the problem exists and to identify the necessary conditions, targets, and strategies for change. After that you can take action to make changes and reflect on how the change process is working for you.

We use this same basic process to create change in organizations and communities. Creating lasting change in organizations and communities requires creating the necessary conditions for change, clearly defining the problem and targets for change, and developing the appropriate actions for change.

creating the necessary conditions for planned second-order change

Creating the necessary conditions for change in organizations and communities requires three things: building **readiness for change**, creating a coalition for change, and grounding the change in shared vision and values.

building readiness for change Systems such as organizations and communities can be at various stages of readiness for change. Those that are open and ready for change are more likely to succeed at transformative change than those which are having change imposed on them. Before any change effort can fully commence, there must be a clear recognition on the part of at least some key players that there is a local problem and that something should be done about it. While it is necessary that leaders in organizations and communities understand change is needed, this is not enough. What's crucial is that a critical mass of individuals in the system feels a sense of urgency for change. This cannot happen when people have little to no awareness of the problem or deny that the problem even exists. Creating readiness involves proactive attempts to influence individuals' beliefs, attitudes, intentions, and behaviour. Developing and delivering a clear message about the need for change and communicating how the current reality is different from desired end states help create readiness (Nadler & Tushman, 1989).

In addition to believing change is desirable, people must believe change is possible. Part of ensuring readiness for change, thus, is helping to create a shared sense among organization and community members that if they act they can make a difference. Armenakis (1993) recommends understanding the difference between individual and organizational readiness. He highlights the importance of opinion leaders and suggests that building readiness in these leaders allows them to act as informal change agents who supply social clues for others in the group. Change-agent characteristics and attributes such as credibility, trustworthiness, sincerity, and expertise also affect how community members receive leaders' readiness-creating messages (Gist, 1987).

Here's an example from the work of the first author and his colleagues (Evans, Hanlin, & Prilleltensky, 2007). At the Oasis Centre, a community-based human services organization in the United States, an undercurrent of dissatisfaction with existing practices needed to be brought to the surface before change could happen. In this case, a presentation by one member of the research team helped create the awareness that change was needed. The presentation's main point was that wellbeing is a balance of individual, relational, and collective wellness, and that working only at the individual and relational levels is insufficient. In the ensuing discussion, Oasis Centre staff members were able to acknowledge that their efforts, as well-intentioned and skilful as they were, were simply not going to make a dent in solving the complex social problems that made life difficult for their clients. One worker noted:

> So I think it really spoke to me because I understood the importance of those systemic factors and the tragedy created by inequality and injustice. Yet, you know we never really talked about, let alone addressed, these larger issues.

The presentation by a trusted friend of the organization generated a great deal of energy and excitement about how the staff members' unique role could help them better address issues at the collective or community level. However, although the presentation did start a fire for change among the organization's members, it was not sufficient to create *organizational* readiness. Several months of internal dialogue and learning were required to build and diffuse a shared sense that there might be different ways to help children and families in the community and that doing so required change in their organization.

creating a coalition for change   Once the need for change is clear, some form of organization is required to promote and manage change. Power for change is accessed through people coming together to mobilize resources and take action: in short, organizing. We can all think of examples where one person or a small group of people decides that change is needed, but after announcing grand plans for change, nothing happens. It's like a classic Dilbert cartoon that shows employees sitting around the conference table where the leader exclaims, 'Our differentiated value-added strategy is transformational change' and then, after a pause, asks 'How was that? Does anyone feel different?' Transformation is often espoused, seldom really attempted, and rarely fully achieved.

Complex change in organizations and communities requires a committed group of people who come together with the skills and motivation to create change. The change team is the engine of change. While some officially leader-less organizations effectively come together to press for change (e.g., the anti-globalization movement), and while we acknowledge that some organizations are overly hierarchical and exploitive, we believe that any change effort capable of transforming power structures needs organization to mobilize resources and sustain energy (McAdam & Scott, 2005). This requires the coordination of effort, organizing processes, and the means for acquiring resources and support.

A diverse and democratic coalition of people with a variety of skills is needed to build power and the momentum for change. In organizations, ideally the change team is a cross-functional team made up of members from different departments, with support and involvement from organizational leaders including the protected time and resources to devote to the cause. In community contexts, neighbourhood residents can come together with local organizations and the help of a community organizer to make plans for action; organizations may train community residents to help build awareness and organizing skills. In the early stages, forming this change team may require skilled facilitation to help establish a group process that best serves the goals and objectives.

Who should be involved in promoting change? In organizations and in communities, this question pertains to values of democratic participation and empowerment. Change can either be top-down or bottom-up. Top-down or community betterment approaches keep decision making and control in the hands of the powerful and risk disempowering community members. **Community empowerment** (Israel, Checkoway, Schulz, & Zimmerman, 1994) or bottom-up approaches shift the balance of power to engage community members as agents of change. This latter approach is more likely to build community capacity, although there are some examples in which top-down (or governmental) approaches were used along with participatory strategies that enhanced community development (Hickey & Mohan, 2004). Preferably, all stakeholders are involved in decision making because 'activating the self-energizing commitment and energy of people around changes they deeply care about has been the key to the many successes that have been achieved' (Senge, 1990: 9). Successful empowering change efforts require strong, skilled, local leadership, a stable democratic organization, a clear sense of mission, and an overall strategy that allows the coalition to build on its defeats and its victories. Success is more likely if change agents involve the various organizational stakeholders to analyse the existing system, set targets for change, plan strategies, and take action (Dimock, 1992).

grounding in vision and values We seek changes in organizations and in communities because we believe that the current state of affairs is unacceptable. We are dissatisfied with the status quo and we want to do something about it. Because a core element of any transformative change effort is making explicit an alternate vision and rooting this vision in shared values, we bring to the foreground the values of collaboration, interdependence, social justice, and equality. Working from a base of shared vision and values is a necessary condition of organizational and community change.

Based upon their study of paradigm change in community mental health, Geoff Nelson and colleagues (Nelson et al., 2001) considered the values clarification process a foundation for planning and implementing organizational change. We can see this also illustrated in the example of the Oasis Centre. At the start of the centre's organizational change project individuals in the organization had myriad beliefs and assumptions; there was no explicitly shared organizational philosophy. As a result, staff practices aiming to help individuals and families cope with their difficult life situations were mostly ameliorative. Many individual staff members cared deeply about social justice issues, but the tacit organizational philosophy blocked their ability to put these values into action. This is an example of the common 'ideology-practice divide' in human service organizations (Delpeche, Jabbar-Bey, Sherif, Taliafero, & Wilder, 2003): organizational practices do not reflect deeply held beliefs. Moving from amelioration to transformation requires making salient transformational values and examining all other beliefs and practices through this lens. Oasis Centre staff did this by asking each other 'what do we care about?' and 'what type of community do we want to see?' Staff members and researchers worked together to fashion responses to these questions into an organizational statement of values that guided the rest of their change process and their new organizational practices. This new philosophy was a clear statement of who they were as an organization and helped to create new standards for what they do and how they do it. And while this outcome was valuable to individuals and to the organization, the process was important as well, as one worker noted:

> I think this process is helping us think critically about what we're doing and state our hopes and dreams. The final statement is going to challenge us to aim high and try out new ways of doing things and new ways of thinking about things. I also think the statement of philosophy is going to be useful in talking with one another and in holding each other and ourselves accountable.

From this shared value base, the Oasis Centre began to consider how to develop ways to practise differently.

_____ *defining the targets of change* _____

Targets of change are the identified beliefs, actions, and conditions that we deem unacceptable and thus aim to modify. How we select our change targets is closely related to how we define the problem situation, and that definition is based on our assumptions about the causes and sources of the problem. Many change efforts fail because of ill-defined problem situations. For example, if organizational members in a non-profit human service organization generally agree that their lack of success is caused by *inefficiencies in their programme delivery*, then the targets of change are *existing programme delivery systems*. Alternatively, if the problem situation is defined as having *too few strategies in place for prevention*, then the target of change becomes the *organizational balance between prevention and treatment*. Ultimately, the choice results in either adjusting the way we are already doing things (first-order changes *within* the existing organizational system) or changing our fundamental approach to reaching organizational goals (second-order changes *to* the existing organizational system). How we individually and collectively understand the problem situation is critical to informing effective action.

Of course, no one definition of a problem situation is fully correct. Analysis of a problem situation often reveals multiple problem definitions and multiple and interdependent targets of change. However, it is important for organizations and community groups to make their assumptions explicit when defining problems and deciding on possible solutions. Actions taken or not taken will likely depend on where our definition of the problem situation locates the causes: within individuals or within the environment (Nelson & Caplan, 1983). Do we believe that the problem situation is best defined as an *individual* problem or as a *social or environmental* one? Do we believe that problems in communities occur because of individual deficits or unjust social conditions? In organizations, do we believe our service delivery is inefficient or do we think our entire organizational philosophy is suspect?

In community organizations, the inability to create lasting impact can be understood as either problems with 'day-to-day' operations or as a more complex problem with the organization's 'deep structures' (Burke, 2002). On the one hand, if day-to-day operations are the source of the problem, then individual or institutional factors such as individual competencies, communication patterns, management practices, organizational climate, and service efficiency are appropriate for change. From this perspective, the way to solve organizational shortcomings is to become more *efficient* in doing what we are already doing. On the other hand, if we understand the problem as a more fundamental concern with the organization's values, goals, and strategies, then the targets for change become shared assumptions, the organizational vision, leadership, strategic actions, and the organizational culture.

One helpful way to understand the ecology of community issues is to consider that all social problems can be defined as being problems at one or more of four levels: individual, institutional, structural, or poststructural (Ife, 2002; Rappaport, 1977). Depending on how we understand the problem situation, we may locate the problem's source in individuals, community organizations and public institutions, community systems and policies (structural), or the dominant discourse (poststructural). Other chapters in this volume provide more detail on the need to understand and change dominant discourse; this chapter focuses more on the organizational and structural levels. Because each level identifies particular aspects of social issues, success will be limited if we focus change efforts only on one level to the exclusion of others. However, 'because of the dominance of class, gender, and race/ethnicity as forms of structural disadvantage, any social or political program that does not specifically question or challenge them is likely (albeit unintentionally) to reinforce these forms of oppression by accepting the dominant order that supports them' (Ife, 2002: 52).

Building a shared understanding about the issues we are attempting to address is an essential component of any change effort. A first step, however, is creating a safe and democratic space to share fundamental differences in beliefs about the issue and about how it should be addressed; if these beliefs remain hidden, substantive change efforts may be significantly hindered or diluted. Thus, it is important to create conditions where various stakeholders can openly discuss their beliefs and assumptions and work to align their understanding of problems and solutions. Approaches to creating spaces for negotiating shared meanings through dialogue include study circles and public conversations (see Sloan's discussion of dialogue in Chapter 19).

_____ *action for change* _____

While the previous sections address the *what* (targets) and *how much* (types) of change, we must also consider *how*. It is essential to connect our *understanding* of organizational or community problems to strategies for *action*. How we define problems and how we understand the boundaries of problem systems leads us to select certain tactics for inducing change. Selecting strategies that are out of alignment with our shared understanding leads to an 'error of logical typing' wherein we take action unlikely to produce the results we desire (Watzlawick et al., 1974). For example, using an individual approach (counselling) to help change a problem we have defined from a structural perspective (poverty) may lead to first-order, ameliorative change, inadvertently blaming the victim of poverty for his or her misfortune.

Considering action for change drives us to an important question: What strategies will help us create the changes we desire?

action for organizational change Any attempt at organizational transformation requires a clear **theory of change** that outlines the building blocks – actions and targets – required to bring about a desired end result. Developing a shared theory helps the change team identify change targets and plan action. A theory of transformative change in organizations should include two basic change targets: individual mindsets and organizational systems. Planned transformative change in human service organizations requires action towards changing both.

Senge (1990) describes how deeply held mental models need to be made explicit and challenged for real learning and change to occur in organizations. Learning and change necessitate acquiring new or different cognitive processes (Agashae & Bratton, 2001). Changing organizations by changing mindsets is a normative-reeducative approach based on the premise that individuals are rational and intelligent and that they conform to, and are committed to, socio-cultural norms (Burke, 2002; Chin & Benne, 1985). Organizational change will only occur as the persons involved change their normative orientations to old patterns and alter old values, beliefs, and assumptions. An organizational change intervention using a normative-reeducative frame begins by having organizational members question individual and shared assumptions regarding the overall organizational purpose and mission. These questions affect individual thought processes which coincide with changes in individual action, organizational interpretive schemes, and organizational practice. These strategies improve the problem-solving capacities of the system through examining the guiding assumptions and subjecting them to critical scrutiny (Argyris & Schon, 1978), learning from action, and fostering growth in individuals in the system.

While we target individuals in organizations for perspective transformation, changing minds is not enough; our objective is to change the norms, conditions, and practices of the organizational system (Burke, 1994; Dimock, 1992). For example, as Oasis Centre members critically examined their individual and shared assumptions about their work, they identified internal and external targets for change. Through sustained dialogue, they identified *intra-organizational targets* such as individual beliefs, organizational policies and procedures, programme structures, shared learning, and the need to diffuse the new organizational philosophy throughout the organization. Because of staff members' heightened awareness of social justice issues, one additional internal target for change became building a more just and democratic organization. They also identified *inter-organizational targets* such as the creation of new and non-traditional partnerships and collaborations in the community. Lastly, because human service organizations depend so heavily on external funding sources, the members identified *extra-organizational targets* such as the local United Way as critical restraining forces in any attempt to implement radically different human service strategies. The Oasis Centre's director committed to working closely with these funding agencies to help raise awareness about the need for new approaches and the appropriate funding to do so (Evans et al., 2007).

action for community change While there are many different ways to approach community change, some of the most popular approaches include **consciousness raising, community organizing**, and **community building**. Consciousness raising or popular education is based on educative critical theory and often attributed to the work and writing of Paulo Freire (1970) through the concept of *conscientization*. Freire describes conscientization, or critical consciousness, as learning to perceive social, political, and economic contradictions and taking action against an oppressive reality. A process of consciousness raising leads to an awareness that a problem one perceives as a personal issue is, in fact, shared by others and thus is really a political issue (Hanisch, 1970). Consciousness-raising approaches strive to help people gain a clearer picture of who they are and how they fit into social hierarchies (enlightenment), to gain the motivation and power that enable and support action (empowerment), and to begin to act politically to liberate themselves from their oppression (emancipation) (Fay, 1987). When consciousness-raising efforts are successful, the personal is made political (Hanisch, 1970). Consequently, this tactic for change is a political action.

At the heart of early consciousness-raising efforts was the act of joining together similarly disempowered individuals who were previously uncon-nected. Those who held power over the participants were excluded. For example, people who were Black excluded those who were White during some early 1960s civil rights meetings; during the US women's liberation movement of that same era, many women organized into groups that did not allow men, even as supporters of the movement, to participate (Sarachild, 1978).

Subsequent to the women's movement, consciousness raising has been used to raise awareness among the general public about a moral or social issue, even if the issue does not directly affect an individual. Thus, consciousness raising strategies can target those who hold more power as well as those who experi-ence less. For example, efforts to raise awareness with non-offending men about domestic violence help women build a broader alliance to eliminate violence against women. In this latter use, the goal is to impact the conscience of others about what is right and wrong within their community. Another illustration is the increased awareness of global climate change and a better understanding of the human impact on climate through behaviours such as burning fossil fuels (e.g., idling cars). This increased awareness has led to changes in individual behaviour as well as organizational and policy change.

Community organizing often starts with an individual or a small group of 'organizers' who may use consciousness raising to increase awareness about the gap between *what is* and *what should be*. Community organizers set out to convince others that there is power in numbers and that together they can make a difference. The 'conflict model' of community organizing promotes confrontational tactics with a specific strategy of engaging those who are poor and disempowered to fight for power by taking it away from those who hold it. In *Rules for Radicals*, Saul Alinsky argued 'the first step in community organization is community disorganization' (1971: 116).

Alinsky's approach was highly confrontational. Those who favour the 'consensus model' of organizing have criticized the conflict model for not including more relational and collaborative strategies (Eichler, 2007; Gittel & Vidal, 1998). Rather than conflict, the consensus model employs participatory and democratic processes to bring all stakeholders into dialogue (Chaskin, Brown, Venkatesh, & Vidal, 2001; Sirianni & Friedland, 2001; Warren, 2001). However, while the organizing strategies of consensus-oriented and confrontation-oriented approaches differ, it is likely a false dichotomy (Kytle, 1977). Successful community change depends on using the right approach at the right time, in the right place, and with the right people (Saegert, 2005). Community organizing as practised today is a vehicle for developing power as well as for building shared identities, mutual respect, and the capacity for collective action (Speer, Hughey, Gensheimer, & Adams-Leavitt, 1995; Warren, 2001).

Effective community organizing practice includes a cycle of four interrelated phases: assessment, research, action, and reflection (Speer et al., 1995). *Assessment* is the process of identifying and defining critical community issues. In the *research* phase, information is gathered about causes and solutions. Then, community groups seek to exercise social power through *action*. The action process includes mobilizing large numbers of community residents to develop strategies and to engage in collective action toward the target. Through the process of *reflection*, members explore the effectiveness of their actions and small wins, discuss the lessons learned, identify the emerging leadership, consider how social power was demonstrated, and plan future actions (Speer & Hughey, 1989).

Community-building approaches engage residents in efforts to address problems and opportunities in their community. Community-building is driven by the belief that the neighbourhood or community is the appropriate focus for change efforts and that the primary objective is to build community capacity (Hyman, 2002). Community capacity is 'the interaction of human, organizational and social capital existing within a given community that can be leveraged to solve collective problems and improve or maintain the well-being of a given community' (Chaskin, Brown, Venkatesh, & Vidal, 2001: 7). The core elements of community-building include 'resident engagement, agenda building, community organizing, community action, and communications and message development' (Hyman, 2002: 196). Community-building efforts seek to improve low-income and marginalized communities through building common purposes, useful relationships, and capacities within the community and through connecting the community to external resources and influence. The ability of neighbourhoods and communities to exert influence on the social and political agenda is a critical component of community-building efforts and is commonly referred to as an indicator of community civic capacity (Hyman, 2002; Saegert, 2005).

In her assessment of community-building strategies, Susan Saegert (2005) identifies four issues that are especially important for enhancing civic capacity: breadth of engagement, democratic processes, centralization of the change agenda, and results in terms of power and resource access. She notes that all the strategies make tradeoffs along these dimensions and that problems such as exclusion, hierarchical decision making, and limited effectiveness occur across strategies as well. An example of community-building for community change can be seen in the efforts of the Coalitions for a Better Acre in Lowell, Massachusetts (NeighborWorks America, 2006). The group spent five years building the capacities of, and connections between, individuals and organizations in the community before launching a powerful grassroots affordable housing and transportation campaign.

Many of these actions for community change can be employed simultaneously or in stages. One might set out to raise consciousness on an issue, reframing it from a personal one to a political one, and then facilitate further organizing, community-building and social action to achieve a goal of community change. A critical psychology approach focuses on building *power* in disempowered communities to influence changes in the social, economic, and physical environments.

critical considerations

We offer four guiding principles for the process and outcomes of any change effort in community-based settings: (a) attend to issues of power; (b) create empowering conditions; (c) build on existing assets; and (d) engage in the cycle of dialogue, action, and reflection. After briefly touching on each of these principles below, we highlight how researchers and consultants can act as 'critical friends' to those engaged in change.

attend to issues of power

Power refers to the capacity and opportunity to fulfil or block personal, relational, and collective needs (Prilleltensky & Nelson, 2002). To understand complex challenges in organizations and communities we must analyse the unequal power relationships that sustain the problem. This power analysis is an essential piece of building a shared understanding of the issue and deciding on the strategies for action. This requires asking difficult questions: Who benefits from keeping things the way they are? What people and groups control participation and decision making on this issue? Who shapes the discourse and thinking on this issue?

We also need to pay attention to issues of power in the change *process*. Participatory decision-making processes and empowerment strategies encourage planning and strategic changes from the bottom up rather than from the top down. These methods increase ownership, commitment, and accountability while capitalizing on creativity and innovation. Powerlessness in the change process, actual and perceived, can inhibit participation and the commitment to change. Nelson and colleagues (2001) had success in shifting paradigms in community mental health organizations using a highly participatory approach to change that involved diverse stakeholders in small groups and action-oriented committees. They also found that these participatory processes helped bring resistance and conflict out into the open where they could be dealt with more effectively. Ignoring issues of power when constructing change targets and action will most certainly block organizational or community transformation.

create empowering conditions

If we value a democratic and participatory change process, then we need to create conditions that promote these principles. Organizational conditions and characteristics are linked to member empowerment, including task focus, inclusive decision making, participatory rewards, and mechanisms that foster intergroup cooperation (Bond & Keys, 1993; Speer & Hughey, 1995). Creating empowering conditions is an intentional effort to create norms, spaces, opportunity structures, and processes that can enable all stakeholders to contribute to and learn from the change effort (Maton & Salem, 1995). It involves removing barriers to participation such as other pressing work demands, inaccessible meetings, a lack of child care support, a lack of transportation, and a lack of information. Empowering conditions in organizations and communities serve as the infrastructure for the human interaction needed for change to occur. They are safe holding environments for people to engage in dialogue, learning, action and reflection. Various organizational structures, policies, processes, and physical locations can promote or block democratic participation in the change effort.

build on assets

Individuals bring with them a variety of skills, experiences, and creative potentials. A strength-based orientation in an organization or change team recognizes people's unique skills, talents, and resources and integrates them into change efforts by providing opportunities to fully utilize and develop their strengths. Change agents are encouraged to take risks. Achievements and accomplishments are celebrated. Missteps are seen as opportunities for learning.

Organizations, neighbourhoods, and communities also have assets upon which substantive change can be built. Identifying these assets empowers employees and residents to recognize and make use of their existing resources to build self-reliance and take control in transforming their organizations and communities. Kretzmann and McKnight suggest the key to neighbourhood regeneration is to 'locate all of the available local assets, to begin connecting them with one another in ways that multiply their power and effectiveness, and to begin harnessing those local institutions that are not yet available for local development purposes' (1993: 6). Even the least powerful of organizations, neighbourhoods, and communities boasts a unique combination of resources upon which to build.

dialogue, action, and reflection

Transformational change requires *dialogical praxis* – the relational activity involving the cycle of dialogue, learning, action, and reflection. The idea of dialogical praxis, which comes from the work of Paulo Freire (1970), is based on the philosophy that knowledge is continually created and recreated as people act and reflect on the world. Engaging in dialogue linking the personal and the political opens up possibilities for action as people become more aware of the structures and the discourses that define and perpetuate oppression (Ife, 2001). Through dialogue, groups gain knowledge and understanding, build a shared theory of change, and engage in action for change. As noted above, reflecting on action increases understanding, helps analyse strategies, and helps plan further action.

While it is important to be strategic and plan adequately to make sure change targets are properly identified, it is also important to act. Real action towards organizational and community change can increase the buy-in for change and reveal new possibilities and new challenges. Engaging in dialogue, raising awareness, building leadership capacities, creating alliances, and making small attempts at innovation are all actions that can build momentum. Although the goal is transformative change, it is also important to achieve small wins. Small wins may be ameliorative change of the first order, but these coordinated small change efforts can remove identified constraints in underlying systems and structures. Small wins are not merely biting small chunks off a larger task, but rather they take advantage of unique opportunities to move forward and promote learning and consciousness raising (Weick, 1984). They can, in the aggregate, approximate radical change or pave the way for revolution (Weick & Westley, 1996). Building on small wins is the focus of several 'mini-grant' programmes in the USA that promote bottom-up community building to address neighbourhood concerns while minimizing frustration and helplessness (Foster-Fishman, Fitzgerald, Brandell, Nowell, Chavis, & Van Egeren, 2006).

At the Oasis Centre, as staff jointly reflected on their new practices and internal processes, dialogues for learning and action continued. This allowed them to co-construct shared meaning from their individual and organizational actions in a process that informed future actions. Dialogue and reflection on action took place in various supportive settings such as team meetings and weekly gatherings. It was critical that the organization's leaders were committed to allowing for spaces to engage in this time-consuming process of reflection and that staff members were willing to struggle through the learning and action process together. Although at the time many felt they were spinning their wheels or just doing a lot of talking without action, this cycle of learning and action proved essential to individual learning and organizational change.

Reflection and learning is a necessary condition for transformative change. Community-based organizations need to operate as *learning organizations* engaged in continuous learning at the systems level. Generating and sharing knowledge within a culture and structure of rapid communication and learning (Senge, 1990), they need to support critical reflection and to respond to lessons in ways that alter organizational action.

the critical friend

We use the term '**critical friend**' to describe the role researchers and consultants can play with organizations and groups engaged in change. Based on trust and mutual respect, this relationship allows external agents to critically reflect with the change team about the process and content of change. A critical friend can be a researcher, consultant, or community organizer who helps to identify assumptions and make issues of power explicit in the change process as well as the change targets. Meg Bond (1999) describes this relationship as one of connected disruption – the process of disrupting organizational culture while staying in relationship to individuals. Critical friends can help a group to consider the power dynamics of organizational and community problems and frame issues in more complex ways. They can also befriend the process by pointing out when people's voices are not being heard and by challenging misguided assumptions, questionable theories of change, erroneous facts, or groupthink.

In the organizational change efforts at the Oasis Centre, we (Scot and his colleagues) often shared personal stories and experiences to help build the relationship. Because the relationship was warm, friendly, and playful, we felt comfortable disagreeing with or questioning assumptions, directions and decisions. In our role as critical friends, we challenged them to find ways to support a broader participation by staff through different mechanisms. We were persistent in driving home the message that living by their shared values internally was important, and that deep, democratic participation would aid buy-in, enrich learning, create new organizational norms, and generate better, more innovative ideas for action. Whether through presenting current research on a relevant issue or holding the group accountable to their vision and values, the quality of the relationship enabled us to contribute as agents of change.

It is a daunting task to cover the complex issues of organizational and community change in one short chapter. We have only scratched the surface. Community-based human service organizations hold great potential for acting as change agents in local communities. Because social power for community change is accessed only through people coming together in an organized way, organizations hold power in communities to the extent that members collectively pursue a common goal or purpose (Galbraith, 1983). There are many more examples of organizations making social change (see, for example, Chetkovich & Kunreuther, 2006) and working to transform the way they do their work in communities. Through joining with these change efforts as action researchers and critical friends, we can learn from their successes and challenges while helping them achieve their vision of the good society.

■ ■ main chapter points ■

1 We highlighted the importance of considering types of change and who is engaged in change.

2 We distinguished between first- and second-order change stressing the need for a focus on change in the 'deep structures' in organizations and the 'root causes' in communities.

3 The necessary conditions for change include building readiness, forming a change team, and grounding the effort in a vision and set of shared values.

4 We highlighted the importance of clearly identifying targets and tactics for planned organizational and community change.

5 Approaching change with a critical value orientation means attending to issues of power in the goals and process of change, utilizing a strengths-based approach, a continuous cycle of dialogue, action, and reflection, and acknowledging the unique role of the critical friend.

glossary

- **community building**: attempts to build community capacity and engage residents of communities in solving shared problems.

- **community empowerment**: bottom-up approaches to community change that shift the balance of power to engage community members as agents of community change.

- **community organizing**: organized people coming together to identify specific obstacles to empowerment and to create constructive conflict to remove these obstacles.

- **consciousness raising**: 'conscientization', or raising critical consciousness, is learning to perceive social, political, and economic contradictions and taking action against an oppressive reality.

- **critical friend**: the role researchers, consultants, and community members can play with organizations and groups engaged in change to help them critically reflect on the role of power in the process and content of change.

- **first-order change**: change within a given system that itself remains unchanged.

- **readiness for change**: a condition in organizations and communities where there is a shared sense that the current state of affairs is unacceptable and a sense of urgency for change exists.

- **second-order change**: alterations made to the fundamental system.

- **targets of change**: those identified beliefs, actions, and conditions that we deem unacceptable and aim to modify.

- **theory of change**: a conceptual model that defines all the building blocks required to bring about a given long-term goal.

- **transformative change** a deliberate, conscious decision to improve the system in a deep, fundamental way.

▪ ▪ reading suggestions ▪

Burke (2002) provides a general overview of organizational change theories. A 2007 special issue of the *American Journal of Community Psychology* devoted to systems change has valuable empirical, theoretical and practical offerings. For organizational change theory and practice specific to the community-based human service organization context, see Proehl (2001) and Evans et al. (2007). Also, for a good analysis of organizations engaged in social change, see Carol Chetovich and Frances Kunreuther's *From the Ground Up: Grassroots Organizations Making Social Change* (2006). Susan Saegert's *Community Building and Civic Capacity* (2005) provides a comprehensive overview and analysis of community change approaches and Davis, McAdam, Scott, and Zald (2005) connect social change and organization theory in their edited volume *Social Movements and Organization Theory*. Lastly, three classic works on community organizing, community building and community change are *Rules for Radicals* (Alinsky, 1971), *The Neighborhood Organizer's Handbook* (Warren & Warren, 1977), and *Dry Bones Rattling: Community Building to Revitalize American Democracy* (Warren, 2001).

- **Action Science** – Concepts, Methods, and Skills for Research and Intervention: www.actiondesign.com/action_science/
- **Aspen Institute Roundtable on Community Change**: www.aspeninstitute.org
- **Aspen Institute Theory of Change**: www.theoryofchange.org
- **The On-Line Conference on Community Organizing and Development**: comm-org.wisc.edu/

 ■ **Questions** ═══════════════════

1 Why is it important to understand organizational and community problems at multiple levels of analysis?

2 What is the difference between first- and second-order types of change?

3 How should we consider issues of power in the process and content of change?

4 How might consciousness raising, community organizing, and community building be used to deal with a community problem such as homelessness?

5 What is the role of values in any change effort?

23

Critical Psychology and the Politics of Resistance

Vicky Steinitz and Elliot G. Mishler

Chapter Topics

which side are you on?

Which side are you on?
They say in Harlan County
There are no neutrals there.
You'll either be a union man
Or a thug for J.H. Blair
Which side are you on?

*Florence Reese's labour anthem for striking
coal miners in the 1930s*

We begin with the question 'Which side are you on?' to announce our perspective on the role of psychologists in political action. We do not think social problems are simple or have only two sides – a right and a wrong one. But we do believe psychologists have something to contribute to the endemic problems of social injustice. This is a core idea of critical psychology, stated in the introductory chapter of this text's first and second editions, which distinguishes critical psychology from mainstream psychology by its emphasis on 'social justice and human welfare' (Fox & Prilleltensky, 1997). This does not mean everything psychologists do is 'political'. Teaching the statistics course or doing research on rapid eyeball movements is a long way from the trenches, but psychologists have often joined with others engaged in struggles against injustice and violence.

We highlight this view of an activist, partisan psychology as an alternative to the standard claim that psychology is a neutral, objective, scientific discipline. Offered as justification for our work as researchers, teachers, and practitioners, the claim of neutrality presumably provides the grounds for trust from our subjects, students, and patients. It also provides a mantle of validity for our research methods and findings, giving psychology an edge among other disciplines in the marketplace of ideas.

As described throughout this book, critical psychologists, among many critics within and outside the discipline, have challenged the assumption of value neutrality. Indeed, rather than being disinterested observers, psychologists often choose topics for research and theory-building which reflect the problematic features of their societies, such as social conformity, domestic violence, and racism, to name a few. In choosing how to study these issues and report their findings, they align themselves – either explicitly or not – with one or another sector of their society that has something at stake in the meaning and use of these findings. It is from this standpoint that we argue that psychologists are often engaged, either directly or indirectly, in some form of political action. The central question is not whether we should or should not be involved in political struggles, but which side we consciously choose to join.

We are inspired, and draw upon work by psychologists and others from sister disciplines who have allied themselves with the poor and oppressed and actively engaged in their struggles for social justice. We rely particularly on the concepts of **liberation psychology** and *the preferential option for the poor* of Ignacio Martín-Baró, a Salvadoran priest and social psychologist assassinated by the Salvadoran army (Martín-Baró, 1994); Brazilian educator Paulo Freire's concept of **critical consciousness** as a necessary precursor to revolutionary action in *Pedagogy of the Oppressed* (Freire & Macedo, 1998; Freire, 1970); and the American medical anthropologist Paul Farmer's concept of **pragmatic solidarity** in his health care and human rights work, which includes providing resources and services for people living in poverty (Farmer, 2005). These three are examples of activists and critical theorists committed to the struggle for social justice and human rights who provide some of the key ideas that inform this chapter. Collectively, their models and analyses re-frame problems of injustice, oppression and violence as the product of socioeconomic and political processes, rather than as the result of individual failings. While many psychologists see themselves as apolitical truth seekers, we are proposing that in answer to the labour anthem's question, we recognize that 'there are no neutrals there'. We envision a critical psychology that allies itself with 'movements of resistance', such as groups engaged in efforts to resist racial discrimination, state-sponsored violence, and various forms of social, political and economic injustice.

We agree with Thomas Teo (Chapter 3) that what psychologists do should be judged by its 'emancipatory relevance', that is, by its contribution to the collective effort to resist and overthrow oppressive social conditions. Psychologists have been involved in this political process both within the field itself and in coalition with activists outside psychology. In this chapter, we begin with the recent controversy within the American Psychological Association about the role of psychologists in the torture of enemy combatants during the ongoing Iraq War. This is followed by brief reviews of a range of psychological organizations with radical political agendas and, then, of traditional psychological studies of problematic social issues such as conformity, discrimination, and authoritarianism. Drawing on Thomas Kuhn's concept of 'exemplars' in his studies of the history of science (Kuhn, 1970; Mishler, 1990), we summarize several emblematic case studies of activist projects. They document the various ways in which psychologists have entered into alliances and collaborations with vulnerable and discriminated-against sectors of society engaged in movements of resistance, using their clinical and research knowledge and skills in the service of political transformation. We conclude with a summary of our argument, emphasizing the complexity of such alliances, the importance of building trust and learning from community activists.

psychologists at war

Psychologists apply their skills and knowledge in all the important social institutions of their societies. They also serve in their wars. In the United States, psychologists' involvement goes back at least to the First World War, when they developed psychological tests to screen draftees for military service and diagnosed and treated soldiers for shell shock and war neuroses. Psychologists' clinical role increased over the course of successive US wars, from the Second World War to the current Iraq war, and is critical to the treatment of disabled and traumatized veterans. During the Second World War, psychologists' theoretical knowledge and research skills were recognized by the Office of Strategic Services, which oversaw US spying operations, and they contributed to analyses of the morale of civilian populations in allied and enemy countries and to propaganda campaigns against the Fascist and Nazi governments (Laurie, 1996; Winks, 1987).

Despite this history, many psychologists and members of the US public were surprised to learn that psychologists played an active role in developing interrogation methods used on enemy combatants in the Iraq war, methods condemned as torture in international laws and covenants signed by the US government. Use of these methods first surfaced when photographs of prisoners being tortured at the US prison in Abu Ghraib appeared in the media in the Spring of 2004. There was widespread shock at this revelation. Initially, the role of psychologists was not public knowledge. We only learned later about the SERE programme (Survival, Evasion, Resistance, Escape), a post-Korean War effort by military psychologists to train soldiers in how to resist breaking down under torture if they were captured. These methods were the source of the abusive techniques used at Abu Ghraib and elsewhere. As this history emerged, controversy surfaced within the American Psychological Association (APA) about the appropriate role of psychologists in the interrogation of prisoners of war (Maruyama & Peterson, 2007).

The APA is a highly diverse professional organization with more than 50 divisions – including Military Psychology and Peace Psychology – that serve the interests of American psychologists through a wide range of activities, including lobbying government agencies to influence public policy. The series of events related to the interrogation issue underlines the inescapable involvement of psychologists in politically relevant activity. It also highlights the interplay between psychological research, the range of values among psychologists, and the institutional interests of psychology's formal leadership.

In early 2005, in response to the Abu Ghraib revelations, the APA leadership appointed a committee on Psychological Ethics and National Security (PENS) with the charge of reviewing whether the 'current Ethics Code adequately addresses the ethical dimensions of psychologists' involvement in national security-related activities' (American Psychological Association, 2005: 1). The APA Board of Directors adopted the PENS report, which listed 12 statements concerning psychologists' ethical obligations. The first seemed to establish a clear limit: 'Psychologists do not engage in, direct, support, facilitate, or offer training in torture or other cruel, inhuman, or degrading treatment' (2005: 1). Other statements, though, created loopholes. For example, one justified psychologists' participation 'in various national security-related roles, such as a consultant to an interrogation', and reminded them to be 'mindful of factors unique to these roles and contexts that require special ethical consideration' (2005: 7).

Controversy over the report surfaced immediately. The Council of the Society for the Psychological Study of Social Issues (SPSSI, Division 9 of the APA) expressed concern that the APA Board of Directors had adopted the PENS report without its review by the APA Council of Representatives, the usual procedure. Physicians for Human Rights criticized the APA for not prohibiting highly coercive interrogations or requiring psychologists 'to adhere to international standards with respect to human rights' (Shinn, 2006: 1). The APA's position was widely criticized, particularly since other major professional organizations, such as the American Medical and American Psychiatric Associations, had adopted more stringent policies and evidence had already surfaced that interrogations often included banned methods of torture.

Claims made by the APA's presidents and senior administrators that there was no evidence psychologists participated in torture or other cruel, inhuman, or degrading treatment were later undermined by the 2007 declassification and release of a 2006 report from the US Department of

Defense's Office of Inspector General. In an open letter to the APA President, a group of psychologists, some of whom later referred to themselves as a 'Coalition for an Ethical Psychology', pointed out that the report provided 'irrefutable evidence' that psychologists who participated in national security interrogations 'systematically violated' the fundamental 'do no harm' principle in the APA's basic code of conduct (3 June 2007). In addition, they documented the role played by military psychologists in writing the PENS report: 'Six of the nine voting psychologist members selected for the task force were from military and intelligence agencies, most with direct connections to national security interrogations'. It was clear, the letter's authors stated, that SERE psychologists were critical to the 'development and migration of abusive interrogation techniques' viewed as 'tantamount to torture' by the International Committee of the Red Cross and other human rights organizations. Within a few weeks, 350 psychologists had added their names to this letter.

At the APA's annual meeting in 2007, a campaign to rescind the PENS report failed to pass. Instead, the APA's Council of Representatives reaffirmed its general position 'against Torture and other cruel, inhuman, or degrading treatment or punishment and its application to individuals defined in the United States Code as Enemy Combatants'. This statement included an 'unequivocal condemnation' of 'all techniques defined as torture or cruel, inhuman, or degrading treatment' by the United Nations and Geneva Conventions against torture. However, this did not end the controversy, in part because the APA did not ban psychologists from working in settings where torture takes place. In February 2008, as we were finishing this chapter, the APA Council of Representatives passed a revised resolution, which closed loopholes in the previous resolution. Briefly, it strikes out the prohibition on abusive interrogation procedures only if they cause 'lasting' or 'significant' harm. Instead, it states an 'unequivocal condemnation' of 'all techniques considered torture or cruel, inhuman or degrading treatment or punishment' as defined by standard international conventions, and an 'absolute prohibition' against the participation or assistance of psychologists in 'the use of all condemned techniques' (http://www.apa.org/governance/resolutions/amend022208.html). This important change is a victory for psychologists who fought for three years for a stronger resolution.

This extended example underlines the complexity of responsibility. It illustrates how findings of psychological research that enter the public domain may be used for a variety of purposes not always anticipated by the discoverer. For example, techniques of sensory deprivation were developed by psychologists who documented their destructive impact on our ability to maintain a stable sense of ourselves as persons in a world with meaning. We lose that sense rather quickly and may break down when placed in isolation with no input from the outside world. The irony is that many 'academic' sensory-deprivation studies were funded, often secretly, by the CIA and military agencies. Although psychologists cannot control who uses their work and for what purposes, we nonetheless believe we have a compelling responsibility to oppose and speak out against the misuse of psychological knowledge.

psychologists as social critics

Psychologists are not strangers to political action. Although activism has not been a central focus of mainstream psychology, efforts to make our work relevant to struggles for equality and social justice are widespread. They run the gamut from research on sociopolitical problems, to the development of radical psychological theories, to the formation of political interest groups within and outside the APA and similar organizations elsewhere in the world. Brief reviews of some classic examples – a US-centred account, reflecting what we are most familiar with – will serve as background to our subsequent discussion of projects explicitly designed to express a pragmatic solidarity with members of oppressed groups.

Within the APA, almost 20 per cent of the divisions have names and programmes that suggest a focus on social or political issues, and 13 divisions have joined together in a loose confederation called Divisions for Social Justice. Psychologists have also founded other organizations with specific sociopolitical aims. For example, Psychologists for Social Responsibility, a US organization with international connections, seeks to use psychological knowledge and skills to promote 'Cultures of Peace'. The Radical Psychology Network, with more than 500 members in three dozen countries, challenges traditional psychology for too often oppressing rather than liberating people. On our own local level, in the mid-1980s we were members of the Mental Health Committee of the Committee for Health Rights in Central America (CHRICA), where we first learned about Martín-Baró's work in El Salvador and FASIC in Chile (described below). We joined with others in forming the Boston Area Psychologists for Peace and Justice as a response to the US government's war fever after the 11 September 2001 attacks. We know of similar groups with specific political agendas in other countries, such as Psychologists Against Apartheid in South Africa; Psychology Politics Resistance, a network of mental health liberationists and critical psychologists in Great Britain; and PsychoActive, a group of Israeli psychotherapists working for human rights, dialogue, and peace. These unofficial groups, doing research and advocacy on political, economic, and social problems such as violence, discrimination, and social injustice, are a significant part of psychology's history and should be recognized as important, legitimate dimensions of the field.

theory and research on social issues

Long before critical psychology became a distinct approach, some of psychology's major theorists directed their work towards fundamental social change.

To illustrate the history and continuity of psychologists' contributions to our understanding of these collective concerns, we have chosen a few influential examples beginning during the Second World War and continuing in its aftermath, primarily from within social psychology (see the related discussion in Chapter 6, this volume). Each reflects a concern with political issues that became dominant during the rise of Fascist regimes in Europe and Asia in the 1930s, such as authoritarianism, conformity, and discrimination.

- Working within the framework of Kurt Lewin's *field theory*, Ronald Lippitt demonstrated how 'democratic' and 'authoritarian' forms of classroom teaching led to markedly different classroom cultures and behaviours (Lippitt, 1939). Lewin observed: 'In the autocracy instead of a cooperative attitude, a hostile and highly personal attitude became prevalent' (1948: 77–78).

- B. F. Skinner's *Walden Two* (Skinner, 1948) was a fictional account of a utopian community functioning primarily through positive reinforcement. Based on his operant conditioning model and experimental laboratory research, Skinner argued that reinforcing or rewarding positive behaviours, in contrast to negative or punishing responses, would reduce hostility and violence and increase cooperative behaviour.

- *The Authoritarian Personality* (Adorno et al., 1950) reported the results of the questionnaires and interviews with more than 2000 respondents focused on what made people susceptible to undemocratic ideas, particularly racial and ethnic prejudice and intolerance. The findings emphasized early childhood experiences, particularly the long-term impact of growing up in families with rigid and harsh child-rearing patterns.

- The US Supreme Court allowed social science evidence for the first time in its 1954 hearings in *Brown vs. Board of Education*, which led to the landmark decision that racially segregated schools were inherently unequal. The Court based its findings, in part, on Mamie and Kenneth Clark's tests of Black children who showed their preference for 'White' over 'Brown' dolls. Asked in court whether the 'type of injury' found would be 'enduring or lasting', Kenneth Clark replied that these children had been 'subjected to an obviously inferior status in the society in which they live … definitely harmed in the development of their personalities' and injured in ways which 'would be as enduring or lasting as the situation endured' (Beggs, 1995: 4).

- Conformity to the demands of authority was a central concern of psychologists after the Second World War. Stanley Milgram's research focused on how much pain people who agreed to participate in the study would inflict on others when ordered to do so by an experimental scientist. The results were startling. In contrast to expectations that only a sadistic few would go beyond a very strong shock, 65 per cent of the subjects in the first series of experiments went through the full cycle of what they had been told were increasingly strong shocks (Milgram, 1963, 1974).

- In Philip Zimbardo's Stanford Prison Experiment, student volunteers were randomly assigned to roles as 'guards' or 'prisoners' in an experimental setting isolated from the outside world. The guards quickly took on their roles – making the prisoners undress, ordering them to do push-ups, moving them into isolation cells if they resisted orders. A rebellion by prisoners was put down quickly. The guards became increasingly sadistic; the prisoners became depressed and showed signs of extreme stress. Designed to run for two weeks, the experiment was ended on the fifth day when Zimbardo realized that, as the 'superintendent' of the prison, he too had taken on his role (Zimbardo, Haney, Banks, & Jaffe, 1974).

This brief review demonstrates that work on politically significant issues is part of psychology's historical record. It also illustrates how the theories and research methods dominant in the post-Second World War period reflected the positivist framework's emphasis on experimental controls, quantitative measures, and statistical analyses. Within this framework 'subjects' were viewed as passive, with their behaviour a product of external influences. None of these studies involved ethnographic approaches; nor did they adopt any features of participatory action research (PAR) where subjects are involved as co-investigators. In all of the studies, experimenters constructed the research conditions and hid the study's purpose from the subjects – there were no Institutional Review Boards or Informed Consent Forms to monitor the ethical treatment of human subjects. Except for the prison experiment, these studies were conducted before the turbulence of the 1960s and the Vietnam War, when many investigators still believed the US was a functioning model of democracy and that the enemy was the authoritarianism and Fascism assumed to characterize other countries. Despite their methodological limitations, these studies played an important role in legitimizing psychological research on social and political problems.

Less positivist approaches to psychological theory and research surfaced in the mid- to late-1960s. These paralleled – and perhaps reflected – widespread currents of alienation and cultural change: the anti-Vietnam War, civil rights, and women's movements; police assaults on protesters at the 1968 Democratic Convention in Chicago; the counter-culture and 1969 Woodstock concert; and the 1970 killing by National Guard troops of Kent State University students protesting at Nixon's invasion of Cambodia. Proposals to change direction in psychology and the other social sciences appeared, including developments in feminist theory and research reflected, for example, in influential books by the psychologists Jean Baker Miller (1976) and Carol Gilligan (1982). Radical approaches were given a hearing in the edited collections *Radical Sociology* (Colfax & Roach, 1971) and *Radical Psychology* (Brown, 1973). In fact, the latter might be viewed as precursors to the Radical Psychology Network in 1993 (Fox, 2001b) and the first edition of this *Critical Psychology* text in 1997.

collaborative political projects

Various forms of collaborative research and action with dispossessed and oppressed groups emerged in the last quarter of the century. Psychologists joined in efforts to support and advocate for groups who had been targets of discrimination and helped develop various institutional and community-based programmes, including Head Start, self-help movements, women's consciousness-raising groups, and the Mental Health Liberation Front. Martín-Baró's preferential option for the poor and Freire's problem-posing approach to raising critical consciousness became models for building alliances while rejecting the dominant victim-blaming paradigm (Ryan, 1971). These developments, reflecting liberation psychology, the pedagogy of the oppressed, and pragmatic solidarity, embody a very different ideological position than that held by psychologists in the earlier post-Second World War period who had focused on the 'enemy without' rather than the 'enemy within'. Participatory action research (PAR) and other approaches that viewed participants as active agents seeking to make sense of their lives took psychologists out of the laboratory and beyond formal research designs. We highlight several examples in this section.

FASIC – Foundation for Aid from Christian Churches in Chile

On 11 September 1973, the democratically elected government of Chile, headed by Salvador Allende, was overturned by a military coup with the not-so-covert aid of the USA. Allende was killed, ushering in 15 years of a brutal dictatorship in which thousands were tortured, 'disappeared', and killed; many others fled into exile. In 1977, Chilean mental health professionals established a clinic within the Catholic Church to 'aid the victims of political persecution whose experiences ranged from the death and disappearance of loved ones to torture, exile, loss of employment, and general harassment' (Cienfuegos & Monelli, 1983: 43).

FASIC's approach was based on the view that the healing process for victims of political repression and torture 'requires restoration of the individuals' capacity to resume their political projects', making 'their previous history – political commitment, personal relationships, work, and social connections – meaningful in the present and the future' (Cienfuegos & Monelli, 1983: 44). Because a central treatment element was the elicitation of 'testimony' from patients during their initial therapeutic contacts, therapists 'encouraged [patients] to tape-record a detailed description of the events leading to their present state of suffering' (1983: 48) and to recall details of their painful experiences, which sometimes included torture. Therapists supported them in this process, not only to help them understand the impact of their trauma but also to 'allow them at the same time to denounce, through a written essay, the violence and injustice to which they have been subjected' (1983: 48). The patient and therapist then reviewed the transcribed text together, producing a jointly revised final document.

An important aspect of the therapeutic process of testimony is that it 'helps patients to integrate the traumatic experience into their lives by identifying its significance in the context of political and social events as well as the context of their personal history' (Cienfuegos & Monelli, 1983: 50). The approach also helps therapists in allowing them to 'tolerate and make therapeutic use of the confession' (1983: 51) in their treatment. Finally, it suggests a broader social and political value to these testimonies since, with the consent of victims, they might be used to document and denounce the crimes – which indeed occurred in Chile several years later. In this way, the therapeutic process serves the political aim of resisting oppression and injustice.

the children's rehabilitation centre (the Philippines)

Shortly after Ignacio Martín-Baró's assassination in El Salvador in November 1989, psychologists inspired by his conception of liberation psychology (Martin-Baró, 1994) established the Ignacio Martín-Baró Fund for Mental Health and Human Rights. The Fund continues his work through grants to community programmes that confront state-sponsored violence and support threatened communities. Many of these programmes transform traditional therapeutic models by incorporating and emphasizing the political process of 'conscientization'. The Children's Rehabilitation Centre (CRC) in the Philippines exemplifies this approach.

Established more than 20 years ago through the efforts of political prisoners and human rights groups, the CRC began as a play group to help the children of prisoners to cope with the trauma of separation from their parents. Over time, it came to serve an ever-widening circle of children affected by state-sponsored violence. Today it works with children who are themselves political detainees as well as with displaced and traumatized children from peasant families targeted by counter-insurgency campaigns. As the Centre's work evolved, it came to focus on the protection of human rights:

> **Human rights are indeed an issue for which we, as development workers, psychologists, and social workers must advocate in our work ... As psychologists, I believe we should go beyond the individual-therapist relationship ... It is extremely important to grasp the meaning and history of our clients' human rights abuses and to be part of the process of claiming their rights through advocacy and public campaigns. (Lamada, 2006: 4)**

Formed during the worst years of repression in the Philippines, the CRC is outspoken in its critique of the current government and stands unequivocally with those in resistance against the so-called war against terrorism. Growing up in this repressive and violent world, children witness physical assaults against their parents, are threatened and harassed by police and military officials and are themselves victims of rapes and assaults. The Centre's treatment and rehabilitation work proceeds in three phases: (1) Diagnostic and Expressive Work, where group activities such as play, arts, summer camp and cultural presentations provide opportunities for revisiting the emotions associated with traumatic experiences; (2) Meaning Construction, where the human rights violation/traumatic experience is contextualized to show the children that they are neither at fault nor alone; and (3) Cognitive Mastery, where activities focus on skills training to build self-esteem, leadership capacities and advocacy skills.

A Children's Collective includes graduates of CRC's therapy programme involved in the centre's advocacy work. They visit schools to speak about human rights abuses; write, produce, and perform plays that portray their experiences; and participate in public rallies to denounce human rights violations. The CRC has found that advocacy activities become part of children's positive coping mechanisms. Their desire to raise awareness and find support from others gives them purpose and inspires them to move on with their lives.

Branded as communists and subjected to frequent military harassment, especially when they go to far-away areas to give 'psychosocial first aid' to rural children, CRC staff coordinate with human rights groups and other local organizations to help ensure their security. The CRC staff believe that their many allies and their capacity 'to make noise' through their campaigns and advocacy work serve, ironically, as a shield against harassment.

Still Present Pasts

Still Present Pasts, an innovative multi-media project, seeks to break what psychologist and project director Ramsay Liem views as the enforced silence surrounding the historical trauma of the Korean War. Drawing on oral history interviews with Korean Americans about their memories of the war, Still Present Pasts created an art exhibition to serve as a form of public remembering. The exhibit, which has toured the USA and been shown in South Korea, combines personal life stories, art, film, the spoken word and history into an interactive experience that lifts the silence shrouding the Korean War with the aim of promoting healing, reconciliation, and restorative justice.

> **For Korean American survivors and their children, the Korean War remains a source of shared, if not publicly expressed, pain and division. To speak openly about the past is to violate a pervasive popular culture that renders the war as 'forgotten', to risk provoking Cold War divisions that linger within Korean American communities, and to expose children and grandchildren to deep personal suffering that survivors, themselves, may not have reconciled. (Liem, 2005: 2)**

From Liem's perspective, the erasure of the Korean War from collective memory and public dialogue was also an ideological achievement of the state which sought to promote the US narrative of the war as a victory against communism while downplaying the US role in the war's devastation. Three years of fighting caused three million civilian deaths, almost two million combat deaths and casualties, and a national division separating ten million Koreans from family members for over half a century. These horrific losses are rarely acknowledged.

Stressing the importance of ending 'over a half century of national division' and moving towards 'empathy for survivors and recognition of our common interest in acting for peace' (Liem, 2005: 2), the exhibit – designed by a collective of Korean American artists, a filmmaker, a historian and a psychologist – brings back silenced memories of the war and raises issues of personal and national reconciliation. It also provides opportunities for visitors to add their own recollections of the war and its aftermath. 'As the pieces grow, they become living art embodying an expanding collective memory of the Korean conflict' (Liem, 2007: 17).

The well-attended exhibit has deeply engaged its visitors. Intergenerational discussions are common. Younger attendees say it is often easier to ask someone else's parent or grandparent about their experiences during the war and its aftermath than their own.

Echoes of Brown

Social psychologist Michelle Fine has documented educational injustices in schools across the USA. Over time, she shifted from ethnographic research, in which young people are the subjects of study, to participatory action research, where they are full participants from the initial choice of research questions through the gathering, analysis and interpretation of data to decisions about how to use the results to bring about change. Fine views 'this subterranean movement of Research Projects by and for youth, across the nation, as an emergent strategy for a mass movement of youth documenting, challenging, resisting, and revising social policies carved on their backs' (Fine, Torre, Burns, & Paine, 2006: 808).

One project, *Echoes of Brown*, exemplifies critical psychological work in the service of the politics of resistance. When several desegregated suburban New York and New Jersey school systems wanted help in responding to the persistent 'achievement gap' 50 years after *Brown v. Board of Education*, Fine and her colleagues recruited more than 100 youth researchers to attend research camps to learn how to conduct interviews, run focus groups, and collect data through participant observation. 'Deconstructing who can do research, what constitutes research and who benefits, they were immersed in methods training and social justice theory' (Fine et al., 2006: 819). At the first meeting, the youth challenged how the research was framed. 'When you call it an achievement gap, that means it's our fault. The real problem is an opportunity gap – let's place the responsibility where it belongs – in society and in the schools' (2006: 819). The name was changed to the Educational Opportunity Gap Project.

The study began with a student-designed national survey of 9000 high school students' views of race and class (in)justice in their schools and the society at large, supplemented by a series of local mini-research projects involving focus groups and individual interviews. Findings confirmed earlier studies that identified public policies and practices that sustain and deepen the gap. Fine and her colleagues refer to these as 'Six Degrees of Segregation': urban/suburban inequities in school financing; the dismantling of desegregation; academic tracking in remaining desegregated schools; race and class differences in students' experiences of respect and support; racial disparities in suspensions and disciplinary actions; and high-stakes testing. To make educators and policy makers aware of the gap's structural and ideological bases, youth researchers led feedback sessions in schools in New York City's surrounding communities and presented their findings to groups of educators and policy makers across the country. These sessions disappointed the research team, as the questions asked invariably assumed that poor youth and youth of colour were responsible for problems in the schools rather than ineffective and inequitable educational practices.

Hoping to have a greater impact as the 50th anniversary of the Brown decision approached, the research team created a performance piece using poetry and movement to dramatize what they had learned. They performed the resulting *Echoes of Brown*, which draws on political history, personal experience, and research findings, before an audience of over 800 in May 2004. A DVD and book on the work came later.

Fine's conclusion emphasizes the need to go beyond simply documenting oppression:

> **In the Echoes project, youth interviewed elders in the Northeast who had been active in struggles for educational civil rights, visited educational organizing groups, and grew, themselves, to be youth researchers, advocates and organizers in the campaign for fiscal equity, the struggle against high-stake testing, and the fight for racially integrated, detracked classrooms. Documenting oppression with youth is significant, but it borders on unethical if decoupled from the study of resistance, possibility, and 'what could be'. (Fine et al., 2006: 825)**

welfare and human rights monitoring project

Despite many years of struggle for authentic welfare reform by a broad-based coalition, in 1995 Massachusetts reduced benefits to welfare recipients, imposed work requirements, and set a two-year time limit and more stringent eligibility requirements. This was the harbinger of the harsh, punitive federal law passed the following year, intended, as President Bill Clinton said, to 'end welfare as we know it'. Unable to prevent these new regulations, the coalition's academic members (including one of us, Vicky Steinitz) began to document their impact, hoping that evidence of the negative effects on poor women might help mobilize the decent majority to rise up and demand that these punitive laws be rescinded. Our experience with the Latin America solidarity movement had introduced us to the power of testimony (see

FASIC, above) as a means of both documenting the atrocities of illegitimate governmental policies and of re-empowering victims.

The new welfare policies violated several articles of the United Nation's Universal Declaration of Human Rights, including civil and political rights, such as the right to protection from arbitrary interference with one's privacy (Art. 12), and economic rights, such as the right to an adequate standard of living (Art. 25). Casting the new regulations as human rights violations, Steinitz sent out a Call for Human Rights Monitors to work with recipient-led welfare rights groups across the state to gather reports of how these violations affected families in poverty. Housed by the Unitarian Universalist Service Committee (UUSC), the monitoring project was planned and carried out in partnership with welfare-rights advocacy and activist groups who agreed with its dual aims: first, to gather documentation to fuel and mobilize opposition to the new laws, and second, to serve as an organizing and educational tool for recipients. Organizers were alert to the dangers of documenting atrocity stories and sought to ensure that project data were not used, as so often happens, to dehumanize and re-victimize oppressed people.

The first project report (Steinitz, 1996) documented five major areas with widespread abuse by case workers and administrators: (a) sanctions on women for failing to provide paternity identification information which, in many cases, they did not have or could not provide without placing themselves at risk; (b) the re-victimization of battered women by forcing them to expose intimate details of their lives; (c) the rigid imposition of teen parent education and group housing regulations, resulting in dropping more than half the mothers under 18 from the rolls; (d) the denial of educational opportunities when students had to drop out of school to meet work requirements; and (e) rampant lawlessness in Department of Transitional Assistance offices when computer or staff 'errors' were used as an excuse for routinely denying benefits to which recipients were legally entitled. After the first year, UUSC assumed major responsibility for the monitoring project and expanded it to three other states. A series of reports directed to state and federal decision-makers continued to document how rules and regulations obstructed due process, imposed unlawful sanctions, and invaded the privacy and dignity of recipients. At the same time, local recipient-led welfare rights groups used the Human Rights Violation Reports to educate their members.

During those years, other groups also used the Universal Declaration of Human Rights to educate, inspire and mobilize low-income people. For example, the Kensington Welfare Rights Union (KWRU), a Philadelphia-based poor people's activist group supported by a network of educators, academics, unions, and faith-based groups, gathered reports of human rights violations while crisscrossing the country in an Economic Human Rights Campaign bus. The bus was filled with people living in poverty who told their stories at each stop along the way and invited others to do the same. The tour culminated in a march to the United Nations where activists presented to the Secretary General caskets filled with Human Rights Violation reports, including those gathered by the Massachusetts monitoring project (http://www.universityofthepoor.org).

joining movements of resistance

In 1967, the founders of RESIST, a progressive foundation that continues to support grassroots organizing for peace, economic, social and environmental justice, circulated a 'Call to Resist Illegitimate Authority'. Signed by more than 20,000 individuals despite the fact that those who signed risked criminal prosecution since it was a misdemeanour, the Call helped mobilize opposition to the Vietnam War and resistance to the draft (http://resistinc.org/thecall.html).

For us, there is a resonance between that statement 40 years ago and our urging psychologists today to align themselves with movements of resistance. The work of Ignacio Martín-Baró and Paolo Freire is grounded in their commitment to resist illegitimate authority. The projects highlighted in this chapter stem from similar convictions. For the Chilean and Filipino therapists, healing the victims of state-sponsored violence was not sufficient. They simultaneously found ways to contribute to the political struggle for social justice and peace. In the case of FASIC, it was by helping political detainees write *testimonios* which documented their experiences. In the case of the CRC, this work of meaning construction was part of a collective therapeutic process that helped child victims understand how the State oppressed their families and violated their rights and also provided them with skills and opportunities to become child advocates in their schools and communities. Similar concerns typified our other examples. Students in the Echoes of Brown research camps met with civil rights leaders, studied the history of desegregation and reflected on their own experiences while creating a performance piece on the legacy of the Brown decision. The Still Present Past multi-media exhibit provided a space for remembrance to help generate a unifying narrative for Korean-Americans whose memories have been silenced. The Welfare and Human Rights Monitoring Project unmasked the illegitimacy of new welfare regulations by documenting their violations of the Universal Declaration of Human Rights.

As we learned from Freire, resistance requires critical consciousness. It is essential to debunk the official story of what is happening and why, and to develop an alternative analysis based on the experiences and perspectives of those who are most directly affected by such injustice. This process was evident in the extended discovery process through which we learned of military psychologists' role in developing interrogation methods widely condemned as torture. The effort of psychologists to ban such methods continues, but the problem is no longer a secret hidden from public view and comment. Collective consciousness-raising in the Freirean mode is critical to building movements of resistance; however, it is not enough. The public support of allies through some form of pragmatic solidarity (Farmer, 2005) is an essential step. For psychologists, this means using one's expertise in the service of those resisting oppression, as exemplified in Martín-Baró's (1994) model of liberation psychology. Such work always involves taking sides in a struggle among different groups and sectors of society. For example, while the FASIC therapists were taking *testimonios* from patients who had been tortured, other Chilean psychologists and psychiatrists were participating in interrogations that included torture.

In making this argument, we are following what we believe is the central thrust of critical psychology, namely, to find ways to use our knowledge and skills in the struggle for a more just society. The examples we selected suggest the range of ways in which psychologists have moved beyond their usual venues – the laboratory, lecture hall, and clinic – to speak out against abuses of psychological knowledge and methods and to join in collective efforts to reduce state-sponsored violence, economic oppression, and racism. Rather than treating communities as sites within which to pursue their own research agendas, these psychologists have allied themselves with groups struggling for change and tried to learn from them how they might put their expertise and knowledge to use.

We are well aware that contributing to effective political action is not an easy task even when, in the course of our training, we learn a great deal about how individuals and groups function. Translating social influence theories, for example, into mobilizing support for a group's political objectives is not automatic. While we may have something to offer, we first need to learn how to become reliable allies, and then how to make our knowledge relevant to the specific goals and programmes of the groups with which we ally ourselves. Group process skills may help facilitate meetings, mediate disputes, and forge alliances across diverse constituencies, but we cannot use them until we demonstrate that we are trustworthy.

Learning how to be of use is a long-term task. A good first step for students and young investigators might take the form of internships on community social change projects. They can learn how to build trust while applying their research and clinical skills to specific tasks such as staffing street clinics and evaluating the effectiveness of particular campaigns. Finding ways to contribute would not only be useful to organizers and activists, but would also alert students to the complexities involved in collaborating with those engaged in the struggle for social justice.

Our own awareness of these issues reflects our involvement over the past five years in a community-led coalition of local residents, academics, scientists, and peace and justice activists in an effort to stop a high-security bioweapons laboratory from being built in a predominantly African-American, inner-city neighbourhood of Boston (Parthasarathi & Steinitz, 2007). The campaign falls into the David vs. Goliath category. It is, therefore, quite remarkable that with little in the way of funds and a generally indifferent press, the coalition has succeeded – through community mobilization, state and federal court decisions, and a critical, external review of the laboratory's environmental impact studies – in bringing to a standstill plans for opening the laboratory.

Our access to professional networks led to an Open Letter opposing the laboratory, signed by 165 faculty members at local universities, which received widespread press attention. We have also helped draft petitions and position papers, testified at public hearings, attended coalition meetings, and joined protest demonstrations. We believe our presence – just being there – has been important in gaining the trust of coalition members. Beyond our particular skills – as psychologists, researchers, and teachers – and our traditional academic stance of scepticism, we have learned from coalition members and leaders the critical importance of believing in our own efficacy, that, in the end, we can win – despite the array of forces against us. What is important is doing whatever can be done to keep the struggle alive.

We began with a labour anthem calling on us to take sides and Thomas Teo's proposal to judge our work by its emancipatory relevance. We end with a stanza from activist folk-singer Ani DiFranco's song, 'Millenium Theatre':

> **Under darkening skies**
> **the resistance is just waiting**
> **to be organized.**

■ ■main chapter points ■

1 Drawing on the concepts of *liberation psychology*, *critical consciousness*, and *pragmatic solidarity*, we argue that critical psychologists should join movements of resistance and find ways to apply their expertise and knowledge in the struggle for social justice.

2 We summarize examples of psychologists' politically relevant work: opposition to psychologist participation in interrogations using torture; experimental studies of authoritarianism and conformity in the post-Second World War period; and collaborative projects with community-based groups engaged in the struggle for social justice.

3 Entering into alliances with community-based groups engaged in campaigns against some form of injustice involves sharing one's resources and expertise and accepting their leadership.

4 Critical psychologists have a responsibility to take public stands against the misuse of psychological knowledge.

glossary

- **critical consciousness**: Paolo Freire's educational programme focused on the development of forms of inquiry about social reality that led to an understanding of the forces that sustain oppression and inequalities. Through a collective process of learning how to 'name' the realities of the world in which they lived, people could achieve a level of 'critical consciousness' which would provide the basis for them to act to gain control of their lives.

- **liberation psychology**: the conception of a psychology that allies itself with the struggles of the poor and oppressed was proposed by Martín-Baró, the Salvadoran priest and social psychologist assassinated in 1989. It involves a view of psychosocial processes from the point of view of those who are dominated; accompanying people living in conditions of economic and social oppression; supporting their efforts to recover their culture and traditions; and joining them in their efforts to liberate themselves.

- **pragmatic solidarity**: there are many ways to align with socially and economically oppressed groups. Paul Farmer suggests that while all forms of support are useful and are welcomed by those in need, acts of 'pragmatic solidarity' which involve providing concrete services and material goods that directly lift the burdens of oppression – such as medical care, food, and housing – are particularly valuable.

▪ ▪ reading suggestions ▪

The work of Paolo Freire is an indispensable starting point to understand how knowledge is politicized and how coming to understand the world is crucial to both the personal liberation and the social transformation of the oppressed. *The Paolo Freire Reader* (Freire & Macedo, 1998) is an excellent collection of his most significant writings. Equally essential is Ignacio Martín-Baró's *Writings for a Liberation Psychology* (1994), which brings together his thoughts on the psychology of politics and the politics of psychology as well as his research on the impact of war and terror on the Salvadoran people. In his collection of essays, *Pathologies of Power* (2005), Paul Farmer documents the close connections between structural violence, poverty, and poor health and argues that the right to good health is an issue of social justice.

; // internet resources /

- **Children's Rehabilitation Centre/CRC** (Philippines): www.childrehab.tripod.com

- **Coalition for an Ethical Psychology**: www.ethicalapa.com

- **Kensington Welfare Rights Union (KWRU)**: www.universityofthepoor.org

- **Psychologists for Social Responsibility (PsySR)**: www.psysr.org

- **Radical Psychology Network (RadPsyNet)**: radpsynet.org

- **'Solidarity Work: Researchers in the Struggle for Social Justice'** – Mishler and Steinitz: www.uga.coe.edu/quig/proceedingsS01_mishler.html

 **Questions**

1 Do psychologists have a responsibility to make sure the results of their research will not be misused? If so, how can that best be accomplished?

2 Are you convinced by this book's argument that there's no such thing as objective, neutral research, and by this chapter's argument that psychologists are always taking sides? Why or why not?

3 A central claim in this chapter is that a primary task for critical psychologists is to find ways to collaborate with groups resisting social injustice in the pursuit of political aims. Do you agree? Why or why not?

Frequently Asked Questions
Dennis Fox

Now that you've read this book, you will have learned a lot about the things critical psychologists find interesting. I hope you've found something that grabs your attention. Still, you probably have a few questions that the book doesn't really answer. And if you're reading this first, before you dive into the substance, you may have even more questions. Maybe you're trying to decide whether to take a critical psychology course. Maybe you're suspicious. Good for you! In any case, I'm going to attempt a few general answers.

Some of what follows I've adapted from my website's Frequently Asked Questions. Since my site has material from this book's first edition along with other critical psychology papers, links, and resources, I get a lot of email from web-surfing students, some who have read the book and many who haven't. I also get email directed to the Radical Psychology Network (radpsynet.org). The FAQ makes things a little more organized. But remember: the answers are brief, informal, personal, incomplete, and changeable. Some get much more attention throughout this book. (My other FAQs touch on issues more or less related to my main interests within critical psychology, especially the interplay among psychology, the law, justice, and anarchism. All this and more at dennisfox.net!).

Q1 What's all this about critical psychology? My psychology professor had never heard of it!

A. Critical psychology is an effort to challenge the forces within mainstream psychology that help sustain unjust political, economic, and other societal structures. At least that's the way I look at it; critical psychologists don't all agree about goals and methods.

One of the most difficult things to confront is the belief of most psychologists that their work is entirely apolitical – they're just trying to help people. In fact, although they are trying to help people, their work often incorporates assumptions they haven't always considered.

Especially in the United States, critical psychology hasn't made much of a dent in mainstream psychology. That's not surprising. The USA is at the centre of mainstream psychology's institutional base. Its textbooks, professional standards, and empirical focus influence the way psychologists in much of the rest of the world teach, do research, and practise, just as other aspects of American culture exert a disproportionate influence. As a result, most psychologists never come across critical psychology in their training. Although a fair amount of critical material is published in mainstream journals (even periodically in the American Psychological Association's main journal, *American Psychologist*), most appears in journals most psychologists don't read, using language and concepts that the majority of psychologists are unfamiliar with. And the truth is, most psychologists are too busy to do much more than skim through the journals they do receive (there are too many journals to actually be able to read them!).

Some psychologists who do come across critical psychology are sympathetic to its goals but don't think it's a smart career move when trying to get academic jobs or fit into a traditional clinical practice. Others consider critical psychology is less 'scientific' by traditional standards, or think it's too 'political'. Of course, plenty of them find nothing wrong with psychology's support for the status quo because they like things pretty much as they are.

As for that professor of yours, give him or her this book!

Q2 Where can I study critical psychology?

A. Good question. There aren't a lot of good answers.

You can always read on your own. You'll probably have to do that even if you're a psychology major, because there are very few courses in the subject. This book is one place to start. (There are plenty of used copies of the still-exciting first edition. No need to send me royalties!) In addition to following up on the references and reading suggestions in this book, my website has a lot of references, a reading list, and links to other lists.

For a formal course of study, outside the USA there are a few university degree programmes and other institutions with a critical focus. In the USA I don't know of any, though some universities offer programmes compatible with, or at least tolerant of, critical perspectives. Circumstances change too frequently to list these programmes in a book, but I try to keep the links on my website reasonably up to date, with links to sites with more complete lists.

Especially at the graduate level, you can contact professors at schools that interest you and ask them how students critical of the mainstream have fared in the past. Get specific here! If you know you want to do qualitative rather than quantitative research, for example, ask if the department would allow that. If you want to study the connection between psychology and justice, find out if that fits in to the department's agenda. Without a professor or two to support your efforts, jumping through the usual graduate school hoops may become unbearable. You might ask professors you communicate with if they plan to remain at the university for the next few years.

Some departments do have significant numbers of psychologists interested in critical issues, though they don't always call themselves 'critical psychologists'. Look through faculty lists, look at the courses they teach, email them, email their students. Find out if professors are involved in off-campus justice organizations. Grad school takes forever. Do some research before you commit!

Another consideration: think hard about which area of psychology you'll specialize in. Adopting critical approaches in community psychology is sometimes easier, because community psychology sees itself as psychology's liberal-activist wing. Theoretical psychology is open to critical theory. There's very little room in social psychology, though; despite the subject matter, traditional methods and assumptions rule. Clinical psychology is also usually difficult for critical people.

Q3 How can I get a job doing critical psychology?

A. Another excellent question with no good answer.

If you want an academic job in a regular psychology department, you'll have to do the kind of research in graduate school that gives you traditional credentials. (I didn't. I ended up in an interdisciplinary legal studies department, with an 'affiliation' in psychology.) Some people can retain a critical edge through years of graduate school, and then job hunting, and then trying to get tenure in a mainstream psychology department. But others never quite get back to their early critical interests, or they persuade themselves they've gotten over being young and impractical. It's a risk.

Here are some options I came up with for a short piece in a UK graduate student journal (adapted from Fox, 2002):

- Address political issues as a small part of your work, spending the bulk of your time doing empirical research on traditional topics.

    Once you succeed on the mainstream's own terms, you have some leeway to raise political questions on the side – you've demonstrated that your political critique isn't based simply on an inability to follow the rules. Of course, it's pretty time-consuming to produce impressive empirical research and also do serious critical work. You may give up, especially if you find the traditional work boring or useless. But who said being critical was going to be easy?

- Do conventional empirical research on politically tinged topics.

    The acceptability of qualitative research has increased, but a nice, neat experimental manipulation demonstrating some dynamic of oppression impresses mainstreamers, especially if published in a prestigious journal. The same is sometimes true for review articles or essays. In both cases, you have to tone down the language to get past reviewers, but if you write a book, you're allowed to admit in the preface that your research was motivated by deep political concerns rather than simple scientific curiosity.

- Find a niche that tolerates political motives and alternative methods.

    This is more easily done in specializations like community or feminist psychology, which began as attacks on societal values and institutions. Although both fields have gone more mainstream, psychologists who see themselves as advocates may still find a home. Outside North America, critical psychology itself is a growing niche, with degree programmes, journals, and conferences. You might make a career publishing in non-mainstream journals. That's a good option for some, though marginal to psychology's core.

- Find a niche outside psychology, perhaps an interdisciplinary department less concerned about psychology's status mania.

    That's what I did. This option lets you present psychology as you see it within a broader context. It also exposes you to work outside psychology. At the same time, though, it moves your focus even further from mainstream psychology and cuts your credibility within the discipline.

Outside academia, if you go into something like clinical psychology you can open your own practice offering any kind of therapy you want. There's a market for feminist therapists, for example. I do know that many clinical students who develop an interest in critical psychology become frustrated with what they have to put up with.

The job question suggests something else to consider: What's your real goal? If you're already a psychologist, it makes sense to try to figure out how you can work in accordance with your critical values. If your main interest is working for justice and social change, though, and especially if you're still a student, you might consider whether psychology is the best field of study. The constraints are pretty significant and the links to social change pretty amorphous despite critical psychology's efforts. You don't need a PhD in psychology to become a political activist! (See Fox, 2005, 2008b.)

Q4 What's the difference between 'critical psychology' and 'radical psychology'?

A. Some of us use the terms more or less interchangeably and find ourselves surprised that others don't see it the same way. *Radical* has a clearer political focus in terms of the scope of social change some of us would like to see; the Radical Psychology Network adopted the term in 1993 to distinguish itself from politically liberal psychologists aiming for more limited social reforms. *Critical* psychology has a more academic than political tone, though as emphasized in this book most critical psychologists advocate transformative social change. However, instead of using the perspectives, styles, and terminology of anarchism, Marxism, or other radical approaches, some work for reforms that, however useful, are more consistent with liberal or progressive politics. I think the term radical leaves less to the imagination, but basically it's a muddle.

Q5   How can I find other critical psychologists?

A. Join RadPsyNet, subscribe to email lists, go to critical psychology conferences, look for the names of critical psychologists at mainstream conferences or at a nearby university, and don't be shy! If you read a book or article you like, email the author. Most academics love it when people approach them about their work. Even as a student you can write articles for critical psychology journals, or less formally for student newsletters or websites. The critical psychology world is a small one - jump right in!

References

A Fairer World: Tasmanian Centre for Global Learning. (2008). Accessed 4 April from http://www.afairerworld.org/_Peace_and_conflict/thehumancostofwar.html.

Abberly, P. (1993). Disabled People and Normality. In J. Swain, V. Finkelstein, S. French and M. Oliver (Eds.), *Disabling Barriers – Enabling Environments* (pp. 107–115). London: Sage.

Aboud, F. E. (1998). *Health Psychology in Global Perspective.* Thousand Oaks, CA: Sage.

Acker, J., Barry, K., & Esseveld, J. (1991). Objectivity and Truth: Problems in Doing Feminist Research. In M. M. Fonow and J. A. Cook (Eds.), *Beyond Methodology: Feminist Scholarship as Lived Research* (pp. 133–153). Indianapolis, IN: Indiana University Press.

Adamson, W. L. (1980). *Hegemony and Revolution: A Study of Antonio Gramsci's Political and Cultural Theory.* Berkeley, CA: University of California Press.

Adler N. E., Epel, E. S., Castellazzo G., & Ickovics, J. R. (2000). Relationship of Subjective and Objective Social Status with Psychological and Physiological Functioning: Preliminary Data in Healthy White Women. *Health Psychology, 19,* 586–592.

Adorno, T. W. (1973). *Negative Dialectics.* New York: Seabury.

Adorno, T. W., Frenkel-Brunswik, E., Levinson, D. J., & Sanford, N. (1950). *The Authoritarian Personality.* New York: Harper & Row.

Agashae, Z., & Bratton, J. (2001). Leader-Follower Dynamics: Developing a Learning Environment. *Journal of Workplace Learning, 13*(3), 89–103.

Agerbak, L. (1991). Breaking the Cycle of Violence: Doing Development in Conflict Situations. *Development in Practice, 1*(3), 151–158.

Albee, G. W. (1977). The Protestant Ethic, Sex, and Psychotherapy. *American Psychologist, 32,* 150–61.

Albee, G. W. (1986). Toward a Just Society: Lessons from Observations on the Primary Prevention of Psychopathology. *American Psychologist, 41,* 891–898.

Albee, G. W. (1990). The Futility of Psychotherapy. *Journal of Mind and Behavior, 11*(3,4), 369–384.

Albrecht, G., Seelman, K., & Bury, M. (Eds.). (2001). *Handbook of Disability Studies.* New York: Sage.

Aldarondo, E. (Ed.). (2007). *Advancing Social Justice Through Clinical Practice.* London: Lawrence Erlbaum.

Alderfer, C. P. (1969). An Empirical Test of a New Theory of Human Needs. *Organizational Behavior and Human Performance, 4,* 142–175.

Alinsky, S. (1971). *Rules for Radicals.* New York: Vintage Books.

Allport, G. (1954). *The Nature of Prejudice.* Garden City, NY: Doubleday.

Allport, G. (1962). Prejudice: Is it Social or Personal? *Journal of Social Issues, 18,* 120–134.

Altemeyer, B. (1988). *Enemies of Freedom: Understanding Right-Wing Authoritarianism.* San Francisco, CA: Jossey Bass.

Alvesson, M., & Deetz, S. (1996). Critical Theory and Postmodernism Approaches to Organizational Studies. In S. R. Clegg, C. Hardy, and W. R. Nord (Eds.), *Handbook of Organization Studies* (pp. 191–217). London: Sage.

American Journal of Community Psychology. (1984). A Tribute to Erich Lindemann, *12*(5), entire issue.

American Psychiatric Association. (2000). *Diagnostic and Statistical Manual of Mental Disorders* (4th edn). Text Revision. Washington, DC: American Psychiatric Association.

American Psychological Association. (2005). *Report of the American Psychological Association Presidential Task Force on Psychological Ethics and National Security.* [Online at http://www.apa.org/releases/PENSTaskForceReportFinal.pdf]

American Psychology-Law Society. (2007). Call for Syllabi – Undergraduate Courses, accessed 21 September 2007 from http://www.ap-ls.org/academics/downloadUnder grad.html

Analyses of Social Issues and Public Policy. (2007). Special Issue on Psychologists and Interrogation, *7*(1), 1–271.

Anderson, I. (2002). Gender, Psychology, and Law: Studies in Feminism, Epistemology, and Science. *Feminism and Psychology, 12,* 379–388.

Anderson, N. (2005). Relationships Between Practice and Research in Personnel Selection: Does the Left Hand Know What the Right is Doing? In A. Evers, N. Anderson, and O. Vosquijl (Eds.), *The Blackwell Handbook of Personnel Selection.* Oxford: Blackwell Publishing.

Anderson, S., Cavanagh, J., Collins, C., Pizzigati, S., & Lapham, M. (2007). *Executive Excess 2007: The Staggering Social Cost of US Business Leadership.* Institute for Policy Studies and United for a Fair Economy. Available from http://www.fairecon omy.org/files/pdf/ExecutiveExcess2007.pdf

Angelique, H., & Culley, M. (2007). History and Theory of Community Psychology: An International Perspective of Community Psychology in the United States: Returning to Political, Critical, and Ecological Roots. In S. Reich, M. Riemer, I. Prilleltensky, and M. Montero (Eds.), *International Community Psychology: History and Theories* (pp. 37–62). New York: Springer.

Angell, M. (2004). *The Truth About the Drug Companies.* New York: Random House.

Antonovsky, A. (1987). *Unraveling the Mystery of Health: How People Manage Stress and Stay Well.* San Francisco, CA: Jossey-Bass.

Applbaum, K. (2006). Pharmaceutical Marketing and the Invention of the Medical Consumer. *PLoS Medicine, 3*(4), e189.

Arena, M. P., & Arrigo, B. A. (2006). *The Terrorist Identity: Explaining the Terrorist Threat.* New York: New York University Press.

Argyris, C., & Schon, D. A. (1978). *Organizational Learning: A Theory of Action Perspective.* San Francisco, CA: Jossey-Bass.

Armenakis, A. A. (1993). Creating Readiness for Organizational Change. *Human Relations, 46*(6), 681–703.

Armstrong, D. (1987). Theoretical Tensions in Biopsychosocial Medicine. *Social Science & Medicine, 25,* 1213–1218.

Armstrong, M. (1996). Privilege In Residential Housing. In S. M. Wildman, with M. Armstrong, A. Davis, and T. Grillo (Eds.), *Privilege Revealed* (pp. 43–65). New York: New York University Press.

Aronson, E., Wilson, T. D., Akert, R. M., & Fehr, B. (2007). *Social Psychology* (3rd Canadian edn). Toronto: Pearson/Prentice Hall.

Arratia, M., & de la Maza, I. (1997). Grounding a Long-Term Deal: Working with the Aymara for Community Development. In S. E. Smith, D. G. Willms, with N. A. Johnson (Eds.), *Nurtured by Knowledge: Learning to Do Participatory Action-Research* (pp. 111–137). New York: The Apex Press.

Arribas-Ayllon, M., & Walkerdine, V. (2008). Foucauldian Discourse Analysis. In C. Willig and W. Stainton Rogers (Eds.), *The SAGE Handbook of Qualitative Research in Psychology* (pp. 91–108). London: Sage.

Arrigo, B. A. (1992). Deconstructing Jurisprudence: An Experiential-Feminist Critique. *Journal of Human Justice, 4*(1): 13–20.

Arrigo, B. A. (1995). The Peripheral Core of Law and Criminology: On Postmodern Social Theory and Conceptual Integration. *Justice Quarterly, 12*, 447–472.

Arrigo, B. A. (2000). Social Justice and Critical Criminology: On Integrating Knowledge. *Contemporary Justice Review, 3*(1), 7–37.

Arrigo, B. A. (2001). Reviewing Graduate Training Models in Forensic Psychology: Implications for Practice. *Journal of Forensic Psychology Practice, 3*, 9–31.

Arrigo, B. A. (2002). *Punishing the Mentally Ill: A Critical Analysis of Law and Psychiatry.* Albany, NY: SUNY Press.

Arrigo, B. A. (2003). Psychology and the Law: The Critical Agenda for Citizen Justice and Radical Social Change. *Justice Quarterly, 20*, 399–444.

Arrigo, B. A. (Ed.). (2004a). *Psychological Jurisprudence: Critical Explorations in Law, Crime, and Society.* Albany, NY: SUNY Press.

Arrigo, B. A. (2004b). The Ethics of Therapeutic Jurisprudence: A Critical and Theoretical Inquiry of Law, Psychology, and Crime. *Psychiatry, Psychology, and Law: An Interdisciplinary Journal, 11*, 23–43.

Arrigo, B. A. (2007). Punishment, Freedom, and the Culture of Control: The Case of Brain Imaging and the Law. *American Journal of Law and Medicine, 33*(2/3), 457–482.

Arrigo, B. A., & Barrett, L. (2008). Philosophical Criminology and Complex Systems Science: Towards A Critical Theory of Justice. *Critical Criminology: An International Journal, 16*(3).

Arrigo, B. A., & Schehr, R. C. (1998). Restoring Justice for Juveniles: A Critical Analysis of Victim-Offender Mediation. *Justice Quarterly, 15*, 629–666.

Arrigo, B. A., Milovanovic, D., & Schehr, R. C. (2005). *The French Connection in Criminology: Rediscovering Crime, Law, and Social Change.* Albany, NY: SUNY Press.

Arthur, W. Jr., Bennett, W. Jr., Edens, P. S., & Bell, S. T. (2003). Effectiveness of Training in Organizations: A Meta-Analysis of Design and Evaluation Features. *Journal of Applied Psychology, 88*(2), 234–245.

Asch, A. (2001). Disability, Bioethics, and Human Rights. In G. Albrecht, K. Seelman, and M. Bury (Eds.), *Handbook of Disability Studies* (pp. 297–326). New York: Sage.

Ash, M. G., & Woodward, W. R. (1987). *Psychology in Twentieth-Century Thought and Society.* Cambridge, MA: Cambridge University Press.

Ashforth, B. E., & Kreiner, G. E. (1999). 'How can you do it?' Dirty Work and the Challenge of Constructing a Positive Identity. *Academy of Management Review, 24*, 413–434.

Askenazy, P. (2004). Shorter Work Time, Hours Flexibility, and Labor Intensification. *Eastern Economic Journal, 30*(4), 603–614.

Augoustinos, M., Tuffin, K., & Every, D. (2005). New Racism, Meritocracy and Individualism: Constraining Affirmative Action in Education. *Discourse & Society, 16*, 315–340.

Austin, J. L. (1962). *How To Do Things With Words.* Cambridge, MA: Harvard University Press.

Austin, S., & Prilleltensky, I. (2001). Contemporary Debates in Critical Psychology: Dialectics and Synthesis. *Australian Psychologist, 36*(1), 75–80.

Ayres, J., Cole, R., Hein, C., Huntington, S., Kobberdahl, W., Leonard, W., & Zetocha, D. (1990). *Take Charge: Economic Development in Small Communities. Empowerment for Rural Communities for the 1990s.* North Central Regional Center for Rural Development, Ames, IA.

Bagdikian, B. H. (1997). *The Media Monopoly* (5th edn). Boston, MA: Beacon Press.

Baier, K. (1973). The Concept of Value. In E. Laszlo and J. B. Wilbur (Eds.), *Value Theory in Philosophy and Social Science* (pp. 1–11). New York: Oxford University Press.

Bakan, D. (1966). *The Duality of Human Existence: An Essay on Psychology and Religion.* Chicago: Rand McNally.

Bakan, D. (1967). Idolatry in Religion and Science. In D. Bakan (Ed.), *On Method: Toward a Reconstruction of Psychological Investigation* (pp. 150–159). San Francisco, CA: Jossey-Bass. (Original work published 1961.)

Baker, T., & Wang, C. (2006). Photovoice: Use of a Participatory Action Research Method to Explore the Chronic Pain Experience in Older Adults. *Qualitative Health Research, 16,* 1405–1413.

Bakunin, M. (1974). *Michael Bakunin: Selected Writings.* New York: Grove.

Bandura, A. (1986). *Social Foundations of Thought and Action.* Englewood Cliffs, NJ: Prentice Hall.

Barclay, H. (1982). *People Without Government: An Anthropology of Anarchism.* London: Kahn & Averill.

Baritz, L. (1974). *The Servants of Power: A History of the Use of Social Science in American Industry.* Greenwood, IL: Greenwood Press.

Barley, S. R., & Knight, D. B. (1992). Toward a Cultural Theory of Stress Complaints. *Research in Organizational Behavior, 14,* 1–48.

Barnes, A. (Ed.). (2006). *Handbook of Women, Psychology, and the Law.* San Francisco, CA: Jossey-Bass.

Barnes, C. (1998). The Social Model of Disability: A Sociological Phenomenon Ignored By Sociologists? In T. Shakespeare (Ed.), *The Disability Reader: Social Science Perspectives* (pp. 65–78). London: Cassell.

Barnes, C., Mercer, M., & Shakespeare, T. (1999). *Exploring Disability: A Sociological Introduction.* Cambridge: Polity Press.

Barr, R. G., Hopkins, B., & Green, J. A. (Eds.). (2000). *Crying as a Sign, Symptom, and A Signal: Clinical, Emotional and Developmental Aspects of Infant and Toddler Crying.* London: Mackeith Press.

Barratt, B. B. (1993). *Psychoanalysis and the Postmodern Impulse: Knowing and Being since Freud's Psychology.* Baltimore: Johns Hopkins University Press.

Barrington, J. M., & Beaglehole, T. H. (1974). *Maori Schools in a Changing Society: An Historical Review.* Wellington: New Zealand Council for Education Research.

Barry, B. (2005). *Why Social Justice Matters.* Malden, MA: Polity.

Bartlett, F. H. (1938). *Sigmund Freud: A Marxian Essay.* London: Victor Gollancz.

Bartlett, K., & Kennedy, R. (1991). Introduction. In K. Bartlett and R. Kennedy (Eds.), *Feminist Legal Theory* (pp. 1–11). Oxford: Westview Press.

Bartol, C. R., & Bartol, A. M. (2006). History of Forensic Psychology. In I. B. Weiner and A. K. Hess (Eds.), *Handbook of Forensic Psychology* (pp. 1–27). Hoboken, NJ: Wiley.

Barton, L. (1998). Sociology, Disability Studies and Education: Some Observations. In T. Shakespere (Ed.), *The Disability Reader: Social Science Perspectives* (pp. 53–64). London: Cassell.

Barton, S. (1994). Chaos, Self-Organization, and Psychology. *American Psychologist, 49,* 5–14.

Bassman, R. (2007). *A Fight To Be: A Psychologist's Experience From both Sides of the Locked Door.* Albany, NY: Tantamount Press.

Bateson, G. (1972). *Steps to an Ecology of the Mind.* New York: Dutton.

Bayer, B., & Malone, K. R. (1998). Feminism, Psychology and Matters of the Body. In H. J. Stam (Ed.), *The Body and Psychology* (pp. 94–199). London: Sage.

Bayoumi, M., & Rubin, A. (Eds.). (2000). *The Edward Said Reader.* London: Granta.

Becker, D., & Lamb, S. (1994). Sex Bias in the Diagnosis of Borderline Personality Disorder and Posttraumatic Stress Disorder. *Professional Psychology: Research and Practice, 25,* 55–61.

Becker, H. (2006). Measuring Health Among People With Disabilities. *Family & Community Health, 29*(1), 70S–77S.

Beggs, G. (1995). Novel Expert Evidence In Federal Civil Rights Litigation. *American University Law Review, 45*(2), 1–65.

Belfield, C., & Levin, H. (Eds.). (2007). *The Price We Pay: Economic and Social Consequences of Inadequate Education.* Washington, DC: Brookings Institution.

Belle, D., & Doucet, J. (2003). Poverty, Inequality, and Discrimination as Sources of Depression Among US Women. *Psychology of Women Quarterly, 27,* 101–113.

Beneke, E. (1845). *Lehrbuch der Psychologie als Naturwissenschaft* (Zweite, vermehrte und verbesserte Auflage) [Textbook of Psychology as a Natural Science (2nd expanded and improved edition)]. Berlin: Mittler. (First edition published 1833.)

Benjamin, J. (1988). *The Bonds of Love.* New York: Basic Books.

Benjamin, L. T., & Crouse, E. M. (2002). The American Psychological Association's Response to Brown v. Board of Education. *American Psychologist, 57,* 38–50.

Bennett, M. (2005). *The Purpose of Counselling and Psychotherapy.* London: Palgrave.

Berger, P. L., & Luckman, T. (1966). *The Social Construction of Reality: A Treatise on the Sociology of Knowledge.* Garden City, NY: Anchor.

Beristain, C. Martín (2006). *Humanitarian Aid Work: A Critical Approach.* Philadelphia: University of Pennsylvania Press.

Berkowitz, L. (1999). Evil is More than Banal: Situationism and the Concept of Evil. *Personality and Social Psychology Review, 3*(3), 246–253.

Bernard, M., & Scharf, T. S. (2007). Critical Perspectives on Ageing Societies. In M. Bernard and T. S. Scharf (Eds.), *Critical Perspectives on Ageing Societies* (pp. 3–12). Bristol: Policy Press.

Bernstein, M. D., & Russo, N. F. (1974). The History of Psychology Revisited: Or, Up With Our Foremothers. *American Psychologist, 29,* 130–134.

Berscheid, E. (2004). The Greening of Relationship Science. In H. Reis and C. Rusbult (Eds.), *Close Relationships* (pp. 25–34). New York: Psychology Press.

Bersoff, D. N., Goodman-Delahunty, J., Grisso, J. T., Hans, V. P., Poythress, N. G., & Roesch, R. G. (1997). Traning in Law and Psychology. *American Psychologist, 52,* 1301–1310.

Best, S., & Kellner, D. (1997). *Postmodern Theory: Critical Interrogations.* New York: Guilford.

Bhagat, R. S. (1983). Effects of Stressful Life Events on Individual Performance Effectiveness and Work Adjustment Processes Within Organizational Settings: A Research Model. *Academy of Management Review, 8,* 660–671.

Billig, M. (1976). *Social Psychology and Intergroup Relations.* Oxford: Basil Blackwell.

Billig, M. (1988). The Notion of 'Prejudice': Some Rhetorical and Ideological Aspects. *Text, 8,* 91–111.

Billig, M. (1991). *Ideology and Opinions.* London: Sage.

Billig, M. (1995). *Banal Nationalism.* London: Sage.

Billig, M., Condor, S., Edwards, C., Gane, M., Middleton, D., & Radley, A. (1989). *Ideological Dilemmas.* London: Sage.

Birdsall, N., & Sabot, R. (1994). Inequality as a Constraint on Growth in Latin America. *Development Policy, Inter-American Development Bank, 3*(3), 1–5. Reprinted in M. A. Seligson and J. T. Passé-Smith (Eds.), (1993–2003). *Development and Underdevelopment: The Political Economy of Global Inequality* (pp. 448–456). Boulder, CO & London: Lynne Reinner.

Birnbaum, M. (1969). A Rationale for the Right. In D. S. Burris (Ed.), *The Right to Treatment* (pp. 77–106). New York: Springer.

Birnbaum, M. (1974). The Right to Treatment: Some Comments on its Development. In F. J. Ayd (Ed.), *Medical, Moral and Legal Issues in Mental Health Care* (pp. 97–141). Baltimore: Williams and Wilkins.

Black, R., & Huygens, I. (2007). Pakeha Culture and Psychology. In I. Evans, J. Rucklidge and M. O'Driscoll (Eds.), *Professional Practice of Psychology in Aotearoa New Zealand* (pp. 49–66). Wellington: New Zealand Psychological Society.

Blaikie, N. (2000). *Designing Social Research.* Cambridge, UK: Polity Press.

Boal, A. (1992). *Games for Actors and Non-Actors* (revised 2002). London: Routledge.

Bohan, J. S. (1997). Regarding Gender: Essentialism, Constructionism and Feminist Psychology. In M. Gergen and S. N. Davis (Eds.), *Toward a New Psychology of Gender: A Reader* (pp. 31–47). New York: Routledge.

Bohm, D. (1996). *On Dialogue.* London: Routledge.

Bond, M. (1999). Gender, Race, and Class in Organizational Contexts. *American Journal of Community Psychology, 27,* 327–356.

Bond, M. A., & Keys, C. B. (1993). Empowerment, Diversity and Collaboration: Promoting Synergy on Community Boards. *American Journal of Community Psychology, 21,* 37–58.

Bornstein, K. (1994). *Gender Outlaw.* New York: Routledge.

Bornstein, K. (1998). *My Gender Workbook: How to Become a Real Man, a Real Woman, the Real You, or Something Else Entirely.* New York: Routledge.

Bourdieu, P. (1986). The Forms of Capital. In J. Richardson (Ed.), *Handbook of Theory and Research for Sociology of Education* (pp. 241–258). New York: Greenwood Press.

Bourdieu, P. (1988). *Outline of a Theory of Practice.* Cambridge: Cambridge University Press.

Boyd, N. M., & Bright, D. S. (2007). Appreciative Inquiry as a Mode of Action Research for Community Psychology. *Journal of Community Psychology, 35,* 1019–1036.

Bracken, P. J., Giller, J. E., & Summerfield, D. (1995). Psychological Responses to War and Atrocity: The Limitations of Current Concepts. *Social Science & Medicine, 40*(8), 1073–1082.

Brahm, E. (2004). Costs of Intractable Conflict. In G. Burgess and H. Burgess (Eds.), *Beyond Intractability.* Conflict Research Consortium, University of Colorado, Boulder. http://www.beyondintractability.org/essay/costs_benefits/.

Bramel, D., & Friend, R. (1981). Hawthorne, the Myth of the Docile Worker, and Class Bias in Psychology. *American Psychologist, 36,* 867–878.

Braun, V., & Kitzinger, C. (2001). Telling it Straight? Dictionary Definitions of Women's Genitals. *Journal of Sociolinguistics, 5,* 214–232.

Breggin, P. R. (1991). *Toxic Psychiatry: Why Therapy, Empathy and Love Must Replace the Drugs, Electroshock, and Biochemical Theories of the 'New Psychiatry'.* New York: St. Martin's Press.

Brewer, N., & Williams, K. D. (Eds.). (2005). *Psychology and Law: An Empirical Perspective.* New York: The Guilford Press.

Briggs, J., & Peat, F. D. (1989). *Turbulent Mirror.* New York: Harper and Row.

Brighouse, H. (2004). *Justice.* Malden, MA: Polity.

Brinkman, S., & Kvale, S. (2008). Ethics in Qualitative Psychological Research. In C. Willig and W. Stainton Rogers (Eds.), *The Sage Handbook of Qualitative Research in Psychology.* London: Sage.

Brion, D. (1993). The Hidden Persistence of Witchcraft. *Law and Critique, 4.*

Brisenden, S. (1998). Independent Living and the Medical Model of Disability. In T. Shakespeare (Ed.), *The Disability Reader: Social Science Perspectives* (pp. 20–27). London: Cassell.

Brock, A. (1993). Something Old, Something New: The 'Reappraisal' of Wilhelm Wundt in Textbooks. *Theory & Psychology, 3,* 235–242.

Brock, A. C. (Ed.). (2006). *Internationalizing the History of Psychology.* New York: New York University Press.

Brohman, J. (1996). *Popular Development: Rethinking the Theory and Practice of Development.* Oxford & Cambridge: Blackwell.

Brooks-Harris, J. (2008). *Integrative Multitheoretical Psychotherapy.* New York: Houghton Mifflin.

Broughton, J. (1986). The Psychology, History and Ideology of the Self. In K. Larsen (Ed.), *Dialectics and Ideology in Psychology* (pp. 128–164). Norwood, NJ: Ablex.

Brown, D. (2001). *Bury my Heart at Wounded Knee: An Indian History of the American West.* New York: Holt Paperbacks.

Brown, L. S. (1994). *Subversive Dialogues: Theory in Feminist Therapy.* New York: Basic Books.

Brown, P. (Ed.). (1973). *Radical Psychology.* New York: Harper.

Brown, S. D. (2001). Psychology and the Art of Living. *Theory and Psychology, 11,* 171–192.

Bruner, J. (1957). On Perceptual Readiness. *Psychological Review, 64,* 123–152.

Bruner, J. (1973). *Going Beyond the Information Given.* New York: Norton.

Brydon-Miller, M. (2004). Using Participatory Action Research to Address Community Health Issues. In M. Murray (Ed.), *Critical Health Psychology* (pp. 187–202). London: Palgrave.

Bucheli, M. (2006). *Good Dictator, Bad Dictator: United Fruit Company and Economic Nationalism in Central America in the Twentieth Century.* University of Illinois at Urbana-Champaign, College of Business Working Papers Series. Working Paper No. 06–0115.

Bullock, H. E. (1995). Class Acts: Middle Class Responses to the Poor. In B. Lott and D. Maluso (Eds.), *The Social Psychology of Interpersonal Discrimination* (pp. 118–159). New York: Guilford Press.

Bullock, H. E., Williams, W. R., & Limbert, W. M. (2003). Predicting Support For Welfare Policies: The Impact of Attributions and Beliefs About Inequality. *Journal of Poverty, 7,* 35–56.

Burke, W. W. (1994). *Organization Development: A Process of Learning and Changing* (2nd ed.). Reading, MA: Addison-Wasley.

Burke, W. W. (2002). *Organization Change: Theory and Practice.* Thousand Oaks, CA: Sage Publications.

Burr, V. (1998). *Gender and Social Psychology.* London: Routledge.

Burr, V. (2003). *Social Constructionism* (2nd edn). London: Psychology Press.

Burton, M., Boyle, S., Harris, C., & Kagan, C. (2007). Community Psychology in Britain. In S. Reich, M. Riemer, I. Prilleltensky, and M. Montero (Eds.), *International Community Psychology: History and Theories* (pp. 219–237). New York: Kluwer/Springer Academic.

Busfield, J. (2006). Pills, Power, People: Sociological Understandings of the Pharmaceutical Industry. *Sociology, 40,* 297–314.

Butler, J. (1990). *Gender Trouble: Feminism and the Subversion of Identity.* New York: Routledge.

Buttny, R (1993). *Social Accountability in Communication.* London: Sage.

Butz, M. (1994). Psychopharmacology: Psychology's *Jurassic Park. Psychotherapy, 31,* 692–698.

Butz, M. (1997). *Chaos and Complexity: Implications for Psychological Theory and Practice.* Bristol, PA: Taylor and Francis.

Buvinic, M. (1997). Women In Poverty: A New Global Underclass. *Foreign Policy, 108,* 38–53.

Camhi, L. (1993). Stealing Femininity: Department Store Kleptomania as Sexual Disorder. *Differences, 5,* 26–50.

Camic, P. (2008). Health Psychology, the Arts and New Approaches to Health Care. *Journal of Health Psychology, 13,* 287–298.

Campbell, C., & Murray, M. (2004). Community Health Psychology: Promoting Analysis and Action for Social Change. *Journal of Health Psychology, 9,* 187–195.

Campos, P., Saguy, A., Ernsberger, P., Oliver, E., & Gaesser, G. (2006). The Epidemiology of Overweight and Obesity: Public Health Crisis or Moral Panic? *International Journal of Epidemiology, 35,* 55–60.

Capshew, J. H. (1999). *Psychologists on the March: Science, Practice, and Professional Identity in America, 1929–1969.* Cambridge: Cambridge University Press.

Carasso, A., Reynolds, G., & Steurle (n.d.). *How Much Does the Federal Government Spend to Promote Economic Mobility and for Whom?* Washington, DC: Economic

Mobility Project. Available: http://www.economicmobility.org/assets/pdfs/EMP_ Mobilty_Budget.pdf.

Carmack, R. M. (Ed.). (1988). *Harvest of Violence: The Maya Indians and the Guatemalan Crisis*. Norman, OK: University of Oklahoma Press.

Carr, S. C., & Sloan, T. (Eds.). (2003). *Poverty and Psychology: From Global Perspective to Local Practice*. New York: Kluwer Academic/Plenum.

Carr, S., McAuliffe, E., & MacLachlan, M. (1998). *Psychology of Aid*. London: Routledge.

Cattell, J. M. (1895). Measurements of the Accuracy of Recollection. *Science, 2,* 761–766.

CEH [Commission for Historical Clarification] (1999). *Guatemala: Memory of Silence. Report of the Commission for Historical Clarification*. Accessed 10 May 2005 from http://shr.aaas.org/guatemala/ceh/report/english/recs1.html.

Center on Budget and Policy Priorities. (2006). *Buying Power of Minimum Wage at 51 Year Low: Congress Could Break Record for Longest Period Without an Increase*. Available: http://www.cbpp.org/6-20-06mw.htm, accessed 20 June.

Chamberlain, K., Stephens, C., & Lyons, A. (1997). Encompassing Experience: Meanings and Methods in Health Psychology. *Psychology & Health, 12,* 691–709.

Chamberlain, L. L. (1994). Future Adventures in Psychology's *Jurassic Park*: The Issue of Psychopharmacology. *Psychotherapy Bulletin, 29,* 47–50.

Chappelle, W., & Lumley, V. (2006). Outpatient Mental Health Care at a Remote U.S. Air Base in Southern Iraq. *Professional Psychology, 37,* 523–530.

Chaskin, R. J., Brown, P., Venkatesh, S., & Vidal, A. (2001). *Building Community Capacity*. New York: Aldine de Gruyter.

Chatman, J. (1991). Matching People and Organizations: Selection and Socialization in Public Accounting Firms. *Administrative Science Quarterly, 36,* 459–484.

Chavis, D. M., & Wolff, T. (1993). *Public Hearing – Community Psychology's Failed Commitment to Social Change: Ten Demandments For Action*. Public meeting held at the biennial conference of the Society for Community Research and Action, Williamsburg, Virginia, June.

Cherry, F. (1995). *The 'Stubborn Particulars' of Social Psychology: Essays on the Research Process*. London: Routledge.

Cherry, F. (2004). Kenneth B. Clark and Social Psychology's Other History. In G. Philogene (Ed.), *Racial Identity in Context: The Legacy of Kenneth B. Clark* (pp. 13–33). Washington, DC: American Psychological Association.

Cherry, F. (2007). *The Peregrinations of Paired Testing: A Brief History*. Paper presented at the First joint meeting of Cheiron and ESSHS, 25 June – 29 July, Dublin, Ireland.

Cherry, F., & Borshuk, C. (1998). Social Action Research and the Commission on Community Interrelations. *Journal of Social Issues, 54,* 119–142.

Cherry, F., Byrne, D., & Mitchell, H. E. (1976). Clogs in the Bogus Pipeline: Demand Characteristics and Social Desirability. *Journal of Research in Personality, 10,* 69–75.

Cherry, F., Mitchell, H. E., & Nelson, D. A. (1973). Helping or Hurting? The Aggression Paradigm. *Proceedings of the 81st Annual Convention, American Psychological Association,* 117–118.

Chesler, P. (1972). *Women and Madness*. Garden City, NY: Doubleday.

Chetovich, C., & Kunreuther, F. (2006). *From the Ground Up: Grassroots Organizations Making Social Change*. Ithaca, NY: Cornell University Press.

Chiang, H. H. (2007). *Effecting Science, Affecting Medicine: Homosexuality, the Kinsey Reports, and the Contested Boundaries of Psychopathology in the United States, 1948–1965*. Unpublished manuscript [winner of John C. Burnham Early Career Award, Forum for the History of the Human Sciences].

Chicuecue, N. M. (1997). Reconciliation: The Role of Truth Commissions and Alternative Ways of Healing. *Development in Practice, 7*(4).

Chin, R., & Benne, K. D. (1985). General Strategies for Effecting Change in Human Systems. In W. G. Bennis, K. D. Benne and R. Chin (Eds.), *The Planning of Change* (4th edn) (pp. 22–43). New York: Rinehart & Winston.

Cienfuegos, A. J., & Monelli, C. (1983). The Testimony of Political Repression as a Therapeutic Instrument. *American Journal of Orthopsychiatry, 53*(1), 43–51.

Cigno, A., Rosati, F. C., & Tzannatos, Z. (2001). *Handbook of Child Labor.* Washington, DC: The World Bank.

Citizens Commission on Human Rights International (Producer) (2006). *Psychiatry: Industry of Death* [motion picture]. Los Angeles, CA: Citizens Commission on Human Rights International.

Ciulla, J. B. (2000). *The Working Life: The Promise and Betrayal of Modern Work.* New York: Times Books.

Clark, K. B. (1953). Desegregation: An Appraisal of the Evidence. *Journal of Social Issues, 9,* 1–77.

Clarke, V. (2007). Man Not Included? A Critical Psychology Analysis of Lesbian Families and Male Influences in Child Rearing. *Journal of GLBT Family Studies: Innovations in Theory, Research and Practice, 3*(4), 309–349.

Clarke, V. (2008). From Outsiders to Motherhood to Reinventing the Family: Constructions of Lesbians as Parents in the Psychological Literature – 1886–2006. *Women's Studies International Forum, 31,* 118–128.

Clarke, V. & Peel, E. (Eds.). (2007). *Out in Psychology: Lesbian, Gay, Bisexual, Trans and Queer Perspectives.* Chichester: Wiley.

Class: But Did They Buy Their Own Furniture? (2006). *The Economist,* 12 August, *380*(8490), 46–47.

Clawson, R. A., & Trice, R. (2000). Poverty As We Know It: Media Portrayals of the Poor. *Public Opinion Quarterly, 64,* 53–64.

Cockburn, C. (1998). *The Space between Us: Negotiating Gender and National Identities in Conflict.* London: Zed Books.

Cohen, C., & Timimi, S. (Eds.). (2008). *Liberatory Psychiatry.* New York: Cambridge University Press.

Cohen, D., & McCubbin, M. (1990). The Political Economy of Tardive Dyskinesia: Asymmetries in Power and Responsibility. *Journal of Mind and Behavior, 11,* 465–488.

Cohen, J., Marecek, J., & Gillham, J. (2006). Is Three a Crowd? Clinicians, Clients, and Managed Care. *American Journal of Orthopsychiatry, 76,* 251–259.

Coker, D. (2001). Crime Control and Feminist Law Reform in Domestic Violence Law. *Buffalo Criminal Law Review, 4,* 801–841.

Colfax, J. D., & Roach, J. L. (Eds.). (1971). *Radical Sociology.* New York: Basic Books.

Collins English Dictionary. (1994). Glasgow: HarperCollins.

Condor, S., Figgou, L., Abell, J., Gibson, S., & Stevenson, C. (2006). 'They're Not Racist …' Prejudice Denial, Mitigation and Suppression in Dialogue. *British Journal of Social Psychology, 45,* 441–462.

Conrad, P. (1992). Medicalization and Social Control. *Annual Review of Sociology, 18,* 209–232.

Conrad, P. (2007). *The Medicalization of Society: On the Transformation of Human Conditions into Treatable Disorders.* Baltimore, MD: Johns Hopkins University Press.

Cooke, B. & Kothari, U. (Eds.). (2001). *Participation: The New Tyranny?* London and New York: Zed Books.

Cooke, B. Mills, A., & Kelly, E. (2005). Situating Maslow in Cold War America: A Recontextualisation of Management Theory. *Group and Organization Management, 30*(2), 129–152.

Coontz, S. (2006). *Marriage, a History: How Love Conquered Marriage.* New York: Penguin.

Cooper, C. L., & Marshall, J. (1976). Occupational Sources of Stress: Review of Literature Relating to Coronary Heart Disease and Mental Ill Health. *Journal of Occupational Psychology, 49,* 11–28.

Cormier, C., & Cormier, W. (1997). *Interviewing Strategies for Helpers: Fundamental Skills and Cognitive Behavioral Interventions.* New York: Brooks/Cole.

Cornish, F. (2006). Challenging the Stigma of Sex Work in India: Material Context and Symbolic Change. *Journal of Community & Applied Social Psychology, 16,* 462–471.

Cornwall, A. (2000). Making a Difference? Gender and Participatory Development. *IDS Discussion Paper 378.*

Cornwall, A. (2007). *Pathways of Women's Empowerment.* openDemocracy. Accesssed 4 April from http://www.opendemocracy.net/node/34188/print.

Cosgrove, L., Krimsky, S., Vijayaraghavana, S., & Schneider, L. (2006). Financial Ties between DSM-IV Panel Members and the Pharmaceutical Industry. *Psychotherapy and Psychosomatics, 75,* 154–160.

Costa, P. T., & McCrae, R. R. (2006). Age Changes in Personality and Their Origins: Comment on Roberts, Walton, and Viechtbauer (2006). *Psychological Bulletin, 132*(1), 26–28.

Costanzo, M. (2004). *Psychology Applied to Law.* Belmont, CA: Wadsworth.

Cowen, E. L. (1985). Person-Centered Approaches to Primary Prevention in Mental Health: Situation-Focused and Competence Enhancement. *American Journal of Community Psychology, 13,* 31–48.

Cowen, E. L. (1991). In Pursuit of Wellness. *American Psychologist, 46,* 404–408.

Cozzarelli, C. A., Wilkinson, A. V., & Tagler, M. J. (2001). Attitudes toward the Poor and Attributions for Poverty. *Journal of Social Issues, 57,* 207–227.

Crawford, R. (1980). Healthism and the Medicalization of Everyday Life. *International Journal of Health Services, 10,* 365–388.

Crawford, R. (2006). Health as a Meaningful Social Practice. *Health: An Interdisciplinary Journal for the Social Study of Health, Illness and Medicine, 10,* 401–420.

Crosby, D. A. (1988). *The Specter of the Absurd: Sources and Criticisms of Modern Nihilism.* Albany, NY: SUNY Press.

Crosby, F. J., Aarti, I., Clayton, S., & Downing, R. A. (2003). Affirmative Action: Psychological Data and the Policy Debates. *American Psychologist, 58*(2), 93–115.

Crossley, M. (2000). *Rethinking Health Psychology.* Buckingham, UK: Open University Press.

Crossley, M. (2001). Do We Need to Rethink Health Psychology? *Psychology, Health & Medicine, 6,* 243–255.

Crow, L. (1996). Including All of Our Lives: Renewing the Social Model of Disability. In J. Morris (Ed.), *Encounters with Strangers: Feminism and Disability* (pp. 206–226). London: The Women's Press.

Culler, J. (1997). *Literary Theory: A Very Short Introduction.* Oxford: Oxford University Press.

Cupchik, W. (1997). *Why Honest People Shoplift or Commit Other Acts of Theft.* Toronto: W. Cupchik.

Curle, A. (1971). *Making Peace.* London: Tavistock Publications.

Curt, B. (1994). *Textuality and Tectonics: The Troubling of Social and Psychological Science.* Buckingham, UK: Open University Press.

Curti, M. W. (1926). The New Lombrosianism. *Journal of Criminal Law and Criminology, 17,* 246–253.

Cushman, P. (1995). *Constructing the Self, Constructing America: A Cultural History of Psychotherapy.* New York: Addison-Wesley.

Cushman, P., & Gilford, P. (2000). Will Managed Care Change Our Way of Being? *American Psychologist, 55,* 985–996.

Dafermos, D., Marvakis, A., & Triliva, S. (Eds.). (2006). Critical Psychology in a Changing World: Contributions from Different Geo-Political Regions. *Annual Review of Critical Psychology, 5* [Special issue]. Available from: http://www.discourseunit.com/arcp/5.htm

Dallaire, B., McCubbin, M., Morin, P., & Cohen, D. (2000). Civil Commitment Due to Mental Illness and Dangerousness: The Union of Law and Psychiatry Within A Treatment-Control System. *Sociology of Health and Illness, 22,* 679–699.

Danziger, K. (1985). The Methodological Imperative in Psychology. *Philosophy of the Social Sciences, 15,* 1–13.

Danziger, K. (1990). *Constructing the Subject: Historical Origins of Psychological Research.* Cambridge, MA: Cambridge University Press.

Danziger, K. (1992). The Project of an Experimental Social Psychology: Historical Perspectives. *Science in Context, 5,* 309–328.

Danziger, K. (1997). *Naming the Mind: How Psychology Found Its Language.* London, UK: Sage.

Davies, M. F. (1997). Belief Persistence after Evidential Discrediting: The Impact of Generated Versus Provided Explanation on the Likelihood of Discredited Outcomes. *Journal of Experimental Social Psychology, 33,* 561–578.

Davis, G. F., McAdam, D. W., Scott, R., & Zald, M. N. (Eds.). (2005). *Social Movements and Organization Theory.* New York: Cambridge University Press.

Davis, S. N., & Gergen, M. (1997). Toward a New Psychology of Gender: Opening Conversations. In M. Gergen and S. N. Davis (Eds.), *Toward a New Psychology of Gender: A Reader* (pp. 1–27). New York: Routledge.

Davison, B. (1992). Columbus: The Bones and Blood of Racism. *Race & Class: Journal for Black and Third World Liberation, 33*(3), 17–25.

De Koning, K., & Martin, M. (1996). *Participatory Research in Health: Issues and Experiences.* Johannesburg: Zed Books Ltd.

Debbink, G., & Ornelas, A. (1997). Cows for Campesinos. In S. E. Smith, D. G. Willms, and N. A. Johnson (Eds.), *Nurtured by Knowledge: Learning to do Participatory Action Research* (pp. 13–33). New York: The Apex Press.

Dehue, T. (1995). *Changing the Rules: Psychology in the Netherlands, 1900–1985.* Cambridge, UK: Cambridge University Press.

Delpeche, H., Jabbar-Bey, R., Sherif, B., Tailafero, J., & Wilder, M. (2003). *Community Development and Family Support: Forging a Practical Nexus to Strengthen Families and Communities.* Newark, DE: Center for community Research and Services.

Denzin, N. (2003). *Performance Ethnography: Critical Pedagogy and the Politics of Culture.* Thousand Oaks, CA: Sage.

Desjarlais, R., Eisenberg, L., Good, B., & Kleinman, A. (1995). *World Mental Health: Problems and Priorities in Low-Income Countries.* New York: Oxford University Press.

Dickason, O. P. (1999). Iron Men, True Men, and the Art of Treaty Making. In D. B. Knight and A. E. Joseph (Eds.), *Restructuring Societies: Insights From the Social Sciences* (pp. 105–122). Ottawa: Carleton University Press.

Dijkers, M. (1999). Correlates of Life Satisfaction Among Persons with Spinal Cord Injuries. *Archives of Physical Medicine and Rehabilitation, 80,* 867–876.

Dilthey, W. (1976). *Selected Writings* (edited, translated, and introduced by H. P. Rickman). Cambridge, MA: Cambridge University Press.

Dimock, H. (1992). *Intervention and Empowerment: Helping Organizations Change.* Concord, Ontario: Captus Press.

Dissanayake, E. (2007). What Art Is and What Art Does: An Overview of Contemporary Evolutionary Hypotheses. In C. Martindale, P. Locher, and V. M. Petrov (Eds.), *Evolutionary and Neurocognitive Approaches to Aesthetics, Creativity and the Arts.* Amityville, NY: Baywood.

Dixon, J. (2006). *Schelling's Checkboard Revisited: The Contact Hypothesis and the Social Psychology of 'Preferential Segregation'*. Keynote Address at the Contact50 conference, Itala, KwaZulu-Natal, South Africa.

Dohoghue, T. (2004, August 25). Maori Strike Gold in Marine Farms. *The Independent*, 1–2.

Dohwenrend, B. P. (1998). *Adversity, Stress, and Psychopathology*. New York, Oxford: Oxford University Press.

Donaldson, L. (1992). The Weick Stuff: Managing Beyond Games. *Organization Science, 3*, 461–466.

Dovidio, J. F., Gaertner, S. L., & Validzic, A. (1998). Intergroup Bias: Status, Differentiation, and a Common In-Group Identity. *Journal of Personality and Social Psychology, 75,* 109–120.

Dreier, O. (2007). *Psychotherapy in Everyday Life*. Cambridge, MA: Cambridge University Press.

Dryden, C. (1999) *Being Married, Doing Gender: A Critical Analysis of Gender Relationships in Marriage*. London: Routledge.

Dunn, D. (2000). Some Social Psychological Issues in Disability. In R. G. Frank and T. R. Elliot (Eds.), *Handbook of Rehabilitation Psychology* (pp. 565–584). Washington, DC: American Psychological Association.

Dunn, D., & Dougherty, S. (2005). Prospects for a Positive Psychology of Rehabilitation. *Rehabilitation Psychology, 50*(3), 305–311.

Dunn, D., & Elliot, T. (2005). Revisiting a Constructivist Classic: Wright's *Physical Disability: A Psychosocial Approach. Rehabilitation Psychology, 50*(2), 183–189.

Durlak, J. A., Taylor, R. D., Kawashima, K., Pachan, M. K., DuPre, E. P., Celio, C. I., Berger, S. R., Dymnicki, A. B., & Weissberg, R. P. (2007). Effects of Positive Youth Development Programs on School, Family, and Community Systems. *American Journal of Community Psychology, 39,* 269–286.

Durrheim, K. (under review). Stereotyping by Implication: The Discourse of Implicit Stereotyping. *British Journal of Social Psychology*.

Durrheim, K., & Dixon, J. (2005a). *Racial Encounter: The Social Psychology of Contact and Desegregation*. London: Routledge.

Durrheim, K., & Dixon, J. (2005b). Studying Talk and Embodied Practices: Toward A Psychology of Materiality of 'Race Relations'. *Journal of Community & Applied Social Psychology, 15*, 446–460.

Eagle, G. T. (1990). Promoting Peace by Integrating Western and Indigenous Healing in Treating Trauma. *Peace and Conflict: Journal of Peace Psychology, 4*(3).

Earnest, W. R. (1992). Ideology Criticism and Interview Research. In G. C. Rosenwald and R. L. Ochberg (Eds.), *Storied Lives* (pp. 250–264). New Haven: Yale University Press.

Eberstadt, M. (2008). Why Ritalin Rules. In R. Heiner (Ed.), *Deviance Across Cultures* (pp. 158–165*)*. New York: Oxford University Press.

Economic Policy Institute (2006). *Wealth Flows to the Wealthiest as the Percentage of Americans Who Own Stock Fall*. Available from: http://www.epi.org/newsroom/releases/2006/08/SWApr-wealth-200608-final.pdf, accessed 29 August.

Ecumenical Women's Team Visit. (1992). *Rape of Women in War*. Geneva: Author.

Edwards, D. (1994). Script Formulations: An Analysis of Event Descriptions in Conversation. *Journal of Language and Social Problems, 13*, 211–247.

Edwards, D. (1997). *Discourse and Cognition*. London: Sage.

Edwards, D. (1999). Emotion Discourse. *Culture and Psychology, 5*, 271–291.

Edwards, D. (2004). Shared Knowledge as a Performative Category in Conversation. *Rivista Italiana di Psicolinguistica Applicata (RiPLA), 4*(2), 41–53. Special Issue edited by A. Fasulo & R. Galatolo, 'L'analisi del parlato in interazione.'

Edwards, D. (2007). Managing Subjectivity in Talk. In A. Hepburn and S. Wiggins (Eds.), *Discursive Research in Practice: New Approaches to Psychology and Interaction* (pp. 31–49). Cambridge: Cambridge University Press.

Edwards, D., Ashmore, M., & Potter, J. (1993). *Death and Furniture: The Rhetoric, Theory and Politics of Bottom Line Arguments Against Relativism.* Mimeograph, Discourse and Rhetoric Group, Loughborough University.

Edwards, D., & Potter, J. (1992). *Discursive Psychology.* London: Sage.

Edwards, P. K. (1992). Industrial Conflict: Themes and Issues in Recent Research. *British Journal of Industrial Relations, 30*, 361–404.

Eichler, M. (2007). *Consensus Organizing: Building Communities of Mutual Self Interest.* Thousand Oaks, CA: Sage Publications.

Ekman, P. (1982). *Emotion in the Human Face.* Cambridge: Cambridge University Press.

Elliot, T., Kurylo, M., & Rivera, P. (2002). Positive Growth Following Acquired Physical Disability. In R. C. Snyder and S. J. Lopez (Eds.), *Handbook of Positive Psychology* (pp. 687–699). New York: Oxford University Press.

Elliot, T., & Warren, A. M. (2007). Why Psychology is Important in Rehabilitation. In P. Kennedy (Ed.), *Psychological Management of Physical Disabilities: A Practitioner's Guide.* New York: Routledge.

Elliott, A. (1992). *Social Theory and Psychoanalysis in Transition.* Oxford: Basil Blackwell.

Engel, G. L. (1977). The Need for a New Medical Model: A Challenge for Biomedicine. *Science, 196,* 129–136.

Entman, R. M. (1995). Television, Democratic Theory and the Visual Construction of Poverty. *Research in Political Sociology, 7,* 139–159.

Epp, J. (1988). *Mental Health for Canadians: Striking a Balance.* Ottawa: Minister of Supplies and Services.

Essed, P. (1990). *Everyday Racism.* Claremon, CA: Hunter House.

Evans, G. W., & Kantrowitz, E. (2002). Socioeconomic Status and Health: The Potential Role of Environmental Risk Exposure. *Annual Review of Public Health, 23,* 303–331.

Evans, S. D., Hanlin, C. E., & Prilleltensky, I. (2007). Blending Ameliorative and Transformative Approaches in Human Services: A Case Study. *Journal of Community Psychology, 35*(3), 329–346.

Eyben, R. (2008). *News at IDS – Being Strategic about the Meanings of Women's Empowerment.* Accessed 4 April from http://www.ids.ac.uk/go/about-ids/news-and-commentary/february-2008-news/meanings-of-women-s-empowerment.

Eyerman, R., & Jamison, A. (1991). *Social Movements: A Cognitive Approach.* University Park, PA: Pennsylvania State University Press.

Facione, P. A., Scherer, D., & Attig, T. (1978). *Values and Society: An Introduction to Ethics and Social Philosophy.* Englewood Cliffs, NJ: Prentice Hall.

Falla, R. *(1994). Massacres in the Jungle: Ixcán, Guatemala, 1975–1982* (Julia Howland, Trans.). Boulder, CO: Westview Press.

Fals Borda, O., & Rahman, M. A. (Eds.). (1991). *Action and Knowledge: Breaking the Monopoly with Participatory Action Research.* New York: Apex Press.

Fancher, R. E. (1988). Henry Goddard and the Kallikak Family Photographs: 'Conscious Skulduggery' or 'Whig History'? *American Psychologist, 42,* 585–590.

Farmer, P. (2005). *Pathologies of Power: Health, Human Rights, and the New War on the Poor.* Berkeley, CA: University of California Press.

Farrington, D. B. (1996). *Understanding and Preventing Youth Crime.* York: Joseph Rowntree Foundation/York Publishing Services.

Fay, B. (1987). *Critical Social Science: Liberation and Its Limits.* Ithaca, NY: Cornell University Press.

Feagin, J. R. (1991). The Continuing Significance of Race: Antiblack Discrimination in Public Places. *American Sociological Review, 56,* 101–116.

Feagin, J. R., & Feagin, C. B. (1978). *Discrimination American Style: Institutional Racism and Sexism.* Englewood Cliffs, NJ: Prentice-Hall.

Ferraro, F., Pfeffer, J., & Sutton, R.I. (2005). Economic Language and Assumptions: How Theories Can Become Self-Fulfilling. *Academy of Management Review, 30*(1), 8–24.

Ferrell, J. (1999). Anarchist Criminology and Social Justice. In B. A. Arrigo (Ed.), *Social Justice/Criminal Justice: The Maturation of Critical Theory in Law, Crime, and Deviance* (pp. 93–108). Belmont, CA: West/Wadsworth.

Fine, M. (1989). Coping with Rape: Critical Perspectives on Consciousness. In R. Unger (Ed.), *Representations: Social Constructions of Gender* (pp. 167–179). New York: Baywood Press.

Fine, M., & Torre, M. E. (2004). Re-membering Exclusions: Participatory Action Research in Public Institutions. *Qualitative Research in Psychology, 1*, 15–37.

Fine, M., Torre, M. E., Burns, A., & Paine, Y. A. (2006). Youth Research/Participatory Methods for Reform. In A. D. C.-S. Thiessen (Ed.), *International Handbook of Student Experience In Elementary and Secondary School* (pp. 805–828). New York: Springer.

Fine, M., & Weis, L. (1998). *The Unknown City: The Lives of Poor and Working-Class Young Adults.* Boston, MA: Beacon Press.

Finison, L. J. (1976). Unemployment, Politics, and the History of Organized Psychology. *American Psychologist, 31*, 747–755.

Fisher, A. (2002). *Radical Ecopsychology: Psychology in the Service of Life.* New York: SUNY Press.

Fiske, S., Bersoff, D. N., Borgida, E., Deaux, K., & Heilman, M. (1991). Social Science Research on Trial: Use of Sex Stereotyping Research in Price Waterhouse v. Hopkins. *American Psychologist, 46*(10), 1049–1060.

Flyvbjerg, B. (2001). *Making Social Science Matter: Why Social Inquiry Fails and How It Can Succeed Again.* Cambridge: Cambridge University Press.

For Whosoever Hath, To Him Shall Be Given, and He Shall Have More. (2007). *The Economist, 384*(8541), 11 August, 36.

Foster, D. (1993). On Racism: Virulent Mythologies and Fragile Threads. In L. J. Nicholas (Ed.), *Psychology and Oppression: Critiques and Proposals*. Braamfontein, South Africa: Skotaville.

Foster-Fishman, P. G., Fitzgerald, K., Brandell, C., Nowell, B., Chavis, D., & Van Egeren, L. A. (2006). Mobilizing Residents for Action: The Role of Small Wins and Strategic Supports. *American Journal of Community Psychology*. Special Issue: Exemplars of Community Practice, *38*(3–4), 143–152.

Foster-Fishman, P. G., Nowell, B., & Yang, H. (2007). Putting the System Back Into Systems Change: A Framework for Understanding and Changing Organizational and Community Systems. *American Journal of Community Psychology, 39,* 197–215.

Foucault, M. (1970). *The Order of Things: An Archaeology of the Human Sciences.* London: Tavistock Publications. (Original work published 1966.)

Foucault, M. (1977). *Discipline and Punish: The Birth of the Prison* (A. Sheridan, Trans.). London: Lane. (Original work published 1975.)

Foucault, M. (1978) (French publication: 1976). *The History of Sexuality, Vol. I: An Introduction* (Robert Hurley, Trans.). New York: Pantheon.

Foucault, M. (1980). *Power/Knowledge: Selected Interviews and Other Writings 1972–1977* (C. Gordon, Ed.). New York: Pantheon.

Foucault, M. (1984). What is Enlightenment? In P. Rabinow (Ed.), *The Foucault Reader.* New York: Pantheon.

Foucault, M. (1987). *Mental Illness and Psychology.* Berkeley, CA: University of California Press.

Foucault, M. (2006). *History of Madness* (Histoire de la folie à l'âge classique). New York: Routledge.

Fox, D. R. (1985). Psychology, Ideology, Utopia, and the Commons. *American Psychologist, 40,* 48–58.

Fox, D. R. (1991). Social Science's Limited Role in Resolving Psycholegal Social Problems. *Journal of Offender Rehabilitation, 17,* 117–124.

Fox, D. R. (1993a). The Autonomy-Community Balance and the Equity-Law Distinction: Anarchy's Task for Psychological Jurisprudence. *Behavioral Sciences and the Law, 11,* 97–109.

Fox, D. R. (1993b). Psychological Jurisprudence and Radical Social Change. *American Psychologist, 48,* 234–241.

Fox, D. R. (1996). The Law Says Corporations are Persons, but Psychology Knows Better. *Behavioral Sciences and the Law, 14,* 339–359.

Fox, D. (1997). Psychology and Law: Justice Diverted. In D. Fox and I. Prilleltensky (Eds.), *Critical Psychology: An Introduction* (pp. 217–232). London: Sage.

Fox, D. R. (1999). Psycholegal Scholarship's Contribution to False Consciousness about Injustice. *Law and Human Behavior, 23,* 9–30.

Fox, D. (2000). The Critical Psychology Project: Transforming Society and Transforming Psychology. In T. Sloan (Ed.), *Critical Psychology: Voices for Change.* New York: St. Martin's Press.

Fox, D. R. (2001a). A Critical-Psychology Approach to Law's Legitimacy. *Legal Studies Forum, 25,* 519–538.

Fox, D. (2001b). Organizing Critical Psychologists: The RadPsyNet Experience. *Radical Psychology Journal.* Online at http://www.radpsynet.org/journal/vol2-2/fox.html.

Fox, D. (2002). The Suitability of Political Debate in Psychology. *PsyPAG Quarterly, 45,* 15–18.

Fox, D. R. (2003). Awareness is Good, but Action is Better. *The Counseling Psychologist, 31,* 299–304.

Fox, D. (2005). Towards Transformative Social Interventions. In G. Nelson and I. Prilleltensky (Eds.), *Community Psychology: In Pursuit of Liberation and Well-being.* London: MacMillan.

Fox, D. (2008a). *Academic Objectivity, Political Neutrality, and Other Barriers to Israeli-Palestinian Reconciliation.* Paper presented at the First International Academic Conference, Israeli-Palestinian Conflict: Pathways to Peace, New Britain, Connecticut, March. [http://www.dennisfox.net/papers/objectivity_israel_palestine.html]

Fox, D. (2008b). Confronting Psychology's Power. *Journal of Community Psychology, 36,* 232–237.

Fox, D., & Prilleltensky, I. (Eds.). (1997). *Critical Psychology: An Introduction.* London: Sage.

Fox, D., & Prilleltensky, I. (2002). Wading through Quicksand: Between the Philosophically Desirable and the Psychologically Feasible. *International Journal of Critical Psychology, 6,* 159–167.

Fox, R. W. (1978). *So Far Disordered in Mind: Insanity in California, 1870–1930.* Berkeley, CA: University of California Press.

Frazier, P. A., & Hunt, J. S. (1998). Research on Gender and Law: Where Are We Going, Where Have We Been? *Law and Human Behavior, 22,* 1–16.

Freedman, J., & Combs, G. (1996). *Narrative Therapy: The Social Construction of Preferred Realities.* New York: Norton.

Freire, A. M. A., & Macedo, D. (Eds.). (1998). *The Paulo Freire Reader.* New York: Continuum.

Freire, P. (1970). *Pedagogy of the Oppressed.* New York: Continuum.

Freire, P. (1973). *Education: The Practice of Freedom.* London: Writers and Readers Publishing Cooperative.

Freire, P. (1975). Cultural Action for Freedom. *Harvard Educational Review Monograph, 1.*

Freire, P. (1981). *Education for Critical Consciousness.* New York: Seabury.

Freire, P. (1995). *Pedagogy of Hope: Reliving Pedagogy of the Oppressed.* New York: Continuum.

Freire, P. (1998). *Pedagogy of Freedom: Ethics, Democracy and Civic Courage* (P. Clarke, Trans.). Lanham, MD: Rowman & Littlefield.

French, S. (1993). Disability, Impairment or Something In Between? In J. Swain, V. Finkelstein, S. French and M. Oliver (Eds.), *Disabling Barriers – Enabling Environments* (pp. 17–25). London: Sage Publications.

Freud, S. (1905/1963). *Dora: An Analysis of a Case of Hysteria*. New York: Collier.

Freud, S. (1917) The History of the Psychoanalytic Movement. *Nervous and Mental Disease Monograph Series* (No. 25).

Freud, S. (1965). *The Interpretation of Dreams*. New York: Avon Books. (Originally published in 1900.)

Friedan, B. (1959). *Memo to Madelin, Barbara, Bob, January 26, 1959*. Folder 708, Betty Friedan papers, Schlesinger Library, Harvard University, Cambridge, MA.

Friedan, B. (1963). *The Feminine Mystique*. New York: Norton.

Friedan, B. (n.d.). *A Study of a Sex in Social Mutation*. Folder 505, Betty Friedan papers, Schlesinger Library, Harvard University, Cambridge, MA.

Fromm, E. (1941). *Escape from Freedom*. New York: Avon.

Fromm, E. (1947). *Man for Himself*. New York: Rinehart.

Fromm, E. (1955). *The Sane Society*. New York: Holt Rinehart Winston.

Fromm, E. (1976) *To Have or To Be*. London: Abacus.

Frosh, S., & Young, L. S. (2008). Psychoanalytic Approaches to Qualitative Psychology. In C. Willig and W. Stainton Rogers (Eds.), *The Sage Handbook of Qualitative Research in Psychology*. London: Sage.

Fulcher, M., Sutfin, E. L., & Patterson, C. J. (2008) Individual Differences in Gender Development: Associations with Parental Sexual Orientation, Attitudes, and Division of Labor. *Sex Roles, 58*(5/6), 330–341.

Furumoto, L. (1989). The New History of Psychology. In I. S. Cohen (Ed.), *The G. Stanley Hall Lecture Series*, v. 9 (pp. 5–34). Washington, DC: American Psychological Association.

Galbraith, J. K. (1983). *The Anatomy of Power*. Boston, MA: Houghton Mifflin.

Garfinkel, H. (1967). *Studies in Ethnomethodology*. Cambridge: Polity Press.

Gavey, N. (1989). Feminist Poststructuralism and Discourse Analysis: Contributions to Feminist Psychology. *Psychology of Women Quarterly, 13*, 459–475.

Gavey, N., & McPhillips, K. (1999). Subject to Romance: Heterosexual Passivity as an Obstacle to Women Initiating Condom Use. *Psychology of Women Quarterly, 23*(2), 349–367.

Gazzaniga, M. S. (2005). *The Ethical Brain*. Washington, DC: The Dana Foundation.

Geary, D. C. (1998). *Male, Female: The Evolution of Human Sex Differences*. Washington, DC: American Psychological Association.

Geertz, C. (1973). *The Interpretation of Cultures*. Basic Books.

Gergen, K. (1973). Social Psychology as History. *Journal of Personality and Social Psychology, 26*, 309–320.

Gergen, K. (1985). The Social Constructionist Movement in Modern Psychology. *American Psychologist, 40*(3), 266–275.

Gilens, M. (1996). Race and Poverty in America: Public Misperceptions and the American News Media. *Public Opinion Quarterly, 60*, 515–541.

Giles, W., de Alwis, M., Klein, E., & Silva, N. (Eds.). (2003). *Feminists Under Fire: Exchanges Across War Zones*. Toronto, Ontario, Canada: Between the Lines Books.

Gill, C. (2001). Divided Understandings: The Social Experience of Disability. In G. Albrecht, K. Seelman, and M. Bury (Eds.), *Handbook of Disability Studies* (pp. 351–372). New York: Sage.

Gill, C., Kewman, D., & Brannon, R. (2003). Transforming Psychological Practice and Society: Policies that Reflect the New Paradigm. *American Psychologist, 58*(4), 305–312.

Gillespie, R. (1991). *Manufacturing Knowledge: A History of the Hawthorne Experiments*. Cambridge: Cambridge University Press.

Gillett, J. (2003). Media Activism and Internet Use by People with HIV/AIDS. *Sociology of Health & Illness, 25*, 608–624.

Gilligan, C. (1982). *In a Different Voice: Psychological Theory and Women's Development*. Cambridge, MA: Harvard University Press.

Gilman, C. P. (1899/1973). *The Yellow Wallpaper*. Brooklyn, NY: The Feminist Press at the City University of New York.

Gist, M. E. (1987). Self-efficacy: Implications for Organizational Behavior and Human Resource Management. *Academy of Managemment Review, 12*, 472–485.

Gittel, R., & Vidal, A. (1998). *Community Organizing: Building Social Capital as a Development Strategy*. Thousand Oaks, CA: Sage Publications.

Glover, M., Dudgeon, P., & Huygens, I. (2005). Colonisation and Racism. In G. Nelson and I. Prilleltensky (Eds.), *Community Psychology: In Pursuit of Liberation and Well-Being* (pp. 521–545). New York: Palgrave MacMillan.

Goerner, S. (1994). *Chaos and the Evolving Ecological Universe*. Langhorne, PA: Gordon and Breach Science.

Goertzen, J. R. (2005). *The Identity of Psychology: A Qualitative Exploration and a Descriptive Account of the Crisis and Unification Literature*. Unpublished Master's Thesis, York University, Canada.

Goffman, E. (1961). *Asylums*. Garden City, NY: Doubleday.

Goffman, E. (1983). Felicity's Condition. *The American Journal of Sociology, 89*(1), 1–53.

Goldfield, M. (1987). *The Decline of Organized Labor in the United States*. Chicago: University of Chicago Press.

Goldstein, B. (1942a). *A Critical Evaluation of the Testing of Intelligence*. Folder 302, Betty Friedan papers, Schlesinger Library, Harvard University, Cambridge, MA.

Goldstein, B. (1942b). *Social Learning: A Reformulation of Freudian Concepts*. Folder 305, Betty Friedan papers, Schlesinger Library, Harvard University, Cambridge, MA.

Golombok, S., Spencer, A., & Rutter, M. (1983). Children in Lesbian and Single-Parent Households: Psychosexual and Psychiatric Appraisal. *Child Psychology and Psychiatry, 24*, 551–572.

Goodley, D., & Lawthom, R. (2006). *Disability & Psychology: Critical Introductions & Reflections*. New York: Palgrave.

Goodman, P. (1979). Reflections on the Anarchist Principle. In T. Stoehr (Ed.), *Drawing the Line: The Political Essays of Paul Goodman* (pp. 176–177). New York: Dutton. (Original work published 1966.)

Goodrich, T. J. (Ed.). (1991). *Women and Power: Perspectives for Family Therapy*. New York: Norton.

Gordon, P. (2001). Psycho-analysis and Racism: The Politics of Defeat. *Race & Class: Journal for Black and Third World Liberation, 42*(4), 17–34.

Gorman, M. (1981). Pre-war Conformity Research in Social Psychology: The Approaches of Floyd H. Allport and Muzafer Sherif. *Journal of the History of the Behavioral Sciences, 17*, 2–14.

Gould, S. J. (1981). *The Mismeasure of Man*. New York: Norton.

Gourevitch, P. (1998). *We Wish to Inform You That Tomorrow We Will be Killed With Our Families: Stories from Rwanda*. New York: Picador.

Graen, G. B., & Scandura, T. A. (1987). Toward a Psychology of Dyadic Organizing. In B. Staw and L. L. Cummings (Eds.), *Research in Organizational Behavior* (Vol. 9, pp. 175–208). Greenwich, CT: JAI Press.

Gramsci, A. (1971). *Selections from the Prison Notebooks*. In Q. Hoare & G. Nowell Smith (Eds.). London: Lawrence and Wishart.

Gray, R., & Sinding, C. (2002). *Standing Ovation: Performing Social Science Research about Cancer*. Walnut Creek, CA: AltaMira.

Green, C. D. (1995). *The Power Hour: Maybe Psychotherapy is Social Control After All.* Unpublished manuscript, York University, Ontario, Canada.

Greenwood, J. D. (2004a). *The Disappearance of the Social in American Social Psychology.* New York: Cambridge University Press.

Greenwood, J. (2004b). What Happened to the 'Social' in Social Psychology? *Journal for the Theory of Social Behaviour, 34,* 19–34.

Gregg, G. (1991). *Self-Representation: Life Narrative Studies in Identity and Ideology.* New York: Greenwood.

Greitens, E. (2001). The Treatment of Children during Conflict. In F. Stewart and V. Fitzgerald (Eds.), *War and Underdevelopment Volume II: The Economic and Social Consequences of Conflict* (pp. 149–167). Oxford: Oxford University Press.

Grieder, W. (1997). *One World, Ready Or Not.* New York: Simon & Schuster.

Griffith, T. L., & Neale, M. A. (2001). Information Processing in Traditional, Hybrid, and Virtual Teams: From Nascent Knowledge to Transactive Memory. *Research in Organizational Behaviour, 23,* 379–421.

Grisso, T. (2005). *Evaluating Competencies: Forensic Assessments and Instruments.* New York: Springer.

Grob, G. N. (1994). The History of the Asylum Revisited: Personal Reflections. In M. S. Micale and R. Porter (Eds.), *Discovering the History of Psychiatry* (pp. 260–281). New York: Oxford University Press.

Guilfoyle, M. (2003). Dialogue and Power: A Critical Analysis of Power in Dialogical Therapy. *Family Process, 42,* 331–343.

Habermas, J. (1972). *Knowledge and Human Interests* (J. J. Shapiro, Trans.). Boston: Beacon Press. (German original published in 1968.)

Habermas, J. (1981). *The Theory of Communicative Action,* Vols. 1 & 2. Boston: Beacon Press.

Hacker, W. (2003). Action Regulation Theory: A Practical Tool for the Design of Modern Work Processes? *European Journal of Work and Organizational Psychology, 12,* 105–130.

Hacking, I. (1995). *Rewriting the Soul: Multiple Personality and the Sciences of Memory.* Princeton, NJ: Princeton University Press.

Hackney, H. L., & Cormier, C. (2005*). The Professional Counselor: A Process Guide to Helping (*5th ed.). New York: Pearson Education.

Hale, C. R. (Ed.). (2008). *Engaging Contradictions: Theory, Politics, and Methods of Activist Scholarship.* Berkeley, CA: University of California Press.

Haney, C. (1980). Psychological and Legal Change: On the Limits of a Factual Jurisprudence. *Law and Human Behavior, 4,* 147–200.

Haney, C. (1993). Psychology and Legal Change: The Impact of a Decade. *Law and Human Behavior, 17,* 371–398.

Haney, C., Banks, C., & Zimbardo, P. (1973). Interpersonal Dynamics in a Simulated Prison. *International Journal of Criminology and Penology, 1*(1), 69–97.

Hanisch, C. (1970). The Personal is Political. In S. Firestone and A. Koedt (Eds.), *Notes from the Second Year: Women's Liberation* (pp. 204–205). New York: Redstockings.

Hanlin, C. E., Bess, K., Conway, P., Evans, S. D., McCown, D., Prilleltensky, I., & Perkins, D. D. (2008). Community Psychology. In C. Willig and W. Stainton Rogers (Eds.), *The Sage Handbook of Qualitative Research in Psychology.* London: Sage.

Hare-Mustin, R. T. (1991). Sex, Lies, and Headaches: The Problem is Power. In T. J. Goodrich (Ed.), *Women and Power.* New York: Norton.

Hare-Mustin, R. T. (1992). Cries and Whispers: The Psychotherapy of Anne Sexton. *Psychotherapy, 29,* 406–409.

Hare-Mustin, R. T., & Marecek, J. (1986). Autonomy and Gender: Some Questions for Therapists. *Psychotherapy: Theory, Practice, and Research, 23,* 205–212.

Hare-Mustin, R. T., & Marecek, J. (1988). The Meaning of Difference: Gender Theory, Postmodernism, and Psychology. *American Psychologist, 43,* 455–464.

Hare-Mustin, R.T., & Marecek, J. (1990). *Making a Difference: Psychology and the Construction of Gender.* New Haven, CT: Yale University Press.

Hare-Mustin, R. T., Marecek, J., Kapan, A. G., & Liss-Levenson, N. (1979). Rights of Clients, Responsibilities of Therapists. *American Psychologist, 34,* 3–16.

Harne, L., & the Rights of Women. (1997). *Valued Families: The Lesbian Mother's Legal Handbook.* London: The Women's Press.

Harper, D. J. (2003). Poverty and Discourse. In S. C. Carr and T. S. Sloan (Eds.), *Poverty and Psychology: From Global Perspective to Local Practice* (pp. 185–204). New York: Kluwer Academic/Plenum.

Harré, R. (1986). An Outline of the Social Constructionist Viewpoint. In R. Harré (Ed.), *The Social Construction of Emotions* (pp. 2–14). Oxford: Blackwell.

Harris, B. (1986) Reviewing Fifty Years of The Psychology of Social Issues. *Journal of Social Issues, 42,* 1–20.

Harris, B. (1994). Century of Progress? *Contemporary Psychology, 39,* 465–468.

Harris, B. (1995). The Benjamin Rush Society and Marxist Psychiatry in the United States, 1944–1951. *History of Psychiatry, 6,* 309–331.

Harris, B. (1997). Repoliticizing the History of Psychology. In D. Fox and I. Prilleltensky (Eds.), *Critical Psychology: An Introduction* (pp. 21–33). London: Sage.

Harris, B., & Curti, M. E. (1999). Margaret Wooster Curti. In J. A. Garraty and M. C. Carnes (Eds.), *American National Biography.* New York: Oxford University Press.

Harris, B., & Nicholson, I. A. M. (Eds.). (1998). Experts in the Service of Social Reform: SPSSI, Psychology and Society, 1936–1996. *Journal of Social Issues, 54*(1).

Harrison, A. E., & McMillan, M. S. (2006). Dispelling Some Myths About Offshoring. *Academy of Management Perspectives, 20*(4), 6–22.

Harrison, T. (2006). Health Promotion for Persons with Disabilities: What Does the Literature Reveal? *Family & Community Health, 29*(1S), 12S–19S.

Harvey, R. J. (1991). Job Analysis. In M. D. Dunnette and L. M. Hough (Eds.), *Handbook of Industrial and Organizational Psychology,* Vol. 2 (2nd ed.) (pp. 71–163). Palo Alto, CA: Consulting Psychologists Press.

Haslam, S. A., & Reicher, S. (2007). Beyond the Banality of Evil: Three Dynamics of an Interactionist Social Psychology of Tyranny. *Personality and Social Psychology Bulletin, 33,* 615–622.

Haslam, S. A., Platow, M. J., Turner, J. C., Reynolds, K. J., McGarty, C., Oakes, P. J., Johnson, S., Ryan, M. K., & Veenstra, K. (2001). Social Identity and the Romance of Leadership: The Importance of Being Seen to be 'Doing it for Us'. *Group Processes Intergroup Relations, 4*(3), 191–205.

Hawken, P. (2007). *Blessed Unrest: How the Largest Movement in the World Came into Being and Why No One Saw It Coming.* New York: Viking.

Hayes, S. C., Barlow, D. H., & Nelson-Gray, R. O. (1999). *The Scientist-Practitioner: Research and Accountability in the Age of Managed Care* (2nd ed.). Boston: Allyn & Bacon.

Held, D. (1980). *Introduction to Critical Theory.* Berkeley, CA: University of California Press.

Henriques, J., Hollway, W., Urwin, C., Venn, C., & Walkerdine, V. (Eds.). (1984). *Changing the Subject.* London: Methuen.

Hepburn, A. (2003). *An Introduction to Critical Social Psychology.* London: Sage.

Hepburn, A. (2004). Crying: Notes on Description, Transcription and Interaction. *Research on Language and Social Interaction, 37*(3), 251–290.

Hepburn, A. (2005). 'You're not taking me seriously': Ethics and Asymmetry in Calls to a Child Protection Helpline. *Journal of Constructivist Psychology* (Special Issue on Constructivist Ethics), *18,* 255–276.

Hepburn, A. (2006). Getting Closer at a Distance: Theory and the Contingencies of Practice. *Theory & Psychology, 16*(3), 325–342.

Hepburn, A., & Potter, J. (2003). Discourse Analytic Practice. In C. Seale, D. Silverman, J. Gubrium, and G. Gobo (Eds.), *Qualitative Research Practice* (pp. 180–196). London: Sage.

Hepburn, A., & Potter, J. (2007). Crying Receipts: Time, Empathy and Institutional Practice. *Research on Language and Social Interaction, 40,* 89–116.

Hepburn, A., & Wiggins, S. (2007). Discursive Research: Themes and Debates. In A. Hepburn and S. Wiggins (Eds.), *Discursive Research In Practice: New Approaches to Psychology and Interaction* (pp. 1–28). Cambridge: Cambridge University Press.

Hepworth, J. (2004). Public Health Psychology: A Conceptual and Practical Framework. *Journal of Health Psychology, 9,* 41–54.

Hepworth, J. (2006a). The Emergence of Critical Health Psychology: Can It Contribute to Promoting Public Health? *Journal of Health Psychology, 11,* 331–341.

Hepworth, J. (2006b). Strengthening Critical Health Psychology: A Critical Action Orientation. *Journal of Health Psychology, 11,* 401–408.

Herman, E. (1995). *The Romance of American Psychology: Political Culture in the Age of Experts.* Berkeley, CA: University of California Press.

Herman, E., & Chomsky, N. (1988). *Manufacturing Consent: The Political Economy of the Mass Media.* New York: Pantheon Books.

Herman, J. (1992). *Trauma and Recovery.* New York: Basic Books.

Herrnstein, R. J. (1971). I.Q. *The Atlantic,* September, pp. 43–64.

Hickey, S., & Mohan, G. (2004). *Participation: From Tyranny to Transformation? – Exploring New Approaches to Participation in Development.* London: Zed Books.

Hill, D. B., & Willoughby, B. L. B. (2005). The Development and Validation of the Genderism and Transphobia Scale. *Sex Roles, 53*(7–8), 531–544.

Hill, M., & Rothblum, E. D. (Eds.). (1996). *Classism and Feminist Therapy: Counting Costs.* New York: Harrington Park Press.

Hoades, U. (2007). The Reproduction of Social Class Inequalities Through Mathematics Pedagogies in South African Primary Schools. *Journal of Curriculum Studies, 39,* 676–706.

Hochschild, J. L. (1995). *Facing Up to the American Dream: Race, Class and the Soul of the Nation.* Princeton, NJ: Princeton University Press.

Hodgetts, D., & Chamberlain, K. (2006). Developing a Critical Media Research Agenda for Health Psychology. *Journal of Health Psychology, 11,* 317–327.

Hodgetts, D., Chamberlain, K., & Radley, A. (2007). Considering Photographs Never Taken During Photo-Production Projects. *Qualitative Research in Psychology, 4,* 263–280.

Hodgetts, D., Radley, A., Chamberlain, K., & Hodgetts, A. (2007). Health Inequalities and Homelessness: Considering Material, Spatial and Relational Dimensions. *Journal of Health Psychology, 12,* 709–725.

Hofrichter, R. (Ed.). (2003). *Health and Social Justice.* San Francisco, CA: Jossey Bass.

Holterman, T., & van Maarseveen, H. (Eds.). (1984). *Law and Anarchism.* Montreal: Black Rose Books.

Holzkamp, K. (1972). *Kritische Psychologie: Vorbereitende Arbeiten [Critical Psychology: Preparatory Works].* Frankfurt am Main, Germany: Fischer.

Holzkamp, K. (1984). Die Menschen sitzen nicht im Kapitalismus wie in einem Käfig [Human are Not Encaged in Capitalism]. *Psychologie heute, 11*(11), 29–37.

Holzkamp, K. (1991). Experience of Self and Scientific Objectivity. In C. W. Tolman and W. Maiers (Eds.), *Critical Psychology: Contributions to an Historical Science of the Subject* (pp. 65–80). Cambridge, MA: Cambridge University Press. (Original work published 1985.)

Holzkamp, K. (1992). On Doing Psychology Critically (C. W. Tolman, Trans.). *Theory and Psychology, 2*(2), 193–204.

Holzkamp-Osterkamp, U. (1991). Personality: Self-Actualization in Social Vacuums. In C. Tolman and W. Maiers (Eds.), *Critical Psychology: Contributions to an Historical Science of the Subject* (pp. 160–179). Cambridge: Cambridge University Press.

Hook, D. (Ed.). (2004). *Critical Psychology*. Lansdowne, South Africa: UCT Press.

Hook, D. (2006). 'Pre-discursive' Racism. *Journal of Community and Applied Social Psychology, 16,* 207–232.

Hook, D. (2008). The 'Real' of Racializing Embodiment. *Journal of Community and Applied Social Psychology, 18,* 140–152.

Hooker, E. (1993). Reflections on a 40 Year Exploration. *American Psychologist, 48,* 450–453.

hooks, b. (2000). *Where We Stand: Class Matters.* New York: Routledge.

Hope, A., and Timmel, S. (1984–2000) *Training for Transformation: A Handbook for Community Workers* (Vols. 1–4). London: Intermediate Technology Publications.

Hopkins, N., Reicher, S., & Levine, M. (1997). On the Parallels Between Social Cognition and The 'New Racism'. *British Journal of Social Psychology, 36,* 305–329.

Horkheimer, M. (1982). *Critical Theory.* New York: Seabury Press.

Horkheimer, M. (1992). Traditional and Critical Theory. In D. Ingram and J. Simon-Ingram (Eds.), *Critical Theory: The Essential Readings* (pp. 239–254). New York: Paragon House. (Original work published 1937.)

Horowitz, D. (1996). Rethinking Betty Friedan and *The Feminine Mystique*: Labor Union Radicalism and Feminism in Cold War America. *American Quarterly, 48,* 1–42.

Horowitz, D. (1998). *Betty Friedan and the Making of The Feminine Mystique.* Amherst, MA: University of Massachusetts Press.

House, R. J., Rousseau, D. M., & Thomas-Hunt, M. (1995). The Meso Paradigm: A Framework for the Integration of Micro and Macro Organizational Behavior. *Research in Organizational Behavior,* (Vol. *17,* pp. 71–114). Greenwich, CT: JAI Press.

Howard, A. (1995). Rethinking the Psychology of Work. In A. Howard (Ed.), *The Changing Nature of Work.* San Francisco, CA: Jossey-Bass.

Howard, G. (1985). The Role of Values in the Science of Psychology. *American Psychologist,* 40, 255–265.

Howarth, C. (2006). A Social Representation is Not a Quiet Thing: Exploring the Critical Potential of Social Representations Theory. *British Journal of Social Psychology, 45,* 65–86.

Howitt, D., & Owusu-Bempah, J. (1994). *The Racism of Psychology.* Hemel Hempstead, UK: Harvester Wheatsheaf.

Huddock, S. D. (1994). The Application of Educational Technology to Occupational Safety and Health Training. *Occupational Medicine, 9,* 201–210.

Human Rights Watch. (2003). *Ill-Equipped: U.S. Prisons and Offenders with Mental Illness.* Accessed 21 April 2008 from http://www.hrw.org/reports/2003/usa1003/index.htm.

Huygens, I. (2006). Discourses for Decolonisation: Affirming Maori Authority in New Zealand Workplaces. *Journal of Community and Applied Social Psychology, 16*(5), 363–378.

Huygens, I. (2007). *Processes of Pakeha Change in Response to the Treaty of Waitangi.* University of Waikato, Hamilton.

Hyman, J. B. (2002). Exploring Social Capital and Civic Engagement to Create a Framework for Community Building. *Applied Developmental Science, 6,* 196–202.

Ibáñez, T., & Iniguez, L. (Eds.). (1997). *Critical Social Psychology.* London: Sage.

Ife, J. W. (2001). *Human Rights and Society Work: Towards Rights-based Practice.* Cambridge, UK: Cambridge University Press.

Ife, J. W. (2002). *Community Development: Community-based Alternatives in an Age of Globalization.* Frenchs Forest, NSW: Pearson Education.

International Rescue Committee (2003). *The Post-Conflict Development Initiative.* Accessed 1 March 2005 from www.theirc.org.

Iraq Body Count. (2008). Accessed 4 April from http://www.iraqbodycount.org.

Isaacs, J. B. (n.d. (a)). *The Economic Mobility of Families Across Generations.* Washington, DC: Economic Mobility Project. Available from http://www.economicmobility.org/assets/pdfs/EMP_FamiliesAcrossGenerations_ChapterI.pdf.

Isaacs, J. B. (n.d.(b)). *International Comparisons of Economic Mobility.* Washington, DC: Economic Mobility Project. Available from http://www.economicmobility.org/ assets/pdfs/EMP_InternationalComparisons_ChapterIII.pdf.

Islam, G., & Zyphur, M. J. (2006). Critical Industrial Psychology: What is it and Where is it? *Psychology in Society, 34,* 17–30.

Islam, G & Zyphur, M. J. (2007). Ways of Interacting: The Standardization of Communication in Medical Training. *Human Relations, 60*(5), 769–792.

Israel, B. A., Checkoway, B., Schulz, A., & Zimmerman, M. (1994). Health Education and Community Empowerment: Conceptualizing and Measuring Perceptions of Individual, Organizational, and Community Control. *Health Education and Behavior, 21*(2), 149–170.

Ivey, A., D'Andrea, M., Ivey, M., & Simek-Morgan, L. (2002). *Counseling and Psychotherapy: A Multicultural Perspective* (5th ed.). Boston, MA: Allyn and Bacon.

Jackson, J. P., Jr. (2001). *Social Scientists for Social Justice: Making the Case Against Segregation.* New York: New York University Press.

Jackson, M. (2003). *Like a Beached Whale: A Consideration of Proposed Crown Action Over Maori Foreshore,* 2003, from http://www.converge.org.nz/pma/ cerd71.htm.

Jacobs, G. C. (2006). Imagining the Flowers, but Working the Rich and Heavy Clay: Participation and Empowerment in Action Research for Health. *Educational Action Research, 14,* 569–581.

Jacoby, R. (1975). *Social Amnesia: A Critique of Contemporary Psychology from Adler to Laing.* Boston, MA: Beacon.

Jana, S., & Banerjee, B. (1999). *Learning to Change: Seven Years' Stint of STD/HIV Intervention Programme at Sonagachi.* Calcutta: SHIP.

Jana, S., Basu, I., Rotheram-Borus, M., & Newman, P. (2004). The Sonagachi Project: A Sustainable Community Intervention Program. *AIDS Education & Prevention, 16*(5), 405–414.

Janzen, R., Nelson, G., Hausfather, N., & Ochocka, J. (2007). Capturing System Level Activities and Impacts of Mental Health Consumer-Run Organizations. *American Journal of Community Psychology, 39,* 287–299.

Jason, L. A., Keys, C. B., Suarez-Balcazar, Y., Taylor, R. R., Davis, M. I., Durlak, J. A., & Isenberg, D. I. (Eds.). (2004). *Participatory Community Research: Theories and Methods in Action.* Washington, DC: American Psychological Association.

Jefferson, G. (1979). A Technique for Inviting Laughter and Its Subsequent Acceptance Declination. In G. Psathas (Ed.), *Everyday Language: Studies in Ethnomethodology* (pp. 79–96). New York: Irvington.

Jefferson, G. (2004). Glossary of Transcript Symbols with an Introduction. In G. H. Lerner (Ed.), *Conversation Analysis: Studies from the First Generation.* (pp. 13–31). Amsterdam/ Philadelphia: John Benjamins.

Jenkins, J. H. (1991). The State Construction of Affect: Political Ethos and Mental Health Among Salvadoran Refugees. *Culture, Medicine and Psychiatry, 15,* 139–165.

Jensen, A. R. (1969). How Much Can We Boost IQ and Scholastic Achievement? *Harvard Educational Review, 39,* 1–123.

Jensen, A. R., & Johnson, F. W. (1994). Race and Sex Differences in Head Size and IQ. *Intelligence, 18,* 309–333.

Johannsen, A.M. (2003). Participatory Action-Research in Post-Conflict Situations: The Example of the War-Torn Societies Project. In M. Fischer, A. Austin, and N. Ropers (Eds.), *Berghof Handbook for Conflict Transformation.* Berlin: Berghof Research Center for Constructive Conflict Management.

Johnston, E., & Johnson, A. (2008). Searching for the Second Generation of American Women Psychologists. *History of Psychology, 11,* 40–72.

Jutel, A. (2006). The Emergence of Overweight as a Disease Entity: Measuring Up Normality. *Social Science & Medicine, 63,* 2268–2276.

Kagan, C., & Burton, M. (2001). *Critical Community Psychology Praxis for the 21st Century.* Paper presented at the British Psychological Society conference, Glasgow.

Kagan, C., Burton, M., & Siddiquee, A. (2008). Action Research. In C. Willig and W. Stainton Rogers (Eds.), *The Sage Handbook of Qualitative Research in Psychology.* London: Sage.

Kairys, D. (Ed.). (1998). *The Politics of Law: A Progressive Critique* (3rd edn). New York: Basic Books.

Kalil, A. (2001). The Role of Social Science in Welfare Reform. *Analyses of Social Issues and Public Policy, 1,* 183–185.

Kamin, L. (1974). *The Science and Politics of I.Q.* Potomac, MD: Erlbaum.

Kaptein, A., & Weinman, J. (2004). Health Psychology: Some Introductory Remarks. In A. Kaptein and J. Weinman (Eds.), *Health Psychology* (pp. 3–18). Oxford: Blackwell.

Kaschak, E., & Tiefer, L. (Eds.). (2001). *A New View of Women's Sexual Problems.* New York: Haworth Press.

Katz, D., & Kahn, R. L. (1978). *The Social Psychology of Organizations.* New York: Wiley.

Kawachi, I., Kennedy, B., & Wilkinson, R. (Eds.). (1999). *The Society and Population Health Reader: Income Inequality and Health.* New York, NY: The New Press.

Keller, E. F. (1985). *Reflections on Gender and Science.* New Haven, CT: Yale University Press.

Kelly, J. G. (1966). Ecological Constraints on Mental Health Services. *American Psychologist, 21,* 535–539.

Kendall, D. (2005). *Framing Class: Media Representations of Wealth and Poverty in America.* Lanham, MD: Rowman and Littlefield.

Keniston, K. (1968). How Community Mental Health Stamped Out the Riots. *Journal of Contemporary Psychotherapy, 1,* 3–12.

Kennedy, D. (1973). Legal Formality. *The Journal of Legal Studies, 2,* 352–398.

Kessler, S. J., & McKenna, W. (1985). *Gender: An Ethnomethodological Approach.* Chicago: University of Chicago Press.

Keyes, C. L. M., & Haidt, J. (Eds.). (2003). *Flourishing: Positive Psychology and the Life Well-Lived.* Washington, DC: American Psychological Association.

Kiernan, V. C. (1993). Colonialism. In W. Outhwaite and T. Bottomore (Eds.), *Dictionary of Twentieth Century Social Thought* (pp. 91–94). Oxford: Blackwell.

Kimble, G. (1984). Psychology's Two Cultures. *American Psychologist, 39,* 833–839.

Kirk, S. A., & Kutchins, H. (1992). *The Selling of DSM: The Rhetoric of Science in Psychiatry.* Hawthorne, NY: Aldine de Gruyter.

Kirp, D. (2007). *The Sandbox Investment.* Cambridge, MA: Harvard University Press.

Kiselica, M. S., & Robinson, M. (2001). Bringing Advocacy Counseling to Life: The History, Issues, and Human Dramas of Social Justice Work in Counseling. *Journal of Counseling and Development, 79*(4), 387–397.

Kitzinger, C. (Ed.). (1994). Should Psychologists Study Sex Differences? *Feminism & Psychology, 4*(4), 501–506.

Kitzinger, C. (1997). Lesbian and Gay Psychology: A Critical Analysis. In D. Fox and I. Prilleltensky (Eds.), *Critical Psychology: An Introduction* (pp. 202–216). London: Sage.

Kitzinger, C., & Wilkinson, S. (2004). Social Advocacy for Equal Marriage: The Politics of 'Rights' and the Psychology of 'Mental Health'. *Analyses of Social Issues and Public Policy, 4*(1), 1–22.

Klein, N. (2007). *The Shock Doctrine: The Rise of Disaster Capitalism.* New York: Metropolitan Books.

Kleinman, A. (1984). *The Illness Narratives.* New York: Basic Books.

Kleinman, A. (1988). *Rethinking Psychiatry: From Cultural Category to Personal Experience.* New York: Free Press.

Kleinman, A. (1995). *Writing at the Margin: Discourse between Anthropology and Medicine.* Berkeley: University of California Press.

Kluegel, J. R., & Smith, E. R. (1986). *Beliefs About Inequality: Americans' Views of What Is and What Ought To Be.* New York: Aldine De Gruyter.

Kluger, R. (2004). *Simple Justice: The History of Brown v. Board of Education and Black America's Struggle For Equality* (rev. ed.). New York: Knopf.

Koch, S. (1985). The Nature and Limits of Psychological Knowledge: Lessons of a Century Qua 'Science'. In S. Koch and D. E. Leary (Eds.), *A Century of Psychology as Science* (pp. 75–97). New York: McGraw-Hill.

Kocsis, R. N. (Ed.). (2007). *The Psychology of Violence and Serial Crime: An International Perspective.* Totowa, NJ: Humana Press.

Kolb, D. A., & Frey, R. (1975) Toward an Applied Theory of Experiential Learning. In C. Cooper (Ed.), *Theories of Group Process.* London: John Wiley.

Komaki, J. L. (1986). Applied Behavioral Analysis and Organizational Behavior: Reciprocal Influences of the Two Fields. In B. M. Staw and L. L. Cummings (Eds.), *Research in Organizational Behavior* (Vol. 8, pp. 297–334). Greenwich, CT: JAI Press.

Koocher, G. P. (2007). 21st Century Ethical Challenges for Psychology. *American Psychologist, 62,* 375–384.

Korten, D. (2001). *When Corporations Rule the World* (2nd ed.). Bloomfield, CT: Berrett-Koehler.

Kraut, R. (2007). *What is Good and Why: The Ethics of Well-being.* Cambridge, MA: Harvard.

Kretzmann, J. P., & McKnight, J. L. (1993). *Building Communities From the Inside Out: A Path Toward Finding and Mobilizing a Community's Assets.* Evanston, IL: Institute for Policy Research.

Kristoff, A. L. (1996). Person-Organization Fit: An Integrative Review of its Conceptualizations, Measurement, and Implications. *Personnel Psychology, 49,* 1–49.

Kroeber, A. L., & Kluckhohn, C. (1952). *Culture: A Critical Review of Concepts and Definitions.* Cambridge, MA: Peabody Museum.

Kropotkin, P. (1902). *Mutual Aid.* Boston, MA: Extending Horizons Books.

Kuhn, T. S. (1962). *The Structure of Scientific Revolutions.* Chicago: University of Chicago Press.

Kuhn, T. S. (1970). *The Structure of Scientific Revolutions* (2nd edn). London: Tavistock.

Kuther, T. L. (2004). *Your Career in Psychology: Psychology and Law.* Belmont, CA: Wadsworth.

Kytle, J. (1977). Ideology and Planned Social Change: A Critique of Two Popular Change Strategies. *Personality and Social Psychology Bulleting, 3,* 697–706.

Lacan, J. (1977). *Ecrits: A Selection* (A. Sheridan, Trans.). New York: Norton.

Lacan, J. (1985). *Feminine Sexuality.* New York: W. W. Norton.

Lacan, J. (1991). *L'envers de la Psychanalyse.* Paris: Editions du Seuil.

Lamada, M. I. (2006). Children's Rehabilitation Center Upholds Human Rights. *The Just Word, XII*(1), 4.

Landrine, H. (1989). The Politics of Personality. *Psychology of Women Quarterly, 13,* 325–340.

Langhout, R. (2006). Where Am I? Locating Myself and its Implications for Collaborative Research. *American Journal of Community Psychology, 37,* 267–274.

Langston, D. (1998). Tired of Playing Monopoly? In M. L. Andersen and P. H. Collins (Eds.), *Race, Class, and Gender: An Anthology* (pp. 126–136). Belmont, CA: Wadsworth Publishing Company.

Laqueur, T. (1990). *Making Sex: Body and Gender from the Greeks to Freud.* Cambridge, MA: Harvard University Press.

Latané, B. (1981). The Psychology of Social Impact. *American Psychologist, 36*(4), 343–356.

Latané, B., & Darley, J. M. (1970). *The Unresponsive Bystander: Why Doesn't He Help?* New York: Meredith.

Latané, B., & Nida, S. (1981). Ten Years of Research on Group Size and Helping. *Psychological Bulletin, 89*, 307–324.

Laurie, C. (1996). *The Propaganda Warriors: America's Crusade Against Nazi Germany.* Lawrence, KS: University Press of Kansas.

Laurier, E., McKie, L., & Goodwin, N. (2000). Daily and Lifecourse Contexts of Smoking. *Sociology of Health and Illness, 22,* 289–309.

Lemme, B. (2006). *Development in Adulthood* (4th edn). New York: Pearson.

Lerner, G. (1979). *The Majority Finds Its Past: Placing Women in History.* New York: Oxford University Press.

Lerner, M. J. (1982). The Justice Motive in Human Relations and the Economic Model of Man: A Radical Analysis of Facts and Fictions. In V. J. Derlega and J. Grzelak (Eds.), *Cooperation and Helping Behavior: Theories and Research* (pp. 249–278). New York: Academic Press.

Levy, B., & Sidel, V. (Eds.). (2006). *Social Injustice and Public Health.* New York: Oxford.

Levy, M. (2007). *Indigenous Psychology in Aotearoa: Realising Maori Aspirations.* Unpublished PhD, University of Waikato, Hamilton.

Lewin, K. (1935). *A Dynamic Theory of Personality.* New York: McGraw-Hill.

Lewin, K. (1946). Action Research and Minority Problems. *Journal of Social Issues, 2*(4), 34–46.

Lewin, K. (1947). Frontiers in Group Dynamics: II. Channels of Group Life, Social Planning and Action Research. *Human Relations, 1*(2), 143–153.

Lewin, K. (1948). *Resolving Social Conflicts: Selected Papers On Group Dynamics.* New York: Harper.

Lewis, J., Arnold, M., House, R., & Toporek. R. (2006). *Advocacy Competencies.* http://www.counseling.org/Files/FD.ashx?guid=680f251e-b3d0-4f77-8aa3-4e360f32f05e.

Lewis, J. A., Lewis, M. D., Daniels, J. A., & D'Andrea, M. J. (2003). *Community Counseling: Empowering Strategies for a Diverse Society* (3rd edn). Pacific Grove, CA: Brooks/Cole-Thomson Learning.

Liem, R. (2005). Creating Still Present Pasts: Korean Americans and the 'Forgotten War'. *Exhibit Brochure: Still Present Pasts.* Boston College, MA.

Liem, R. (2007). Silencing Historical Trauma: The Politics and Psychology of Memory and Voice. *Peace and Conflict: Journal of Peace Psychology, 13*(2), 1–22.

Linton, S. (1998). *Claiming Disability: Knowledge and Identity.* New York: New York University Press.

Lippitt, R. (1939). Field Theory and Experiment in Social Psychology: Autocratic and Democratic Group Atmospheres. *American Journal of Sociology, 45*, 26–49.

Liu, W. M., Ali, S. R., Soleck, G., Hopps, J., Dunston, K., & Pickett, T. (2004). Using Social Class in Counseling Psychology Research. *Journal of Counseling Psychology, 51*, 3–18.

Livneh, H. (2001). Psychosocial Adaptation to Chronic Illness and Disability: A Conceptual Framework. *Rehabilitation Counseling Bulletin, 44*(3), 151–160.

Livneh, H., & Antonak, R. F. (2005). Psychological Adaptation to Chronic Illness and Disability: A Primer for Counselors. *Journal of Counseling and Development, 83*, 12–20.

Locke, A., & Edwards, D. (2003). Bill and Monica: Memory, Emotion and Normativity in Clinton's Grand Jury Testimony. *British Journal of Social Psychology, 42*, 239–256.

Locke, E. A. (2002). The Dead End of Postmodernism, *American Psychologist, 57,* 458.

Locke, E. A., & Latham, G. P. (1990). Work Motivation and Satisfaction: Light at the End of the Tunnel. *Psychological Science, 1*, 240–246.

Loehlin, J. C. (1992). *Genes and Environment in Personality Development.* Newbury Park, CA: Sage.

Longenecker, C. O., & Gioia, D. A. (1992). The Executive Appraisal Paradox. *Academy of Management Executive, 6*(2), 18–28.

Lord, J., & Hutchison, P. (1993). The Process of Empowerment: Implications for Theory and Practice. *Canadian Journal of Community Mental Health, 12*(1), 5–22.

Lord, J., & Hutchison, P. (2007). *Pathways to Inclusion: Building a New Story With People and Communities.* Concord, ON: Captus Press Inc.

Lord, R. G., & Maher, K. J. (1991). *Leadership and Information Processing: Linking Perceptions and Performance.* London: Unwin Hyman.

Lott, B. (2002). Cognitive and Behavioral Distancing from the Poor. *American Psychologist, 57,* 100–110.

Lott, B., & Bullock, H. E. (2007). *Psychology and Economic Injustice: Personal, Professional, and Political Intersections.* Washington, DC: American Psychological Association.

Lubek, I., Wong, M. L., McCourt, M., Chew, K., Dy, B. C., Kros, S., Pen, S., Chhit, M., Touch, S., Lee, T. N., & Mok, V. (2002). Collaboratively Confronting the Current Cambodian HIV/AIDS Crisis in Siem Reap: A Cross-disciplinary, Cross-cultural Participatory Action Research Project in Consultative, Community Health Change. *Asian Psychologist, 3,* 21–28.

Luhrmann, T. M. (2000). *Of Two Minds: The Growing Disorder in Psychiatry.* New York: Alfred A. Knopf.

Lui, M., Robles, B., Leondar-Wright, B., Brewer, R., & Adamson, R. (2006). *The Color of Wealth: The Story Behind the US Racial Wealth Divide.* New York: New Press.

Lukács, G. (1967). *History and Class Consciousness.* London: Merlin Press. [Originally published 1923.]

Luthar, S. S., Cicchetti, D., & Becker, B. (2000). The Construct of Resilience: A Critical Evaluation and Guidelines for Future Work. *Child Development, 71,* 543–562.

Lykes, M. B. (2000). Possible Contributions of a Psychology of Liberation: Whither Health and Human Rights? *Journal of Health Psychology, 5,* 383–397.

Lykes, M. B. (2001). Human Rights Violations as Structural Violence. In D. J. Christie, R. V. Wagner and D. DuN. Winter (Eds.), *Peace, Conflict and Violence: Peace Psychology for the 21st Century* (pp. 158–167). Upper Saddle River, NJ: Prentice Hall.

Lykes, M. B., & Coquillon, E. (2006). Participatory and Action Research and Feminisms: Towards Transformative Praxis. In S. Hesse-Biber (Ed.), *Handbook of Feminist Research: Theory and Praxis* (pp. 297–326). Thousand Oaks, CA: Sage Publications.

Lykes, M. B., & Mallona, A. (2008). Towards Transformational Liberation: Participatory Action Research and Activist Praxis. In P. Reason and H. Bradbury (Eds.), *The SAGE Handbook of Action Research II* (pp. 260–292). London: SAGE Publications Ltd.

Lykes, M. B., & Mersky, M. (2006). Reparations and Mental Health: Psychosocial Interventions Towards Healing, Human Agency, and Rethreading Social Realities. In Pablo de Greiff (Ed.), *The Handbook of Reparations* (pp. 589–622). Oxford: Oxford University Press.

Lykes, M. B., in collaboration with Mateo, A.C., Anay, J. C., Caba, A.L., Ruiz, U., & Williams, J. W. (1999). Telling Stories-Rethreading Lives: Community Education, Women's Development, and Social Change Among the Maya Ixil. *International Journal of Leadership in Education: Theory and Practice, 2*(3), 207–227.

Lynch, M., & Bogen, D. (1996). *The Spectacle of History: Speech, Text and Memory at the Iran-Contra Hearings.* Durham, NC: Duke University Press.

Lynch, R. (2007). *Enriching Children, Enriching the Nation: Public Investment in High Quality Prekindergarten.* Washington, DC: Economic Policy Institute.

Lyons, A., & Chamberlain, K. (2006). *Health Psychology: A Critical Introduction.* Cambridge: Cambridge University Press.

Macleod, C. (2004). Writing into Action: The Critical Research Endeavour. In D. Hook (Ed.), *Critical Psychology.* Cape Town, South Africa: University of Cape Town Press.

Macleod, C., & Bhatia, S. (2008). Postcolonialism and Psychology. In C. Willig and W. Stainton Rogers (Eds.), *The Sage Handbook of Qualitative Research in Psychology.* London: Sage.

Maddux, J. E. (2002). Stopping the Madness: Positive Psychology and the Deconstruction of the Illness Ideology and the DSM. In C.R. Snyder and S.J. Lopez (Eds.), *Handbook of Positive Psychology* (pp. 13–25). New York: Oxford University Press.

Madison, D. S. (2005). *Critical Ethnography: Method, Ethics and Performance.* Thousand Oaks, CA: Sage.

Mainiero, L.A., & Sullivan, S.E. (2006). *The Opt-Out Revolt: Why People Are Leaving Companies to Create Kaleidoscope Careers.* Mountain View, CA: Davies-Black Publishing.

Manning, R., Levine, M., & Collins, A. (2007). The Kitty Genovese Murder and the Social Psychology of Helping: The Parable of the 38 Witnesses. *American Psychologist, 62*(6), 555–562.

Mantsios, G. (1998). Media Magic: Making Class Invisible. In P. S. Rothenberg (Ed.), *Race, Class, and Gender in the United States: An Integrated Study* (4th edn) (pp. 510–519). New York: St. Martin's Press.

Marcus, E. (2002). *Making Gay History: The Half-Century Fight for Lesbian and Gay Rights.* New York: Perennial.

Marcuse, H. (1955). *Eros and Civilization: A Philosophical Inquiry into Freud.* Boston, MA: Beacon.

Marcuse, H. (1964). *One-Dimensional Man: Studies in the Ideology of Advanced Industrial Society.* Boston, MA: Beacon.

Marecek, J. (1993). Disappearances, Silences, and Anxious Rhetoric: Gender in Abnormal Psychology Textbooks. *Journal of Theoretical and Philosophical Psychology, 13,* 114–123.

Marks, D. F. (2002). Editorial Essay: Freedom, Responsibility and Power: Contrasting Approaches to Health Psychology. *Journal of Health Psychology, 7,* 5–19.

Marks, D. F. (2004). Rights to Health, Freedom from Illness: A Life and Death Matter. In M. Murray (Ed.), *Critical Health Psychology* (pp. 61–82). Basingstoke, UK: Palgrave.

Marmor, J. (1949). Psychoanalysis. In R. W. Sellars (Ed.), *Philosophy for the Future: The Quest of Modern Materialism* (pp. 317–339). New York: Macmillan.

Marmot, M. (1999). Introduction. In M. Marmot and R. Wilkinson (Eds.), *Social Determinants of Health* (pp. 1–16). New York: Oxford.

Marmot, M. (2004). *The Status Syndrome: How Social Standing Affects Our Health and Longevity.* New York: Owl Books.

Marmot, M. G., Bosma, H., Hemingway, H., Brunner, E., & Stansfeld, S. (1997). Contribution of Job Control & Other Risk Factors to Social Variations in Coronary Heart Disease Incidence. *Lancet, 350,* 235–239.

Marshall, B. (2002). 'Hard Science': Gendered Constructions of Sexual Dysfunction in the 'Viagra Age'. *Sexualities, 5*(2), 131–158.

Martin, J., Sugarman, J. H., & Thompson, J. (2003). *Psychology and the Question of Agency.* Albany, NY: Suny Press.

Martin, P. P., Lounsbury, D. W., & Davidson, W. S. (2004). AJCP as a Vehicle for Improving Community Life: An Historic-Analytic Review of the Journal's Contents. *American Journal of Community Psychology, 34,* 163–173.

Martín-Baró, I. (1994). *Writings For A Liberation Psychology* (A. Aron and S. Corne, Trans.). Cambridge, MA: Harvard.

Maruyama, G., & Peterson, J. J. (2007). Editor's Forward to 'Psychologists and the Use of Torture In Interrogations' and Invited Comments about that article. *Analyses of Social Issues and Public Policy, 7*(1), 1–6.

Marx, K. (1906). *Capital: A Critique of Political Economy, Vol. 1.* Chicago: Kerr.

Marx, K. (1970). Theses on Feuerbach. In K. Marx and F. Engels, *The German Ideology.* New York: International.

Marx, K., & Engels, F. (1848/2001). *The Communist Manifesto.* London: ElecBook.

Maslow, A. (1943). A Theory of Human Motivation. *Psychological Review, 50*, 370–396.

Maslow, A. H. (1963). *Letter to Betty Friedan, January 15, 1963.* Folder 715, Betty Friedan papers, Schlesinger Library, Harvard University, Cambridge, MA.

Matarazzo, J. D. (1980). Behavioral Health and Behavioral Medicine: Frontiers for a New Health Psychology. *American Psychologist, 35*, 807–817.

Matarazzo, J. D. (1982). Behavioral Health's Challenge to Academic, Scientific and Professional Psychology. *American Psychologist, 37*, 1–14.

Maton, K. I., & Salem, D. (1995). Organizational Characteristics of Empowering Community Settings: A Multiple Case Study Approach. *American Journal of Community Psychology, 23*, 631–656.

Maxwell, S. E., & Arvey, R. D. (1993). The Search for Predictors with High Validity and Low Adverse Impact: Compatible or Incompatible Goals? *Journal of Applied Psychology, 78*(3), 433–437.

Mazowiecki, T. (1993). United Nations Commission on Human Rights: Situation of Human Rights in the Territory of the former Yugoslavia. New York: United Nations.

McAdam, D., & Scott, R. (2005). Organizations and Movements. In G. F. Davis, D. McAdam, W. R. Scott, and M. N. Zald (Eds.), *Social Movements and Organization Theory* (pp. 4–40). New York: Cambridge University Press.

McAdams, D. P., & Ochberg, R. L. (Eds.). (1988). Psychobiography and Life Narratives. *Journal of Personality, 56*(1).

McClelland, D. C., & Boyatzis, R. E. (1982). Leadership Motivation Pattern and Long Term Success in Management. *Journal of Applied Psychology, 67*, 737–743.

McCrae, R. R., & Costa, P. T. (1997). Personality Trait Structure as a Human Universal. *American Psychologist, 52*(5), 509–516.

McCrae, R. R., & John, O. P. (1992). An Introduction to the Five-Factor Model and its Applications. *Journal of Personality, 60*, 175–215.

McCreanor, T. N. (1993). Mimiwhangata: Media Reliance on Pakeha Commonsense in the Interpretation of Maori Actions. *Sites, 26*, 79–90.

McCreanor, T. N. (1997). When Racism Stepped Ashore: Antecedents of Anti-Maori Discourse in New Zealand. *New Zealand Journal of Psychology, 26*(1), 36–44.

McCreanor, T. N. (2005). 'Sticks and stones may break my bones ...': Talking Pakeha Identities. In J. Liu, T. McCreanor, T. McIntosh and T. Te Aiwa (Eds.), *New Zealand Identities: Departures and Destinations* (pp. 52–68). Wellington, New Zealand: Victoria University Press.

McCubbin, M. (1994). Deinstitutionalization: The Illusion of Disillusion. *Journal of Mind and Behavior, 15*, 35–53.

McCubbin, M., & Labonte, R. (2002). Toward Psychosocial Theory for an Understanding of the Health and Well-Being of Populations. *Ethical Human Sciences and Services, 4*, 47–61.

McCubbin, M., & Weisstub, D. N. (2001). 'Meeting the Needs of the Mentally Ill': A Case Study of the 'Right To Treatment' as Legal Rights Discourse in the U.S.A. *Academy for the Study of the Psychoanalytic Arts* (online archives). Available from: http://www.academyanalyticarts.org/cnmccweiss.html

McDermott, M. J. (1992). The Personal is Empirical: Research Methods and Criminal Justice Education. *Journal of Criminal Justice Education, 3*, 237–249.

McLean, C., Carey, M., & White, C. (Eds.). (1996). *Men's Ways of Being.* Boulder, CO: Westview Press.

McPherson, P. (2003). Revisionist Historians. *AHA Perspectives Online, September.*

McTaggart, R. (Ed.). (1997). *Participatory Action Research: International Contexts and Consequences.* Albany, NY: SUNY Press.

McVittie, C. (2006). Critical Health Psychology, Pluralism and Dilemmas: The Importance of Being Critical. *Journal of Health Psychology, 11*, 373–377.

Meek, V. L. (1988). Organizational Culture: Origins and Weaknesses. *Organization Studies, 9*(4), 453–473.

Mehryar, A.H. (1984). The Role of Psychology in National Development: Wishful Thinking and Reality. *International Journal of Psychology, 19,* 159–167.

Meindl, J. R., Ehrlich, S. B., & Dukerich, J. M. (1985). The Romance of Leadership. *Administrative Science Quarterly, 30,* 78–102.

Melton, G. B. (1990). Law, Science, and Humanity: The Normative Foundation of Social Science in Law. *Law and Human Behavior, 14,* 315–332.

Melton, G. B. (1992). The Law Is a Good Thing (Psychology Is, Too). Human Rights in Psychological Jurisprudence. *Law and Human Behavior, 16,* 381–398.

Melton, G. B., & Saks, M. J. (1986). The Law as an Instrument of Socialization and Social Structure. In G. B. Melton (Ed.), *The Law as a Behavioral Instrument* (pp. 235–277). Lincoln: University of Nebraska.

Memmi, A. (1965). *The Colonizer and the Colonized* (H. Greenfield, Trans.). Boston, MA: Beacon Press.

Merleau-Ponty, M. (1962). *Phenomenology of Perception* (C. Smith, Trans.). London: Routledge and Kegan. (Original work published 1945.)

Merry, S. E. (2006). Transnational Human Rights and Local Activism: Mapping the Middle. *American Anthropologist, 108*(1), 38–51.

Messer, E. (1995). Anthropology and Human Rights in Latin America. *Journal of Latin American Anthropology, 1*(1), 48–97.

Meyer, J. W., Ramirez, F. O., Frank, D. J., & Schofer, E. (2006). *Higher Education as an Institution.* CDDRL Working Papers, 57.

Meyerowitz, J. (1993). Beyond the Feminine Mystique: A Reassessment of Postwar Mass Culture, 1946–1958. *Journal of American History, 79,* 1455–1482.

Meyerowitz, J. (2004). Hooker, Evelyn. In S. Ware (Ed.), *Notable American Women: A Biographical Dictionary Completing the Twentieth Century* (pp. 308–309). Cambridge, MA: Harvard University Press.

Meyerson, D. E. (1994). Interpretations of Stress in Institutions: The Cultural Production of Ambiguity and Burnout. *Administrative Science Quarterly, 39,* 628–653.

Mielewczyk, F., & Willig, C. (2007). Old Clothes and an Older Look: The Case for a Radical Makeover in Health Behaviour Research. *Theory & Psychology, 17,* 811–837.

Milgram, S. (1963). Behavioral Study of Obedience. *Journal of Abnormal & Social Psychology, 67,* 371–378.

Milgram, S. (1974). *Obedience to Authority: An Experimental View.* New York: Harper Collins.

Miller, D. (1978). *Social Justice.* Oxford: Clarendon.

Miller, D. (1999). *Principles of Social Justice.* Cambridge, MA: Harvard University Press.

Miller, J. B. (1976). *Toward A New Psychology of Women.* Boston, MA: Beacon.

Miller, K. E., & Rasco, L. M. (Eds.). (2004). *The Mental Health of Refugees: Ecological Approaches to Healing and Adaptation.* Mahwah, NJ: Lawrence Erlbaum.

Milovanovic, D. (Ed.). (1997). *Chaos, Criminology, and Social Justice: The New Orderly (Dis)Order.* Westport, CT: Praeger.

Milovanovic, D. (2003). *An Introduction to the Sociology of Law* (3rd edn). Monsey, NY: Criminal Justice Press.

Milovanovic, D. (2002). *Critical Criminology at the Edge: Postmodern Perspectives, Integration, and Applications.* Westport, CT: Praeger.

Ministry of Justice. (2008). *Main Elements of Foreshore and Seabed Act.* Retrieved 22 March 2008, from http://www.justice.govt.nz/foreshore/main2.html

Minton, H. L. (2002). *Departing from Deviance; A History of Homosexual Rights and Emancipatory Science in America.* Chicago, IL: University of Chicago Press.

Mishler, E.G. (1990). Validation in Inquiry-Guided Research: The Role of Exemplars in Narrative Studies. *Harvard Educational Review, 60,* 415–442.

Mitchell, T. R. (1974). Expectancy Models of Job Satisfaction, Occupational Preference, and Effort: A Theoretical, Methodological, and Empirical Appraisal. *Psychological Bulletin, 81,* 1053–1077.

Mkhize, N. (2004). Psychology: An African Perspective. In D. Hook (Ed.), *Critical Psychology* (pp. 24–52). Lansdowne, South Africa: UCT Press.

Moane, G. (1999). *Gender and Colonialism: A Psychological Analysis of Oppression and Liberation.* Houndmills: Macmillan Press.

Moane, G. (2003). Bridging the Personal and the Political: Practices for a Liberation Psychology. *American Journal of Community Psychology, 31,* 91–101.

Moewaka-Barnes, A., Gregory, M., McCreanor, T., Nairn, R., Pega, F., & Rankine, J. (2005). *Media and Te Tiriti o Waitangi 2004.* Tamaki Makaurau/Auckland: Kupu Taea: Media and Te Tiriti Project.

Mollica, R. F., Lopes Cardozo, B., Osofsky, H. J., Raphael, B., Ager, A., & Salama, S. (2004). Mental Health in Complex Emergencies. *The Lancet, 364*(9450), 2058.

Mona, L., Cameron, R., & Fuentes, A. (2006). Broadening Paradigms of Disability Research to Clinical Practice: Implications for Conceptualization and Application. In K. Hagglund and A. Heinemann (Eds.), *Handbook of Applied Disability and Rehabilitation Research.* New York: Springer Publishing Company.

Monahan, J., & Walker, L. (1991). Judicial Use of Social Science Research. *Law and Human Behavior, 15,* 571–584.

Monsebraaten, L. (2008). GTA Middle Class Struggles: Gap Between Rich and Poor Widens While the Centre Lags, Census Figures Show. *The Toronto Star.* Available from http://www.thestar.com/article/420670, accessed 2 May.

Montero, M., & Christlieb, P. F. (Eds.). (2003). Critical Psychology in Latin America. *Critical Psychology: The International Journal of Critical Psychology, 9.*

Morawski, J. G., & Bayer, B. M. (2003). Social Psychology. In I. B. Weiner (Ed.), *Handbook of Psychology: History of Psychology, Vol. 1* (pp. 223–247). New York: Wiley.

Morawski, J. S. (1984). Not Quite New Worlds: Psychologists' Conceptions of the Ideal Family in the Twenties. In M. Lewin (Ed.), *In The Shadow of the Past: Psychology Portrays the Sexes* (pp. 97–125). New York: Columbia University Press.

Moreland, D. (1997). *Demanding the Impossible: Human Nature and Politics in Nineteenth Century Social Anarchism.* Washington, DC: Cassell.

Moreno, C., Laje, G., Blanco, C., Jiang, H., Schmidt, A. B., & Olfson, M. (2007). National Trends in the Outpatient Diagnosis and Treatment of Bipolar Disorder in Youth. *Archives of General Psychiatry, 64,* 1032–1039.

Morgan, A. (2000). *What is Narrative Therapy? An Easy-To-Read Introduction.* Adelaide, South Australia: Dulwich Centre Publications.

Morris, E. (2004). *The Foreshore and Seabed Act: A Sad End to a Sorry Spectacle*, from http://www.converge.org.nz/pma/fs191104a.htm

Morrow, R. A., & Brown, D. D. (1994). *Critical Theory and Methodology.* Thousand Oaks, CA: Sage.

Morsillo, J., & Prilleltensky, I. (2007). Social Action with Youth: Interventions, Evaluation, and Psychopolitical Validity. *Journal of Community Psychology, 35,* 725–740.

Morss, J. (1996). *Growing Critical: Alternatives to Developmental Psychology.* London: Routledge.

Moss, P., & Teghtsoonian, K. (Eds.). (2008). *Contesting Illness: Processes and Practices.* Toronto: University of Toronto Press.

Moynihan, R., & Cassels, A. (2005). *Selling Sickness.* New York: Nation Books.

Moynihan, R., & Henry, D. (2006). The Fight Against Disease Mongering: Generating Knowledge for Action. *PLoS Medicine, 3*(4), e191.

Münch, R. (1988). *Understanding Modernity.* London: Routledge.

Munsterberg, H. (1901/1981). *On the Witness Stand: Essays on Psychology and Crime.* Littleton, CO: Fred B. Rothman & Co.

Murray, M. (Ed.). (2004). *Critical Health Psychology.* Basingstoke, UK: Palgrave Macmillan.

Murray, M., & Campbell, C. (2003). Living in a Material World: Reflecting on Some Assumptions of Health Psychology. *Journal of Health Psychology, 8,* 231–236.

Murray, M., & Chamberlain, K. (Eds.). (1998). Qualitative Research [Special Issue]. *Journal of Health Psychology, 8*(2).

Murray, M., & Chamberlain, K. (1999a). Health Psychology and Qualitative Research. In M. Murray and K. Chamberlain (Eds.), *Qualitative Health Psychology: Theories and Methods* (pp. 3–15). London: Sage.

Murray, M., & Chamberlain, K. (Eds.). (1999b). *Qualitative Health Psychology: Theories and Methods.* London: Sage.

Murray, M., & Gray, N. (Eds.). (2008). Health Psychology and the Arts [Special Issue]. *Journal of Health Psychology, 13*(2).

Murray, M., & Poland, B. (2006). Health Psychology and Social Action. *Journal of Health Psychology, 11*, 379–384.

Murray, M., & Tilley, N. (2006). Using Community Arts to Promote Awareness of Safety in Fishing Communities: An Action Research Study. *Safety Science, 44*, 797–808.

Mustakova-Possardt, E. (2003). *Critical Consciousness: A Study of Morality in Global, Historical Context.* London: Praeger.

Myers, T. (2003). *Slavoj Žižek.* London: Routledge.

Nadler, D. A., & Tushman, M. L. (1989). Organizational Frame Bending: Principles for Managing Reorientation. *Academy of Management Executive 3*(3), 194–204.

Nairn, M. (1990). *Understanding Colonization.* Unpublished manuscript, Auckland.

Nairn, R., & McCreanor, T. (1991). Race Talk and Commonsense: Patterns in Pakeha Discourse on Maori/Pakeha Relations in New Zealand. *Journal of Language and Social Psychology, 10*(4), 245–262.

National Commission on Excellence in Education (1983). *A Nation At Risk: The Imperative for Educational Reform.* Washington, DC: US Government Printing Office.

Neckerman, K. M., & Torche, F. (2007). Inequality: Causes and Consequences. *Annual Review of Sociology, 33*, 335–357.

Nehru, J. (1946). The Discovery of India. In I. Wallerstein (Ed.), *Social Change: The Colonial Situation* (1966) (pp. 62–67). New York: John Wiley.

NeighborWorks America. (2006). *Community Building and Organizing Initiative* (Annual Report July 2005–June 2006). Boston, MA.

Nelson, G. (1994). The Development of a Mental Health Coalition: A Case Study. *American Journal of Community Mental Health, 22*, 229–255.

Nelson, G., Lord, J., & Ochocka, J. (2001). *Shifting the Paradigm in Community Mental Health: Towards Empowerment and Community.* Toronto: University of Toronto Press.

Nelson, G., Pancer, S., Hayward, K., & Peters, R. (2005). *Partnerships for Prevention: The Story of the Highfield Community Enrichment Project.* Toronto: University of Toronto Press.

Nelson, G., & Prilleltensky, I. (Eds.). (2005). *Community Psychology: In Pursuit of Liberation and Well-being.* Basingstoke, UK: Palgrave MacMillan.

Nelson, G., Prilleltensky, I., & MacGillivary, H. (2001). Building Value-based Partnerships: Toward Solidarity with Oppressed Groups. *American Journal of Community Psychology, 29*, 649–677.

Nelson, J. K. (2000). Clinical Assessment of Crying and Crying Inhibition Based on Attachment Theory. *Bulletin of the Menninger Clinic, 64*, 509–529.

Nelson, S. D., & Caplan, N. (1983). Social Problem Solving and Social Change. In D. Perlman and P. C. Cozby (Eds.), *Social Psychology* (pp. 503–532). New York: Holt, Rinehart.

Nelson, T. E., & Kinder, D. R. (1996). Issue Frames and Group-Centrism in American Public Opinion. *The Journal of Politics, 58*, 1055–1078.

New Zealand Press Association. (2008). Minor Parties Coy on Post-Election Ties. *New Zealand Herald*, 31 March.

Nicholson, I. A. M. (2001). 'GIVING UP MALENESS': Abraham Maslow, Masculinity, and the Boundaries of Psychology. *History of Psychology, 4*, 79–91.

Nicholson, I. A. M. (2003). *Inventing Personality: Gordon Allport and the Science of Selfhood.* Washington, DC: APA Books.

Nietzsche, F. W. G. (1966). *Beyond Good and Evil.* New York: Vintage Books.

Nikora, L., Levy, M., Masters, B., & Waitoki, M. (2006). Origins and Development of Indigenous Psychologies: An International Analysis. *International Journal of Psychology, 41*(4), 243–268.

No Hiding Place: Human Rights – A World Report. (1998). *The New Internationalist,* January–February, *298.*

Nordstrom, C. (1997). *A Different Kind of War Story.* Philadelphia, PA: University of Pennsylvania Press.

Nussbaum, M. (1999). *Sex and Social Justice.* Oxford: Oxford University Press.

Nussbaum, M. (2002). Women's Capabilities and Social Justice. In M. Molyneaux and S. Razavi (Eds.), *Gender Justice, Development, and Rights* (pp. 45–77). Oxford: Oxford University Press.

Nussbaum, M. (2006). *Frontiers of Justice: Disability, Nationality, Species Membership.* Cambridge, MA: Harvard.

Obeyesekere, G. (1984). Depression, Buddhism and the Work of Culture in Sri Lanka. In A. Kleinman and B. Good (Eds.), *Culture and Depression* (pp. 134–152). Berkeley, CA: University of California Press.

Ogden, J. (1997). The Rhetoric and Reality of Psychosocial Theories: A Challenge to Biomedicine. *Journal of Health Psychology, 2,* 21–29.

Ogloff, J. R. P., Tomkins, A. J., & Bersoff, D. N. (1996). Education and Training in Psychology and Law/Criminal Justice: Historical Foundations, Present Structures, and Future Developments. *Criminal Justice and Behavior, 23,* 200–235.

Oliver, K. (2004). *The Colonization of Psychic Space: A Psychoanalytic Social Theory of Oppression.* Minneapolis, MN: University of Minnesota Press.

Oliver, M. (1996). A Sociology of Disability or a Disabled Sociology? In L. Barton (Ed.), *Disability & Society: Emerging Issues and Insights* (pp. 18–42). London: Longman.

Olkin, R. (1999). *What Therapists Should Know About Disability.* New York: The Guilford Press.

Olkin, R., & Pledger, C. (2003). Can Disability Studies and Psychology Join Hands? *American Psychologist, 58*(4), 296–304.

Ostrove, J. M., & Cole, E. R. (2003). Privileging Class: Toward a Critical Psychology of Social Class in the Context of Education. *Journal of Social Issues, 59,* 677–692.

Ostrove, J. M., & Long, S. M. (2007). Social Class and Belonging: Implications for College Adjustment. *Review of Higher Education, 30,* 363–389.

Otto, M. (2007). For Want of a Dentist: Pr. George's Boy Dies After Bacteria from Tooth Spread to Brain. Available: http://www.washingtonpost.com/wp-dyn/content/article/2007/02/27/AR2007022702116.html, accessed 28 February.

Ouchi, W. G. (1981). *Theory Z.* Reading, MA: Addison-Wesley.

Oullette, S. C. (2008). Notes for a Critical Personality Psychology: Making Room under the Critical Psychology Umbrella. *Social and Personality Psychology Compass, 2*(1), 1–20.

Owens, G. (2001). Is Critical Health Psychology Sufficiently Self-Critical? *Psychology, Health & Medicine, 6,* 259–264.

Pacht, W., Fox, R., Zimbardo, P., & Antonuccio, D. (2007). Corporate Funding and Conflicts of Interest: A Primer for Psychologists. *American Psychologist, 62,* 1005–1015.

Pancer, M. (1997). Social Psychology: The Crisis Continues. In D. Fox and I. Prilleltensky (Eds.), *Critical Psychology: An Introduction.* London: Sage.

Papineau, D. (1996). *Citizen Empowerment Through Community Economic Development in a Multiethnic Neighborhood.* Unpublished Dissertation. Université de Montreal, Canada.

Paranjpe, A. C. (1998). *Self and Identity in Modern Psychology and Indian Thought.* New York: Plenum.

Pare, D., & Larner, G. (Eds.). (2004). *Collaborative Practice in Psychology and Therapy.* London: The Haworth Press.

Parker, D. F., & DeCotiis, T. A. (1983). Organizational Determinants of Job Stress. *Organizational Behavior and Human Performance, 32,* 160–177.

Parker, I. (1989). *The Crisis in Modern Social Psychology – and How to End It.* London: Routledge.

Parker, I. (1997). *Psychoanalytic Culture: Psychoanalytic Discourse in Western Society.* London: Sage.

Parker, I. (2003). Jacques Lacan, Barred Psychologist. *Theory and Psychology, 13*(1), 95–115.

Parker, I. (2007). Critical Psychology: What It Is and What It Is Not. *Social and Personality Psychology Compass, 1*(1), 1–15.

Parker, I., & Burmann, E. (1993). Against Discursive Imperialism, Empiricism and Constructionism: Thirty-Two Problems With Discourse Analysis. In I. E. Burman and I. Parker (Eds.), *Discourse Analytic Research: Repertoires and Readings of Texts in Action.* London: Routledge.

Parker, I., & Spears, R. (Eds.). (1996). *Psychology and Society: Radical Theory and Practice.* London, UK: Pluto.

Parthasarathi, P., & Steinitz, V. (2007) Bioweapons Lab Opposed in Boston. *Resist, 16*(3), 6–7.

Patrinos, H. A., Skoufias, E., & Lunde, T. (2007). Indigenous Peoples in Latin America: Economic Opportunities and Social Networks. Available from http://www-wds.world bank.org/external/default/WDSContentServer/WDSP/IB/2007/05/03/000016406_2007 0503093331/Rendered/PDF/wps4227.pdf

Pawelski, J., & Prilleltensky, I. (2005). That At Which All Things Aim: Wellness, Happiness, and the Ethics of Organizational Life. In R. Giacalone (Ed.), *Positive Psychology in Business Ethics and Corporate Social Responsibility* (pp. 191–208). Charlotte, NC: InfoAge.

Pears, I. (1992). The Gentleman and the Hero: Wellington and Napoleon in the Nineteenth Century. In R. Porter (Ed.), *Myths of the English* (pp. 216–236). Cambridge: Polity Press.

Peirce, C. S. (1940). Abduction and Induction. In J. Bulchder (Ed.), *The Philosophy of Peirce: Selected Writings.* London: Routledge and Keegan Paul. (Republished in 1955 as *Philosophical Writings of Peirce.* New York: Dover.)

Perkins, D. D., Hughey, J., & Speer, P. W. (2002). Community Psychology Perspectives on Social Capital Theory and Community Development Practice. *Journal of the Community Development Society, 33,* 33–52.

Perlin, M. L. (1991). Power Imbalances in Therapeutic and Forensic Relationships. *Behavioral Sciences and the Law, 9,* 111–128.

Peter, M., Vingerhoets, J. J. M., & Van Heck, G. L. (2001). Personality, Gender and Crying. *European Journal of Personality, 15,* 19–28.

Pfeffer, J. (1981). Management as Symbolic Action: The Creation and Maintenance of Organizational Paradigms. *Research in Organizational Behavior,* Vol. 31 (pp. 1–52). Greenwich, CT: JAI Press.

Phillips, D. C. (1987). *Philosophy, Science and Social Inquiry.* Oxford: Pergamon.

Phillipson, C., & Walker, A. (1987). The Case for a Critical Gerontology. In S. DeGregorio (Ed.), *Social Gerontology: New Directions* (pp. 1–15). London: Croon Helm.

Pieterman, R. (2007). The Social Construction of Fat: Care and Control in the Public Concern for Healthy Behaviour. *Sociology Compass, 1/1,* 309–321.

Pilgrim, D. (1992). Psychotherapy and Political Evasions. In W. Dryden and C. Feltham (Eds.), *Psychotherapy and its Discontents* (pp. 225–242). Bristol, PA: Open University Press.

Pledger, C. (2003). Discourse on Disability and Rehabilitation Issues: Opportunities for Psychology. *American Psychologist, 58,* 279–288.

Politzer, G. (1928). *Critique des Fondements de la Psychologie.* Paris: Editions Rieder.

Politzer, G. (1994). *Critique of the Foundations of Psychology: The Psychology of Psychoanalysis.* Pittsburgh, PA: Duquesne University Press.

Pols, H. (2007). Psychological Knowledge in a Colonial Context: Theories on the Nature of the 'Native Mind' in the Former Dutch East Indies. *History of Psychology, 10,* 111–131.

Porter, E. (2006). Study Finds Wealth Inequality is Widening Worldwide. *The New York Times,* 6 December. Available from http://www.nytimes.com/2006/12/06/business/world business/06wealth.html?ref=business

Portes, A. (1998). Social Capital: Its Origins and Applications in Modern Sociology. *Annual Review of Sociology, 24,* 1–24.

Potter, J. (1996). *Representing Reality: Discourse, Rhetoric and Social Construction.* London: Sage.

Potter, J., & Hepburn, A. (2005). Qualitative Interviews in Psychology: Problems and Possibilities. *Qualitative Research in Psychology, 2,* 281–307.

Potter, J., & Wetherell, M. (1987). *Discourse and Social Psychology: Beyond Attitudes and Behavior.* London: Sage.

Potts, A. (2008). The Female Sexual Dysfunction Debate: Different 'Problems', New Drugs – More Pressures? In P. Moss and K. Teghtsoonian (Eds.), *Contesting Illness: Processes and Practices* (pp. 259–280). Toronto: University of Toronto Press.

Potts, A., & Tiefer, L. (2006). Introduction: Special Issue on 'Viagra Culture'. *Sexualities, 9,* 267–272.

Potts, R. G. (2003). Emancipatory Education versus School-Based Prevention in African-American Communities. *American Journal of Community Psychology, 31,* 173–183.

Pratt, M. G. (2000). The Good, the Bad, and the Ambivalent: Managing Identification among Amway Distributors. *Administrative Science Quarterly, 45,* 456–493.

President's New Freedom Commission on Mental Health (2003). *Final Report for the President's New Freedom Commission on Mental Health.* Available from www.mental healthcommission.gov/reports/reports.html (accessed 28 April 2008).

Pressman, J. (1998). *Last Resort.* New York: Cambridge University Press.

Prilleltensky, I. (1993). The Immigration Experience of Latin-American Families: Research and Action on Perceived Risk and Protective Factors. *Canadian Journal of Community Mental Health, 12*(2), 101–116.

Prilleltensky, I. (1994). *The Morals and Politics of Psychology: Psychological Discourse and the Status Quo.* Albany, NY: SUNY Press.

Prilleltensky, I. (1997). Values, Assumptions, and Practices: Assessing the Moral Implications of Psychological Discourse and Action. *American Psychologist, 52*(5), 517–535.

Prilleltensky, I. (2000). Bridging Agency, Theory and Action: Critical Links in Critical Psychology. In T. Sloan (Ed.), *Critical Psychology: Voices for Change* (pp. 67–81). London: MacMillan.

Prilleltensky, I. (2001). Value-based Praxis in Community Psychology: Towards Psychopolitical Validity. *American Journal of Community Psychology, 29,* 195–201.

Prilleltensky, I. (2003). Poverty and Power. In S. C. Carr and T. S. Sloan (Eds.), *Poverty and Psychology: From Global Perspective to Local Practice* (pp. 19–44). New York: Kluwer Academic.

Prilleltensky, I. (2008). The Role of Power In Wellness, Oppression, and Liberation: The Promise of Psychopolitical Validity. *Journal of Community Psychology, 36,* 116–136.

Prilleltensky, I., & Fox, D. (2007). Psychopolitical Literacy for Wellness and Justice. *Journal of Community Psychology, 35*(6), 793–806.

Prilleltensky, I., & Gonick, L. (1996). Polities Change, Oppression Remains: On the Psychology and Politics of Oppression. *Political Psychology, 17,* 127–147.

Prilleltensky, I., & Nelson, G. (2002). *Doing Psychology Critically: Making a Difference in Diverse Settings.* New York: Palgrave Macmillan.

Prilleltensky, I., Nelson, G., & Sanchez, L. A. (2000). Value-based Smoking Prevention Program With Latin American Youth: Program Evaluation. *Journal of Ethnic and Cultural Diversity in Social Work, 9*(1-2), 97–117.

Prilleltensky, I., & Prilleltensky, O. (2003). Towards a Critical Health Psychology Practice. *Journal of Health Psychology, 8,* 197–210.

Prilleltensky, I., & Prilleltensky, O. (2006). *Promoting Well-Being: Linking Personal, Organizational, and Community Change.* Hoboken, NJ: Wiley.

Prilleltensky, O. (2004). *Motherhood and Disability: Children and Choices.* New York: Palgrave Macmillan.

Prince, T. (2004). Multicultural Psychology, Community Mental Health and Social Transformation. *Challenge, 11,* 1–16.

Proehl, R. A. (2001). *Organizational Change in the Human Services.* Thousand Oaks, CA: Sage Publications.

Psychosocial Working Group (2003). *Psychosocial Intervention in Complex Emergencies: A Conceptual Framework.* Edinburgh: Authors. Accessed 9 May 2005 from http://www.forcedmigration.org/psychosocial/papers/Conceptual%20Framework.pdf

Pupavac, V. (2000). Securing the Community? An Examination of International Psychosocial Intervention. Paper presented at 'Balkan Security: Visions of the Future Conference', The Centre for South-East European Studies, School of Slavonic and East European Studies, University College London, 16–17 June.

Putnam, M., Greenen, S., Powers, L., Saxton, M., Finney, S., & Dautel, P. (2003). Health and Wellness: People with Disabilities Discuss Barriers and Facilitators to Well Being. *Journal of Rehabilitation, I*(1), 37–45.

Putnam, R. (2000). *Bowling Alone: The Collapse and Revival of American Community.* New York: Simon and Schuster.

Putzke, J., Richards, S., Hicken, B., & DeVivo, M. (2002). Predictions of Life Satisfaction. A Spinal Cord Injury Research Study. *Archives of Physical Medicine and Rehabilitation, 83,* 555–561.

Rabinow, P. (Ed.). (1984). *The Foucault Reader.* New York: Pantheon.

Radley, A. (1994). *Making Sense of Illness: The Social Psychology of Health and Disease.* London: Sage.

Radley, A. (2000). Health Psychology, Embodiment and the Question of Vulnerability. *Journal of Health Psychology, 5,* 297–304.

Rappaport, J. (1977). *Community Psychology: Values, Research, and Action.* New York: Holt, Rinehart, & Winston.

Rappaport, J. (1981). In Praise of Paradox: A Social Policy of Empowerment over Prevention. *American Journal of Community Psychology, 9,* 1–25.

Rappaport, J., & Stewart, E. (1997). A Critical Look at Critical Psychology: Elaborating the Questions. In D. Fox and I. Prilleltensky (Eds.), *Critical Psychology: An Introduction* (pp. 301–317). London: Sage.

Rawls, J. (1972). *A Theory of Justice.* New York: Oxford University Press.

Reason, P., & Bradbury, H. (Eds.). (2001). *Handbook of Action Research: Participative Inquiry and Practice.* London: Sage.

Reay, D. (1996a). Insider Perspectives or Stealing the Words Out of Women's Mouths: Interpretation in the Research Process. *Feminist Review, 53,* 57–73.

Reay, D. (1996b). Dealing With Difficult Differences: Reflexivity and Social Class in Feminist Research. *Feminism & Psychology, 6,* 443–456.

Reay, D. (1999). 'Class Acts': Educational Involvement and Psycho-Sociological Class Processes. *Feminism & Psychology, 9,* 89–106.

Reay, D. (2005). Beyond Consciousness? The Psychic Landscape of Social Class. *Sociology, 39,* 911–928.

Reeve, D. (2002). Negotiating Psycho-Emotional Dimensions of Disability and their Influence on Identity Constructions. *Disability & Society, 15*(5), 493–508.

Reeve, D. (2006). Towards a Psychology of Disability: The Emotional Effects of Living in a Disabling Society. In D. Goodley and R. Lawthom (Eds.), *Disability & Society: Critical Introductions & Reflections* (pp. 94–107). New York: Palgrave MacMillan.

Regional Income Distribution. (2008). *The Economist, 387*(8576), 19 April, 118.

Reich, S., Riemer, M., Prilleltensky, I., & Montero, M. (Eds.). (2007). *International Community Psychology: History and Theories*. New York: Kluwer.

Reich, W. (1972). *Character Analysis* (3rd ed.). New York: Simon and Schuster.

Reicher, S. D., & Haslam, S. A. (2006). Rethinking the Psychology of Tyranny: The BBC Prison Study. *British Journal of Social Psychology, 45*, 1–40.

Reimers, F. A. (2007). Putting It All Together: A Content Analysis and Methodological Review of Intersections of Class, Race, and Gender in the Counseling Literature (Doctoral Dissertation, Texas Woman's University). *Dissertation Abstracts, 68*, 1B.

Rein, M. (1976). *Social Science and Public Policy*. New York: Penguin.

Remenyi, J. (2004). Poverty and Development: The Struggle to Empower the Poor. In D. Kingsbury, J. Remenyi, J. McKay and J. Hunt (Eds.), *Key Issues in Development* (pp. 190–220). New York: Palgrave MacMillan.

Richards, G. (1997). *Race, Racism and Psychology: Towards A Reflexive History*. London: Routledge.

Richardson, F. C., Rogers, A., & McCarroll, J. (1998). Toward a Dialogical Self. *American Behavioral Scientist, 41*(4), 496–515.

Richardson, J. T. E. (2003). Howard Andrew Knox and the Origins of Performance Testing on Ellis Island, 1912–1916. *History of Psychology, 6*(2), 143–170.

Riggs, D. W., & Augoustinos, M. (2004). Projecting Threat: Managing Subjective Investments in Whiteness. *Psychoanalysis, Culture & Society, 9*, 219–236.

Riggs, D. W., & Augoustinos, M. (2005). The Psychic Life of Colonial Power: Racialised Subjectivities, Bodies, and Methods. *Journal of Community and Applied Social Psychology, 15*, 461–477.

Roback, A. A. (1961). *History of Psychology and Psychiatry*. New York: Philosophical Library.

Roberts, B. W., Walton, K. E., & Viechtbauer, W. (2006). Patterns of Mean-Level Change in Personality Traits Across the Life Course: A Meta-Analysis of Longitudinal Studies. *Psychological Bulletin, 132*(1), 1–25.

Roberts, H., & Gidley, R. (2000). *Memory and Monuments: The Fight Against Impunity in Guatemala*. Publication for Catholic Institute for International Relations.

Robertson, J., & Fitzgerald, L. F. (1990). The (Mis)Treatment of Men: Effects of Client Gender Role and Life-Style on Diagnosis and Attribution of Pathology. *Journal of Counseling Psychology, 37*, 3–9.

Rogler, L. H. (1997). Making Sense of Historical Changes in the *Diagnostic and Statistical Manual of Mental Disorders*: Five Propositions. *Journal of Health and Social Behavior, 38*, 9–20.

Rose, N. (1996). *Inventing our Selves: Psychology, Power, and Personhood*. Cambridge, UK: Cambridge University Press.

Rose, N. (2004). Becoming Neurochemical Selves. In N. Stehr (Ed.), *Biotechnology, Commerce and Civil Society* (pp. 89–128). New York: Transaction Press.

Rose, N. (2006). *The Politics of Life Itself: Biomedicine, Power, and Subjectivity in the Twenty-First Century*. Princeton, NJ: Princeton University Press.

Rose, N. (2007). Molecular Biopolitics, Somatic Ethics and the Spirit of Biocapital. *Social Theory & Health, 5*, 3–29.

Rosenberg, R. (1982). *Beyond Separate Spheres: Intellectual Roots of Modern Feminism*. New Haven, CT: Yale University Press.

Rosenhan, D. L. (1973). On Being Sane In Insane Places. *Science, 179*(4070), 250–258.

Rosenwald, G. C. (1985). Hypocrisy, Self-deception, and Perplexity: The Subject's Enhancement as Methodological Criterion. *Journal of Personality and Social Psychology, 49*, 682–703.

Rosenwald, G. C. (1988). Toward a Formative Psychology. *Journal for the Theory of Social Behavior, 18*, 1–32.

Rosenwald, G. C., & Ochberg, R. L. (Eds.). (1992). *Storied Lives: The Cultural Politics of Self-understanding*. New Haven, CT: Yale University Press.

Ross, L., Lepper, M., & Hubbard, M. (1975). Perseverance in Self Perception and Social Perception: Biased Attributional Processes in the Debriefing Paradigm. *Journal of Personality and Social Psychology, 32*, 880–892.

Roth, W. M., & Lee, Y. J. (2007). 'Vygotsky's Neglected Legacy': Cultural-Historical Activity Theory. *Review of Educational Research, 77*(2), 186–232.

Rothman, R. A. (2005). *Inequality and Stratification: Race, Class, and Gender* (5th ed.). Upper Saddle River, NJ: Prentice Hall.

Rutherford, A. (2006). Mother of Behavior Therapy and Beyond: Mary Cover Jones and the Study of the 'Whole Child'. In D. A. Dewsbury, L. T. Benjamin and M. Wertheimer (Eds.), *Portraits of Pioneers in Psychology,* vol. 6 (pp. 189–204). Washington, DC: APA Books.

Ryan, W. (1971). *Blaming the Victim*. New York: Vintage Books.

Saegert, S. (2005). *Community Building and Civic Capacity*. Aspen Institute.

Saegert, S. C., Adler, N. E., Bullock, H. E., Cauce, A. M., Lui, W. M., & Wyche, K. F. (2007). *Report of the APA Task Force Report on Socioeconomic Status*. Washington, DC: American Psychological Association.

Said, E. (1978). *Orientalism*. New York: Pantheon.

Said, E. (1988). Yeats and Decolonization. Reprinted in M. Bayoumi & A. Rubin (Eds.), (2000) *The Edward Said Reader* (pp. 291–313). London: Granta.

Salancik, G. R., & Pfeffer, J. (1977). An Examination of Need-Satisfaction Models of Job Attitudes. *Administrative Science Quarterly, 22*, 427–456.

Salas, E., & Cannon-Bowers, J. A. (2001). The Science of Training: A Decade of Progress. *Annual Review of Psychology, 52,* 471–499.

Samelson, F. (1974). History, Origin Myth, and Ideology: Comte's 'Discovery' of Social Psychology. *Journal for the Theory of Social Behavior, 4*, 217–231.

Samelson, F. (1975). On the Science and Politics of the IQ. *Social Research, 42,* 467–488.

Samelson, F. (1992). Rescuing the Reputation of Sir Cyril [Burt]. *Journal of the History of the Behavioral Sciences, 28*, 221–233.

Sampson, E. E. (1983). *Justice and the Critique of Pure Psychology*. New York: Plenum.

Sampson, E. E. (1989). The Challenge of Social Change for Psychology: Globalization and Psychology's Theory of the Person. *American Psychologist, 44*, 914–921.

Sampson, E. E. (1991). *Social Worlds: Personal Lives: An Introduction to Social Psychology*. San Diego, CA: Harcourt Brace Jovanovich.

Sandoval, C. (2000). *Methodology of the Oppressed*. Minneapolis, MN: University of Minnesota Press.

Sarachild, K. [Karthie Amatniek] (1978). Consciousness Raising: A Radical Weapon. In *Redstockings of the Women's Liberation Movement, Feminist Revolution: An Abridged Edition with Additional Writings,* pp. 144–50. New York: Random House.

Sarafino, E. P. (2005). *Health Psychology: Biopsychosocial Interactions* (5th edn). New York: Wiley.

Sarason, S. B. (1974). *The Psychological Sense of Community: Prospects for a Community Psychology*. San Francisco, CA: Jossey-Bass.

Sarason, S. B. (1976). Community Psychology and the Anarchist Insight. *American Journal of Community Psychology, 4*, 243–261.

Sarason, S. B. (1981). *Psychology Misdirected*. New York: Free Press.

Sarat, A., & Kearns, T. (1992). *Law's Violence*. Ann Arbor, MI: Michigan University Press.

Satin, D. G. (1982). Erich Lindemann: The Humanist and the Era of Community Mental Health. *Proceedings of the American Philosophical Society, 126*(4), 327–346.

Savin-Baden, M., & Wimpenny, K. (2007). Exploring and Implementing Participatory Action Research. *Journal of Geography in Higher Education, 31,* 331–343.

Scarborough, E., & Furumoto, L. (1987). *Untold Lives: The First Generation of American Women Psychologists.* New York: Columbia University Press.

Schein, E. (1990). Organizational Culture. *American Psychologist, 45,* 109–119.

Schein, E. (2006). From Brainwashing to Organizational Therapy: A Conceptual and Empirical Journey in Search of 'Systemic' Health and a General Model of Change Dynamics. A Drama in Five Acts. *Organization Studies, 27*(2), 287–301.

Schiller, B. R. (2003). *The Economics of Poverty and Discrimination* (8th edn). Upper Saddle River, NJ: Prentice Hall.

Schmidt, J. (2000). *Disciplined Minds: A Critical Look at Salaried Professionals and the Soul-Battering System that Shapes their Lives.* Lanham, MD: Rowman & Littlefield.

Schmiechen, R. (Director) (1992). *Changing our Minds: The Story of Dr. Evelyn Hooker* [motion picture]. San Francisco, CA : Frameline.

Schnarch, B. (2004). Ownership, Control, Access, and Possession (OCAP) or Self-Determination Applied to Research: A Critical Analysis of Contemporary First Nations Research and Some Options for First Nations Communities. *The Journal of Aboriginal Health, 1,* 80–95.

Schnittker, J., & McLeod, J. D. (2005). The Social Psychology of Health Disparities. *Annual Review of Sociology, 31,* 105–125.

Schram, S. F., Soss, J., & Fording, R. C. (Eds.), (2003). *Race and the Politics of Welfare Reform.* Ann Arbor, MI: University of Michigan Press.

Schriner, K. (2001). A Disability Studies Perspective on Employment Issues and Policies for Disabled People: An International View. In G. Albrecht, K. Seelman, and M. Bury (Eds.), *Handbook of Disability Studies* (pp. 642–662). New York: Sage.

Schroeder, J. L. (1998). *The Vestal and the Fasces: Hegel, Lacan, Property, and the Feminine.* Berkeley, CA: University of California Press.

Schultz, D. P. (1969). *A History of Modern Psychology.* New York: Academic Press.

Schwartz, B. (1986). *The Battle For Human Nature.* New York: Norton.

Scott, J., & Leonhardt, D. (2005). Shadowy Lines That Still Divide. *The New Times,* 15 May, 1.1.

Seale, C. (2005). New Directions for Critical Internet Health Studies: Representing Cancer Experience on the Web. *Sociology of Health & Illness, 27,* 515–540.

Seider, R. (2001). War, Peace, and the Politics of Memory in Guatemala. In N. Biggar (Ed.), *Burying the Past: Making Peace and Doing Justice after Civil Conflict* (pp. 184–206). Washington, DC: Georgetown University Press.

Seidman, E. (1988). Back to the Future, Community Psychology: Unfolding a Theory of Social Intervention. *American Journal of Community Psychology, 16*(1), 3–21.

Seligman, M. E. (2002a). Positive Psychology, Positive Prevention, and Positive Therapy. In C. R. Snyder and S. J. Lopez (Eds.), *Handbook of Positive Psychology* (pp. 3–9). New York: Oxford University Press.

Seligman. M. E. (2002b). *Authentic Happiness: Using the New Positive Psychology to Realize Your Potential for Lasting Fulfillment.* New York: The Free Press.

Sen, A. (1999). *Development as Freedom.* New York: Anchor Books.

Senge, P. M. (1990). *The Fifth Discipline: The Art and Practice of the Learning Organization* (1st ed.). New York: Doubleday.

Sève, L. (1978). *Man in Marxist Theory and the Psychology of Personality.* Atlantic Highlands, NJ: Humanities Press.

Shakespeare, T. (2006). *Disability Rights and Wrongs.* New York: Routledge.

Shank, G. (1998). The Extraordinary Powers of Abductive Reasoning. *Theory & Psychology, 8*(6), 841–860.

Sherman, D. K., & Kim, H. S. (2002). Affective Perseverance: The Resistance of Affect to Cognitive Invalidation. *Personality and Social Psychology Bulletin, 28,* 224–237.

Shields, S. (2007). Passionate Men, Emotional Women: Psychology Constructs Gender Differences in the Late 19th Century. *History of Psychology, 10,* 92–110.

Shinn, B. (2006). Psychologists and Torture: APA, PENS, SPSSI, and DSJ. *Forward/SPSSI* (229), 1–2, 20.

Shon, P. (2000). 'He you c'me here!' Subjectivization, Resistance, and the Interpellative Violence of Self-Generated Police Citizen Encounters. *International Journal for the Semiotics of Law, 13,* 159–179.

Shon, P., & Arrigo, B. A. (2006). Reality-Based TV and Police-Citizen Encounters: The Intertextual Construction and Situated Meaning of Mental Illness-as-Punishment. *Punishment & Society: The International Journal of Penology, 8,* 59–85.

Sirianni, S., & Friedland, L. (2001). *Civic Innovation in America: Community Empowerment, Public Policy, and the Movement for Civic Renewal.* Berkeley, CA: University of California Press.

Skinner, B. F. (1948). *Walden Two.* New York: Macmillan.

Skinner, B. F. (1971). *Beyond Freedom and Dignity.* New York: Knopf.

Slife, B. D., Reber, J. S., & Richardson, F. C. (2005). *Critical Thinking About Psychology: Hidden Assumptions and Plausible Alternatives.* Washington, DC: American Psychological Association.

Sloan, T. (1986). Breaking the Objectivist Hold on Personality Psychology. *Annals of Theoretical Psychology, 4,* 226–231.

Sloan, T. (1987). Lucien Sève: Foundations for a Critical Psychology of Personality. In R. Hogan and W. Jones (Eds.), *Perspectives on Personality, 2,* 125–142. Greenwich, CT: JAI Press.

Sloan, T. (1994). La Personalidad como Construcción Ideológica. In M. Montero (Ed.), *Construcción y Crítica de la Psicología Social* (pp. 177–188). Barcelona: Anthropos.

Sloan, T. (1996a). *Damaged Life: The Crisis of the Modern Psyche.* London: Routledge.

Sloan, T. (1996b). *Life Choices: Understanding Dilemmas and Decisions.* Boulder, CO: Westview.

Sloan, T. (2000). (Ed.). *Critical Psychology: Voices for Change.* London: Macmillan.

Sloan, T. (2005). Globalization, Poverty and Social Justice. In G. Nelson and I. Prilleltensky (Eds.), *Community Psychology: In Pursuit of Liberation and Well-being* (pp. 309–329). New York: Palgrave Macmillan.

Small, M. A. (1993). Advancing Psychological Jurisprudence. *Behavioral Sciences and the Law, 11,* 3–16.

Smedslund, J. (1988). *Psycho-Logic.* Berlin: Springer.

Smith, C. (2007). *The Cost of Privilege: Taking On the System of White Supremacy and Racism.* Fayetteville, NC: Camino Press.

Smith, D. J. (2005). The Effectiveness of the Juvenile Justice System. *Criminology and Criminal Justice, 6*(2), 239–257.

Smith, D., Langa, K., Kabeto, M., & Ubel, P. (2005). Health, Wealth and Happiness: Financial Resources Buffer Subjective Wellbeing after Onset of a Disability. *Psychological Science, 16*(9), 663–666.

Smith, L. (2005). Psychotherapy, Classism, and the Poor: Conspicuous by their Absence. *American Psychologist, 60,* 687–696.

Smith, L. T. (1999). *Decolonising Methodologies: Research and Indigenous Peoples.* Auckland, New Zealand: Zed.

Sobell, L., Ellingstad, T., & Sobell, M. (2000). Natural Recovery from Alcohol and Drug Problems: Methodological Review of the Research with Suggestions for Future Directions. *Addiction, 95,* 749–764.

Speer, P. W., & Hughey, J. (1995). Community Organizing: An Ecological Route to Empowerment and Power. *American Journal of Community Psychology, 23*(5), 729–748.

Speer, P. W., Hughey, J., Gensheimer, L. K., & Adams-Leavitt, W. (1995). Organizing for Power: A Comparative Case Study. *Journal of Community Psychology, 23,* 57–73.

Spence, R. (1999). The Centrality of Community-Led Recovery. In G. Harris (Ed.), *Recovery from Armed Conflict in Developing Countries: An Economic and Political Analysis* (pp. 204–222). London: Routledge.

Spicer, J., & Chamberlain, K. (1996). Developing Psychosocial Theory in Health Psychology: Problems and Prospects. *Journal of Health Psychology, 1,* 161–171.

Spivak, G. C. (1988). Can the Subaltern Speak? In N. Cary and L. Grossberg (Eds.), *Marxism and the Interpretation of Culture.* Urbana, IL: University of Illinois Press.

Spring, J. (1998). *Education and the Rise of the Global Economy.* Mahwah, NJ: Lawrence Erlbaum.

St. James-Roberts, I. (1988, October). Persistent Crying in the First Year of Life: A Progress Report. *Newsletter of the Association for Child Psychology and Psychiatry, 10,* 28–29.

Stacey, H. (1996). Lacan's Split Subjects: Raced and Gendered Transformations. *Legal Studies Forum, 20,* 277–293.

Stainton Rogers, W. (2003). *Social Psychology: Experimental and Critical Approaches.* Maidenhead: Open University Press.

Stam, H. J. (2000). Theorizing Health and Illness: Functionalism, Subjectivity and Reflexivity. *Journal of Health Psychology, 5,* 273–284.

Stam, H. J. (2006). Physician Health Thyself: The Fate of the Professional Cum Critic. *Journal of Health Psychology, 11,* 385–389.

Stampp, K. (1956). *The Peculiar Institution of Slavery in the Ante-Bellum South.* New York: Alfred Knopf.

Starcevic, V., & Durdic, S. (1993). Post-traumatic Stress Disorder: Current Conceptualization, An Overview of Research and Treatment. *Psihijatrija Danas, 25* (1–2), 9–22.

Stavenhagen, R. (2006). *Mission to New Zealand: Report by Special Rapporteur on the Situation of Human Rights and Fundamental Freedoms of Indigenous Peoples.* Accessed 1 December 2007 from http://www.converge.org.nz/pma/srnzmarch06.pdf

Staw, B. M., & Boettger, R. D. (1990). Task Revision: A Neglected Form of Work Performance. *Academy of Management Journal, 33,* 534–559.

Steinitz, V. (1996). *Interim Report: Welfare and Human Rights Monitoring Project.* Cambridge, MA: Unitarian Universalist Service Committee.

Stephens, N. M., Markus, H. R., & Townsend, S. S. M. (2007). Choice as an Act of Meaning: The Case of Social Class. *Journal of Personality and Social Psychology, 93*(5), 814–830.

Stephenson, N., & Kippax, S. (2008). Memory Work. In C. Willig and W. Stainton Rogers (Eds.), *The Sage Handbook of Qualitative Research in Psychology.* London: Sage.

Sternberg, R. J. (2005). There are No Public Policy Implications: A Reply to Rushton and Jensen (2005). *Psychology, Public Policy, and Law, 11*(2), 295–301.

Stevenson, M. (1992). Columbus and the War on Indigenous Peoples. *Race & Class: Journal for Black and Third World Liberation, 33*(3), 27–45.

Stewart, G. L. (2003). Toward an Understanding of the Multilevel Role of Personality in Teams. In M. R. Barrick and A. M. Ryan (Eds.), *Reconsidering the Role of Personality in Organizations.* San Francisco, CA: Jossey-Bass.

Stewart, S., Riecken, T., Scott, T., Tanaka, M., & Riecken, J. (2008). Expanding Health Literacy: Indigenous Youth Creating Videos. *Journal of Health Psychology, 13,*180–189.

Stolle, D. P. (2000). *Practicing Therapeutic Jurisprudence.* Durham, NC: Carolina Academic Press.

Stone, J. [Judd Marmor]. (1946). Theory and Practice of Psychoanalysis. *Science & Society, 10,* 54–79.

Stout, L. (1996). *Bridging the Class Divide and Other Lessons for Grassroots Organizing.* Boston, MA: Beacon Press.

Strakowski, S. M., Lonczak, H. S., Sax, K. W., West, S. A., Crist, A., Mehta, R., & Thienhaus, O. J. (1995). The Effects of Race on Diagnosis and Disposition from a Psychiatric Emergency Service. *Journal of Clinical Psychiatry, 56,* 101–107.

Subramanian S. V., & Kawachi, I. (2006). Whose Health is Affected by Income Inequality? A Multilevel Interaction Analysis of Contemporaneous and Lagged Effects of State Income Inequality on Individual Self-Rated Health in the United States. *Health & Place, 12,* 141–156.

Sue, D. W., Arredondo, P., & McDavis, R. J. (1992). Multicultural Counseling Competencies and Standards: A Call to the Profession. *Journal of Counseling and Development, 70,* 477–486.

Sullivan, J., Petronella, S., Brooks, E., Murillo, M., Primeau, L., & Ward, J. (2008). Theatre of the Oppressed and Environmental Justice Communities: A Transformational Therapy for the Body Politic. *Journal of Health Psychology, 13,* 166–179.

Sullivan, N. (2003). *A Critical Introduction to Queer Theory.* Edinburgh: Edinburgh University Press.

Suls, J., & Rothman, A. (2004). Evolution of the Biopsychosocial Model: Prospects and Challenges for Health Psychology. *Health Psychology, 23,* 119–125.

Sveaass, N., & Lavik, N. J. (2000). Psychological Aspects of Human Rights Violations: The Importance of Justice and Reconciliation. *Nordic Journal of International Law, 69,* 35–52.

Swain, J., Griffiths, C., & French, S. (2006). Counseling with the Social Model: Challenging Therapy's Pathologies. In D. Goodley and R. Lawthom (Eds.), *Disability & Society: Critical Introductions & Reflections* (pp. 155–169). New York: Palgrave MacMillan.

Swiss, S., & Giller, J. E. (1993). Rape as a Crime of War: A Medical Perspective. *Journal of the American Medical Association, 270,* 612–615.

Sylvestre, J., Nelson, G., Durbin, J., George, L., Aubry, T., & Ollenberg, M. (2006). Housing for People with Serious Mental Illness: Challenges for System-Level Development. *Community Development: Journal of the Community Development Society, 37,* 35–45.

Sylvestre, J., Nelson, G., Sabloff, A., & Peddle, S. (2007). Housing for People with Serious Mental Illness: A Comparison of Values and Research. *American Journal of Community Psychology, 40,* 125–137.

Szasz, T. (1962). Bootlegging Humanistic Values through Psychiatry. *Antioch Review, 22,* 341–349.

Szasz, T. (1974). *The Myth of Mental Illness: Foundations of a Theory of Personal Conduct* (rev.). New York: Harper & Row.

Tamasese, K., & Waldegrave, C. (1996). Culture and Gender Accountability in the 'Just Therapy' Approach. In C. McLean, M. Carey, and C. White (Eds.), *Men's Ways of Being* (pp. 51–62). Boulder, CO: Westview Press.

Tancredi, L. R. (2005). *Hardwired Behavior: What Neuroscience Reveals About Morality.* New York: Cambridge University Press.

Tapp, J. L. (1974). The Psychological Limits of Legality. In J. R. Pennock and J. W. Chapman (Eds.), *The Limits of Law: Nomos xv* (pp. 46–75). New York: Lieber-Atherton.

Tapp, J. L., & Levine, F. J. (Eds.). (1977). *Law, Justice, and the Individual in Society: Psychological and Legal Issues.* New York: Holt, Rinehart.

Tate, D., & Pledger, C. (2003). An Integrative Conceptual Framework of Disability: New Directions for Research. *American Psychologist, 58*(4), 289–295.

Tavris, C. (1993). The Mismeasure of Woman. *Feminism & Psychology, 3,* 149–168.

Taylor, S. E., & Fiske, S. T. (1975). Point of View and Perceptions of Causality. *Journal of Personality and Social Psychology, 32*(3), 439–445.

Teo, T. (2005). *The Critique of Psychology: From Kant to Postcolonial Theory.* New York: Springer.

Teo, T. (2008). From Speculation to Epistemological Violence in Psychology: A Critical-Hermeneutic Reconstruction. *Theory & Psychology, 18*(1), 47–67.

Teo, T., & Febbraro, A. (2003). Ethnocentrism as a Form of Intuition in Psychology. *Theory and Psychology, 13*, 673–694.

Terre Blanche, M., & Durrheim, K. (Eds.). (1999). *Research in Practice: Applied Methods for the Social Sciences*. Cape Town, South Africa: University of Cape Town Press.

Thomas, C. (1999). *Female Forms: Experiencing and Understanding Disability*. Buckingham: Open University Press.

Thompson, J. (1984). *Studies in the Theory of Ideology*. Berkeley: University of California Press.

Thompson Woolley, H. (1910). A Review of the Recent Literature on the Psychology of Sex. *Psychological Bulletin, 7*, 335–342.

Thorndike, R. L. (1986). The Role of General Ability in Prediction. *Journal of Vocational Behavior, 29*, 322–339.

Tiefer, L. (2004). *Sex is Not a Natural Act & Other Essays* (2nd ed.). Boulder, CO: Westview Press.

Tiefer, L. (2006). Female Sexual Dysfunction: A Case Study of Disease Mongering and Activist Resistance. *PLoS Medicine, 3*(4), e178.

Tiefer, L., Brick, P., & Kaplan, M. (2003). *A New View of Women's Sexual Problems: A Teaching Manual*. New York: The Campaign for a New View.

Tolman, C. W. (1994). *Psychology, Society, and Subjectivity: An Introduction to German Critical Psychology*. London: Routledge.

Tolman, C. W., & Maiers, W. (Eds.). (1991). *Critical Psychology: Contributions to an Historical Science of the Subject*. Cambridge, MA: Cambridge University Press.

Tolman, D. L., & Brydon-Miller, M. (2001). *From Subjects to Subjectivities: A Handbook of Interpretive and Participatory Methods*. New York: New York University Press.

Toporek, R., Gerstein, L., Fouad, N., Roysircar-Sodowsky, G., & Israel, T. (Eds.). (2006). *Handbook for Social Justice in Counseling Psychology: Leadership, Vision, and Action*. London: Sage.

Toulmin, S., & Leary, D. E. (1985). The Cult of Empiricism in Psychology, and Beyond. In S. Koch and D. E. Leary (Eds.), *A Century of Psychology as Science* (pp. 594–617). New York: McGraw-Hill.

Townley, B. (1993). Foucault, Power/Knowledge, and its Relevance for Human Resource Management. *The Academy of Management Review, 18*, 518–545.

Trice, H. M., & Beyer, J. (1984) Studying Organizational Cultures Through Rites and Ceremonials. *Academy of Management Review, 9*(4), 653–669.

Trickett, E. J., & Ryerson Espino, S. L. (2004). Collaboration and Social Inquiry: Multiple Meanings of a Construct and Its Role in Creating Valid and Useful Knowledge. *American Journal of Community Psychology, 34*, 125–137.

Tsui, A. S., & O'Reilly, C. A. (1989). Beyond Simple Demographic Effects: The Importance of Relational Demography in Superior-Subordinate Dyads. *Academy of Management Journal, 32*, 402–423.

Tuffin, K. (2004). *Understanding Critical Social Psychology*. London: Sage.

Tuhiwai Smith, L. (1999). *Decolonizing Methodologies: Research and Indigenous Peoples*. London: Zed Books.

Tushnet, M. (1986). Critical Legal Studies: An Introduction to its Origins and Underpinnings. *Journal of Legal Education, 36*, 505–517.

Tyler, T., Degoey, P., & Smith, H. (1996). Understanding Why the Justice of Group Procedures Matters: A Test of the Psychological Dynamics of the Group-Value Model. *Journal of Personality and Social Psychology, 70*, 913–930.

Ubel, P., Lowenstein, G., & Jepson, C. (2005). Disability and Sunshine: Can Hedonic Predictions Be Improved by Drawing Attention to Focusing Illusions or Emotional Adaptations? *Journal of Applied Experimental Psychology, 11*(2), 111–123.

Unger, R. (1996). Using the Master's Tools: Epistemology and Empiricism. In S. Wilkinson (Ed.), *Feminist Social Psychologies: International Perspectives* (pp. 165–181). Buckingham: Open University Press.

Unger, R. M. (1984). *Passion: An Essay on Personality.* New York: Free Press.

UNICEF. (2005). Patterns in Conflict: Civilians Are Now the Targets. Information: Impact of Armed Children in Conflict. http://www.unicef.org/graca/patterns.htm, accessed 25 May.

US Census Bureau. (2007). *Income, Poverty, and Health Insurance Coverage in the United States: 2006.* Available: http://www.census.gov

Uvin, P. (2004). *Human Rights and Development.* Bloomfield, CT: Kumarian Press, Inc.

Van Dijk, T. A. (1992). Discourse and the Denial of Racism. *Discourse & Society, 3,* 87–118.

Van Dijk, T. A. (1993). *Elite Discourse and Racism.* Newbury Park, CA: Sage.

Van Eenwyk, J. (1991). Archetypes: The Strange Attractors of the Psyche. *Journal of Analytical Psychology, 36,* 1–25.

Van Maanen, J. (1973). Observations on the Making of Policemen. *Human Organizations, 32,* 404–418.

Van Maanen, J., & Schein, E. H. (1979). Toward a Theory of Organizational Socialization. *Research in Organizational Behavior, 1,* 209–264.

Venn, C. (1984). The Subject of Psychology. In J. Henriques, W. Hollway, C. Urwin, C. Venn, and V. Walkerdine (Eds.), *Changing the Subject: Psychology, Social Regulation, and Subjectivity* (pp. 119–152). London: Methuen.

Vermeire, E., Hearnshaw, H., Van Royen, P., & Denekens, J. (2001). Patient Adherence to Treatment: Three Decades of Research. A Comprehensive Review. *Journal of Clinical Pharmacy & Therapeutics, 26,* 331–342.

Vinck, J., & Meganck, J. (2004). Do We Need Critical Health Psychology or Rather Critical Health Psychologists? *Journal of Health Psychology, 11,* 391–393.

Vranesic, M. (2003). *IMC Mental Health Project in Afghanistan.* Accessed from 9 May http://www.imcworldwide.org/fn_mentalHeatlthmelin.shtml

Vroom, V. H. (1964). *Work and Motivation.* New York: Wiley.

Vygotsky, L. S. (1978). *Mind in Society: The Development of Higher Psychological Processes.* Cambridge, MA: Harvard University Press.

Wainer, J., & Chesters, J. (2000). Rural Mental Health: Neither Romanticism nor Despair. *Australian Journal of Rural Health, 8*(3), 141.

Waitangi Tribunal. (2004). *WAI 1071 Urgent Hearings into the Crown's Foreshore and Seabed Policy.* Wellington: Department of Justice.

Waldegrave, C. (2003). Just Therapy. In C. Waldegrave, K. Tamases, F. Tuhaka, and W. Campbell (Eds.), *Just Therapy: A Journey.* Adelaide, South Australia: Dulwich Centre Publications.

Walkerdine, V. (1996). Subjectivity and Social Class: New Directions for Feminist Psychology. *Feminism & Psychology, 6,* 355–360.

Walkerdine, V. (Ed.). (2002). *Challenging Subjects: Critical Psychology for a New Millennium.* New York: Palgrave Macmillan.

Walkerdine, V. (2003). Reclassifying Upward Mobility: Femininity and the Neo-Liberal Subject. *Gender and Education, 15,* 237–248.

Wang, C. (2003). Using Photovoice as a Participatory Assessment and Issue Selection Tool: A Case Study with the Homeless in Ann Arbor. In M. Minkler and N. Wallerstein (Eds.), *Community Based Participatory Research for Health* (pp. 179–196). San Francisco, CA: Jossey-Bass.

Wang, C., Burris, M., & Xiang, Y. P. (1996). Chinese Village Women as Visual Anthropologists: A Participatory Approach to Reaching Policymakers. *Social Science and Medicine, 42,* 1391–1400.

Ward, S. C. (2002). *Modernizing the Mind: Psychological Knowledge and the Remaking of Society.* Westport, CT: Praeger.

Warren, M. R. (2001). *Dry Bones Rattling: Community Building to Revitalize American Democracy*. Princeton: Princeton University Press.

Warren, R. B., & Warren, D. I. (1977). *The Neighborhood Organizer's Handbook*. Notre Dame, IN: University of Notre Dame Press.

Washington, O., & Moxley, D. (2008). Telling My Story: From Narrative to Exhibit in Illuminating the Lived Experience of Homelessness among Older African American Women. *Journal of Health Psychology, 13,* 154–165.

Watson, G., & Williams, J. (1992). Feminist Practice in Therapy. In J. M. Ussher and P. Nicholson (Eds.), *Gender Issues in Clinical Psychology* (pp. 212–236). London: Routledge.

Watts, R. J. (1992). Elements of a Psychology of Human Diversity. *Journal of Community Psychology, 20,* 116–131.

Watts, R. J., & Serrano-García, I. (2003). The Quest for a Liberating Community Psychology: An Overview. *American Journal of Community Psychology, 31,* 73–78.

Watts, R. J., Griffith, D. M., & Abdul-Adil, J. (1999). Sociopolitical Development as an Antidote for Oppression – Theory and Action. *American Journal of Community Psychology, 27,* 255–272.

Watzlawick, P., Weakland, J. H., & Fisch, R. (1974). *Change: Principles of Problem Formation and Problem Resolution* (1st ed.). New York: Norton.

Webb, S. M. (2004). 'America is a Middle-Class Nation': The Presentation of Class in the Pages of *Life*. In D. Heider (Ed.), *Class and News* (pp. 167–198). Lanham, MD: Rowman & Littlefield.

Webster, B. H. Jr., & Bishaw, A. (2007). *Income, Earnings, and Poverty Data From the 2006 American Community Survey*. Washington, DC: US Census Bureau.

Weick, K. E. (1984). Small Wins: Redefining the Scale of Social Problems. *American Psychologist, 39*(1), 40–49.

Weick, K. E., & Westley, F. (1996). Organizational Learning: Affirming an Oxymoron. In S. R. Clegg, C. Hardy and W. R. Nord (Eds.), *Handbook of Organization Studies* (pp. 440–458). London: Sage.

Weiner, I. B., & Hess, A. K. (Eds.). (2006). *The Handbook of Forensic Psychology*. New York: Wiley.

Weiss, H. M., & Kurek, K. E. (2003). Dispositional Influences on Affective Experiences at Work. In M. R. Barrick and A. M. Ryan (Eds.), *Reconsidering the Role of Personality in Organizations*. San Francisco: Jossey-Bass.

Weiss, T., & Collins, C. (2000). *Humanitarian Challenges & Interventions* (2nd ed.). Boulder, CO: Westview Press.

Weisstein, N. (1968). *Kinder, Küche, Kirche As Scientific Law: Psychology Constructs the Female*. Boston, MA: New England Free Press.

Weisstein, N. (1993). Psychology Constructs the Female; Or, the Fantasy Life of the Male Psychologist (with some Attention to the Fantasies of his Friends, the Male Biologist and the Male Anthropologist). *Feminism & Psychology, 3,* 195–210.

Weller, C. E., & Staub, E. (2006). *Middle Class in Turmoil: Economic Risks Up Sharply For Most Families Since 2001*. Washington, DC: Center for American Progress and Service Employees International Union. Available from http://www.americanprogress.org/issues/2006/09/MidClassReport.pdf, accessed 28 September.

Wessells, M. (2006a). A Living Wage: The Importance of Livelihood in Reintegrating Former Child Soldiers. United Nations Protection of Civilians: Child Protection. Accessed 5 April 2008 from http://protection.unsudanig.org/index.php?fid=child

Wessells, M. (2006b). *Child Soldiers: From Violence to Protection*. Cambridge, MA: Harvard University Press.

Wessells, M. G., & Monteiro, C. (2000). Healing Wounds of War in Angola. In D. Donald, A. Dawes, and J. Louw (Eds.), *Addressing Childhood Adversity* (pp. 176–201). Cape Town: David Philip.

Wessells, M., & Jonah, D. (2005). Reintegration of Former Youth Soldiers in Sierra Leone: Challenges of Reconciliation and Post-Accord Peacebuilding. In S. McEvoy (Ed.), *Youth and Post-accord Peacebuilding*. South Bend, IN: University of Notre Dame Press.

Wetherell, M. S., & Potter, J. A. (1992). *Mapping the Language of Racism: Discourse and the Legitimation of Exploitation*. Hertfordshire: Harvester Wheatsheaf.

Wexler, D. B. (1993). Therapeutic Jurisprudence and Changing Conceptions of Legal Scholarship. *Behavioral Sciences and the Law, 11,* 17–29.

Wexler, D. B., & Winick, B. J. (Eds.). (1996). *Law in a Therapeutic Key: Developments in Therapeutic Jurisprudence*. Durham, NC: Carolina Academic Press.

Wexler, P. (1996). *Critical Social Psychology*. New York: Peter Lang Publishing.

Wheary, J., Shapiro, T. M., & Draut, T. (2007). *By A Thread: The New Experience of America's Middle Class*. Demos and the Institute on Assets and Social Policy. Available from http://www.demos.org/pubs/BaT112807.pdf

White, M. (1995). *Re-Authoring Lives: Interviews and Essays*. Adelaide, Australia: Dulwich Centre Publications.

White, M., & Epston, D. (1990). *Narrative Means to Therapeutic Ends*. New York: Norton Press.

Whiteneck, G., Meade, M., Dijkers, M., Tate, D., Bushnik, T., & Forchheimer, M. (2004). Environmental Factors and their Role in Participation and Life Satisfaction after Spinal-Cord Injury. *Archives of Physical Medicine & Rehabilitation, 85,* 1793–1803.

Wiener, R. L., Watts, B. A., & Stolle, D. P. (1993). Psychological Jurisprudence and the Information Processing Paradigm. *Behavioral Sciences and the Law, 11,* 79–96.

Wierzbicka, A. (1999). *Emotions Across Languages and Cultures: Diversity and Universals*. Cambridge: Cambridge University Press.

Wilkinson, S. (1997a). Feminist Psychology. In D. Fox and I. Prilleltensky (Eds.), *Critical Psychology: An Introduction* (pp. 247–264). London: Sage.

Wilkinson, S. (1997b). Prioritizing the Political: Feminist Psychology. In T. Ibáñez and L. Íñiguez (Eds.), *Critical Social Psychology* (pp. 178–194). London: Sage.

Williams, C. R. (2004). Anarchic Insurgencies: The Mythos of Authority and the Violence of Mental Health. In B. A. Arrigo (Ed.), *Psychological Jurisprudence: Critical Exploration in Law, Crime, and Society* (pp. 43–74). Albany, NY: SUNY Press.

Williams, C. R., & Arrigo, B. A. (2001). Anarchaos and Order: On the Emergence of Social Justice. *Theoretical Criminology: An International Journal, 5*(2), 223–252.

Williams, C. R., & Arrigo, B. A. (2002). *Law, Psychology, and Justice: Chaos Theory and the New (Dis)Order*. Albany, NY: SUNY Press.

Williams, C. R., & Arrigo, B. A. (2007). Drug-taking Behavior, Compulsory Treatment, and Desistance: Implications of Self-Organization and Natural Recovery for Policy and Practice. *Journal of Offender Rehabilitation, 46*(1/2), 57–80.

Williams, D. (1999). *Te Kooti Tango Whenua: The Native Land Court 1864–1909*. Wellington: Huia.

Willig, C. (1998). Constructions of Sexual Activity and their Implications for Sexual Practice. *Journal of Health Psychology, 3,* 383–392.

Willig, C. (2001). *Introducing Qualitative Research in Psychology: Adventures in Theory and Method*. Maidenhead: Open University Press.

Willig, C., & Stainton Rogers, W. (Eds.). (2008). *The Sage Handbook of Qualitative Research in Psychology*. London: Sage.

Willinsky, J. (1987). Learning the Language of Difference: The Dictionary in High School. *English Education, 19*(3), 146–158.

Willy, R. (1899). *Die Krisis in der Psychologie [The Crisis in Psychology]*. Leipzig: Reisland.

Wilson, H., Hutchinson, S., & Holzemer, W. (2002). Reconciling Incompatibilities: A Grounded Theory of HIV Medication Adherence and Symptom Management. *Qualitative Health Research, 12,* 1309–1322.

Wilson, M. (1993). DSM-III and the Transformation of American Psychiatry: A History. *American Journal of Psychiatry, 150*, 399–410.

Winick, B. J., & Wexler, D. B. (Eds.). (2003). *Judging in a Therapeutic Key: Therapeutic Jurisprudence and the Courts*. Durham, NC: Carolina Academic Press.

Winks, R. (1987). *Cloak and Gown Scholars in the Secret War, 1939–1961*. New York: Morrow.

Wise, T. (2005). *White Like Me: Reflections on Race from a Privileged Son*. Brooklyn, NY: Soft Skull Press.

Wittgenstein, L. (1961). *Notebooks, 1914–1916*. Oxford: Blackwell.

Women of Photovoice/ADMI & Lykes, M. B. (2000). *Voces e imágenes: Mujeres Mayas Ixiles de Chajul/Voices and images: Mayan Ixil women of Chajul*. Guatemala: MagnaTerra.

Woodward, W., & Ash, M. G. (Eds.). (1982). *The Problematic Science: Psychology in Nineteenth-Century Thought*. New York: Praeger.

World Resources Institute (1998). *World Resources 1998–1999: Environmental Change and Human Health*. Available from http://population.wri.org/pubs_content_text.cfm.contentID=1374, accessed 12 June 2005.

Wright, B. (1960). *Physical Disability: A Psychological Approach*. New York: Harper & Row.

Wright, B. A., & Lopez, S. J. (2002). Widening the Diagnostic Focus: A Case for Including Human Strengths and Environmental Resources. In C. R. Snyder and S. J. Lopez (Eds.), *Handbook of Positive Psychology* (pp. 26–44). New York: Oxford University Press.

Wrzesniewski, A., & Dutton, J. E. (2001). Crafting a Job: Revisioning Employees as Active Crafters of their Work. *Academy of Management Review, 26*(2), 179–201.

Wylie, M. S. (1995). Diagnosing for Dollars: The Power of *DSM-IV*. *Psychotherapy Networker*, May/June, 23–33 and 65–69.

Young, F. (2006). Social Problems: A Focus for a New Branch of Public Health. *Social Theory & Health, 4*, 264–274.

Zenderland, L. (1998). *Measuring Minds: Henry Herbert Goddard and the Origins of American Intelligence Testing*. New York: Cambridge University Press.

Zimbardo, P. G., Haney, C., Banks, W. C., & Jaffe, D. (1974). The Psychology of Imprisonment: Privation, Power, and Pathology. In Z. Rubin (Ed.), *Doing Unto Others: Explorations in Social Behavior* (pp. 61–73). New Jersey: Prentice-Hall.

Zimmerman, J. L., & Dickerson, V. C. (1996). *If Problems Talked: Adventures in Narrative Therapy*. New York: Guilford.

Zimmerman, M. (2000). Empowerment Theory: Psychological, Organizational, and Community Levels of Analysis. In J. Rappaport and E. Seidman (Eds.), *Handbook of Community Psychology* (pp. 43–63). New York: Kluwer Academic/Plenum.

Zinn, H. (1980). *A People's History of the United States*. New York: Harper & Row.

Index

Please note that page numbers relating to Figures and Tables will be in *italic* print; titles of publications beginning with 'A' or 'The' will be filed under the first significant word.

Human Resource Management techniques 115
human resources technologies 114–17
human rights and capabilities 287–8
human sciences, and natural sciences 41
humanistic psychologists 60
Huygens 14, 140
hypotheses 43, 339
hysteria 84

iatrogenesis 308
ICF see International Classification of Functioning
ideological processes 68–9
ideologization 69, 73
ideology 62, 69
    definitions/concepts 9, 332
    dialogue theory 328
    managerial 116
    role 9–10
Ideology and Consciousness (journal) 329
ideology criticism 328
'ideology-practice divide' 378
IDS see Institute of Development Studies
if-then-statements 45
IMF see International Monetary Fund
immigration laws (1920s) 25
imperialism 269, 271, 281
implementer, role 370
inclusive host, role of 366–7
Independent Living Movement 254
indigenous people 198, 270
individual differences
    personality theories 64–5
    work context 64–5
individual tragedy model 255
individual values 133
individualism
    and meaninglessness 5–8
    and psychology 176
    and social class 221
individuals
    current diagnostic system based on 77
    focus on, in clinical psychology 85–6
    individual differences 64–5
    in organizational context, psychology 112–14
individual/society dualism 70
Industrial and Labour Relations 111
industrial/organizational psychology (IO) 110–23
inequality
    and discursive psychology 180–2
    discursive psychology 180–2
    and oppression 8–10
    social class 219–20
    see also social class
    Third World nations 269–70
infantalization of mentally ill 302, 308
informed consent 351
Innocence Project 160
insider-outsider distinction 257
Institute of Development Studies (IDS) 292
intellectual history 21
intelligence testing
    Binet on 159
    psychological concepts 41
    and revisionism 24–6, 28

intention 11
interaction 177
interactionism 103
International Classification of Functioning (ICF) 258
International Monetary Fund (IMF) 269
internationalization 51
inter-organizational targets 381
Interpretative Phenomenological Analysis 178
interpretive repertoires 203, 213
intersectionality 234
intersubjectivity 68, 328, 332
interventions
    arts-based participatory 151
    and community mental health 88
    community psychology 129
    culture, class and gender 86
    Dora, case of 85
    individual, focus on 85–6
    personality theories 64
    power hour 87
    praxis 140
    psychosocial interventions and psychotherapy 85–7
IO see industrial/organizational psychology
    as 'applied' science 111
    careers, changing nature 119–20
    human resources technologies 114–17
    implications/recommendations 121–3
    individual differences at work 112–13
    Industrial and Labour Relations 111
    job analysis 115
    leadership 114
    macro approach 121
    microsociological approach 121
    motivation 113
    organization and culture 120–1
    Organization Studies 111
    psychology of individuals in organizational context 112–14
    selection and recruitment 116–17
    training and socialization 117
    work-environment issues 118–21
    work stress 7, 85–6, 118–19
IQ see intelligence testing
Iraq War 393
Irish Suppression of Rebellion Act (1799) 273

Jacoby, R. 67–8
James, William 21
Jefferson, Gail 186, 187
Jensen, Arthur 24, 25, 26
job analysis 115
Jung, Carl 60, 320
jurisprudence, psychological 162–3
Just Therapy model 84
justice, search for 171–3

Kabeto, M. 259
Kagan, Carol 342–3
Kagan, Carolyn 130, 280–1
Kallikak family 25, 28
Kamin, Leon 24–6, 27
Kant, Immanuel 36
Kawachi, I. 224
Keller, E. F. 46

Kelly, Jim 127
Kendall, D. 221
Kennedy, D. 165
Kennedy, President John F. 88
Kensington Welfare Rights Union (KWRU) 404
Kerner Commission 29
Kinder, Küche, Kirsche as Scientific Law: Psychology Constructs the Female (Weisstein) 27
Kinsey, Alfred 32
Kitzinger, Celia 245
kleptomania 81–2
Knight 118, 119
knowledge
    action-oriented 206
    critique of 165
    implicit shared 206
    politics of 77
    social context 76
    tacit 206
Koch, S. 43
Korean War 401
Kretzmann, J. P. 386
Kuhn, Thomas 43, 340
    on 'exemplars' 393
Kvale 350–1
KWRU see Kensington Welfare Rights Union

labels, psychiatric 76, 301
Lacan, Jacques 166
Langa, K. 259
language
    see also discourse analysis
    and discursive psychology 178
    genital parts, dictionary definitions 243–5
    limitations 70
    and postmodernism 166
    and psychology 178
    of science 46
    and social construction 76
    subject matter of psychology 40
    traditional view, in mainstream psychology 244
Laqueur, T
Laqueur, T. 242
Latané, B. 103
Latin America, oppressed people of 47
Latin American Educational Group 128
Laurier, E. 148
Lawthom, R. 262
leadership 114
learning organizations 387
legal psychology 159–73
    advocacy, and rights-claiming 173
    anarchism 167–9
    applied empirical research 161–2
    chaos theory 169–71
    crime of policy, and search for justice 171–3
    critical perspectives 163–71
    education and training 172
    forensic clinician as expert witness 161
    legal psychology 161–2
    postmodernism 165–7
    psychological jurisprudence 162–3
    race, gender and class 172–3